Beginning JavaS 

CSS Development

Beginning
JavaScript® and CSS Development with jQuery

Beginning
JavaScript® and CSS Development with jQuery

Richard York

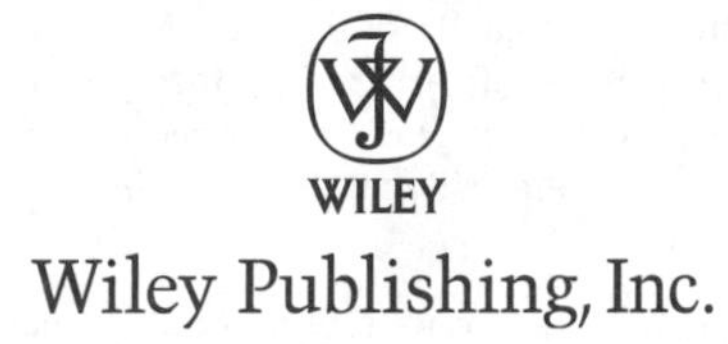

Wiley Publishing, Inc.

Beginning JavaScript® and CSS Development with jQuery

Published by
Wiley Publishing, Inc.
10475 Crosspoint Boulevard
Indianapolis, IN 46256
www.wiley.com

Published simultaneously in Canada

ISBN: 978-0-470-22779-4

Manufactured in the United States of America

10 9 8 7 6 5 4 3 2

Library of Congress Cataloging-in-Publication Data

York, Richard.
Beginning JavaScript and CSS development with jQuery / Richard York.
p. cm.
Includes index.
ISBN 978-0-470-22779-4 (paper/website)
1. JavaScript (Computer program language) 2. Web sites--Design. 3. Cascading style sheets. I. Title.
QA76.73.J38Y67 2009
006.7'6--dc22
2009005636

About the Author

Richard York is a web developer and author of three Wrox books in addition to this: *Beginning CSS: Cascading Style Sheets for Web Design* (Wiley, 2007), *CSS Instant Results* (Wiley, 2006), and *Beginning CSS: Cascading Style Sheets for Web Design*, 2nd ed (Wiley, 2007).

Website: `www.deadmarshes.com`

Credits

Senior Development Editor
Tom Dinse

Technical Editor
Sam Judson

Senior Production Editor
Debra Banninger

Copy Editor
Cate Caffrey

Editorial Manager
Mary Beth Wakefield

Production Manager
Tim Tate

Vice President and Executive Group Publisher
Richard Swadley

Vice President and Executive Publisher
Barry Pruett

Associate Publisher
Jim Minatel

Project Coordinator, Cover
Lynsey Stanford

Compositor
James D. Kramer,
Happenstance Type-o-Rama

Proofreader
Nancy Carrasco

Indexer
J & J Indexing

Contents

Introduction

The jQuery JavaScript framework is a rising star in the world of web development. JavaScript frameworks in general have grown to become immensely popular in the past few years in parallel with the ever-increasing presence of JavaScript-driven, so-called Web 2.0 websites that make heavy use of technologies like AJAX and JavaScript in general for slick graphical enhancements that would be impossible or much more cumbersome to incorporate without JavaScript.

jQuery's mission as a JavaScript library is simple — it strives to make the lives of web developers easier by patching over certain portions of cross-browser development and by making other tasks commonly needed by developers much easier. jQuery has the real, proven ability to reduce many lines of plain-vanilla JavaScript to just a few lines, and, in many cases, just a single line. jQuery strives to remove barriers to JavaScript development by removing redundancy wherever possible and normalizing cross-browser JavaScript development in key areas where browsers would otherwise differ, such as Microsoft's Event API and the W3C Event API, and other, more remedial tasks like getting the mouse cursor's position when an event has taken place.

jQuery is a compact, lightweight library that currently works in Microsoft's Internet Explorer browser from version 6 on, Firefox from version 1.5 on, Safari from version 2.0.2 on, Opera from version 9 on, and Google's new Chrome browser from version 0.2 on. Getting started with jQuery is very easy — all you have to do is include a single link of markup in your HTML or XHTML documents that includes the library. Throughout this book, I demonstrate jQuery's API (Application Programming Interface) components in detail and show you how all the nuts and bolts of this framework come together to enable you to rapidly develop client-side applications.

I also cover the jQuery UI library, which makes redundant user-interface (UI) tasks on the client side ridiculously easy and accessible to everyday web developers who might not have much JavaScript programming expertise. Have you ever wanted to create an animated accordion effect like the one found on Apple's Mac home page at `www.apple.com/mac`? With jQuery, not only can you create this effect with your own look and feel, but also it's dead simple to boot.

Have you ever wondered how websites make virtual pop-up windows using JavaScript, HTML, and CSS? The jQuery UI library provides the ability to create these pop-up windows and includes the ability to animate transitions like fading the window on and off, or having it re-size from very small to full sized. The jQuery UI library gives you the ability to use animations and transitions using JavaScript, markup, and CSS that you may have thought previously could only have been done with Adobe's Flash player.

The jQuery framework itself has enjoyed a great deal of mainstream exposure. It has been used by Google, Dell, Digg, NBC, CBS, Netflix, The Mozilla Foundation, and the popular WordPress and Drupal PHP frameworks.

jQuery is fast — superfast — and it has a small footprint. It's only 15 KB, using the compressed and gzipped version.

jQuery gives you the ability to provide complex, professional, visually driven user interfaces and effects with very few lines of code. What may have taken other developers days or even weeks to accomplish can be done with jQuery in just a few hours.

Who This Book Is For

This book is for anyone interested in doing more with less code! You should have a basic understanding of JavaScript. I review some basic JavaScript programming concepts, such as the Event API, but I do not go into great detail about the JavaScript language itself. You'll want to have at least a basic grasp of the Document Object Model, or DOM, and basic JavaScript programming syntax. Additionally, you'll need to know your way around CSS and HTML, since knowledge of those technologies is also assumed. A complete beginner might be able to grasp what is taking place in the examples in this book but might not understand certain terminology and programming concepts that would be presented in a beginner's JavaScript guide, so if you are a beginner and insist with pressing forward, I recommend doing so with a beginning JavaScript book on hand as well. Specifically, I recommend the following Wrox books for more help with the basics:

- *Beginning Web Programming with HTML, XHTML, and CSS*, 2nd ed. (2008), by Jon Duckett
- *Beginning CSS: Cascading Style Sheets for Web Design*, 2nd ed. (2007), also written by yours truly.
- *Beginning JavaScript*, 3rd ed. (2007), by Paul Wilton and Jeremy McPeak

For further knowledge of JavaScript above and beyond what is covered in this book, I recommend *Professional JavaScript for Web Developers*, 2nd ed. (2009), by Nicholas C. Zakas.

What This Book Covers

This book covers the jQuery JavaScript framework and the jQuery UI JavaScript framework and demonstrates in great detail how to use the jQuery framework to get more results more quickly out of JavaScript programming. I cover each method exposed by jQuery's API, which contains methods to make common, redundant tasks go much more quickly in less code. Some examples are methods that help you to select elements from a markup document through the DOM and methods that help you to traverse through those selections and filter them using jQuery's fine-grained controls. This makes working with the DOM easier and more effortless. I also cover how jQuery eliminates certain cross-browser, cross-platform development headaches like the event model; not only does it eliminate these headaches, but it also makes it easier to work with events by reducing the amount of code that you need to write to attach events. It even gives you the ability to simulate events.

Later in the book, I cover how you can leverage the jQuery UI library to make graphically driven UI widgets. jQuery gives you the ability to break content up among multiple tabs in the same page. You have the ability to customize the look and feel of the tabs, and even to create a polished look and feel by providing different effects that come in when you mouse over tabs and click on them. The jQuery UI library also makes it easy to create accordion sidebars, like the one on Apple's Mac website. These sidebars have two or more panels, and when you mouse over an item, one pane transitions to another via a smooth, seamless animation wherein the preceding pane collapses and the proceeding pane expands.

The jQuery UI library also gives you the ability to make any element draggable with the mouse; by clicking and holding and moving the mouse, you can move elements around on a page. It also makes it really easy to create drag-and-drop user interfaces. This can be used to make a dropping zone where you take elements from other parts of the page and drop them in another, as you would in your operating system's file manager when you want to move a folder from one place to another. You can also make lists that are sortable via drag-and-drop, rearranging elements based on where you drop them. You can also have a user interface where you drag the mouse cursor to make a selection, as you would in your operating system's file manager when you want to select more than one file. Then jQuery UI also exposes the ability to re-size elements on a page using the mouse. All of those neat things that you can do on your computer's desktop, you can also do in a web browser with jQuery UI.

jQuery UI also provides a widget for entering a date into a field using a nice, accessible JavaScript-driven calendar that pops up when you click on an input field.

You can also make custom pop-up dialogues that are like virtual pop-up windows, except they don't open a separate browser window — they come up using markup, CSS, and JavaScript.

Another widget that jQuery UI provides is a graphical slider bar, similar to your media player's volume control.

As jQuery has done for JavaScript programming in general, jQuery UI strives to do for redundant graphical user interface (GUI) tasks. jQuery UI gives you the ability to make professional user-interface widgets with much less development effort.

If you're interested in reading news about jQuery, how it's evolving, and topics related to web development, you may be interested in reading the official jQuery blog at `blog.jquery.com`, or jQuery's creator, John Resig's blog, at `www.ejohn.org`.

If you are in need of help, you can participate in programming discussion at `p2p.wrox.com`, which you can join for free to ask programming questions in moderated forums. There are also programming forums provided by the jQuery community, which you can learn more about at `http://docs.jquery.com/Discussion`.

Finally, I maintain a blog and website at `www.deadmarshes.com`, where you can contact me directly with your thoughts about the book or read about the web development projects I'm working on.

How This Book Is Structured

This book is divided into two parts: The first half of the book covers the basic API exposed by the jQuery library, and the second half covers the jQuery UI library.

Part 1: jQuery API

- **Chapter 1: Introduction to jQuery** — In this first chapter, I discuss a little of where jQuery came from and why it was needed. Then I walk you through downloading and creating your first jQuery-enabled JavaScript.

- **Chapter 2: Selecting and Filtering** — This chapter introduces jQuery's selector engine, which uses selectors like you will have used with CSS to make selections from the DOM. Then I talk about the various methods that jQuery exposes for working with a selection, to give you fine-grained control over what elements you're working with from the DOM. I talk about methods that let you select, ancestor elements, parent elements, sibling elements, descendent elements, how to remove elements from a selection, how to add elements to a selection, and how to reduce a selection to a specific subset of elements.
- **Chapter 3: Events** — In this chapter, I begin by reviewing the event model as you find it in plain-vanilla JavaScript. You have the traditional event model, the W3C's event model, and Microsoft's event model. I discuss the differences between these and why jQuery needed an entirely new Event API to make the situation easier for web developers. Then I present jQuery's Event API and how you use it.
- **Chapter 4: Manipulating Content and Attributes** — In Chapter 4, you learn how to use the methods that jQuery exposes for working with content, text and HTML, and element attributes. jQuery provides methods for doing just about everything you'd want to do to an element.
- **Chapter 5: Arrays and Iteration** — In Chapter 5, I talk about how you can enumerate over a selection of elements or an array using jQuery. As with everything else, jQuery provides an easier way that requires fewer lines of code to loop over the contents of an array or a selection of elements from the DOM.
- **Chapter 6: CSS** — In this chapter, you learn about the methods that jQuery exposes for working with CSS properties and declarations. jQuery provides intuitive and versatile methods that let you manipulate CSS in a variety of ways.
- **Chapter 7: AJAX** — Chapter 7 elaborates on the methods that jQuery exposes for making AJAX requests from a server, which allows you to request server content without working directly with the `XMLHttpRequest` object and supports handling server responses in a variety of formats.
- **Chapter 8: Effects** — In Chapter 8, I discuss some helper methods that jQuery exposes for discovering what browser and browser version you're working with, whether you're working with a browser that supports the standard W3C box model for CSS, and a variety of odds and ends methods for working with objects, arrays, functions, and strings.
- **Chapter 9: Plugins** — In this chapter, I describe how you can make your own plugins for jQuery.

Part II: jQuery UI

- **Chapter 10: Implementing Drag-and-Drop** — In Chapter 10, I begin my coverage of the jQuery UI library by discussing how you make individual elements draggable and how you make a drag-and-drop interface where you take one element and place it on top of another to create a complete drag-and-drop sequence.
- **Chapter 11: Drag-and-Drop Sorting** — In Chapter 11, I discuss how you make lists sortable using drag-and-drop.
- **Chapter 12: Selection by Drawing a Box** — In Chapter 12, I cover the portion of the jQuery UI library that lets you make a selection by drawing a box with your mouse, just like you would do in your OS's file management application.
- **Chapter 13: Accordion UI** — In this chapter, I discuss how to make a really neat, polished-looking sidebar that has panes that transition like an accordion. When you mouse over an element, one pane collapses via a slick animation, and another one expands, also via an animation.

- **Chapter 14: Datepicker** — In Chapter 14, I cover how you make a standard form input field into a Datepicker, using jQuery's Datepicker widget.
- **Chapter 15: Dialogs** — In Chapter 15, I talk about how you create virtual pop-up windows, using the jQuery UI library, that look and act like real pop-up windows but are entirely contained in the same web page that launches them and are built using pure markup, CSS, and JavaScript.
- **Chapter 16: Tabs** — In Chapter 16, I discuss the jQuery UI tab component, which allows you to take a document and split it into several tabs and navigate between those tabs without needing to load another page.
- **Appendixes** — Appendix A contains the answers to chapter exercises. Appendix B through Appendix S contain reference materials for jQuery and jQuery UI.

What You Need to Use This Book

To make use of the examples in this book, you need the following:

- Several Internet browsers to test your web pages
- Text-editing software or your favorite IDE

Designing content for websites requires being able to reach more than one type of audience. Some of your audience may be using different operating systems or different browsers other than those you have installed on your computer. This book focuses on the most popular browsers available at the time of this writing as supported:

- Microsoft Internet Explorer 6 or newer for Windows
- Safari for Mac OS X, version 2 or newer
- Mozilla Firefox for Mac OS X, Windows, or Linux
- Opera for Mac OS X, Windows and Linux, version 9 or newer

Conventions

To help you get the most from the text and keep track of what's happening, I've used a number of conventions throughout the book.

First, be aware that not all the figures referenced in the text actually appear in print. This means, for example, that the screenshots that actually do appear in a chapter might not be numbered in strict sequence. For example, if you look only at the screenshots in Chapter 3, the first is Figure 3-1, and the second is Figure 3-3. There is a reference to Figure 3-2 in the text, but the actual screenshot is not printed. These "missing" screenshots aren't really missing, though — they are generated by the code download. It's just that for all intents and purposes, they are identical to the screenshots that are printed before or after them and are therefore not needed in the text.

Try It Out

The *Try It Out* is an exercise you should work through, following the text in the book.

1. It usually consists of a set of steps.
2. Each step has a number.
3. Follow the steps through with your copy of the database.

> **Boxes like this one hold important, not-to-be forgotten information that is directly relevant to the surrounding text.**

Notes, tips, hints, tricks, and asides to the current discussion are offset and placed in italics like this.

As for styles in the text:

- We *highlight* with italics new terms and important words when we introduce them.
- We show keyboard strokes like this: *Ctrl+A*.
- We show URLs and code within the text like so: `persistence.properties`.
- We present code in the following way:

```
We use a monofont type with no highlighting for most code examples.
```

Also, Visual Studio's code editor provides a rich color scheme to indicate various parts of code syntax. That's a great tool to help you learn language features in the editor and to help prevent mistakes as you code. To reinforce Visual Studio's colors, the code listings in this book are colorized using colors similar to what you would see on screen in Visual Studio working with the book's code. In order to optimize print clarity, some colors have a slightly different hue in print from what you see on screen. But all of the colors for the code in this book should be close enough to the default Visual Studio colors to give you an accurate representation of the colors.

Source Code

As you work through the examples in this book, you may choose either to type in all the code manually or to use the source code files that accompany the book. All of the source code used in this book is available for download at `www.wrox.com`. Once at the site, simply locate the book's title (either by using the Search box or by using one of the title lists) and click on the Download Code link on the book's detail page to obtain all the source code for the book.

Because many books have similar titles, you may find it easiest to search by ISBN; this book's ISBN is 978-0-470-22779-4.

Once you download the code, just decompress it with your favorite compression tool. Alternatively, you can go to the main Wrox code download page at `www.wrox.com/dynamic/books/download.aspx` to see the code available for this book and all other Wrox books.

Errata

We make every effort to ensure that there are no errors in the text or in the code. However, no one is perfect, and mistakes do occur. If you find an error in one of our books, like a spelling mistake or faulty piece of code, we would be very grateful for your feedback. By sending in errata you may save another reader hours of frustration, and at the same time, you will be helping us provide even higher quality information.

To find the errata page for this book, go to `www.wrox.com` and locate the title using the Search box or one of the title lists. Then, on the Book Search Results page, click on the Errata link. On this page, you can view all errata that have been submitted for this book and posted by Wrox editors.

A complete book list including links to errata is also available at `www.wrox.com/misc-pages/booklist.shtml`.

If you don't spot "your" error on the Errata page, click on the Errata Form link and complete the form to send us the error you have found. We'll check the information and, if appropriate, post a message to the book's Errata page and fix the problem in subsequent editions of the book.

p2p.wrox.com

For author and peer discussion, join the P2P forums at `p2p.wrox.com`. The forums are a Web-based system for you to post messages relating to Wrox books and related technologies and interact with other readers and technology users. The forums offer a subscription feature to e-mail you topics of interest of your choosing when new posts are made to the forums. Wrox authors, editors, other industry experts, and your fellow readers are present on these forums.

At `http://p2p.wrox.com`, you will find several different forums that will help you not only as you read this book, but also as you develop your own applications. To join the forums, just follow these steps:

1. Go to `p2p.wrox.com` and click on the Register link.
2. Read the terms of use and click Agree.
3. Complete the required information to join as well as any optional information you wish to provide and click Submit.
4. You will receive an e-mail with information describing how to verify your account and complete the joining process.

You can read messages in the forums without joining P2P, but in order to post your own messages, you must join.

Once you join, you can post new messages and respond to messages other users post. You can read messages at any time on the Web. If you would like to have new messages from a particular forum e-mailed to you, click on the "Subscribe to this Forum" icon by the forum name in the forum listing.

For more information about how to use the Wrox P2P, be sure to read the P2P FAQs for answers to questions about how the forum software works as well as many common questions specific to P2P and Wrox books. To read the FAQs, click the FAQ link on any P2P page.

Part I
jQuery API

Introduction to jQuery

JavaScript frameworks have arisen as necessary and useful companions for client-side web development. Without JavaScript frameworks, client-side programming becomes a crater-filled minefield of cross-browser, cross-platform inconsistencies and idiosyncrasies. JavaScript frameworks pave over those craters and inconsistencies to create a seamless, enjoyable client-side programming experience.

The most important hole filled by a JavaScript framework is inconsistencies between Internet Explorer's and the W3C's standard Event APIs. jQuery fills in this hole by making a cross-browser Event API that is very similar to the W3C's, adding some original helpful extensions of its own.

Another hole filled by most of the popular client-side JavaScript frameworks is the ability to select and traverse through nodes in the Document Object Model (DOM) using more than the very remedial selection and traversal APIs that are provided by browsers' default DOM implementations.

jQuery provides a selection mechanism that uses selector syntax like that used in cascading style sheets. However, not content to support only the standard selectors supported in CSS and even the new Selectors API implementations supported by WebKit and Internet Explorer 8, jQuery again extends the standard to support new, innovative, and useful selectors that make sense when using selectors to select DOM nodes.

In a nutshell, jQuery reduces significantly the amount of JavaScript programming and Q/A (quality assurance) you have to undertake. It takes what might take several lines of code to write, and more often than not reduces that to just one or a few lines of code. jQuery makes your JavaScript more intuitive and easier to understand. jQuery takes JavaScript programming (which at one time had a higher barrier of entry due to complexity and cross-browser, cross-platform idiosyncrasies) and makes it easier and more attractive to average web developers.

Throughout this book, I will discuss jQuery's Application Programming Interface, or API. We'll look in depth and up close at each little bit of programming syntax that enables jQuery to do what it does. With each new bit, I also provide simple, to-the-point examples that demonstrate how that bit works. I show you how to write JavaScript applications using jQuery, and by the end of this book, you too will be able to create Web 2.0 applications that function seamlessly across multiple browsers and platforms.

In this chapter, I begin discussion of jQuery by introducing what you get out of jQuery, who develops jQuery, how you obtain jQuery, and how you install jQuery and test that it is ready to use.

As I mentioned in the Introduction, I do not assume that you are a JavaScript expert in this book, but I do assume that you are familiar with basic JavaScript concepts, such as the DOM and attaching events. I will do my best to keep examples simple and to the point and avoid layering on thick programming jargon.

What Does jQuery Do for Me?

jQuery makes many tasks easier. Its simplistic, comprehensive API has the ability to completely change the way you write JavaScript, with the aim of consolidating and eliminating as many common and redundant tasks as possible. jQuery really shines in the following areas:

- jQuery makes iterating and traversing the DOM much easier via its various built-in methods for doing the same.
- jQuery makes selecting items from the DOM easier via its sophisticated, built-in ability to use selectors, just like you would use in CSS.
- jQuery makes it really easy to add your own custom methods via its simple-to-understand plug-in architecture.
- jQuery helps reduce redundancy in navigation and UI functionality, like tabs, CSS and markup-based pop-up dialogues, animations, and transitions, and lots of other things.

jQuery won't do your laundry, walk the dog, or broker world peace (yet), but it does bring a lot to the table in terms of making client-side website development easier.

Is jQuery the only JavaScript framework? — no, certainly not. You can pick from several JavaScript frameworks: base2, Yahoo UI, Prototype, SproutCore, Dojo, and so on. I picked jQuery for this book simply because I enjoy its simplicity and lack of verbosity. On the other hand, among the other frameworks, you'll find that there is a lot of similarity and each provides its own advantages in terms of unifying Event APIs, providing sophisticated selector and traversal implementations, and providing simple interfaces for redundant JavaScript-driven UI tasks.

In the past, I've been a big fan of base2, simply for its commitment to supporting W3C-sanctioned and de facto standard APIs seamlessly. But I have decided to focus on jQuery exclusively and exhaustively for this book because I think its popularity merits comprehensive coverage, which I'm able to present in a way that is more befitting novice programmers.

In a nutshell, jQuery blurs and even erases lines in some places that existed as barriers for true cross-browser, cross-platform development. It gives you a standard Event API, a standard Selectors API, useful traversal and enumeration methods, and a very useful UI library that work across the board in Internet Explorer, Safari, Firefox, and Opera on Windows, Mac, and Linux platforms.

That's not to say that you won't ever encounter cross-browser issues with your programs, but jQuery makes it much less likely and eliminates a hefty chunk of compatibility issues.

Who Develops jQuery?

I won't spend a lot of time talking about the history of JavaScript frameworks, why they exist, and so on. I prefer to get straight to the point. That said, a brief mention of the people involved with developing jQuery is in order.

jQuery's lead developer and creator is John Resig, whose website is located at `www.ejohn.org`. John resides in Boston, Massachusetts and is a JavaScript Evangelist for the Mozilla Corporation.

There are also several other people who have contributed to jQuery and continue to assist with its development. You can learn more about these people and what roles they played in jQuery's development at `http://docs.jquery.com/About/Contributors`.

Obtaining jQuery

jQuery is a free, Open Source JavaScript Framework. The current stable, production release version, as of this writing, is 1.2.6. I use version 1.2.6 throughout the course of this book. Getting jQuery is easy — all you have to do is go to `www.jquery.com` and click on the "Download" link. You'll see three options for downloading: a packed and gzipped version, an uncompressed version, and a packed version; these all refer to the same jQuery script. Download "uncompressed" if you want to be able to look at jQuery's source code. Download "packed" if you, for whatever reason, are unable to use gzip compression. The packed version is the same JavaScript code minus all comments, white space, and line breaks. Otherwise, for the best possible download performance, the packed and gzipped version is the best.

Installing jQuery

Throughout this book, I will refer to the jQuery script as though it is installed at the following path: `www.example.com/Library/jquery/jquery.js`.

Therefore, if I were using the domain `example.com`, jQuery would have this path from the document root, /Source Code/jquery/jquery.js. You do not have to install jQuery at this exact path.

The following "Try It Out" assists you with installing jQuery by giving you an alternative dialogue when the script is properly installed.

Try It Out Installing and Testing jQuery

Example 1-1

To install and test jQuery, follow these steps.

1. Download the jQuery script from `www.jquery.com`. Alternatively, I have also provided the jQuery script in this book's source code download materials available for free from `www.wrox.com`.
2. Enter the following XHTML document, and save the document as *Example 1-1.html*. Adjust your path to jQuery appropriately; the path that I use reflects the path needed for the example to

work when opened in a browser via the source code materials download made available for this book from `www.wrox.com`.

```
<!DOCTYPE html PUBLIC "-//W3C//DTD XHTML 1.0 Transitional//EN"
    "http://www.w3.org/TR/2002/REC-xhtml1-20020801/DTD/xhtml1-transitional.dtd">
<html xmlns='http://www.w3.org/1999/xhtml' xml:lang='en'>
  <head>
    <meta http-equiv='content-type' content='text/html; charset=utf-8' />
    <meta http-equiv='content-language' content='en-us' />
    <title>Link</title>
    <script type='text/javascript'
            src='../../../Source Code/jQuery/jQuery.js'>
    </script>
    <script type='text/javascript' src='Example 1-1.js'></script>
    <link type='text/css' href='Example 1-1.css' rel='stylesheet' />
  </head>
  <body>
    <p>
        jQuery is not loaded.
    </p>
  </body>
</html>
```

3. Enter the following JavaScript document, and save the document as *Example 1-1.js*:

```
if ($) {
  $(document).ready(
    function() {
      $('p').addClass('tmpFrameworkLoaded');
      $('p').text('jQuery successfully loaded and running!');
    }
  );
}
```

4. Enter the following CSS document, and save the document as *Example 1-1.css*:

```
body {
    font: 16px sans-serif;
}
p {
    color: red;
    border: 1px solid red;
    padding: 5px;
    margin: 5px;
}
p.tmpFrameworkLoaded {
    color: green;
    border: 1px solid green;
}
```

The preceding code results in the screenshot that you see in **Figure 1-1**, if the installation was unsuccessful; and the screenshot in **Figure 1-2**, if the installation was successful.

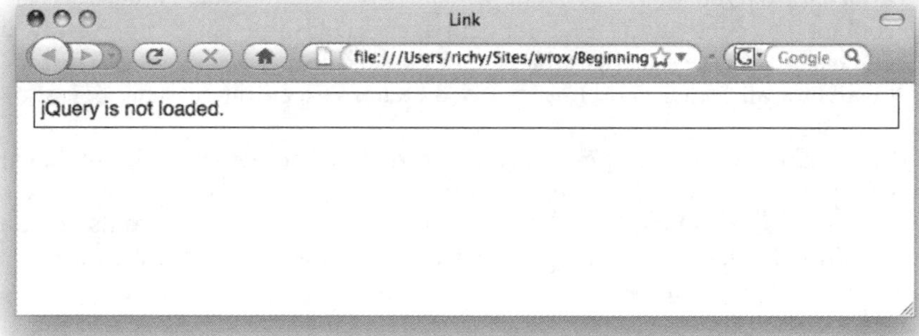

Figure 1-1

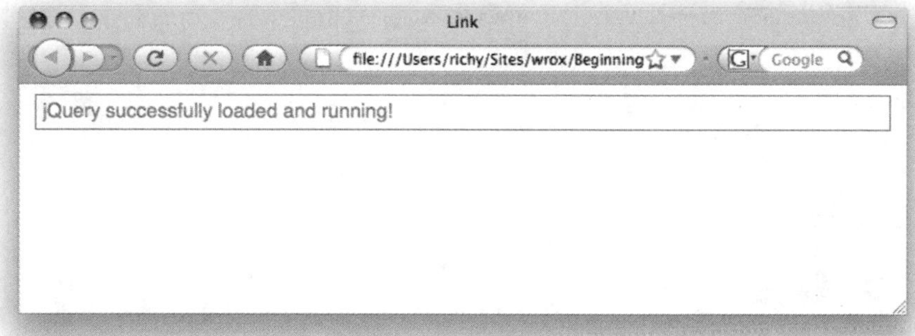

Figure 1-2

In the preceding example, you installed and tested your installation of the jQuery framework. The XHTML document references a style sheet and a test JavaScript. The XHTML document contains just a single <p> element that contains the text "jQuery is not loaded." The style sheet has a rule that makes that text red with a red border around the <p> element.

The JavaScript that you included first looks for the jQuery object, which is contained in a single dollar sign. That one dollar sign contains all of jQuery's functionality, which makes jQuery statements really short. If that's too short for you, you can also substitute "jQuery" for the dollar sign, which would have made that JavaScript example look like this:

```
if (jQuery) {
  jQuery(document).ready(
    function() {
      jQuery('p').addClass('tmpFrameworkLoaded');
      jQuery('p').text('jQuery successfully loaded and running!');
    }
  );
}
```

An event is attached to jQuery's `ready` event, which is executed as soon as the DOM is fully loaded, or all markup content, JavaScript and CSS, but not images. In old-time JavaScript, you would have made your JavaScript execute at page load, or the `onload` event. The `onload` event can be much slower, however, since it waits for all content and images to load before executing, instead of just content.

With an event attached to the `ready` event, you're ready to do something with the document. In this case, once the document is loaded, jQuery selects the `<p>` element and gives it the class name *tmpFrameworkLoaded*. Then jQuery selects the `<p>` element again and changes its text content to say "jQuery successfully loaded and running!" The addition of the class name results in the `<p>` element having green text with a green border around the element.

The preceding is a pretty simple, cut-and-dry test of jQuery's existence, and with this simple example, you see a huge difference with traditional, framework-less JavaScript. Without the jQuery framework, this is what the preceding example would have looked like:

```
window.onload = function() {
  var $p = document.getElementsByTagName('p')[0];

  $p.className = 'tmpFrameworkLoaded';

  if ($p.innerText) {
    $p.innerText = 'jQuery successfully loaded and running!';
  } else {
    $p.textContent = 'jQuery successfully loaded and running!';
  }
};
```

Programming Conventions

In web development, it's common for professional web designers, web developers — and anyone with a job title whose day-to-day activities encompass the maintenance of source code — to adopt standards and conventions with regard to how the source code is written. Standardization bodies like the W3C, who define the languages that you use to create websites, already decide on some standards for you. Some standards are not written, but are rather de facto standards. *De facto standards* are standards that have become accepted throughout the industry, despite not appearing in any official document developed by a standards organization.

Throughout this book, I talk about standards, de facto and official, and how to develop and design web-based documents and even web-based applications that take those standards into account. For example, I talk extensively about how to separate behavior (JavaScript) from presentation (CSS) and structure (XHTML). JavaScript written in this way is commonly referred to as *non-intrusive* JavaScript — it's non-intrusive because it supplements the content of a web document, and, were it turned off, the document would still be functional. CSS is used to handle all the presentational aspects of the document. And the structure of the document lives in semantically written XHTML. XHTML that is *semantically written* is organized meaningfully with the right markup elements and contains very little, if any at all, presentational components directly in the markup.

In addition to standards, I discuss how to develop web-based documents, taking into account different browser inconsistencies, discrepancies, and idiosyncrasies. There is some interactive functionality that nearly every browser handles differently; in those situations, other web professionals have already pioneered de facto standards that are used to bring all browsers into accord. The idea of a JavaScript foundational framework has become more popular and increasingly a dependency for so-called Web 2.0 applications, like the ones you'll learn to develop using the jQuery framework.

Before I begin the discussion of jQuery, in the coming sections, I provide a generalized overview of programming conventions and good practice that should be followed.

XHTML and CSS Conventions

It's important that your web documents be well-organized, cleanly written, and appropriately named and stored. This requires discipline and even an obsessive attention to the tiniest of details.

The following is a list of rules to abide by when creating XHTML and CSS documents:

- Catch errors in XHTML and CSS.
- When selecting ID and Class names, make sure that they are descriptive and are contained in a namespace. You never know when you might need to combine one project with another — namespaces will help you to prevent conflicts.
- When defining CSS, avoid using generic type selectors. Make your CSS more specific. This will also help with preventing conflicts.
- Organize your files in a coherent manner. Group files from the same project in the same folder; separate multiple projects with multiple folders. Avoid creating huge file dumps that make it difficult to locate and associate files.
- Avoid inaccessible markup. Stay away from frames, where possible. Organize your markup using semantically appropriate elements. Place paragraphs in `<p>` elements. Place lists in `<ul>` or `<ol>` elements. Use `<h1>` through `<h6>` for headings, and so on.
- If you are able to, also consider the loading efficiency of your documents. For development, use small, modularized files organized by the component; combine and compress those modularized files for a live production site.

In the following sections, I present some examples of why the preceding list of rules is important.

Catching Errors in XHTML and CSS

There are certain times when you won't be able to easily spot markup or style errors. More often than not, getting into a routine of indenting and spacing markup documents and style sheets will make it much easier to spot errors during the initial development of a document, and much easier to perform ongoing maintenance. However, neat and tidy development of a document isn't always an option. Maybe you've inherited an old content management system or have to deal with some other piece of software that generates your source code for you. Next I'll talk about what you can do to more easily detect and repair errors.

Markup Errors in XHTML and HTML

Markup errors typically come about from simple human error. You may forget to type in a closing tag for an element. You may forget to encode certain special characters. You may use an ID name more than once in a document by mistake.

If a web document contains errors, the browser may carry on as if everything is just fine and dandy, and it may not be obvious that it contains errors. Some errors go undetected because browsers are designed to handle errors in HTML as they are found. The browser decides what to do with an error when it comes to it and then simply moves on with processing the HTML document. (For example, it may be able to guess where a closing tag is supposed to be.) When an error is found, the browser tries to continue on and display a document to the end-user, and more often than not, it succeeds.

In some cases, you may notice a visual glitch and see clearly that something is out of place, but it's also possible that something not so obvious has been affected by the error. For example, you may try attaching an event with JavaScript, and the event doesn't fire. You may try manipulating the document with script by removing or inserting elements and find that the elements aren't being inserted, or are being inserted in the wrong place. The effects of markup errors like this are much more subtle. Markup errors do not appear in your browser's error console. The only place where a structural markup error will show up is in a validation of the document using the W3C's markup validation service located at `http://validator.w3.org`.

XHTML, on the other hand, is not forgiving of markup errors, and assuming that the browser properly supports XHTML, the browser won't attempt any kind of error correction when it encounters an error in an XHTML document. One type of markup error that will bring processing to a halt is an incorrectly specified MIME (Multipurpose Internet Mail Extensions) type.

The MIME standard is used by browsers and Web Servers to facilitate the automatic identification and handling of files, which is to say that a MIME type is part of what a browser uses to identify the contents of a document. XHTML documents are supposed to be served with an `application/xhtml+xml` MIME type. The following is one way of setting the MIME type for an XHTML document:

```
<!DOCTYPE html PUBLIC "-//W3C//DTD XHTML 1.0 Strict//EN"
                      "http://www.w3.org/TR/xhtml1/DTD/xhtml1-strict.dtd">
 <html xmlns='http://www.w3.org/1999/xhtml' xml:lang='en'>
   <head>
     <meta http-equiv='Content-Type'
           content='application/xhtml+xml; charset=UTF-8' />
   </head>
   <body>
```

In the preceding code example, the XHTML MIME type is set using a `<meta />` element that's included in the document headers. The `http-equiv` attribute included in a `<meta />` element is used to set HTTP headers within the markup document itself. In the preceding code example, the `Content-Type` HTTP header is being set, which, when supported by the browser, will force the browser to interpret an XHTML document as `application/xhtml+xml`, rather than `text/html`.

An XHTML document properly served with the `application/xhtml+xml` MIME type with markup errors like mismatched tags, or missing tags, or any markup error of any kind will result in what's commonly called the XML *yellow screen of death* (YSOD). The name *yellow screen of death* was coined because Mozilla's (and later, Firefox's) XML error messages appear against a yellow background, and XML error messages prevent the display of the document, which prevents the user from seeing a web page, hence the "death" part. Of course, the XML/XHTML error message isn't yellow in every browser, but the point is that, in properly served XHTML, one error could make a document unviewable by the end-user.

The yellow screen of death is also related to another error message, the blue screen of death, *which, of course, is the de facto name for error messages in the Windows Operating System that result in a complete system crash — at the time of the crash, an error message with white lettering on a blue screen is seen.*

XHTML 1.0 documents are not typically served with the correct, intended MIME type. Rather, they are usually served as an HTML document — which isn't technically illegal, as long as they are XHTML 1.0 documents. XHTML 1.1, on the other hand, must be served as `application/xhtml+xml`**.**

It's a good idea, if you're going the XHTML route, to properly serve the document with the `application/xhtml+xml` MIME type. Setting the XHTML MIME type is the best, most compatible approach, since browsers like IE that don't understand the XHTML MIME type will carry on and interpret the document as plain-old HTML, while Firefox, Safari, and the like will correctly interpret the XHTML document. If errors are present, these browsers won't show a rendered document but, rather, will show an error message complaining that something is awry in the document.

If you're going the XHTML route, keeping the document neat becomes a matter of keeping the document maintainable, and thus a matter of personal preference. Typically, dynamic websites strip the markup source of excess white space in order to reduce the size of the document for performance advantages, and even in the age of ubiquitous broadband connections, it's still a good idea to optimize a document for very slow dial-up connections, which are still in widespread use in rural areas. Dynamic websites typically also have the best of both worlds in place. That is to say, on a pre-production server, the website may serve uncompressed markup, while on a production server, the website serves compressed markup.

For your own sanity as a programmer, I strongly recommend that you maintain neat and organized markup, check your markup documents for validation errors using the W3C validation service, and consider using XHTML. Ultimately, however, XHTML or HTML is a matter of personal preference. Both are perfectly acceptable Internet standards for the creation of web documents. The examples in this book use the XHTML standard — however, these examples will work equally well with the HTML standard.

Errors in CSS

Errors in style sheets usually make themselves known by not displaying the style you applied.

However, errors in CSS can also be more subtle and difficult to spot. To catch errors in CSS, I recommend one of the two following approaches:

- ❑ Use Mozilla Firefox (or another browser that reports CSS errors), and look for CSS errors in the browser's Error Console. In Firefox, that's located in Tools?Error Console.
- ❑ Use the W3C's CSS validation service at `http://jigsaw.w3.org/css-validator`.

Either of these solutions will assist you in locating and extinguishing style-sheet errors.

It's also good practice to get into the habit of writing neat and organized CSS. Indent your style sheets with white space, and use line breaks to make the style sheets more maintainable. The browser doesn't care what your style sheet looks like, as long as the basic syntax is correct. You may add or remove white space to your heart's content.

I continue to revisit the topics of neat and organized source code throughout this book by way of example.

ID and Class Naming Conventions

Most web developers don't think too much about the topics of *namespacing* and *naming conventions*. Naming conventions are just as important in your markup ID and class names as namespacing is important in programming languages.

First, what is namespacing, and why do you need to do it? *Namespacing* is the concept of making your programs, source code, and so on tailored to a particular naming convention, in an effort to make your programs more portable and more capable of living in diverse, foreign programming environments. In other words, if you want to be able to directly insert a web application into your document, you want to be sure that the class and ID names, style sheets and script, and all the bits that make your web application what it is do not conflict with any applications that are already present in the document. Your applications should be fully self-contained and self-sufficient and not collide or conflict with any elements already present in a document.

What are some common ID names that people use in style sheets? Think first about what the typical components of a web application are. There's a body. There may be one or more columns. There may be a header and a footer, and there are lots of components that can potentially be identified as generic, redundant pieces that all web applications may have. Then, it stands to reason that plenty of websites are probably using ID and class names like *body, header, footer, column, left, right,* and the like. If you name an element with the ID or class name *body,* you have a very good chance of conflicting with an overwhelming majority of websites in existence today. To avoid this type of conflict, it's considered good practice to prefix ID and class names within a web application to avoid conflicts and namespace collisions. If you write an application called *tagger,* you might namespace that application by prefixing all of your ID and class names with the word *tagger.* For example, you might have *taggerBody, taggerHeader, taggerFooter,* and so on. It may be possible, however, that someone has already written an application called *tagger.* To be safe, you might do a Web search on the name you've chosen for your application to make sure that no one's already using that name. Typically, simply prefixing your ID and class names with your application's name is enough.

Additionally, it also helps to prefix ID and class names with type selectors in style sheets. *Type selectors* help you narrow down what to look for when modifying or maintaining a document. For example, the ID selector `#thisID` is ambiguous. You don't know what kind of element `thisID` is, and thus would likely have to scan the entire document to find it. But `div#thisID` is more specific. By including the `div` in the selector, you instantly know you're looking for a `<div>` element. Including the type in the selector also helps you in another way: When dealing with class names, you can have the same class name applied to different types of elements. While I may not condone that as good practice, at least in the style sheet, you can control which element gets which style. `span.someClass` and `div.someClass` are selectors that differentiate style based on the type of element, whereas `.someClass` is more ambiguous and applies to any element.

ID and class names should also be descriptive of their purpose in a semantically meaningful way. Keep in mind that an ID name can potentially be used in a URL as an HTML anchor. Which is better:

www.example.com/index.html#left or www.example.com/index.html#exRelatedDocuments? The latter ID anchor is namespaced ex for *example.com*, and RelatedDocuments is the name of the element; thus, the latter URL includes more information about what purpose the element serves and greatly increases the maintainability of the document in a very intuitive way. Additionally, the latter has more benefit in terms of search engine optimization (SEO). The former is too ambiguous and won't provide much in the way of SEO. Think of each of your ID and class names as though it is part of the URL of your document. Give each ID and class name that you create semantic names that convey meaning and purpose.

Generic Type Selectors

Generic type selectors are style-sheet rules that look something like this:

```
a {
    color: #29629E;
}
```

In the preceding style-sheet rule, you see what's probably a pretty common scenario, changing the color of every link in a document via a generic type selector that refers to all <a> elements. Generic type selectors should be avoided for the same reason that it is good to namespace ID and class names within a document, avoiding conflicts when multiple scripts or style sheets are combined in the same document. Instead, it's best practice to apply ID or class names to these elements, or at the very least, place them in a container that has an ID or class name, and only use descendent selectors when referencing those elements via a style sheet.

```
div#tmpBanner a {
    color: #29629E;
}
```

The preceding example avoids the pitfalls introduced by using a blanket, generic selector style-sheet rule by limiting the scope of the style-sheet rule's application. Now, only <a> elements that are descendants of a <div> with the ID name *tmpBanner* will receive the declaration color: #29629E;.

Storing and Organizing Files

How files are organized and stored is important to the maintainability of a document. You should maintain your documents in an easy-to-understand, easy-to-learn directory hierarchy. Different people have different approaches to storing and organizing files, obviously. What matters is that there is an organization scheme, rather than none at all. Some choose to store documents by type and then separate them by application, while others prefer to separate by application first, then sort by type.

Avoid Making Documents Inaccessible

Accessibility is also an important factor to consider in the design of a web document. You should do your best to make your JavaScript non-intrusive, but also avoid taking away a document's accessibility by either script or markup.

- ❑ Avoid using frames.
- ❑ Limit the number of images to those that actually contribute to the content of a document (as opposed to the design). Try to contain as much of the design as possible in CSS background

images, and keep images that contribute to the content in `<img />` elements. Be sure to include alt attributes that describe the image for each `<img />` element.

- Place content in semantically appropriate markup containers — use `<p>` for paragraphs, `<h1>` through `<h6>` for headings, for example.
- Make the design high contrast. Imagine what the document would look like in black and white through the eyes of someone with poor vision. Can you easily read the content?
- Avoid wandering too far away from established user-interface conventions. Can you distinguish hyperlinks from normal content?
- Make the content keyboard-accessible. Can you navigate without a pointing device?
- Make the content unobtrusive. Can you use the website without flash and JavaScript functionality? JavaScript and flash should enhance web content in a complementary way, not be a requirement.
- Avoid placing a large number of links at the beginning of every document. If you were listening to the content being read to you, rather than seeing it visually, would the experience be enjoyable?

Accessibility should be practiced to the point of becoming an automatic reflex. It should be cemented in your development practices in a fundamental way in the same way that namespacing, file organization, and validation are; but while other best practices can become second nature easily, it's also very easy to get into the habit of ignoring accessibility, so a conscious effort must be made to periodically review accessibility and ingrain accessibility in the development process.

Efficiency in Markup and CSS

Markup and CSS in a complex website can easily become large and bloated and drag down overall loading and execution times more and more. This can become particularly troublesome as the overall popularity of a site increases. As the complexity of a website increases, it becomes necessary to look into ways of streamlining the content. It's best to limit the number of external files being loaded, but all CSS and JavaScript should be included in at least one external file. Were JavaScript and CSS included directly in a document, the initial loading time would improve, but you'd also lose the advantage of caching JavaScript and CSS on the client side.

For the best of the best in efficiency, combine the following concepts:

- Server-side gzip compression
- Client-side caching
- Automatic compression of markup content
- Automatic compression and consolidation of multiple CSS and JavaScript files

When the preceding items are combined, you make the loading times of a web document the best possible; however, there are some caveats to consider that may at first seem contradictory:

- Maintainable markup should be written in a neat and organized manner. It should be well-spaced and indented and contain line breaks where appropriate.
- Good programming practice means modularized development, so break up your CSS and JavaScript by component and application. Make small, easy-to-digest chunks. This will speed up your ability to maintain and extend projects.

- Client-side caching can lead to headaches when updates are made to CSS or script files. Browsers will continue to use the old version of the CSS and script files after an update is made, when caching is working correctly.

The good news is, all of the preceding caveats can be overcome. The bad news is, it's not particularly easy to overcome them.

The best way to implement efficiency in markup, JavaScript, and CSS documents is to make the efficiency automatic. That is to say, write server-side applications that handle efficiency tasks for you. A well-designed professional content management system will work out those bits for you. It will allow you to make your JavaScript, markup, and CSS documents modularized, and separate them based on the task each is designed to perform, but automatically combine and compress those documents for you.

Unfortunately, not everyone can use a professional content management system to serve their content. For those individuals, there are some compromises to be made:

- JavaScript and CSS can be hand-compressed using a web-based utility like Dean Edwards's packer, `http://dean.edwards.name/packer`. Development can continue to be modularized, and the compression and consolidation portion of development simply becomes a manual task.
- You can limit the amount of white space you use in a document. Indent content with two spaces instead of four.

Overcoming the headaches with document caching, on the other hand, is a much easier task. You can force a browser to update a document by changing its path. For example, say you have the following script included in your markup:

```
<script src='/script/my.js' type='text/javascript'></script>
```

You change the path from /script/my.js to /script/my.js?lastModified=09/16/07. The latter references the same, my.js, but is technically a different path to the browser and, consequently, will force the browser into refreshing its cached copy of the document. The *?lastModified=09/16/07* portion of the path is what's called the *query string* portion of the path. The query string begins with a question mark and then contains one or more query string variables. Query string variables are used by a server-side programming language or client-side JavaScript to pass information from one document to another. In this example, there is no information being passed per se. You're including the time of the last modification, although I could have just as easily included the revision, or even a random string of characters. The inclusion of a query string in this example has only one purpose: to force the browser into refreshing the cached version of the document.

The same can be done with CSS:

```
<link type='text/css' rel='stylesheet' href='/styles/my.css?lastModified=09/16/07' />
```

In the preceding snippet of markup that includes an external CSS document, the query string is used to force a refresh of the browser's cached copy of the style sheet `my.css`.

In the next section, I talk about some conventions specific to JavaScript.

JavaScript Conventions

In JavaScript, there are several things that should be considered bad practice and avoided:

- **Include All Script in External Documents** — JavaScript code should only be included in external script files. Script should not be embedded in markup documents or be included inline, directly on markup elements.
- **Write Clean, Consistent Code** — JavaScript code should be neatly formatted and organized in a consistent, predicable way.
- **Namespace JavaScript Code** — JavaScript variables, functions, objects, and the like should be namespaced to minimize potential namespace conflicts and collisions with other JavaScript applications.
- **Avoid Browser Detection** — Browser detection should be avoided where possible. Instead, detect specific browser features.

In the next sections, I present cursory, generalized overviews of each of the preceding concepts.

Include All Script in External Documents

Part of making JavaScript non-obtrusive means making JavaScript complementary and supplemental, rather than required and mandatory. This concept is explored in detail throughout this book; however, it should be noted why this is the best approach.

Consider the following code example:

```
<!DOCTYPE html PUBLIC "-//W3C//DTD XHTML 1.0 Strict//EN"vvvvvv
                      "http://www.w3.org/TR/xhtml1/DTD/xhtml1-strict.dtd">
<html xmlns="http://www.w3.org/1999/xhtml" xml:lang="en">
    <head>
        <meta http-equiv="Content-Type"
              content="application/xhtml+xml; charset=UTF-8"/>
        <title>Inline JavaScript</title>
        <link rel='stylesheet' type='text/css' href='style.css' />
    </head>
    <body>
        <p>
            <img src='pumpkin.jpg' alt='Pumpkin' />
            <a href='javascript:void(0);'
               onclick='window.open(
                   "pumpkin.jpg",
                   "picture",
                   "scrollbars=no,width=300,height=280,resizable=yes"
               );'>Open Picture</a>
        </p>
    </body>
</html>
```

Combine the preceding markup with the following style sheet:

```
img {
    display: block;
```

```
        margin: 10px auto;
        width: 100px;
        border: 1px solid rgb(128, 128, 128);
    }
    body {
        font: 14px sans-serif;
    }
    p {
        width: 150px;
        text-align: center;
    }
```

The preceding code gives you something like what you see in **Figure 1-1**.

In **Figure 1-1**, you see what is probably a pretty common scenario: You have a thumbnail, and you can click to see a bigger version of the thumbnail. This is the kind of thing that JavaScript works well for — giving you the bigger version in a separate pop-up window that doesn't have any controls.

Now let's examine why what I did in **Figure 1-1** was the wrong way to go about adding this functionality.

Here are the problems with this approach:

- If JavaScript is disabled, viewing the larger picture doesn't work.
    - JavaScript can be disabled out of personal preference.
    - JavaScript can be disabled because of company policy.
    - JavaScript can be disabled if the end-user is using a handheld device or viewing the site through any kind of alternative medium.
- Search bots may not understand the JavaScript, so Search Engines may not properly index this content.
- Placing the JavaScript directly in the markup document adds unnecessary bloat and complexity to the markup document.

The overwhelming point in all of this is that inline JavaScript is a really bad way to approach adding complementary, interactive functionality to a web document.

Here is a better approach to the application presented in **Figure 1-1**. First, you take the inline JavaScript out of the markup and replace it with a reference to an externally loaded JavaScript. In the following example, I've named the externally loaded JavaScript `thumb.js`:

```
<!DOCTYPE html PUBLIC "-//W3C//DTD XHTML 1.0 Strict//EN"
                      "http://www.w3.org/TR/xhtml1/DTD/xhtml1-strict.dtd">
<html xmlns="http://www.w3.org/1999/xhtml" xml:lang="en">
    <head>
        <meta http-equiv="Content-Type"
              content="application/xhtml+xml; charset=UTF-8"/>
        <title>Inline JavaScript</title>
        <link rel='stylesheet' type='text/css' href='style.css' />
        <script type='text/javascript' src='thumb.js'></script>
```

```
    </head>
    <body>
        <p>
            <img src='pumpkin.jpg' alt='Pumpkin' />
            <a href='pumpkin.jpg'>Open Picture</a>
        </p>
    </body>
</html>
```

Then in the externally loaded JavaScript you do something like the following:

```
window.onload = function()
{
    var $nodes = document.getElementsByTagName('a');

    for (var $i = 0, $length = $nodes.length; $i < $length; $i++) {
        $nodes[$i].onclick = function($e) {
            window.open(
                this.href,
                "picture",
                "scrollbars=no,width=300,height=280,resizable=yes"
            );

            $e? $e.preventDefault() : (window.event.returnValue = false);
        };
    }
};
```

With the preceding bits of code, you get the same results that you saw in **Figure 1-1**, and an example of non-obtrusive JavaScript. Non-obtrusive JavaScript provides extended, interactive functionality within a web document, but does not do so in a way that obstructs using the document in a plain-vanilla manner. That is to say, with JavaScript disabled, you are still able to use the website and get what you need from it.

In the preceding example, the JavaScript is moved to an external document called *thumb.js*. thumb.js gets all <a> elements present in the document with `document.getElementsByTagName('a')`. Each <a> element is placed in an array called `$nodes`, and then a `for` loop is used to iterate through every <a> element present in the `$nodes` variable. This is done by making a counter, variable `$i`; then the number of <a> elements is assigned to a variable called `$length` via the `$nodes.length` property. Now the `for` loop will execute once for every <a> element present, and the variable `$i` will increment by a count of 1 each time. When the variable `$i` contains a count that's more than the number of <a> elements, execution of the `for` loop will end.

Inside the `for` loop, you have an `onclick` event that's assigned to each <a> element present in the `$nodes` array. An anonymous `function` is assigned to the `onclick` event. When a user clicks on an <a> element, the anonymous `function` will be executed. Within the anonymous `function`, the <a> element's properties are available in a special object called `this`. You see a call to the `window.open` method; the `href` property of the <a> element is passed as the path to open in the new window (`this.href`), then the window name and some window parameters are defined.

So far, the user clicks on an <a> element and gets a pop-up window. You want the window to pop up instead of initiating the default action that occurs when a user clicks on a link (which is for the browser to navigate to the document defined in the `href` attribute of the <a> element). Stopping the default action, unfortunately, depends on what browser you're using. IE has its way, and all the others have a standard way. The JavaScript code accounts for both in the following line:

```
$e? $e.preventDefault() : (window.event.returnValue = false);
```

The preceding line says that if the variable `$e` evaluates to a Boolean `true` value, execute the `preventDefault` method of the event object, as in, `$e.preventDefault();`, otherwise, if `$e` evaluates to a `false` value, evaluate this expression: `(window.event.returnValue = false)`. So if `$e` is true, use the standard W3C method for preventing the default action; if `$e` is false, use Microsoft's method for preventing the default action.

In this very simple example, you've seen how a really simple example can balloon into something much more complex. All of the concepts I've presented in this example are ones I continue to revisit throughout this book, but you get a pretty good idea of some of the challenges that non-obtrusive JavaScript prevents. You run into situations in which one browser has one way of doing things, and another has its way of doing things, and sometimes all of the popular browsers differ on how to go about accomplishing a given task. Therefore, doing JavaScript the right way often involves quite a bit more thought and planning. The good thing about this additional thought and planning is that it becomes second nature once you understand how to account for all of the browser differences. The good news is that there are people out there looking out for you, and who've already braved all the deep, dark corners of browser inconsistencies, incompatibilities, and lack of common, coherent standards.

At this point, you might be asking yourself, so what are the benefits of going through all of this hassle to get non-obtrusive, multiplatform JavaScript? I'm glad you asked.

- In the preceding example, if JavaScript had been disabled, the end-user could still have clicked on the link to see a larger version of the thumbnail image. This makes your website much more accessible.
- When JavaScript is included in an externally loaded file, you get a speed boost, since the JavaScript only has to be loaded once, and from there on is cached by the client browser.
- While it takes some planning, the cross-browser inconsistencies and incompatibilities can be completely overcome.
- You can achieve better search rankings, since search engines can now access and see all of your content.
- You'll appear more hip, all the girls (or guys) will like you, a pretty butterfly will land on your shoulder, there will be world peace, and so on.

Well, maybe not that last one, but non-obtrusive JavaScript is, simply, A Good Thing™.

Write Clean, Consistent Code

It's important to follow some predetermined criteria for producing clean, consistent, well-organized code. In the professional world, most programmers have a particular way they like to see their code formatted. Earlier in this section, I talked about how indenting and spacing markup and CSS documents can help you more easily catch errors in those documents and make those documents more maintainable. Well, the same can be applied to JavaScript, although, with JavaScript and other programming languages, programming conventions are typically much more defined, down to a very fine-grained level of detail. Here I talk about each of the programming conventions that I follow for writing JavaScript source code.

Indenting and Line Length

It's a good idea to indent your code so that it's easier to read and maintain. Take the following, for example:

```
window.onload=function(){var $nodes=document.getElementsByTagName('a');
for(var $i=0,$length=$nodes.length;$i<$length;$i++){$nodes[$i].onclick=function($e){
window.open(this.href,"picture","scrollbars=no,width=300,height=280,resizable=yes");
$e? $e.preventDefault():(window.event.returnValue=false);};}};
```

In the preceding block of code, you see the contents of thumb.js presented above in this section, formatted without any indenting or spacing. Now, imagine that the preceding code is 10,000 lines of code spread out over many files, all formatted the same way. It's not a bad idea to reduce spacing for a live, production script; in fact, many professionals use compression routines specifically for this. But those same professionals don't maintain their scripts in the compressed format and often have a rigid programming standard to which every script they produce must conform.

A common, fairly universal programming standard is setting the size of an indentation to four spaces, although some use just two spaces. This is in addition to setting a blanket rule that tabs cannot be used in place of individual spaces, even though, technically, a tab character results in less bytes added to a file when compared to four individual space characters. The "no tab" rule exists because of the wide variance in the interpretation of what a tab character is in text applications. Some text applications say that a tab character is equal to eight individual spaces. Some text applications say that a tab character is equal to four individual spaces, while others still let you explicitly define how big a tab character is. These variances have led to the tab character being unreliable. Most professional integrated developer environments (IDEs) let you define the [Tab] key on a keyboard as individual spaces, in addition to letting you define how many spaces to insert.

Some examples of IDEs are Adobe Dreamweaver, Zend Studio, and Microsoft Visual Studio: These are all development environments for either directly writing or generating source code. Additionally, most IDEs try to guess what you mean when writing a source document, by intelligently adjusting the number of spaces. For example, when you press [Return] to begin a new line in your source code document, the IDE can indent the new line with at least as much space as the preceding line. Most IDEs behave this way by default. Dreamweaver automatically inserts two spaces when you hit the [Tab] key. Zend Studio can be configured to insert spaces instead of tab characters when you press the [Tab] key.

Throughout this book, I try to use four characters for a [Tab] key, although limited space may sometimes require that I use two characters. Generally, the professional standard for client-side source code is two characters, since four characters makes file sizes much larger. I've stuck with four because concerns about file size and bandwidth usage can be addressed by compressing your source code when it's used on a production website.

Control Structures

Control structures include programming statements that begin with the keywords *if, if else, switch, case, else, for, while, try, catch,* and the like. Control structure programming statements are the building blocks of any programming language. Let's see how control structure statements should be formatted with regard to popular programming standards and guidelines.

Although, ultimately, different people have different preferences for how to write source code, there are two prevailing methods for formatting control structures in use by the majority of the professional programming community.

The following convention, which is formally called *K&R Style*, is included in Sun's Coding Standards Guidelines for Java:

```
if ($condition) {
    $something = 1;
} else if ($another) {
    $something = 2;
} else {
    $something = 3;
}
```

In the preceding code example, you see that the curly braces and the parentheses are used as markers for indention.

Compare the preceding to the next convention, which is known as *Allman Style*, which is the default in Microsoft Visual Studio:

```
if ($condition)
{
    $something = 1;
}
else if ($another)
{
    $something = 2;
}
else
{
    $something = 3;
}
```

In Allman Style, all the curly braces line up in the source code, which makes it easier to detect when one is missing, in addition to preventing typos like missing curly braces from occurring in the first place, since you have a visual aid for their placement.

When function calls, like `window.open` in the example, are very long, sometimes the function call is broken up over multiple lines to make it easier to read. To the browser,

```
window.open(
    this.href,
    "picture",
    "scrollbars=no,width=300,height=280,resizable=yes"
);
```

and

```
window.open(this.href, "picture", "scrollbars=no,width=300,height=280,resizable=yes");
```

are exactly the same. The former example just makes it easier for humans to parse the arguments present in the function call.

Sometimes these two conventions are mixed to form a third convention, which is known as the *One True Brace* convention. This convention is defined in the Coding Standards Guidelines for PHP's PEAR repository.

```
window.onload = function()
{
    var $nodes = document.getElementsByTagName('a');

    for (var $i = 0, $length = $nodes.length; $i < $length; $i++) {
        $nodes[$i].onclick = function($e) {
            window.open(
                this.href,
                "picture",
                "scrollbars=no,width=300,height=280,resizable=yes"
            );
            $e? $e.preventDefault() : (window.event.returnValue = false);
        };
    }
};
```

In the One True Brace convention, the function assigned to `window.onload` follows the Allman Style, while the code within it follows K&R Style. This is the convention that I prefer for writing JavaScript, since it's more compact and leads to smaller file size, although I prefer the Allman Style for writing non-JavaScript code for its greater readability, since with other languages, file size is less of an issue.

Which programming convention you use is a matter of personal taste. Often which convention to use can lead to endless battles among programming teams, since sometimes people have different tastes. You should use whichever convention makes the most sense for you. Although the three I've showcased are the most popular, there are a multitude of variations that exist out in the wild. More information about programming indention styles can be found on Wikipedia at `http://en.wikipedia.org/wiki/Indent_style`.

Optional Curly Braces and Semicolons

In the conventions above, you'll note that there is always a single space between the keyword that begins the control structure, like `if`, and the opening parenthesis. The following is a `switch` control structure using the first convention:

```
switch ($variable) {
    case 1:
        $condition = 'this';
        break;

    case 2:
        $condition = 'that';
        break;

    default:
        $condition = 'those';
}
```

Note in the preceding that no break statement appears in the default case. As the default, a break is implied, and it is necessary to include the break statement. I tend to deviate from the norm with how I prefer `switch` control structures to be written.

```
switch ($variable) {
    case 1:
    {
        $condition = 'this';
        break;
    };
    case 2:
    {
        $condition = 'that';
        break;
    };
    default:
    {
        $condition = 'those';
    };
}
```

I like to add curly braces around each case in the `switch` statement; I do this because I believe it makes the `switch` statement easier to read; however, ultimately, these are not necessary. Concerning optional curly braces, I always include them, even if they're technically optional. The same goes for semicolons. Terminating each line with a semicolon is technically optional in JavaScript, although there are some circumstances in which you won't be able to omit it. I include all optional semicolons and curly braces, as I think that this not only makes the code cleaner, more organized, and consistent, but also gives you a technical benefit. If you want to compress your code to remove all additional white space, comments, and so on, these optional bits suddenly are no longer optional, but needed to keep the program functional once it's been compressed. In the following example, you can see what I mean by optional components:

```
if ($condition)
    $something = 1
else if ($another)
    $something = 2
else
    $something = 3
```

In JavaScript, the preceding code is perfectly valid. The semicolon is implied where there is a line break. And as long as there is only a single statement being executed, technically you don't have to include curly braces. However, the above fails when it is compressed:

```
if ($condition) $something = 1 else if ($another) $something = 2 else $something = 3
```

The preceding fails with a syntax error when you try to execute it. It fails because the script interpreter has no idea where you intend one statement to end and the next to begin. The language could probably be extended to guess in some circumstances, but it's better to just be as explicit as possible.

Something else that you might think is odd is the inclusion of a semicolon after some function definitions. You'll see this in JavaScript because a function can be a type of data, just like a number is a type of data or a string is a type of data. In JavaScript, it's possible to pass a function around as you would a number or a string. You can assign a function to a variable and execute the function later. You've already seen an example of this, and here it is again in the following code example:

```
window.onload = function()
{
    var $nodes = document.getElementsByTagName('a');

    for (var $i = 0, $length = $nodes.length; $i < $length; $i++) {
        $nodes[$i].onclick = function($e) {
            window.open(
                this.href,
                "picture",
                "scrollbars=no,width=300,height=280,resizable=yes"
            );
            $e? $e.preventDefault() : (window.event.returnValue = false);
        };
    }
};
```

In the preceding code example, you can see that a function is being assigned to the `onload` event of the `window` object. The function definition is terminated with a semicolon. Again, that semicolon is technically optional in this example, but I include it because I want the code to work if it gets compressed, and I think that it makes the code more consistent, organized, and easier to follow.

Naming Variables, Functions, Objects, . . .

Variable naming is also accounted for in the coding standards I follow throughout this book. I always use the camelCase convention when naming variables, functions, objects, or anything that I can potentially invent a name for. I like to append a dollar sign ($) to local variable names (variables that are executed within the scope of the currently executing function or object method). I name global variables without a dollar sign to indicate that they are global. The dollar sign is technically optional in JavaScript. You aren't required to begin variable names with it, but I use it to assist with identifying variable scope. Also, it's worth noting that my use of the dollar sign originates from my roots as a PHP programmer, where the dollar sign is a required prefix for variable names. Some people find this convention odd, so, again, I implore you to do what makes the most sense to you.

Namespace JavaScript Code

It's important to think about the big picture when writing an application. Whether you're writing an application for your own use or writing an application that will be deployed in varying environments that you have no control over, you're likely to run into one problem at some point in your career: naming conflicts. I touched on this topic when I talked about namespacing class and ID names in your CSS and markup. The same principles I talked about there are also applicable to JavaScript. Your script applications need to run without invading the global namespace too much. I say "too much," because you'll need to invade it somewhat, but you need to do so in a controlled and intelligent way. As you may have done for your markup and CSS, namespacing your JavaScript may be as simple as sticking to object-oriented code, wrapping all of your programs in just one, or a handful of objects and then naming those objects in the global namespace in a non-invasive way. A common approach is to namespace those objects with a prefix of some kind that doesn't infringe on some other existing project. One example is how the jQuery JavaScript framework is namespaced. jQuery does a lot, but for all of the code that's included in jQuery, there are precious few intrusions made on the global namespace, the "jQuery" object, and the dollar sign method the jQuery object is aliased to. All of the functionality that jQuery provides is provided through those objects.

Without a well-thought-out approach to the namespacing problem, it's possible that your application may cause conflicts with others. It's best to just assume that everything you place in the global namespace will cause a conflict, and thus set out to make as minimal as possible an intrusion into the global namespace.

Avoid Browser Detection

Browser detection can be a real annoyance. You're surfing the Web using your favorite browser, and you hit a website that locks you out — not because your web browser is technically incapable, but because it didn't match what the website's creators presupposed would be capable. So, I propose the following:

- Make no assumptions about the capabilities of a visitor's browser.
- Test for feature compatibility, rather than a browser name or browser version.
- Account for the official standards and the de facto standards. (Official standards should take precedence — de facto standards will either become or be replaced by the former.)
- The world is always changing — what's most popular today may not remain the most popular in the months and years to come.
- It may be time to turn to a framework for some compatibility bridging.

Anyone remember a little company called Netscape? At one time, Netscape was the dominant, de facto standard. Now Netscape holds just under 0.6 percent of world market share, and Microsoft's IE is dominant. At its most popular, IE held more than 90 percent of the market. Now IE holds around 70 percent; Firefox holds 21 percent; and Safari holds roughly 7 percent, Opera and others have around 2 percent combined. The browsing market can and does fluctuate. In the real world, there are lots of people who use less popular browsers. And 2 percent may sound small at first glance, but keep in mind that is 2 percent of a very large number. According to `www.internetworldstats.com`, in 2008, as I write this, there are just over 1.4 billion Internet users world-wide, which is 21.9 percent of the world's population. Therefore, the so-called less popular browsers aren't really doing too shabby in the grand scheme of things, and while 2 percent sounds small, it's actually a pretty large base of users.

Summary

jQuery takes what would otherwise be a more complex or verbose task in plain-vanilla JavaScript, and it makes it much easier, sometimes reducing many lines to one or a few. Throughout this book, you will learn about what jQuery has to offer and how to use its simple, easy-to-understand API to write spectacular, professional-appearing web applications that have all the polish and sparkle of a Fortune 500 company.

In this chapter, I talked a little about what jQuery is, where it comes from, and who develops and maintains it; and I showed you how to install it and begin using it. In the next chapter, you get right down to business, learning about jQuery's powerful implementation of the Selectors API and its world-class Event API.

If you are interested in learning more about jQuery's origins, visit `www.jquery.com` and `www.ejohn.org`.

This chapter also covered some things that a good programmer will want to get into the habit of doing, such as adopting a formal programming convention and avoiding conflicts with others' code through using a namespace of some sort (whether that be via a feature provided by the language, or through prefixing the names that you use that make an impact on the global namespace). I've shown a few of the practices that I have adopted for myself, although I should emphasize that it doesn't matter what programming convention that you adopt, but rather that you adopt one. The premise of a programming convention is that you have a set of rules that you can follow to format your code so that it is neat, organized, and easy to follow. My conventions might not be what you want, but there are many others to choose from.

You should avoid detecting the user's browser, especially when it may lead to one group or another being locked out from functionality.

Your code should take advantage of client-side caching and the increase in performance it provides.

In my opinion, it is better to write code in neatly organized modules and combine those into a larger script later using server-side programming.

Finally, it is also important that you adopt standards for the presentation and maintenance of client-side markup and CSS. Choose either XHTML or HTML, since both are accepted standards. I personally use XHTML, although XHTML may be too strict for your taste. Use the W3C's validation services to discover errors in your markup or your CSS, as sometimes errors in CSS or markup can cause errors in your JavaScript.

2

Selecting and Filtering

In this chapter, I talk about jQuery's sophisticated implementation of a Selectors API, which provides the ability to select elements in the DOM using selectors just like you use in CSS. jQuery's Selectors API allows you to select one or more elements from the DOM using a selector, then you can either use that result set, or you can pass those elements on to be filtered down to a more specific result set.

If you've never heard of a selector before, then I recommend that you have a look at my book, *Beginning CSS: Cascading Style Sheets for Web Design*, 2nd ed. (Wrox, 2004; ISBN 978-0-7645-7642-3), which has extensive coverage of selectors.

In CSS, you can apply style to one or more elements by writing a style sheet. You choose which elements to style based on the syntax that appears in the first part of a CSS rule, before the first curly brace, which is known as the *selector*. Here is a sample CSS selector:

```
body form#hProductSummaryDialogue {
    display: block;
    position: absolute;
    z-index: 1;
    top: 22px;
    left: 301px;
    right: 0;
    bottom: 24px;
    width: auto;
    margin: 0;
    border: none;
    border-bottom: 1px solid rgb(180, 180, 180);
}
```

Using markup and CSS, you are able to assign IDs and class names to elements, and you are able to control the presentational aspects of elements very specifically using selectors. In jQuery, that concept of selectors as applied to CSS is also applied to the concept of the *DOM*, or *Document Object Model*. In the DOM, you have available to you every element that exists in the markup of your document, and you are able to travel the DOM and select the elements you want to work with using selectors, just like you use in your CSS style sheets.

Once you've selected elements from the DOM, you can apply behavior to them. You can make something happen when a user clicks on an element, for example. You can make something happen when the user's mouse cursor comes over or leaves an element. Basically, you can make your web documents look and behave more like desktop applications. You are no longer limited to static content as you are with markup and CSS alone — you can apply behavior as well.

In this chapter, I describe how to use jQuery's Selectors API to retrieve elements from a document, in addition to providing some practical examples of usage. I also describe how you can chain calls in jQuery. One use for this is filtering elements, which you would do to reduce a larger selection of elements down to a smaller selection. Finally, I discuss how jQuery's Event API works in relation to the W3C's Event API and Microsoft's.

The Origin of the Selectors API

The concept of a *Selectors API* was first dreamed up by Dean Edwards, a JavaScript guru, who first created a Selectors API in JavaScript in a free, Open Source package he called *cssQuery*. Not long after Dean pioneered the idea and produced a working, proof-of-concept implementation of that idea, it was taken up and expanded upon by John Resig (and other JavaScript framework authors, mutually exclusive to John's efforts) and implemented in his jQuery framework. This led to some back-and-forth collaboration and competition between Dean, John, and other JavaScript framework authors, which resulted in much needed performance boosts in these ad hoc implementations, which at their conception were quite slow in some scenarios.

Not long after Dean came up with the concept of a Selectors API, W3C members and editors Anne van Kesteren and Lachlan Hunt drafted it into a specification for the W3C. The official W3C Selectors API involves two methods, one for selecting a single element called `document.querySelector()` and one for selecting multiple elements called `document.querySelectorAll()`.

The names for the official API were under considerable debate for quite some time, as no browser makers could agree on the names used. The names were finally put to a vote, with these names being the ones decided on. The controversy surrounding the names was not without merit, as this API is quite possibly the most important change to JavaScript that will have a lasting impact for years to come. It's important in that, in one fell swoop, it replaces methods like `document.getElementById`, `document.all`, *and* `document.getElementsByTagName`, *which are no longer really needed — since these methods let you use selector syntax, you can select by ID, by tag name, by class name, or by context, via whatever selectors the browser already supports for CSS.*

As I write this, the W3C version is a Candidate Recommendation, and `document.querySelector` and `document.querySelectorAll` are implemented natively in Internet Explorer 8, Safari 3, Firefox 3.1, and Opera 10. For once, a new feature is present and accounted for in the latest releases of all of the major browsers!

The great thing about jQuery and other JavaScript frameworks is that they had their own versions of the Selectors API already implemented prior to its native inclusion in browsers, which allows them to use the native implementation, if it is available. Using the native implementation makes selecting elements screamingly fast. Otherwise, if the user has an older browser, the framework can fall back on its own, slower, JavaScript-based implementation. This means that when using a JavaScript framework like jQuery, the Selectors API is ubiquitously available across all platforms it supports. jQuery is officially compatible with IE 6+, Firefox 1.5+, Safari 2.0.2+, and Opera 9+.

Using the Selectors API

Using the Selectors API in jQuery is very easy. First, you must know that everything you want to do with jQuery originates from a single, very simply named object that is called `$`. That's right, its name is a single dollar sign. As I mentioned back in Chapter 1, you can also use "jQuery" in place of the dollar sign, but from here on throughout this book, I will use only the dollar sign, and I will refer to it either as "the dollar sign object" or "the dollar sign method," depending on context, because it is really both a method and an object at the same time.

The dollar sign is both a method and an object because it can be used like a function call, but it also has member properties and methods that you can call. The dollar sign is named after a single dollar sign for one reason only, and that is to reduce the amount of code that you have to write. This is why a dollar sign is used instead of, say, `document.getElementsBySelector()`, which is very long, verbose, and annoying to type out.

Here's a very simple example of how you would use this method with a selector to add a click behavior to a collection of links. Basically, the object of the following code is to force the links to open in a new window, instead of using the "target" attribute, which does not validate under XHTML Strict.

Let's say that you have a markup document that looks like this:

```
<!DOCTYPE html PUBLIC "-//W3C//DTD XHTML 1.0 Strict//EN"
    "http://www.w3.org/TR/xhtml1/DTD/xhtml1-strict.dtd">
<html xmlns='http://www.w3.org/1999/xhtml' xml:lang='en'>
  <head>
    <meta http-equiv='content-type' content='text/html; charset=utf-8' />
    <meta http-equiv='content-language' content='en-us' />
    <title>Link</title>
    <script type='text/javascript'
            src='../../../Source Code/jQuery/jQuery.js'>
    </script>
    <script type='text/javascript' src='Figure 2-1.js'></script>
    <link type='text/css' href='Figure 2-1.css' rel='stylesheet' />
  </head>
  <body>
    <ul id='tmpFavorites'>
        <li><a href='http://www.wrox.com'>Wrox</a></li>
        <li><a href='http://www.gizmodo.com'>Gizmodo</a></li>
        <li><a href='http://www.apple.com'>Apple</a></li>
        <li><a href='http://www.jquery.com'>jQuery</a></li>
    </ul>
  </body>
</html>
```

In the preceding markup document, you have a simple unordered list that contains four links. You take that markup and put it with the following CSS:

```
body {
    font: 16px sans-serif;
}
ul {
    list-stlye: none;
```

```
        margin: 0;
        padding: 0;
    }
    a {
        text-decoration: none;
    }
```

The preceding CSS document does little more than make that list look a little prettier — it neither really adds to nor takes away from the example.

Finally, you add the following JavaScript document to the markup:

```
var tmpExample = {
  ready : function() {
    // Get all links...
    $('ul#tmpFavorites li a').click(
      function($e) {
        $e.preventDefault();
        window.open(this.href, 'FavoriteLink', '');
      }
    );
  }
};

$(document).ready(tmpExample.ready);
```

The preceding code, all put together, should look something like what you see in **Figure 2-1**.

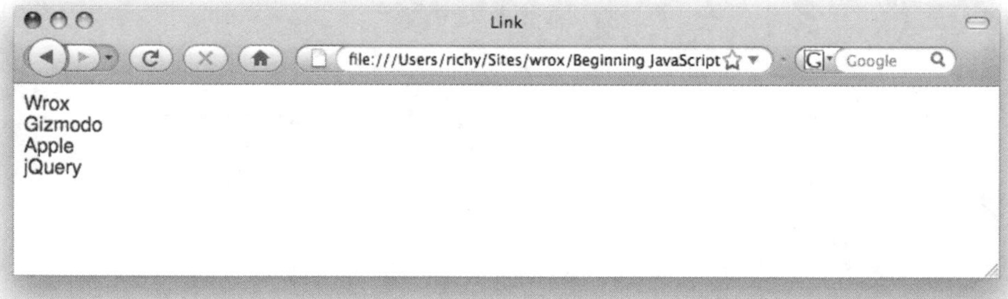

Figure 2-1

When you click on a link in the example, you should see the link open in a new window or tab, depending on how you have your browser's preferences set up to handle pop-up windows.

In the preceding example, you're using JavaScript to force the links in the `<ul>` element with ID name *tmpFavorites* to open in a new window or tab. To do this, in the JavaScript, you created a JavaScript Object Literal, which isn't the only way to create a new object — there are lots of ways to do this, but I just happen to like this one. The new object is called `tmpExample`, and it has one member method, called `ready`; then inside the `ready` method are all the things you want to do when the document is ready.

I don't go into much detail on the topic of object-oriented JavaScript, preferring instead to stick to the topic of jQuery. If you'd like to learn more about object-oriented JavaScript, I recommend Nicholas C. Zakas's excellent, critically acclaimed Professional JavaScript for Web Developers, *also from Wrox Press (2005; 2nd ed., 2009).*

As I touched on briefly in Chapter 1, jQuery provides its own event called `ready`, which is fired as soon as the DOM has finished loading, which is different from the `onload` or `load` event, in that with the `load` event, you have to wait for all the images to load too before that event will fire. Most of the time, you don't need to wait so long; you just want to start working with the document and adding behavior as soon as the DOM has finished loading. That's what the last line of code does:

```
$(document).ready(tmpExample.ready);
```

The preceding line of code attaches an event that fires when the DOM has finished loading, at which time the function `tmpExample.ready` is called and executed. Note that when you reference `tmpExample.ready`, you do so without adding parentheses to the function reference — parentheses cause the function reference to be executed immediately, whereas without the parentheses you are simply referencing the function. In this case, you want the function reference to be executed when the document is ready, instead of immediately, so you assign the function to the event by referencing it without parentheses. With parentheses, you are assigning the return value of the executed function, instead of the function itself.

Now that the DOM is loaded, you want to add behaviors to the document using script. The first item is an example of jQuery's Selectors API in action: it is a function call to the dollar sign method that uses a selector that picks a `<ul>` element with the ID name *tmpFavorites* that looks for descendant `<li>` elements within that `<ul>` element, then looks for descendant <a> elements within the `<li>` elements.

```
$('ul#tmpFavorites li a')
```

Once those <a> elements are selected, you more than likely want to do something with them. In this example, you add a `click` event to each of the <a> elements that you selected. The `click` event is added via a `click` method that is unique to jQuery:

```
  $('ul#tmpFavorites li a').click();
```

What you see here is an example of how jQuery lets you chain methods together. First, you selected a bunch of <a> elements; now, you're applying a `click` event directly to each of those <a> elements via a new method called `click()` that's chained to the end of your selection.

Within the `click()` method, you are passing a single anonymous (i.e., nameless) function that contains the programming that you want to be executed when each <a> element is clicked on by a user.

```
  $('ul#tmpFavorites li a').click(
    function($e) {
      $e.preventDefault();
      window.open(this.href, 'FavoriteLink', '');
    }
  );
```

The anonymous function contains one argument called $e, which represents the event object. The event object is just like what you would use with the standard W3C Event API, and works even in Internet Explorer, which does not natively support the W3C Event API at the time of this writing. Internet Explorer is able to use the standard API because jQuery has patched the problem areas and created a seamless API behind the scenes. No browser upgrade required!

Next, the function call `$e.preventDefault();` prevents the default action from occurring. The default action varies depending on what element you're referring to. In the case of the `<a>` element, the default action would be to navigate the window the user is using to the link specified in the `href` attribute of the `<a>` element. `$e.preventDefault()` prevents that default action from occurring, since you want the link to open in a new window or tab instead. If you were to omit that line, `$e.preventDefault();`, you would find that the link opens in a new window or tab in addition to the main window where the user clicked on the link, and also navigates to that page.

Finally, the code includes the line that causes the link to open in a new window or tab:

```
window.open(this.href, 'FavoriteLink', '');
```

The `window.open()` method is called with the value of the `href` attribute as its first value, followed by the name of the window or tab, followed by the arguments used for controlling the presentation of the window; an empty string causes this method to behave similarly to the `target` attribute with a value of `_blank`.

The following "Try It Out" takes what you've just learned about jQuery and the Selectors API and gives you an opportunity to try it out for yourself. (Remember, this book's source code for all of the "Try It Out" exercises, and the examples of each section, is available via download for free from www.wrox.com.)

Try It Out Using the Selectors API

Example 2-1

For a hands-on demonstration of jQuery's Selectors API, follow these steps:

1. Create the following markup document in your text editor, and save the document as *Example 2-1.html*:

```
<!DOCTYPE html PUBLIC "-//W3C//DTD XHTML 1.0 Strict//EN"
    "http://www.w3.org/TR/xhtml1/DTD/xhtml1-strict.dtd">
<html xmlns='http://www.w3.org/1999/xhtml' xml:lang='en'>
  <head>
    <meta http-equiv='content-type' content='text/html; charset=utf-8' />
    <meta http-equiv='content-language' content='en-us' />
    <title>Link</title>
    <script type='text/javascript'
            src='../../../Source Code/jQuery/jQuery.js'>
    </script>
    <script type='text/javascript' src='Example 2-1.js'></script>
    <link type='text/css' href='Example 2-1.css' rel='stylesheet' />
  </head>
  <body id='tmpDialogueExample'>
    <form action='javascript:void(0);' method='post'>
      <p>
```

```
          In jQuery, the selector API allows you to select elements from
          the DOM, just like you do in CSS stylesheets.  This simple dialogue
          contains a few selector API examples.
        </p>
        <p>
          <input type='submit' name='tmpDialogueOpen'
                 id='tmpDialogueOpen' value='Open Dialogue' />
        </p>
        <div id='tmpDialogue'>
          <input type='submit' name='tmpDialogueClose'
                 id='tmpDialogueClose' value='Close Dialogue' />
        </div>
      </form>
    </body>
  </html>
```

2. Create the following CSS document in your text editor, and save the CSS document in the same folder where you saved the previous HTML document, as *Example 2-1.css*:

```
body {
    font: 16px sans-serif;
}
div#tmpDialogue {
    display: none;
    position: absolute;
    top: 50%;
    left: 50%;
    width: 500px;
    height: 500px;
    margin: -251px 0 0 -251px;
    border: 1px solid blue;
    background: lightblue;
}
body#tmpDialogueExample div.tmpDialogueOn {
    display: block;
}
input#tmpDialogueClose {
    position: absolute;
    bottom: 5px;
    right: 5px;
    width: 100px;
}
```

3. Enter the following JavaScript, and save this as yet another document in the same folder as your HTML and CSS as *Example 2-1.js*:

```
var tmpExample = {
  ready : function() {
    $('input#tmpDialogueOpen').click(
      function($e) {
        $e.preventDefault();
        $('div#tmpDialogue').addClass('tmpDialogueOn');
      }
```

```
            );

            $('input#tmpDialogueClose').click(
              function($e) {
          $e.preventDefault();
          $('div#tmpDialogue').removeClass('tmpDialogueOn');
        }
      );
    }
  };

  $(document).ready(tmpExample.ready);
```

Keep in mind that the examples that you create and the examples I demonstrate in each section must also take into account your path to jQuery that you made back in Example 1-1 in Chapter 1, when you installed and tested jQuery. If all is right and good, you should see something like the screenshot in **Figure 2-2**.

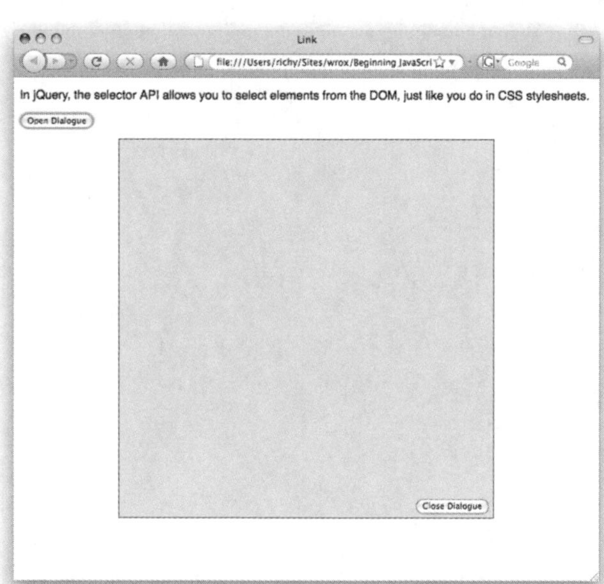

Figure 2-2

In Example 2-1, you see a little more of what jQuery can do with selectors (and a little beyond selectors even). What you have is a very simple implementation of a markup and CSS-driven pop-up.

In the markup, you lay the structural groundwork for your pop-up.

```
<form action='javascript:void(0);' method='post'>
  <p>
    In jQuery, the selector API allows you to select elements from
```

```
        the DOM, just like you do in CSS stylesheets.  This simple dialogue
        contains a few selector API examples.
      </p>
      <p>
        <input type='submit' name='tmpDialogueOpen'
               id='tmpDialogueOpen' value='Open Dialogue' />
      </p>
      <div id='tmpDialogue'>
        <input type='submit' name='tmpDialogueClose'
             ' id='tmpDialogueClose' value='Close Dialogue' />
      </div>
    </form>
```

It should be noted that you don't really need a `<form>` element to make this work, and you also don't really need name attributes on your `<input>` elements — these are included simply to make things validate. Also, a more responsible implementation will also take into account that some people don't have JavaScript enabled, whether by paranoia or by strict IT policy. You should account for that in your design — however, to keep things simple, I've ignored that requirement.

Structurally speaking, things are pretty simple; you have a button to open your dialogue. You have a `<div>` element that contains the dialogue itself, and within that dialogue you have a button to close the dialogue. It doesn't look particularly pretty, but it works.

In the CSS, you see how things really come together, "presentationally" speaking. First, you have a rule that sets the font and font size for the `<body>` element; then, you have a rule that positions the `<div>` element with ID name *tmpDialogue* absolutely and then offsets the position by 50 percent on the top and left sides. You have a static width and height set, which is required, so that you can offset the top and left margin to center the dialogue. Centering is achieved by positioning top and left 50 percent, then applying a negative margin to the top and left sides that is equal to half of the width + left and right padding + left and right borders, and half of the height + top and bottom padding + top and bottom borders. In this case, the width is 500 pixels, and there is 1 pixel (px) of border on the left and right sides. So the value you want to divide by 2 is 502, which comes to 251. The height value is also 502, so that also comes to 251. You apply a negative margin of 251 pixels to the top and left sides, which results in the dialogue being perfectly centered.

```
div#tmpDialogue {
    display: none;
    position: absolute;
    top: 50%;
    left: 50%;
    width: 500px;
    height: 500px;
    margin: -251px 0 0 -251px;
    border: 1px solid blue;
    background: lightblue;
}
```

The dialogue is also set to `display: none;` by default, which makes it invisible. To make the dialogue visible, you use JavaScript to add a class name to the `<div>` element with ID name *tmpDialogue*. The class name you add is *tmpDialogueOn*. To make the `display: block;` declaration work in the next rule, you have to think about specificity in CSS. An ID is more specific than a class name, so to make the dialogue visible, you have to reference an ID name in the CSS rule. The approach I take is to give the `<body>`

element an ID name, in this case, *tmpDialogueExample*, and then reference the class name for the `<div>` for the dialogue via a descendant selector. This makes the selector `body#tmpDialogueExample div.tmpDialogueOn` more specific than `div#tmpDialogue`, which means that when the class name *tmpDialogueOn* is present, the dialogue is on, and when it is not, the dialogue is off.

```
body#tmpDialogueExample div.tmpDialogueOn {
    display: block;
}
```

The last rule in the style sheet is very simple: It positions the `<input>` element with ID name *tmpDialogueClose* to the lower right-hand corner of the dialogue, 5 pixels from the bottom and 5 pixels from the left. A fixed width is set to correct a sizing glitch in IE7 and IE6.

```
input#tmpDialogueClose {
    position: absolute;
    bottom: 5px;
    right: 5px;
    width: 100px;
}
```

That brings me to the JavaScript. Like the example you saw earlier in this section, I set up an object literal called `tmpExample` with one method called `ready`, and that method is set to execute using jQuery's `ready` event. The method in the object literal can actually have any name, but I like using *ready* because it's more semantically correct. Some people like to call the method loaded when the document is ready `init` (short for "initiate") — use whatever makes sense for you. As to why I set up an object literal, and not a stand-alone function, I like to minimize pollution of the global namespace as much as possible. This helps to avoid naming conflicts with third-party scripts.

Within the `ready` method, two things happen: An event is set to happen when the user clicks on the `<input>` element with ID name *tmpDialogueOpen*, and another event is set to happen when the user clicks on the `<input>` element with ID name *tmpDialogueClose*.

First, I select the `<input>` element with the dollar sign method:

```
$('input#tmpDialogueOpen')
```

Then, I directly add a `click` event to that element using jQuery's `click()` method. The function call to the `click` method is chained right to the back of the selection.

```
$('input#tmpDialogueOpen').click();
```

The `click` method receives a single argument, which is an anonymous function:

```
function($e) {
  $e.preventDefault();
  $('div#tmpDialogue').addClass('tmpDialogueOn');
}
```

This function is executed every time a click occurs on the `<input>` element. The function takes one argument, which contains the event object; in this example, the event object is placed in the variable named `$e`. The event object lets you get information about the event that occurred and control the outcome of the event. In this case, you want to prevent the default action from occurring. The default action for an `<input>` element with the `type` attribute set to `submit` results in the form being submitted to the URL referenced in the action attribute of the `<form>` element. Of course, for this example, I set the action attribute to `javascript:void(0);`, which also prevents the form from being submitted, so preventing the default action isn't technically needed. But what if I were to return to this `<form>` later and change the `action` attribute? Let's say I wanted to be a responsible JavaScript programmer and account for situations in which the user does not have JavaScript enabled. One thing I could do is set the `action` attribute to a new page that contains the data I would have displayed in the JavaScript-driven pop-up dialogue. I could add a `target="_blank"` attribute to the `<form>` element, which would result in the pop-up dialogue being opened in a new window, and allow my content to continue to function in the absence of JavaScript. Of course, I would also have to use an XHTML Transitional Doctype instead of Strict, since the target attribute isn't allowed in XHTML Strict. So, in any case, thinking about how you would continue to build on and expand your web page in the future — it's good practice to provision for as much as possible when writing your script.

With the default action canceled, the next thing that happens is making the dialogue visible. To do that, you use the dollar sign method to select the `<div>` element with ID name *tmpDialogue*. And next you chain another jQuery method to the end of the selection called `addClass()`. As the name implies, `addClass()` adds a class name to the element; in this case, the class name you're adding is *tmpDialogueOn*. Remembering the style sheet that you created, adding this class name to the dialogue makes it visible.

Then for the Close Dialogue button, you do the same as you did for the Open Dialogue button; but this time, you're removing the class name to make the dialogue invisible again.

```
$('input#tmpDialogueClose').click(
  function($e) {
    $e.preventDefault();
    $('div#tmpDialogue').removeClass('tmpDialogueOn');
  }
);
```

As you can see, jQuery can help with something trivial like making a pop-up dialogue. In this case, however, jQuery could have done even more because as you will see later on the book, in Chapter 15, jQuery can provide just about everything you need to do a pop-up dialogue like this, even including fancy animated transitions — all you have to do is provide the content that you want to use and how you want it to look.

jQuery supports more selectors than browsers support natively for CSS. For example, jQuery supports many advanced selectors defined in the CSS 2.1 and CSS 3 specifications. In addition to advanced selector support, jQuery introduces some selectors of its own that are impractical for CSS.

Appendix B contains a reference table of all selectors supported by jQuery.

Filtering a Selection

jQuery has a very innovative feature, in that, every method it provides returns the jQuery object. In previous examples, you saw how this works by making a selection, and then doing something with that selection, like adding a `click` event.

There are lots of ways you can take a larger selection of elements and narrow it down in jQuery. In this section, I present some of the ways you can narrow a selection.

Searching within a Selection with find()

jQuery's find() method lets you perform a selection within a selection. This concept is illustrated in the following example. Let's say you have the following markup:

```
<!DOCTYPE html PUBLIC "-//W3C//DTD XHTML 1.0 Strict//EN"
    "http://www.w3.org/TR/xhtml1/DTD/xhtml1-strict.dtd">
<html xmlns='http://www.w3.org/1999/xhtml' xml:lang='en'>
  <head>
    <meta http-equiv='content-type' content='text/html; charset=utf-8' />
    <meta http-equiv='content-language' content='en-us' />
    <title>Link</title>
    <script type='text/javascript'
            src='../../../Source Code/jQuery/jQuery.js'>
    </script>
    <script type='text/javascript' src='Figure 2-3.js'></script>
    <link type='text/css' href='Figure 2-3.css' rel='stylesheet' />
  </head>
  <body>
    <ul id='tmpFavorites'>
        <li><a href='http://www.wrox.com'>Wrox</a></li>
        <li><a href='http://www.gizmodo.com'>Gizmodo</a></li>
        <li><a href='http://www.apple.com'>Apple</a></li>
        <li><a href='http://www.jquery.com'>jQuery</a></li>
    </ul>
  </body>
</html>
```

The preceding markup is that familiar list of hyperlinks from earlier in this chapter. Combine the preceding markup with the following CSS:

```
body {
    font: 16px sans-serif;
}
ul#tmpFavorites {
    list-style: none;
    margin: 0;
    padding: 0;
}
ul#tmpFavorites li {
    margin: 1px;
    padding: 3px;
}
a {
    text-decoration: none;
}
li.tmpFound {
    background: yellowgreen;
}
```

Then, the following JavaScript is added:

```
var tmpExample = {
  ready : function() {
    $('ul#tmpFavorites').find('li').addClass('tmpFound');
  }
};

$(document).ready(tmpExample.ready);
```

The source code in the preceding examples results in the output that you see in **Figure 2-3**.

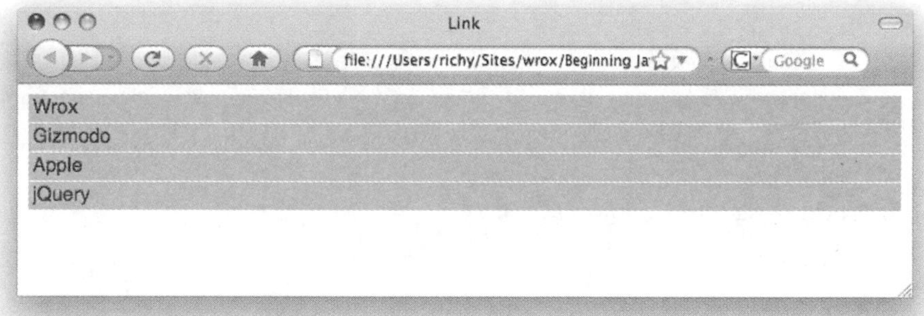

Figure 2-3

In the preceding example, you see an example of jQuery's `find()` method. Basically, `find()` lets you take a selection and refine it. In this example, first you selected the `<ul>` element with ID name *tmpFavorites*; then, once you had that selection, you looked at the `<ul>`'s descendants to find every `<li>` element within it. Once you had those `<li>` elements, you added the class name *tmpFound* to each of them. This method would be more useful if, for example, you wanted to take the `<ul>` element and add some events to it, and then do something with each of its children `<li>` elements. In that scenario, you can assign the selection of the original `<ul>` element to a variable, perform some actions on the `<ul>` element using that variable, and then reuse that selection to find the `<li>` elements and do something with those.

The `find()` method gives you the ability to search for elements within a selection you've already made.

Finding an Element's Siblings with `siblings()`

The next method I demonstrate shows you how to find all of one element's siblings using the `siblings()` method. You begin with the following markup:

```
<!DOCTYPE html PUBLIC "-//W3C//DTD XHTML 1.0 Strict//EN"
    "http://www.w3.org/TR/xhtml1/DTD/xhtml1-strict.dtd">
<html xmlns='http://www.w3.org/1999/xhtml' xml:lang='en'>
  <head>
    <meta http-equiv='content-type' content='text/html; charset=utf-8' />
    <meta http-equiv='content-language' content='en-us' />
    <title></title>
```

```
        <script type='text/javascript'
                src='../../../Source Code/jQuery/jQuery.js'>
        </script>
        <script type='text/javascript' src='Figure 2-4.js'></script>
        <link type='text/css' href='Figure 2-4.css' rel='stylesheet' />
      </head>
      <body>
        <h4>Places in Middle-Earth</h4>
        <ul id='tmpPlaces'>
          <li>Mordor</li>
          <li>Gondor</li>
          <li>Rohan</li>
          <li>Moria</li>
          <li>Lothlorien</li>
          <li>Dead Marshes</li>
          <li class='tmpExampleCity'>Minas Tirth</li>
        </ul>
      </body>
    </html>
```

A little style is added with the following CSS:

```
body {
    font: 16px sans-serif;
}
h4 {
    font-size: 16px;
    margin: 0 0 5px 0;
}
ul#tmpPlaces {
    list-style: none;
    margin: 0;
    padding: 0;
}
ul#tmpPlaces li {
    margin: 1px;
    padding: 3px;
}
li.tmpSiblings{
    background: khaki;
}
```

Then, the following JavaScript:

```
var tmpExample = {
  ready : function() {
    $('ul#tmpPlaces li.tmpExampleCity').siblings().addClass('tmpSiblings');
  }
};

$(document).ready(tmpExample.ready);
```

The preceding source code gives you the output you see in **Figure 2-4**.

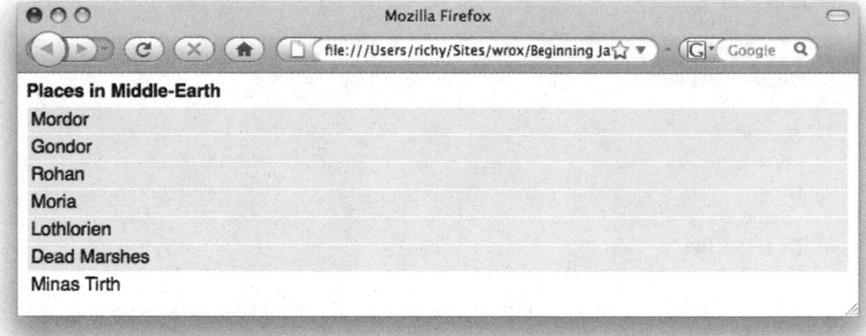

Figure 2-4

In the preceding example, you see another method that's very similar to the `find()` method that you saw in the last section; only this time, the selection is filtered to include all of the element's siblings. First, you select the `<li>` element with class name *tmpExampleCity* via the selector `ul#tmpPlaces li.tmpExampleCity`. Then the selection is filtered to include all of the `<li>` elements with class name *tmpExampleCity*'s siblings, or in other words, all of the `<li>` elements except that one.

The `siblings()` method, like the `find()` method, could also include a selector to filter even more. First, let's modify the markup of the last example to include more class names:

```
<h4>Places in Middle-Earth</h4>
<ul id='tmpPlaces'>
  <li>Mordor</li>
  <li class='tmpRealmOfMen'>Gondor</li>
  <li class='tmpRealmOfMen'>Rohan</li>
  <li>Moria</li>
  <li class='tmpRealmOfElves'>Lothlorien</li>
  <li>Dead Marshes</li>
  <li class='tmpExampleCity'>Minas Tirth</li>
</ul>
```

Then modify the JavaScript of the last example, so that it looks for only siblings that have the class name *tmpRealmOfMen*:

```
var tmpExample = {
 ready : function() {
  $('ul#tmpPlaces li.tmpExampleCity')
    .siblings('.tmpRealmOfMen')
    .addClass('tmpSiblings');
 }
};

$(document).ready(tmpExample.ready);
```

This time you get output like that shown in **Figure 2-5**.

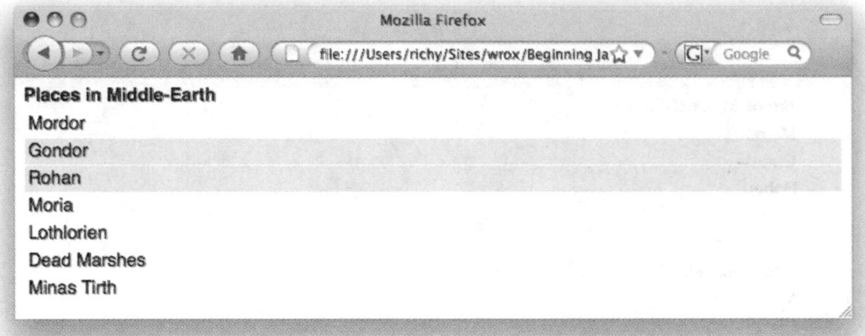

Figure 2-5

So, in **Figure 2-5**, you see that only the `<li>` elements with the class name *tmpRealmOfMen* have been given the class name *tmpSiblings*, and thus a colored background.

> *When you add a class name using* `addClass`*, that class name is applied in addition to previous class names. In **Figure 2-5**, the* `<li>` *elements with class name* tmpRealmOfMen *have that class, in addition to the class name* tmpSiblings.

Selecting Specific Siblings

Going back to the topic of siblings, jQuery has yet more methods that provide you with fine-grained control over sibling selection. In a preceding section, you saw how jQuery's `siblings()` method allows you to select all siblings or a specific set of siblings using a selector. jQuery also gives you the ability to select siblings based on whether they appear before or after an element, using the following methods: `next()`, `prev()`, `nextAll()`, and `prevAll()`. These methods work similarly to the `siblings()` method. The following example demonstrates the `next()` method:

```
<!DOCTYPE html PUBLIC "-//W3C//DTD XHTML 1.0 Strict//EN"
    "http://www.w3.org/TR/xhtml1/DTD/xhtml1-strict.dtd">
<html xmlns='http://www.w3.org/1999/xhtml' xml:lang='en'>
  <head>
    <meta http-equiv='content-type' content='text/html; charset=utf-8' />
    <meta http-equiv='content-language' content='en-us' />
    <title></title>
    <script type='text/javascript'
            src='../../../Source Code/jQuery/jQuery.js'>
    </script>
    <script type='text/javascript' src='Figure 2-6.js'></script>
    <link type='text/css' href='Figure 2-6.css' rel='stylesheet' />
  </head>
  <body>
    <h4>Colors</h4>
    <ul id='tmpColors'>
      <li>Red</li>
      <li>Blue</li>
      <li>Green</li>
```

```
      <li id='tmpYellow'>Yellow</li>
      <li>Orange</li>
      <li>Purple</li>
    </ul>
  </body>
</html>
```

The following CSS is included with the preceding markup:

```
body {
    font: 16px sans-serif;
}
h4 {
    font-size: 16px;
    margin: 0 0 5px 0;
}
ul#tmpColors {
    list-style: none;
    margin: 0;
    padding: 0;
}
ul#tmpColors li {
    margin: 1px;
    padding: 3px;
}
li.tmpSibling {
    background: #165b91;
    color: white;
}
```

The following JavaScript demonstrates the `next()` method.

```
var tmpExample = {
  ready : function() {
    $('li#tmpYellow').next().addClass('tmpSibling');
  }
};

$(document).ready(tmpExample.ready);
```

In **Figure 2-6**, you see that the `<li>` element containing the word *Orange* has a dark-blue background with white text, which is a result of that element receiving the *tmpSibling* class name, which is the next element appearing after the `<li>` element with ID name *tmpYellow*.

The following demonstrates what happens if you replace `next()` with `prev()`:

```
var tmpExample = {
  ready : function() {
    $('li#tmpYellow').prev().addClass('tmpSibling');
  }
};

$(document).ready(tmpExample.ready);
```

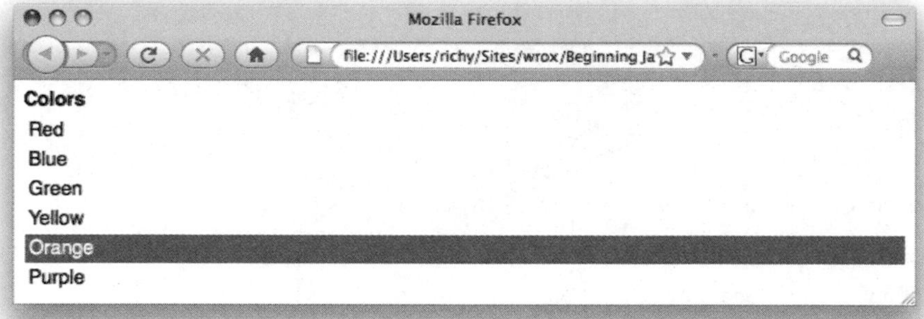

Figure 2-6

In **Figure 2-7**, you see that the `<li>` element containing the word *Green* has the class name *tmpSibling*, indicating that the element immediately preceding the `<li>` element with ID name *tmpYellow* has been selected.

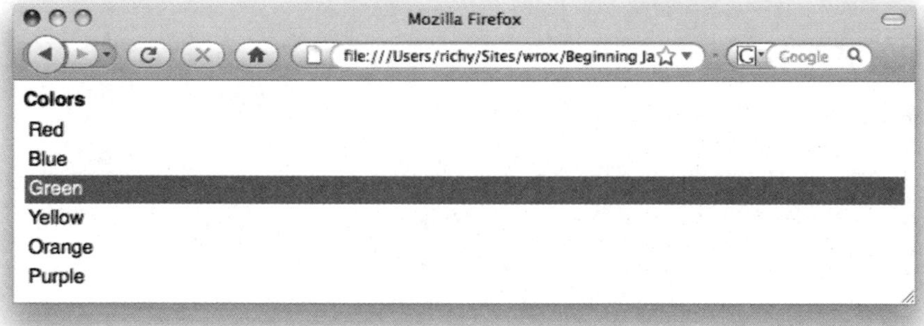

Figure 2-7

Next, I demonstrate what happens when `prev()` is replaced with the method `nextAll()`:

```
var tmpExample = {
  ready : function() {
    $('li#tmpYellow').nextAll().addClass('tmpSibling');
  }
};

$(document).ready(tmpExample.ready);
```

In **Figure 2-8**, you see that `<li>` elements containing the words *Orange* and *Purple* have the *tmpSibling* class name, indicating that all elements following the `<li>` element with ID name *tmpYellow* have been selected.

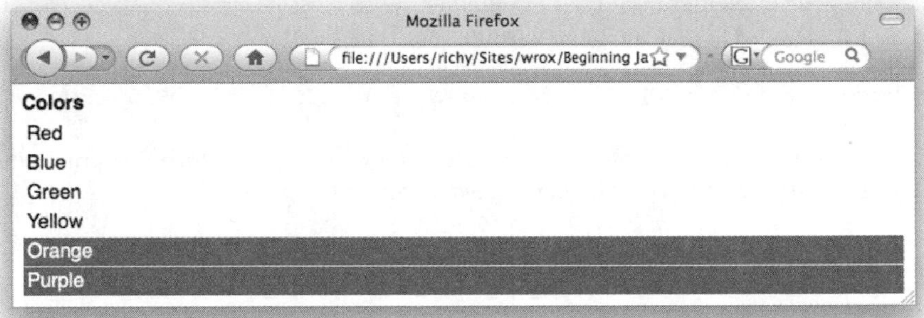

Figure 2-8

Finally, the last sibling-related method that I demonstrate is the `prevAll()` method, which, as you might have expected, selects all previous siblings:

```
var tmpExample = {
  ready : function() {
    $('li#tmpYellow').prevAll().addClass('tmpSibling');
  }
};

$(document).ready(tmpExample.ready);
```

In **Figure 2-9**, the `<li>` elements with the words *Red, Blue,* and *Green* have the *tmpSibling* class name, indicating that all elements previous to the `<li>` element with ID name *tmpYellow* have been selected.

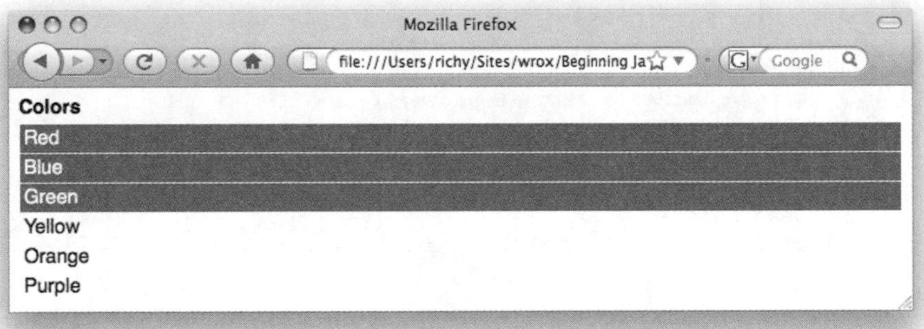

Figure 2-9

Each of the methods, `prev()`, `prevAll()`, `next()`, and `nextAll()` also accepts a selector as the first argument, which allows you to filter the selection. For example, calling `next()` like so:

```
$('li#tmpYellow').next('li.someClassName').addClass('tmpSibling');
```

only selects the `next()` element if it is a <li> element with class name *someClassName*. Likewise, calling the `nextAll()` method with a selector also limits which elements are selected.

```
$('li#tmpYellow').nextAll('li.someClassName').addClass('tmpSibling');
```

The preceding code selects elements that come after the <li> element with ID name *tmpYellow*, but only if they are <li> elements with the class name *someClassName*.

Searching Ancestors Using the `parents()` and `parent()` Methods

As you can select siblings and descendants, you can also go up the DOM tree and select ancestor elements. The following markup builds on the example you saw in **Figures 2-4** and **2-5**:

```
<!DOCTYPE html PUBLIC "-//W3C//DTD XHTML 1.0 Strict//EN"
    "http://www.w3.org/TR/xhtml1/DTD/xhtml1-strict.dtd">
<html xmlns='http://www.w3.org/1999/xhtml' xml:lang='en'>
  <head>
    <meta http-equiv='content-type' content='text/html; charset=utf-8' />
    <meta http-equiv='content-language' content='en-us' />
    <title></title>
    <script type='text/javascript'
            src='../../../Source Code/jQuery/jQuery.js'>
    </script>
    <script type='text/javascript' src='Figure 2-10.js'></script>
    <link type='text/css' href='Figure 2-10.css' rel='stylesheet' />
  </head>
  <body id='tmpExample'>
    <h4>Places in Middle-Earth</h4>
    <div id='tmpPlacesWrapper'>
      <ul id='tmpPlaces'>
        <li>Mordor</li>
        <li class='tmpRealmOfMen'>Gondor</li>
        <li class='tmpRealmOfMen'>Rohan</li>
        <li>Moria</li>
        <li class='tmpRealmOfElves'>Lothlorien</li>
        <li>Dead Marshes</li>
        <li class='tmpExampleCity'>Minas Tirth</li>
      </ul>
    </div>
  </body>
</html>
```

The CSS file has a few modifications too; the new document looks like this:

```
body {
    font: 16px sans-serif;
}
h4 {
    font-size: 16px;
    margin: 0 0 5px 0;
}
ul#tmpPlaces {
```

```
        list-style: none;
        margin: 0;
        padding: 0;
    }
    ul#tmpPlaces li {
        margin: 1px;
        padding: 3px;
    }
    div#tmpPlacesWrapper {
        padding: 5px;
        border: 1px solid rgb(200, 200, 200);
        background: rgb(240, 240, 240);
    }
    body#tmpExample div.tmpParent {
        background: rgb(174, 211, 248);
    }
```

Then, the JavaScript looks like this:

```
var tmpExample = {
  ready : function() {
    $('li.tmpExampleCity').parents('div#tmpPlacesWrapper').addClass('tmpParent');
  }
};

$(document).ready(tmpExample.ready);
```

In **Figure 2-10**, you see how you are able to select an element's ancestors using a selector, although in this example, you are only selecting a single parent, the `<div>` with ID name *tmpPlacesWrapper*. You can select multiple ancestors if more than one ancestor matches the selector that you supply to the `parents()` method. Giving that `<div>` element a class name of *tmpParent* causes the background to change to RGB 174, 211, 248, or a nice shade of sky-blue. If the *tmpParent* class name were not added, the background color would have been RGB 200, 200, 200, or light gray.

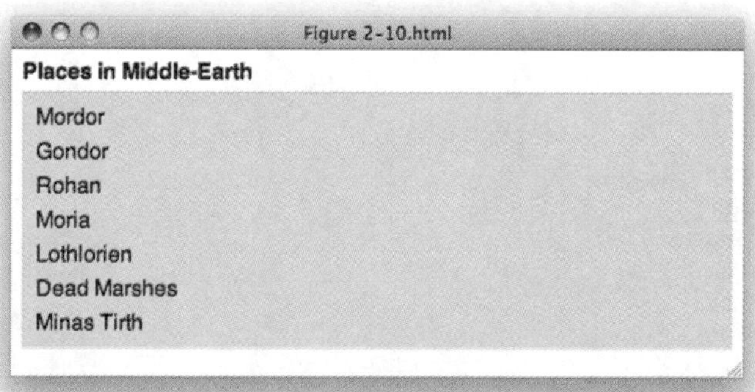

Figure 2-10

In the previous example, if you exclude the selector, all ancestor elements are selected:

```
$('li.tmpExampleCity').parents().addClass('tmpParent');
```

The `parents()` method has the ability to look at all of an element's ancestors, all the way back to the root element. If you only want to look at the immediate parent, you can use the `parent()` method instead. The following code gives you the same result as **Figure 2-10**:

```
$('ul#tmpPlaces').parent().addClass('tmpParent');
```

The preceding code selects the `<ul>` element with ID name *tmpPlaces* immediate parent, which is the `<div>` element with the ID name *tmpPlacesWrapper*.

Additionally, you may also use a selector to limit the `parent()` method to matching a more specific element:

```
$('ul#tmpPlaces').parent('div#tmpPlacesWrapper').addClass('tmpParent');
```

The preceding code limits the `parent()` method to making a match only when the `<ul>` with the ID element `tmpPlaces` has a parent `<div>` element with the ID name *tmpPlacesWrapper*.

Selecting Children Elements

You can also select an element's children with jQuery using the `children()` method. The following demonstrates the `children()` method:

```
<!DOCTYPE html PUBLIC "-//W3C//DTD XHTML 1.0 Strict//EN"
    "http://www.w3.org/TR/xhtml1/DTD/xhtml1-strict.dtd">
<html xmlns='http://www.w3.org/1999/xhtml' xml:lang='en'>
  <head>
    <meta http-equiv='content-type' content='text/html; charset=utf-8' />
    <meta http-equiv='content-language' content='en-us' />
    <title></title>
    <script type='text/javascript'
            src='../../../Source Code/jQuery/jQuery.js'>
    </script>
    <script type='text/javascript' src='Figure 2-11.js'></script>
    <link type='text/css' href='Figure 2-11.css' rel='stylesheet' />
  </head>
  <body>
    <h4>Fruit</h4>
    <ul>
       <li>Apple</li>
       <li>Cherry</li>
       <li>Orange</li>
       <li>Lemons</li>
       <li>Limes</li>
       <li>Grapes</li>
    </ul>
  </body>
</html>
```

The following style sheet is included with the preceding markup:

```
body {
    font: 16px sans-serif;
}
```

```
h4 {
    font-size: 16px;
    margin: 0 0 5px 0;
}
ul {
    list-style: none;
    margin: 0;
    padding: 0;
}
ul li {
    margin: 1px;
    padding: 3px;
}
li.tmpChild {
    background: #cf0c35;
    color: white;
}
```

The following JavaScript demonstrates how every `<li>` element is selected using jQuery's `children()` method:

```
var tmpExample = {
  ready : function() {
    $('ul').children().addClass('tmpChild');
  }
};

$(document).ready(tmpExample.ready);
```

Figure 2-11 shows that each of the `<li>` elements has the class name *tmpChild*. Each `<li>` element was selected by first selecting the `<ul>` element, then calling jQuery's `children()` method.

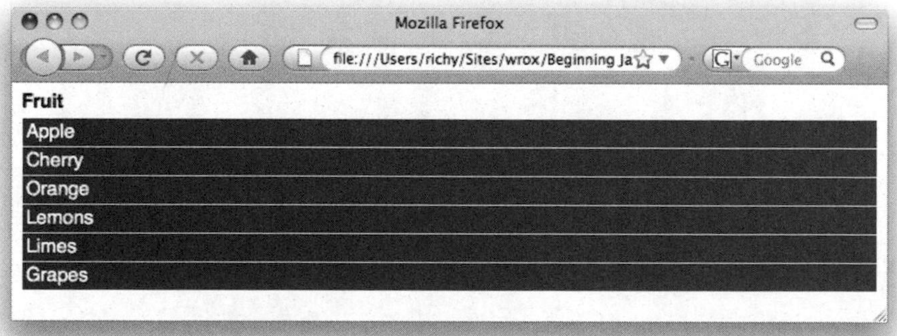

Figure 2-11

Like the other methods I've demonstrated throughout this chapter, you can also pass a selector to the `children()` method to limit which elements are included:

```
$('ul').children('li.tmpCitrus').addClass('tmpChild');
```

In the preceding code snippet, passing the selector `li.tmpCitrus` limits the selection to `<li>` elements that have a class name of *tmpCitrus*.

Selecting Elements via What You Don't Want

The next method gives you the ability to select elements based on what you *don't* want included in the selection. This markup document sets up the structure for the demonstration:

```
<!DOCTYPE html PUBLIC "-//W3C//DTD XHTML 1.0 Strict//EN"
    "http://www.w3.org/TR/xhtml1/DTD/xhtml1-strict.dtd">
<html xmlns='http://www.w3.org/1999/xhtml' xml:lang='en'>
  <head>
    <meta http-equiv='content-type' content='text/html; charset=utf-8' />
    <meta http-equiv='content-language' content='en-us' />
    <title></title>
    <script type='text/javascript'
            src='../../../Source Code/jQuery/jQuery.js'>
    </script>
    <script type='text/javascript' src='Figure 2-7.js'></script>
    <link type='text/css' href='Figure 2-7.css' rel='stylesheet' />
  </head>
  <body id='tmpExample'>
    <h4>Slapstick Comedians</h4>
    <ul id='tmpSlapstick'>
      <li class='tmpMarxBrothers'>Groucho</li>
      <li class='tmpMarxBrothers'>Chico</li>
      <li class='tmpMarxBrothers'>Harpo</li>
      <li class='tmpMarxBrothers'>Zeppo</li>
      <li class='tmpThreeStooges'>Moe</li>
      <li class='tmpThreeStooges'>Larry</li>
      <li class='tmpThreeStooges'>Curly</li>
      <li class='tmpThreeStooges'>Shemp</li>
      <li class='tmpAbbottAndCostello'>Abbott</li>
      <li class='tmpAbbottAndCostello'>Costello</li>
    </ul>
  </body>
</html>
```

The preceding markup is styled by the following CSS:

```
body {
    font: 16px sans-serif;
}
h4 {
    font-size: 16px;
    margin: 0 0 5px 0;
}
ul#tmpSlapstick {
    list-style: none;
    margin: 0;
    padding: 0;
}
ul#tmpSlapstick li {
```

```
        margin: 1px;
        padding: 3px;
    }
    li.tmpFunny {
        background: rgb(174, 211, 248);
    }
```

Next, the following JavaScript demonstrates how you can exclude elements from the result set using jQuery's `:not()` method:

```
var tmpExample = {
  ready : function() {
    $('ul#tmpSlapstick li').not('li.tmpThreeStooges').addClass('tmpFunny');
  }
};

$(document).ready(tmpExample.ready);
```

In **Figure 2-12**, you can see that all of the slapstick comedians except those with the class name *tmpThreeStooges* have been given a *tmpFunny* class name. To come to this result, first you selected every element using the selector `ul#tmpSlapstick li`; then you filtered out what you didn't want to select using jQuery's `not()` method, whereas every `<li>` element that did not have the class name *tmpThreeStooges* was given the *tmpFunny* class name. Just kidding — by the way, the Stooges are great.

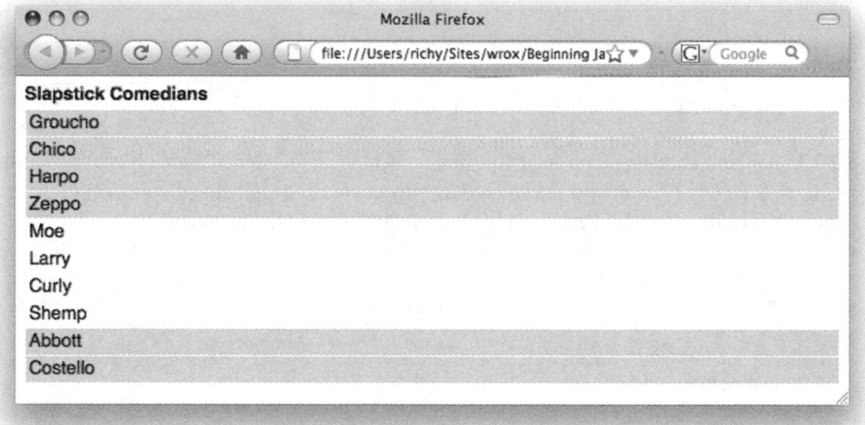

Figure 2-12

Selecting a Snippet of the Results

So far you've seen how jQuery's Selectors API allows you to do all kinds of contextual selection up and down the DOM and sideways and upside down. The next method I demonstrate shows you how to select a snippet of the results set with a method called `slice()`. Taking the same slapstick comedians example from the last section, and modifying the CSS ever so slightly:

```
body {
    font: 16px sans-serif;
}
h4 {
    font-size: 16px;
    margin: 0 0 5px 0;
}
ul#tmpSlapstick {
    list-style: none;
    margin: 0;
    padding: 0;
}
ul#tmpSlapstick li {
    margin: 1px;
    padding: 3px;
}
li.tmpReallyFunny {
    background: #fcc16e;
}
```

In the following JavaScript, you see how the `slice()` method is tacked onto the end of a selection to filter the results:

```
var tmpExample = {
  ready : function() {
    $('ul#tmpSlapstick li').slice(0, 4).addClass('tmpReallyFunny');
  }
};

$(document).ready(tmpExample.ready);
```

In **Figure 2-13**, you see that the first four list items have been selected, which corresponds to the Marx Brothers. jQuery's `slice()` method takes two arguments, the position of the first element that you want to select, and the position of the last element you want to select. The numbering is offset from zero.

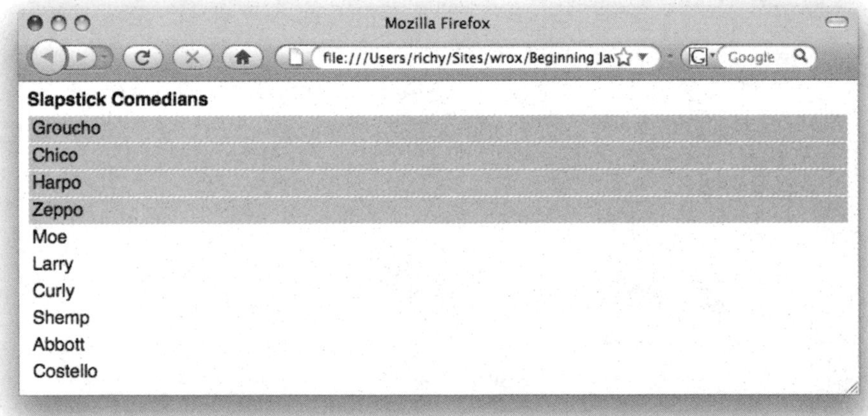

Figure 2-13

The `slice()` method's second argument is optional. The following JavaScript demonstrates what shows the `slice()` method with the second argument left off:

```
var tmpExample = {
  ready : function() {
    $('ul#tmpSlapstick li').slice(5).addClass('tmpReallyFunny');
  }
};

$(document).ready(tmpExample.ready);
```

In the preceding JavaScript, the `slice()` method receives a single argument, `5`. In **Figure 2-14**, you see the outcome of this modification.

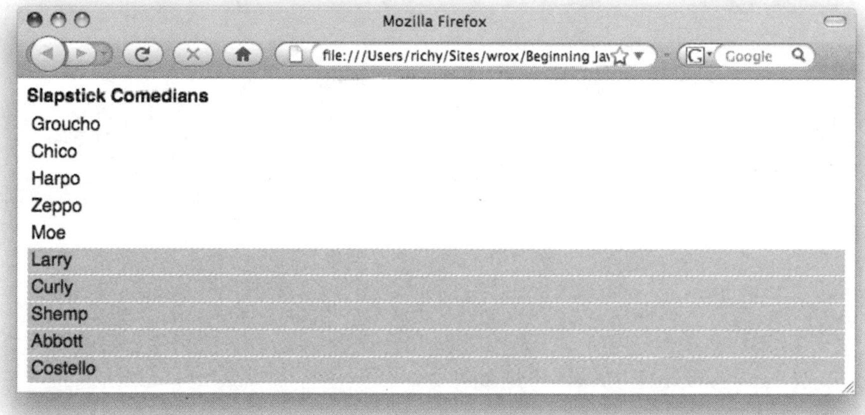

Figure 2-14

When you specify just one argument, the `slice()` method selects from the specified index, which is numbered offset from zero, and goes to the end. In the Slapstick Comedians example, that results in numbers 6, 7, 8, 9, and 10 being selected.

Adding More Elements to a Selection

Sometimes when you make a selection, you may need to `add()` more elements. jQuery gives you the ability to do this with the `add()` method. So, continuing to build on the Slapstick Comedians example, you modify the markup to look like so:

```
<!DOCTYPE html PUBLIC "-//W3C//DTD XHTML 1.0 Strict//EN"
    "http://www.w3.org/TR/xhtml1/DTD/xhtml1-strict.dtd">
<html xmlns='http://www.w3.org/1999/xhtml' xml:lang='en'>
  <head>
    <meta http-equiv='content-type' content='text/html; charset=utf-8' />
    <meta http-equiv='content-language' content='en-us' />
    <title></title>
    <script type='text/javascript'
```

```
            src='../../../Source Code/jQuery/jQuery.js'>
    </script>
    <script type='text/javascript' src='Figure 2-10.js'></script>
    <link type='text/css' href='Figure 2-10.css' rel='stylesheet' />
  </head>
  <body id='tmpExample'>
    <h3>Slapstick Comedians</h3>
    <h4>The Marx Brothers</h4>
    <ul id='tmpMarxBrothers'>
      <li>Groucho</li>
      <li>Chico</li>
      <li>Harpo</li>
      <li>Zeppo</li>
    </ul>
    <h4>The Three Stooges</h4>
    <ul id='tmpThreeStooges'>
      <li>Moe</li>
      <li>Larry</li>
      <li>Curly</li>
      <li>Shemp</li>
    </ul>
    <h4>Abbott &amp; Costello</h4>
    <ul id='tmpAbbottAndCostello'>
      <li>Abbott</li>
      <li>Costello</li>
    </ul>
  </body>
</html>
```

The style sheet has a few modifications as well:

```
body {
    font: 16px sans-serif;
}
h3 {
    font-size: 18px;
    margin: 0 0 5px 0;
}
h4 {
    font-size: 16px;
    margin: 5px 0;
}
ul {
    list-style: none;
    margin: 0;
    padding: 0;
}
ul li {
    margin: 1px;
    padding: 3px;
}
li.tmpReallyFunny {
    background: #88fac6;
}
```

The following JavaScript shows how you add elements to a selection using jQuery's `add` method:

```
var tmpExample = {
 ready : function() {
   $('ul#tmpMarxBrothers li')
     .add('ul#tmpAbbottAndCostello li')
     .addClass('tmpReallyFunny');
 }
};

$(document).ready(tmpExample.ready);
```

Figure 2-15 shows, as you might expect, that the `<li>` elements within the `<ul>` element with ID name *tmpMarxBrothers* and the `<li>` elements within the `<ul>` element with ID name *tmpAbbottAndCostello* all have the `seagreen` background (#88fac6).

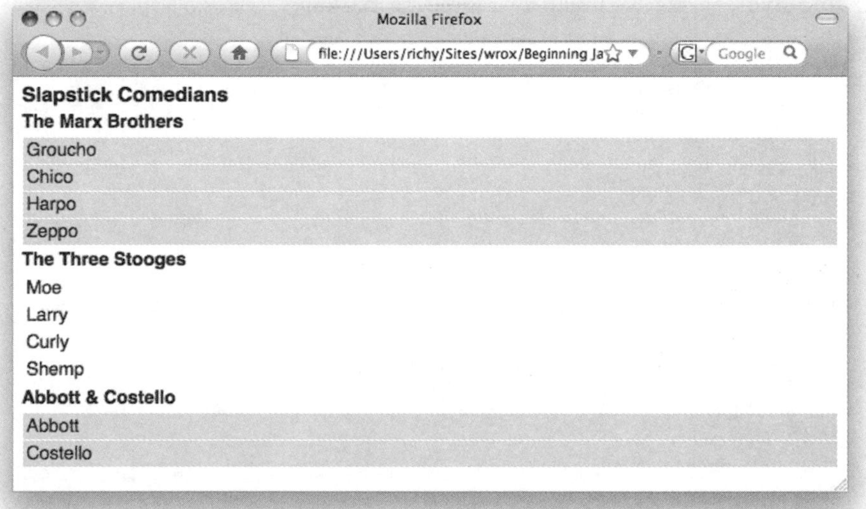

Figure 2-15

Selecting One Specific Element from a Result Set

jQuery's `eq()` method (short for "equals") gives you the ability to select an element based on its position within a result set. The following source code demonstrates how this method is used:

```
<!DOCTYPE html PUBLIC "-//W3C//DTD XHTML 1.0 Strict//EN"
    "http://www.w3.org/TR/xhtml1/DTD/xhtml1-strict.dtd">
<html xmlns='http://www.w3.org/1999/xhtml' xml:lang='en'>
  <head>
    <meta http-equiv='content-type' content='text/html; charset=utf-8' />
    <meta http-equiv='content-language' content='en-us' />
    <title></title>
```

```
    <script type='text/javascript'
            src='../../../Source Code/jQuery/jQuery.js'>
    </script>
    <script type='text/javascript' src='Figure 2-11.js'></script>
    <link type='text/css' href='Figure 2-11.css' rel='stylesheet' />
  </head>
  <body>
    <h3>Brilliant Muscians</h3>
    <ul>
      <li>Brian Wilson</li>
      <li>Paul McCartney</li>
      <li>John Lennon</li>
      <li>Freddie Mercury</li>
    </ul>
  </body>
</html>
```

The following style sheet is used with the preceding markup:

```
body {
    font: 16px sans-serif;
}
h3 {
    font-size: 18px;
    margin: 0 0 5px 0;
}
ul {
    list-style: none;
    margin: 0;
    padding: 0;
}
ul li {
    margin: 1px;
    padding: 3px;
}
li.tmpQueen {
    background: #cdb6ed;
}
```

Then, the following JavaScript demonstrates how the `eq()` method is used to pick just one element from a result set based on its position offset from zero:

```
var tmpExample = {
  ready : function() {
    $('ul li').eq(3).addClass('tmpQueen');
  }
};

$(document).ready(tmpExample.ready);
```

The preceding source code gives you the results that you see in **Figure 2-16**.

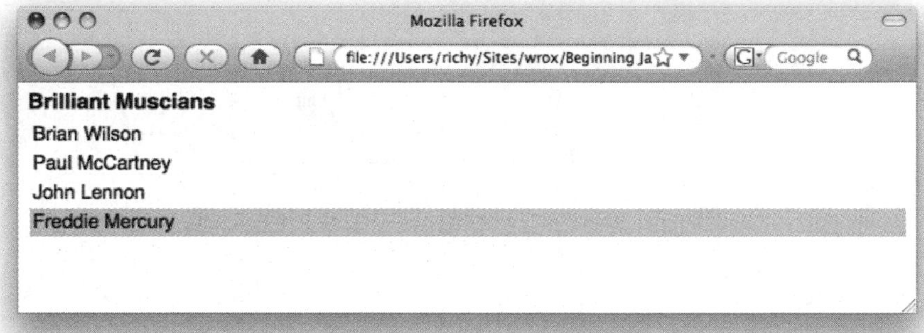

Figure 2-16

As you saw with the `slice()` method, the `eq()` method picks a specific element from the result set. jQuery, and just about any JavaScript library you find, selects elements from the DOM based on what order they appear in the markup. So, in this example, *Brian Wilson* is contained within `<li>` element `0`, and *Freddie Mercury* is contained within `<li>` element `3`.

The following "Try It Out" recaps all the methods jQuery provides for filtering a selection. You can try this example out for yourself to aid you in remembering how each method works and what each method might be used for. If you feel that you have a sufficient understanding of the material, then you may want to skip ahead to the section on events.

All source code examples within this book are downloadable for free from `www.wrox.com`.

Try It Out — Filtering a Selection

Example 2-2

To recap selection filtering, follow these steps:

1. Create the following markup document as *Example 2-2.html*:

```
<!DOCTYPE html PUBLIC "-//W3C//DTD XHTML 1.0 Strict//EN"
    "http://www.w3.org/TR/xhtml1/DTD/xhtml1-strict.dtd">
<html xmlns='http://www.w3.org/1999/xhtml' xml:lang='en'>
  <head>
    <meta http-equiv='content-type' content='text/html; charset=utf-8' />
    <meta http-equiv='content-language' content='en-us' />
    <title>Link</title>
    <script type='text/javascript'
            src='../../../Source Code/jQuery/jQuery.js'>
    </script>
    <script type='text/javascript' src='Example 2-2.js'></script>
    <link type='text/css' href='Example 2-2.css' rel='stylesheet' />
  </head>
  <body id='tmpDialogueExample'>
    <div id='tmpSelection'>
      <div class='tmpList'>
          <h4>Edible Plants</h4>
```

```
        <ul id='tmpPlants'>
          <li class='tmpVegetables' id='tmpOnion'>Onion</li>
          <li class='tmpVegetables' id='tmpBroccoli'>Broccoli</li>
          <li class='tmpVegetables' id='tmpPepper'>Pepper</li>
          <li class='tmpVegetables' id='tmpCarrot'>Carrot</li>
          <li class='tmpFruits'>Apple</li>
          <li class='tmpFruits'>Cherry</li>
          <li class='tmpFruits' id='tmpOrange'>Orange</li>
          <li class='tmpFruits'>Lemon</li>
        </ul>
    </div>
    <div class='tmpList'>
        <h4>Animals</h4>
        <ul id='tmpAnimals'>
          <li id='tmpChicken'>Chicken</li>
          <li id='tmpCow'>Cow</li>
          <li id='tmpBuffalo'>Buffalo</li>
          <li id='tmpSheep'>Sheep</li>
          <li id='tmpRabbit'>Rabbit</li>
        </ul>
    </div>
  </div>
  <div id='tmpRecap'>
    <p>
       <a href='#' id='tmpFind'>
          Find all &lt;li&gt; elements inside of &lt;ul&gt; elements.
       </a>
    </p>
    <p>
      <a href='#' id='tmpSiblings'>
          Find all siblings of the &lt;li&gt; element with id tmpCarrot.
      </a>
    </p>
    <p>
      <a href='#' id='tmpNext'>
          Select the &lt;li&gt; sibling element after the &lt;li&gt; element
          with id name tmpBroccoli.
      </a>
    </p>
    <p>
      <a href='#' id='tmpPrev'>
          Select the &lt;li&gt; sibling element before the &lt;li&gt; element
           with id name tmpBroccoli.
      </a>
    </p>
    <p>
      <a href='#' id='tmpNextAll'>
          Select all &lt;li&gt; sibling elements after the &lt;li&gt; element
          with id name tmpBroccoli.
      </a>
    </p>
    <p>
      <a href='#' id='tmpPrevAll'>
          Select all &lt;li&gt; sibling elements before the &lt;li&gt; element
          with id name tmpOrange.
      </a>
```

```
          </p>
          <p>
            <a href='#' id='tmpVegetables'>
                Select only &lt;li&gt; sibling elements before the &lt;li&gt;
                element with id name tmpOrange that are vegetables.
            </a>
          </p>
          <p>
            <a href='#' id='tmpParents'>
                Find the parent &lt;div&gt; element, with id tmpSelection.
            </a>
          </p>
          <p>
            <a href='#' id='tmpParent'>
                Find parent &lt;ul&gt; elements of &lt;li&gt; elements.
            </a>
          </p>
          <p>
            <a href='#' id='tmpChildren'>
                Find children &lt;h4&gt; elements of parent &lt;div&gt; elements with
                class name tmpList.
            </a>
          </p>
          <p>
            <a href='#' id='tmpNot'>
                Select children &lt;li&gt; elements of parent &lt;ul&gt; elements,
                except for vegetables.
            </a>
          </p>
          <p>
            <a href='#' id='tmpSlice'>
                Select &lt;li&gt; elements beginning with Cow and ending with Sheep.
            </a>
          </p>
          <p>
            <a href='#' id='tmpAdd'>
                Select all animal &lt;li&gt; elements, then add Pepper and Broccoli.
            </a>
          </p>
          <p>
            <a href='#' id='tmpEq'>
                Select all &lt;li&gt; elements, and reduce to only Buffalo.
            </a>
          </p>
        </div>
      </body>
    </html>
```

2. Create the following CSS document as *Example 2-2.css*:

```
body {
    font: 16px sans-serif;
}
ul {
    list-style: none;
    padding: 0;
```

```
        margin: 0;
        width: 200px;
    }
    li {
        padding: 3px;
        margin: 3px;
    }
    div.tmpList {
        float: left;
        margin: 0 20px;
    }
    div#tmpRecap {
        clear: left;
        padding: 10px;
    }
    .tmpExample {
        border: 1px solid rgb(200, 200, 200);
        background: #cbe5f8;
    }
    div#tmpSelection {
        overflow: hidden;
    }
```

3. Create the following JavaScript document as *Example 2-2.js*:

```
var tmpExample = {
  ready : function() {
    // Find all <input> elements and add a click
    // event.
    $('a').click(tmpExample.findElements);
  },

  findElements : function($e)
  {
    // Prevent the default action, navigating to the link.
    $e.preventDefault();

    // Reset the example before applying the next.
    $('*').removeClass('tmpExample');

    switch (this.id)
    {
      case 'tmpFind':
      {
        // If the id of "this" <input> element contains "Find",
        // Do the find() example.
        $('ul').find('li').addClass('tmpExample');
        break;
      }
      case 'tmpSiblings':
      {
        $('li#tmpCarrot').siblings().addClass('tmpExample');
        break;
      }
      case 'tmpNext':
```

```
{
  $('li#tmpBroccoli').next().addClass('tmpExample');
  break;
}
case 'tmpPrev':
{
  $('li#tmpBroccoli').prev().addClass('tmpExample');
  break;
}
case 'tmpNextAll':
{
  $('li#tmpBroccoli').nextAll().addClass('tmpExample');
  break;
}
case 'tmpPrevAll':
{
  $('li#tmpOrange').prevAll().addClass('tmpExample');
  break;
}
case 'tmpVegetables':
{
  $('li#tmpOrange').prevAll('li.tmpVegetables').addClass('tmpExample');
  break;
}
case 'tmpParents':
{
  $('li#tmpCarrot').parents('div#tmpSelection').addClass('tmpExample');
  break;
}
case 'tmpParent':
{
  $('li').parent('ul').addClass('tmpExample');
  break;
}
case 'tmpChildren':
{
  $('div.tmpList').children('h4').addClass('tmpExample');
  break;
}
case 'tmpNot':
{
  $('ul li').not('li.tmpVegetables').addClass('tmpExample');
  break;
}
case 'tmpSlice':
{
  $('ul#tmpAnimals li').slice(1, 4).addClass('tmpExample');
  break;
}
case 'tmpAdd':
{
  $('ul#tmpAnimals li')
    .add('li#tmpBroccoli, li#tmpPepper')
    .addClass('tmpExample');
```

```
            break;
          }
          case 'tmpEq':
          {
            $('ul li').eq(10).addClass('tmpExample');
            break;
          }
        }
      }
    };

    $(document).ready(tmpExample.ready);
```

The preceding document looks something like what you see in **Figure 2-17**. Clicking on each link in the example results in a different section of the top portion of the document being highlighted, depending on the description provided for each <a> element.

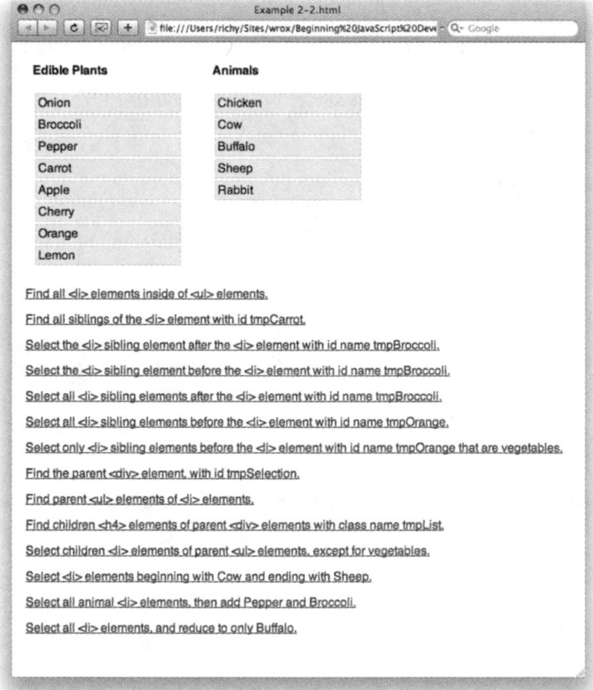

Figure 2-17

The preceding example is one big recap of all the ways jQuery provides for selecting elements and filtering elements you've already selected. When you click on a link, some JavaScript is executed to demonstrate what is described in the link.

First, each <a> element has a `click` event attached to it, so that when you click on a link, that event is handled by the `findElements()` method of the `tmpExample` object. This is as easy as having one line of code execute once the `ready()` method of the `tmpExample` object executes:

```
$('a').click(tmpExample.findElements);
```

Inside the `findElements()` method, the first thing done prevents the default action from occurring, which in the case of an <a> element is navigating to the document specified in the `href` attribute. Of course, in this case, that wouldn't have happened anyway, since the value of the `href` attribute for each <a> element is a hash character (or pound sign), but the default action is canceled nevertheless, since you're never really sure how your script might evolve.

The next thing that happens is that every element in the document is selected via the universal selector (the asterisk), and the class name *tmpExample* is removed. This re-sets the document to its original state so that each time you click on a new link, you're only seeing the elements that match that link's description.

```
    // Reset the example before applying the next.
$('*').removeClass('tmpExample');
```

Then, a big, long switch statement is executed; each case is an ID name for an individual <a> element in the markup document.

The first <a> element with ID name *tmpFind* locates all `<li>` elements within all `<ul>` elements in the document using jQuery's `find()` method. Thus, clicking on the following link:

```
    <a href='#' id='tmpFind'>
        Find all &lt;li&gt; elements inside of &lt;ul&gt; elements.
  </a>
```

results in this code being executed in the JavaScript:

```
  case 'tmpFind':
  {
    // If the id of "this" <input> element contains "Find",
    // Do the find() example.
    $('ul').find('li').addClass('tmpExample');
    break;
}
```

subsequently results in all of the `<li>` elements having a gray border and sky-blue background, as is defined in the style sheet for the class name *tmpExample.*

```
.tmpExample {
    border: 1px solid rgb(200, 200, 200);
    background: #cbe5f8;
}
```

The jQuery selector selects all `<li>` elements, regardless of what `<ul>` element they appear in. This is because you first made a selection using `$('ul')`, which is a type selector, resulting in the selection of all `<ul>` elements. Chaining the `find()` method to the selection changed the selection to include all `<li>` elements instead, since you supplied a type selector to the `find()` method, as `find('li')`.

The next link triggers a selection of all sibling elements of the `<li>` element with ID name *tmpCarrot*:

```
        <a href='#' id='tmpSiblings'>
            Find all siblings of the &lt;li&gt; element with id tmpCarrot.
        </a>
```

Clicking on the preceding link executes the following JavaScript within Example 2-2.js:

```
      case 'tmpSiblings':
      {
        $('li#tmpCarrot').siblings().addClass('tmpExample');
        break;
      }
```

Using jQuery's `siblings()` method causes all `<li>` elements that are adjacent to Carrot to be selected. Therefore, Onion, Broccoli, Pepper, Apple, Cherry, Orange, and Lemon are selected. Since you're selecting Carrot's siblings, all `<li>` elements within the same `<ul>` element except Carrot are selected.

When you click the following link, the `<li>` element that comes after the `<li>` element with ID name *tmpBroccoli* is selected using jQuery's `next()` method, which is Pepper:

```
        <a href='#' id='tmpNext'>
            Select the &lt;li&gt; sibling element after the &lt;li&gt; element
            with id name tmpBroccoli.
        </a>
```

The preceding link triggers the following JavaScript when you click on it:

```
      case 'tmpNext':
      {
        $('li#tmpBroccoli').next().addClass('tmpExample');
        break;
      }
```

The following link does the opposite; it selects the `<li>` element that comes before Broccoli, which is the Carrot `<li>` element. This is done via jQuery's `prev()` method.

```
        <a href='#' id='tmpPrev'>
            Select the &lt;li&gt; sibling element before the &lt;li&gt; element
            with id name tmpBroccoli.
        </a>
```

The preceding link executes the following JavaScript when you click it:

```
      case 'tmpPrev':
      {
        $('li#tmpBroccoli').prev().addClass('tmpExample');
        break;
      }
```

In the next snippet, you select all <li> elements following Broccoli using jQuery's `nextAll()` method:

```
case 'tmpNextAll':
{
  $('li#tmpBroccoli').nextAll().addClass('tmpExample');
  break;
}
```

Then, you select all the elements preceding the Orange <li> element with jQuery's `prevAll()` method:

```
$('li#tmpOrange').prevAll().addClass('tmpExample');
```

In the next case, you look through all of the ancestor elements of the <li> element with ID name *tmpCarrot* to find the <div> element with ID name *tmpSelection*, and add the class name *tmpExample* to it.

```
$('li#tmpCarrot').parents('div#tmpSelection').addClass('tmpExample');
```

In the next example, you select the immediate parent of any <li> element, which would be the <ul> elements. The selector `'ul'` ensures that the parent is only selected if it is a <ul> element, a moot point in this case, since it would be a <ul> element anyway, but demonstrative of your option to pass a selector to jQuery's `parent()` method if you so choose.

```
$('li').parent('ul').addClass('tmpExample');
```

The next example selects all children of the <div> element with ID name *tmpList* that are <h4> elements using jQuery's `children()` method:

```
$('div.tmpList').children('h4').addClass('tmpExample');
```

Subsequently, you create an example that selects all <li> elements that are descendant of <ul> elements, but remove all <li> elements with class name `tmpVegetables` from the selection using jQuery's `not()` method:

```
$('ul li').not('li.tmpVegetables').addClass('tmpExample');
```

In the following snippet, you use jQuery's `slice()` method to select <li> elements based on their position in the selection, where each number represents the element's sequential position in the selection offset from zero. The following selects Cow, Buffalo, and Sheep:

```
$('ul#tmpAnimals li').slice(1, 4).addClass('tmpExample');
```

Next, you see how jQuery's `add()` method can be used to add to a selection you've already made. The following selects all <li> elements descendant of the <ul> element with ID name *tmpAnimals*, then adds the <li> elements with ID names *tmpBroccoli* and *tmpPepper*:

```
$('ul#tmpAnimals li')
  .add('li#tmpBroccoli, li#tmpPepper')
  .addClass('tmpExample');
```

In the last example, you select a `<li>` element based on its offset position in the selection. Each element is assigned a number, starting with `0`; the following selects Buffalo, because it is `<li>` element number `10` in the selection:

```
$('ul li').eq(10).addClass('tmpExample');
```

Appendix C provides a reference for all of jQuery's selection and filtering methods.

Summary

In this chapter, you've seen some remedial examples that give you a comprehensive overview of jQuery's selection and filtering abilities. You learned how jQuery provides ridiculously fine-grained control over selecting elements from the DOM, so fine-grained, that you'll often find that there are multiple ways to achieve the same results.

jQuery's selection and filtering methods go much farther than what you get with plain-vanilla JavaScript, which more often than not would take several lines of code to come to the same level of control over a selection.

jQuery harnesses the power, ease, familiarity, and convenience of selectors to help you get anywhere in the DOM you want to go. The selector syntax, you'll find, is the same as what you're used to using for CSS; jQuery even supports a few extensions of its own. See Appendix B for a full listing of selector syntax supported by jQuery.

jQuery's filtering methods let you select descendants using the `find()` method; ancestors using the `parents()` method; and siblings using the `siblings()`, `prev()`, `prevAll()`, `next()`, and `nextAll()` methods. You can add elements using the `add()` method or ignore elements using the `not()` method. And you can also get even more specific using the `slice()` and `eq()` methods. See Appendix C for a full list of methods related to selection and filtering.

Exercises

1. What other client-side technology does jQuery have a lot in common with in terms of its fine-grained control over the selection of elements from the markup source?
2. If you wanted to select an element from the DOM using jQuery based on an ancestral relationship, which method would you use?
3. Let's say you wanted to swap an element's position in the DOM with its preceding sibling. What jQuery method would help with that application?
4. If you have selected an element and want to select one of that element's descendants from the DOM, what methods does jQuery expose that would give you the results you seek?
5. If you made a selection but later wanted to remove one or more elements from that selection, what jQuery method would you use?

6. If you only wanted to select a single element from a broader selection, what jQuery method would you use?
7. List all of the methods that jQuery provides for working with sibling elements.
8. How would you add elements to a selection using jQuery?
9. Internet Explorer 8 does not support the `:nth-child` selector from the CSS 3 specification. Would that selector work in that browser using jQuery?

Events

One of John Resig's primary motivations for creating jQuery was the need to make support for certain scripting features more seamless across browsers in a way that is as efficient and performance-aware as is possible. John has managed pretty well — his Event API not only works across all the popular, modern browsers, but it also simplifies events in very intuitive ways, reducing the amount of code that you need to write to bind events to objects.

That said, to truly appreciate what John has done to bridge the gap in jQuery, a brief review of how events work without a framework is in order. This chapter reiterates how event handling works in JavaScript via the traditional event model, the W3C event model, and Microsoft's JScript event model, followed by a demonstration of how events work with jQuery.

Long a thorn in the sides of web developers everywhere is the rift in the event model supported by Internet Explorer, and the event model standardized by the W3C. Over the years, developers have come up with all sorts of creative ways to unite these different event models to have an extensible, reliable, and easy-to-use Event API. To truly understand the challenge that a developer faces when attempting to bridge the compatibility gaps in event handling, you have to understand the subtle nuisances that created the compatibility gap in the first place. In this chapter, I look at the different methods for attaching an event in more detail by providing a recap on how each of the different event-handling methods work, and some of those subtle nuances that make cross-browser event handling a challenge, although I do not go into great detail on those nuances, since that discussion can get quite advanced, and we don't really need that kind of detail to convey the point.

Assigning an Event with the Traditional Event Model

Most browsers ever made that support JavaScript also support the so-called *traditional event model*, a relic of Netscape's original JavaScript design. This event model lets you assign a single event of the same type to the same element. For example, if you wanted to assign an `onclick` event to an HTML element, you'd only be able to assign just one `onclick` event to that element. If you tried to assign another onclick event to the same element, subsequent assignments would overwrite previous ones, and you'd be left in a situation wherein only the last onclick event that you assigned is the one fired when you click on the element.

Most of the time, this limitation presents no problem at all, because you usually only need one event of the same type on the same element, but there are enough use cases in which you want to be able to assign the same event to the same element multiple times for this to become a very big limitation of event handling. The most common example is attaching an onload event to the window object. In a modularized development environment where script is separated into more manageable chunks based on its purpose and loaded via external scripts, the traditional event model becomes very difficult to deal with. In every script that you load, you'll need to attach document events, and to attach those events, you'll need to wait until the document is fully loaded; so you need to attach a function to the onload event. With the traditional event model, you can only attach one function to the onload event. Capable programmers could use some programming creativity to overcome the limitations of the traditional event model, but this leads to bloated scripts, and fortunately standards bodies have already recognized this limitation and come up with a superior solution — the W3C event model.

The following example demonstrates how the traditional event model works with a very simple example that's very common on the Web — a search box that has its label included as its initial value. Typically, the value of the search input is *Search* or *Search Example.com*, or *Search Company*. When you click on the input, the value is removed so that you can enter your query. When the input loses focus (the onblur event), if the user has entered a query, his or her query stays entered in the input box; otherwise, the label returns to the search box. This is an easy and convenient way to save space by combining the input's label with the input itself.

```
<!DOCTYPE html PUBLIC "-//W3C//DTD XHTML 1.0 Transitional//EN"
    "http://www.w3.org/TR/2002/REC-xhtml1-20020801/DTD/xhtml1-transitional.dtd">
<html xmlns='http://www.w3.org/1999/xhtml' xml:lang='en'>
 <head>
  <meta http-equiv='content-type' content='text/html; charset=utf-8' />
  <meta http-equiv='content-language' content='en-us' />
  <title></title>
  <script type='text/javascript' src='Figure 2-18.js'></script>
  </head>
  <body>
     <input type='text' name='q' id='tmpSearch' value='Search' />
  </body>
</html>
```

The following JavaScript demonstrates the traditional event model, which limits you to a single event being assigned to the same element. In the context of the following JavaScript, that would mean that you could not have additional onfocus events attached to the same element, since subsequent assignments would overwrite the first.

```
window.onload = function()
{
    document.getElementById('tmpSearch').onfocus = function() {
        if (this.value == 'Search') {
            this.value = '';
        }
```

```
    };

    document.getElementById('tmpSearch').onblur = function() {
        if (!this.value) {
            this.value = 'Search';
        }
    };
};
```

The preceding looks like what you see in **Figure 3-1** when you load it into a browser.

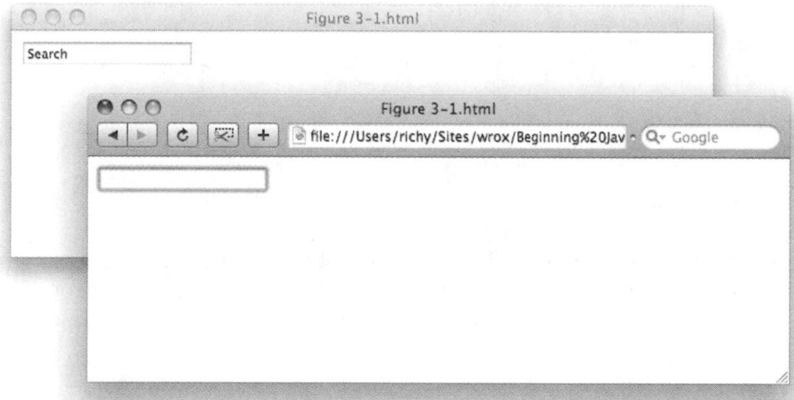

Figure 3-1

In **Figure 3-1** you see three objects: the HTML document (Figure 3-1.html), the JavaScript document (Figure 3-1.js), and the rendered output of the HTML and JavaScript in Safari. In the JavaScript, there is an event that fires once the document is loaded, via a function assigned to `window.onload`. Within the function that's executed `onload`, there is an `onfocus` and an `onblur` event being applied to the `<input>` element with ID name *tmpSearch*. When the `<input>` element receives focus and its value is *Search*, the value is set to `null`. When the element is blurred (loses focus) and if it has no value, its value again becomes *Search*. This is a common technique used to make a search box's label its initial value.

There is one big limitation to this method of assigning events, however. Let's say that you have a separate JavaScript library being loaded and that library applies `onfocus` and `onblur` events of its own, or even more common, that you have multiple external scripts that need to create events at `onload`. With the traditional event model, you can only assign one of the same events to the same object. Were you to create additional assignments to `window.onload`, in the `window.onload = function()` fashion, your subsequent assignments would override previous ones, and you'd end up with a system in which not all of your events are being assigned.

Of course, with the right planning, you could overcome this limitation of the traditional event model. Having also recognized this limitation of the traditional event model, the W3C created a new event model to give developers more flexibility.

Assigning Events with the W3C Event Model

With the W3C's event model, you can assign as many of the same events to the same element that you like. The following is an example of the concept presented in **Figure 3-1**, but using the W3C's event model rather than the traditional event model:

```
<!DOCTYPE html PUBLIC "-//W3C//DTD XHTML 1.0 Transitional//EN"
    "http://www.w3.org/TR/2002/REC-xhtml1-20020801/DTD/xhtml1-transitional.dtd">
<html xmlns='http://www.w3.org/1999/xhtml' xml:lang='en'>
 <head>
  <meta http-equiv='content-type' content='text/html; charset=utf-8' />
  <meta http-equiv='content-language' content='en-us' />
  <title>Contacts</title>
  <script type='text/javascript' src='Figure 3-2.js'></script>
  </head>
  <body>
     <input type='text' name='q' id='tmpSearch' value='Search' />
  </body>
</html>
```

In contrast to the traditional event model, the W3C event model lets you assign as many events of the same type to the same element as you like. In the following JavaScript, I can theoretically assign as many `focus` and `blur` events to the `<input>` element as I like — well, within reason, of course!

```
window.addEventListener(
    'load',
    function() {
        document.getElementById('tmpSearch').addEventListener(
            'focus',
            function() {
                if (this.value == 'Search') {
                    this.value = '';
                }
            }, false
        );

        document.getElementById('tmpSearch').addEventListener(
            'blur',
            function() {
                if (!this.value) {
                    this.value = 'Search';
                }
            }, false
        );
    }, false
);
```

This will produce **Figure 3-2** when run, although that figure is not actually shown here.

It results in the same document that you saw in **Figure 3-1**, the only difference being how events are assigned. The W3C's event model works by calling the `addEventListener()` method on the object you want to assign an event to. In the preceding code, the first instance of attaching an event with `addEventListener()` is calling that method on the `window` object to attach a `load` event. In **Figure 3-1**, the event was `onload`, and the W3C's event model dispenses with the *on* prefix of event names; otherwise, the events are the same. The `addEventListener()` method accepts three arguments:

```
object.addEventListener(event, function, useCapture);
```

The second argument of `addEventListener()` is the function that you want to execute when the event takes place. The argument that you provide to `addEventListener()` can be the name of the function, or, as you see in the preceding JavaScript, the argument can also be an anonymous function. Anonymous functions do not have a name, as in this example, so the nameless function definition is passed as the second argument to `addEventListener()`. You will see many more examples of anonymous functions versus named functions throughout this book, so I won't go into great detail about that here.

The third argument, called `useCapture`, is almost never needed, although there are a handful of situations that call for its use. `useCapture` has to do with the concept of event capturing. Because event capturing is a feature that few JavaScript developers use or need, I've chosen not to explore this concept in depth, since this is really a fringe feature with few actual use cases justifying its existence — in fact, it is such a fringe feature that jQuery does not provide for it in the majority of its publically exposed Event API. For the most part, the value of the `useCapture` argument should always be `false`.

The `this` Object

The `this` object has special meaning in JavaScript, and its meaning can change depending on the context it's used in, and even the browser it's used in. Because of how its meaning can change depending on context, the `this` object can be confusing to JavaScript newcomers. In the preceding two examples demonstrating the traditional Event API and the W3C Event API, `this` is used to modify properties of the element to which events are applied.

Some of you may be saying, hold on — technically, `this` *is a keyword! I think it helps to think of* `this` *as an object, since it usually is. And technically, it isn't necessarily incorrect to call it an object. If you're interested in more nuts-and-bolts discussion about* `this`*, I recommend you pick up Nicholas C. Zakas's* Professional JavaScript for Web Developers, *also from Wrox Press (2005; 2nd ed., 2009).*

Let's say you've added an event to an element. If you used the traditional event model, `this` always refers to the element you added the event to, and the same is true when you're using the `addEventListener` function. An example of `this` appears in the following documents ... literally and figuratively:

```
<!DOCTYPE html PUBLIC "-//W3C//DTD XHTML 1.0 Transitional//EN"
    "http://www.w3.org/TR/2002/REC-xhtml1-20020801/DTD/xhtml1-transitional.dtd">
<html xmlns='http://www.w3.org/1999/xhtml' xml:lang='en'>
  <head>
    <meta http-equiv='content-type' content='text/html; charset=utf-8' />
    <meta http-equiv='content-language' content='en-us' />
    <title>Contacts</title>
    <script type='text/javascript' src='Figure 3-3.js'></script>
    <link rel='stylesheet' href='Figure 3-3.css' type='text/css' />
  </head>
  <body>
    <input type='text' name='q' id='tmpSearch' value='Search' />
  </body>
</html>
```

The following style sheet is included in the preceding markup document:

```
input.tmpInputFocused {
    background: red;
    color: white;
}
```

Finally, the following JavaScript is also included in the preceding document. It demonstrates how `this` refers to the `<input />` element in the markup document. When you're working with an event that you've attached to an element, `this` always refers to the element to which you've attached the event — that is, if you're working with the W3C or the traditional Event API. Unfortunately, Internet Explorer has a different idea of what `this` should mean. In fact, it should also be noted that Internet Explorer does not support the W3C event, so this example and the last example won't work in IE.

```
window.addEventListener(
    'load',
    function() {
        document.getElementById('tmpSearch').addEventListener(
            'focus',
            function($e) {
                this.className = 'tmpInputFocused';
            }, false
        );

        document.getElementById('tmpSearch').addEventListener(
            'blur',
            function($e) {
                this.className = '';
            }, false
        );

    }, false
);
```

In **Figure 3-3**, the correlation between the `this` object and the element is highlighted; the `this` object when using the traditional event model, or the W3C event model, is an HTML node object, and whatever properties or methods that are exposed for the particular HTML node object you've attached an event to are available in the `this` object. In **Figure 3-3**, `this` refers to the `<input>` element in Figure 3-3.html. **Figure 3-3** shows you what happens when you load Figure 3-3.html in Safari and focus the `<input>` element. (Note that the figure references in the book's source code don't always match up with the figure numbers in the book itself.)

In **Figure 3-3**, you see that when the `<input>` element gains focus, the class name, *tmpInputFocused*, becomes the value of the `<input>` element's `class` attribute by assigning that class name to the `<input>` element's `className` property. From the style sheet in the preceding source code, you can see that makes the `<input>` element's background red, and its text is white. **Figure 3-4** shows what happens when the `<input>` element loses focus, or is blurred.

In **Figure 3-4**, you see that the red background and white text styles are no longer applied, and that's because the class name *tmpInputFocused* was removed upon the `<input>` element losing focus or becoming blurred.

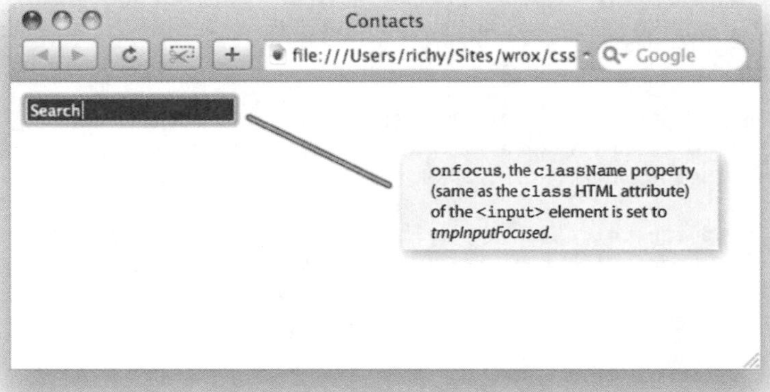

Figure 3-3

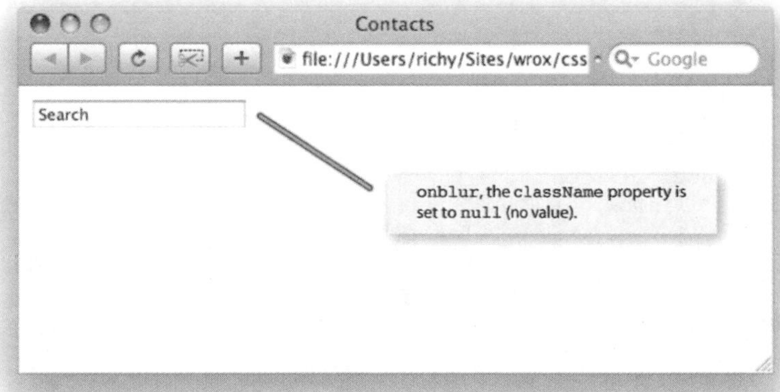

Figure 3-4

The `this` object can also refer to other objects depending on what context that you use it in. What you've seen so far is the `this` object in relation to the traditional event model and the W3C event model, but those are not the only situations in which you can use the `this` object. Having said that, you will see more examples of how the `this` object can be used throughout this book.

The `event` Object

When you're handling an event, sometimes you want to intercept or prevent another action from occurring. For example, let's say that you have existing links on a web page. When you click on a link, your browser takes you to the document referenced in the `href` attribute of the `<a>` element. With JavaScript it's possible to intercept a click on a hyperlink. If you want to prevent the default action from occurring, that is, the browser navigating to the document referenced in the `href` attribute, you need to access methods of an `event` object that can be passed as the first argument in any function acting as an event listener (a function assigned via the W3C event model, or the traditional event model). To prevent the default action, you need to call the `preventDefault()` method of the `event` object. An example of this appears in the following code:

```
<!DOCTYPE html PUBLIC "-//W3C//DTD XHTML 1.0 Transitional//EN"
    "http://www.w3.org/TR/2002/REC-xhtml1-20020801/DTD/xhtml1-transitional.dtd">
<html xmlns='http://www.w3.org/1999/xhtml' xml:lang='en'>
  <head>
    <meta http-equiv='content-type' content='text/html; charset=utf-8' />
    <meta http-equiv='content-language' content='en-us' />
    <title>Link</title>
    <script type='text/javascript' src='Figure 3-5.js'></script>
  </head>
  <body>
    <a href='http://p2p.wrox.com'>Wrox&reg; Programmer to Programmer&trade;</a>
  </body>
</html>
```

The following JavaScript is included in the preceding markup:

```
window.addEventListener(
    'load',
    function() {
        document.getElementsByTagName('a')[0].addEventListener(
            'click',
            function($event) {
                window.open(this.href, 'P2P', 'width=500,height=500');
                $event.preventDefault();
            }, false
        );
    }, false
);
```

In the preceding source code, you see a simple markup document with a single hyperlink. In the referenced JavaScript, a `click` event is attached to that one hyperlink, by getting all <a> elements and adding the `click` event to the first <a> element returned via `document.getElementsByTagName('a')[0]`. An anonymous function is used to handle the `click` event, and it has one argument defined, `$event`. That argument can have whatever name you like; most developers use a variable named `e` or `$e` to save time typing. With that argument in place, when the `click` event fires, the browser passes the `event` object to the event-handling function.

The `event` object carries with it a few predefined methods and properties that give you more control over an event. You can use that object to learn more about the event or the object that the event is attached to relative to the event, or to control what happens after your event-handling function has finished executing. In the case of the preceding code, you want to intercept a `click` on an <a> element. Instead of the browser navigating to the location specified in the `href` property as soon as the user has clicked on the <a> element, you're telling the browser to open a pop-up window at the location specified in the `href` property of the <a> element, and not to navigate the main window to that location by calling the `preventDefault()` method of the `event` object. **Figure 3-5** is a demonstration of what happens when you execute the code above.

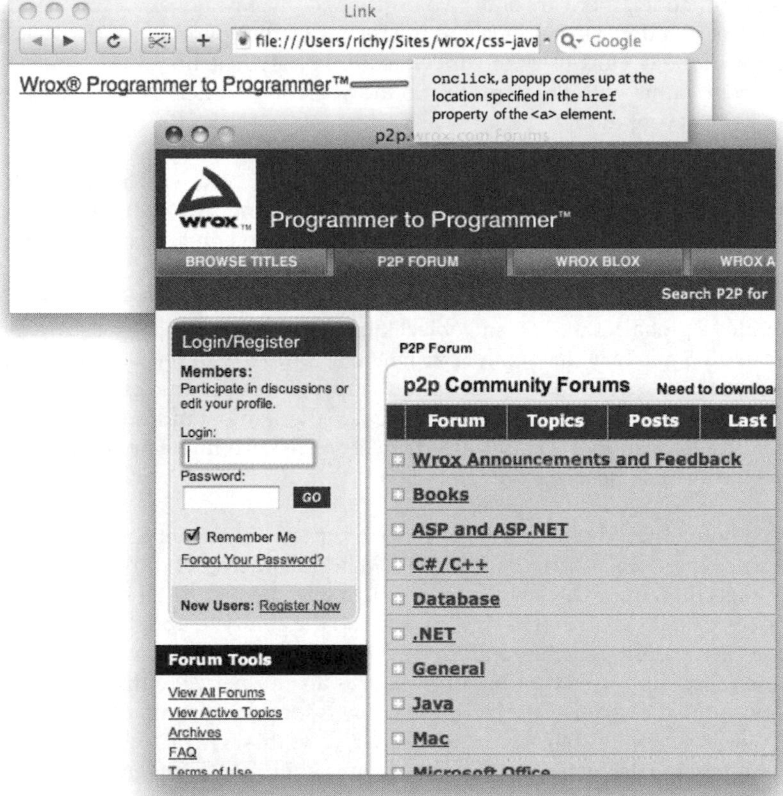

Figure 3-5

In the case of attaching `click` events to hyperlinks, the default action is the browser navigating to the location specified in the `href` property. The default action changes depending on the event and the object the event is being applied to.

There are other methods and properties that the `event` object provides, but for the purpose of introducing you to the `event` object or refreshing your memory on the `event` object, that's the gist of what it is. I continue to revisit the `event` object throughout this book.

The Microsoft JScript Event Model

Up till now I've been talking about the W3C event model and the traditional event model. Microsoft's JScript supports a substantially different event model, of Microsoft's own design. The API for Microsoft's event model looks like this:

```
object.attachEvent(event, function);
```

In Microsoft's event model, there are only two arguments, `event` and `function`. At first glance, this may give you the impression that the JScript event model has feature parity with the W3C event model, save the `useCapture` argument. However, there is not feature parity. The first difference is that its event argument takes the event name with the *on* prefix. So the Microsoft model uses the same event names verbatim as the traditional event model.

In Microsoft's event model, when events are attached via `attachEvent()`, `this` points to the `window` object, not the object the event is attached to, a pretty big deviation from the handling of `this` in the traditional event model, which Microsoft does support in its implementation of the traditional event model.

Microsoft does not allow the `event` object to be passed as the first argument of listener functions. Instead, Microsoft provides a global `window.event` object. So, rather than calling `$event.preventDefault();` as you saw in **Figure 3-5** above, you'd set the `returnValue` property of the `window.event` object to `false`, as in `window.event.returnValue = false`, and that provides the same outcome in Internet Explorer. Additionally, Microsoft's `event` object does not provide the same, standardized, methods that the `event` objects in other browsers support. This is also true of Microsoft's implementation of the traditional event model — the `event` object is *always* global.

It should also be noted that Microsoft's JScript, as supported in Internet Explorer, has not seen much revision at all since the release of IE6 back in 2001. Whereas Microsoft did provide a few CSS improvements in IE7 — less than many had hoped for — there was precious little in the way of JScript enhancements or bug fixes, despite Microsoft having always had the ability to update JScript without updating IE. Sure, there have been security patches, and they gave us a native implementation of the `XMLHttpRequest` object in IE7, the same supported by other browsers, as an alternative to the ActiveX object provided by previous versions of IE. Otherwise, the JScript of today is the same one that IE has used since the release of IE6 in 2001. With Microsoft's latest browser release, as of this writing, IE8, the JavaScript side does see a few notable improvements: faster performance, more stability, and implementation of the Selectors API. Unfortunately, however, there is still no support for the W3C's Event API, and a rift remains between the Event API of Microsoft's browsers and the standard W3C Event API supported by everyone else.

While there are some nooks and crannies of JavaScript where browser makers are so fragmented that each has its own particular way of doing one particular thing, the rift in support between Microsoft's event model and the W3C's is the single biggest annoyance, since it is an incompatibility that has to be dealt with each and every time you want to attach and handle events, the most common task a JavaScript developer will embark upon.

Creating a Universal Event API

Despite the differences, for the most part developers have coped, using home-brewed solutions that bridge compatibility. As I mentioned earlier in this chapter, such home-brewed solutions must take quite a heavy load into account. Here is a reiteration of the ingredients required to make your own home-brewed `addEventListener()/attachEvent()` method:

- Don't leak memory. A memory leak occurs when your browser claims memory (RAM) for a script. Your script uses the memory, but the memory is never released when the browser is finished using it. The next time the browser needs memory, it claims more memory instead of reusing or releasing what it already claimed. Your JavaScript can become a black hole, sucking up more memory to sit in a useless limbo. Be careful, though: Memory leaks can be difficult to recognize. Slowly, over multiple page loads, your browser will become more and more sluggish and less stable. Depending on the severity of the leak, it could lead to your browser crashing. At this time, IE6 has the biggest problem with runaway memory use. IE7 fixed some of this, but some problems remain. And IE8 fixes still more. Firefox and other browsers have been known to suffer from this problem too, so this is not an infliction that's limited to IE alone.

- You must fix the `this` object in IE. `this` should point to the object that the event is attached to, rather than the `window` object.
- You must fix the `event` object in IE and provide feature parity with the `event` object that other browsers support.
- You need to be able to attach multiple events to the same element.
- You need to be able to remove attached events from an element. That is, remember which events are assigned to which elements so you can unassign them, if needed.

It may not seem like it, but to implement that list is actually a bit of a tall order. You need lots of testing and expert JavaScript knowledge, and most times less experienced programmers fail on one or more of the necessary points needed for a truly fluid and stable Event API implementation.

Average web developers, for the most part, shouldn't have to worry or care about memory usage, at least not at that low level. Of course, you need to keep memory usage in mind. You need to avoid crashing the browser because your JavaScript application wants to load megabytes upon megabytes of data, and you want to find ways to make average performing scripts faster and more efficient.

Thankfully, you don't have to develop your own event-handling method. In 2005, Dean Edwards and other prominent JavaScript experts came together to fix the event problem. Pioneered mostly by Dean's effort, a solution called `addEvent()` was born. Later, John Resig drew inspiration from the fundamentals of Dean's script, while bringing in his own innovations to create jQuery's Event API. John did away with much of the verbosity and unnecessary complexity of the Event API.

jQuery supports events through the following APIs:

- The `bind()` method, which can be thought to be just like the W3C's Event API, minus that mostly useless `useCapture` argument
- Via individual event methods, like `click()`, `change()`, `focus()`, `blur()`, and so on, which make the code required to attach an event even less verbose. To use this API, all you have to do is pass a reference to a function, or an anonymous function as the first and only argument to one of these individual methods. This is just like you've seen earlier in this chapter, and in Chapter 1, with the `click()` and `ready()` methods.
- An event can be simulated programmatically very easily. All you have to do is call the event method without any arguments.

The next few sections describe the preceding APIs in a little more detail.

For a full reference of what jQuery supports in terms of events, see Appendix D.

Binding Events with jQuery's `bind()` *Method*

As I mentioned in the previous section, jQuery's `bind()` method works similarly to the W3C's standard Event API. Aside from it having a much shorter name, the only other difference is that it omits the mostly useless `useCapture` argument. The `useCapture` argument is so useless that I have decided not to even discuss it in this book, except to say that it is useless. Well, actually, to be fair, there are a precious few fringe cases where this feature of the W3C's Event API is useful, but 99 percent of the time you won't run into them. If you absolutely must know more about this, then, fear not, you can find some coverage of this in Nicholas C. Zakas's *Professional JavaScript for Web Developers*, also from Wrox Press (2005; 2nd ed., 2009).

The following example demonstrates the `bind()` method:

```
<!DOCTYPE html PUBLIC "-//W3C//DTD XHTML 1.0 Strict//EN"
    "http://www.w3.org/TR/xhtml1/DTD/xhtml1-strict.dtd">
<html xmlns='http://www.w3.org/1999/xhtml' xml:lang='en'>
  <head>
    <meta http-equiv='content-type' content='text/html; charset=utf-8' />
    <meta http-equiv='content-language' content='en-us' />
    <title></title>
    <script type='text/javascript'
            src='../../../Source Code/jQuery/jQuery.js'>
    </script>
    <script type='text/javascript' src='Figure 3-6.js'></script>
    <link rel='stylesheet' href='Figure 3-6.css' type='text/css' />
  </head>
  <body>
    <div></div>
    <div></div>
    <div></div>
    <div></div>
    <div></div>
    <div></div>
  </body>
</html>
```

The preceding document is linked to the following style sheet:

```
div {
    border: 1px solid rgb(200, 200, 200);
    width: 100px;
    height: 100px;
    margin: 5px;
    float: left;
}
div.tmpExampleOver {
    background: #5092c5;
}
div.tmpExampleOn {
    background: #165b91;
}
```

and the following JavaScript:

```
$(document).bind(
  'ready',
  function() {
    $('div').bind(
      'mouseover',
      function() {
        $(this).addClass('tmpExampleOver');
      }
    );

    $('div').bind(
      'mouseout',
      function() {
        $(this).removeClass('tmpExampleOver');
      }
    );

    $('div').bind(
      'click',
      function() {
        if ($(this).hasClass('tmpExampleOn')) {
          $(this).removeClass('tmpExampleOn');
        } else {
          $(this).addClass('tmpExampleOn');
        }
      }
    );
  }
);
```

The preceding source code demonstrates how you use jQuery's `bind()` method to attach events, and from the example earlier in this chapter, you can see that it works just like the W3C's `addEventListener()` method (minus that one `useCapture` argument), in that the method is called on the object you want to attach events to, then you pass the name of the event and a function that acts as an event listener. In this case, you attached a `mouseover` and `mouseout` event that result in each `<div>` element turning blue when you pass your mouse cursor over each box by attaching the class name *tmpExampleOver* to the `<div>` element. Then you attach a `mouseout` event that removes the *tmpExampleOver* class name from the `<div>` element, reverting it to have no background. Finally, you attach a `click` event that toggles the class name *tmpExampleOn* to be present every other click. The preceding gives you the output shown in **Figure 3-6**.

The `bind()` method is useful when you need to attach an event that jQuery does not provide a method for. Some examples would be Microsoft's `onselectstart` event, or `ondrag` event, which are only supported by Internet Explorer and Safari at present. Those events would be passed to the `bind()` method, minus the *on* prefix, as `selectstart` or `drag`.

You'll also note the way in which I have called the `hasClass()`, `addClass()`, and `removeClass()` methods, which are all methods provided by jQuery, within the event-handling functions. In the event-handling function, by default, jQuery provides the `this` object just like the standard W3C Event API does; it is an object representing the element that the event is attached to. To access jQuery methods, you have to wrap `this` in a call to the jQuery object, that is, `$(this)`; then you have access to all of jQuery's methods.

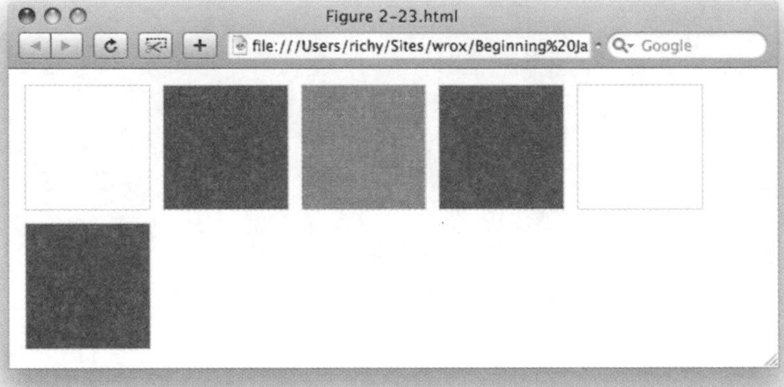

Figure 3-6

Binding Events with jQuery's Event Methods

John Resig and the jQuery team didn't stop at building a unified, cross-browser Event API into jQuery, but they saw an opportunity to make event binding even simpler by making individual methods for each event, similar to the traditional event model, but with two big differences. John dropped the *on* prefix for each event name, as is done for the W3C Event API, and he made the events methods instead of properties, so that you could attach multiple events of the same type to the same element. The following example demonstrates the example you saw in the previous section rewritten to use jQuery's individual event methods, using the same markup and style sheet, with the following JavaScript:

```
$(document).ready(
  function() {
    $('div').mouseover(
      function() {
        $(this).addClass('tmpExampleOver');
      }
    );

    $('div').mouseout(
      function() {
        $(this).removeClass('tmpExampleOver');
      }
    );

    $('div').click(
      function() {
        if (!$(this).hasClass('tmpExampleOn')) {
          $(this).addClass('tmpExampleOn');
        } else {
          $(this).removeClass('tmpExampleOn');
        }
      }
    );
  }
);
```

The preceding has the same functionality as the example that you saw that uses the `bind()` method in **Figure 3-6** but is slightly less verbose, since it uses individual event methods to attach each function. This example produces **Figure 3-7** (not shown).

Additionally, jQuery accounts for a few patterns that occasionally come up when attaching events, such as when you attach a `mouseover` event, you also tend to attach a `mouseout` event. Well, why not make an event that can attach both at once? That's exactly what they did — the jQuery method that allows attaching both a `mouseover` event and a `mouseout` event is called `hover()`. jQuery also accounts for another pattern that alternates between attached functions every other click; this method is called `toggle()`. The preceding example is refined further to use these two methods.

```
$(document).ready(
  function() {
    $('div').hover(
      function() {
        $(this).addClass('tmpExampleOver');
      },
      function() {
        $(this).removeClass('tmpExampleOver');
      }
    );

    $('div').toggle(
      function() {
        $(this).addClass('tmpExampleOn');
      },
      function() {
        $(this).removeClass('tmpExampleOn');
      }
    );
  }
);
```

The preceding source code produces **Figure 3-8** (not shown) and it does the same thing as the last two examples in still less code. The `hover()` method's first argument is a function that is bound to the element's `mouseover` event, and the second argument is a function that is bound to the element's `mouseout` event. Then the `toggle()` method accepts a minimum of two methods: Each method is alternated with each click — upon the first click, the first function is executed; upon the second click, the second function is executed; upon the third click, it goes back to the first function; and so on. A minimum of two functions is required, but you can supply an unlimited number of methods to alternate between.

Triggering Events

The functions that you bind to events with jQuery's Event API can be triggered independent of any event taking place rather easily. The concept allows you to reuse functions bound to events for other purposes. You can even pass arguments to the function without much fuss. The following demonstrates how you trigger an event in jQuery using the `trigger()` method:

```
<!DOCTYPE html PUBLIC "-//W3C//DTD XHTML 1.0 Strict//EN"
    "http://www.w3.org/TR/xhtml1/DTD/xhtml1-strict.dtd">
<html xmlns='http://www.w3.org/1999/xhtml' xml:lang='en'>
  <head>
```

```
        <meta http-equiv='content-type' content='text/html; charset=utf-8' />
        <meta http-equiv='content-language' content='en-us' />
        <title></title>
        <script type='text/javascript'
                src='../../../Source Code/jQuery/jQuery.js'>
        </script>
        <script type='text/javascript' src='Figure 3-9.js'></script>
        <link rel='stylesheet' href='Figure 3-9.css' type='text/css' />
      </head>
      <body>
        <form method='post' action='javascript:void(0);'>
          <div>
            <input type='text' name='tmpExample' value='Example' size='25' />
          </div>
        </form>
      </body>
    </html>
```

The following style sheet is included in the preceding markup document:

```
input.tmpFocused {
    background: #5092c5;
    color: white;
}
```

The following JavaScript demonstrates jQuery's `trigger()` method:

```
$(document).ready(
  function() {
    $('input').focus(
      function() {
        $(this).addClass('tmpFocused');
      }
    );

    $('input').blur(
      function() {
        $(this).removeClass('tmpFocused');
      }
    );

   $('input').trigger('focus');
  }
);
```

In the preceding example, you see a simple focus and blur event combination: When the `<input />` element is focused, the class name *tmpFocused* is added to it; when it is blurred, it is taken away. Upon page load, the `focus` event is triggered, giving the `<input />` element focus by default. This should look something like the screenshot in **Figure 3-9**.

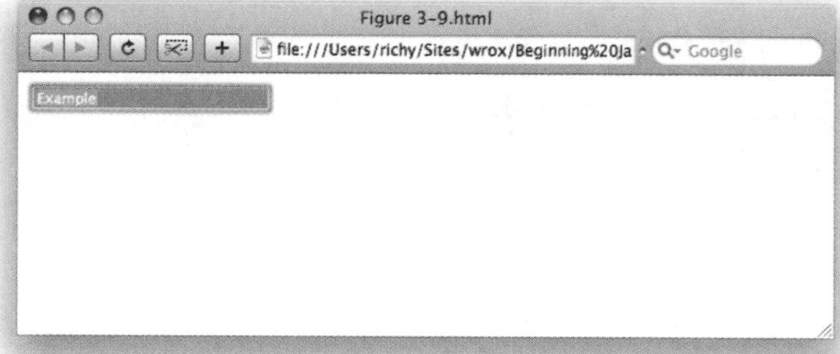

Figure 3-9

In the preceding example, you see how the `trigger()` element complements the `bind()` method, by giving you the ability to artificially simulate an event, without actually needing the event to take place. However, like the `bind()` method, jQuery also makes event simulation even easier, and you can also simulate an event in jQuery by simply calling the event method without any arguments. The following JavaScript demonstrates this concept by modifying the JavaScript that you saw in the last example:

```
$(document).ready(
  function() {
    $('input').focus(
      function() {
        $(this).addClass('tmpFocused');
      }
    );

    $('input').blur(
      function() {
        $(this).removeClass('tmpFocused');
      }
    );

   $('input').focus();
  }
);
```

In the preceding JavaScript, which produces **Figure 3-10** (not shown), instead of calling the `trigger()` method to simulate the focus event, you simply call the `focus()` method without passing any arguments to it, and this gives you the same result that you observed in **Figure 3-9.**

As I mentioned at the beginning of this section, if you need to, you can also pass arguments to the simulated event. You can do this by passing a second argument to the `trigger()` method, called the *data argument*. The data that you pass to the `trigger()` method is made available in the function acting as the event handler via its second argument, which can have whatever name you like. This is demonstrated in the following document:

```
<!DOCTYPE html PUBLIC "-//W3C//DTD XHTML 1.0 Strict//EN"
    "http://www.w3.org/TR/xhtml1/DTD/xhtml1-strict.dtd">
<html xmlns='http://www.w3.org/1999/xhtml' xml:lang='en'>
  <head>
    <meta http-equiv='content-type' content='text/html; charset=utf-8' />
    <meta http-equiv='content-language' content='en-us' />
    <title></title>
    <script type='text/javascript'
            src='../../../Source Code/jQuery/jQuery.js'>
    </script>
    <script type='text/javascript' src='Figure 3-11.js'></script>
    <link rel='stylesheet' href='Figure 3-11.css' type='text/css' />
  </head>
  <body>
    <form method='post' action='javascript:void(0);'>
      <div>
        <input type='text' name='tmpExample' value='Example' size='25' />
      </div>
    </form>
  </body>
</html>
```

The preceding markup document links to the following style sheet:

```
input.tmpFocused {
    background: #89130a;
    color: white;
}
input.tmpFocusedOnLoad {
    background: #acd1ed;
}
```

In the following JavaScript, you see how the `trigger()` method can pass additional information to the event handler. To access the information being passed to it, the event handler must define a second argument, which can have whatever name you like. In the following example, the information is passed to the event handler via the `$data` argument:

```
$(document).ready(
  function() {
    $('input').focus(
      function($e, $data) {
        if (typeof($data) != 'undefined' && $data.thisIsOnLoad) {
          $(this).addClass('tmpFocusedOnLoad');
        } else {
          $(this).addClass('tmpFocused');
        }
      }
    );

    $('input').blur(
```

```
          function() {
            $(this).removeClass('tmpFocusedOnLoad');
            $(this).removeClass('tmpFocused');
          }
        );

      $('input').trigger('focus', {thisIsOnLoad: true});
    }
  );
```

The preceding source code comes together to give you what you see in **Figure 3-11**. When the page first loads, the `<input />` element is given the class name *tmpFocusedOnLoad* and receives focus. Upon losing focus, or blurring, it loses that class name. Then on subsequent focuses, the `<input />` element receives the class name *tmpFocused*.

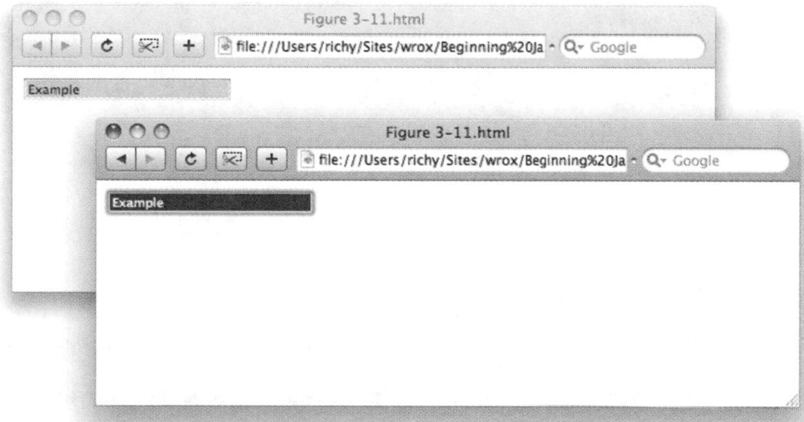

Figure 3-11

The following "Try It Out" reviews jQuery's Event API.

Try It Out — Reviewing jQuery's Event API

Example 3-1

For a comprehensive review of jQuery's Event API, follow these steps:

1. Create the following HTML document as *Example 3-1.html*:

```
<!DOCTYPE html PUBLIC "-//W3C//DTD XHTML 1.0 Strict//EN"
    "http://www.w3.org/TR/xhtml1/DTD/xhtml1-strict.dtd">
<html xmlns='http://www.w3.org/1999/xhtml' xml:lang='en'>
  <head>
    <meta http-equiv='content-type' content='text/html; charset=utf-8' />
    <meta http-equiv='content-language' content='en-us' />
```

```
    <title></title>
    <script type='text/javascript'
            src='../../../Source Code/jQuery/jQuery.js'>
    </script>
    <script type='text/javascript' src='Example 3-1.js'></script>
    <link rel='stylesheet' href='Example 3-1.css' type='text/css' />
  </head>
  <body>
    <p>
        jQuery's event API is modeled after the standard event API put
        forth by the W3C.  It's bind() method simplifies this API,
        by requiring less code, and dropping a mostly unneeded argument.
    </p>
    <div class='tmpBind'>
       <div></div>
       <div></div>
       <div></div>
    </div>
    <p>
        jQuery doesn't stop there, however, you can also use individual
        event methods to bind events.
    </p>
    <div class='tmpIndividual'>
        <div></div>
        <div></div>
        <div></div>
    </div>
    <p>
        And if that weren't enough, jQuery also provides two methods that
        accommodate applying both a mouseover and mouseout event in the
        same method, and a method that makes toggling easier and
        more intuitive.
    </p>
    <div class='tmpPattern'>
        <div></div>
        <div></div>
        <div></div>
    </div>
    <p>
        You can also programmatically trigger events, like automatically
        focusing the following &lt;textarea&gt; element on page load.
    </p>
    <div class='tmpTrigger'>
        <textarea name='tmpExample' cols='50' rows='5'>Example</textarea>
    </div>
    <p>
        Even triggering an event is made easier, you can use individual
        event methods with no arguments to do that too.
    </p>
  </body>
</html>
```

2. Create the following style sheet as *Example 3-1.css*:

```
body {
    font: 16px sans-serif;
}
div.tmpBind,
div.tmpIndividual,
div.tmpPattern {
    height: 100px;
}
div.tmpBind div,
div.tmpIndividual div,
div.tmpPattern div {
    height: 88px;
    width: 88px;
    border: 1px solid rgb(200, 200, 200);
    float: left;
    margin: 0 3px;
    background: #cfdbe5;
}
body div.tmpExampleOver {
    background: #acd1ed;
}
body div.tmpExampleOn {
    background: #7e93a4;
}
textarea.tmpFocused {
    background: #acd1ed;
    color: white;
}
```

3. Create the following JavaScript as *Example 3-1.js*:

```
$(document).ready(
  function() {
    $('div.tmpBind').bind(
      'mouseover',
      function() {
        $(this).find('div').addClass('tmpExampleOver');
      }
    ).bind(
      'mouseout',
      function() {
        $(this).find('div').removeClass('tmpExampleOver');
      }
    ).bind(
      'click',
      function() {
        if ($(this).find('div').hasClass('tmpExampleOn')) {
          $(this).find('div').removeClass('tmpExampleOn');
        } else {
          $(this).find('div').addClass('tmpExampleOn');
        }
      }
```

```
        );

        $('div.tmpIndividual').mouseover(
          function() {
            $(this).find('div').addClass('tmpExampleOver');
          }
        ).mouseout(
          function() {
            $(this).find('div').removeClass('tmpExampleOver');
          }
        ).click(
          function() {
            if ($(this).find('div').hasClass('tmpExampleOn')) {
              $(this).find('div').removeClass('tmpExampleOn');
            } else {
              $(this).find('div').addClass('tmpExampleOn');
            }
          }
        );

        $('div.tmpPattern').hover(
          function() {
            $(this).find('div').addClass('tmpExampleOver');
          },
          function() {
            $(this).find('div').removeClass('tmpExampleOver');
          }
        ).toggle(
          function() {
            $(this).find('div').addClass('tmpExampleOn');
          },
          function() {
            $(this).find('div').removeClass('tmpExampleOn');
          }
        );

        $('div.tmpTrigger textarea').focus(
          function($e) {
            $(this).addClass('tmpFocused');
          }
        ).blur(
          function() {
            $(this).removeClass('tmpFocused');
          }
        );

        $('div.tmpTrigger textarea').focus();
      }
    );
```

The preceding example should look like the screenshot in **Figure 3-12** when you load it into a browser.

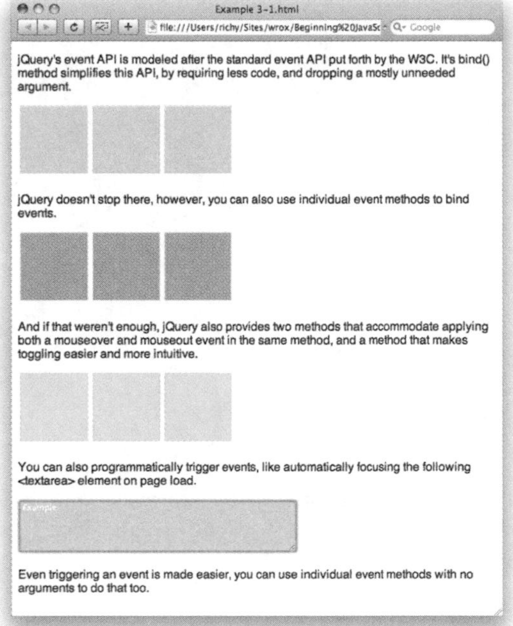

Figure 3-12

The preceding example lumps in almost everything you learned about jQuery's Event API in this chapter — the most important bits, at least. I introduced some minor deviations from the previous examples to keep things interesting.

The biggest deviation is that I demonstrated how you can reduce jQuery code even more by chaining the events together one after the other. Once you've made a selection in jQuery, most jQuery methods also return that selection, or a filtered selection, if you've opted to do that; even the event methods return your previous selection so that you can keep doing things with that selection. This is one thing about jQuery that has contributed to its immense popularity: It lets you chain methods one after the other to save you even more lines of code than it already does otherwise. Of course, you don't have to use this innovation, but it is one more thing you have available at your disposal.

The rest of the example reiterates the different ways that you can use jQuery's Event API to attach events to each element. The first chain of jQuery methods utilizes the `bind()` method to attach events to the following markup:

```
    <div class='tmpBind'>
      <div></div>
      <div></div>
      <div></div>
</div>
```

The preceding markup is styled by the following CSS:

```
div.tmpBind,
div.tmpIndividual,
div.tmpPattern {
    height: 100px;
}
div.tmpBind div,
div.tmpIndividual div,
div.tmpPattern div {
    height: 88px;
    width: 88px;
    border: 1px solid rgb(200, 200, 200);
    float: left;
    margin: 0 3px;
    background: #cfdbe5;
}
```

The preceding CSS puts those `<div>` elements side-by-side and makes them perfectly square boxes with a gray border and murky sky-blue backgrounds. The following JavaScript adds some remedial `mouseover`, `mouseout`, and `click` interactions:

```
$('div.tmpBind').bind(
  'mouseover',
  function() {
    $(this).find('div').addClass('tmpExampleOver');
  }
).bind(
  'mouseout',
  function() {
    $(this).find('div').removeClass('tmpExampleOver');
  }
).bind(
  'click',
  function() {
    if ($(this).find('div').hasClass('tmpExampleOn')) {
      $(this).find('div').removeClass('tmpExampleOn');
    } else {
      $(this).find('div').addClass('tmpExampleOn');
    }
  }
);
```

The `bind()` method in the preceding code takes two arguments: the type of event you want to attach and the function you want to use as an event listener. In this case, you're adding `mouseover`, `mouseout`, and `click` events to the `<div>` element with class name *tmpBind*. Upon `mouseover`, the class name *tmpExampleOver* is added to each of the child `<div>` elements, and upon `mouseout`, the class name is removed. The *tmpExampleOver* class name makes each child `<div>` element have a brighter sky-blue background. Upon clicking on the `<div>` element, the class name *tmpExampleOn* is added to each child `<div>` element, which makes each `<div>` element have a darker blue background. Clicking again removes the class name.

The next chunk of code does the same thing, but instead of using the `bind()` method to attach each event, you attach each event using the individual `mouseover()`, `mouseout()`, and `click()` event methods.

Then, in the chunk of code after that, you consolidate the event handlers for the `mouseover()` and `mouseout()` events into a single `hover()` method, and you split the event handler for the previous `click()` method into two methods that are passed to the `toggle()` method.

Finally, you add focus and blur events to the `<textarea>` element, and you trigger the `focus()` event handler for the `<textarea>` at page load.

Summary

Previous to JavaScript frameworks, the Event API was pretty fragmented between browsers. Microsoft had its own way of doing things, and everyone else had theirs. Through the past several years, cross-browser development potholes like this one helped to keep JavaScript down and relegated to the realm of novelty in mainstream web development … and worse, it contributed to the close-minded IE-only development policies put forth by many IT departments. The popularity of Firefox and Safari has challenged that mindset and pushed change on the status quo, and even forced Microsoft to return to serious development of its flagship browser.

JavaScript experts like Dean Edwards, Peter-Paul Koch, John Resig, and others have been instrumental in developing entirely JavaScript-driven patch-jobs that pave over JavaScript's rough edges to make development in JavaScript much more seamless and accessible to the average web developer.

jQuery's Event API makes dealing with events in JavaScript much easier and takes away the constant, tedious cross-browser bits that plagued the JavaScript of old and normalized events in JavaScript mostly on the W3C's superior event model. No longer do you have to worry about what object `this` refers to, or how to cancel the browser's default action for an event.

jQuery's `bind()` method mirrors the W3C `addEventListener()` closely, but makes it less verbose and drops the need to specify the third argument that barely ever gets any use. Additionally, jQuery innovates even further by providing individual event methods that further reduce the amount of code that you need to write, and makes it very easy to simulate an event.

Exercises

1. In the traditional event model, is it possible to attach multiple events of the same type to the same element?
2. What was the biggest shortcoming of the traditional event model that was addressed by the W3C's `addEventListener()` API?
3. In terms of the names of events, what is the difference in how events are named between the traditional event model, the W3C `addEventListener()` API, and Microsoft's event model?
4. What method does jQuery provide that is very similar to the W3C's `addEventListener()` API, and what are the differences?
5. What methods would you use if you wanted to simulate a `focus` event on a form `<input>` field?
6. If you wanted to attach both `mouseover` and `mouseout` events to an element, what would be the best method for doing so?

Manipulating Content and Attributes

jQuery is a thorough library, and it provides everything you can imagine for working with content from the DOM. In Chapter 2, you saw how jQuery made it really easy to fetch elements from the DOM via its fine-grained support for selecting and filtering selections. Then in Chapter 3, you saw how jQuery built on the W3C event model and made it less verbose while providing more methods that you can use in every browser today. This chapter continues the discussion of jQuery's API components with an in-depth look at the methods that jQuery makes available for manipulating content and attributes. No longer do you have to worry about whether a browser supports the `innerText` or `textContent` properties, or the `outerHTML` property, or what the standard DOM method of removing an element from a document is. jQuery paves right over these frighteningly verbose and sometimes fragmented methods with a rock-solid API that just works.

In this chapter, I cover how you can shuffle DOM content around, doing things like replacing one element with another, inserting new text or HTML, appending or prepending content, cloning content, and getting rid of content.

I also cover how you manipulate attributes using jQuery, another area that fringe use cases in some browsers (cough, IE) can make difficult.

Or maybe you've had occasion to want to save custom data with an element, without having to mess around with creating custom attributes or hidden elements. jQuery provides this too.

Setting and Accessing Attributes

Working with attributes is very easy with jQuery. Like everything you do with jQuery, first you make a selection, and then once you've made a selection, you can do something with that selection, like setting or accessing an attribute. Setting an attribute on a selection sets the attribute on every element that you've selected, which can be one or more elements. Accessing an attribute's value is also easy — once you've made a selection, accessing an attribute's value will provide you with the attribute value of the first element in the selection. The following document demonstrates these concepts in source code:

```
<!DOCTYPE html PUBLIC "-//W3C//DTD XHTML 1.0 Strict//EN"
    "http://www.w3.org/TR/xhtml1/DTD/xhtml1-strict.dtd">
<html xmlns='http://www.w3.org/1999/xhtml' xml:lang='en'>
  <head>
    <meta http-equiv='content-type' content='text/html; charset=utf-8' />
    <meta http-equiv='content-language' content='en-us' />
    <title></title>
    <script type='text/javascript'
            src='../../../Source Code/jQuery/jQuery.js'>
    </script>
    <script type='text/javascript' src='Figure 4-1.js'></script>
    <link type='text/css' href='Figure 4-1.css' rel='stylesheet' />
  </head>
  <body>
     <div>Mouse over to change this element's id.</div>
  </body>
</html>
```

The following style sheet is linked to the preceding document:

```
body {
    font: 16px sans-serif;
}
div {
    width: 350px;
    padding: 10px;
    border: 1px solid rgb(200, 200, 200);
    background: #93cdf9;
    margin: 5px;
}
div#tmpExample {
    background: #6faddd;
}
```

And the following JavaScript is also linked to the preceding document:

```
$(document).ready(
  function() {
    $('div').hover(
      function() {
        // Set the id attribute
        $(this).attr('id', 'tmpExample');

        // Get the id attribute
        $(this).text('This element\'s ID is: ' + $(this).attr('id'));
      },
      function() {
        $(this).attr('id', '');
        $(this).text('This element\'s ID has been removed.');
      }
    );
  }
);
```

The preceding example demonstrates how you use jQuery's `attr()` method to set the `id` attribute in the document. It's pretty easy: All you have to do is specify the name of the attribute you want to set in the first argument and the value you want to set in the second argument. Retrieving the attribute's value is also easy: Just call the `attr()` method with the name as the first argument, and do not specify a second argument. The preceding gives what you see in **Figure 4-1**.

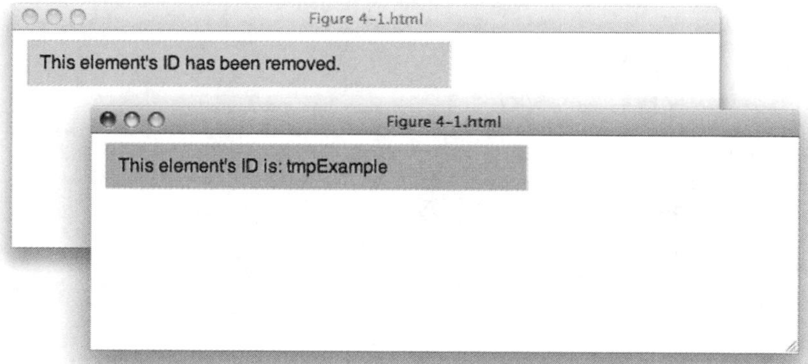

Figure 4-1

jQuery's `attr()` method can also have slightly different syntax — you can also pass an object literal to the method defining attributes in key, value pairs. This would look like the following:

```
$('a').attr({
  id:    'tmpExample',
  title: 'Some Tooltip Text',
  href:  'http://www.example.com'
});
```

Note the inclusion of the curly braces above. The opening curly brace comes after the opening parenthesis, letting JavaScript know that what follows is an object literal. Each property appears as the attribute name followed by a colon, then followed by the value. If the value is a string, it is, of course, enclosed in quotes; then you put in a comma and the next attribute key, value pair, and so on; then a closing curly brace completes the object. In this example, you set three separate attributes, the `id`, `title`, and `href` attributes. The alteration of the DOM would produce corresponding HTML that looks like this:

```
<a href='http://www.example.com' title='Some Tooltip Text' id='tmpExample'>A link
</a>
```

Taking away attributes is also easy — for that you use the `removeAttr()` method. This method takes the name of an attribute, then deletes that attribute from each selected element. So, if you were to run the following jQuery on the preceding markup:

```
$('a').removeAttr('title');
```

As you would expect, you would have the following markup instead:

```
<a href='http://www.example.com' id='tmpExample'>A link</a>
```

jQuery's `attr()` method lets you do one other thing, and that's set attributes using a callback function. This concept is demonstrated in the following document:

```
<!DOCTYPE html PUBLIC "-//W3C//DTD XHTML 1.0 Strict//EN"
    "http://www.w3.org/TR/xhtml1/DTD/xhtml1-strict.dtd">
<html xmlns='http://www.w3.org/1999/xhtml' xml:lang='en'>
  <head>
    <meta http-equiv='content-type' content='text/html; charset=utf-8' />
    <meta http-equiv='content-language' content='en-us' />
    <title></title>
    <script type='text/javascript'
            src='../../../Source Code/jQuery/jQuery.js'>
    </script>
    <script type='text/javascript' src='Figure 4-2.js'></script>
    <link type='text/css' href='Figure 4-2.css' rel='stylesheet' />
  </head>
  <body>
      <ul>
          <li>Jupiter</li>
          <li>Saturn</li>
          <li>Uranus</li>
          <li>Neptune</li>
      </ul>
  </body>
</html>
```

The following style sheet is included in the preceding document:

```
body {
    font: 16px sans-serif;
}
ul {
    list-style: none;
    padding: 0;
    margin: 0;
}
ul li {
    margin: 3px;
    padding: 3px;
}
li#tmpJupiter {
    background: #d7b05b;
}
li#tmpSaturn {
    background: #d3988a;
}
li#tmpUranus {
    background: #8ad3a6;
}
li#tmpNeptune {
    background: #8aa9d3;
}
```

The following JavaScript shows how each <li> element is selected; then an `id` attribute is added using jQuery's `attr()` method. An anonymous function is provided in the second argument, which is executed in the context of each selected <li> element. That means the anonymous function is executed four times, since there are four <li> elements. Within that function, an ID is created and returned by taking the prefix *tmp*, and the text content of the <li> element is retrieved using jQuery's `text()` method (which I discuss later in this chapter) and glued to that prefix. So, each <li> element receives a unique ID: The first <li> element is given the ID name *tmpJupiter*; the second, *tmpSaturn*; the third, *tmpUranus*; and the fourth, *tmpNeptune*.

```
$(document).ready(
  function() {
    $('li').attr(
      'id',
      function() {
        return 'tmp' + $(this).text();
      }
    );
  }
);
```

So jQuery's `attr()` method can accept a callback function, which is executed in the context of each selected element; the value returned by that function becomes the attribute value. **Figure 4-2** shows the example as it appears in a browser.

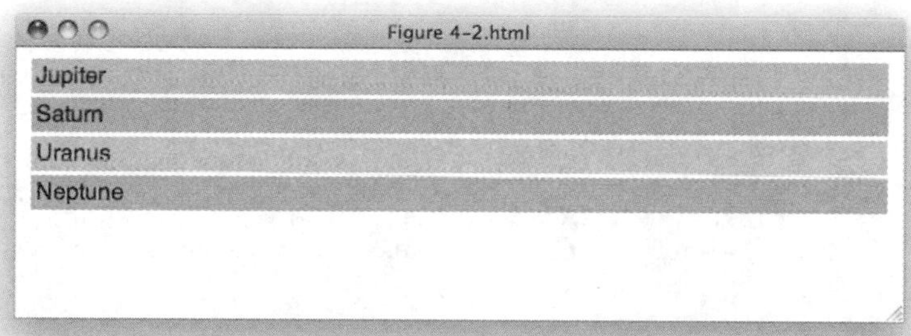

Figure 4-2

The following "Try It Out" recaps all you've learned about jQuery's attribute manipulation abilities.

Try It Out Manipulating Attributes

Example 4-1

To review attribute manipulation in jQuery, follow these steps:

1. Enter the following markup document into your text editor:

```
<!DOCTYPE html PUBLIC "-//W3C//DTD XHTML 1.0 Strict//EN"
    "http://www.w3.org/TR/xhtml1/DTD/xhtml1-strict.dtd">
<html xmlns='http://www.w3.org/1999/xhtml' xml:lang='en'>
```

```
<head>
  <meta http-equiv='content-type' content='text/html; charset=utf-8' />
  <meta http-equiv='content-language' content='en-us' />
  <title></title>
  <script type='text/javascript'
          src='../../../Source Code/jQuery/jQuery.js'>
  </script>
  <script type='text/javascript' src='Example 4-1.js'></script>
  <link type='text/css' href='Example 4-1.css' rel='stylesheet' />
</head>
<body>
   <p>
     Setting an attribute value with jQuery's attr() method is
     really easy, all you have to do is supply the name of the
     attribute and a value.
   </p>
   <span class='tmpSetAttr'>
     The id attribute of this element is set to <i>tmpSetID</i>.
   </span>
   <p>
     You can also set multiple attributes by supplying an object
     literal to the attr() method.
   </p>
   <span class='tmpSetMultipleAttr'>
     The title of this element is set to <i>Hello, World!</i> and
     the id attribute of this element is set to <i>tmpHelloWorld</i>.
   </span>
   <p>
     Getting an attribute value is just as intuitive, all you need
     to do is call the attr() method with the name of the attribute
     you want to get the value for.
   </p>
   <span class='tmpGetAttr' title='Foo'>
     This element's title attribute has a value of <span></span>.
   </span>
   <p>
     An attribute can be removed from an element using the
     removeAttr() method.
   </p>
   <span class='tmpRemoveAttr'>
     This element's class attribute is removed.
   </span>
   <p>
     Element attributes may also be set via a callback function.
   </p>
   <ul>
     <li>I</li>
     <li>Me</li>
     <li>Mine</li>
   </ul>
 </body>
</html>
```

2. Save the preceding document as *Example 4-1.html*.

3. Enter the following style sheet into your text editor:

```
body {
  font: 16px sans-serif;
}
span#tmpSetID {
  background: yellow;
  border: 1px dashed rgb(128, 128, 128);
  padding: 3px;
}
span#tmpHelloWorld {
  background: green;
  padding: 3px;
  border: 1px dashed yellowgreen;
  color: yellowgreen;
}
span.tmpGetAttr {
  background: blue;
  padding: 3px;
  border: 1px dashed lightblue;
  color: lightblue;
}
span.tmpRemoveAttr {
  background: red;
  padding: 3px;
  border: 1px dashed pink;
  color: pink;
}
ul {
  list-style: none;
  padding: 0;
  margin: 5px;
}
li#tmpI,
li#tmpMe,
li#tmpMine {
  padding: 3px;
}
li#tmpI {
  background: orange;
}
li#tmpMe {
  background: purple;
}
li#tmpMine {
  background: magenta;
}
```

4. Save the preceding document as *Example 4-1.css*.

5. Enter the following JavaScript document:

```
$(document).ready(
  function() {
    $('span.tmpSetAttr').attr('id', 'tmpSetID');

    $('span.tmpSetMultipleAttr').attr({
```

```
        title: 'Hello, World!',
        id: 'tmpHelloWorld'
      });

      $('span.tmpGetAttr').find('span').text(
        $('span.tmpGetAttr').attr('title')
      );

      $('span.tmpRemoveAttr').removeAttr('class');

      $('li').attr(
        'id',
        function() {
          return 'tmp' + $(this).text();
        }
      );
    }
  );
```

6. Save the preceding document as *Example 4-1.js*.

The preceding document gives you something like what you see in **Figure 4-3**.

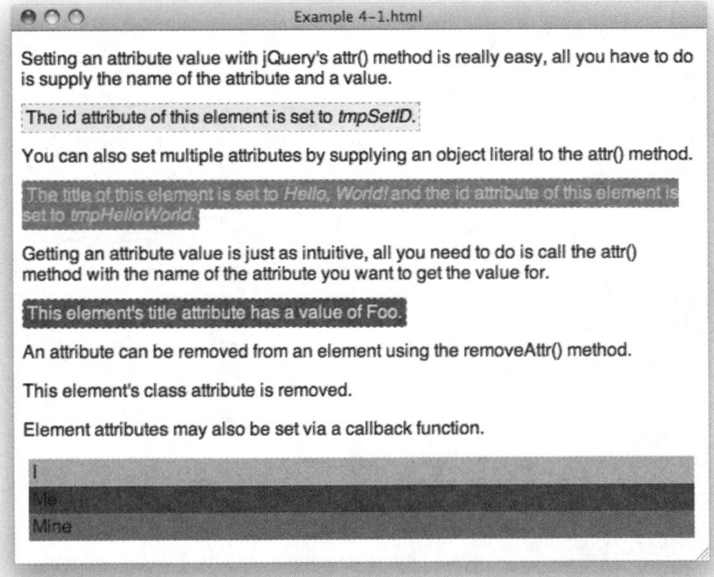

Figure 4-3

In Example 4-1, you reviewed all the ways that jQuery's API provides for direct manipulation of attribute values.

In the first example, you set the following <span> element's ID attribute to *tmpSetID*:

```
<span class='tmpSetAttr'>
  The id attribute of this element is set to <i>tmpSetID</i>.
</span>
```

The id attribute of the <span> element is set with the following JavaScript, by first selecting the <span> element with the selector span.tmpSetAttr, and then setting the id attribute by using jQuery's attr() method with two values, the first value being the attribute you want to set and the second value being the value you want to give to that attribute.

```
$('span.tmpSetAttr').attr('id', 'tmpSetID');
```

Adding the ID *tmpSetID* to the preceding <span> element triggers the following style-sheet rule to be applied to the <span> element:

```
span#tmpSetID {
  background: yellow;
  border: 1px dashed rgb(128, 128, 128);
  padding: 3px;
}
```

Subsequently, you set both the id and title attributes of the following <span> element:

```
<span class='tmpSetMultipleAttr'>
  The title of this element is set to <i>Hello, World!</i> and
  the id attribute of this element is set to <i>tmpHelloWorld</i>.
</span>
```

You set both the id and title attributes at the same time by providing an object literal to the attr() method, containing multiple attributes in key, value pairs.

```
$('span.tmpSetMultipleAttr').attr({
  title: 'Hello, World!',
  id: 'tmpHelloWorld'
});
```

The preceding application of the ID *tmpHelloWorld* results in the following style-sheet rule being applied to that <span> element:

```
span#tmpHelloWorld {
  background: green;
  padding: 3px;
  border: 1px dashed yellowgreen;
  color: yellowgreen;
}
```

In the next example, you simply retrieve the value of the title attribute and insert that value within a nested <span> element.

```
<span class='tmpGetAttr' title='Foo'>
  This element's title attribute has a value of <span></span>.
</span>
```

Setting the value of the nested `<span>` element is done with the following script. The outer `<span>` element is selected with the selector `span.tmpGetAttr`, then the nested `<span>` element is selected using `find('span')`, and the `text()` method is used to set the text value of that nested `<span>` element. The outer `<span>` is selected again, and the value of its `title` attribute is retrieved using the method `attr('title')`.

```
$('span.tmpGetAttr').find('span').text(
  $('span.tmpGetAttr').attr('title')
);
```

In the next example, you remove an attribute completely using jQuery's `removeAttr()` method.

```
<span class='tmpRemoveAttr'>
  This element's class attribute is removed.
</span>
```

The `class` attribute is removed completely using the following script:

```
$('span.tmpRemoveAttr').removeAttr('class');
```

The removal of the `class` attribute results in the following style-sheet rule *not* being applied:

```
span.tmpRemoveAttr {
  background: red;
  padding: 3px;
  border: 1px dashed pink;
  color: pink;
}
```

Then, the final example that you see demonstrates how you can use a callback function to set an element's attribute. You take the text values of the following `<li>` elements, and turn those into ID names.

```
<li>I</li>
<li>Me</li>
<li>Mine</li>
```

The following script selects each `<li>` element, and sets the `id` attribute of each `<li>` element to *tmpI, tmpMe, tmpMine*, respectively:

```
$('li').attr(
  'id',
  function() {
    return 'tmp' + $(this).text();
  }
);
```

The execution of the preceding script results in the following style-sheet rules being applied:

```
li#tmpI,
li#tmpMe,
li#tmpMine {
  padding: 3px;
}
```

```
li#tmpI {
  background: orange;
}
li#tmpMe {
  background: purple;
}
li#tmpMine {
  background: magenta;
}
```

In the next section, I continue the discussion of attribute manipulation in jQuery with the API jQuery offers for manipulating class names.

Manipulating Class Names

In earlier chapters, you've already seen examples of the `addClass()`, `hasClass()`, and `removeClass()` methods that jQuery uses to manipulate class names. It is considered best practice in client-side web development to avoid placing style declarations directly in your JavaScript code, and instead maintain a separation of behavior and presentation by placing styles in your CSS and manipulating the class names of elements for situations in which you require a manipulation of style. This is considered best practice for a reason: It makes the most sense. Since all of your presentation is neatly contained in CSS, and your behaviors in JavaScript, and your structure in HTML, your documents become much easier to manage, since it's more predictable where to look to make a modification. If your styles are scattered inline in HTML, in the JavaScript, and in actual style sheets, then it becomes an order of magnitude more difficult to change the presentation of a document.

Class names are very flexible and allow you to specify one or more class names for the same element. Multiple class names are separated by a single space in the attribute like so:

```
<div class='thisClassName otherClassName stillAnotherClassName'>
  Some content…
</div>
```

In the preceding example, the `<div>` element has three separate class names, any one of which can be used to delegate style from style sheets. CSS also specifies the ability to chain class names together in the style sheet, like so:

```
div.thisClassName.otherClassName.stillAnotherClassName {
    color: red;
}
```

The preceding isn't used very much, though, since IE6 only applies style to the last class name specified in the chain. This was fixed in IE7, and other browsers have long supported this. However, you don't have to chain the class names in the style sheet; you can specify the styles separately, using only one class name at a time, and utilize CSS's specificity and cascading rules to make sure the right style is applied.

```
div.thisClassName {
    color: red;
}
div.otherClassName {
    color: maroon;
```

```
}
div.stillAnotherClassName {
    color: crimson;
}
```

In the preceding example, the style for the <div> element will be crimson, since its selector has the same specificity as the preceding two, and thanks to the cascade, since it is last, its styles take precedence over the preceding two. Since you're applying behavior using JavaScript, you can use these rules to your advantage to create effects that happen on `click`, or on `mouseover` or `mouseout`, dynamically swapping the class names assigned to an element.

If these CSS topics are foreign to you, you might consider picking up a copy of my book Beginning CSS: Cascading Style Sheets for Web Design, *2nd ed. (Wiley, 2007), in which I discuss the preceding concepts in great detail.*

In the following "Try It Out" you review jQuery's class name manipulation API.

Try It Out — Manipulating Class Names

Example 4-2

To review the methods jQuery provides for manipulating class names, follow these steps:

1. Enter the following markup in a new document in your text editor:

```
<!DOCTYPE html PUBLIC "-//W3C//DTD XHTML 1.0 Strict//EN"
    "http://www.w3.org/TR/xhtml1/DTD/xhtml1-strict.dtd">
<html xmlns='http://www.w3.org/1999/xhtml' xml:lang='en'>
  <head>
    <meta http-equiv='content-type' content='text/html; charset=utf-8' />
    <meta http-equiv='content-language' content='en-us' />
    <title></title>
    <script type='text/javascript'
            src='../../../Source Code/jQuery/jQuery.js'>
    </script>
    <script type='text/javascript' src='Example 4-2.js'></script>
    <link type='text/css' href='Example 4-2.css' rel='stylesheet' />
  </head>
  <body>
      <p>
        jQuery's class name manipulation API can be used to add or
        remove a class name from multiple elements at once, using
        the addClass(), removeClass(), or toggleClass() methods.
      </p>
      <table>
        <tbody>
          <tr>
            <td></td>
            <td></td>
            <td></td>
          </tr>
          <tr>
            <td></td>
```

```
                <td></td>
                <td></td>
              </tr>
              <tr>
                <td></td>
                <td></td>
                <td></td>
              </tr>
            </tbody>
          </table>
      </body>
    </html>
```

2. Save the preceding markup document as *Example 4-2.html.*

3. Enter the following style sheet in yet another new document in your text editor:

```
body {
  font: 16px sans-serif;
}
td {
  width: 100px;
  height: 100px;
  border: 1px solid rgb(200, 200, 200);
}
td.tmpHover {
  background: yellow;
}
td.tmpSelected {
  background: orange;
}
```

4. Save the preceding document as *Example 4-2.css.*

5. Enter the following JavaScript in another new document:

```
$(document).ready(
  function() {
    $('table').hover(
      function() {
        $('td').addClass('tmpHover');
      },
      function() {
        $('td').removeClass('tmpHover');
      }
    )
    .click(
      function() {
        $('td').toggleClass('tmpSelected');
      }
    );
  }
);
```

6. Save the preceding document as *Example 4-2.js.*

The preceding document results in the screenshot that you see in **Figure 4-4** when you hover your mouse cursor over the table, and the screenshot that you see in **Figure 4-5** when you click on the table.

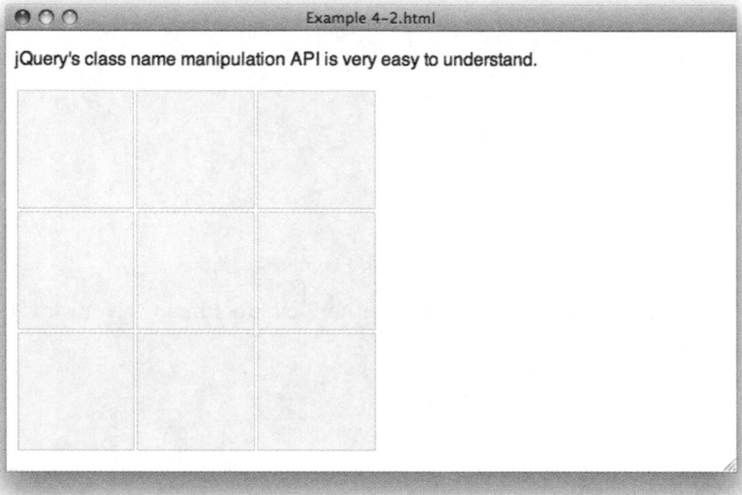

Figure 4-4

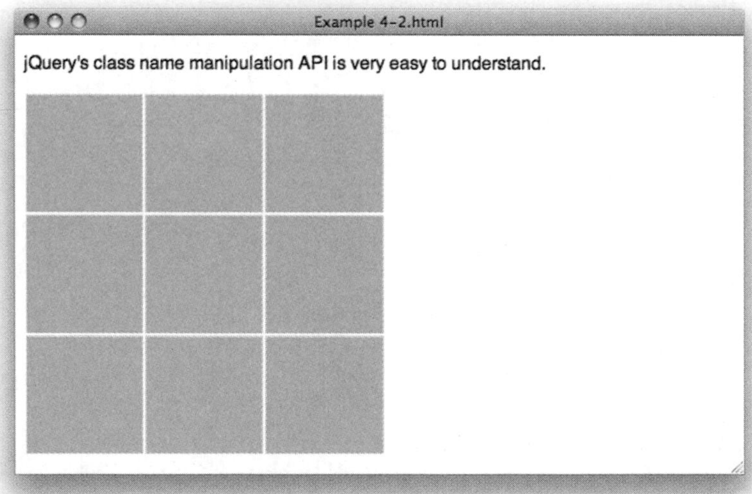

Figure 4-5

In Example 4-2, you did a quick review of the class name manipulation methods provided by jQuery. You attached two events to the `<table>` element, a `hover` event and a `click` event. When your mouse cursor hovers over the `<table>` element, the following script is executed:

```
$('table').hover(
  function() {
    $('td').addClass('tmpHover');
  },
  function() {
    $('td').removeClass('tmpHover');
  }
)
```

When the mouse is over the `<table>` element, the class name *tmpHover* is added to all nine `<td>` elements, using jQuery's `addClass()` method. When the mouse leaves the `<table>` element, the class name *tmpHover* is removed from all nine `<td>` elements using jQuery's `removeClass()` method. Adding the class name *tmpHover* to each `<td>` element triggers the following style-sheet rule to be applied to each `<td>` element:

```
td.tmpHover {
  background: yellow;
}
```

Finally, when you click on the `<table>`, the class name *tmpSelected* is toggled on and off (added and removed from each `<td>` element) with each alternate click.

```
.click(
  function() {
    $('td').toggleClass('tmpSelected');
  }
);
```

Adding the *tmpSelected* class name triggers the following style to be applied:

```
td.tmpSelected {
  background: orange;
}
```

jQuery's class-name manipulation methods make it much easier to add, remove, and toggle class names, in addition to checking for the presence of a class name. Making class-name manipulation easier, in turn, makes it easier for you to maintain separation of style and behavior, keeping your presentation in style sheets and your behavior in JavaScript.

Manipulating HTML and Text Content

jQuery provides a method for just about everything. Its unique, innovative approach to JavaScript programming reinvents how you program JavaScript. Reinventing JavaScript is required since jQuery methods define some ground rules that can be expected to be universal among all of its methods. For example, one ground rule that becomes more obvious as you learn more about how jQuery works is how wherever it is possible, its methods work on one or more elements. You never have to distinguish between whether you want to work with just one or lots of elements, since jQuery always assumes the possibility of an array.

Since jQuery always assumes the possibility of an array, it eliminates redundant code that has historically always been required to do an iteration over an array or list of several elements. You can chain methods onto one another, and you can perform complex operations on just one or many elements at the same time. One thing you may ask yourself while working with jQuery is, how do I access standard or de facto standard DOM methods and properties? In many cases, you don't need to directly access DOM properties or methods, since jQuery provides equivalent, and in most cases, less verbose methods that are designed to work seamlessly with jQuery's chainable model of programming. And not only are jQuery's methods less verbose, they also attempt to fix as many cross-browser stability and reliability issues as possible.

One such property that jQuery replaces is the de facto standard `innerHTML` property. The `innerHTML` property and many of Microsoft's extensions to the DOM are on their way to standardization in the HTML5 specification. The `innerHTML` property is one of the few Microsoft extensions to the DOM that has been ubiquitously adopted among browser makers.

Rather than relying exclusively on the implementation of Microsoft's de facto standard `innerHTML` property and similar properties, jQuery provides a variety of methods that assist you in manipulating HTML and text content. In this section, I discuss the following methods offered in jQuery's API:

- The `html()` method sets or gets the HTML content of one or more elements.
- The `text()` method gets or sets the text content for one or more elements.
- The `append()` and `prepend()` methods let you append or prepend content. I also talk about how these methods are actually better than the native de facto standard alternative, `innerHTML`.
- The `after()` and `before()` methods let you place content beside other elements (as opposed to appending or prepending the content inside of those elements).
- `insertAfter()` and `insertBefore()` methods let you modify a document by taking one selection of elements and inserting those elements beside another selection of elements.
- The `wrap()`, `wrapAll()`, and `wrapInner()` methods give you the ability to wrap one or more elements with other elements.

In the following sections, I describe and demonstrate how the preceding methods work, to give you expertise in understanding how content manipulation in jQuery works.

Getting, Setting, and Removing Content

The simplest methods that jQuery provides for content manipulation are the `html()` and `text()` methods. If you make a selection and call one of these methods without any arguments, jQuery simply returns the text or HTML content of the first matched element in a jQuery selection. The following document demonstrates how this works:

```
<!DOCTYPE html PUBLIC "-//W3C//DTD XHTML 1.0 Strict//EN"
    "http://www.w3.org/TR/xhtml1/DTD/xhtml1-strict.dtd">
<html xmlns='http://www.w3.org/1999/xhtml' xml:lang='en'>
```

```
  <head>
    <meta http-equiv='content-type' content='text/html; charset=utf-8' />
    <meta http-equiv='content-language' content='en-us' />
    <title></title>
    <script type='text/javascript'
            src='../../../Source Code/jQuery/jQuery.js'>
    </script>
    <script type='text/javascript' src='Figure 4-6.js'></script>
    <link type='text/css' href='Figure 4-6.css' rel='stylesheet' />
  </head>
  <body>
    <p>
      Before I speak, I have something important to say. <i>- Groucho Marx</i>
    </p>
  </body>
</html>
The preceding document is linked to the following stylesheet:
body {
    font: 16px sans-serif;
}
```

The following script demonstrates how you use the `html()` and `text()` methods and what to expect in the output that you get back:

```
$(document).ready(
  function() {
   alert(
     'HTML: ' + $('p').html() + "\n" +
     'Text: ' + $('p').text()
   )
  }
);
```

In **Figure 4-6**, you see that the `html()` method has returned the `<i>` element in the results, but the `text()` method has left that out. In this sense, you find that the `html()` method is similar to the `innerHTML` property, and the `text()` method is similar to the `innerText` or `textContent` properties.

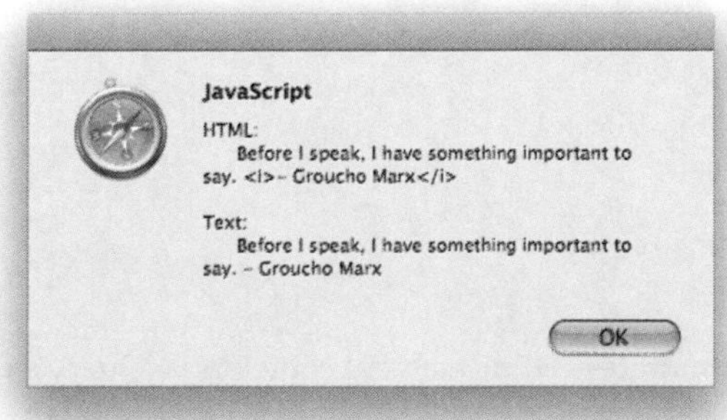

Figure 4-6

Setting Text or HTML Content

Setting content works similarly: All you have to do is provide the content that you want to set as the value for the element (or elements) in the first argument to the `text()` or `html()` method. Which method you use, of course, depends on whether or not you want HTML tags to be expanded as HTML. The following document demonstrates how to set text or HTML content:

```
<!DOCTYPE html PUBLIC "-//W3C//DTD XHTML 1.0 Strict//EN"
    "http://www.w3.org/TR/xhtml1/DTD/xhtml1-strict.dtd">
<html xmlns='http://www.w3.org/1999/xhtml' xml:lang='en'>
  <head>
    <meta http-equiv='content-type' content='text/html; charset=utf-8' />
    <meta http-equiv='content-language' content='en-us' />
    <title></title>
    <script type='text/javascript'
            src='../../../Source Code/jQuery/jQuery.js'>
    </script>
    <script type='text/javascript' src='Figure 4-7.js'></script>
    <link type='text/css' href='Figure 4-7.css' rel='stylesheet' />
  </head>
  <body>
    <p>
      Before I speak, I have something important to say. <i>- Groucho Marx</i>
    </p>
    <p class='tmpQuote' id='tmpQuote-1'>
    </p>
    <p class='tmpQuote' id='tmpQuote-2'>
    </p>
  </body>
</html>
```

The following style sheet is applied to the preceding HTML document:

```
body {
    font: 16px sans-serif;
}
p {
    padding: 5px;
    margin: 5px;
}
p.tmpQuote {
    background: lightblue;
}
p#tmpQuote-2 {
    background: lightgreen;
}
```

The following script demonstrates setting element content via jQuery's `text()` and `html()` methods:

```
$(document).ready(
  function() {
    $('p#tmpQuote-1').text(
      "Getting older is no problem. You just have to " +
```

```
            "live long enough. <i>- Groucho Marx</i>"
        );

        $('p#tmpQuote-2').html(
            "I have had a perfectly wonderful evening, but " +
            "this wasn't it. <i>- Groucho Marx</i>"
        );
    }
);
```

Figure 4-7 shows how the content applied via the `text()` method results in the HTML tags being ignored, and showing through in the rendered output of the <p> element with ID name *tmpQuote-1*. It also shows how the HTML tags are expanded in the content of the <p> element with ID name *tmpQuote-2*, which is applied using jQuery's `html()` method.

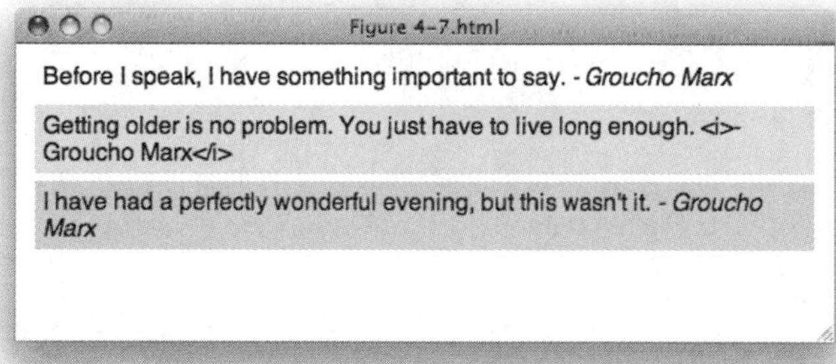

Figure 4-7

Setting Text or HTML Content for Multiple Items

Although you probably usually think about text or HTML content being applied only to a single element at a time, jQuery's `text()` and `html()` methods will apply that text or HTML content to one or more elements. The following document is essentially the same document that you saw in **Figure 4-7**, with some minor changes to demonstrate what happens when you apply HTML content to a selection that includes multiple elements:

```
<!DOCTYPE html PUBLIC "-//W3C//DTD XHTML 1.0 Strict//EN"
    "http://www.w3.org/TR/xhtml1/DTD/xhtml1-strict.dtd">
<html xmlns='http://www.w3.org/1999/xhtml' xml:lang='en'>
  <head>
    <meta http-equiv='content-type' content='text/html; charset=utf-8' />
    <meta http-equiv='content-language' content='en-us' />
    <title></title>
    <script type='text/javascript'
            src='../../../Source Code/jQuery/jQuery.js'>
    </script>
    <script type='text/javascript' src='Figure 4-8.js'></script>
    <link type='text/css' href='Figure 4-8.css' rel='stylesheet' />
  </head>
```

```
    <body>
      <p>
        Before I speak, I have something important to say. <i>- Groucho Marx</i>
      </p>
      <p class='tmpQuote' id='tmpQuote-1'>
      </p>
      <p class='tmpQuote' id='tmpQuote-2'>
      </p>
    </body>
  </html>
```

The following CSS is linked to the preceding HTML document:

```
body {
    font: 16px sans-serif;
}
p {
    padding: 5px;
    margin: 5px;
    background: lightgreen;
}
```

The following script applies HTML content to all of the <p> elements in the document:

```
$(document).ready(
  function() {
    $('p').html(
      "Quote me as saying I was mis-quoted.  " +
      "<i>- Groucho Marx</i>"
    );
  }
);
```

Figure 4-8 shows a screenshot of the output. You see that the quote applied in the script has been applied to all three <p> elements, replacing whatever content was present previously.

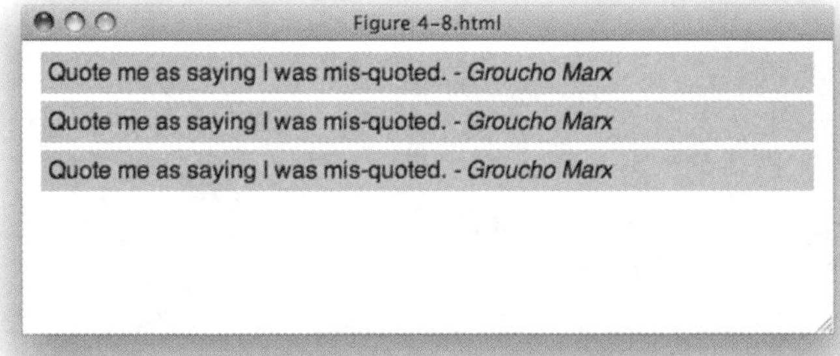

Figure 4-8

As you can see in **Figure 4-8**, jQuery applies the HTML content depending on your selection. If you've selected several elements, you'll find that the content modification has been applied to several elements, and if you've only selected a single element, you'll find that your content modifications have only been applied to a single element.

Removing Content

Removing content can also be done with jQuery's `text()` and `html()` elements. All you have to do to remove an element is to call either method with an empty string, that is, `text('')` or `html('')`, and that's all there is to it. That isn't the only way to remove content from a document, however, and you'll see alternative methods for doing this later in this chapter.

Appending and Prepending Content

One of the nuisances that jQuery patches over, leaving new jQuery developers completely oblivious to browser idiosyncrasies, is IE's Read Only limitation of `<table>` elements. When you use properties like `innerHTML` or `outerHTML` on `<table>` elements, the *table* designation encompasses any element used inside of `<table>` tag: `<tbody>`, `<thead>`, `<tfoot>`, `<tr>`, `<td>`, and `<th>`. As you develop more complex applications in which you require HTML tables for the layout of tabular data, this limitation becomes a painful roadblock that stifles innovation. Working around this limitation isn't too terribly difficult; any creative programmer can imagine a work-around where the table is completely rebuilt. Thankfully, jQuery paves right over this annoying IE bug, as is demonstrated with the following code:

```
<!DOCTYPE html PUBLIC "-//W3C//DTD XHTML 1.0 Strict//EN"
    "http://www.w3.org/TR/xhtml1/DTD/xhtml1-strict.dtd">
<html xmlns='http://www.w3.org/1999/xhtml' xml:lang='en'>
  <head>
    <meta http-equiv='content-type' content='text/html; charset=utf-8' />
    <meta http-equiv='content-language' content='en-us' />
    <title></title>
    <script type='text/javascript'
            src='../../../Source Code/jQuery/jQuery.js'>
    </script>
    <script type='text/javascript' src='Figure 4-9.js'></script>
    <link type='text/css' href='Figure 4-9.css' rel='stylesheet' />
  </head>
  <body>
      <h4>John Lennon Albums</h4>
      <table>
        <thead>
          <tr>
            <th>Title</th>
            <th>Year</th>
          </tr>
        </thead>
        <tbody>
          <tr>
            <td>John Lennon/Plastic Ono Band</td>
            <td>1970</td>
          </tr>
          <tr>
            <td>Imagine</td>
            <td>1971</td>
          </tr>
```

```
            <tr>
              <td>Some Time in New York City</td>
              <td>1972</td>
            </tr>
            <tr>
              <td>Mind Games</td>
              <td>1973</td>
            </tr>
            <tr>
              <td>Walls and Bridges</td>
              <td>1974</td>
            </tr>
            <tr>
              <td>Rock 'n Roll</td>
              <td>1975</td>
            </tr>
          </tbody>
        </table>
      </body>
    </html>
```

The preceding code is linked to the following style sheet:

```
body {
    font: 16px sans-serif;
}
h4 {
    margin: 5px;
}
table {
    width: 100%;
    background: lightgreen;
}
th {
    background: green;
    color: lightgreen;
}
```

Then the following JavaScript demonstrates IE's `innerHTML` Read Only limitation:

```
$(document).ready(
  function() {
    $('table tbody')[0].innerHTML +=
        "<tr>\n" +
        "  <td>Double Fantasy</td>\n" +
        "  <td>1980</td>\n" +
        "</tr>\n";
  }
);
```

As you can see in **Figure 4-9**, the new row including the album *Double Fantasy* is not present when this document is loaded in IE, but it is present when you load the document in Safari (or Firefox or Opera).

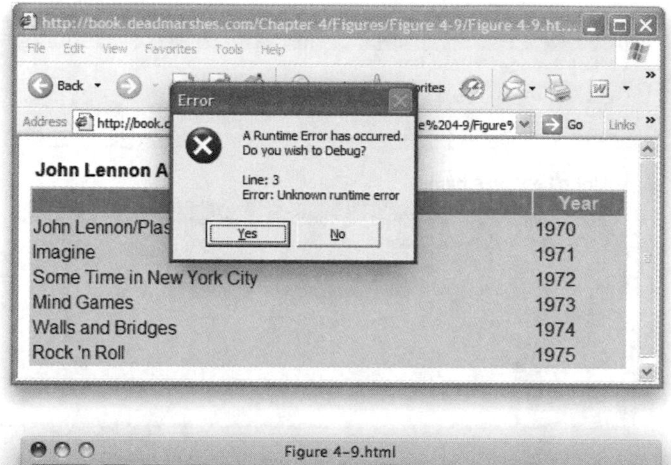

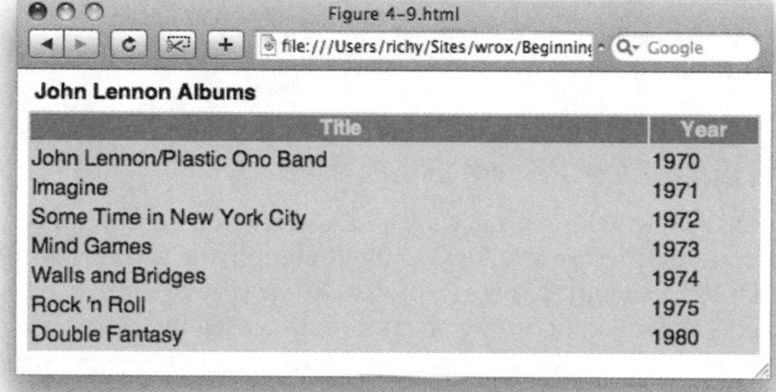

Figure 4-9

Figure 4-10 shows the same document in IE, with the following modifications made to the JavaScript:

```
$(document).ready(
  function() {
    $('table tbody').append(
      "<tr>\n" +
      "  <td>Double Fantasy</td>\n" +
      "  <td>1980</td>\n" +
      "</tr>\n"
    );
  }
);
```

In the preceding example, instead of directly using the `innerHTML` property to append HTML content to the `<tbody>` element, instead, you use jQuery's `append()` method. Since jQuery's `append()` method automatically fixes the Read Only limitation of the `innerHTML` property, appending the HTML to the table works this time, and you see *Double Fantasy* added to the table in IE6.

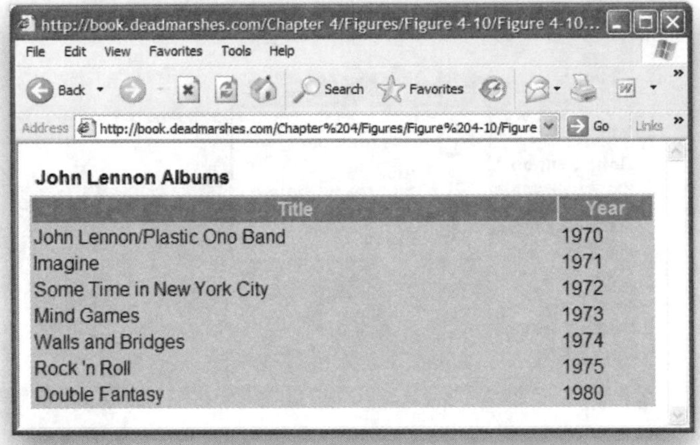

Figure 4-10

Fixing Firefox's `innerHTML` Form Bugs

In the previous section you saw how jQuery's `append()` function is superior to IE's native support for `innerHTML`, since it does not impose any Read Only limitation and actively works around that limitation. Another browser that has `innerHTML` bugs is Firefox. In the case of Firefox, a bug manifests while using `innerHTML` on elements that contain form elements, and you see the bug in action when you attempt to use `innerHTML` to append new content. When you do this, Firefox re-sets form elements and does not retain their values. Here again, jQuery comes to the rescue and actively fixes the issue, so you don't have to work around it.

The following document modifies the example that you saw in **Figures 4-9** and **4-10** so that the table now contains form elements:

```
<!DOCTYPE html PUBLIC "-//W3C//DTD XHTML 1.0 Strict//EN"
    "http://www.w3.org/TR/xhtml1/DTD/xhtml1-strict.dtd">
<html xmlns='http://www.w3.org/1999/xhtml' xml:lang='en'>
  <head>
    <meta http-equiv='content-type' content='text/html; charset=utf-8' />
    <meta http-equiv='content-language' content='en-us' />
    <title></title>
    <script type='text/javascript'
            src='../../../Source Code/jQuery/jQuery.js'>
    </script>
    <script type='text/javascript' src='Figure 4-11.js'></script>
    <link type='text/css' href='Figure 4-11.css' rel='stylesheet' />
  </head>
  <body>
    <h4>John Lennon Albums</h4>
    <table>
      <thead>
        <tr>
          <th>Title</th>
          <th>Year</th>
```

```
          </tr>
        </thead>
        <tbody>
          <tr>
            <td>
              <select>
                <option value='0'>0</option>
                <option value='0'>1</option>
              </select>
              <input type='text' value='John Lennon/Plastic Ono Band' size='25' />
            </td>
            <td>1970</td>
          </tr>
          <tr>
            <td>
              <input type='text' value='Imagine' size='25' />
            </td>
            <td>1971</td>
          </tr>
          <tr>
            <td>
              <input type='text' value='Some Time in New York City' size='25' />
            </td>
            <td>1972</td>
          </tr>
          <tr>
            <td>
              <input type='text' value='Mind Games' size='25' />
            </td>
            <td>1973</td>
          </tr>
          <tr>
            <td>
              <input type='text' value='Walls and Bridges' size='25' />
            </td>
            <td>1974</td>
          </tr>
          <tr>
            <td>
              <input type='text' value='Rock &#039;n Roll' size='25' />
            </td>
            <td>1975</td>
          </tr>
        </tbody>
      </table>
      <input type='submit' value='Add Album' id='tmpAddAlbum' />
  </body>
</html>
```

The preceding HTML document is linked to the same CSS document that you saw in **Figure 4-9**.

```
body {
    font: 16px sans-serif;
}
```

```
h4 {
    margin: 5px;
}
table {
    width: 100%;
    background: lightgreen;
}
th {
    background: green;
    color: lightgreen;
}
```

The JavaScript in **Figure 4-11** demonstrates a scripting scenario that trips the Firefox bug. Like the example that you saw in **Figure 4-9**, this example also does not work in IE because of its Read Only limitation.

```
$(document).ready(
  function() {
    $('input#tmpAddAlbum').click(
      function($e) {
        $e.preventDefault();

        $('table tbody')[0].innerHTML +=
          "<tr>\n" +
          "  <td>\n" +
          "    <input type='text' value='Double Fantasy' size='25' />\n" +
          "  </td>\n" +
          "  <td>1980</td>\n" +
          "</tr>\n";
      }
    );
  }
);
```

In **Figure 4-11**, you see that when you select the option “1” from the dropdown list in the first row, then click on the “Add Album” button, the select box in the first row reverts to option “0.”

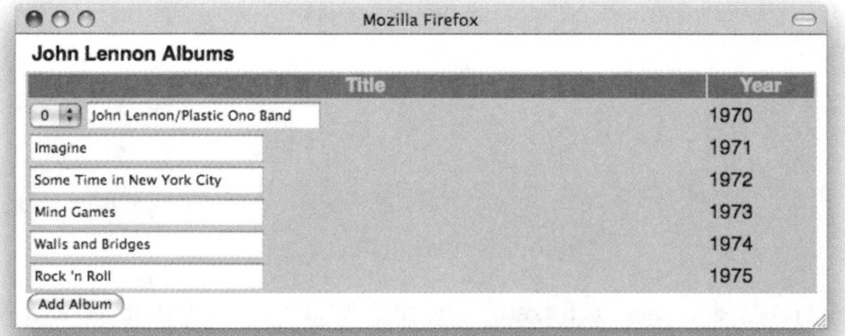

Mozilla Firefox

John Lennon Albums

Title	Year
0 John Lennon/Plastic Ono Band	1970
Imagine	1971
Some Time in New York City	1972
Mind Games	1973
Walls and Bridges	1974
Rock 'n Roll	1975

Add Album

Figure 4-11

In **Figure 4-12**, you see that the option "1" is selected, and the "Add Album" button is pressed.

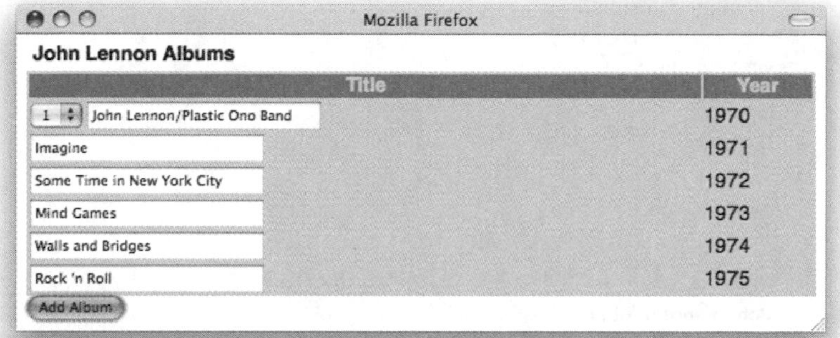

Figure 4-12

Figure 4-13 shows that the select box has reverted to option "0" after the row containing *Double Fantasy* is added.

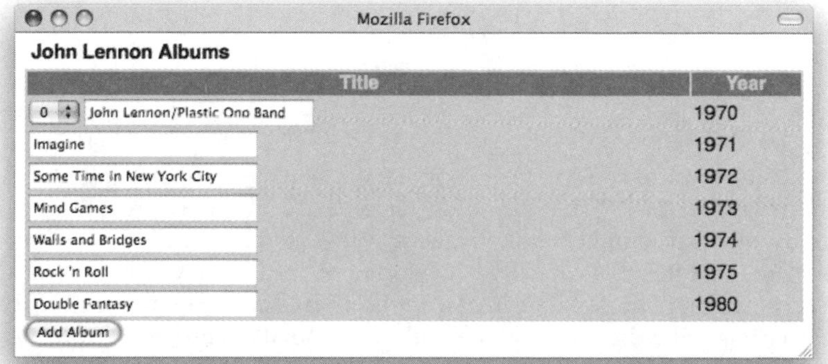

Figure 4-13

Again, jQuery's `append()` method works around this bug that's long been present in Firefox and is still present in Firefox 3 as I write this. The following script demonstrates how changing the JavaScript so that jQuery's `append()` method is used instead of directly working with the `innerHTML` method fixes the bug. **Figure 4-14** shows that the right outcome has been achieved upon pressing the "Add Album" button.

```
$(document).ready(
  function() {

    $('input#tmpAddAlbum').click(
      function($e) {
        $e.preventDefault();

        $('table tbody').append(
```

```
                "<tr>\n" +
                "  <td>\n" +
                "    <input type='text' value='Double Fantasy' size='25' />\n" +
                "  </td>\n" +
                "  <td>1980</td>\n" +
                "</tr>\n"
            );
        }
    );
  }
);
```

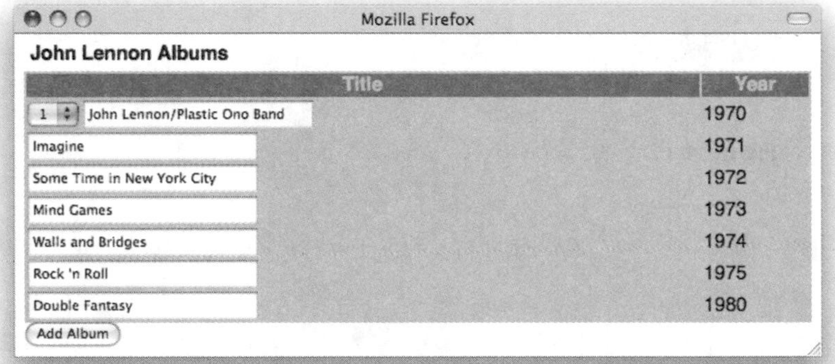

Figure 4-14

With the previous examples, you can see that jQuery doesn't just superfluously replace standard and de facto standard JavaScript API methods like `innerHTML`. It also fixes cross-browser bugs that act as roadblocks to smooth and seamless cross-browser web-based application development. You don't have to worry about the idiosyncrasies of native development, like those you've seen in the preceding examples, and you can ever more increasingly make applications that are guaranteed to just work everywhere. Aside from fixing bugs like the ones you see with the `innerHTML` property, however, you also find that jQuery's API is also more universally consistent in the way that it always lets you work with one or more items (where that makes sense and is possible). jQuery uses a standard method of selecting elements in a document, and it applies that standard, *selectors,* everywhere you need the ability to select an element. Browser makers and the authors of standardized JavaScript have much to learn from jQuery's clean, consistent, and smooth API.

Of course, even though you may have less to worry about in the realm of JavaScript, you're still stuck with Internet Explorer's badly outdated and undersupported CSS capabilities. As I am also an avid supporter of CSS, I look at a few of the challenges that you face with CSS as well, throughout this book.

Prepending Content

The word *prepend* is a term more or less invented by the technical programming world (although it does have some use outside of that world). It means to prefix or add some content to the beginning of something else. In fact, you won't find the word *prepend* in many dictionaries, and if you do, you'll find that the definition offered — "(transitive) To premeditate; to weigh up mentally" — doesn't really match up with the way it's used in the technical programming community, where this word is meant to be the opposite of *append*, which, of course, means "to add to the end of something."

This term has come out of the technical programming world by virtue of the flexible nature of computing when compared to the world of print. In the print world, modifying a hardcopy body of work is very difficult to do. You have to renumber pages, possibly renumber chapters, and rewrite table of contents and indexes. Without a computer, that's an enormous amount of work. So in the print world, it's easier to add to a printed body of work by *appending*, or tacking on new content to the end. It's not always done that way, but it's one possible explanation for why the world never really needed a word like *prepend* until the existence of computers made the action a necessity. In the technical world, it's easy to glue something onto the beginning of something else, so we made a new word to describe that action.

In the preceding sections discussing various bugs with modifying content via the `innerHTML` property, you learned how jQuery can modify content, tack on new content to the end of other content, via a method called `append()`. jQuery also offers a method that lets you prepend content, add content to the beginning of other content, and that is done with the method `prepend()`.

Inserting Beside Content

With the `append()` and `prepend()` methods, you're adding to content *within* an element. With the `before()` and `after()` methods, you are inserting content *beside* an element. The `before()` and `after()` methods are demonstrated in the following document:

```
<!DOCTYPE html PUBLIC "-//W3C//DTD XHTML 1.0 Strict//EN"
    "http://www.w3.org/TR/xhtml1/DTD/xhtml1-strict.dtd">
<html xmlns='http://www.w3.org/1999/xhtml' xml:lang='en'>
  <head>
    <meta http-equiv='content-type' content='text/html; charset=utf-8' />
    <meta http-equiv='content-language' content='en-us' />
    <title></title>
    <script type='text/javascript'
            src='../../../Source Code/jQuery/jQuery.js'>
    </script>
    <script type='text/javascript' src='Figure 4-15.js'></script>
    <link type='text/css' href='Figure 4-15.css' rel='stylesheet' />
  </head>
  <body>
      <p>
        Why, I'd horse-whip you if I had a horse.
      </p>
  </body>
</html>
```

The following style sheet is applied to the preceding document:

```
body {
    font: 16px sans-serif;
}
```

```
h4 {
    margin: 5px;
}
p {
    margin: 5px;
}
p.tmpAttribution {
    text-align: right;
}
```

The following JavaScript demonstrates how content can be inserted before and after the <p> element, via the respective `before()` and `after()` methods:

```
$(document).ready(
  function() {
    $('p')
      .before(
        "<h4>Quotes</h4>"
      )
      .after(
        "<p class='tmpAttribution'>\n" +
        " - Groucho Marx\n" +
        "</p>\n"
      );
  }
);
```

Figure 4-15 shows what happens when you load the preceding document in a browser.

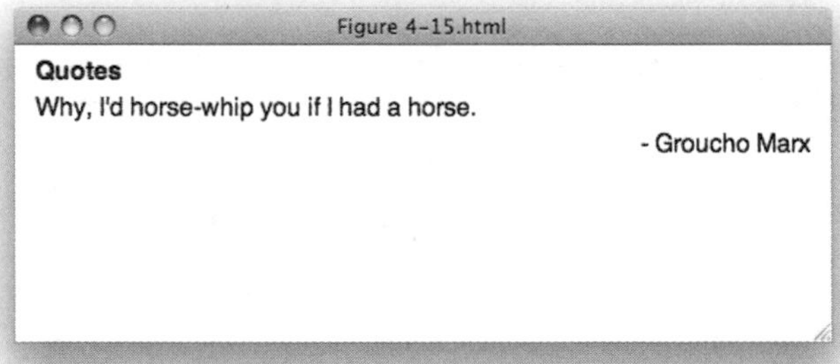

Figure 4-15

Figure 4-15 shows no real surprises. The content passed to the `before()` method is inserted before the <p> element, and the content passed to the `after()` method is inserted after the <p> element. The following markup shows what the source code looks like upon execution of this JavaScript:

```
<!DOCTYPE html PUBLIC "-//W3C//DTD XHTML 1.0 Strict//EN"
    "http://www.w3.org/TR/xhtml1/DTD/xhtml1-strict.dtd">
<html xmlns='http://www.w3.org/1999/xhtml' xml:lang='en'>
  <head>
    <meta http-equiv='content-type' content='text/html; charset=utf-8' />
```

```
    <meta http-equiv='content-language' content='en-us' />
    <title></title>
    <script type='text/javascript'
            src='../../../Source Code/jQuery/jQuery.js'>
    </script>
    <script type='text/javascript' src='Figure 4-15.js'></script>
    <link type='text/css' href='Figure 4-15.css' rel='stylesheet' />
  </head>
  <body>
     <h4>Quotes</h4>
     <p>
       Why, I'd horse-whip you if I had a horse.
     </p>
     <p class='tmpAttribution'>
      - Groucho Marx
     </p>
  </body>
</html>
```

Inserting Beside Content via a Selection

The `before()` and `after()` methods are used to insert content beside elements. The `insertBefore()` and `insertAfter()` methods do the same function, but instead of passing content directly to these methods, as you did with the `before()` and `after()` methods, you use a selector to reference another element in your document that you want inserted beside another element. In addition, the logic is reversed in how you write the script that does the insert beside action. The following document demonstrates how you might use the `insertBefore()` and `insertAfter()` methods:

```
<!DOCTYPE html PUBLIC "-//W3C//DTD XHTML 1.0 Strict//EN"
    "http://www.w3.org/TR/xhtml1/DTD/xhtml1-strict.dtd">
<html xmlns='http://www.w3.org/1999/xhtml' xml:lang='en'>
  <head>
    <meta http-equiv='content-type' content='text/html; charset=utf-8' />
    <meta http-equiv='content-language' content='en-us' />
    <title></title>
    <script type='text/javascript'
            src='../../../Source Code/jQuery/jQuery.js'>
    </script>
    <script type='text/javascript' src='Figure 4-16.js'></script>
    <link type='text/css' href='Figure 4-16.css' rel='stylesheet' />
  </head>
  <body>
     <!--  Template Items -->
     <table id='tmp'>
       <thead>
         <tr>
           <th>Title</th>
           <th>Year</th>
         </tr>
       </thead>
       <tfoot>
         <tr>
           <th>Title</th>
```

```
      <th>Year</th>
    </tr>
  </tfoot>
</table>

<!--  Main Content -->
<h4>John Lennon '70s Albums</h4>
<table class='tmpAlbums'>
 <tbody>
  <tr>
   <td>John Lennon/Plastic Ono Band</td>
   <td>1970</td>
  </tr>
  <tr>
   <td>Imagine</td>                <td>1971</td>
  </tr>
  <tr>
   <td>Some Time in New York City</td>
   <td>1972</td>
  </tr>
  <tr>
   <td>Mind Games</td>             <td>1973</td>
  </tr>
  <tr>
   <td>Walls and Bridges</td>      <td>1974</td>
  </tr>
  <tr>
   <td>Rock &#039;n Roll</td>      <td>1975</td>
  </tr>
 </tbody>
</table>
<h4>Paul McCartney '70s Albums</h4>
<table class='tmpAlbums'>
 <tbody>
  <tr>
   <td>McCartney</td>              <td>1970</td>
  </tr>
  <tr>
   <td>RAM</td>                    <td>1971</td>
  </tr>
  <tr>
   <td>Wild Life</td>              <td>1971</td>
  </tr>
  <tr>
   <td>Red Rose Speedway</td>      <td>1973</td>
  </tr>
  <tr>
   <td>Band on the Run</td>        <td>1973</td>
  </tr>
  <tr>
   <td>Venus and Mars</td>         <td>1975</td>
  </tr>
  <tr>
   <td>At the Speed of Sound</td>  <td>1976</td>
```

```
        </tr>
        <tr>
          <td>Thrillington (As Percy Thrillington)</td>
          <td>1977</td>
        </tr>
        <tr>
          <td>Londontown</td>            <td>1978</td>
        </tr>
        <tr>
          <td>Wings Greatest</td>        <td>1978</td>
        </tr>
        <tr>
          <td>Back To The Egg</td>       <td>1979</td>
        </tr>
      </tbody>
    </table>
  </body>
</html>
```

The following style sheet is applied to the preceding markup document:

```
body {
    font: 16px sans-serif;
}
h4 {
    margin: 5px;
}
table {
    width: 100%;
    background: lightblue;
}
th {
    background: royalblue;
    color: lightblue;
    font-weight: normal;
}
table#tmp {
    display: none;
}
```

The following script demonstrates how you use the `insertBefore()` and `insertAfter()` methods with selectors to duplicate content in a document:

```
$(document).ready(
  function() {
    $('table#tmp thead').insertBefore('table.tmpAlbums tbody');
    $('table#tmp tfoot').insertAfter('table.tmpAlbums tbody');
  }
);
```

Figure 4-16 shows the results of the preceding document in Safari.

Figure 4-16

In the preceding example, you can see that the `<thead>` and `<tfoot>` elements contained within the hidden `<table>` element with ID name *tmp* are duplicated to the other two `<table>` elements using jQuery. You start the script with the logic reversed; that is to say, you do the opposite of what you did with the `before()` and `after()` methods, where you first selected the element that you wanted to insert content beside and then provided the content to be inserted beside the selected element(s) within the `before()` or `after()` methods. This time, you begin with a selection of existing content within the document that you want to insert beside another element. In the script, you have the following:

```
$('table#tmp thead').insertBefore('table.tmpAlbums tbody');
```

The preceding line begins with selecting the `<thead>` element contained in the `<table>` with ID name *tmp*. You want to duplicate that `<thead>` element to the other two tables and use that content as a template. To do that, you call the `insertBefore()` method, then pass a selector to that method. The selector that you pass is the element before which you want the original selection, `<thead>`, to be inserted. The selector first references `<table>` elements with the class name *tmpAlbums*, then selects the descendent `<tbody>` element. So, in plain English, the script says, "Take the `<thead>` element in the hidden table and duplicate and insert that `<thead>` element before the `<tbody>` elements of the other two tables containing discography information for 1970s era albums of two former Beatles." The other line:

```
$('table#tmp tfoot').insertAfter('table.tmpAlbums tbody');
```

does the same thing, but this time, you take the `<tfoot>` element from the hidden table and duplicate and insert that element after the `<tbody>` element of the other two tables.

Essentially, the `insertBefore()` and `insertAfter()` methods make it easier to do templating.

Wrapping Content

In jQuery, *wrapping* an element means creating a new element and placing an existing element within a document inside that new element.

jQuery provides a few methods for wrapping content, that is to say, methods that take one or more elements and place those elements within container elements to change the structural hierarchy of a document. The methods that jQuery provides that let you wrap content are `wrap()`, `wrapAll()`, and `wrapInner()`. In the following sections, I demonstrate how to use these methods.

Wrapping a Selection of Elements Individually

jQuery's `wrap()` method is used to wrap each element matched in a selection individually. That is, if your selection matches five different elements, jQuery's `wrap()` method makes five separate wrappers. To better illustrate how this works, the following code demonstrates how the `wrap()` method is used to wrap three <p> elements within `<div>` elements:

```
<!DOCTYPE html PUBLIC "-//W3C//DTD XHTML 1.0 Strict//EN"
    "http://www.w3.org/TR/xhtml1/DTD/xhtml1-strict.dtd">
<html xmlns='http://www.w3.org/1999/xhtml' xml:lang='en'>
  <head>
    <meta http-equiv='content-type' content='text/html; charset=utf-8' />
    <meta http-equiv='content-language' content='en-us' />
    <title></title>
    <script type='text/javascript'
            src='../../../Source Code/jQuery/jQuery.js'>
    </script>
    <script type='text/javascript' src='Figure 4-17.js'></script>
    <link type='text/css' href='Figure 4-17.css' rel='stylesheet' />
  </head>
  <body>
    <h4>Mitch Hedberg Quotes</h4>
    <p>
      Dogs are forever in the push up position.
    </p>
    <p>
      I haven't slept for ten days, because that would be too long.
    </p>
    <p>
      I once saw a forklift lift a crate of forks. And it was way
      too literal for me.
    </p>
  </body>
</html>
```

The following style sheet is applied to the preceding markup document:

```
body {
    font: 16px sans-serif;
}
```

```
h4, p {
    margin: 5px;
}
div {
    background: #fedd58;
    border: 1px solid #ebcb49;
    margin: 3px;
}
```

The following script demonstrates jQuery's `wrap` method:

```
$(document).ready(
  function() {
    $('p').wrap('<div></div>');
  }
);
```

In **Figure 4-17**, you see that each <p> element is wrapped in a <div> element, which is made obvious by the styles applied in the style sheet. Each <div> has a distinct border, margin, and background color applied to make it obvious that a <div> exists.

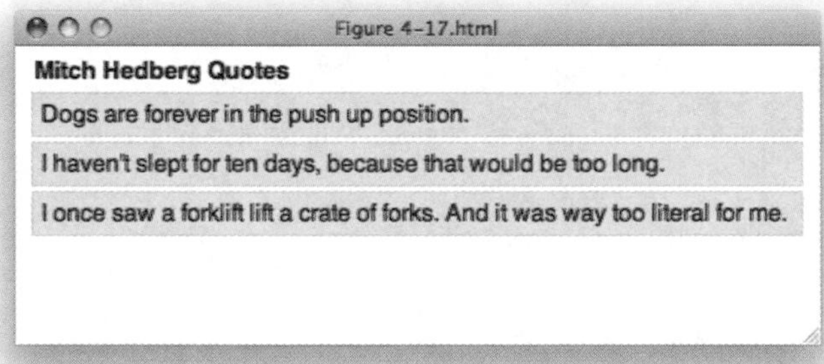

Figure 4-17

The preceding example makes it obvious that jQuery's `wrap()` method is used to wrap each element present in a selection individually.

Wrapping a Collection of Elements

Whereas the `wrap()` method wraps each item present in a selection individually, jQuery's `wrapAll()` method wraps all items present in a selection within a single wrapper. The following document presents the same markup and style sheet as you saw in the last section for the demonstration of the `wrap()` method. The only item that is changed is that the `wrapAll()` method is used instead of the `wrap()` method.

```
<!DOCTYPE html PUBLIC "-//W3C//DTD XHTML 1.0 Strict//EN"
    "http://www.w3.org/TR/xhtml1/DTD/xhtml1-strict.dtd">
<html xmlns='http://www.w3.org/1999/xhtml' xml:lang='en'>
```

```
    <head>
      <meta http-equiv='content-type' content='text/html; charset=utf-8' />
      <meta http-equiv='content-language' content='en-us' />
      <title></title>
      <script type='text/javascript'
              src='../../../Source Code/jQuery/jQuery.js'>
      </script>
      <script type='text/javascript' src='Figure 4-18.js'></script>
      <link type='text/css' href='Figure 4-18.css' rel='stylesheet' />
    </head>
    <body>
      <h4>Mitch Hedberg Quotes</h4>
      <p>
        Dogs are forever in the push up position.
      </p>
      <p>
        I haven't slept for ten days, because that would be too long.
      </p>
      <p>
        I once saw a forklift lift a crate of forks. And it was way
        too literal for me.
      </p>
    </body>
  </html>
  The following stylesheet is applied to the preceding markup.
  body {
      font: 16px sans-serif;
  }
  h4, p {
      margin: 5px;
  }
  div {
      background: #fedd58;
      border: 1px solid #ebcb49;
      margin: 3px;
  }
```

In the following script, you see that the `wrap()` method has been swapped out for the `wrapAll()` method:

```
$(document).ready(
  function() {
    $('p').wrapAll('<div></div>');
  }
);
```

Figure 4-18 shows that instead of each <p> element being individually wrapped in a <div> element, you find that all three <p> elements are wrapped with a single <div> element, as made obvious again by the styles used in your style sheet.

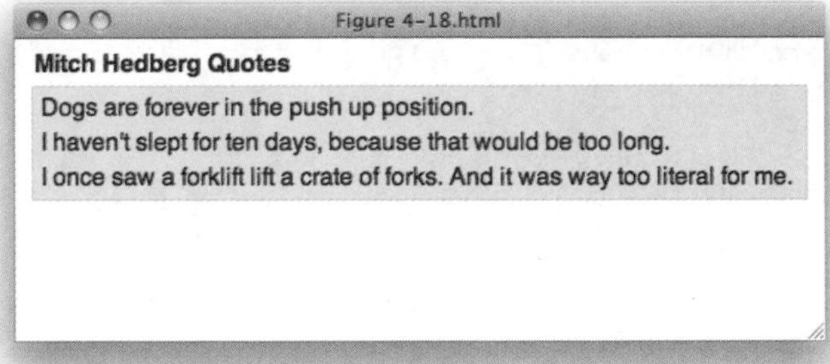

Figure 4-18

As you can see in the preceding example, the `wrapAll()` method takes a selection of elements and collectively wraps the whole selection with a single wrapper element.

Wrapping an Element's Contents

The last wrapper method that I demonstrate is the `wrapInner()` method, which is used to wrap an element's contents. This method works similarly to the `wrap()` method, in that a wrapper is applied to each item in a selection, but instead of the selected element being placed in a wrapper, its contents are placed in a wrapper. The following document, which is the same document you saw in the last two examples, demonstrates how the `wrapInner()` method compares and contrasts with the `wrap()` and `wrapAll()` methods:

```
<!DOCTYPE html PUBLIC "-//W3C//DTD XHTML 1.0 Strict//EN"
    "http://www.w3.org/TR/xhtml1/DTD/xhtml1-strict.dtd">
<html xmlns='http://www.w3.org/1999/xhtml' xml:lang='en'>
  <head>
    <meta http-equiv='content-type' content='text/html; charset=utf-8' />
    <meta http-equiv='content-language' content='en-us' />
    <title></title>
    <script type='text/javascript'
            src='../../../Source Code/jQuery/jQuery.js'>
    </script>
    <script type='text/javascript' src='Figure 4-19.js'></script>
    <link type='text/css' href='Figure 4-19.css' rel='stylesheet' />
  </head>
  <body>
    <h4>Mitch Hedberg Quotes</h4>
    <p>
      Dogs are forever in the push up position.
    </p>
    <p>
      I haven't slept for ten days, because that would be too long.
    </p>
    <p>
      I once saw a forklift lift a crate of forks. And it was way
      too literal for me.
    </p>
  </body>
</html>
```

The following style sheet is applied to the preceding markup document:

```
body {
    font: 16px sans-serif;
}
h4, p {
    margin: 5px;
}
```

In the following script, you see that the only change from the preceding two examples is that the `wrapInner()` method is used instead of the `wrap()` or `wrapAll()` methods:

```
$(document).ready(
  function() {
    $('p').wrapInner('<i></i>');
  }
);
```

In **Figure 4-19**, you see that the contents of all three `<p>` elements are each wrapped with `<i>` tags, making the contents of each `<p>` element styled in italics. Of course, this example is meant simply to convey how the `wrapInner()` method works. Even though what you see is a change to style invoked from JavaScript, which I personally consider to be bad practice, you should keep all style changes contained in your style sheet, but you see how the `wrapInner()` method technically works.

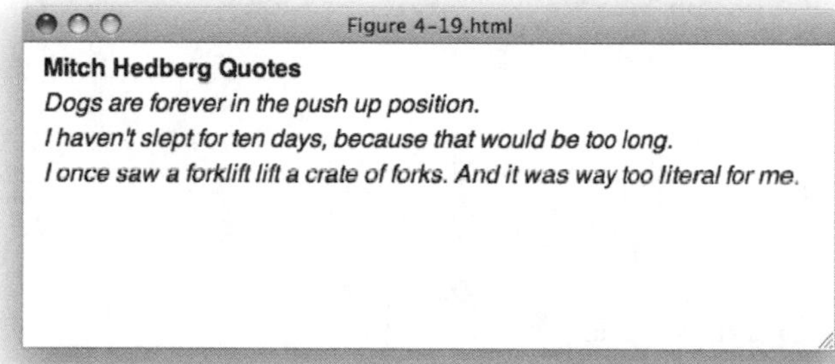

Figure 4-19

As demonstrated by what you see in **Figure 4-19**, the `wrapInner()` method takes the contents of each individual element present in a selection and places that content in a wrapper.

Wrapping Elements Using an Object Reference

The last item that I cover with regard to wrapping elements can be applied to any of the three wrapper methods — `wrap()`, `wrapAll()`, or `wrapInner()`. Specifically, you don't have to use a string of HTML in the argument passed to each of these methods, but you can also use a JavaScript object reference to a valid DOM element. The following document demonstrates what I mean by this:

```
<!DOCTYPE html PUBLIC "-//W3C//DTD XHTML 1.0 Strict//EN"
    "http://www.w3.org/TR/xhtml1/DTD/xhtml1-strict.dtd">
<html xmlns='http://www.w3.org/1999/xhtml' xml:lang='en'>
```

```
    <head>
      <meta http-equiv='content-type' content='text/html; charset=utf-8' />
      <meta http-equiv='content-language' content='en-us' />
      <title></title>
      <script type='text/javascript'
              src='../../../Source Code/jQuery/jQuery.js'>
      </script>
      <script type='text/javascript' src='Figure 4-20.js'></script>
      <link type='text/css' href='Figure 4-20.css' rel='stylesheet' />
    </head>
    <body>
      <h4>Mitch Hedberg Quotes</h4>
      <p>
        I saw a human pyramid once. It was very unnecessary. It
        did not need to exist.
      </p>
      <p>
        I used to be a hot-tar roofer. Yeah, I remember that… day.
      </p>
      <p>
        I want to get a vending machine, with fun sized candy bars,
        and the glass in front is a magnifying glass. You'll be mad,
        but it will be too late.
      </p>
    </body>
  </html>
  The following CSS is applied to the preceding markup document.
  body {
      font: 16px sans-serif;
  }
  h4, p {
      margin: 5px;
  }
  div {
      background: #70d6f0;
      border: 3px solid #7ac3d5;
      margin: 3px;
  }
```

In the following script, you see that instead of the string `<div></div>`, you pass `document.createElement('div')` to the `wrapAll()` method, which provides essentially the same effect that was demonstrated in **Figure 4-18**:

```
$(document).ready(
  function() {
    $('p').wrapAll(document.createElement('div'));
  }
);
```

Figure 4-20 shows that using a JavaScript object reference to an element provides the same result as passing a raw string of HTML to jQuery's `wrapAll()` method.

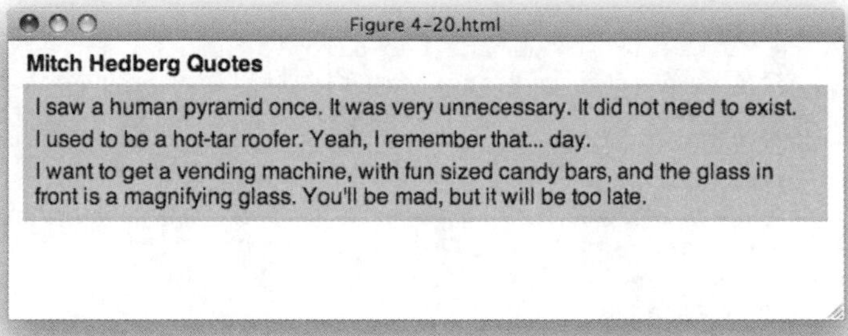

Figure 4-20

In the following "Try It Out," you recap all that you've learned about jQuery's document manipulation API:

Try It Out — Manipulating HTML and Text Content

Example 4-3

To review jQuery's document manipulation API, follow these steps:

1. Enter the following HTML into your text editor:

```
<!DOCTYPE html PUBLIC "-//W3C//DTD XHTML 1.0 Strict//EN"
    "http://www.w3.org/TR/xhtml1/DTD/xhtml1-strict.dtd">
<html xmlns='http://www.w3.org/1999/xhtml' xml:lang='en'>
  <head>
    <meta http-equiv='content-type' content='text/html; charset=utf-8' />
    <meta http-equiv='content-language' content='en-us' />
    <title></title>
    <script type='text/javascript'
            src='../../../Source Code/jQuery/jQuery.js'>
    </script>
    <script type='text/javascript' src='Example 4-3.js'></script>
    <link type='text/css' href='Example 4-3.css' rel='stylesheet' />
  </head>
  <body>
    <p>
      jQuery's <b>html()</b> method can be used to get HTML content.
    </p>
    <input type='submit' id='tmpGetHTML' value='Get HTML' />
    <p>
      jQuery's <b>text()</b> method can be used to get text content.
    </p>
    <input type='submit' id='tmpGetText' value='Get Text' />
    <p>
      The <b>html()</b> method can also be used to set HTML content,
      which is done by passing HTML to its first argument.
    </p>
    <input type='submit' id='tmpSetHTML' value='Set HTML' />
```

```
<p>
  The <b>text()</b> method can also be used to set text content,
  which is done by passing text to its first argument.
</p>
<input type='submit' id='tmpSetText' value='Set Text' />
<p class='tmpSetMultiple'>
  Text or HTML can be set on just one or many elements.
  <span></span>
  <span></span>
  <span></span>
</p>
<input type='submit' id='tmpSetMultiple' value='Set Multiple' />
<p>
  The <b>append()</b> method is used to append content.
</p>
<input type='submit' id='tmpAppend' value='Append HTML' />
<p>
  The <b>prepend()</b> method is used to prepend content.
</p>
<input type='submit' id='tmpPrepend' value='Prepend HTML' />
<p>
  The <b>before()</b> and <b>after()</b> methods are used
  to insert content beside other content.
</p>
<div class='tmpBeside'>
  <span class='tmpReference'></span>
</div>
<input type='submit' id='tmpBefore' value='Insert Before' />
<input type='submit' id='tmpAfter' value='Insert After' />
<span class='tmpReferenceBefore tmpTemplate'></span>
<span class='tmpReferenceAfter tmpTemplate'></span>
<p>
  The <b>insertBefore()</b> and <b>insertAfter()</b> methods are
  used to insert existing content beside other content via a
  selector.
</p>
<div class='tmpBesideSelection'>
  <span class='tmpReference'></span>
</div>
<input type='submit' id='tmpBeforeSelection' value='Insert Before' />
<input type='submit' id='tmpAfterSelection' value='Insert After' />
<p>
  The <b>wrap()</b> method is used to wrap each item in a selection
  with individual wrapper elements.
</p>
<input type='submit' id='tmpWrap' value='Wrap' />
<p>
  The <b>wrapAll()</b> method wraps an entire selection of elements
  in a single wrapper.
</p>
<input type='submit' id='tmpWrapAll' value='Wrap All' />
<p>
  The <b>wrapInner()</b> method wraps the contents of every element
  in a selection with individual wrapper elements.
</p>
```

```
    <input type='submit' id='tmpWrapInner' value='Wrap Inner' />
  </body>
</html>
```

2. Save the preceding document as *Example 4-3.html.*

3. Enter the following CSS in a new document in your text editor:

```
body {
  font: 16px sans-serif;
}
p {
  margin: 5px;
}
p.tmpSetMultiple span {
  display: block;
  margin: 5px;
}
div.tmpBeside,
div.tmpBesideSelection {
  clear: both;
  height: 62px;
}
span.tmpReference,
span.tmpReferenceBefore,
span.tmpReferenceAfter {
  float: left;
  width: 50px;
  height: 50px;
  margin: 5px;
}
span.tmpTemplate {
  display: none;
}
div span.tmpReference,
div span.tmpReferenceBefore,
div span.tmpReferenceAfter {
  display: block;
}
span.tmpReference {
  background: blue;
  border: 1px solid lightblue;
}
span.tmpReferenceBefore {
  background: green;
  border: 1px solid lightgreen;
}
span.tmpReferenceAfter {
  background: red;
  border: 1px solid pink;
}
div.tmpWrapper {
  background: #fdee8a;
  border: 3px solid #f3e270;
  margin: 5px;
```

```
}
div.tmpWrapAll {
  background: #bdfae2;
  border: 3px solid #a1e8cc;
}
span.tmpWrapInner {
  background: #b8def8;
}
```

4. Save the preceding document as *Example 4-3.css*.

5. Enter the following JavaScript in a new document in your text editor:

```
$(document).ready(
  function() {
    $('input').click(
      function($e) {
        $e.preventDefault();

        switch (this.id) {
          case 'tmpGetHTML': {
            alert($(this).prev().html());
            break;
          }
          case 'tmpGetText': {
            alert($(this).prev().text());
            break;
          }
          case 'tmpSetHTML': {
            $(this).prev().html(
              "<b>Set HTML Content.</b>"
            );
            break;
          }
          case 'tmpSetText': {
            $(this).prev().text(
              "<b>Set Text Content.</b>"
            );
            break;
          }
          case 'tmpSetMultiple': {
            $(this).prev().find('span').html(
              "<b>Set content on multiple items.</b>"
            );
            break;
          }
          case 'tmpAppend': {
            $(this).prev().append(
              " <b>This content is appended.</b>"
            );
            break;
          }
```

```
          case 'tmpPrepend': {
            $(this).prev().prepend(
              "<b>This content is prepended.</b> "
            );
            break;
          }
          case 'tmpBefore': {
            $('div.tmpBeside').find('span.tmpReference').before(
              "<span class='tmpReferenceBefore'></span>"
            );
            break;
          }
          case 'tmpAfter': {
            $('div.tmpBeside').find('span.tmpReference').after(
              "<span class='tmpReferenceAfter'></span>"
            );
            break;
          }
          case 'tmpBeforeSelection': {
            $('span.tmpReferenceBefore.tmpTemplate').insertBefore(
              'div.tmpBesideSelection span.tmpReference'
            );
            break;
          }
          case 'tmpAfterSelection': {
            $('span.tmpReferenceAfter.tmpTemplate').insertAfter(
              'div.tmpBesideSelection span.tmpReference'
            );
            break;
          }
          case 'tmpWrap': {
            $('p').wrap("<div class='tmpWrapper'></div>");
            break;
          }
          case 'tmpWrapAll': {
            $('body > *').wrapAll("<div class='tmpWrapAll'></div>");
            break;
          }
          case 'tmpWrapInner': {
            $('p').wrapInner("<span class='tmpWrapInner'></span>");
            break;
          }
        }
      }
    );
  }
);
```

6. Save the preceding document as *Example 4-3.js*.

The preceding example results in the document that you see in **Figure 4-21**.

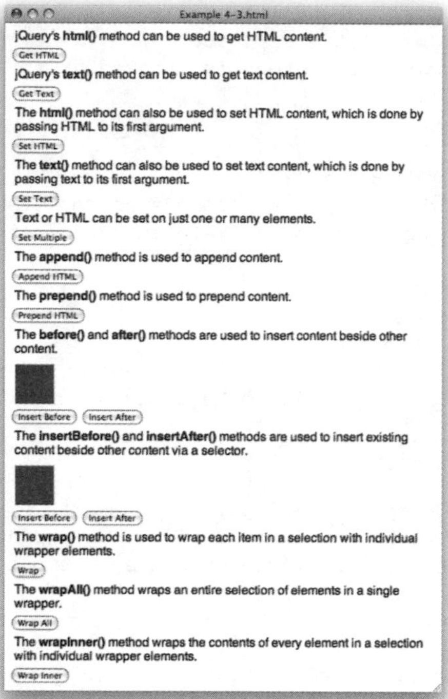

Figure 4-21

Example 4-3 reviews the various methods that jQuery provides for manipulating a document. Following is a line-by-line review of the code used in this example.

The first method that you review is jQuery's `html()` method. When you use this method without any arguments, you retrieve an element's HTML contents.

```
<p>
  jQuery's <b>html()</b> method can be used to get HTML content.
</p>
<input type='submit' id='tmpGetHTML' value='Get HTML' />
```

When you press the button labeled "Get HTML," you get an alert message that contains the contents of the `<p>` element that precedes that `<input>` element.

```
case 'tmpGetHTML': {
  alert($(this).prev().html());
  break;
}
```

In the alert message, you can see that the <b> tags are present, which lets you know that you retrieved the <p> element's content with HTML tags intact.

The next method that you review is the `text()` method. When you press the button in the following snippet, you get an alert message that contains the text content of the <p> element:

```
<p>
  jQuery's <b>text()</b> method can be used to get text content.
</p>
<input type='submit' id='tmpGetText' value='Get Text' />
```

This time, the <b> tags are not present in the alert message, which lets you know that you retrieved just the text content, ignoring all of the HTML tags.

Subsequently, you observe setting HTML content, also using the `html()` method.

```
<p>
  The <b>html()</b> method can also be used to set HTML content,
  which is done by passing HTML to its first argument.
</p>
<input type='submit' id='tmpSetHTML' value='Set HTML' />
```

When you press the `<input>` button associated with the preceding snippet, you replace the contents of the <p> element with the string `<b>Set HTML Content.</b>`.

```
case 'tmpSetHTML': {
  $(this).prev().html(
    "<b>Set HTML Content.</b>"
  );
  break;
}
```

Then, you observe setting text content using the `text()` method:

```
<p>
  The <b>text()</b> method can also be used to set text content,
  which is done by passing text to its first argument.
</p>
<input type='submit' id='tmpSetText' value='Set Text' />
```

This time, you set the contents of the <p> element to the string <b>`Set Text Content.`</b> using the `text()` method, upon pressing the `<input>` button. When you do this, you see that the raw unrendered HTML <b> tags appear as text.

```
case 'tmpSetText': {
  $(this).prev().text(
    "<b>Set Text Content.</b>"
  );
  break;
}
```

In the next example, you observe how using jQuery's manipulation methods work on multiple elements, if multiple elements are present in the selection. In this example, you see how this is true of the `html()` method, but it is true of all of jQuery's manipulation methods.

```
<p class='tmpSetMultiple'>
  Text or HTML can be set on just one or many elements.
  <span></span>
  <span></span>
  <span></span>
</p>
<input type='submit' id='tmpSetMultiple' value='Set Multiple' />
```

This time when you press the `<input>` button, you set the string `<b>Set content on multiple items .</b>` on the three `<span>` elements in the preceding snippet.

```
      case 'tmpSetMultiple': {
        $(this).prev().find('span').html(
          "<b>Set content on multiple items.</b>"
        );
        break;
      }
```

The next example demonstrates how the `append()` method is used to, ahem, append content.

```
<p>
  The <b>append()</b> method is used to append content.
</p>
<input type='submit' id='tmpAppend' value='Append HTML' />
```

When you press the button labeled "Append HTML," the string `<b>This content is appended.</b>` is tacked onto the end of the content of the `<p>` element.

```
      case 'tmpAppend': {
        $(this).prev().append(
          " <b>This content is appended.</b>"
        );
        break;
      }
```

Then, you observe the opposite, `prepend()` method, to, you guessed it, prepend content:

```
<p>
  The <b>prepend()</b> method is used to prepend content.
</p>
<input type='submit' id='tmpPrepend' value='Prepend HTML' />
```

When you press the button labeled "Prepend HTML," the string `<b>This content is prepended.</b>` is tacked onto the front of the content of the `<p>` element.

```
      case 'tmpPrepend': {
        $(this).prev().prepend(
          "<b>This content is prepended.</b> "
```

```
      );
      break;
    }
```

Consequentially, that leads to the next example, where you observe the `before()` and `after()` methods.

```
<p>
  The <b>before()</b> and <b>after()</b> methods are used
  to insert content beside other content.
</p>
<div class='tmpBeside'>
  <span class='tmpReference'></span>
</div>
<input type='submit' id='tmpBefore' value='Insert Before' />
<input type='submit' id='tmpAfter' value='Insert After' />
```

When you click on the button labeled "Insert Before," you insert a <span> element with class name *tmpReferenceBefore* before the <span> element with class name *tmpReference*. The <span> element inserted is styled with a green background, and the reference <span> is styled with a blue background.

```
    case 'tmpBefore': {
      $('div.tmpBeside').find('span.tmpReference').before(
        "<span class='tmpReferenceBefore'></span>"
      );
      break;
    }
```

First, you select the <div> with class name *tmpBeside*, then you use jQuery's `find()` method to locate the <span> with class name *tmpReference* (the blue <span>), and then you use jQuery's `before()` method to insert the new <span> with the green background before it.

When you click the button labeled "Insert After," you insert a <span> element with class name *tmpReferenceAfter*, after the <span> element with class name *tmpReference*. The new <span> is styled with a red background.

```
    case 'tmpAfter': {
      $('div.tmpBeside').find('span.tmpReference').after(
        "<span class='tmpReferenceAfter'></span>"
      );
      break;
    }
```

The next methods that you review are the `insertBefore()` and `insertAfter()` methods.

```
<span class='tmpReferenceBefore tmpTemplate'></span>
<span class='tmpReferenceAfter tmpTemplate'></span>
<p>
  The <b>insertBefore()</b> and <b>insertAfter()</b> methods are
  used to insert existing content beside other content via a
  selector.
</p>
<div class='tmpBesideSelection'>
  <span class='tmpReference'></span>
```

```
</div>
<input type='submit' id='tmpBeforeSelection' value='Insert Before' />
<input type='submit' id='tmpAfterSelection' value='Insert After' />
```

When you click the button labeled "Insert Before," the following script is executed:

```
case 'tmpBeforeSelection': {
  $('span.tmpReferenceBefore.tmpTemplate ').insertBefore(
    'div.tmpBesideSelection span.tmpReference'
  );
  break;
}
```

In the preceding script, you select the <span> with class name *tmpReferenceBefore,* then you call the `insertBefore()` method, which takes that <span> element, duplicates it, and inserts it before the <span> with class name *tmpReference,* which is contained within the <div> with class name *tmpBesideSelection.*

The following script does the name thing, only this time, you take the <span> with class name *tmpReferenceAfter,* duplicate it, and insert that <span> element after the <span> element with class name *tmpReference*:

```
case 'tmpAfterSelection': {
  $('span.tmpReferenceAfter.tmpTemplate ').insertAfter(
    'div.tmpBesideSelection span.tmpReference'
  );
  break;
}
```

Then, you review the various wrapper methods. The first wrapper method that you review is the `wrap()` method.

```
<p>
  The <b>wrap()</b> method is used to wrap each item in a selection
  with individual wrapper elements.
</p>
<input type='submit' id='tmpWrap' value='Wrap' />
```

When you click the button labeled "Wrap," the following script takes each <p> element and wraps it with a <div> with class name *tmpWrapper*:

```
case 'tmpWrap': {
  $('p').wrap("<div class='tmpWrapper'></div>");
  break;
}
```

Wrapping each <p> element in that <div> element triggers the following style-sheet rule to be applied:

```
div.tmpWrapper {
  background: #fdee8a;
  border: 3px solid #f3e270;
  margin: 5px;
}
```

Each <div> element has a yellow background with a darker yellow border.

Then, you review the wrapAll() method.

```
<p>
  The <b>wrapAll()</b> method wraps an entire selection of elements
  in a single wrapper.
</p>
<input type='submit' id='tmpWrapAll' value='Wrap All' />
```

When you click on the "Wrap All" button, the following script takes all children of the <body> element and wraps all of those elements in a single <div> element with class name *tmpWrapAll*:

```
case 'tmpWrapAll': {
  $('body > *').wrapAll("<div class='tmpWrapAll'></div>");
  break;
}
```

Wrapping everything in that <div> element triggers the application of the following style-sheet rule:

```
div.tmpWrapper {
  background: #fdee8a;
  border: 3px solid #f3e270;
  margin: 5px;
}
```

This <div> element has a sea-green colored background, with a darker sea-green border.

The final method that you review in Example 4-3 is the wrapInner() method:

```
<p>
  The <b>wrapInner()</b> method wraps the contents of every element
  in a selection with individual wrapper elements.
</p>
<input type='submit' id='tmpWrapInner' value='Wrap Inner' />
```

When you click the button labeled "Wrap Inner," the following script takes the content of each <p> element in a <span> element with class name *tmpWrapInner*:

```
case 'tmpWrapInner': {
  $('p').wrapInner("<span class='tmpWrapInner'></span>");
  break;
}
```

The addition of that <span> element results in the application of the following style-sheet rule:

```
span.tmpWrapInner {
  background: #b8def8;
}
```

The preceding style-sheet rule results in a light-blue colored background being applied to the text content of each <p> element.

Replacing Elements

In this section, I discuss two methods, jQuery's `replaceWith()` and `replaceAll()` methods. jQuery's `replaceWith()` method replaces a selection with whatever HTML content that you specify. This works very similarly to jQuery's `html()` method, but whereas the `html()` method sets an element's contents, jQuery's `replaceWith()` method replaces the element and its content. This can be thought to be similar to Microsoft's de facto standard `outerHTML` property. The following document demonstrates how jQuery's `replaceWith()` method works:

```
<!DOCTYPE html PUBLIC "-//W3C//DTD XHTML 1.0 Strict//EN"
    "http://www.w3.org/TR/xhtml1/DTD/xhtml1-strict.dtd">
<html xmlns='http://www.w3.org/1999/xhtml' xml:lang='en'>
  <head>
    <meta http-equiv='content-type' content='text/html; charset=utf-8' />
    <meta http-equiv='content-language' content='en-us' />
    <title></title>
    <script type='text/javascript'
            src='../../../Source Code/jQuery/jQuery.js'>
    </script>
    <script type='text/javascript' src='Figure 4-22.js'></script>
    <link type='text/css' href='Figure 4-22.css' rel='stylesheet' />
  </head>
  <body>
    <h4><i>More</i> Mitch Hedberg Quotes</h4>
    <div>
      <input type='submit' id='tmpQuote1' value='View Quote' />
    </div>
    <div>
      <input type='submit' id='tmpQuote2' value='View Quote' />
    </div>
  </body>
</html>
```

The following style sheet is applied to the preceding HTML:

```
body {
    font: 16px sans-serif;
}
h4, p {
    margin: 5px;
}
div {
    background: #70d6f0;
    border: 3px solid #7ac3d5;
    margin: 3px;
}
```

The following script demonstrates how jQuery's `replaceWith()` method is used to replace elements:

```
$(document).ready(
  function() {
    $('input#tmpQuote1').click(
```

```
        function($e) {
          $e.preventDefault();

          $(this).replaceWith(
            "<p>\n" +
            "  I would imagine that if you could understand \n" +
            "  Morse code, a tap dancer would drive you crazy.\n" +
            "</p>\n"
          );
        }
      );

      $('input#tmpQuote2').click(
        function($e) {
          $e.preventDefault();

          $(this).replaceWith(
            "<p>\n" +
            "  I'd like to get four people who do cart wheels \n" +
            "  very good, and make a cart.\n" +
            "</p>\n"
          );
        }
      );
    }
  );
```

Figure 4-22 shows the results of the preceding document. When you click on either of the buttons, you see that the button is replaced with the quote.

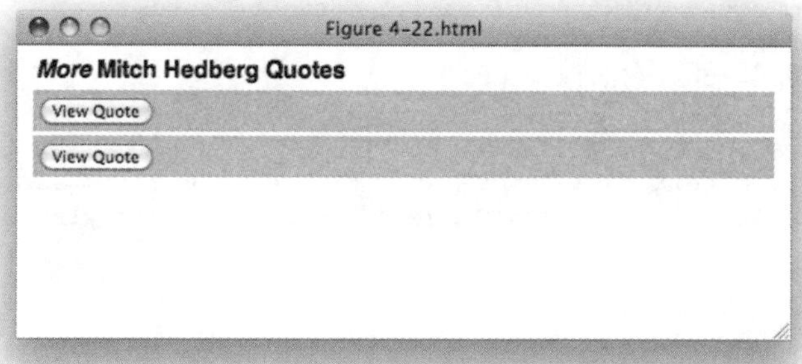

Figure 4-22

Figure 4-23 shows the buttons have been replaced with the quotes.

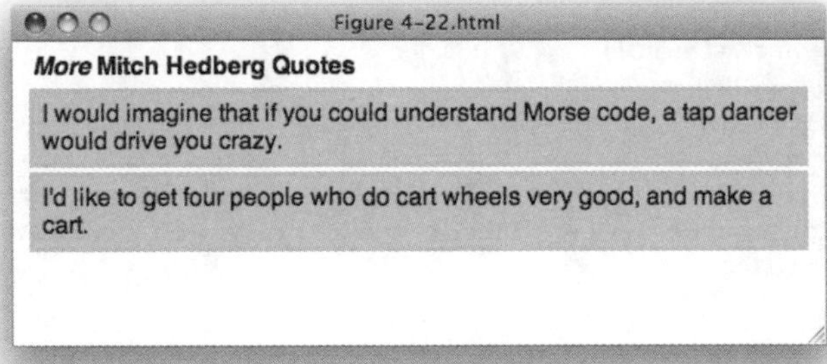

Figure 4-23

In the preceding example, you see that a `click` event is attached to each button, and upon clicking either button, you make a call to `$(this).replaceWith()`, which causes the `<input>` element to be replaced with the HTML content passed to the `replaceWith()` method.

The second method that I present in this section is jQuery's `replaceAll()` method, which works similarly to jQuery's `insertBefore()` and `insertAfter()` methods that you learned about previously in this chapter. jQuery's `replaceAll()` method takes a selector, instead of a string. The following document takes essentially the same content that you saw in **Figure 4-22**, but uses the `replaceAll()` method, instead of the `replaceWith()` method:

```
<!DOCTYPE html PUBLIC "-//W3C//DTD XHTML 1.0 Strict//EN"
    "http://www.w3.org/TR/xhtml1/DTD/xhtml1-strict.dtd">
<html xmlns='http://www.w3.org/1999/xhtml' xml:lang='en'>
  <head>
    <meta http-equiv='content-type' content='text/html; charset=utf-8' />
    <meta http-equiv='content-language' content='en-us' />
    <title></title>
    <script type='text/javascript'
            src='../../../Source Code/jQuery/jQuery.js'>
    </script>
    <script type='text/javascript' src='Figure 4-24.js'></script>
    <link type='text/css' href='Figure 4-24.css' rel='stylesheet' />
  </head>
  <body>
    <div id='tmp'>
      <p id='tmpQuoteText1'>
        I'm sick of following my dreams. I'm just going to ask them
        where they're goin', and hook up with them later
      </p>
      <p id='tmpQuoteText2'>
        My fake plants died because I did not pretend to water them.
      </p>
    </div>
    <h4><i>Even More</i> Mitch Hedberg Quotes</h4>
```

```
      <div>
        <input type='submit' id='tmpQuote1' value='View Quote' />
      </div>
      <div>
        <input type='submit' id='tmpQuote2' value='View Quote' />
      </div>
    </body>
  </html>
```

The following style sheet is applied to the preceding markup document:

```
body {
    font: 16px sans-serif;
}
h4, p {
    margin: 5px;
}
div {
    background: #acf7d0;
    border: 3px solid #96dab6;
    margin: 3px;
}
div#tmp {
    display: none;
}
```

The following script demonstrates how the `replaceAll()` method is used to replace content:

```
$(document).ready(
  function() {
    $('input#tmpQuote1').click(
      function($e) {
        $e.preventDefault();
        $('p#tmpQuoteText1').replaceAll(this);
      }
    );

    $('input#tmpQuote2').click(
      function($e) {
        $e.preventDefault();
        $('p#tmpQuoteText2').replaceAll(this);
      }
    );
  }
);
```

Figure 4-24 shows that you get a document similar to the one you saw in **Figure 4-22**. You have two buttons, and when you click on either button, a new Hedberg quote is revealed.

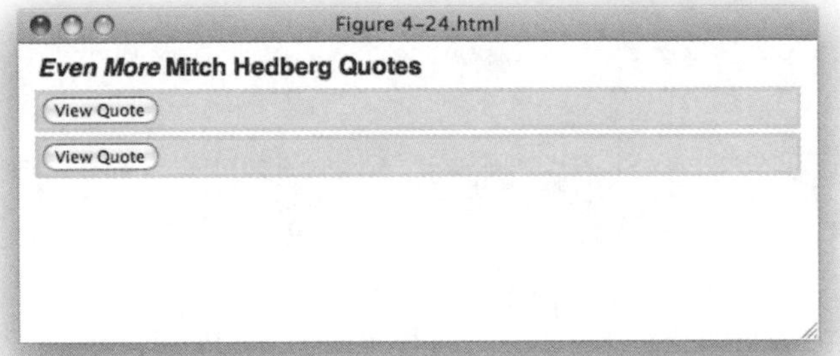

Figure 4-24

Figure 4-25 shows the results of clicking on each button.

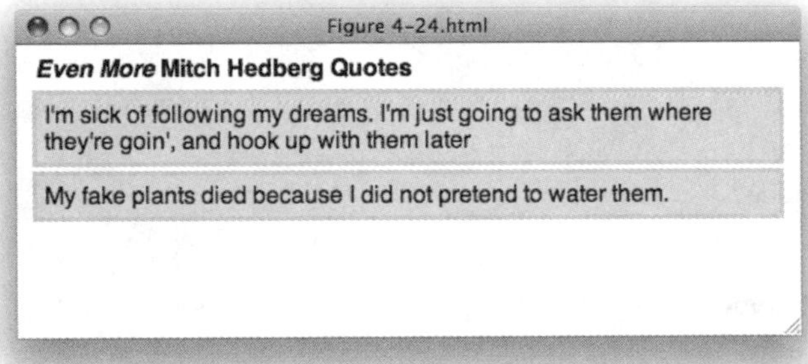

Figure 4-25

In the preceding example, you see that when you click on a button, a `click` event is executed. The content you want to use for replacement is selected, as `p#tmpQuoteText1`, for example, then the `replaceAll()` method is called, and you provide the item you want to replace as an argument to that method. In the preceding example, you pass the `this` keyword, but you can also use a selector. Essentially, you find that the logic is reversed from the `replaceWith()` method demonstrated earlier in this section.

Removing Content

Removing content can be done in a variety of ways. You can, for example, use the `replaceWith()` or `html()` methods in conjunction with an empty string. But jQuery also provides methods that are specifically designated for the removal of content, the `empty()` and the `remove()` methods. The following document demonstrates how both of these methods are used:

```
<!DOCTYPE html PUBLIC "-//W3C//DTD XHTML 1.0 Strict//EN"
    "http://www.w3.org/TR/xhtml1/DTD/xhtml1-strict.dtd">
<html xmlns='http://www.w3.org/1999/xhtml' xml:lang='en'>
  <head>
```

```
    <meta http-equiv='content-type' content='text/html; charset=utf-8' />
    <meta http-equiv='content-language' content='en-us' />
    <title></title>
    <script type='text/javascript'
            src='../../../Source Code/jQuery/jQuery.js'>
    </script>
    <script type='text/javascript' src='Figure 4-26.js'></script>
    <link type='text/css' href='Figure 4-26.css' rel='stylesheet' />
  </head>
  <body>
    <h4>John Lennon Albums</h4>
    <table>
      <thead>
        <tr>
          <th>Title</th>
          <th>Year</th>
        </tr>
      </thead>
      <tbody>
        <tr>
          <td>John Lennon/Plastic Ono Band</td>
          <td>1970</td>
        </tr>
        <tr>
          <td>Imagine</td>
          <td>1971</td>
        </tr>
        <tr>
          <td>Some Time in New York City</td>
          <td>1972</td>
        </tr>
        <tr>
          <td>Mind Games</td>
          <td>1973</td>
        </tr>
        <tr>
          <td>Walls and Bridges</td>
          <td>1974</td>
        </tr>
        <tr>
          <td>Rock 'n Roll</td>
          <td>1975</td>
        </tr>
        <tr>
          <td>Double Fantasy</td>
          <td>1980</td>
        </tr>
      </tbody>
    </table>
    <input type='submit' id='tmpEmptyTable' value='Empty Table' />
    <input type='submit' id='tmpDelete' value='Delete Content' />
  </body>
</html>
```

The following style sheet is applied to the preceding markup document:

```
body {
    font: 16px sans-serif;
}
h4 {
    margin: 5px;
}
table {
    width: 100%;
    background: lightgreen;
    margin-bottom: 5px;
}
th {
    background: green;
    color: lightgreen;
}
```

The following script demonstrates both the `empty()` and the `remove()` methods:

```
$(document).ready(
  function() {
    $('input#tmpEmptyTable').click(
      function($e) {
        $e.preventDefault();
        $('td').empty();
      }
    );

    $('input#tmpDelete').click(
      function($e) {
        $e.preventDefault();
        $('h4, table').remove();
      }
    );
  }
);
```

Figure 4-26 shows the result of the preceding example.

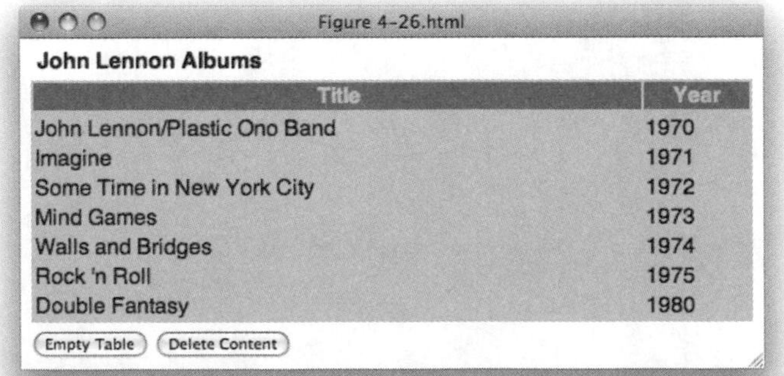

Figure 4-26.html

John Lennon Albums

Title	Year
John Lennon/Plastic Ono Band	1970
Imagine	1971
Some Time in New York City	1972
Mind Games	1973
Walls and Bridges	1974
Rock 'n Roll	1975
Double Fantasy	1980

Empty Table | Delete Content

Figure 4-26

Figure 4-27 shows what happens when you click on the button labeled "Empty Table": Each `<td>` element has its content removed.

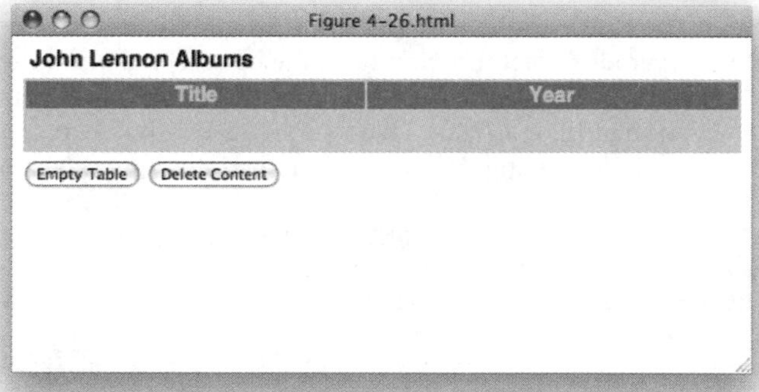

Figure 4-27

Figure 4-28 shows what happens when you click on the button labeled "Delete Content." Both the `<h4>` and the `<table>` element are removed from the document.

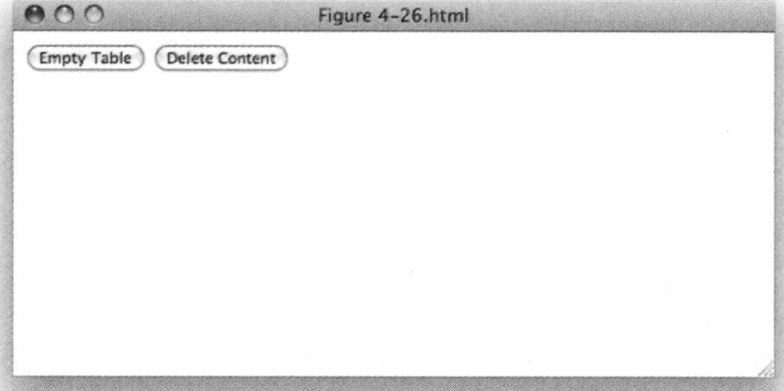

Figure 4-28

The preceding example shows what happens when you use jQuery's `empty()` method. This is essentially the same as passing an empty string to the `html()` method — all of the element's children elements, whether HTML elements or text, are removed.

The preceding example also demonstrates jQuery's `remove()` method, which deletes the items specified in the selection. It should be noted, however, that those items still exist within jQuery, and you can continue to work with those items by chaining subsequent jQuery methods to the `remove()` method. You can also pass a selector to the `remove()` method, which acts as a filter. Any items specified in a selector provided to the `remove()` method are preserved and are not removed from the document.

Cloning Content

jQuery provides a method called `clone()` for cloning (copying) content. jQuery's `clone()` method, unlike the DOM `cloneNode()` method, automatically assumes that you want to copy the element and all of its descendants, so you don't have to worry about specifying whether you want to clone descendant elements. Also unlike the DOM `cloneNode()` method, you have the option of cloning the element's event handlers (as well as those of descendant elements), which cannot be done with plain-vanilla JavaScript. If you want to clone the element's event handlers, all you have to do is specify Boolean `true` as the first argument to jQuery's `clone()` method. The following document demonstrates jQuery's `clone()` method:

```
<!DOCTYPE html PUBLIC "-//W3C//DTD XHTML 1.0 Strict//EN"
    "http://www.w3.org/TR/xhtml1/DTD/xhtml1-strict.dtd">
<html xmlns='http://www.w3.org/1999/xhtml' xml:lang='en'>
  <head>
    <meta http-equiv='content-type' content='text/html; charset=utf-8' />
    <meta http-equiv='content-language' content='en-us' />
    <title></title>
    <script type='text/javascript'
            src='../../../Source Code/jQuery/jQuery.js'>
    </script>
    <script type='text/javascript' src='Figure 4-29.js'></script>
    <link type='text/css' href='Figure 4-29.css' rel='stylesheet' />
  </head>
  <body>
     <h4>My Form</h4>
     <form action='javascript:void(0);' method='post'>
       <table>
         <thead>
           <tr>
             <th>Title</th>
             <th>Selected</th>
           </tr>
         </thead>
         <tbody>
           <tr id='tmp'>
             <td><input type='text' name='tmpTitle[]' value='0' /></td>
             <td><input type='checkbox' name='tmpTitleChecked[]' value='1' /></td>
           </tr>
           <tr>
             <td><input type='text' name='tmpTitle[]' value='0' /></td>
             <td><input type='checkbox' name='tmpTitleChecked[]' value='1' /></td>
           </tr>
           <tr>
             <td><input type='text' name='tmpFirst[]' value='0' /></td>
             <td><input type='checkbox' name='tmpTitleChecked[]' value='1' /></td>
           </tr>
         </tbody>
       </table>
       <input type='submit' id='tmpAddRow' value='Add a Row' />
     </form>
  </body>
</html>
```

The following style sheet is linked to the preceding document:

```
body {
    font: 16px sans-serif;
}
h4 {
    margin: 5px;
}
table {
    width: 100%;
    background: #b6d9f6;
    margin-bottom: 5px;
}
th {
    background: #8dc3f0;
}
tr#tmp {
    display: none;
}
```

The following script demonstrates jQuery's `clone()` method:

```
$(document).ready(
  function() {
    $('input#tmpAddRow').click(
      function($e) {
        $e.preventDefault();
        $('tr#tmp').clone(true).removeAttr('id').appendTo('tbody');
      }
    );

    $('tr input[type=text]').focus(
      function() {
        $(this).addClass('tmpFocused');
      }
    ).blur(
      function() {
        $(this).removeClass('tmpFocused');
      }
    );
  }
);
```

Figure 4-29 shows a screenshot of the preceding example. When you click on the "Add a Row" button, a new row is added to the form.

The script adds a `click` event to the `<input>` element. When the `<input>` element receives a `click` event, the `<tr>` with ID name *tmp* is selected, then the `clone()` method is called with the first argument set to `true`. Setting that argument to `true` causes the `clone()` method to also clone any event handlers present on the element being cloned, or any that element's children elements. Setting the first argument to `true` causes the `focus` and `blur` events attached to the text `<input>` element to be cloned along with the structural markup. The next method in the chain removes the `id` attribute from the cloned element by calling `removeAttr('id')`. Otherwise, the cloned row would be hidden. Then, the new cloned row is inserted into the document using jQuery's `appendTo()` method, which has the selector `tbody` specified, causing the new row to be appended to the `<tbody>`, thus adding a new row to the form.

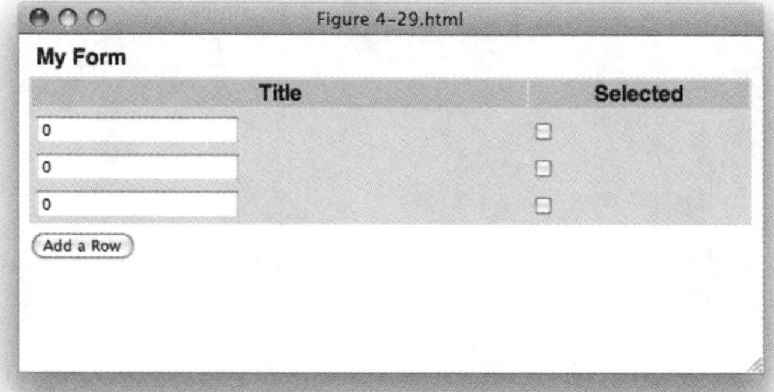

Figure 4-29

The following "Try It Out" recaps everything you've learned about jQuery's `replaceAll()`, `replaceWith()`, `empty()`, `remove()`, and `clone()` methods:

Try It Out — Replacing, Removing, and Cloning Content

Example 4-4

To recap replacing, removing, and cloning content with jQuery's manipulation API, follow these steps:

1. Enter the following markup into a new document in your text editor:

```
<!DOCTYPE html PUBLIC "-//W3C//DTD XHTML 1.0 Strict//EN"
    "http://www.w3.org/TR/xhtml1/DTD/xhtml1-strict.dtd">
<html xmlns='http://www.w3.org/1999/xhtml' xml:lang='en'>
  <head>
    <meta http-equiv='content-type' content='text/html; charset=utf-8' />
    <meta http-equiv='content-language' content='en-us' />
    <title></title>
    <script type='text/javascript'
            src='../../../Source Code/jQuery/jQuery.js'>
    </script>
    <script type='text/javascript' src='Example 4-4.js'></script>
    <link type='text/css' href='Example 4-4.css' rel='stylesheet' />
  </head>
  <body>
    <div class='tmpWrapper'>
      <input type='submit' id='tmpReplaceWith' value='Replace With' />
    </div>
    <div class='tmpWrapper'>
      <p id='tmpReplaceAllContent'>
        jQuery's replaceAll() method takes existing content and
        replaces it.
      </p>
```

```
        <input type='submit' id='tmpReplaceAll' value='Replace All' />
      </div>
      <div class='tmpWrapper'>
        <p>
          jQuery's empty() method removes all children elements (including
          text) from selected items. jQuery's remove() method completely
          removes the selected items.
        </p>
        <ul>
          <li>replaceAll()</li>
          <li>replaceWith()</li>
          <li>empty()</li>
          <li>remove()</li>
          <li>clone()</li>
        </ul>
        <input type='submit' id='tmpEmpty' value='Empty' />
        <input type='submit' id='tmpRemove' value='Remove' />
      </div>
      <div class='tmpWrapper'>
        <p>
          jQuery's clone() method can be used to duplicate elements.  Setting
          its first argument to true also duplicates those elements' event
          handlers.
        </p>
        <form action='javascript:void(0);' method='post'>
          <div id='tmp' class='tmpRow'>
            <input type='text' name='tmpItem' value='' size='25' />
          </div>
          <div>
            <input type='submit' id='tmpAddInput' value='Add Input' />
          </div>
        </form>
      </div>
    </body>
  </html>
```

2. Save the preceding document as *Example 4-4.html.*

3. Key the following CSS into another new document in your text editor:

```
body {
  font: 16px sans-serif;
}
p {
  margin: 5px;
}
p#tmpReplaceAllContent {
  display: none;
}
div.tmpWrapper,
form div {
  padding: 5px;
}
input.tmpFocused {
  background: lightblue;
}
```

4. Save the preceding document as *Example 4-4.css*.

5. Enter the following JavaScript into your text editor:

```
$(document).ready(
  function() {
    $('input#tmpReplaceWith').click(
      function($e) {
        $e.preventDefault();

        $(this).replaceWith(
          "<p>\n" +
          "  jQuery's replaceWith() method is used to completely \n" +
          "  replace one or more elements with the specified content.\n" +
          "</p>\n"
        );
      }
    );

    $('input#tmpReplaceAll').click(
      function($e) {
        $e.preventDefault();

        $('p#tmpReplaceAllContent')
          .replaceAll(this)
          .removeAttr('id');
      }
    );

    $('input#tmpEmpty').click(
      function($e) {
        $e.preventDefault();

        $('ul li').empty();
      }
    );

    $('input#tmpRemove').click(
      function($e) {
        $e.preventDefault();

        $('ul').remove();
      }
    );

    $('input#tmpAddInput').click(
      function($e) {
        $e.preventDefault();

        $('div#tmp')
          .clone(true)                    // Copy the <div>
          .removeAttr('id')               // Remove the id
          .insertAfter('div.tmpRow:last') // Insert after the last <div>
          .find('input')                 // Get the input
          .val('');                       // Remove the value
```

```
        }
      );

      $('input[type=text]')
        .focus(
          function() {
            $(this).addClass('tmpFocused');
          }
        )
        .blur(
          function() {
            $(this).removeClass('tmpFocused');
          }
        );
    }
  );
```

6. Save the preceding document as *Example 4-4.js*.

The documents you created in the preceding example result in the screenshot that you see in **Figure 4-30**.

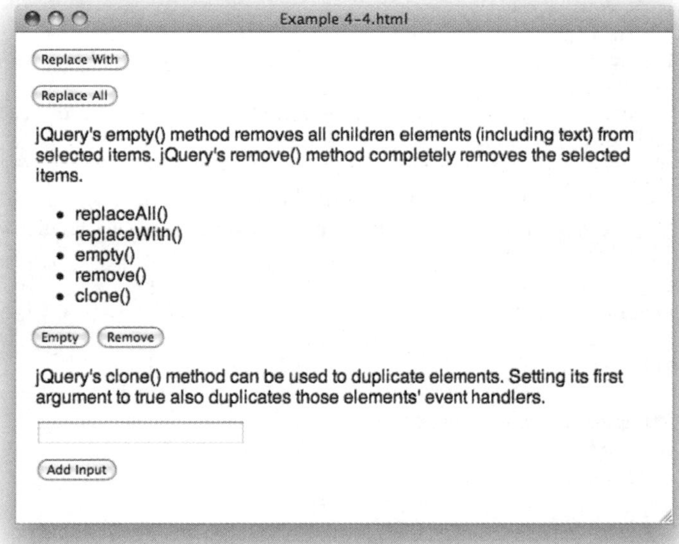

Figure 4-30

In Example 4-4, you reviewed the remaining jQuery manipulation methods that I cover in this chapter. You began the example by reviewing jQuery's `replaceWith()` method.

```
<div class='tmpWrapper'>
  <input type='submit' id='tmpReplaceWith' value='Replace With' />
</div>
```

When you press the preceding `<input>` button labeled "Replace With," the following script is executed:

```
$('input#tmpReplaceWith').click(
  function($e) {
    $e.preventDefault();

    $(this).replaceWith(
      "<p>\n" +
      "  jQuery's replaceWith() method is used to completely \n" +
      "  replace one or more elements with the specified content.\n" +
      "</p>\n"
    );
  }
);
```

In the preceding script, the `<input>` element that the user clicks on is completely removed from the document and replaced with the `<p>` element and its text content using the `replaceWith()` method.

The second method that you review in this example is jQuery's `replaceAll()` method.

```
<div class='tmpWrapper'>
  <p id='tmpReplaceAllContent'>
    jQuery's replaceAll() method takes existing content and
    replaces it.
  </p>
  <input type='submit' id='tmpReplaceAll' value='Replace All' />
</div>
```

When the `<input>` button in the preceding markup, labeled "Replace All" is clicked, the `<input>` element is completely removed from the document and replaced with the `<p>` element with ID name *tmpReplaceAllContent*.

```
$('input#tmpReplaceAll').click(
  function($e) {
    $e.preventDefault();

    $('p#tmpReplaceAllContent')
      .replaceAll(this)
      .removeAttr('id');
  }
);
```

After the `<input>` element is replaced with the `<p>` element, the `id` attribute is removed from the `<p>` element, which also makes that content visible. As you can see in this script and remember from previous discussions in this chapter, the `replaceAll()` method works with the logic reversed from the `replaceWith()` method. You first select the content that you want to use for replacement. You can also provide content directly to the dollar sign method, if you so choose; then you call the `replaceAll()` method with its first argument being a selector that references the content that you want to replace.

Next, you review jQuery's `empty()` and `remove()` methods.

```
<div class='tmpWrapper'>
  <p>
```

```
      jQuery's empty() method removes all children elements (including
      text) from selected items. jQuery's remove() method completely
      removes the selected items.
    </p>
    <ul>
      <li>replaceAll()</li>
      <li>replaceWith()</li>
      <li>empty()</li>
      <li>remove()</li>
      <li>clone()</li>
    </ul>
    <input type='submit' id='tmpEmpty' value='Empty' />
    <input type='submit' id='tmpRemove' value='Remove' />
  </div>
```

When you click on the <input> button labeled "Empty" in the preceding snippet of markup, you execute the following script:

```
$('input#tmpEmpty').click(
  function($e) {
    $e.preventDefault();

    $('ul li').empty();
  }
);
```

The preceding script demonstrates how `empty()` is used to remove the content of each `<li>` element.

When you click on the <input> button labeled "Remove" in the preceding snippet of markup, you execute this script:

```
$('input#tmpRemove').click(
  function($e) {
    $e.preventDefault();

    $('ul').remove();
  }
);
```

The preceding script demonstrates how jQuery's `remove()` method removes the `<ul>` element and all of its children.

Finally, the last method that you review in this example is jQuery's `clone()` method.

```
<div class='tmpWrapper'>
  <p>
    jQuery's clone() method can be used to duplicate elements.  Setting
    its first argument to true also duplicates those elements' event
    handlers.
  </p>
  <form action='javascript:void(0);' method='post'>
    <div id='tmp' class='tmpRow'>
      <input type='text' name='tmpItem' value='' size='25' />
    </div>
```

```
      <div>
        <input type='submit' id='tmpAddInput' value='Add Input' />
      </div>
    </form>
  </div>
```

When you click on the button labeled "Add Input" in the preceding snippet of markup, the following script is executed:

```
$('input#tmpAddInput').click(
  function($e) {
    $e.preventDefault();

    $('div#tmp')
      .clone(true)                      // Copy the <div>
      .removeAttr('id')                 // Remove the id
      .insertAfter('div.tmpRow:last')  // Insert after the last <div>
      .find('input')                    // Get the input
      .val('');                         // Remove the value
  }
);
```

In the preceding script, you begin by selecting the `<div>` element with ID name *tmp*, which is used as a template for duplicating the text input fields. Calling `clone(true)` duplicates the `<div>` element, its descendents, its event handlers, and the event handlers of its descendents, which means that the focus and blur events attached to the text `<input>` elements are copied as well. The `id` attribute is removed with the `removeAttr()` method, which maintains the uniqueness of the IDs used in the document and thus also prevents unwanted bugs from popping up. The new copied and modified `<div>` element is then inserted after the last `<div>` element with class name *tmpRow*. jQuery's special `:last` pseudo-class is invoked so that the last element in the selection is the one selected, ensuring that the new `<div>` element being inserted is always last. Then the `<div>` element's `<input>` element is selected using jQuery's `find()` method, and its value is removed, which ensures that the new `<input>` element is pristine and unused.

Summary

In this chapter, you learned about a variety of jQuery's manipulative abilities. The content discussed in this chapter is documented in detail in the Quick Reference appearing in Appendix E. You began this chapter by learning about jQuery's attribute manipulation method `attr()`, which lets you specify attributes in a variety of ways, with the attribute as the first argument, and the value as the second, or via an object literal specifying arguments in key, value pairs, and also by using callback functions. jQuery's `removeAttr()` method can be used to remove attributes completely.

You also learned how jQuery helps you immensely with manipulating class names. jQuery's `addClass()` method can be used to add a class name to an element. Its `hasClass()` method can be used to determine whether a class name is present. Its `removeClass()` method can be used to remove a class name. And its `toggleClass()` method can be used to toggle a class name on and off.

You learned about various jQuery methods used to manipulate text and HTML content. You can get or set text or HTML content for elements using jQuery's `text()` and `html()` methods. You can append or prepend HTML content to other elements using jQuery's `append()` or `prepend()` methods. jQuery's `after()`, `before()`, `insertAfter()`, and `insertBefore()` methods can all be used to insert content beside other content. And jQuery's `wrap()`, `wrapAll()`, and `wrapInner()` methods can be used to wrap elements with wrapper elements.

Finally, jQuery's `replaceWith()` and `replaceAll()` methods can be used to completely replace one or more elements with other content. Its `empty()` method can be used to completely remove an element's children and descendants. Its `remove()` methods can be used to completely delete an element and all of its contents. And its `clone()` method can be used to duplicate content, and optionally, event handlers that exist within that content.

Exercises

1. Write sample code that might be used to set both the value and the class attributes of an `<input>` element.
2. If you want to set the `href` attribute for an `<a>` element to `www.example.com` using jQuery, what might the JavaScript look like?
3. What jQuery method is used to completely remove attributes from elements?
4. What jQuery method would you use to determine whether a class name is present for an element?
5. If an element contains HTM content and you retrieve the content of that element using jQuery's `text()` method, will the HTML tags be present in the returned value?
6. If you set an element's content using jQuery's `text()` method and that content contains HTML tags, will the HTML tags be visible in the rendered output displayed in your browser's viewport?
7. Describe one bug that jQuery's `append()` and `prepend()` methods work around in IE when compared to `innerHTML`.
8. Describe one bug that jQuery's `append()` and `prepend()` methods work around in Firefox when compared to `innerHTML`.
9. If you want to insert existing content within a document before other existing content within a document, what jQuery method might be best suited for this task?
10. What jQuery method might you use if you needed to wrap multiple items in a document in a single element?
11. jQuery's `replaceWith()` method is most similar to what de facto standard JavaScript property?
12. What jQuery method would you use if you want to completely remove an item and all of its children from your document?
13. What jQuery function call would you make if you wanted to duplicate an element and its event handlers and insert the duplicate element elsewhere in the document?

Arrays and Iteration

In this chapter, I talk about the methods that jQuery provides that help you work with arrays. Historically, working with arrays in JavaScript often required you to come up with your own helper methods and to deal with writing tedious redundant code every time you wanted to enumerate over the contents of an array.

As you saw in Chapter 4, jQuery provides a rich, robust, and helpful API for various tasks associated with manipulating the content in a document. In this chapter, you see that jQuery also does not leave much to be desired in what it offers for dealing with arrays.

Basic Iteration

In this section, you learn a whole new way to approach the task of iterating over an array of values using jQuery's `$.each()` method. Up to now, when it comes to looking at each individual value contained within an array, you're probably used to dealing with a loop that looks something like this:

```
var $items = document.getElementsByTagName('div');

for (var $i = 0; $i < $items.length; $i++) {
  // Do something with each item
  alert($item[$i].innerHTML);
}
```

You have an array of items, or a static node list, or a live node list. Then you make a `for` loop, you define a counter, and you proceed to iterate over the contents of your array or list.

jQuery makes this completely unnecessary, by providing a way to iterate over an array or list using a function call instead of a `for` loop, and a callback function that's used to actually look at each individual item. The function that jQuery uses, again, is called `each()`, and it is demonstrated in the following document:

```
<!DOCTYPE html PUBLIC "-//W3C//DTD XHTML 1.0 Strict//EN"
    "http://www.w3.org/TR/xhtml1/DTD/xhtml1-strict.dtd">
<html xmlns='http://www.w3.org/1999/xhtml' xml:lang='en'>
  <head>
    <meta http-equiv='content-type' content='text/html; charset=utf-8' />
    <meta http-equiv='content-language' content='en-us' />
    <title></title>
    <script type='text/javascript'
            src='../../../Source Code/jQuery/jQuery.js'></script>
    <script type='text/javascript' src='Figure 5-1.js'></script>
    <link type='text/css' href='Figure 5-1.css' rel='stylesheet' />
  </head>
  <body>
     <ul>
     </ul>
  </body>
</html>
```

The preceding markup document is linked to the following style sheet:

```
body {
    font: 16px sans-serif;
}
The following script demonstrates jQuery's each() method.
$(document).ready(
  function() {
    var $items = [
      'John Lennon',
      'Paul McCartney',
      'George Harrison',
      'Ringo Starr'
    ];

    $($items).each(
      function() {
        $('ul').append("<li>" + this + "</li>");
      }
    );
  }
);
```

In the preceding script, you create an ad hoc array and assign that array to the variable `$items`. The variable `$items` is passed to jQuery's dollar sign method, then jQuery's `each()` method is chained onto the end of that. You pass an anonymous function to jQuery's `each()` method, which is executed once for each item in the array; upon each execution, the current item is passed to the anonymous function within the `this` keyword.

Figure 5-1 shows that the `<ul>` element is populated with four new `<li>` items via script.

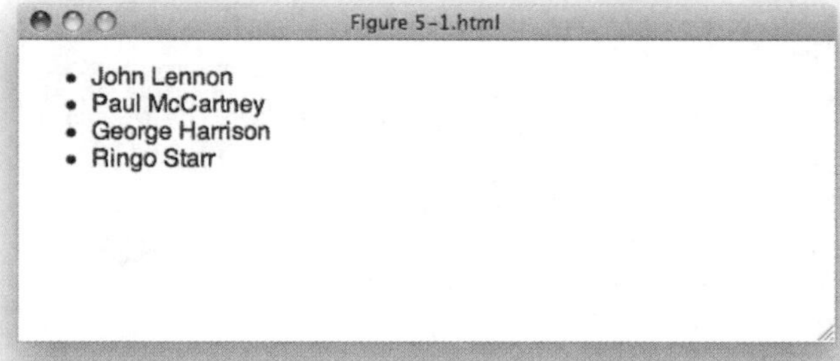

Figure 5-1

In the preceding example, you see how jQuery is able to eliminate the traditional `for` construct that you'd typically use for iterating the contents of an array or list. Instead, you pass an array to jQuery's dollar sign method, so that you have the full power of jQuery at your disposal for use with that array. Then you chain a call to jQuery's `each()` method, which takes a callback function as its one and only argument. That callback function then is executed once for each item in the array, eliminating the need for a counter, since the current item is passed to the function with each iteration in the `this` keyword.

Calling `each()` *Directly*

You don't have to write a call to `each()` exactly like you see in the preceding example; however, you can also pass your array to a direct call to jQuery's `each()` method. The following document demonstrates this variation:

```
<!DOCTYPE html PUBLIC "-//W3C//DTD XHTML 1.0 Strict//EN"
    "http://www.w3.org/TR/xhtml1/DTD/xhtml1-strict.dtd">
<html xmlns='http://www.w3.org/1999/xhtml' xml:lang='en'>
  <head>
    <meta http-equiv='content-type' content='text/html; charset=utf-8' />
    <meta http-equiv='content-language' content='en-us' />
    <title></title>
    <script type='text/javascript'
            src='../../../Source Code/jQuery/jQuery.js'></script>
    <script type='text/javascript' src='Figure 5-2.js'></script>
    <link type='text/css' href='Figure 5-2.css' rel='stylesheet' />
  </head>
  <body>
     <ul>
     </ul>
  </body>
</html>
```

The preceding document is linked to the following style sheet:

```
body {
    font: 16px sans-serif;
}
```

The following script demonstrates how you call `each()` directly.

```
$(document).ready(
  function() {
    $.each(
      ['Groucho', 'Chico', 'Harpo', 'Zeppo'],
      function() {
        $('ul').append("<li>" + this + "</li>");
      }
    );
  }
);
```

In the preceding example, you call the `each()` method directly, using `$.each()`, and you pass the array you want to iterate over as its first value and the callback function as its second value. **Figure 5-2** shows the preceding example rendered in a browser.

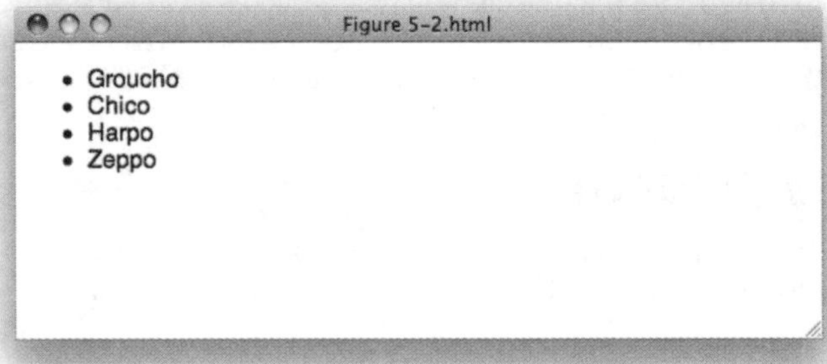

Figure 5-2

It doesn't really matter which way you use jQuery's `each()` method. Use whichever way makes the most sense for you.

Variable Scope

Scope can be a tricky thing since different languages define scope differently. In a nutshell, *scope* limits what variables you can access depending on the context in which they're used. Variables defined globally in JavaScript (with or without the `var` keyword) — *globally* meaning outside a function, object, or closure — can be accessed anywhere in your document, globally or from within any function. Variables that are defined locally within a function without a `var` keyword are also considered to be global variables. Variables that you define locally, within a function with the `var` keyword, can only be accessed within that function … or from within anonymous functions defined within that function.

Knowing how scope works helps you cope much more easily with using jQuery's `each()` method for array iteration, since you find that you can access local variables defined outside the anonymous function you pass to the `each()` method.

The following document demonstrates the concept of variable scope:

```
<!DOCTYPE html PUBLIC "-//W3C//DTD XHTML 1.0 Strict//EN"
    "http://www.w3.org/TR/xhtml1/DTD/xhtml1-strict.dtd">
<html xmlns='http://www.w3.org/1999/xhtml' xml:lang='en'>
  <head>
    <meta http-equiv='content-type' content='text/html; charset=utf-8' />
    <meta http-equiv='content-language' content='en-us' />
    <title></title>
    <script type='text/javascript'
            src='../../../Source Code/jQuery/jQuery.js'></script>
    <script type='text/javascript' src='Figure 5-3.js'></script>
    <link type='text/css' href='Figure 5-3.css' rel='stylesheet' />
  </head>
  <body>
     <ul>
     </ul>
  </body>
</html>
```

The following style sheet is linked to the preceding markup document:

```
body {
    font: 16px sans-serif;
}
ul {
    list-style: none;
}
```

The following script demonstrates variable scope as it applies to locally defined variables and anonymous functions that are defined in the same function:

```
$(document).ready(
  function() {
    var $append = " Marx";

    $(['Groucho', 'Chico', 'Harpo', 'Zeppo'])
      .each(
        function() {
          $('ul').append("<li>" + this + $append + "</li>");
        }
      );
  }
);
```

In the preceding script, you see that the `$append` variable is defined with the string Marx; then the `each()` method is used to iterate over the contents of an array. In the anonymous function that is passed to the `each()` method, you see that you are able to access the `$append` variable from within that separately defined function. **Figure 5-3** shows the rendered output of the preceding JavaScript, CSS, and HTML documents.

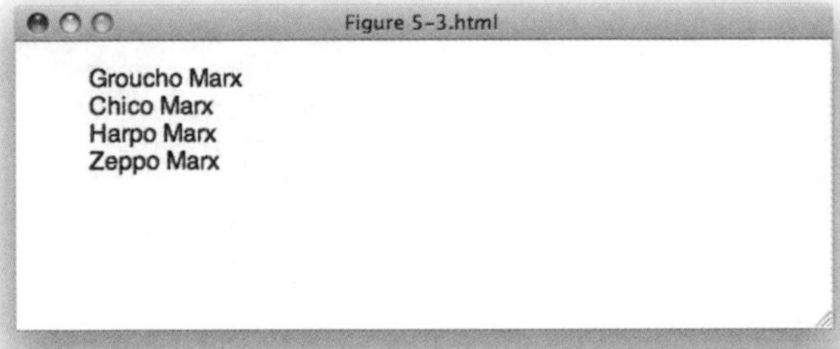

Figure 5-3

Aside from being able to access locally defined variables from within your iterator function, there are two items left to talk about that you're used to doing in traditional `for` constructs: using the `break` and `continue` keywords, which are the topics discussed in the next section.

Emulating `break` *and* `continue`

Emulating the functionality of the `break` and `continue` keywords in jQuery's `each()` method is handled in a very intuitive way. All you have to do is write a return statement in your anonymous function. Returning Boolean `false` stops the iteration, just like using a `break` keyword in a normal loop, and returning Boolean `true` continues the iteration, just like using a `continue` keyword. The following document demonstrates how the `break` and `continue` keywords are emulated using jQuery's `each()` method:

```
<!DOCTYPE html PUBLIC "-//W3C//DTD XHTML 1.0 Strict//EN"
    "http://www.w3.org/TR/xhtml1/DTD/xhtml1-strict.dtd">
<html xmlns='http://www.w3.org/1999/xhtml' xml:lang='en'>
  <head>
    <meta http-equiv='content-type' content='text/html; charset=utf-8' />
    <meta http-equiv='content-language' content='en-us' />
    <title></title>
    <script type='text/javascript'
            src='../../../Source Code/jQuery/jQuery.js'></script>
    <script type='text/javascript' src='Figure 5-4.js'></script>
    <link type='text/css' href='Figure 5-4.css' rel='stylesheet' />
  </head>
  <body>
     <ul>
     </ul>
  </body>
</html>
```

The following style sheet is linked to the preceding markup document:

```
body {
    font: 16px sans-serif;
}
ul {
    list-style: none;
}
```

The following script demonstrates how Boolean `return` values are used to simulate the `continue` and `break` keywords:

```
$(document).ready(
  function() {
    $(['Groucho', 'Chico', 'Harpo', 'Zeppo'])
      .each(
        function() {
          if (this == 'Groucho') {
            // Continue
            return true;
          }

          $('ul').append(
            "<li>" + this + "</li>"
          );
        }
      );

    $(['John', 'Paul', 'George', 'Ringo'])
      .each(
        function() {
          if (this == 'Ringo') {
            // Break
            return false;
          }

          $('ul').append(
            "<li>" + this + "</li>"
          );
        }
      );
  }
);
```

In the preceding script, you see with the first array that the script looks to see if the current array value is *Groucho,* in which case the function returns `true`, which causes `each()` to proceed directly to the next value in the array. In the second array iteration, the script checks to see if the current value is *Ringo,* in which case the function returns `false`, which simulates a break, and `each()` ceases iteration. **Figure 5-4** shows the rendered output of the preceding Javascript, CSS, and HTML documents.

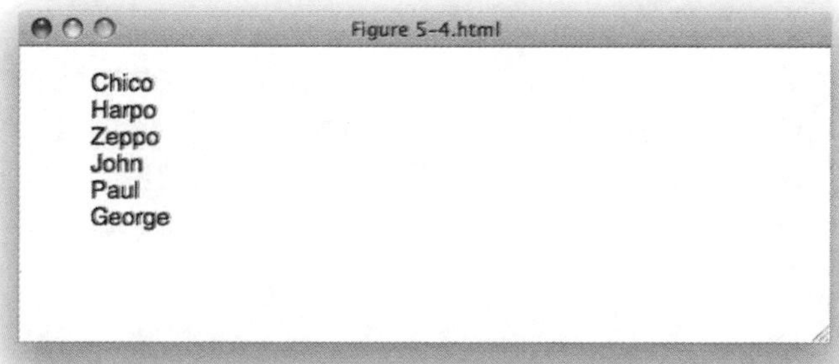

Figure 5-4

Iterating a Selection

jQuery's `each()` method doesn't have to be applied to an array; however, it can also be applied to a selection of elements. The following document demonstrates how `each()` can be used to iterate over a selection of elements:

```
<!DOCTYPE html PUBLIC "-//W3C//DTD XHTML 1.0 Strict//EN"
    "http://www.w3.org/TR/xhtml1/DTD/xhtml1-strict.dtd">
<html xmlns='http://www.w3.org/1999/xhtml' xml:lang='en'>
  <head>
    <meta http-equiv='content-type' content='text/html; charset=utf-8' />
    <meta http-equiv='content-language' content='en-us' />
    <title></title>
    <script type='text/javascript'
            src='../../../Source Code/jQuery/jQuery.js'></script>
    <script type='text/javascript' src='Figure 5-5.js'></script>
    <link type='text/css' href='Figure 5-5.css' rel='stylesheet' />
  </head>
  <body>
     <h4>Rubber Soul</h4>
     <ul>
       <li>Drive My Car</li>
       <li>Norwegian Wood (This Bird Has Flown)</li>
       <li>You Won't See Me</li>
       <li>Nowhere Man</li>
       <li>Think for Yourself</li>
       <li>The Word</li>
       <li>Michelle</li>
       <li>What Goes On</li>
       <li>Girl</li>
       <li>I'm Looking Through You</li>
       <li>In My Life</li>
       <li>Wait</li>
       <li>If I Needed Someone</li>
       <li>Run for Your Life</li>
     </ul>
  </body>
</html>
```

The following style sheet is applied to the preceding markup document:

```
body {
    font: 16px sans-serif;
}
h4 {
    margin: 0;
}
ul {
    list-style: none;
    margin: 5px;
    padding: 0;
}
li.tmpSong {
    background: #a0cde5;
    border: 4px solid #99c6dd;
}
```

In the following script, you see that jQuery's `each()` method can be chained onto a selection like any other method, and you are able to iterate over the items of the selection:

```
$(document).ready(
  function() {
    $('li').each(
      function() {
        $(this).addClass('tmpSong');
      }
    );
  }
);
```

Iterating a selection is essentially the same as iterating an array, only this time, when you're working with the callback function, the `this` keyword contains an individual element from the selection. If you want to use jQuery methods within the callback function, you'll have to wrap the `this` keyword with a call to the dollar sign method. In the example, each `<li>` element is selected, iterated using the `each()` method, and given the class name *tmpSong*. Figure 5-5 shows a screenshot of the preceding example in a browser.

Figure 5-5

Filtering Selections and Arrays

There are two methods that can be associated with filtering an array or a selection in jQuery's API. One method is called `filter()`, and it is used for filtering items from a selection exclusively. The other method is called `grep()`, and it is used for filtering items from an array exclusively.

Filtering a Selection

`filter()` is used to remove items from a selection using a selector or a callback function. The following document demonstrates how `filter()` can use a selector to reduce items in a selection:

```
<!DOCTYPE html PUBLIC "-//W3C//DTD XHTML 1.0 Strict//EN"
    "http://www.w3.org/TR/xhtml1/DTD/xhtml1-strict.dtd">
<html xmlns='http://www.w3.org/1999/xhtml' xml:lang='en'>
  <head>
    <meta http-equiv='content-type' content='text/html; charset=utf-8' />
    <meta http-equiv='content-language' content='en-us' />
    <title></title>
    <script type='text/javascript'
            src='../../../Source Code/jQuery/jQuery.js'></script>
    <script type='text/javascript' src='Figure 5-6.js'></script>
    <link type='text/css' href='Figure 5-6.css' rel='stylesheet' />
  </head>
  <body>
      <h4>Rubber Soul</h4>
      <ul>
        <li class='Paul'>Drive My Car</li>
        <li class='John'>Norwegian Wood (This Bird Has Flown)</li>
        <li class='Paul'>You Won't See Me</li>
        <li class='John'>Nowhere Man</li>
        <li class='George'>Think for Yourself</li>
        <li class='John'>The Word</li>
        <li class='Paul'>Michelle</li>
        <li class='John'>What Goes On</li>
        <li class='John'>Girl</li>
        <li class='Paul'>I'm Looking Through You</li>
        <li class='John'>In My Life</li>
        <li class='John'>Wait</li>
        <li class='George'>If I Needed Someone</li>
        <li class='John'>Run for Your Life</li>
      </ul>
  </body>
</html>
```

The preceding markup document includes the following style sheet:

```
body {
    font: 16px sans-serif;
}
h4 {
    margin: 0;
}
ul {
    list-style: none;
    margin: 5px;
    padding: 0;
}
li.tmpSelected {
    background: #a1e6b2;
    border: 4px solid #93daa4;
}
```

The following script demonstrates how the `filter()` method uses a selector to indicate which items should be in the selection:

```
$(document).ready(
  function() {
    $('li')
      .filter('.George')
      .addClass('tmpSelected');
  }
);
```

In the preceding script, the selector `.George` reduces the selection to include only the `<li>` elements that have a class name of *George*; then the class name *tmpSelected* is added to each of those `<li>` elements. **Figure 5-6** shows a screenshot of this example in Safari.

Figure 5-6

Filtering a Selection with a Callback Function

The `filter()` method can also be used with a callback function. When it is used in this way, `filter()` is very similar to `each()`, in that it allows a callback function to be specified that is subsequently executed once for every item present in a selection.

With the `each()` method, you learned that returning a Boolean value simulates `continue` and `break` statements. With the `filter()` method, returning a Boolean value decides whether an item should be kept or removed from the selection. Returning `true` keeps the item in the selection, and returning `false` removes the item from the selection. Using `filter()` with a callback function is demonstrated in the following document:

```
<!DOCTYPE html PUBLIC "-//W3C//DTD XHTML 1.0 Strict//EN"
    "http://www.w3.org/TR/xhtml1/DTD/xhtml1-strict.dtd">
<html xmlns='http://www.w3.org/1999/xhtml' xml:lang='en'>
  <head>
    <meta http-equiv='content-type' content='text/html; charset=utf-8' />
```

```
        <meta http-equiv='content-language' content='en-us' />
        <title></title>
        <script type='text/javascript'
                src='../../../Source Code/jQuery/jQuery.js'></script>
        <script type='text/javascript' src='Figure 5-7.js'></script>
        <link type='text/css' href='Figure 5-7.css' rel='stylesheet' />
      </head>
      <body>
         <h4>Rubber Soul</h4>
         <ul>
           <li class='Paul'>Drive My Car</li>
           <li class='John'>Norwegian Wood (This Bird Has Flown)</li>
           <li class='Paul'>You Won't See Me</li>
           <li class='John'>Nowhere Man</li>
           <li class='George'>Think for Yourself</li>
           <li class='John'>The Word</li>
           <li class='Paul'>Michelle</li>
           <li class='John'>What Goes On</li>
           <li class='John'>Girl</li>
           <li class='Paul'>I'm Looking Through You</li>
           <li class='John'>In My Life</li>
           <li class='John'>Wait</li>
           <li class='George'>If I Needed Someone</li>
           <li class='John'>Run for Your Life</li>
         </ul>
      </body>
    </html>
```

The preceding markup document links to the following style sheet:

```
body {
    font: 16px sans-serif;
}
h4 {
    margin: 0;
}
ul {
    list-style: none;
    margin: 5px;
    padding: 0;
}
li.tmpSelected {
    background: #a1e6b2;
    border: 4px solid #93daa4;
}
```

The following script demonstrates how jQuery's `filter()` method can use a callback function to reduce items present in a selection:

```
$(document).ready(
  function() {
    $('li')
      .filter(
        function() {
          return $(this).hasClass('John') || $(this).hasClass('Paul');
```

```
            }
        )
        .addClass('tmpSelected');
    }
);
```

In the preceding script, the `filter()` method iterates over each item present in the original selection. It looks at each individual `<li>` element and checks to see if the `<li>` element has a class name of *John* or a class name of *Paul;* if either class name is present, the callback function returns `true`, indicating that the item should be kept in the selection. Each item kept in the selection then receives a class name of *tmpSelected*. Figure 5-7 shows a screenshot of this example in Safari. Each song written primarily by John or Paul has a green background with a slightly darker green border.

Figure 5-7

Filtering an Array

As I indicated previously, arrays are filtered using a different method called `grep()`. The `grep()` method can only be called directly, which is to say, you may only call it as `$.grep()` or `jQuery.grep()`. Wrapping an array in the dollar sign method and then calling `grep()` doesn't work, at least as of the version of jQuery I'm using as I write this. The following document demonstrates how `grep()` is used to filter arrays:

```
<!DOCTYPE html PUBLIC "-//W3C//DTD XHTML 1.0 Strict//EN"
    "http://www.w3.org/TR/xhtml1/DTD/xhtml1-strict.dtd">
<html xmlns='http://www.w3.org/1999/xhtml' xml:lang='en'>
  <head>
    <meta http-equiv='content-type' content='text/html; charset=utf-8' />
    <meta http-equiv='content-language' content='en-us' />
    <title></title>
    <script type='text/javascript'
            src='../../../Source Code/jQuery/jQuery.js'></script>
    <script type='text/javascript' src='Figure 5-8.js'></script>
```

```
    <link type='text/css' href='Figure 5-8.css' rel='stylesheet' />
  </head>
  <body>
    <h4>Rubber Soul</h4>
    <ul id='tmpAlbum'>
      <li class='Paul'>Drive My Car</li>
      <li class='John'>Norwegian Wood (This Bird Has Flown)</li>
      <li class='Paul'>You Won't See Me</li>
      <li class='John'>Nowhere Man</li>
      <li class='George'>Think for Yourself</li>
      <li class='John'>The Word</li>
      <li class='Paul'>Michelle</li>
      <li class='John'>What Goes On</li>
      <li class='John'>Girl</li>
      <li class='Paul'>I'm Looking Through You</li>
      <li class='John'>In My Life</li>
      <li class='John'>Wait</li>
      <li class='George'>If I Needed Someone</li>
      <li class='John'>Run for Your Life</li>
    </ul>
    <ul id='tmpFiltered'>
    </ul>
  </body>
</html>
```

The preceding markup document is linked to the following style sheet:

```
body {
    font: 16px sans-serif;
}
h4 {
    margin: 0;
}
ul {
    list-style: none;
    margin: 5px;
    padding: 0;
}
```

The following script demonstrates the `grep()` method:

```
$(document).ready(
  function() {
    var $items = [];

    $('li').each(
      function() {
        $items.push($(this).text());
      }
    );

    var $filtered = $.grep(
      $items,
      function($value, $key) {
        return ($value.indexOf('You') != -1);
```

```
          }
        );

        $('ul#tmpAlbum').hide();

        $($filtered).each(
          function() {
            $('ul#tmpFiltered').append("<li>" + this + "</li>\n");
          }
        );
      }
    );
```

The preceding script begins by creating a new array and assigning that array to the variable `$items`. The script then selects all `<li>` elements and assigns the text of each `<li>` element as a new item in the `$items` array using `push()`. The end result is that the `$items` array contains the titles for all the songs on *Rubber Soul*.

Then, a new variable is created called `$filtered`, which will contain the filtered array. The `grep()` method is called directly as `$.grep()`, with the `$items` array as the first argument and a callback function as the second argument. In the callback function, you return a Boolean value to indicate whether each item should be kept in the array or removed. Returning `true` indicates that the value should be kept; returning `false` indicates that the item should be discarded. You can also change the value being kept as well — simply return the replacement value you want to use, and it will replace any previous value.

In the example, the callback function checks to see if each song title contains the word *you*, using JavaScript's `indexOf()` method. If it does, the song title is kept; if not, the song title is discarded.

The `<ul>` element with ID name *tmpAlbum* is hidden by selecting it, then making a call to jQuery's `hide()` method.

Finally, the script iterates over the new `$filtered` array using `each()`, and the four song titles containing the word *you* are appended as new `<li>` elements to the `<ul>` element with ID name *tmpFiltered*. **Figure 5-8** shows the results of the preceding example in a browser.

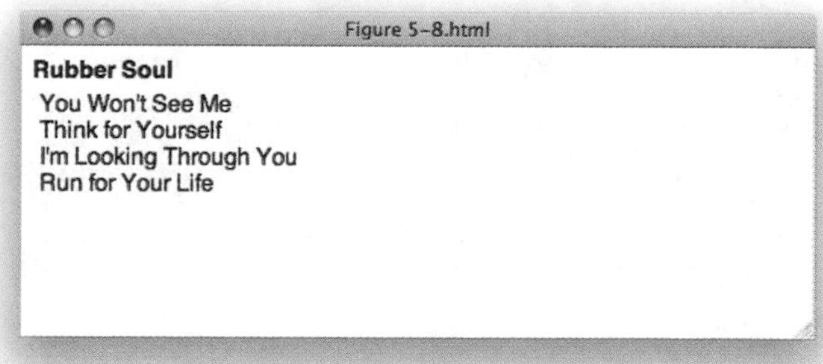

Figure 5-8

The `grep()` method also allows an optional third argument called `invert` to be specified; if it is set to `true`, the values of the filtered array are reversed.

Mapping a Selection or an Array

As was the case with filtering, there are two different contexts in which you can map one collection of items to another, in a selection or with an arbitrary array of items. This time, however, both contexts use a function that goes by the same name, `map()`. In the following sections, you learn more about the `map()` method as applied within either context.

Mapping a Selection

The concept of *mapping* is taking one set of values and modifying one or more of those values to create a new set of values. No items are removed from the set during a mapping, so it's expected that you'll have a set of values of the same length when you finish mapping as when you started — the idea being more or less that you can arbitrarily replace values as needed with new ones. The following document demonstrates how you'd map a selection with jQuery:

```
<!DOCTYPE html PUBLIC "-//W3C//DTD XHTML 1.0 Strict//EN"
    "http://www.w3.org/TR/xhtml1/DTD/xhtml1-strict.dtd">
<html xmlns='http://www.w3.org/1999/xhtml' xml:lang='en'>
  <head>
    <meta http-equiv='content-type' content='text/html; charset=utf-8' />
    <meta http-equiv='content-language' content='en-us' />
    <title></title>
    <script type='text/javascript'
            src='../../../Source Code/jQuery/jQuery.js'></script>
    <script type='text/javascript' src='Figure 5-9.js'></script>
    <link type='text/css' href='Figure 5-9.css' rel='stylesheet' />
  </head>
  <body>
      <h4>Rubber Soul</h4>
      <ul id='tmpAlbum'>
        <li class='Paul'>Drive My Car</li>
        <li class='John'>Norwegian Wood (This Bird Has Flown)</li>
        <li class='Paul'>You Won't See Me</li>
        <li class='John'>Nowhere Man</li>
        <li class='George'>Think for Yourself</li>
        <li class='John'>The Word</li>
        <li class='Paul'>Michelle</li>
        <li class='John'>What Goes On</li>
        <li class='John'>Girl</li>
        <li class='Paul'>I'm Looking Through You</li>
        <li class='John'>In My Life</li>
        <li class='John'>Wait</li>
        <li class='George'>If I Needed Someone</li>
        <li class='John'>Run for Your Life</li>
      </ul>
      <ul id='tmpMapped'>
      </ul>
  </body>
</html>
```

The preceding markup document is styled with the following style sheet:

```
body {
    font: 16px sans-serif;
}
h4 {
    margin: 0;
}
ul {
    list-style: none;
    margin: 5px;
    padding: 0;
}
ul li {
    position: relative;
    background: #eff557;
    border: 1px solid black;
    padding: 3px;
    margin: 2px 0;
}
i {
    position: absolute;
    top: 3px;
    right: 3px;
}
```

The following script demonstrates how a selection is mapped to a new array:

```
$(document).ready(
  function() {
    var $mapped = $('li').map(
      function($key) {
        switch (true) {
          case ($(this).hasClass('John')): {
            return $(this).text() + " <i>John Lennon</i>";
          }
          case ($(this).hasClass('Paul')): {
            return $(this).text() + " <i>Paul McCartney</i>";
          }
          case ($(this).hasClass('George')): {
            return $(this).text() + " <i>George Harrison</i>";
          }
        }
      }
    );

    $('ul#tmpAlbum').hide();

    $($mapped).each(
      function() {
        $('ul#tmpMapped').append("<li>" + this + "</li>\n");
      }
    );
  }
);
```

The preceding script begins by selecting all `<li>` elements in the document. Then a call to the `map()` method is chained onto that selection, and a callback function is provided as the first argument to the `map()` method.

The callback function provided to the `map()` method, as with the other methods you've observed in this chapter, passes each item to its callback function in the `this` keyword. If you need to reference it, the index or key or counter (whatever you choose to call it) is accessible in the first argument that you provide to your callback function. Each item is numbered offset from zero, and that counter is accessible in that first argument. In the preceding example, I named the first argument `$key`.

Inside the callback function, a `switch` construct looks to see what class name each `<li>` element has. If a `<li>` element has a class name of *John*, for example, the callback function returns the name of the song with the HTML `<i>John Lennon</i>` appended to the end. The callback function attaches the name of the more prominent writer of each song for each song present, building a new array that is assigned to the variable `$mapped`.

The first `<ul>` list with ID name *tmpAlbum* is then hidden by selecting it and making a call to jQuery's `hide()` method.

The `each()` method is then used to iterate the contents of the `$mapped` variable, appending each mapped value to the second `<ul>` element with the ID name *tmpMapped*. Figure 5-9 shows the final product.

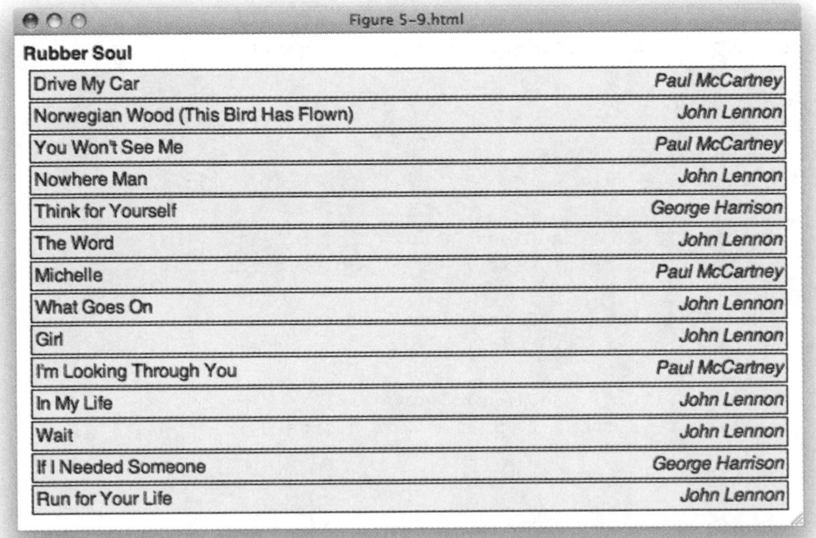

Figure 5-9.html

Rubber Soul

Drive My Car	*Paul McCartney*
Norwegian Wood (This Bird Has Flown)	*John Lennon*
You Won't See Me	*Paul McCartney*
Nowhere Man	*John Lennon*
Think for Yourself	*George Harrison*
The Word	*John Lennon*
Michelle	*Paul McCartney*
What Goes On	*John Lennon*
Girl	*John Lennon*
I'm Looking Through You	*Paul McCartney*
In My Life	*John Lennon*
Wait	*John Lennon*
If I Needed Someone	*George Harrison*
Run for Your Life	*John Lennon*

Figure 5-9

Mapping an Array

Mapping an array basically employs the same logic that you observed in **Figure 5-9** with mapping a selection — you're just using an array instead of a selection. So, you can call jQuery's `map()` method with an array, the same way that you were able to call the `each()` method, by either passing an array to the dollar sign method or by calling the `map()` method directly, with an array as its first argument and a callback function as its second argument. The following document shows an example of the `map()` method as it is applied to an array:

```
<!DOCTYPE html PUBLIC "-//W3C//DTD XHTML 1.0 Strict//EN"
    "http://www.w3.org/TR/xhtml1/DTD/xhtml1-strict.dtd">
<html xmlns='http://www.w3.org/1999/xhtml' xml:lang='en'>
  <head>
    <meta http-equiv='content-type' content='text/html; charset=utf-8' />
    <meta http-equiv='content-language' content='en-us' />
    <title></title>
    <script type='text/javascript'
            src='../../../Source Code/jQuery/jQuery.js'></script>
    <script type='text/javascript' src='Figure 5-10.js'></script>
    <link type='text/css' href='Figure 5-10.css' rel='stylesheet' />
  </head>
  <body>
     <h4>Revolver</h4>
     <ul id='tmpMapped'>
     </ul>
  </body>
</html>
```

The following style sheet is applied to the preceding markup:

```
body {
    font: 16px sans-serif;
}
h4 {
    margin: 0;
}
ul {
    list-style: none;
    margin: 5px;
    padding: 0;
}
ul li {
    position: relative;
    background: #a9c1ff;
    border: 2px solid #9ab6fc;
    padding: 3px;
}
```

The following script demonstrates how jQuery's `map()` method is used with an array instead of a selection:

```
$(document).ready(
  function() {
    var $items = [
      'Taxman',
      'Eleanor Rigby',
      'I\'m Only Sleeping',
      'Love You To',
      'Here, There and Everywhere',
      'Yellow Submarine',
      'She Said, She Said',
      'Good Day Sunshine',
      'And Your Bird Can Sing',
      'For No One',
      'Doctor Robert',
      'I Want to Tell You',
      'Got to Get You into My Life',
      'Tomorrow Never Knows'
    ];

    var $i = 0;

    var $mapped = $($items).map(
      function($key) {
        $i++;
        return ($i < 10? '0' + $i : $i) + ' ' + this;
      }
    );

    $($mapped).each(
      function() {
        $('ul#tmpMapped').append("<li>" + this + "</li>\n");
      }
    );
  }
);
```

In the preceding script, an array of song titles of the Beatles' album *Revolver* are placed in an array and assigned to the variable `$items`. Then a new variable named `$i` is created and set to a value of zero.

The `$items` variable is then passed to a call to the dollar sign method, and the `map()` method is called.

In the callback function passed to the `map()` method, the `$i` variable is incremented; it's going to be used as a counter. The callback function then checks to see if `$i` is less than 10 using a ternary expression; if it is, a leading zero is prepended to the value; otherwise, no leading zero is prepending. This portion becomes the track number.

A single space is inserted between the track number and the song title, and the new array containing song titles with track numbers prefixed is assign to the variable `$mapped`.

Finally, the array assigned to the `$mapped` variable is iterated using the `each()` method, and the modified song titles with track name prefixes are appended as `<li>` elements to the `<ul>` element in the document. The result of the preceding example appears in **Figure 5-10**.

Figure 5-10

The following "Try It Out" reiterates the various methods used for iteration that you've learned about up to this point:

Try It Out A Review of Iteration

Example 5-1

To review the array iteration methods that you've been learning about, follow these steps:

1. Enter the following HTML document in a new document in your text editor:

```
<!DOCTYPE html PUBLIC "-//W3C//DTD XHTML 1.0 Strict//EN"
    "http://www.w3.org/TR/xhtml1/DTD/xhtml1-strict.dtd">
<html xmlns='http://www.w3.org/1999/xhtml' xml:lang='en'>
  <head>
    <meta http-equiv='content-type' content='text/html; charset=utf-8' />
    <meta http-equiv='content-language' content='en-us' />
    <title></title>
    <script type='text/javascript'
            src='../../../Source Code/jQuery/jQuery.js'></script>
    <script type='text/javascript' src='Example 5-1.js'></script>
    <link type='text/css' href='Example 5-1.css' rel='stylesheet' />
  </head>
```

```
<body>
  <div class='tmpAlbum tmpAlbumBeatles'>
    <h4>The Beatles' Sgt. Pepper's Lonely Hearts Club Band</h4>
    <ul class='tmpBeatles'>
      <li>Sgt. Pepper's Lonely Hearts Club Band</li>
      <li>With a Little Help from My Friends</li>
      <li>Lucy in the Sky With Diamonds</li>
      <li>Getting Better</li>
      <li>Fixing a Hole</li>
      <li>She's Leaving Home</li>
      <li>Being for the Benefit of Mr. Kite</li>
      <li>Within You, Without You</li>
      <li>When I'm Sixty-Four</li>
      <li>Lovely Rita</li>
      <li>Good Morning, Good Morning</li>
      <li>Sgt. Pepper's Lonely Hearts Club Band (Reprise)</li>
      <li>A Day in the Life</li>
    </ul>
    <ul class='tmpBeatlesMapped'>
    </ul>
  </div>
  <div class='tmpAlbum tmpAlbumELO'>
    <h4>Electric Light Orchestra's Time</h4>
    <ul class='tmpELO'>
      <li>Prologue</li>
      <li>Twilight</li>
      <li>Yours Truly, 2095</li>
      <li>Ticket to the Moon</li>
      <li>The Way Life's Meant To Be</li>
      <li>Another Heart Breaks</li>
      <li>Rain Is Falling</li>
      <li>From the End of the World</li>
      <li>The Lights Go Down</li>
      <li>Here Is the News</li>
      <li>21st Century Man</li>
      <li>Hold On Tight</li>
      <li>Epilogue</li>
      <li>The Bouncer</li>
      <li>When Time Stood Still</li>
      <li>Julie Don't Live Here</li>
    </ul>
    <ul class='tmpELOMapped'>
    </ul>
  </div>
  <div class='tmpActions'>
    <p>
      jQuery's each() method can be used to arbitrary iterate over
      an array or a selection.
    </p>
    <input type='submit' id='tmpEach' value='Each' />
    <p>
      jQuery's filter() method can be used to remove items from a
      selection using a selector.
    </p>
```

```
      <input type='submit' id='tmpFilter' value='Filter' />
      <p>
        jQuery's filter() method can also be used to remove items from
        a selection using a callback function.
      </p>
      <input type='submit' id='tmpFilterCallback' value='Filter Callback' />
      <p>
        jQuery's grep() method() can be used to remove items from an
        array.
      </p>
      <input type='submit' id='tmpGrep' value='Filter Array' />
      <p>
        jQuery's map() method can be used to translate a selection into an
        array.
      </p>
      <input type='submit' id='tmpMap' value='Map Selection' />
      <p>
        jQuery's map() method can also be used to translate an array
        into another array.
      </p>
      <input type='submit' id='tmpMapArray' value='Map Array' />
    </div>
  </body>
</html>
```

2. Save the preceding document as *Example 5-1.html*.

3. Enter the following CSS document in a new document in your text editor:

```
body {
    font: 16px sans-serif;
}
body,
html {
    padding: 0;
    margin: 0;
}
div.tmpAlbum {
    width: 50%;
    float: left;
    position: relative;
}
div.tmpActions {
    clear: left;
    padding: 5px;
}
h4 {
    margin: 5px;
}
ul {
    margin: 5px;
    padding: 0;
    list-style: none;
    border: 1px solid black;
}
```

```
ul.tmpBeatlesFiltered {
    border: 1px solid blue;
    color: blue;
}
ul.tmpELOFiltered {
    border: 1px solid crimson;
    color: crimson;
}
ul li {
    padding: 3px;
}
ul.tmpBeatles li.tmpSong {
    background: #a6c7fa;
}
ul.tmpELO li.tmpSong {
    background: #dba6fa;
}
li.tmpContainsThe {
    opacity: 0.6;
}
ul.tmpBeatlesMapped {
    background: lightblue;
    border: 1px solid #000;
    display: none;
}
ul.tmpELOMapped {
    background: pink;
    border: 1px solid #000;
    display: none;
}
```

4. Save the preceding document as *Example 5-1.css.*
5. Enter the following JavaScript document in a new document in your text editor:

```
$(document).ready(
  function() {
    $('input#tmpEach').click(
      function($e) {
        $e.preventDefault();

        $('li').each(
          function() {
            $(this).addClass('tmpSong');
          }
        );
      }
    );

    $('input#tmpFilter').click(
      function($e) {
        $e.preventDefault();

        $('ul')
          .filter('ul.tmpBeatles')
```

```
        .addClass('tmpBeatlesFiltered');
    }
);

$('input#tmpFilterCallback').click(
    function($e) {
        $e.preventDefault();

        $('ul')
            .filter(
                function() {
                    return $(this).hasClass('tmpELO');
                }
            )
            .addClass('tmpELOFiltered');
    }
);

$('input#tmpGrep').click(
    function($e) {
        $e.preventDefault();

        var $items = $('li').get();

        var $filtered = $.grep(
            $items,
            function($value, $key) {
                return (
                    $($value).text().indexOf('the') != -1 ||
                    $($value).text().indexOf('The') != -1
                ) ;
            }
        );

        $($filtered).each(
            function() {
                $(this).addClass('tmpContainsThe');
            }
        );
    }
);

$('input#tmpMap').click(
    function($e) {
        $e.preventDefault();

        var $songs = $('ul.tmpBeatles li').map(
            function($i) {
                $i++;
                return ($i < 10? '0' + $i : $i) + '. ' + $(this).text();
            }
        );

        $('ul.tmpBeatles').hide();
```

```
            $('ul.tmpBeatlesMapped').show();

            $($songs).each(
              function() {
                $('ul.tmpBeatlesMapped').append("<li>" + this + "</li>");
              }
            );

          }
        );

        $('input#tmpMapArray').click(
          function($e) {
            $e.preventDefault();

            var $songs = [
              'Eldorado Overture',
              'Can\'t Get It Out of My Head',
              'Boy Blue',
              'Laredo Tornado',
              'Poor Boy (The Greenwood)',
              'Mister Kingdom',
              'Nobody\'s Child',
              'Illusions in G Major',
              'Eldorado',
              'Eldorado Finale',
              'Eldorado Instrumental Medley',
              'Dark City'
            ];

            var $mapped = $($songs).map(
              function($i) {
                $i++;
                return ($i < 10? '0' + $i : $i) + '. ' + this;
              }
            );

            $('ul.tmpELO').hide();
            $('ul.tmpELOMapped').show();

            $($mapped).each(
              function() {
                $('ul.tmpELOMapped').append("<li>" + this + "</li>");
              }
            );

            $('div.tmpAlbumELO h4').text('Electric Light Orchestra\'s Eldorado');
          }
        );
      }
    );
```

6. Save the preceding document as *Example 5-1.js*.

The preceding example should look something like what you see in **Figure 5-11**.

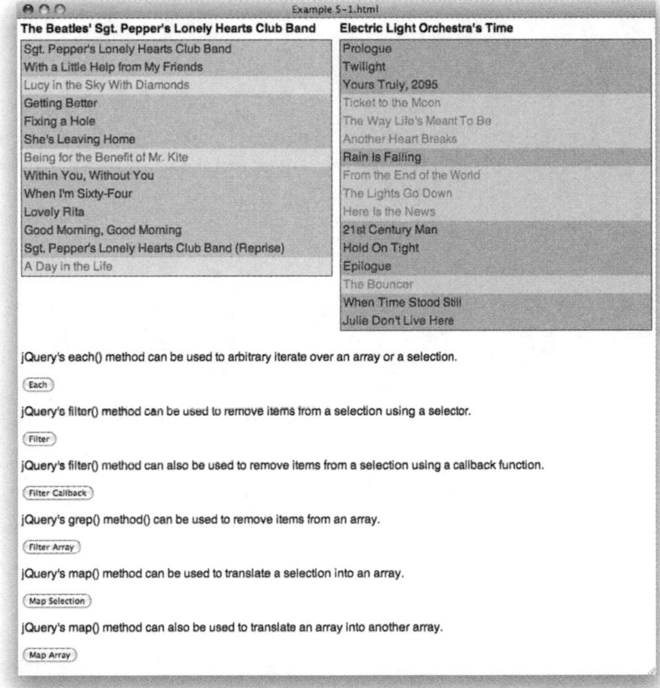

Figure 5-11

In Example 5-1, you reviewed the various array iteration methods provided by jQuery, which again uses song names from popular albums to help demonstrate each method's purpose.

The first method that you review is jQuery's `each()` method.

```
<p>
  jQuery's each() method can be used to arbitrary iterate over
  an array or a selection.
</p>
<input type='submit' id='tmpEach' value='Each' />
```

When you click on the button labeled "Each" in the preceding snippet of markup, you execute the following section of JavaScript:

```
$('input#tmpEach').click(
  function($e) {
    $e.preventDefault();

    $('li').each(
```

```
            function() {
              $(this).addClass('tmpSong');
            }
          );
        }
      );
```

In the preceding script, you iterate over each <li> element present in the document, adding the class name *tmpSong*. Upon adding the class name to each element, the following style-sheet rules are applied:

```
ul.tmpBeatles li.tmpSong {
    background: #a6c7fa;
}
ul.tmpELO li.tmpSong {
    background: #dba6fa;
}
```

The second method that you review in Example 5-1 is jQuery's `filter()` method when used with a selector.

```
<p>
  jQuery's filter() method can be used to remove items from a
  selection using a selector.
</p>
<input type='submit' id='tmpFilter' value='Filter' />
```

When you click on the button labeled "Filter" in the preceding snippet of markup, the following script is executed:

```
$('input#tmpFilter').click(
  function($e) {
    $e.preventDefault();

    $('ul')
      .filter('ul.tmpBeatles')
      .addClass('tmpBeatlesFiltered');
  }
);
```

First, you select each <ul> element in the document; there are four total. Then you call the `filter()` method with the selector `ul.tmpBeatles` as its first argument, which removes any <ul> element that does not have a class name of *tmpBeatles*, which leaves just one <ul> element. That <ul> element then receives the class name *tmpBeatlesFiltered*, which applies the following style-sheet rule:

```
ul.tmpBeatlesFiltered {
    border: 1px solid blue;
    color: blue;
}
```

The third method that you review in the preceding example is jQuery's `filter()` method when used with a callback function.

```
<p>
  jQuery's filter() method can also be used to remove items from
  a selection using a callback function.
</p>
<input type='submit' id='tmpFilterCallback' value='Filter Callback' />
```

When you click the button labeled "Filter Callback" in the preceding snippet of markup, the following script is executed:

```
$('input#tmpFilterCallback').click(
  function($e) {
    $e.preventDefault();

    $('ul')
      .filter(
        function() {
          return $(this).hasClass('tmpELO');
        }
      )
      .addClass('tmpELOFiltered');
  }
);
```

Each `<ul>` element is selected again. That's four total, and each is passed to the `filter()` method's callback function. Only those `<ul>` elements with a class name of *tmpELO* are allowed to remain in the selection, leaving just one `<ul>` element. The remaining `<ul>` element receives the class name *tmpELOFiltered*, which results in the application of the following style-sheet rule:

```
ul.tmpELOFiltered {
    border: 1px solid crimson;
    color: crimson;
}
```

The next method that you review in this example is jQuery's `grep()` method.

```
<p>
  jQuery's grep() method() can be used to remove items from an
  array.
</p>
<input type='submit' id='tmpGrep' value='Filter Array' />
```

When you click on the button labeled "Filter Array" in the preceding snippet of markup, the following script is executed:

```
$('input#tmpGrep').click(
  function($e) {
```

```
            $e.preventDefault();

            var $items = $('li').get();

            var $filtered = $.grep(
              $items,
              function($value, $key) {
                return (
                  $($value).text().indexOf('the') != -1 ||
                  $($value).text().indexOf('The') != -1
                );
              }
            );

            $($filtered).each(
              function() {
                $(this).addClass('tmpContainsThe');
              }
            );
          }
        );
```

In the preceding script, an array of all `<li>` elements is stored in the `$items` variable. Then, the `$items` array is filtered based on whether each element's text contains the word *the* or *The*, which is necessary since `indexOf()` is case-sensitive. If either variation is present, the callback function provided to `grep()` returns `true`, and the item is placed in the array assigned to the variable `$filtered`; if not, the element is discarded. Finally, you iterate over each item present in the array stored in the `$filtered` variable, adding the class name *tmpContainsThe* to each `<li>` element making the final cut, which results in the application of the following style-sheet rule:

```
li.tmpContainsThe {
    opacity: 0.6;
}
```

Next, you review jQuery's `map()` method, as it is applied to a selection.

```
        <p>
          jQuery's map() method can be used to translate a selection into an
          array.
        </p>
        <input type='submit' id='tmpMap' value='Map Selection' />
```

When you click on the button labeled "Map Selection" in the preceding snippet of markup, the following script is executed:

```
        $('input#tmpMap').click(
          function($e) {
            $e.preventDefault();

            var $songs = $('ul.tmpBeatles li').map(
              function($i) {
                $i++;
                return ($i < 10? '0' + $i : $i) + '. ' + $(this).text();
              }
```

```
      );

      $('ul.tmpBeatles').hide();
      $('ul.tmpBeatlesMapped').show();

      $($songs).each(
        function() {
          $('ul.tmpBeatlesMapped').append("<li>" + this + "</li>");
        }
      );
    }
  );
```

In the preceding script, you begin by selecting each `<li>` element that is a descendant of the `<ul>` element with class name *tmpBeatles* (or all of the Beatles songs). Then you call the `map()` method. In the callback function passed to the `map()` method, the first argument is named `$i`, which indicates the `<li>` element's offset position within the selection. The variable `$i` is incremented so that it can be used for the track number (since it would ordinarily begin numbering from zero). The callback function returns the song title with the track number prepended, including the leading zero. Each of the modified song titles is stowed away in the variable `$songs`.

Next, the `<ul>` element with class name *tmpBeatles* is hidden with a call to `hide()`, and the `<ul>` with class name *tmpBeatlesMapped* is revealed with a call to `show()`.

Then, each of the modified song titles is appended to the `<ul>` element with class name *tmpBeatlesMapped*.

Finally, you review jQuery's `map()` method, as it is used with an array.

```
<p>
  jQuery's map() method can also be used to translate an array
  into another array.
</p>
<input type='submit' id='tmpMapArray' value='Map Array' />
```

When you click on the button labeled "Map Array" in the preceding snippet of markup, the following script is executed:

```
$('input#tmpMapArray').click(
  function($e) {
    $e.preventDefault();

    var $songs = [
      'Eldorado Overture',
      'Can\'t Get It Out of My Head',
      'Boy Blue',
      'Laredo Tornado',
      'Poor Boy (The Greenwood)',
      'Mister Kingdom',
      'Nobody\'s Child',
      'Illusions in G Major',
      'Eldorado',
      'Eldorado Finale',
```

```
            'Eldorado Instrumental Medley',
            'Dark City'
          ];

          var $mapped = $($songs).map(
            function($i) {
              $i++;
              return ($i < 10? '0' + $i : $i) + '. ' + this;
            }
          );

          $('ul.tmpELO').hide();
          $('ul.tmpELOMapped').show();

          $($mapped).each(
            function() {
              $('ul.tmpELOMapped').append("<li>" + this + "</li>");
            }
          );

          $('div.tmpAlbumELO h4').text('Electric Light Orchestra\'s Eldorado');
        }
      );
```

In the preceding script, you begin by creating a new array of songs for a completely different ELO album, *Eldorado*. Each song title is stored in the variable named `$songs`. Next, you pass the `$songs` variable to the dollar sign method and chain a call to `map()` onto it. In the callback function that you pass to `map()`, you do the same thing you did with the Beatles album, prepend the track number to each song title, storing the modified song titles in a new variable called `$mapped`.

Then, like with the last example, you hide the `<ul>` element with class name *tmpELO* with a call to `hide()` and show the `<ul>` element with class name *tmpELOMapped* with a call to `show()`.

And finally, you append each of the modified song titles as new `<li>` elements under the `<ul>` with class name *tmpELOMapped*, and you change the text of the `<h4>` element to reflect the new album's name.

Array Utility Methods

jQuery also provides a few utility methods that are useful for probing information from an array. In the following sections, I briefly cover each of jQuery's utility methods:

- `$.makeArray(`*`data`*`)` — Transforms any data into a true array.
- `$.inArray(needle, haystack)` — Finds the index associated with the first occurrence of needle within the haystack.
- `$.merge(first, second)` — Merges two arrays together.
- `$.unique(array)` — Removes any duplicate values from the array.
- `get()` — Retrieves a selection as an array.
- `concat()` — Joins an array to another.

Most of jQuery's array utility methods must be called directly, using the dollar sign dot function name, as you see documented in the preceding list, with the exception of `get()` and `concat()`. All of the methods covered in this chapter are documented in the Quick Reference that appears in Appendix F, with the exception of the `filter()` method, which is documented in Appendix C.

Making an Array

jQuery's `makeArray()` method does just what the name implies — it takes any data and transforms it into a true array. The following example shows how a string can be made into an array using this method:

```
    var $item = 'The Beatles';

    var $transformed = $.makeArray($item);

alert(typeof($transformed.push));
```

The preceding code puts up the JavaScript alert that you see in **Figure 5-12**.

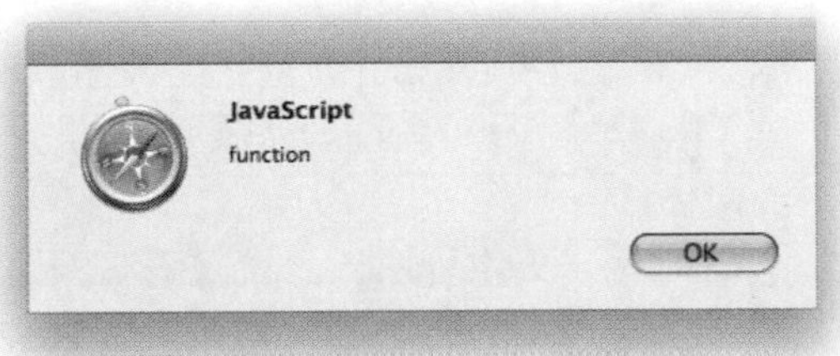

Figure 5-12

In the script, the string *The Beatles* is assigned to the variable `$item`. The variable `$item` is passed to `makeArray()`, and the result is assigned to the variable `$transformed`. Then, you check the `typeof` of the object `$transformed.push`. If the value assigned to `$transformed` is truly an array, the function `push` will be present, since that's a method that is always available on array objects, and the alert dialogue will say *function*, which it does.

Finding a Value within an Array

jQuery's `inArray()` method works just like JavaScript's `indexOf()` method. It returns the position of an item within an array. If it is present, offset from zero, and if the item is not present, the function returns minus one. The following example demonstrates how jQuery's `inArray()` method works:

```
var $items = [
  'Taxman',
  'Eleanor Rigby',
  'I\'m Only Sleeping',
  'Love You To',
  'Here, There and Everywhere',
  'Yellow Submarine',
  'She Said, She Said',
```

```
        'Good Day Sunshine',
        'And Your Bird Can Sing',
        'For No One',
        'Doctor Robert',
        'I Want to Tell You',
        'Got to Get You into My Life',
        'Tomorrow Never Knows'
      ];

      alert($.inArray('Love You To', $items));

    alert($.inArray('Strawberry Fields Forever', $items));
```

The preceding script throws the respective JavaScript alerts that you see in **Figure 5-13**.

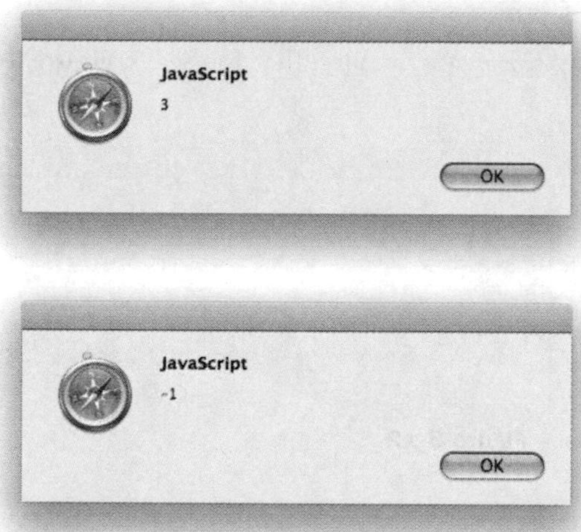

Figure 5-13

Merging Two Arrays

jQuery's `$.merge()` method can be used to glue two arrays together, to make a single array. The following script demonstrates how this works:

```
$(document).ready(
  function() {
    var $vegetables = [
      'Carrots',
      'Tomatoes',
      'Lettuce'
    ];

    var $fruits = [
      'Oranges',
      'Apples',
```

```
        'Cherries'
      ];

      $merged = $.merge($vegetables, $fruits);

      var $string = '';

      $($merged).each(
        function() {
          $string += this + "\n";
        }
      );

      alert($string);
    }
  );
```

The preceding script results in the alert dialogue that you see pictured in **Figure 5-14**.

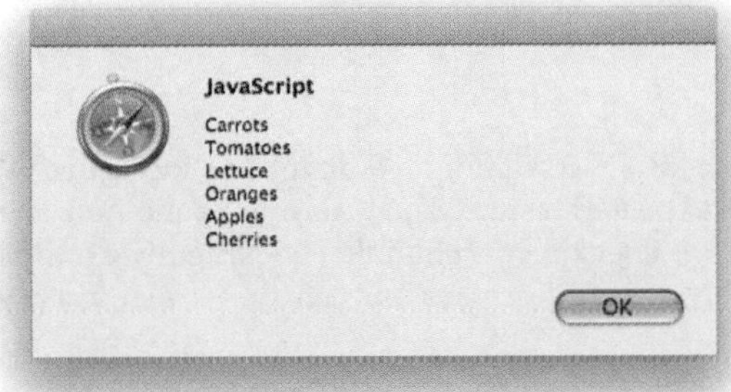

Figure 5-14

As you can see, jQuery's `merge()` method is pretty straightforward.

Removing Duplicate Items

Finally, jQuery's `$.unique()` method, at first glance, would seem to have the purpose of removing duplicate items from any array. The following script tests this hypothesis:

```
$(document).ready(
  function() {
    var $vegetables = [
      'Carrots',
      'Tomatoes',
      'Lettuce',
      'Tomatoes'
    ];

    var $before = '';

    $($vegetables).each(
```

```
          function() {
            $before += this + "\n";
          }
        );

        var $vegetables = $.unique($vegetables);

        var $after= '';

        $($vegetables).each(
          function() {
            $after += this + "\n";
          }
        );

        alert(
          "Before:\n" +
            $before + "\n" +
          "After:\n" +
            $after
        );
      }
    );
```

The preceding script throws the alert dialogue that you see in **Figure 5-15**, where you see that the script did not produce the expected results. The `$.unique()` method does not remove the duplicate item *tomatoes* from the array. After checking and double-checking my example script, I read jQuery's official documentation more closely, which describes its `$.unique()` method as having the following purpose:

> *Remove all duplicate elements from an array of elements.*

The key word in that statement is *elements*. jQuery's `$.unique()` method is only intended to remove duplicate items from an array of *elements*.

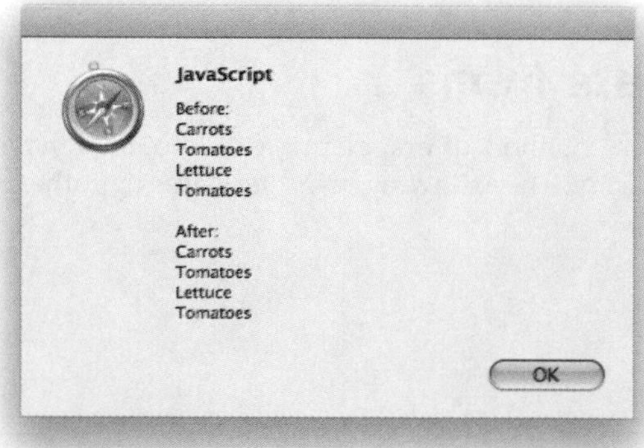

Figure 5-15

The following document demonstrates jQuery's `$.unique()` method as it is intended to be used … to remove duplicate items from an array of elements:

```
<!DOCTYPE html PUBLIC "-//W3C//DTD XHTML 1.0 Strict//EN"
    "http://www.w3.org/TR/xhtml1/DTD/xhtml1-strict.dtd">
<html xmlns='http://www.w3.org/1999/xhtml' xml:lang='en'>
  <head>
    <meta http-equiv='content-type' content='text/html; charset=utf-8' />
    <meta http-equiv='content-language' content='en-us' />
    <title></title>
    <script type='text/javascript'
            src='../../../Source Code/jQuery/jQuery.js'></script>
    <script type='text/javascript' src='Figure 5-16.js'></script>
    <link type='text/css' href='Figure 5-16.css' rel='stylesheet' />
  </head>
  <body>
    <p id='tmpParagraph-1'>
      Lorem ipsum dolor sit amet, consectetuer adipiscing elit.
      Ut convallis orci et felis feugiat suscipit. Etiam euismod
      mattis nunc. Pellentesque justo. Morbi commodo mattis velit.
      Aliquam nulla felis, fringilla nec, pharetra in, sollicitudin
      quis, erat.
    </p>
    <p id='tmpParagraph-2'>
      Vestibulum rutrum dapibus felis. Sed non urna quis pede
      convallis sodales.
    </p>
    <p id='tmpParagraph-3'>
      Aenean vel nisl nec tellus sollicitudin tempus. Donec risus
      est, gravida in, dapibus ac, gravida nec, sapien.
    </p>
  </body>
</html>
```

The preceding markup document links to the following style sheet:

```
body {
    font: 16px sans-serif;
}
```

The following script demonstrates how to remove duplicate items from an array with `$.unique()`, in addition to jQuery's `get()` and `concat()` methods:

```
$(document).ready(
  function() {
    var $p = $('p').get();

    var $before = "Before:\n";

    $($p).each(
```

```
            function() {
              $before += this.id + "\n";
            }
          );

          $p = $p.concat(
            $('#tmpParagraph-1, #tmpParagraph-2').get()
          );

          var $merged= "\nMerged:\n";

          $($p).each(
            function() {
              $merged += this.id + "\n";
            }
          );

          $p = $.unique($p);

          var $after = "\nAfter\n";

          $($p).each(
            function() {
              $after += this.id + "\n";
            }
          );

          alert(
            $before + $merged + $after
          );
        }
      );
```

The preceding script introduces a few new methods. The script begins with the following line:

```
var $p = $('p').get(
```

The `get()` method in the preceding line retrieves the jQuery selection as a true array and assigns that array to a new variable, `$p`.

The next few lines record what's in the `$p` variable so far, by taking the ID of each <p> element and storing it in the variable named `$before`:

```
var $before = "Before:\n";

$($p).each(
  function() {
    $before += this.id + "\n";
  }
);
```

At this point, the `$p` variable should contain three elements; each of the <p> elements present in the markup document and the variable `$before` should contain three ID names for each of those <p> elements.

In the next few lines, jQuery's `concat()` method is used to merge a new array from a new selection in with the three items that were already present in the variable `$p`:

```
$p = $p.concat(
  $('#tmpParagraph-1, #tmpParagraph-2').get()
);
```

After the preceding code, the variable `$p` should contain five elements, the three originally selected and two duplicates.

The next few lines record what the array stored in the `$p` variable looks like so far. Each ID of each <p> element present in the array stored in the `$p` variable is recorded as a string in the variable `$merged`.

```
var $merged= "\nMerged:\n";

$($p).each(
  function() {
    $merged += this.id + "\n";
  }
);
```

In the next line, duplicate elements are removed from the array stored in the `$p` variable using jQuery's `$.unique()` method.

```
$p = $.unique($p);
```

Since two duplicate items were intentionally added to the array, the array should now contain only three items again.

In the next few lines, you look at what the array stored in the `$p` variable looks like after making it unique by storing each ID from each <p> element as a string in a new variable called `$after`:

```
var $after = "\nAfter\n";

$($p).each(
  function() {
    $after += this.id + "\n";
  }
);
```

Finally, an alert dialogue is summoned (see **Figure 5-16**) so that the values stored in the `$before`, `$merged`, and `$after` variables can be viewed, which you see in **Figure 5-17**.

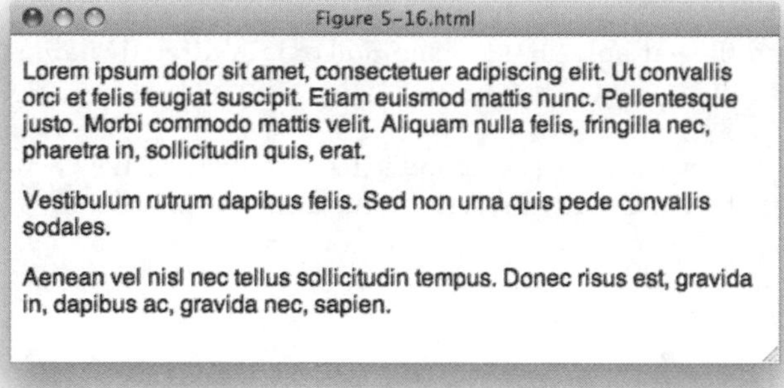

Figure 5-16

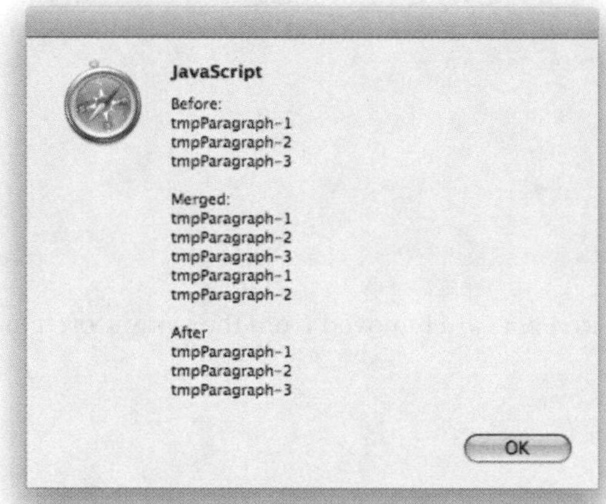

Figure 5-17

Finally, vis-à-vis the text in the alert dialogue displayed in **Figure 5-17**, you see that jQuery's `$.unique()` method does work, when used for its stated purpose.

Summary

In this chapter, I presented several methods associated with iterating and working with arrays and selections.

You learned how jQuery's `each()` method is a less-verbose, easier-to-use alternative for iterating over an array or selection when compared to using a `for` construct and a counter. You learned how to emulate `break` and `continue` keywords with the `each()` method by returning a Boolean value. You learned that jQuery's `each()` method can be called directly or chained to a selection or an array that's wrapped in a call to the dollar sign method. You learned that you don't have to worry about variable scope with anonymous callback functions, and that you can access variables defined within the scope of the function an anonymous function is contained within. For more in-depth discussions about topics like variable scope, I again recommend Nicholas C. Zakas's excellent book *Professional JavaScript for Web Developers* (Wiley, 2005; 2nd ed., 2009).

You learned how a selection can be filtered using jQuery's `filter()` method with either a selector or a callback function. An array can be filtered using jQuery's `grep()` method, which must be called directly.

You learned how one array can be mapped to another array and how one selection can be mapped to an array using jQuery's `map()` method, which exists to translate one set of values to another set of values.

Finally, you learned about jQuery's various array utility methods. `$.makeArray()` is used to turn any data into a true array. `$.inArray()` is used to find the position of a value within an array, offset from zero, and works just like JavaScript's `indexOf()` method, with –1 (minus one) indicating that a value is not present within the array. `$.merge()` is used to glue two separate arrays together into just one array. `$.unique()` is used to remove duplicate elements from an array of elements, the key word there being *elements*: `$.unique()` does not work on arrays consisting of values that are not elements. `$.get()` is used to return a jQuery selection as a true array. `$.concat()` can be used on an array created by jQuery to join one array to another, similar to jQuery's `$.merge()` method.

Exercises

1. What might the JavaScript code look like if you wanted to iterate over the following collection of elements using jQuery's `each()` method?

   ```
   $elements = document.getElementsByTagName('div');
   ```

2. What statement would you write inside a callback function provided to jQuery's `each()` method if you wanted to simulate a `break` statement?
3. When filtering a selection using `filter()`, what does providing a selector to the `filter()` method do?
4. When filtering a selection using `filter()` with a callback function, what does returning `true` do?
5. What value does a callback function provided to jQuery's `grep()` method have to return in order to keep an item in the array?
6. What happens to the value returned by a callback function provided to jQuery's `map()` method?
7. What does –1 (minus one) mean when returned by jQuery's `$.inArray()` method?
8. Describe the purpose of jQuery's `$.unique()` method.

CSS

When working with CSS from JavaScript, there are a few minor points of verbosity and inconsistency where jQuery lends a helping hand. First, jQuery makes it easier to manipulate CSS from JavaScript. jQuery's approach allows you to define styles for multiple CSS properties at once, or one CSS property at a time. But instead of setting CSS properties one element at a time, you can set the style on one or many elements at once.

As I mentioned in Chapter 4 and in Chapter 1, it's generally good practice to avoid mixing style (CSS) with behavior (JavaScript) and/or structure (HTML). You want to keep CSS, JavaScript, and HTML partitioned as cleanly as possible into their respective documents.

In some cases, however, it is unavoidable to bring presentation into your JavaScript programming. In these cases, the style changes dynamically in such a way that it is impractical and unreasonable to keep CSS only in a style sheet, and not directly modify style with JavaScript programming. In this short chapter, I cover the methods that jQuery exposes that let you work with style-sheet properties and values.

The `css()` Method

Instead of messing around with the `style` property as you're used to doing with traditional JavaScript, when you want to access style information or modify style information with jQuery, you use jQuery's `css()` method. The `css()` method can be used in three different ways:

- To return a property's value from the first element matched in a selection
- To set a property's value on one or more elements
- To set multiple properties on one or more elements

When you simply want to get a property's value for an element, this is what you do:

```
var $backgroundColor = $('div').css('backgroundColor');
```

Once you've made a selection, you call the `css()` method chained to the selection with the property that you want the value for. Properties are accessed in the same way that you would use were you using the `style` property directly; that is to say, hyphenated properties are named with camelCase instead of hyphens, so, for example, the property "`background-color`" is accessed as "`backgroundColor`." The snippet of code here returns the `backgroundColor` for the first `<div>` element of the selection, so if there are five `<div>` elements present in a document, the preceding code would return the `backgroundColor` for the first one.

If you want to set a single property, that's done like this:

```
$('div').css('backgroundColor', 'lightblue');
```

In the preceding example, the `backgroundColor` of all `<div>` elements in the document is set to `lightblue`.

Setting multiple properties for multiple elements is done like this:

```
$('div').css({
  backgroundColor: 'lightblue',
  border: '1px solid lightgrey',
  padding: '5px'
});
```

An object literal with key, value pairs is passed to the `css()` method. In the preceding example, the `backgroundColor` is set to `lightblue`, the `border` is set to `1px solid lightgrey`, and the `padding` is set to `5px` for all of the `<div>` elements in the document.

The outerWidth() and outerHeight() Methods

In traditional JavaScript, when you want to get the width of an element — which includes the CSS width, in addition to border width, and padding width — you use the property `offsetWidth`. Using jQuery, this information is available when you call the method `outerWidth()`, which provides the `offsetWidth` of the first element in a selection. This gives you a pixel measurement including width, border, and padding. The following example illustrates how these methods work:

```
<!DOCTYPE html PUBLIC "-//W3C//DTD XHTML 1.0 Strict//EN"
    "http://www.w3.org/TR/xhtml1/DTD/xhtml1-strict.dtd">
<html xmlns='http://www.w3.org/1999/xhtml' xml:lang='en'>
  <head>
    <meta http-equiv='content-type' content='text/html; charset=utf-8' />
    <meta http-equiv='content-language' content='en-us' />
    <title></title>
    <link type='text/css' href='Figure 6-1.css' rel='stylesheet' />
    <script type='text/javascript'
            src='../../../Source Code/jQuery/jQuery.js'></script>
    </script>
    <script type='text/javascript' src='Figure 6-1.js'></script>
  </head>
  <body>
    <div></div>
  </body>
</html>
```

The following style sheet is included in the preceding document:

```
body {
    font: 16px sans-serif;
}
div {
    width: 200px;
    height: 200px;
    padding: 10px;
    border: 1px solid rgb(200, 200, 200);
    background: lightblue;
}
```

The following JavaScript outputs the values returned by the `outerHeight()` and the `outerWidth()` methods for the `<div>` element:

```
$(document).ready(
  function() {
    alert(
      'outerWidth: '  + $('div').outerWidth() + "\n" +
      'outerHeight: ' + $('div').outerHeight()
    );
  }
);
```

The preceding example results in the document that you see in **Figure 6-1**.

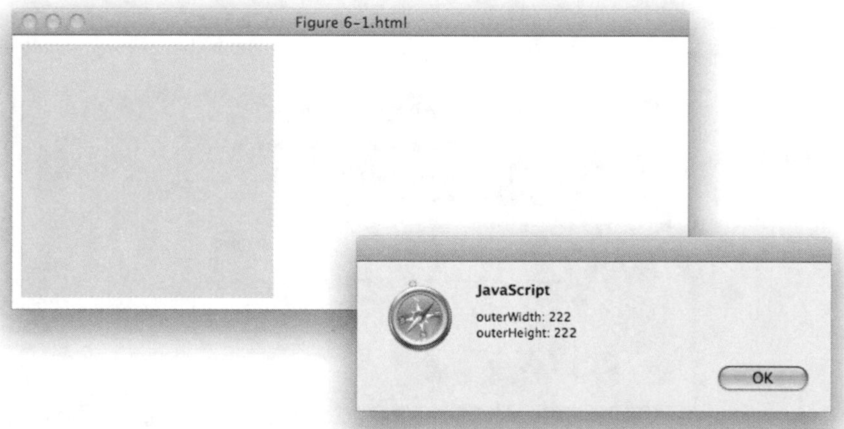

Figure 6-1

In the preceding example, you see that the script puts up an alert dialogue that outputs the values for `outerHeight()` and `outerWidth()`. Each value is `222`, which takes the width, 200 pixels, plus 10 pixels of padding on each side, or 20 pixels, and 1 pixel of border on each side, or 2 pixels, for 222 pixels total. Then the same is done to get the `outerHeight()`. If you want the element's margin to be accounted for as well, you can provide an argument to each method that tells each method to put in the margin as well. The preceding example's CSS is modified so that some margin is specified for the `<div>` element:

```
body {
    font: 16px sans-serif;
}
div {
    width: 200px;
    height: 200px;
    padding: 10px;
    border: 1px solid rgb(200, 200, 200);
    background: lightblue;
    margin: 10px;
}
```

Then the JavaScript is also modified to specify that `margin` should be returned as part of the value:

```
$(document).ready(
  function() {
    alert(
      'outerWidth:  '  + $('div').outerWidth({margin: true}) + "\n" +
      'outerHeight: '  + $('div').outerHeight({margin: true})
    );
  }
);
```

The example changes only slightly — an object literal is passed to both the `outerWidth()` and `outerHeight()` methods with an option `margin: true` to indicate that `margin` should be included in the return value. This gives you the output that you see in **Figure 6-2**.

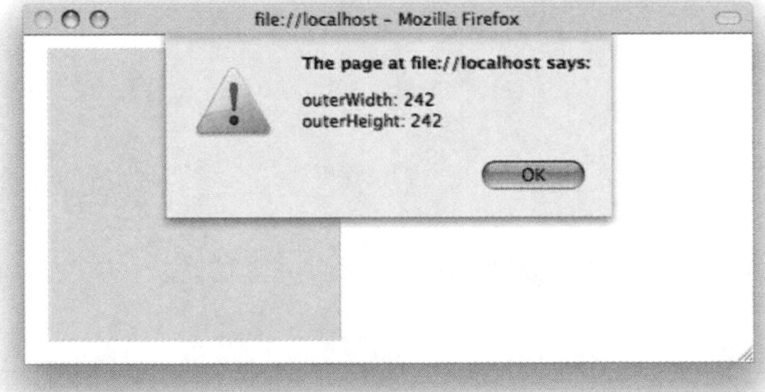

Figure 6-2

The preceding output is shown in Firefox because a bug in the current version of jQuery reports an incorrect value for `outerWidth()` when run in Safari or Google Chrome. jQuery developers are already working to resolve this bug. The new value output in the alert dialogue shows 242 pixels, which includes the 10 pixels of left and right margin that you added to the style sheet.

To demonstrate how you would use the `css()`, `outerWidth()`, and `outerHeight()` methods in a real-world-oriented example, the following "Try It Out" shows you how to make a custom context menu that leverages these methods to set a custom context menu's position within the document. The *context menu* is the menu your browser provides when you click on the right button on a three-button mouse, when you click and hold, or when you hold down the [Ctrl] key and click on older Mac systems. This menu always pops up at the location of your mouse cursor.

Try It Out Making a Custom Context Menu

Example 6-1

To make a custom context menu, follow these steps:

1. Create the following XHTML document as *Example 6-1.html*:

```
<!DOCTYPE html PUBLIC "-//W3C//DTD XHTML 1.0 Strict//EN"
    "http://www.w3.org/TR/xhtml1/DTD/xhtml1-strict.dtd">
<html xmlns='http://www.w3.org/1999/xhtml' xml:lang='en'>
  <head>
    <meta http-equiv='content-type' content='text/html; charset=utf-8' />
    <meta http-equiv='content-language' content='en-us' />
    <title></title>
    <link type='text/css' href='Example 6-1.css' rel='stylesheet' />
    <script type='text/javascript'
            src='../../../Source Code/jQuery/jQuery.js'></script>
    </script>
    <script type='text/javascript' src='Example 6-1.js'></script>
  </head>
  <body>
    <div id='tmpContextMenu'></div>
    <div class='tmpContextItem'></div>
    <div class='tmpContextItem'></div>
    <div class='tmpContextItem'></div>
    <div class='tmpContextItem'></div>
    <div class='tmpContextItem'></div>
    <div class='tmpContextItem'></div>
  </body>
</html>
```

2. Create the following CSS as *Example 6-1.css*:

```
body {
    font: 16px sans-serif;
}
div.tmpContextItem {
    width: 100px;
    height: 100px;
    padding: 10px;
    border: 1px solid rgb(200, 200, 200);
    background: lightblue;
    margin: 10px;
    float: left;
}
div#tmpContextMenu {
    width: 150px;
    height: 150px;
    background: yellowgreen;
    border: 1px solid rgb(128, 128, 128);
```

```
    padding: 10px;
    position: absolute;
    left: 0;
    right: 0;
    display: none;
}
```

3. Create the following JavaScript as *Example 6-1.js*:

```
var tmpContextMenuOn = false;

$(document).ready(
  function() {
    $('div.tmpContextItem').bind(
      'contextmenu',
      function($e) {
        $e.preventDefault();

        // The contextmenu doesn't work in Opera.
        // Guess those four users will just have to do without.
        var $menu = $('div#tmpContextMenu');

        $menu.show();

        // The following bit gets the dimensions of the viewport
        var $vpx, $vpy;

        if (self.innerHeight) {
          // all except Explorer
          $vpx = self.innerWidth;
          $vpy = self.innerHeight;
        } else if (document.documentElement &&
                   document.documentElement.clientHeight) {
          // Explorer 6 Strict Mode
          $vpx = document.documentElement.clientWidth;
          $vpy = document.documentElement.clientHeight;
        } else if (document.body) {
          // other Explorers
          $vpx = document.body.clientWidth;
          $vpy = document.body.clientHeight;
        }

        // Reset offset values to their defaults
        $menu.css({
          top:    'auto',
          right:  'auto',
          bottom: 'auto',
          left:   'auto'
        });

        /**
        * If the height or width of the context menu is greater than the amount
        * of pixels from the point of click to the right or bottom edge of the
        * viewport adjust the offset accordingly
        */
```

```
          if ($menu.outerHeight() > ($vpy - $e.pageY)) {
            $menu.css('bottom', ($vpy - $e.pageY) + 'px');
          } else {
            $menu.css('top', $e.pageY + 'px');
          }

          if ($menu.outerWidth() > ($vpx - $e.pageX)) {
            $menu.css('right',  ($vpx - $e.pageX) + 'px');
          } else {
            $menu.css('left', $e.pageX + 'px');
          }
        }
      );

      $('div#tmpContextMenu').hover(
        function() {
          tmpContextMenuOn = true;
        },
        function() {
          tmpContextMenuOn = false;
        }
      );

      $(document).mousedown(
        function() {
          if (!tmpContextMenuOn) {
            $('div#tmpContextMenu').hide();
          }
        }
      );
    }
  );
```

The preceding example produces output similar to the screenshot in **Figure 6-3**.

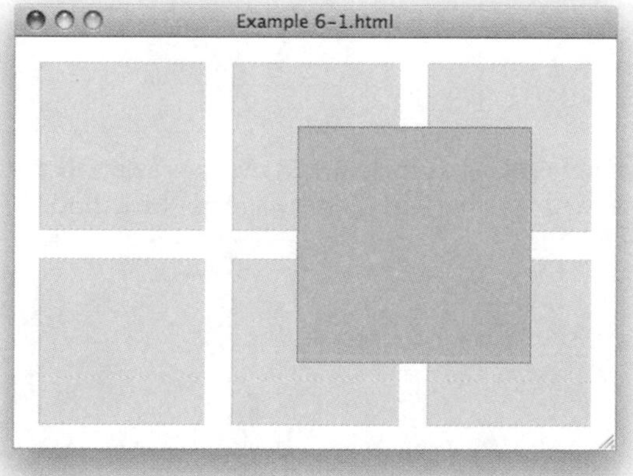

Figure 6-3

Before I explain the concepts in this example, I put forth one word of warning... . While replacing the context menu that your browser provides can be used to provide useful functionality that can go much further in making your web-based applications look and feel like desktop applications, you should be cautious about the scenarios that you choose to invoke custom context menu functionality. The context menu is also heavily used by browser users to do simple things like navigate forward or backward from their present location, to reload the current page, or to do other useful tasks associated with using the browser. But if your web application recklessly takes control of the context menu, you risk alienating or annoying your user base, since your application prevents the user from accessing and interacting with his or her browser in the way he or she normally would. Additionally, disabling the browser's context menu will not prevent users from seeing your application's source code, since you can still go to the browser's main menu and click on the View Source option. More savvy users can bypass JavaScript by disabling it, or even directly access your source code through other means, such as via your browser's cache or by accessing the source code from your website directly from the command line or a script. If you're considering disabling the context menu for this purpose, you may want to reconsider publishing your web application for public consumption, as this method of preventing access to your website's source code is ineffective and is subject to numerous work-arounds. Remember, content you place on the Web is, by design, made to be publicly consumed and transportable to browsers of all kinds residing on platforms of all kinds.... The key thing to keep in mind is that rendering your markup and executing your JavaScript is entirely optional.

That said, the preceding example takes a `<div>` with perfectly square dimensions that takes the place of your browser's default context menu. When you click on one of the six `<div>` elements with class name *tmpContextItem*, the `<div>` acting as the context menu is repositioned based on where the click occurred.

First, you set up the event that fires when the user accesses the context menu. This is done using jQuery's `bind()` method, since jQuery does not provide a `contextmenu()` method. It should also be noted that the Opera browser does not support the `contextmenu` event, and `contextmenu` events can be disabled in Firefox, although they are enabled by default.

The following code thus far disables the browser's default context menu when the user tries to access the context menu with the mouse cursor over one of the `<div>` elements with class name *tmpContextItem*:

```
$('div.tmpContextItem').bind(
  'contextmenu',
  function($e) {
    $e.preventDefault();
```

Next, the `<div>` element that will act as the context menu is selected and assigned to the `$menu` variable, and that `<div>` element is made visible with jQuery's `show()` method.

```
      // The contextmenu doesn't work in Opera.
      // Guess those four users will just have to do without.
      var $menu = $('div#tmpContextMenu');

  $menu.show();
```

When you're creating your own context menu, you want to have the position of your context menu change depending on where in the browser window the context menu is accessed. If the user accesses the context menu close to the left and top sides of the window, you want your context menu to position itself from the left and the top. If the user accesses the context menu from the right and bottom of the window, then you want the context menu to intelligently reposition from the right and bottom, and do this without any part of the context menu being obstructed. In order to make the context menu so that it dynamically repositions itself depending on where it is accessed, you need to do a little bit of math. The first bits of data that you need to do that math are the dimensions of the viewport. You'll use the dimensions of the viewport to help determine how the context menu should be positioned relative to the place where the user accesses it. Getting the viewport's dimensions, unfortunately, is one of those fringe areas where different browsers differ, but frameworks like jQuery don't yet provide a neat, unified method of patching over those differences. The following code intelligently obtains the viewport's dimensions depending on the browser's implementation:

```
    // The following bit gets the dimensions of the viewport
    var $vpx, $vpy;

    if (self.innerHeight) {
      // all except Explorer
      $vpx = self.innerWidth;
      $vpy = self.innerHeight;
    } else if (document.documentElement &&
               document.documentElement.clientHeight) {
      // Explorer 6 Strict Mode
      $vpx = document.documentElement.clientWidth;
      $vpy = document.documentElement.clientHeight;
    } else if (document.body) {
      // other Explorers
      $vpx = document.body.clientWidth;
      $vpy = document.body.clientHeight;
}
```

Before you actually position the context menu, you need to re-set your context menu's offset positions to the defaults. All four offsets have to be re-set, because the next portion of code will set at least two of the offset properties to the right values, and the two that are set can vary depending on where the user accesses the context menu. You don't, for example, want the positions you set the last time the user accessed the context menu to persist to this time, since that may create a conflict. In order to re-set each offset position, you use jQuery's `css()` method to set the `top`, `right`, `bottom`, and `left` offset properties back to each property's default value, `auto`.

```
    // Reset offset values to their defaults
    $menu.css({
      top:    'auto',
      right:  'auto',
      bottom: 'auto',
      left:   'auto'
});
```

Now you're ready to mathematically determine the proper position for the context menu. To get the right position, you want to know if the `offsetHeight` of the `<div>` element you're using for the menu exceeds the browser's viewport height minus the vertical point of the mouse cursor's position, relative to the document. If the `offsetHeight` [provided by jQuery's `outerHeight()` method] is bigger than this calculation, it means that the menu should be positioned from the `bottom`, rather than from the `top`; otherwise, the menu would be clipped.

```
/**
 * If the height or width of the context menu is greater than the amount
 * of pixels from the point of click to the right or bottom edge of the
 * viewport adjust the offset accordingly
 */
if ($menu.outerHeight() > ($vpy - $e.pageY)) {
  $menu.css('bottom', ($vpy - $e.pageY) + 'px');
} else {
  $menu.css('top', $e.pageY + 'px');
}
```

The same calculation is done for the horizontal portion. If the `offsetWidth` [provided by jQuery's `outerWidth()` method] of the menu is greater than the width of the viewport minus the horizontal coordinate of the mouse cursor's position, relative to the document, the menu should be positioned from the `right`, rather than the `left`; otherwise, the menu would be clipped horizontally.

```
    if ($menu.outerWidth() > ($vpx - $e.pageX)) {
      $menu.css('right',  ($vpx - $e.pageX) + 'px');
    } else {
      $menu.css('left', $e.pageX + 'px');
}
```

As far as positioning the context menu correctly depending on where the user clicks in the document, that's all there is to it. The additional code handles revealing and hiding the context menu at the right moments. At the beginning of the document, you declare the following variable:

```
var tmpContextMenuOn = false;
```

The preceding variable is used to track whether or not the user's mouse cursor is over the context menu when it is active. When the user's mouse cursor leaves the context menu, this variable is set to `false`; when the user's mouse cursor is present, this variable is set to `true`. This Boolean value is then used to toggle the menu off when the user clicks on an area outside of the context menu, and keeps the menu active when the user clicks on the menu itself.

The following code handles the part that sets the `tmpContextMenuOn` variable to either `true` or `false` via passing two event handlers to jQuery's `hover()` method:

```
  $('div#tmpContextMenu').hover(
    function() {
      tmpContextMenuOn = true;
    },
    function() {
      tmpContextMenuOn = false;
    }
);
```

Then the following code hides the menu when the user clicks anywhere outside of the menu, since the variable is `false` in that case, and keeps the menu on when the user actually clicks on the menu.

```
$(
  document).mousedown(
  function() {
    if (!tmpContextMenuOn) {
      $('div#tmpContextMenu').hide();
    }
  }
);
```

jQuery's API as it relates to CSS is documented in Appendix H.

Summary

In this chapter, you learned how to get the value of an element's CSS property using jQuery's `css()` method. You also learned how to manipulate an element's style using the same `css()` method, which can be done by passing a property and value to the `css()` method as two separate strings, or by passing an object literal with one or more property, value pairs.

jQuery provides the `offsetHeight` and `offsetWidth` properties by calling the methods `outerHeight()` or `outerWidth()`. These methods return an element's pixel width or height, including padding and borders. You can also specifically add `margin` to the value returned by these methods, but adding `margin` does not work in the Safari or Google Chrome browsers at the time of this writing.

Finally, I reiterated these methods with a real-world-oriented example that shows you how to replace the browser's default context menu with your own. In this situation, you want to use jQuery's `css()` method to set CSS property values, rather than a style sheet, since the values being set are set dynamically.

Exercises

1. What script would you use if you wanted to obtain the value of the color property for a `<div>` element using jQuery?
2. If you wanted to set the background color of a web page using jQuery, what code would you use?
3. If you needed to set padding, margin, and a border on a set of `<div>` elements using jQuery, what would the code look like?
4. What is the jQuery method that returns an element's pixel width, including border and padding dimensions, called?
5. If you wanted to obtain a `<div>` element's pixel height, including border, padding, and margins, using jQuery, what would the code look like?

AJAX

AJAX is the technology that encompasses the ability to make arbitrary HTTP requests from JavaScript to obtain new data without the need for reloading a document. *AJAX* stands for "Asynchronous JavaScript and XML." The name is misleading, though, since you don't have to use XML at all. XML is just one of many possible formats that you can use to transmit data from a server to a client-side JavaScript.

Using AJAX it becomes possible to make web documents behave much less like documents and much more like completely self-contained desktop applications. The advantages of web-based applications have come to be recognized en masse in recent years with the mainstream adoption in ever-greater frequency of AJAX to make seamless, cross-platform, ubiquitously available web-based portals like Google's gmail service and numerous other web-based offerings, or Apple's MobileMe service. With a web-based application, updates are much easier to propagate, since everyone upgrades immediately upon their next visit to the website. No longer do companies have to worry about maintaining legacy software and users — with a web-based application, everyone is pushed to the latest version. It also becomes easier for a user to access these applications. Since a separate installation is not required on every computer where the application's use is desired, all that is required is a capable browser on top of moderately capable hardware. Browsers strive to blur the line between desktop applications and web-based applications even more, since browsers like Firefox and Google's Chrome browser make it easier to make a web-based application available as a desktop application via placing an icon on the user's desktop, dock, start menu, or quick-launch bar. In Firefox's case, this functionality is experimental, but in the case of Chrome, the feature is already a reality. Then there is Adobe's AIR run time, which allows you to develop desktop applications using Web standards. Since AIR is built on top of WebKit — which is the rendering engine used in Safari, Chrome, Android, iPhone, and Apple's OSX Dashboard, among others — AIR is capable of making sophisticated, complex desktop applications using a robust standards-compliant rendering engine. So, if these companies have anything to say about it, web-based applications will become more popular and increasingly take over certain tasks that desktop applications once served.

Another advantage of web-based application development, which some people may perceive as nefarious, is that web-based applications are immune to piracy, at least in the traditional sense. It's impossible to obtain a web-based application's services without payment, since a user can simply be locked out if payment is not made. Up until now, this aspect hasn't been much of a problem, though, since web-based applications are often supported with advertisements that make them free.

Then another advantage still is that you can make a web-based application available to many more operating systems and browsers than you might have otherwise with a self-contained desktop application. You can target Safari, Chrome, Firefox, Internet Explorer, and Opera and reach more than 99 percent of your browsing audience easily. Frameworks like jQuery make this even easier since it eliminates many browser inconsistencies and headaches that might otherwise present as roadblocks to cross-browser development.

AJAX has become a powerful and increasingly essential component of web development; in this chapter, I cover jQuery's built-in methods for making AJAX requests. As you would expect, jQuery takes something that is moderately verbose and complex and boils it down into a much simpler, easier-to-grasp API that gets you started writing AJAX-capable web applications much more quickly.

Making a Server Request

As you're probably already aware, the Web works through a protocol called HTTP. When you navigate to a web page, your browser fires off a request to a remote HTTP server that's running Apache or Microsoft IIS or some other HTTP server software, using the HTTP communication protocol. AJAX makes it so that you can fire off those HTTP requests programmatically, without having to reload the entire web page again. Once your JavaScript makes a request and receives a response, you can then take that data and manipulate the content that's in front of the user based on the response that you receive. Using the HTTP protocol, there are two ways that you can request data from the server — the GET and the POST methods.

What's the Difference between GET and POST?

At face value, the GET and POST methods seem identical: Both allow you to request a web page and send data along with that request. Most of the time, for AJAX requests, you want to use the GET method since it is slightly faster from a performance standpoint where AJAX in concerned, but there are other differences that you should be aware of that address semantic differences between the two, as well as technical and security differences. The following outlines these differences:

- The GET method is intended for requests that have no tangible, lasting effect on the state of anything (the HTTP specification calls this type of request *idempotent*). For example, when you make a request and you're simply retrieving data from a database, GET is properly suited for this type of request. If a request results in a change to the database via an insertion, update, or delete — for example, when managing content or making an order or uploading data — the POST method is best suited. This difference, however, is merely semantic.
- Using the POST method will cause a browser to automatically prevent re-submitting a form if the user navigates back to a submitted form using the browser's Back button, since the `POST` method is intended to be used for situations in which manipulation occurs. This is a technical difference put in place to prevent re-submission of form data. But this automatic prevent is ineffective since you still have to design your server-side programs to account for possible re-submissions … anything that can go wrong, will! Users can be impatient and click the Submit button multiple times or refresh submitted forms, ignoring a browser's warnings. On the other hand, the GET method provides no automatic protection against re-submission. This difference is mostly inconsequential to AJAX programming because there is no way for a user to re-submit a POST request without you specifically designing the ability into your program.

- The GET method has a much lower limitation on request length imposed than the POST method. This difference is a technical difference that can have an effect on your applications. The limitation of the length a GET request can be varies among browsers, but RFC 2068 states that servers should be cautious about depending on URI lengths greater than 255 bytes. Since GET request data is included as part of the URI (the web page's address), then the GET request is really limited by the length of the URI a browser supports. Internet Explorer can support a URL up to 2,083 characters in length, which is ridiculously long. The POST method, on the other hand, theoretically has no limitation on length other than what your server is configured to accept. PHP, for example, is configured to accept a POST request that's 8 MB or less in size, by default. This setting and others, such as how long a script can execute and how much memory it can consume, collectively define how big your POST requests can be; on the client side, however, a POST request has no hard limitation defined, other than the limits of the client's hardware, network, and server capabilities.
- The POST and GET methods can be encoded differently, again a technical difference. I'm not going to go into this difference in great detail, since it is outside the scope of this book. This difference applies when you want to upload files via the POST method, but since AJAX is incapable of handling file uploads, this difference does not apply to AJAX. I cover how to upload a file using an AJAX-like technique later in this chapter.

The distinction between the POST and GET methods is mostly moot when it comes to making a request originating from an AJAX script. Since the user is not involved with the request, the automatic protection portion becomes unnecessary, which leaves only the semantic differences and the limitations in length. For the most part, you can get away with making GET requests for everything, which has been said to have a slight performance advantage over the POST method. Personally, I tend to honor the semantic differences out of simple habit from years of working with forms in client-side programming. More information about the performance aspect is available on the Yahoo Developer website at `http://developer.yahoo.com/performance/rules.html`.

Formats Used to Transport Data with an AJAX Request

Although the name implies that you use XML to transport data with an AJAX Request, this is entirely optional. Besides XML, there are two other common ways that data is transmitted from the server to a client-side JavaScript application: JSON (or JavaScript Object Notation) and HTML. You are not limited to these formats, however, since you can conceivably take any data you like from the server and transmit it to the client. These formats are the most popular because JavaScript provides you with tools for working with these types of data. XML can be easily queried using DOM tools and methods. HTML can be sent in incomplete snippets that can be effortlessly inserted into a document using the `innerHTML` property, or via jQuery's `html()` method.

You can also transmit JavaScript from the server and the JavaScript will be be evaluated in the client-side application, executing it and making whatever variables, functions, objects, and so on available. JSON is a subset of the syntax allowed for JavaScript Object Literals, and therefore a subset of JavaScript itself. It is considered to be its own format for data transmission, however. Many popular languages have the ability to both read and send JSON-formatted data.

There are potential security issues that are associated with the JSON format that you should consider that result from using `eval()` to execute JavaScript code from the server. `eval()` should only be used if you are certain that the data being eval'd cannot be manipulated and cannot contain malicious code. In the case of your web application, you should take precautions before using the `eval()` method to execute anything that has been user-provided, since it's possible that a user can have malicious intentions. Since a portion of your code is available for all to see on the client side, any user can discover what methods you use to transmit and receive data. If you're using JSON to transmit user-supplied data that originates from your input forms, a user could maliciously craft the data submitted in your forms to be executed alongside your JSON-formatted code. One exploit a malicious user could take advantage of in this way would be to execute JavaScript that takes other users' session data and transmits that data back to the malicious user's server. This type of exploit is known as an *XSS*, or *Cross-Site Scripting vulnerability*, alternatively known as *Cross-Site Scripting Forgery*. Since session data is not tied to a user's computer but, instead, relies on very long strings of numbers and letters that are mathematically difficult to reproduce, once a malicious user obtains another user's session ID, it then becomes possible for that malicious user to impersonate other users and steal their sensitive data or log in to your server and obtain privileged information. So great care and thought must be placed into what code is safe to `eval()` and what code is not.

Throughout this chapter, I provide examples of all three popular methods for transmitting data with AJAX. For more information about this and other AJAX-related topics, pick up a copy of Nicholas C. Zakas, Jeremy McPeak, and Joe Fawcett's excellent, critically acclaimed *Professional AJAX*, 2nd ed. (Wiley, 2007).

Making a GET Request with jQuery

Having talked about some of the nuts and bolts of what an AJAX Request is, the next topic up for discussion is making your first GET request with AJAX using jQuery.

Of course, AJAX is typically used to create dynamic web applications that have a server-side component written in something like PHP, Java, ASP.NET, Ruby, or whatever. The server-side portion of this is outside the scope of this book, so, instead of linking an AJAX Request to a server-side application, I link these requests to hard-coded documents that provide the same response every time. If you'd like to learn more about the server-side components that are involved, Wrox has an excellent selection of books covering just about every language under the sun.

That said, jQuery makes a few methods available that initiate a GET request from a server; the method that you use depends on the data you're getting. The generic method, which you can use to make any type of GET request, is called, easily enough, `get()`. Each method is a member of the jQuery object, so you'd call the `get()` method like this: `$.get()`.

Requesting Data Formatted in XML

The first example I demonstrate shows you how to request data from a server that formats the response as XML. The following source code demonstrates an input form for an address in which the country field causes the state field to be dynamically updated when the country selection is changed, and the country's flag to change as well. Each list of states is dynamically fetched from the server using an AJAX Request. However, this only happens for three of the country selections — the United States, Canada, and the United Kingdom — since the information is being fed from static XML files, rather than a database-driven server. If I were to create an XML file for all 239 country options, I would at least be able to change the flag for that country, even if no administrative subdivision similar to a state exists for that country. The following is the HTML portion of this example:

```
<!DOCTYPE html PUBLIC "-//W3C//DTD XHTML 1.0 Strict//EN"
    "http://www.w3.org/TR/xhtml1/DTD/xhtml1-strict.dtd">
<html xmlns='http://www.w3.org/1999/xhtml' xml:lang='en'>
```

```
<head>
  <meta http-equiv='content-type' content='text/html; charset=utf-8' />
  <meta http-equiv='content-language' content='en-us' />
  <title></title>
  <script type='text/javascript'
          src='../../../Source Code/jQuery/jQuery.js'>
  </script>
  <script type='text/javascript' src='Figure 7-1.js'></script>
  <link type='text/css' href='Figure 7-1.css' rel='stylesheet' />
</head>
<body>
   <form action='javascript:void(0);' method='post'>
     <fieldset>
       <legend>Address</legend>
     <div id='hLocationCountryIDWrapper'>
       <label for='hLocationCountryID'>
         <img src='../../../Images/Flags/us.png' alt='Country' />
       </label>
       <select id='hLocationCountryID' size='1'
               name='hLocationCountryID' class='hFormSelectInput'>
         <option value='0'>Please select a country</option>
         <option value='1'>Afghanistan</option>
         <option value='2'>Albania</option>
         <option value='3'>Algeria</option>
         <option value='4'>American Samoa</option>
         <option value='5'>Andorra</option>
```

The very long list of countries has been snipped out. The complete file is available as part of this book's free source code download materials available from `www.wrox.com`.

```
         <option value='222'>United Kingdom</option>
         <option value='223' selected='selected'>United States</option>
         <option value='224'>United States Minor Outlying Islands</option>
         <option value='225'>Uruguay</option>
         <option value='226'>Uzbekistan</option>
         <option value='227'>Vanuatu</option>
         <option value='228'>Vatican City State (Holy See)</option>
         <option value='229'>Venezuela</option>
         <option value='230'>Vietnam</option>
         <option value='231'>Virgin Islands (British)</option>
         <option value='232'>Virgin Islands (U.S.)</option>
         <option value='233'>Wallis and Futuna Islands</option>
         <option value='234'>Western Sahara</option>
         <option value='235'>Yemen</option>
         <option value='236'>Yugoslavia</option>
         <option value='237'>Zaire</option>
         <option value='238'>Zambia</option>
         <option value='239'>Zimbabwe</option>
       </select>
     </div>
     <div>
       <label for='hLocationStreetAddress'>Street Address:</label>
       <textarea name='hLocationStreetAddress'
                 id='hLocationStreetAddress' rows='2' cols='50'></textarea>
```

```
        </div>
        <div>
          <label for='hLocationCity'>City:</label>
          <input type='text' name='hLocationCity' id='hLocationCity' size='25' />
        </div>
        <div>
          <label for='hLocationStateID'>State:</label>
          <select name='hLocationStateID' id='hLocationStateID'>
          </select>
        </div>
        <div>
          <label for='hLocationPostalCode'>Postal Code:</label>
          <input type='text' name='hLocationPostalCode'
                 id='hLocationPostalCode' size='10' />
        </div>
        <div id='hLocationButtonWrapper'>
          <input type='submit' id='hLocationButton'
                 name='hLocationButton' value='Save' />
        </div>
        </fieldset>
      </form>
    </body>
  </html>
```

The preceding HTML is styled with the following CSS:

```
body {
    font: 16px sans-serif;
}
fieldset {
    background: #93cdf9;
    border: 1px solid rgb(200, 200, 200);
}
fieldset div {
    padding: 10px;
    margin: 5px;
}
fieldset label {
    float: left;
    width: 200px;
    text-align: right;
    padding: 2px 5px 0 0;
}
div#hLocationCountryIDWrapper img {
    position: relative;
    top: -4px;
}
```

Then, the following JavaScript is included in the preceding HTML document:

The following JavaScript does not function in Internet Explorer without accessing the entire example via an HTTP server, that is, opening and executing the documents locally in IE causes the AJAX portion of the code to fail. However, this code works fine in Firefox, Safari, and so on, without the aid of an HTTP server.

```
$(document).ready(
  function() {
    $('select#hLocationCountryID').click(
      function() {
        $.get(
          'Figure 7-1 ' + this.value + '.xml',
          function($xml) {
            // Make the XML query-able with jQuery
            $xml = $($xml);

            // Get the ISO2 value, that's used for the
            // file name of the flag.
            var $iso2 = $xml.find('hLocationCountryISO2').text();

            // Swap out the flag image
            $('img[alt=Country]').attr(
              'src',
              '../../../Images/Flags/' + $iso2.toLowerCase() + '.png'
            );

            // Remove all of the options
            $('select#hLocationStateID').empty();

            // Set the states...
            $xml.find('hLocationState').each(
              function() {
                $('select#hLocationStateID').append(
                  "<option value='" + $(this).attr('hLocationStateID') + "'>" +
                  $(this).text() +
                  "</option>"
                );
              }
            );

            // Change the label
            $('label[for=hLocationStateID]').text(
              $xml.find('hLocationStateLabel').text() + ':'
            );
          },
          'xml'
        );
      }
    );
  }
);
```

Then for the AJAX Requests to succeed, you need to create some XML files for the response content. When you change the country in the `<select>` element, an AJAX Request is sent off via the GET method for the file Figure 7-1`<CountryID>`.xml, where `<CountryID>` is the numeric ID of the country selected from the dropdown list. I've prepared XML files for three countries with the IDs 38, 222, and 223, those being the respective IDs of Canada, the United Kingdom, and the United States. Each XML file looks similar to the following, which is Canada's:

```
<?xml version="1.0" encoding="UTF-8" standalone="yes"?>
<response>
  <hLocationCountryISO2>CA</hLocationCountryISO2>
  <hLocationCountryISO3>CAN</hLocationCountryISO3>
  <hLocationStateLabel>Province</hLocationStateLabel>
  <hLocationState hLocationStateID='0'> </hLocationState>
  <hLocationState hLocationStateID="66">Alberta</hLocationState>
  <hLocationState hLocationStateID="67">British Columbia</hLocationState>
  <hLocationState hLocationStateID="68">Manitoba</hLocationState>
  <hLocationState hLocationStateID="69">Newfoundland</hLocationState>
  <hLocationState hLocationStateID="70">New Brunswick</hLocationState>
  <hLocationState hLocationStateID="71">Nova Scotia</hLocationState>
  <hLocationState hLocationStateID="72">Northwest Territories</hLocationState>
  <hLocationState hLocationStateID="73">Nunavut</hLocationState>
  <hLocationState hLocationStateID="74">Ontario</hLocationState>
  <hLocationState hLocationStateID="75">Prince Edward Island</hLocationState>
  <hLocationState hLocationStateID="76">Quebec</hLocationState>
  <hLocationState hLocationStateID="77">Saskatchewan</hLocationState>
  <hLocationState hLocationStateID="78">Yukon Territory</hLocationState>
</response>
```

Each XML file is structured identically, providing an ISO2 and ISO3 country code, a label, and the list of administrative subdivisions, which I have simply called *states*, even though that's not always technically correct.

The preceding example looks like what you see in **Figure 7-1**, when you select United Kingdom from the country dropdown.

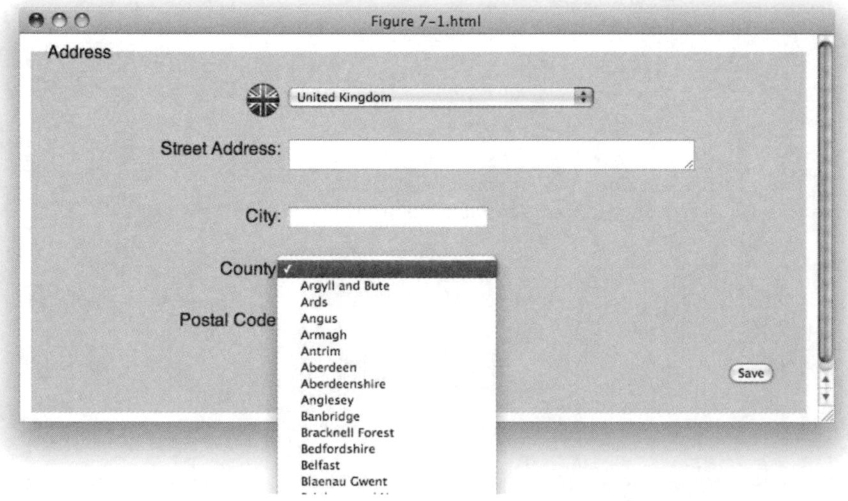

Figure 7-1

In the JavaScript file, things get under way with adding a `click` event to the `<select>` element with ID name *hLocationCountryID*. Within the handler for the `click` event, you begin your AJAX Request using jQuery's `$.get()` method. The first argument specifies the path that you want to request, which is the XML file, dynamically substituting the country ID in the filename. The second argument is a callback function that you want to execute when your script has received the server's response, and the third argument is the type of AJAX Request that you want to make. For a complete overview of the API of the `$.get()` method, see Appendix G.

The callback method that you specified has one argument specified, `$xml`. This variable contains the XML data that the server has sent back. This data is then made into a jQuery object, which makes it much easier to extract data from it:

```
// Make the XML query-able with jQuery
$xml = $($xml);
```

The next thing to do is to fetch the ISO2 code from the XML document, which is used to fetch the updated flag for the selected country:

```
var $iso2 = $xml.find('hLocationCountryISO2').text();
```

Just as you would do in a normal HTML document, you are able to use jQuery's `find()` method to locate the XML element `<hLocationCountryISO2>` and retrieve its text content via jQuery's `text()` method. In the context of the three countries I've created XML files for, the `$iso2` variable would contain CA for Canada, GB for the United Kingdom, or US for the United States. The next step is to set the `src` attribute of the `<img>` element referencing the country flag:

```
// Swap out the flag image
$('img[alt=Country]').attr(
  'src',
  '../../../Images/Flags/' + $iso2.toLowerCase() + '.png'
);
```

The `<img>` element is located by querying the DOM for an `<img>` element with an `alt` attribute having the value *Country*. Then the `<img>` element's `src` attribute is set using jQuery's `attr()` method, and the path is defined taking into account the structure of files in this book's source code download materials. Then the filename is appended, and the ISO2 code is converted to lowercase, since each flag image is named using lowercase characters. This may not be a problem for some servers, like Windows or some Mac servers that are case-insensitive, but UNIX and Linux servers, including some Mac servers (depending on how the Macs have been formatted) are case-sensitive, and having the incorrect case for the filename would cause the image to fail to load.

The next step is to remove all state options. First you query for the `<select>` element with ID name *hLocationStateID*, then call jQuery's `empty()` method to remove all options.

```
// Remove all of the options
$('select#hLocationStateID').empty();
```

The next step is to add the administrative subdivisions from the XML file as options. jQuery's `find()` method locates all of the `<hLocationState>` elements in the XML file. Then you enumerate over each `<hLocationState>` element using the `each()` method.

```
// Set the states...
$xml.find('hLocationState').each(
  function() {
  }
);
```

Now you create each `<option>` element and append each element to the `<select>` element:

```
$('select#hLocationStateID').append(
  "<option value='" + $(this).attr('hLocationStateID') + "'>" +
  $(this).text() +
  "</option>"
);
```

Since you're working within the callback function provided to the `each()` method, each `<hLocationState>` element is passed to that callback function as `this`. Now to access jQuery's methods, you have to wrap `this` in a call to the jQuery object, like so: `$(this)`. You set the value attribute for each `<option>` element, which will be the unique numeric ID passed in each `<hLocationState>` element as the attribute `hLocationStateID="0"`, where zero is the unique ID. To get to that ID, all you have to do is call jQuery's `attr()` method with the attribute's name as the first argument. Then all that's left to do is set the option's label, which is done with a simple call to jQuery's `text()` method, which retrieves the text content of the `<hLocationState>` element.

The last item is to set the label for the "state." Since Canadians use provinces, Britons use counties, and Americans use states, you need to use the right label, which is provided in the XML file as the `<hLocationStateLabel>` element. To find the `<label>` element you want to change, you query the DOM for the `<label>` element with a `for` attribute having the value *hLocationStateID*. Then you set that `<label>` element's text content to the text content of the `<hLocationStateLabel>` element from the XML document.

```
$('label[for=hLocationStateID]').text(
  $xml.find('hLocationStateLabel').text() + ':'
);
```

As you can see with the preceding example, jQuery does not disappoint with its well-thought-out AJAX-handling abilities. With traditional JavaScript and DOM methods, the preceding would have been much more verbose and much more difficult to get working. jQuery's ability to *bind* itself to an XML response makes parsing and working with XML documents just like working with HTML documents, dead easy.

The iTunes-like flags included in the source code download originated from the following website, where you may also obtain higher-quality images:

`www.bartelme.at/journal/archive/flag_button_devkit/.`

Sending Data along with a Request

Let's say in that last example that you were really working with a database-driven server; in that case, how you would have constructed the request would be slightly different in the preceding example. Instead of dynamically creating the filename of the XML file you want to retrieve using the country's ID, you would instead need to pass that information separately. jQuery accommodates passing data in the `$.get()` method. In the context of the preceding example, you started out making a call to the `$.get()` method, that looked like this, with the extra code snipped out to made the example easier to understand:

```
$.get('Figure 7-1.xml', function($xml) {}, 'xml');
```

The first argument is the path of the file you're requesting — this can be any URL value. Typically, you'll want to reference some server-side script that can output data for you. The second argument is the callback function that the server's response XML will be passed to, and the third argument is the type of request being made, which is one of `xml`, `html`, `script`, `json`, `jsonp`, or `text`. This argument is set depending on the type of data that you expect coming back from the server.

When you want to send additional data with the request, another argument is added:

```
$.get(
  'Figure 7-1.xml',
  {hLocationCountryID: this.value}
  function($xml) {

  },
  'xml'
);
```

The new argument comes after the filename and before the function reference, and this is an object literal that contains the data you want to pass along in the GET request to the server. In the preceding example, I've modified the filename to be simply *Figure 7-1.xml*, and I've created an object literal with one property, `hLocationCountryID`, and its value becomes `this.value`, as passed from the `<select>` element. So, behind the scenes, this modification will cause the request to the server to look like this: `Figure 7-1.xml?hLocationCountryID=223`. jQuery takes the items in the object literal and builds the GET request. Since GET requests include data as part of the URL that you are calling, that data gets appended to the end of the URL. The question mark in the URL indicates that what follows is GET request data; then values are passed in name/value pairs, where each name and value is separated by an equals sign; and then if there is more than one value, additional values are appended subsequently by appending an ampersand character to the last name/value pair, like so:

```
Figure 7-1.xml?hLocationCountryID=223&someThingElse=thisothervalue
```

Then this data is also specially encoded for transport to the HTTP server. Once at the HTTP server, how this data is read depends on the server-side language that you're using to read it.

Requesting JSON Formatted Data

In this section, I revisit the example of the last section, but this time use JSON as the format for data transport, instead of XML. I could use the same jQuery method, `$.get()`, to do this, and change the last argument from `xml` to `json`, but as it turns out, jQuery offers another method called `$.getJSON()` for retrieving JSON-formatted data. This method is just like the `$.get()` method, except that the data format returned by the server is obviously expected to be JSON.

Using JSON as the data transportation format makes the code even leaner and easier to work with than XML, in addition to significantly reducing the size of the response from the server as well. The following example is the same example that you saw in the last section, where when you select Canada, the United States, or the United Kingdom from the dropdown, the flag, administrative subdivisions, and administrative subdivision label all swap out, presenting data relevant to the country you're looking at. The HTML portion remains the same, and just a few modifications are made to the JavaScript portion.

```
$(document).ready(
  function() {
    $('select#hLocationCountryID').click(
      function() {
        $.getJSON(
          'Figure 7-2 ' + this.value + '.json',
          function(json) {
            // Get the ISO2 value, that's used for the
            // file name of the flag.
            // Swap out the flag image
            $('img[alt=Country]').attr(
              'src',
              '../../../Images/Flags/' + json.ISO2.toLowerCase() + '.png'
            );

            // Remove all of the options
            $('select#hLocationStateID').empty();

            // Set the states...
            $.each(
              json.states,
              function() {
                var $state = this.split(':');
                $('select#hLocationStateID').append(
                  "<option value='" + $state[0] + "'>" +
                  $state[1] +
                  "</option>"
                );
              }
            );

            // Change the label
            $('label[for=hLocationStateID]').text(json.label + ':');
          }
        );
      }
    );
  }
);
```

In the preceding JavaScript, things function similarly to the example that you saw in the last section where the server response was formatted as XML, only this time you're initiating an AJAX Request using the `$.getJSON()` method instead of the `$.get()` method. These two methods are very similar, except that you don't have to specify the last argument, specifying the format of the server response with the `$.getJSON()` method. Another difference is that you are requesting a file with a `.json` extension instead of `.xml`, and also, like in the last example, the file requested depends on which country is selected from the dropdown menu. The JSON object is formatted like so in the file being requested:

```
{
  ISO2: 'CA',
  ISO3: 'CAN',
  label : 'Province',
  states : [
    '0: ',
    '66:Alberta',
    '67:British Columbia',
    '68:Manitoba',
    '69:Newfoundland',
    '70:New Brunswick',
    '71:Nova Scotia',
    '72:Northwest Territories',
    '73:Nunavut',
    '74:Ontario',
    '75:Prince Edward Island',
    '76:Quebec',
    '77:Saskatchewan',
    '78:Yukon Territory'
  ]
}
```

As you can see, the JSON format uses object literal syntax that you're already familiar with in JavaScript. The whole object is wrapped in curly braces but isn't itself assigned a name, which makes it easy for frameworks like jQuery to take the JSON-formatted data and assign it directly to an object. In the JavaScript, the preceding JSON was passed to the event handler for the `$.getJSON()` method as the `json` argument. All the data that you see in the JSON-formatted document is available inside of that `json` variable. You access the ISO2 information as `json.ISO2`, the label as `json.label`, and the states array as `json.states`. Using JSON, you've removed a step that would otherwise be required if you were working with XML data, which is querying the data within the response; with JSON, the data is fed directly to an object and is available immediately. You'll also note how much leaner the JSON file is compared to the verbose XML document. (Admittedly, the XML document didn't have to be that verbose — the example you saw was formatted based on the structure of my database, which is heavily namespaced with various name prefixes.)

Like the `$.get()` method, if you want to pass data to the server, you can provide that data in the same optional data argument.

```
$.getJSON(
  'Figure 7-2.json',
  {hLocationCountryID: this.value}
  function($xml) {

  }
);
```

The preceding produces **Figure 7-2** (not shown here) and is identical to what you would have done for the `$.get()` method, should you have had the need to send additional data along with the request, minus the inclusion of the last argument.

Making a POST Request

POST requests are identical to GET requests in jQuery, save the name of the method. Instead of `$.get()`, you use `$.post()`. Since a POST method request is reserved for modifying the state of the data in some way, you're probably more often than not going to want to pass some data along with your POST request, and that data will probably come from a form of some kind. It just so happens that jQuery makes it really easy to grab form data and pass that along to the server. The method jQuery provides for this is called the `serialize()` method. The `serialize()` method takes data for the input elements that you specify (which encompasses `<input>`, `<textarea>`, and `<select>` elements) and processes the values in those fields into a query string. This is demonstrated by adding a new event to the JavaScript that you've seen demonstrated in the last two sections for GET and JSON requests. The following is what the updated JavaScript looks like:

```
$(document).ready(
  function() {
    $('select#hLocationCountryID').click(
      function() {
        $.getJSON(
          'Figure 7-3 ' + this.value + '.json',
          function(json) {
            // Get the ISO2 value, that's used for the
            // file name of the flag.
            // Swap out the flag image
            $('img[alt=Country]').attr(
              'src',
              '../../../Images/Flags/' + json.ISO2.toLowerCase() + '.png'
            );

            // Remove all of the options
            $('select#hLocationStateID').empty();

            // Set the states...
            $.each(
              json.states,
              function() {
                var $state = this.split(':');
                $('select#hLocationStateID').append(
                  "<option value='" + $state[0] + "'>" +
                  $state[1] +
                  "</option>"
                );
              }
            );

            // Change the label
            $('label[for=hLocationStateID]').text(json.label + ':');
          }
        );
      }
    );

    $('input#hLocationButton').click(
      function($e) {
        $e.preventDefault();
```

```
            $.post(
              'Figure 7-3.xml',
              $('form :input').serialize(),
              function(xml) {
                // Process the server's response
                if (parseInt($(xml).text()) > 0) {
                  alert('Data successfully posted!');
                }
              },
              'xml'
            );
          }
        );
      }
    );
```

When you make the preceding modifications, load up the new document, and click on the Save button, you should see something like the screenshot that you see in **Figure 7-3**.

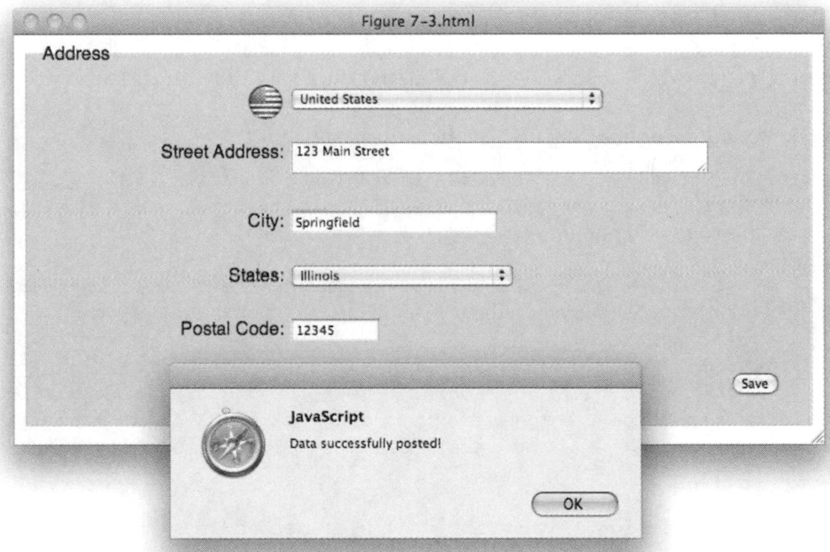

Figure 7-3

You've added a new event to the `<input>` element with ID name *hLocationButton*. When you click on the `<input>` element, a POST request is initiated using jQuery's `$.post()` method. Of course, you have no HTTP server set up to transmit this data to, so, instead, you simply reference a static XML file that lets you know the POST request succeeded at least as far as requesting the specified document. In the second argument to the `$.post()` method, you supply the data that you want to transmit to the server, just like you can do with the `$.get()` and `$.getJSON()` methods that you saw in the previous two sections. However, instead of passing an object literal, this time you search the document for all `<input>` elements by using a special, jQuery-specific selector, `form :input`. The selector says to find all input elements that are descendent of the `<form>` element, via specifying jQuery's `:input` pseudo-class, which applies to all input elements, which is to say, `<input>` elements (and all of its variants, like password, checkbox, radio, etc.), `<textarea>`, and `<select>` elements; these are all considered input elements. That selection is then passed to jQuery's `serialize()` method, which finds the right names and values from the various input elements, formatting that data like so:

```
hLocationCountryID=223&hLocationStreetAddress=123+Main+Street&hLocationCity=
Springfield&hLocationStateID=23&hLocationPostalCode=12345
```

This data is now ready to be posted to the server, so all you have to do is pass this formatted data in the data argument of the `$.post()` method. This also works for jQuery's other AJAX Request methods as well, and jQuery is smart enough to know when you're passing an object literal, as I demonstrated previously, and when you're passing a formatted query string, like you are here. Then, on the server side, all you have to do is access the posted data as you would normally work with POST request data. Again, if you're not versed in server-side programming, Wrox Press offers many books on a plethora of server-side programming languages that can help get you right up to speed.

Try It Out Working with AJAX Requests

Example 7-1

For a recap of jQuery's AJAX capabilities as discussed thus far, follow these steps:

1. Enter the following markup document as *Example 7-1.html*:

```
<!DOCTYPE html PUBLIC "-//W3C//DTD XHTML 1.0 Strict//EN"
    "http://www.w3.org/TR/xhtml1/DTD/xhtml1-strict.dtd">
<html xmlns='http://www.w3.org/1999/xhtml' xml:lang='en'>
  <head>
    <meta http-equiv='content-type' content='text/html; charset=utf-8' />
    <meta http-equiv='content-language' content='en-us' />
    <title></title>
    <script type='text/javascript'
            src='../../../Source Code/jQuery/jQuery.js'></script>
    <script type='text/javascript' src='Example 7-1.js'></script>
    <link type='text/css' href='Example 7-1.css' rel='stylesheet' />
  </head>
  <body>
     <form action='javascript:void(0);' method='post'>
       <fieldset>
         <legend>jQuery AJAX Recap</legend>
         <p>
           jQuery's $.get() method can be used to retrieve XML-formatted
           data, which jQuery makes incredibly easy to work with by
           allowing you to use jQuery's rich selector API on XML documents.
         </p>
         <div>
           <label for='tmpFirstName'>First Name:</label>
           <input type='text' name='tmpFirstName'
                  id='tmpFirstName' size='25' />
         </div>
```

```
            <div>
              <label for='tmpLastName'>Last Name:</label>
              <input type='text' name='tmpLastName'
                     id='tmpLastName' size='25' />
            </div>
            <div class='tmpButton'>
              <input type='submit' name='tmpFetchName'
                     id='tmpFetchName' value='Fetch Name' />
            </div>
            <p>
              jQuery also has first-class support for JSON, a data trasport
              format that is fast-rising in popularity and use.
              JSON-formatted requests are even easier and less verbose to
              work with.
            </p>
            <div>
              <label for='tmpTitle'>Title:</label>
              <input type='text' name='tmpTitle'
                     id='tmpTitle' size='25' />
            </div>
            <div>
              <label for='tmpCompany'>Company:</label>
              <input type='text' name='tmpCompany'
                     id='tmpCompany' size='25' />
            </div>
            <div class='tmpButton'>
              <input type='submit' name='tmpFetchOther'
                     id='tmpFetchOther' value='Fetch Title &amp; Company' />
            </div>
            <p>
              Finally, jQuery makes it very easy to post data back to the
              server, via its serialize() method.
            </p>
            <div class='tmpButton'>
              <input type='submit' name='tmpPostData'
                     id='tmpPostData' value='Post Data' />
            </div>
            <div id='tmpPostedData'>

            </div>
          </fieldset>
        </form>
      </body>
    </html>
```

2. Enter the following CSS as *Example 7-1.css*:

```
body {
    font: 16px sans-serif;
}
```

```
fieldset {
    border: 1px solid rgb(200, 200, 200);
    background: yellow;

}
fieldset div {
    padding: 10px;
    margin: 5px;
}
fieldset label {
    float: left;
    width: 200px;
    text-align: right;
    padding: 2px 5px 0 0;
}
div#hLocationCountryIDWrapper img {
    position: relative;
    top: -4px;
}
div.tmpButton {
    text-align: right;
}
```

3. Enter the following JavaScript as *Example 7-1.js*:

```
$(document).ready(
  function() {
    $('input#tmpFetchName').click(
      function($e) {
        $e.preventDefault();
        $.get(
          'Example 7-1.xml',
          function(xml) {
            $('input#tmpFirstName').val($(xml).find('firstName').text());
            $('input#tmpLastName').val($(xml).find('lastName').text());
          }
        );
      }
    );

    $('input#tmpFetchOther').click(
      function($e) {
        $e.preventDefault();
        $.getJSON(
          'Example 7-1.json',
          function(json) {
            $('input#tmpTitle').val(json.title);
            $('input#tmpCompany').val(json.company);
          }
        );
      }
```

```
      );

      $('input#tmpPostData').click(
        function($e) {
          $e.preventDefault();

          var $data = $('form :input').serialize();

          $('div#tmpPostedData').html(
            "<h4>Posted Data:</h4>" +
            $data
          );

          $.post(
            'Example 7-1 Post.xml',
            $data,
            function(xml) {
              if (parseInt($(xml).text()) > 0) {
                alert('Data successfully posted!');
              }
            }
          );
        }
      );
    }
  );
```

4. Create the following XML document as *Example 7-1.xml*:

```
<?xml version="1.0" encoding="UTF-8" standalone="yes"?>
<response>
  <firstName>John</firstName>
  <lastName>Doe</lastName>
</response>
```

5. Create the following JSON document as *Example 7-1.json*:

```
{
  company : 'Springfield Electronics',
  title : 'Chief Widget Maker'
}
```

6. Finally, create the following document as *Example 7-1 Post.xml*:

```
<?xml version="1.0" encoding="UTF-8" standalone="yes"?>
<response>1</response>
```

When you run the preceding documents in a browser, you should see something like what you see in **Figure 7-4**.

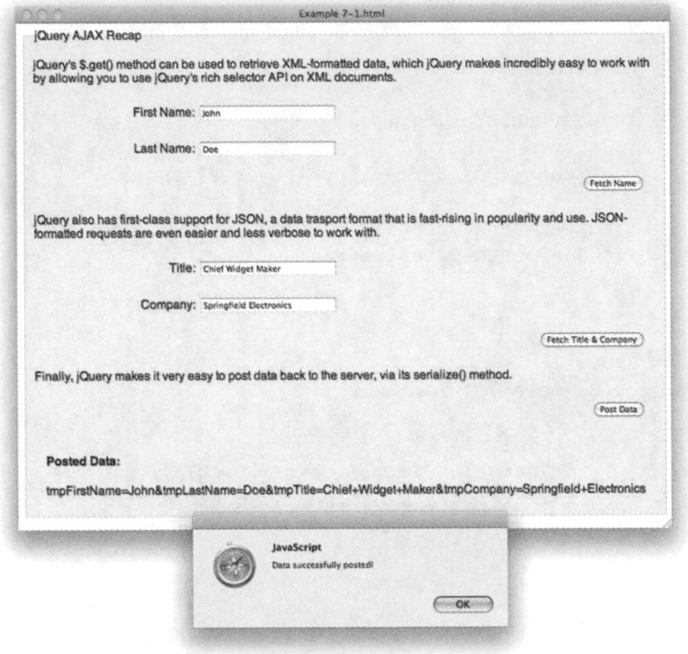

Figure 7-4

In this example, you recap everything you've learned about jQuery's AJAX capabilities up to this point. You begin with a demonstration of requesting an XML-formatted document via the GET method with jQuery's `$.get()` method. The HTML side sets up two input fields and a button:

```
<div>
  <label for='tmpFirstName'>First Name:</label>
  <input type='text' name='tmpFirstName'
         id='tmpFirstName' size='25' />
</div>
<div>
  <label for='tmpLastName'>Last Name:</label>
  <input type='text' name='tmpLastName'
         id='tmpLastName' size='25' />
</div>
<div class='tmpButton'>
  <input type='submit' name='tmpFetchName'
         id='tmpFetchName' value='Fetch Name' />
</div>
```

In the JavaScript, a `click` event is attached to the button. When it is clicked, a GET request is initiated for the Example 7-1.xml document, which defines two elements, `<firstName>` and `<lastName>` for Mr. John Doe.

```
    $('input#tmpFetchName').click(
      function($e) {
        $e.preventDefault();
        $.get(
          'Example 7-1.xml',
          function(xml) {
            $('input#tmpFirstName').val($(xml).find('firstName').text());
            $('input#tmpLastName').val($(xml).find('lastName').text());
          }
        );
      }
);
```

Retrieving the data contained in the XML document is effortless because jQuery allows you to query the XML document with its various selection and filtering methods. The text content of the `<firstName>` element is assigned as the value of the `<input>` element with ID name *tmpFirstName*, via jQuery's `val()` method, and the same is done with the `<lastName>` element, placing its text content in the value of the `<input>` element with ID name *tmpLastName*.

In the next set of input elements, you have a field for title and a field for company, and when you click on the button labeled "Fetch Title & Company," another AJAX Request is made, this time using jQuery's `getJSON()` method.

```
    $('input#tmpFetchOther').click(
      function($e) {
        $e.preventDefault();
        $.getJSON(
          'Example 7-1.json',
          function(json) {
            $('input#tmpTitle').val(json.title);
            $('input#tmpCompany').val(json.company);
          }
        );
      }
    );
```

This time you fetch the Example 7-1.json document, which contains two bits of data — the company and the title. The JSON example is easier to work out and less verbose since it requires less overhead than the XML method. jQuery automatically makes the object that you defined in Example 7-1.json available in the callback function as its first argument, which in this example is named `json`. The title is available as `json.title` and `json.company`, respectively, and each is assigned as the value of the appropriate `<input>` element.

The last example demonstrates posting the data of your input form back to the server, although again, since you're not working with an actual HTTP server, we'll have to pretend that the data is actually passed on and simulate how the server might respond, which is what the purpose of the Example 7-1 Post.xml document is.

```
$('input#tmpPostData').click(
  function($e) {
    $e.preventDefault();

    var $data = $('form :input').serialize();

    $('div#tmpPostedData').html(
      "<h4>Posted Data:</h4>" +
      $data
    );

    $.post(
      'Example 7-1 Post.xml',
      $data,
      function(xml) {
        if (parseInt($(xml).text()) > 0) {
          alert('Data successfully posted!');
        }
      }
    );
  }
);
```

The first thing that you do, after preventing the default action of the button (so the form isn't actually submitted), is grab all the data present in the various input elements in the form. You do this by crafting a special selector syntax that uses jQuery's `:input` pseudo-class to grab all the `<input>`, `<select>`, and `<textarea>` elements. Then that selection is passed to the `serialize()` method, which actually grabs all the relevant names and values from the form and constructs a query string that you can then pass in the second argument to the `$.post()` method. But before you pass that data on to the `$.post()` method, first you output the serialized data to the web page by setting the `innerHTML` of the `<div>` element with ID name *tmpPostedData*. This allows you to see what happens when the `serialize()` method is called and see for yourself all the heavy lifting that jQuery is doing on your behalf.

Finally, after passing the data to the `$.post()` method, a JavaScript alert lets you know that the AJAX Request completed successfully.

The various methods covered in this chapter are documented in the API reference that appears in Appendix G.

Loading HTML Snippets from the Server

In the previous sections, you've seen how to request data from the server using the XML and JSON data transport formats. The other popular way of transporting data from the server to the client asynchronously is via HTML snippets. Using this method, you request small chunks of HTML as you need them, without the `<html>`, `<head>`, and `<body>` tags.

The following example demonstrates how to load snippets of HTML with jQuery's `load()` method:

```
<!DOCTYPE html PUBLIC "-//W3C//DTD XHTML 1.0 Strict//EN"
    "http://www.w3.org/TR/xhtml1/DTD/xhtml1-strict.dtd">
<html xmlns='http://www.w3.org/1999/xhtml' xml:lang='en'>
  <head>
    <meta http-equiv='content-type' content='text/html; charset=utf-8' />
    <meta http-equiv='content-language' content='en-us' />
    <title></title>
    <script type='text/javascript'
            src='../../../Source Code/jQuery/jQuery.js'></script>
    <script type='text/javascript' src='Figure 7-5.js'></script>
    <link type='text/css' href='Figure 7-5.css' rel='stylesheet' />
  </head>
  <body>
    <div id='hFinderTree'>
<ul class='hFinderTree'>
  <li>
    <div class='hFinderTreeDirectory hFinderTreeRoot'
         id='hFinderTreeDirectory-1' title='/'>
      <span>Macintosh HD</span>
    </div>
    <ul class='hFinderTreeDirectoryBranchOn' id='hFinderTreeDirectoryBranch-1'>
      <li class='hFinderTreeDirectoryBranch'>
        <div class='hFinderTreeDirectory' id='hFinderTreeDirectory-5175'
             title='/Applications'>
          <div class='hFinderTreeIcon'></div>
          <span>Applications</span>
        </div>
        <img src='../../../Images/Finder/Right.png' class='hFinderTreeHasChildren'
             id='hFinderTreeIcon-5175' alt='+' title='Click to expand.' />
        <div class='hFinderTreeBranchWrapper'>
        </div>
      </li>
      <li class='hFinderTreeDirectoryBranch hFinderTreeServer'>
        <div class='hFinderTreeDirectory' id='hFinderTreeDirectory-5198'
             title='/Library'>
          <div class='hFinderTreeIcon'></div>
          <span>Library</span>
        </div>
        <img src='../../../Images/Finder/Right.png' class='hFinderTreeHasChildren'
             id='hFinderTreeIcon-5198' alt='+' title='Click to expand.' />
        <div class='hFinderTreeBranchWrapper'></div>
      </li>
      <li class='hFinderTreeDirectoryBranch'>
        <div class='hFinderTreeDirectory' id='hFinderTreeDirectory-3667'
             title='/System'>
          <div class='hFinderTreeIcon'></div>
          <span>System</span>
        </div>
        <img src='../../../Images/Finder/Right.png' class='hFinderTreeHasChildren'
             id='hFinderTreeIcon-5198' alt='+' title='Click to expand.' />
        <div class='hFinderTreeBranchWrapper'></div>
      </li>
```

```
        <li class='hFinderTreeDirectoryBranch'>
          <div class='hFinderTreeDirectory' id='hFinderTreeDirectory-5185'
               title='/Users'>
            <div class='hFinderTreeIcon'></div>
            <span>Users</span></div>
            <img src='../../../Images/Finder/Right.png'
class='hFinderTreeHasChildren'
                 id='hFinderTreeIcon-5185' alt='+' title='Click to expand.' />
            <div class='hFinderTreeBranchWrapper'>
          </div>
        </li>
      </ul>
    </li>
  </ul>
        </div>
    </body>
  </html>
```

This markup is styled with the following style sheet:

```
body {
    font: 13px "Lucida Grande", Arial, sans-serif;
    background: rgb(214, 221, 229);
}
div#hFinderTree ul {
    list-style: none;
    padding: 0;
    margin: 0;
}
div.hFinderTreeRoot {
    height: 28px;
    background: url('../../../Images/Finder/Hard Drive.png') no-repeat left;
    padding: 4px 0 0 35px;
}
li.hFinderTreeDirectoryBranch {
    position: relative;
    padding: 0 0 0 20px;
    zoom: 1;
}
img.hFinderTreeHasChildren {
    position: absolute;
    top: 3px;
    left: 0;
}
div.hFinderTreeIcon {
    background: url('../../../Images/Finder/Folder.png') no-repeat left;
    width: 16px;
    height: 16px;
    margin: 0 5px 0 0;
    float: left;
}
div.hFinderTreeBranchWrapper {
    display: none;
}
```

Then the following JavaScript demonstrates how folders in a tree structure are loaded asynchronously. Each folder is an HTML snippet that loads separately from the server, which makes the initial download much smaller and the overall application much more efficient.

```
$(document).ready(
  function() {
    $('img.hFinderTreeHasChildren').click(
      function() {
        if (!$(this).next().children('ul').length) {
          $(this).next().load(
            'AJAX%20Request%20Documents/' +
              $(this).prev().attr('id').split('-').pop() + '.html',
            function() {
              $(this).show();
              $(this).prev().attr(
                'src',
                '../../../Images/Finder/Down.png'
              );
            }
          );
        } else {
          $(this).next().toggle();

          $(this).attr(
            'src',
            '../../../Images/Finder/' +
              ($(this).attr('src').indexOf('Down') != -1? 'Right' : 'Down') + '.png'
          );
        }
      }
    );
  }
);
```

All put together, the preceding code looks like **Figure 7-5** when it is tested in a browser.

In the preceding script, a `click` event is attached to each `<img>` element in the HTML document. When the user clicks on the `<img>` element, which is a gray arrow; the script first checks to see whether the folder's contents have already been requested. The script checks to see if a folder's contents have already been requested by checking to see if the `<img>` element's next sibling, the `<div>` element with class name *hFinderTreeBranchWrapper*, has a child `<ul>` element. Whether or not that `<ul>` element exists is determined by the following expression:

```
!$(this).next().children('ul').length
```

The `next()` method traverses the selection from the `<img>` to the `<div>` element, and the `children()` method looks at the children of the `<div>` method. Then the `length` property is used to determine how many children `<ul>` elements exist. If there is a `<ul>` element, that means that the folder's contents have already been requested from the server and loaded into the document. If there is not a `<ul>` element, then the folder's contents are requests from the server.

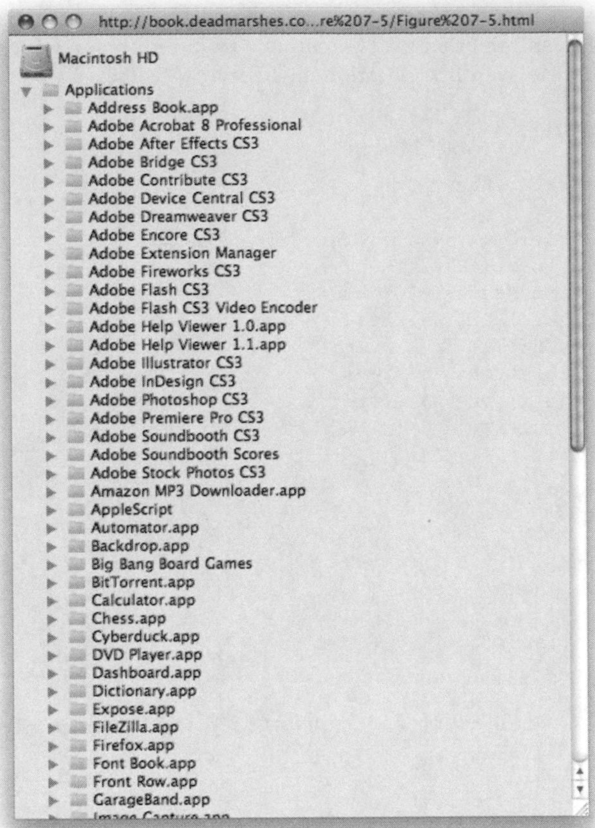

Figure 7-5

Loading directly in the document is done based on a selection. In this script, you select the `<div>` element with the class name *hFinderTreeBranchWrapper*, which is done with the call to `$(this).next()`. `this` references the `<img>` element, and `next()` causes the next sibling element to be selected, which is the `<div>` element. Then the `load()` method is chained directly to that selection. By chaining the `load()` method to the selection, you're telling jQuery where you want the HTML snippet to be inserted in the DOM.

The `load()` method otherwise works similarly to the other AJAX Request methods that jQuery provides: You specify the URL of the document you want to request in the first argument. You can include an optional second argument that includes data that you want to send to the server via a GET request, and the third parameter is a callback function that is executed upon success of the request. Both providing data to send to the server and specifying a callback function are optional — if you like, you can simply call the `load()` method with only a URL, and that will work just fine as well.

The server responds with a snippet of HTML that is loaded directly into the document. The following is what the HTML snippet being loaded looks like:

```
<ul id="hFinderTreeDirectoryBranch-31490s">
  <li class="hFinderTreeDirectoryBranch">
    <div class="hFinderTreeDirectory" id="hFinderTreeDirectory-31491s"
         title="/Users/Shared">
      <div class="hFinderTreeIcon"></div>
      <span>Shared</span>
    </div>
    <img src="../../../Images/Finder/Right.png" class="hFinderTreeHasChildren"
         id="hFinderTreeIcon-31491s" alt="+" title="Click to expand.">
    <div class="hFinderTreeBranchWrapper"></div>
  </li>
  <li class="hFinderTreeDirectoryBranch hFinderTreeServer">
    <div class="hFinderTreeDirectory" id="hFinderTreeDirectory-698482s"
         title="/Users/johnappleseed">
      <div class="hFinderTreeIcon"></div>
      <span>johnappleseed</span>
    </div>
    <img src="../../../Images/Finder/Right.png" class="hFinderTreeHasChildren"
         id="hFinderTreeIcon-698482s" alt="+" title="Click to expand.">
    <div class="hFinderTreeBranchWrapper"></div>
  </li>
</ul>
```

The preceding is the HTML snippet that is loaded upon clicking on the arrow for the /Users folder. I've prepared HTML snippets for each of the top-level folders. In the source code download for this book, each of these is named using a numeric directory ID. For example, /Applications has the ID 5175, and /Library has the ID 5198, and so on. Each of these numeric IDs is embedded in the id attribute of the <div> element with class name *hFinderTreeDirectory* that is present in the structure for each folder. Upon requesting the folder contents, the embedded numeric ID is extracted with the following:

```
$(this).prev().attr('id').split('-').pop()
```

The preceding starts out at the <img> element, where the click originated, which is the `$(this)` portion of the code. Then you navigate to the preceding sibling with the `prev()` method and access its `id` attribute with `attr('id')`. Then you split the `id` along the hyphens, creating an array. The `pop()` method returns the last item from that array, which leaves you with just the numeric portion of the `id` attribute. That's used to construct the filename of the HTML snippet to be loaded, which again wouldn't normally be requested as a static HTML file — for this kind of thing, you really want a server-side script to do the heavy lifting. Each HTML snippet is located in a subfolder called *AJAX Request Documents.* Note the spaces in that filename. I'm very fond of naming items in a realistic, human-readable way. Many web professionals avoid allowing spaces in the names of web-based content, not really because of any technical limitation, but because some browsers uglify spaces in filenames by URL-encoding `%20` in their place. Firefox is one that lets the spaces be spaces and simply encodes the spaces with `%20` transparently, behind the scenes, and keeps the spaces in the address bar as spaces, which I like a lot. In any case, however you prefer to name your files, you should be aware that jQuery doesn't allow spaces to be placed directly in the URL of this method, and if you want spaces in the URL, you'll have to encode them yourself. This is not true of jQuery's other AJAX Request methods. The reason for the difference here is that jQuery allows you to include a selector in the URL that you pass to the `load()` method, which is then, in turn, used to filter the selection that you've made. Personally, I think this is overkill, since jQuery already offers so many methods for filtering, but the functionality is there if you desire it.

Once the request is made, the following callback function is executed:

```
function() {
  $(this).show();
  $(this).prev().attr(
    'src',
    '../../../Images/Finder/Down.png'
  );
}
```

The callback function is executed within the context of the `<div>` element with class name *hFinderTreeBrachWrapper*; `this` refers to that `<div>` element. By default, all of the `<div>` elements with class name *hFinderTreeBranchWrapper* are hidden by the inclusion of `display: none` in the style sheet; calling jQuery's `show()` method makes the `<div>` visible. Now all that's left to do is to change the orientation of the arrow from pointing right to pointing down to indicate that the folder is open, which is what the second bit of code in the callback function does — it changes the image referenced in the `src` attribute of the `<div>` element's preceding sibling, which is the `<img>` element housing the arrow.

That leaves what happens if the folder is already loaded:

```
} else {
    $(this).next().toggle();

    $(this).attr(
      'src',
      '../../../Images/Finder/' +
        ($(this).attr('src').indexOf('Down') != -1? 'Right' : 'Down') + '.png'
    );
  }
}
```

If the folder already exists, then you want to toggle the display of the folder on and off with each click of the arrow. The call to `$(this).next().toggle()` does exactly that: If the `<div>` element is visible, it's made invisible, and vice versa. The second bit of code toggles the orientation of the arrow by toggling between the `Right.png` and `Down.png` images.

The following "Try It Out" exercise takes the `load()` method that you've learned about in this section and puts it in the context of a more real-world-oriented example, which is the beginnings of a web-based Apple iCal clone.

> **Reminder: You can obtain full source code examples in this book's source code download materials available free from** `www.wrox.com`**.**

Try It Out — Loading HTML Snippets Asynchronously

Example 7-2

To recap jQuery's `load()` method, follow these steps:

1. Create the following HTML document as *Example 7-2.html*:

```
<!DOCTYPE html PUBLIC "-//W3C//DTD XHTML 1.0 Strict//EN"
    "http://www.w3.org/TR/xhtml1/DTD/xhtml1-strict.dtd">
<html xmlns='http://www.w3.org/1999/xhtml' xml:lang='en'>
  <head>
    <meta http-equiv='content-type' content='text/html; charset=utf-8' />
    <meta http-equiv='content-language' content='en-us' />
    <title></title>
    <script type='text/javascript'
            src='../../../Source Code/jQuery/jQuery.js'></script>
    <script type='text/javascript' src='Example 7-2.js'></script>
    <link type='text/css' href='Example 7-2.css' rel='stylesheet' />
    <link type='text/css' href='Exanple 7-2 Controls.css' rel='stylesheet' />
    <!--[if lt IE 8]>
      <link type='text/css' href='Example 7-2.IE.css' rel='stylesheet' />
    <![endif]-->
  </head>
  <body id='hCalendarTemplate'>
<div id='hCalendar'>
  <table class='hCalendar'>
    <thead>
      <tr>
        <th class='hCalendarMonth' colspan='7'>
          <span class='hCalendarMonth'>September</span>
          <span class='hCalendarYear'>2008</span>
        </th>
      </tr>
      <tr>
        <th class='hCalendarWeekday'>Sunday</th>
        <th class='hCalendarWeekday'>Monday</th>
        <th class='hCalendarWeekday'>Tuesday</th>
        <th class='hCalendarWeekday'>Wednesday</th>
        <th class='hCalendarWeekday'>Thursday</th>
        <th class='hCalendarWeekday'>Friday</th>
        <th class='hCalendarWeekday'>Saturday</th>
      </tr>
    </thead>
    <tbody>
      <tr>
        <td class='hCalendarDay hCalendarLastMonth'>
          <span class='hCalendarDay'>31</span>
        </td>
        <td class='hCalendarDay hCalendarThisMonth hCalendarFirst'>
          <span class='hCalendarDay'>1</span>
        </td>
        <td class='hCalendarDay hCalendarThisMonth'>
          <span class='hCalendarDay'>2</span>
        </td>
```

```
    <td class='hCalendarDay hCalendarThisMonth'>
      <span class='hCalendarDay'>3</span>
    </td>
    <td class='hCalendarDay hCalendarThisMonth'>
      <span class='hCalendarDay'>4</span>
    </td>
    <td class='hCalendarDay hCalendarThisMonth'>
      <span class='hCalendarDay'>5</span>
    </td>
    <td class='hCalendarDay hCalendarThisMonth'>
      <span class='hCalendarDay'>6</span>
    </td>
  </tr>
  <tr>
    <td class='hCalendarDay hCalendarThisMonth'>
      <span class='hCalendarDay'>7</span>
    </td>
    <td class='hCalendarDay hCalendarThisMonth'>
      <span class='hCalendarDay'>8</span>
    </td>
    <td class='hCalendarDay hCalendarThisMonth'>
      <span class='hCalendarDay'>9</span>
    </td>
    <td class='hCalendarDay hCalendarThisMonth'>
      <span class='hCalendarDay'>10</span>
    </td>
    <td class='hCalendarDay hCalendarThisMonth'>
      <span class='hCalendarDay'>11</span>
    </td>
    <td class='hCalendarDay hCalendarThisMonth'>
      <span class='hCalendarDay'>12</span>
    </td>
    <td class='hCalendarDay hCalendarThisMonth'>
      <span class='hCalendarDay'>13</span>
    </td>
  </tr>
  <tr>
    <td class='hCalendarDay hCalendarThisMonth'>
      <span class='hCalendarDay'>14</span>
    </td>
    <td class='hCalendarDay hCalendarThisMonth'>
      <span class='hCalendarDay'>15</span>
    </td>
    <td class='hCalendarDay hCalendarThisMonth'>
      <span class='hCalendarDay'>16</span>
    </td>
    <td class='hCalendarDay hCalendarThisMonth'>
      <span class='hCalendarDay'>17</span>
    </td>
    <td class='hCalendarDay hCalendarThisMonth'>
      <span class='hCalendarDay'>18</span>
    </td>
    <td class='hCalendarDay hCalendarThisMonth'>
      <span class='hCalendarDay'>19</span>
    </td>
```

```
          <td class='hCalendarDay hCalendarThisMonth'>
            <span class='hCalendarDay'>20</span>
          </td>
        </tr>
        <tr>
          <td class='hCalendarDay hCalendarThisMonth'>
            <span class='hCalendarDay'>21</span>
          </td>
          <td class='hCalendarDay hCalendarThisMonth'>
            <span class='hCalendarDay'>22</span>
          </td>
          <td class='hCalendarDay hCalendarThisMonth'>
            <span class='hCalendarDay'>23</span>
          </td>
          <td class='hCalendarDay hCalendarThisMonth'>
            <span class='hCalendarDay'>24</span>
          </td>
          <td class='hCalendarDay hCalendarThisMonth'>
            <span class='hCalendarDay'>25</span>
          </td>
          <td class='hCalendarDay hCalendarThisMonth'>
            <span class='hCalendarDay'>26</span>
          </td>
          <td class='hCalendarDay hCalendarThisMonth'>
            <span class='hCalendarDay'>27</span>
          </td>
        </tr>
        <tr>
          <td class='hCalendarDay hCalendarThisMonth'>
            <span class='hCalendarDay'>28</span>
          </td>
          <td class='hCalendarDay hCalendarThisMonth'>
            <span class='hCalendarDay'>29</span>
          </td>
          <td class='hCalendarDay hCalendarThisMonth hCalendarLast'>
            <span class='hCalendarDay'>30</span>
          </td>
          <td class='hCalendarDay hCalendarNextMonth'>
            <span class='hCalendarDay'>1<span>
          </td>
          <td class='hCalendarDay hCalendarNextMonth'>
            <span class='hCalendarDay'>2<span>
          </td>
          <td class='hCalendarDay hCalendarNextMonth'>
            <span class='hCalendarDay'>3<span>
          </td>
          <td class='hCalendarDay hCalendarNextMonth'>
            <span class='hCalendarDay'>4<span>
          </td>
        </tr>
      </tbody>
    </table>
  </div>
  <div id='hCalendarControls'>
    <div id='hCalendarControlPrevious'></div>
    <div class='hCalendarSeparator' id='hCalendarSeparatorOne'></div>
```

```
  <div id='hCalendarControlDay' class='hCalendarControlToggle'></div>
  <div class='hCalendarSeparator' id='hCalendarSeparatorTwo'></div>
  <div id='hCalendarControlWeek' class='hCalendarControlToggle'></div>
  <div class='hCalendarSeparator' id='hCalendarSeparatorThree'>
    <div></div>
  </div>
  <div id='hCalendarControlMonth' class='hCalendarControlToggle'>
    <div class='hCalendarControlOn'></div>
  </div>
  <div class='hCalendarSeparator' id='hCalendarSeparatorFour'>
    <div></div>
  </div>
  <div id='hCalendarControlNext'></div>
</div>
  </body>
</html>
```

2. Create the following style sheet as *Example 7-2.css*:

```
body {
    font: 12px "Lucida Grande", Arial, sans-serif;
    background: rgb(200, 200, 200);
    color: rgb(50, 50, 50);
}
div#hCalendar {
    position: absolute;
    top: 10px;
    right: 10px;
    bottom: 40px;
    left: 190px;
    background: #fff;
    border: 1px solid rgb(128, 128, 128);
    overflow: hidden;
}
div#hCalendar table.hCalendar {
    width: 100%;
    height: 100%;
    border-collapse: collapse;
}
div#hCalendar table.hCalendar tbody td {
    overflow: hidden;
    border: 1px solid rgb(200, 200, 200);
    font-size: 12px;
    height: 15%;
    width: 14.28%;
}
div#hCalendar table.hCalendar td.hCalendarDay {
    vertical-align: top;
    padding: 5px;
    text-align: right;
}
div#hCalendar table.hCalendar td.hCalendarLastMonth,
div#hCalendar table.hCalendar td.hCalendarNextMonth {
    color: rgb(200, 200, 200);
    background: rgb(244, 244, 244);
}
```

```
div#hCalendar table.hCalendar th.hCalendarMonth {
    height: 25px;
    font-size: 17px;
}
div#hCalendar table.hCalendar th.hCalendarWeekday {
    height: 16px;
    font-weight: normal;
    font-size: 11px;
}
```

3. Create the following style sheet as *Example 7-2 Controls.css*:

```
div#hCalendarControls {
    position: absolute;
    left: 50%;
    bottom: 8px;
    width: 188px;
    height: 25px;
    margin: 0 0 0 -94px;
}
div#hCalendarControls div {
    position: absolute;
    height: 25px;
    top: 0;
    left: 0;
    background: url('../../../Images/Calendar/Navigation.png') no-repeat top left;
}
div#hCalendarControls div div {
    width: 100%;
    height: 100%;
    background: url('../../../Images/Calendar/Navigation.png') no-repeat top left;
}
div div#hCalendarControlPrevious {
    width: 23px;
}
div div#hCalendarControlPrevious div {
    background-position: 0 -50px;
}
div div#hCalendarControlDay {
    width: 46px;
    left: 24px;
    background-position: -24px 0;
}
div div#hCalendarControlDay div.hCalendarControlOn {
    background-position: -24px -25px;
}
div div#hCalendarControlDay div {
    background-position: -24px -50px;
}
div div#hCalendarControlWeek {
    width: 46px;
    left: 71px;
    background-position: -71px 0;
}
```

```
div div#hCalendarControlWeek div.hCalendarControlOn {
    background-position: -71px -25px;
}
div div#hCalendarControlWeek div {
    background-position: -71px -50px;
}
div div#hCalendarControlMonth {
    width: 46px;
    left: 118px;
    background-position: -118px 0;
}
div div#hCalendarControlMonth div.hCalendarControlOn {
    background-position: -118px -25px;
}
div div#hCalendarControlMonth div {
    background-position: -118px -50px;
}
div div#hCalendarControlNext {
    width: 23px;
    left: 165px;
    background-position: -165px 0;
}
div div#hCalendarControlNext div {
    background-position: -165px -50px;
}
div#hCalendarControls div.hCalendarSeparator {
    left: 23px;
    width: 1px;
    background-position: -23px 0;
}
div#hCalendarControls div.hCalendarSeparator div {
    background-position: -23px -50px;
}
div#hCalendarControls div#hCalendarSeparatorTwo {
    left: 70px;
}
div#hCalendarControls div#hCalendarSeparatorThree {
    left: 117px;
}
div#hCalendarControls div#hCalendarSeparatorFour {
    left: 164px;
}
```

4. Create the following style sheet as *Example 7-2.IE.css*:

```
html, body {
    padding: 0;
    margin: 0;
    width: 100%;
    height: 100%;
}
div#hCalendar {
    height: expression(document.body.offsetHeight - 50);
    width: expression(document.body.offsetWidth - 200);
}
```

5. Create the following JavaScript as *Example 7-2.js*:

```
$(document).ready(
  function() {
    $('div#hCalendarControls > div').mousedown(
      function() {
        if (!$(this).hasClass('hCalendarSeparator')) {
          $(this).html("<div></div>");
          $(this).prev().html("<div></div>");
          $(this).next().html("<div></div>");
        }
      }
    ).mouseup(
      function() {
        if (!$(this).hasClass('hCalendarSeparator')) {
          if ($(this).hasClass('hCalendarControlToggle')) {
            $('div#hCalendarControls div').not(this).empty();
            $(this).find('div').addClass('hCalendarControlOn');
            $(this).prev().html("<div></div>");
            $(this).next().html("<div></div>");
          } else {
            $(this).empty();

            if (!$(this).prev().prev().find('div').length) {
              $(this).prev().empty();
            }

            if (!$(this).next().next().find('div').length) {
              $(this).next().empty();
            }

            var $isNext = ($(this).attr('id').indexOf('Next') != -1);

            $('div#hCalendar').load(
              'Example%207-2%20' + ($isNext? 'Next' : 'Previous') + '.html'
            );
          }
        }
      }
    );
  }
);
```

6. Using the structure in Example 7-2.html, create calendar tables for August and October 2008. Name the table for August *Example 7-2 Previous.html* and the table for October *Example 7-2 Next .html*. The structure for August 2008 is provided in the following code; use the same code to create October 2008, editing the relevant days, class names, and so on. These files are also provided in this book's source code download.

```
<table class="hCalendar">
  <thead>
    <tr>
      <th class="hCalendarMonth" colspan="7">
        <span class="hCalendarMonth">August</span>
        <span class="hCalendarYear">2008</span>
```

```
        </th>
      </tr>
      <tr>
        <th class="hCalendarWeekday">Sunday</th>
        <th class="hCalendarWeekday">Monday</th>
        <th class="hCalendarWeekday">Tuesday</th>
        <th class="hCalendarWeekday">Wednesday</th>
        <th class="hCalendarWeekday">Thursday</th>
        <th class="hCalendarWeekday">Friday</th>
        <th class="hCalendarWeekday">Saturday</th>
      </tr>
    </thead>
    <tbody>
      <tr>
        <td class="hCalendarDay hCalendarLastMonth">
          <span class="hCalendarDay">27</span>
        </td>
        <td class="hCalendarDay hCalendarLastMonth">
          <span class="hCalendarDay">28</span>
        </td>
        <td class="hCalendarDay hCalendarLastMonth">
          <span class="hCalendarDay">29</span>
        </td>
        <td class="hCalendarDay hCalendarLastMonth">
          <span class="hCalendarDay">30</span>
        </td>
        <td class="hCalendarDay hCalendarLastMonth">
          <span class="hCalendarDay">31</span>
        </td>
        <td class="hCalendarDay hCalendarThisMonth hCalendarFirst">
          <span class="hCalendarDay">1</span>
        </td>
        <td class="hCalendarDay hCalendarThisMonth">
          <span class="hCalendarDay">2</span>
        </td>
      </tr>
      <tr>
        <td class="hCalendarDay hCalendarThisMonth">
          <span class="hCalendarDay">3</span>
        </td>
        <td class="hCalendarDay hCalendarThisMonth">
          <span class="hCalendarDay">4</span>
        </td>
        <td class="hCalendarDay hCalendarThisMonth">
          <span class="hCalendarDay">5</span>
        </td>
        <td class="hCalendarDay hCalendarThisMonth">
          <span class="hCalendarDay">6</span>
        </td>
        <td class="hCalendarDay hCalendarThisMonth">
          <span class="hCalendarDay">7</span>
        </td>
        <td class="hCalendarDay hCalendarThisMonth">
          <span class="hCalendarDay">8</span>
        </td>
```

```
    <td class="hCalendarDay hCalendarThisMonth">
      <span class="hCalendarDay">9</span>
    </td>
  </tr>
  <tr>
    <td class="hCalendarDay hCalendarThisMonth">
      <span class="hCalendarDay">10</span>
    </td>
    <td class="hCalendarDay hCalendarThisMonth">
      <span class="hCalendarDay">11</span>
    </td>
    <td class="hCalendarDay hCalendarThisMonth">
      <span class="hCalendarDay">12</span>
    </td>
    <td class="hCalendarDay hCalendarThisMonth">
      <span class="hCalendarDay">13</span>
    </td>
    <td class="hCalendarDay hCalendarThisMonth">
      <span class="hCalendarDay">14</span>
    </td>
    <td class="hCalendarDay hCalendarThisMonth">
      <span class="hCalendarDay">15</span>
    </td>
    <td class="hCalendarDay hCalendarThisMonth">
      <span class="hCalendarDay">16</span>
    </td>
  </tr>
  <tr>
    <td class="hCalendarDay hCalendarThisMonth">
      <span class="hCalendarDay">17</span>
    </td>
    <td class="hCalendarDay hCalendarThisMonth">
      <span class="hCalendarDay">18</span>
    </td>
    <td class="hCalendarDay hCalendarThisMonth">
      <span class="hCalendarDay">19</span>
    </td>
    <td class="hCalendarDay hCalendarThisMonth">
      <span class="hCalendarDay">20</span>
    </td>
    <td class="hCalendarDay hCalendarThisMonth">
      <span class="hCalendarDay">21</span>
    </td>
    <td class="hCalendarDay hCalendarThisMonth">
      <span class="hCalendarDay">22</span>
    </td>
    <td class="hCalendarDay hCalendarThisMonth">
      <span class="hCalendarDay">23</span>
    </td>
  </tr>
  <tr>
    <td class="hCalendarDay hCalendarThisMonth">
      <span class="hCalendarDay">24</span>
    </td>
```

```
        <td class="hCalendarDay hCalendarThisMonth">
          <span class="hCalendarDay">25</span>
        </td>
        <td class="hCalendarDay hCalendarThisMonth">
          <span class="hCalendarDay">26</span>
        </td>
        <td class="hCalendarDay hCalendarThisMonth">
          <span class="hCalendarDay">27</span>
        </td>
        <td class="hCalendarDay hCalendarThisMonth">
          <span class="hCalendarDay">28</span>
        </td>
        <td class="hCalendarDay hCalendarThisMonth">
          <span class="hCalendarDay">29</span>
        </td>
        <td class="hCalendarDay hCalendarThisMonth">
          <span class="hCalendarDay">30</span>
        </td>
      </tr>
      <tr>
        <td class="hCalendarDay hCalendarThisMonth hCalendarLast">
          <span class="hCalendarDay">31</span>
        </td>
        <td class="hCalendarDay hCalendarNextMonth">
          <span class="hCalendarDay">1</span>
        </td>
        <td class="hCalendarDay hCalendarNextMonth">
          <span class="hCalendarDay">2</span>
        </td>
        <td class="hCalendarDay hCalendarNextMonth">
          <span class="hCalendarDay">3</span>
        </td>
        <td class="hCalendarDay hCalendarNextMonth">
          <span class="hCalendarDay">4</span>
        </td>
        <td class="hCalendarDay hCalendarNextMonth">
          <span class="hCalendarDay">5</span>
        </td>
        <td class="hCalendarDay hCalendarNextMonth">
          <span class="hCalendarDay">6</span>
        </td>
      </tr>
    </tbody>
  </table>
```

The preceding example results in the rendering that you see in **Figure 7-6**.

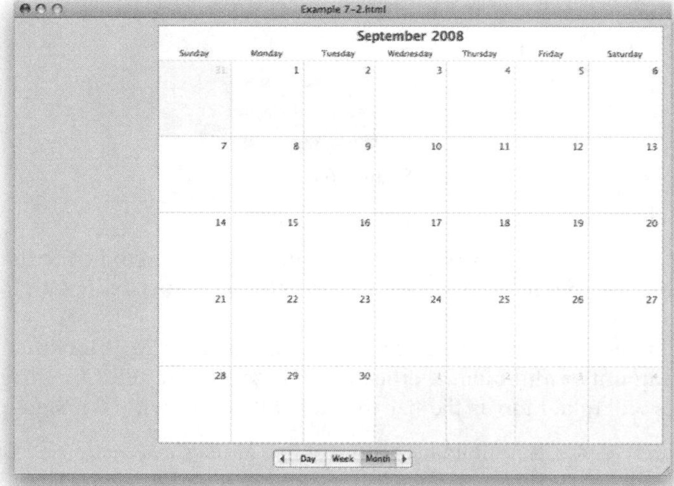

Figure 7-6

As you've probably figured out by now, the preceding example does a little more than just demonstrate another way that you can use jQuery's `load()` method. What you see is the beginnings of a web-based iCal clone, which I refer back to in later examples in this book. This example is incomplete; you can only navigate one month forward or one month backward. It is assumed that the calendar is generated on the server side, since you're using the `load()` method to request the previous or next month via an AJAX Request. You could forego the server-side part and force your calendar to be generated on the client side with JavaScript too, which really is a matter of personal taste. Since it is assumed that the server will generate this calendar, the example crudely simulates what might happen if you had a server-side language involved.

It's difficult to convey one concept, like AJAX, without also showing others — at least to make examples that are in any way useful and representative of the real world. So in addition to demonstrating another way you might use AJAX, in providing a server-generated calendar, you also see some of the design challenges that you face in styling such an application. So this admittedly long, but very worthwhile example shows a few of the challenges that you confront on the design side. One challenge is getting the calendar to display as intended in all the popular browsers. You'll have noticed, for example, that a few hacks were required to get IE to display the calendar correctly.

Another challenge I've demonstrated is an advanced CSS concept that works with jQuery to make the bottom row of buttons provide different states, depending on user interaction, and that concept is *CSS sprites*. CSS sprites were originally introduced to the web development world in an article on the "A List Apart" website way back in 2004 by Dave Shea. *Sprites* are several smaller images stuck in the same image file together, then individually displayed in a program without separating the images into smaller files. I defer to the "A List Apart" article for further esoteric reasoning for sprites, and further defaults on the origin of sprites: `http://alistapart.com/articles/sprites`.

Figure 7-7 shows the sprites image file used in Example 7-2.

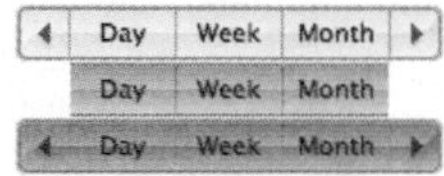

Figure 7-7

Each of the states for the bottom row of buttons is contained in the single file that you see in **Figure 7-7**. The immediate, tangible benefit of sprites for web development has to do with three things primarily:

- Individual image files suck up more file space and bandwidth. Individual image files each require a certain amount of minimum overhead simply to create a file. One image sliced into many individual files will total more in file size than all of those individual images placed into the same file.
- Toggling between different images in response to user interaction becomes much more responsive since the browser doesn't have to download images at the time a user clicks on a button or mouses over something — since each state is contained in the same image file, you don't have to.
- More HTTP requests from the server results in more lag, since every HTTP request that you make has some overhead and latency associated with it. A slightly larger file size in a single request loads much more quickly than several individual files in several individual requests.

jQuery's role in making the user states demonstrated in these buttons functional is minimal. The brunt of the work needed to make functional buttons actually takes place in the style sheet. But first things first: The following HTML sets up the skeleton structure that your buttons will occupy:

```
<div id='hCalendarControls'>
  <div id='hCalendarControlPrevious'></div>
  <div class='hCalendarSeparator' id='hCalendarSeparatorOne'></div>
  <div id='hCalendarControlDay' class='hCalendarControlToggle'></div>
  <div class='hCalendarSeparator' id='hCalendarSeparatorTwo'></div>
  <div id='hCalendarControlWeek' class='hCalendarControlToggle'></div>
  <div class='hCalendarSeparator' id='hCalendarSeparatorThree'>
    <div></div>
  </div>
  <div id='hCalendarControlMonth' class='hCalendarControlToggle'>
    <div class='hCalendarControlOn'></div>
  </div>
  <div class='hCalendarSeparator' id='hCalendarSeparatorFour'>
    <div></div>
  </div>
  <div id='hCalendarControlNext'></div>
</div>
```

The preceding snippet of HTML takes a collection of `<div>` elements and wraps them in a single `<div>` element with ID name *hCalendarControls*. Within that `<div>` element, individual `<div>` elements exist for each individual sprite. To loyally simulate Apple's user interface, each button must have a 1-pixel-wide separator that changes color depending on the state of the buttons around it, so there are `<div>` elements for each separator as well. The Day, Week, and Month buttons have the ability to be activated and remain turned on. In iCal, these buttons are used to change the view of the calendar. Since these buttons have an extra state compared to the Previous and Next buttons, you need some way to be able to pick out those buttons from the rest, so they receive a class name, *hCalendarControlToggle*. The default view, `Month`, is made active by default by adding a child `<div>` element with the class name *hCalendarControlOn*. As I explain the JavaScript and CSS portions of this example, the reasoning behind this HTML structure will become clearer. The style sheet Example 7-2 Controls.css contains all the CSS handling the presentational aspects of these buttons, and the high wire act that splits the CSS sprite image into smaller images via some well-placed kung-fu kicks. So, let's review each rule in that style sheet to see how that works. The first rule doesn't do much of anything special. It takes the `<div>` element with ID name *hCalendarControls*, and it centers it along the bottom of the window. If you remember from Chapter 2, that's done by positioning from the left 50 percent, then setting a negative left margin equal to half of the fixed width.

```
div#hCalendarControls {
    position: absolute;
    left: 50%;
    bottom: 8px;
    width: 188px;
    height: 25px;
    margin: 0 0 0 -94px;
}
```

The next rule lays the foundation for CSS sprites. Each child `<div>` element contained in the `<div>` element with ID name *hCalendarControls* is positioned absolutely. Then you give each a fixed height of 25 pixels, which is equal to the height of an individual sprite image. Each row of images in the image in **Figure 7-7** has a height of 25 pixels. Finally, you set the background of each individual `<div>` element to that one image that contains all of the individual sprites.

```
div#hCalendarControls div {
    position: absolute;
    height: 25px;
    top: 0;
    left: 0;
    background: url('../../../Images/Calendar/Navigation.png') no-repeat top left;
}
```

Then the subsequent rule styles a nested `<div>` element, its dimensions are set to 100 percent of its parent, and it too is given a background image that contains the master sprites image. This nested `<div>` element will be used to display the toggled on and the mousedown (or active) image states present in the master file.

```
div#hCalendarControls div div {
    width: 100%;
    height: 100%;
    background: url('../../../Images/Calendar/Navigation.png') no-repeat top left;
}
```

The following two rules set up the first button, the Previous button. All you have to do to display the default image is set the width of the `<div>` element to 23 pixels. To display the mousedown state, its only other state, all you have to do is adjust the background position of the *Y*-axis by –50 pixels. This adjustment causes the last row of images to be displayed from the master sprite file, and with jQuery's help, that means that the image displayed for the button changes when the user presses the button.

```
div div#hCalendarControlPrevious {
    width: 23px;
}
div div#hCalendarControlPrevious div {
    background-position: 0 -50px;
}
```

And that's the secret to making sprites with CSS — all you have to do is adjust the background position to the portion of the master image that you want to display.

The following three rules define the Day button: It has one extra rule, since it has one more state than the Previous button. In addition to the mousedown state, it can also be toggled on. The first rule defines the location of the button within its parent `<div>` container. So that you don't overlap the Previous button, you set the `left` property to 24 pixels, which accounts for the width of the Previous button, plus 1 pixel for the separator that appears between the two. The width of the Day button is 46 pixels in the master sprite file, so you set the width of this `<div>` element to 46 pixels. Finally, to display the right part of that master sprite file, you adjust the horizontal position of the background image, –24 pixels, which is the same as your offset left position, again accounting for the position of the Previous button. The other two rules adjust the background position for each of the other states. Toggled on adjusts the vertical position of the background image by –25 pixels, and it is given a class name, *hCalendarControlOn*, to distinguish it from the mousedown state. And like you did for the Previous button, you create another rule for the mousedown state that adjusts the vertical position of the background image by –50 pixels.

```
div div#hCalendarControlDay {
    width: 46px;
    left: 24px;
    background-position: -24px 0;
}
div div#hCalendarControlDay div.hCalendarControlOn {
    background-position: -24px -25px;
}
div div#hCalendarControlDay div {
    background-position: -24px -50px;
}
```

This concept would be much less verbose if browsers ubiquitously supported the ability to independently adjust the background position via the `background-position-x` and `background-position-y` properties. These properties were originally proprietary to IE but have since been defined in the CSS3 Borders and Backgrounds draft specification. When all browsers support the `background-position-y` properties, it'll be possible to make a simpler style sheet that doesn't have so much redundancy.

In the next block, you do the same thing that you did for the Day button, but position further to the left to account for the preceding buttons and separators. At this point, it might help to get out a calculator to help you determine the correct `left` offset position and the correct `background` offset position for each button.

```
div div#hCalendarControlWeek {
    width: 46px;
    left: 71px;
    background-position: -71px 0;
}
```

```
div div#hCalendarControlWeek div.hCalendarControlOn {
    background-position: -71px -25px;
}
div div#hCalendarControlWeek div {
    background-position: -71px -50px;
}
div div#hCalendarControlMonth {
    width: 46px;
    left: 118px;
    background-position: -118px 0;
}
div div#hCalendarControlMonth div.hCalendarControlOn {
    background-position: -118px -25px;
}
div div#hCalendarControlMonth div {
    background-position: -118px -50px;
}
```

For the next two rules, you complete the strip of buttons with the addition of the Next button. These rules are just like the other ones that you've done, but like the Previous button, there is no toggled on state, so you only need two rules.

```
div div#hCalendarControlNext {
    width: 23px;
    left: 165px;
    background-position: -165px 0;
}
div div#hCalendarControlNext div {
    background-position: -165px -50px;
}
```

The final block of rules positions each of the individual separators:

```
div#hCalendarControls div.hCalendarSeparator {
    left: 23px;
    width: 1px;
    background-position: -23px 0;
}
div#hCalendarControls div.hCalendarSeparator div {
    background-position: -23px -50px;
}
div#hCalendarControls div#hCalendarSeparatorTwo {
    left: 70px;
}
div#hCalendarControls div#hCalendarSeparatorThree {
    left: 117px;
}
div#hCalendarControls div#hCalendarSeparatorFour {
    left: 164px;
}
```

All that's left to do is make the buttons functional with jQuery. But, before I describe how the JavaScript portion works, let's rewind to the main focus of this example — the big calendar that takes up most of the window! In terms of the CSS and markup structure, there isn't anything truly advanced or out of the ordinary about this example, save a few rendering quirks that present themselves when loading up the calendar in IE. The visual goal is pretty simple: You want a calendar that can expand and contract in response to resizing the window. Each cell of the table should resize in proportion to its available space, and that's easy enough to accommodate. The first thing you do is create the `<div>` element with ID name *hCalendar*. It's absolutely positioned and uses the four offset properties to imply its dimensions, that is, specifying both the `top` and `bottom` properties in tandem results in the `<div>` being stretched to both the top and bottom positions that you specify. And the same thing for the `left` and `right` properties — specifying both causes the `<div>` to be stretched horizontally to both of the positions that you specify. Then once you have that, you can set the `<table>` element that holds the calendar information to have 100 percent width and height, so that it takes up the whole `<div>` element it is contained within, and presto, you have a calendar that expands and contracts in response to the browser window being resized, and a calendar that looks very similar to Apple's native desktop-based iCal software, or even Outlook's calendar.

```
div#hCalendar {
    position: absolute;
    top: 10px;
    right: 10px;
    bottom: 40px;
    left: 190px;
    background: #fff;
    border: 1px solid rgb(128, 128, 128);
    overflow: hidden;
}
```

There are a few flaws in this logic when you want to render the example in IE, though. IE6 doesn't support specifying opposing offset properties to imply width or height. So, putting both a `top` and a `bottom` property on the same `<div>` element with a pixel position doesn't result in the `<div>` getting stretched in IE6. To overcome this glitch, I use CSS expressions to specify the width and height of the `<div>` using JavaScript within a condition comment style sheet that only IE6 and IE7 can see. Another problem that presents itself is that IE6 and IE7 don't display the `<table>` correctly and don't make it take up 100 percent of the height of its containing `<div>`. It turns out that setting the `width` and `height` of the containing `<div>` element using a CSS expression also helps to fix this problem. Oddly enough, even though the `<div>` element clearly has explicit `width` and `height` set, you also have to set the `width` and `height` of the `<html>` and `<body>` elements to 100 percent … then the table is fixed up properly and takes up 100 percent of the height of its parent `<div>` element.

```
html, body {
    padding: 0;
    margin: 0;
    width: 100%;
    height: 100%;
}
div#hCalendar {
    height: expression(document.body.offsetHeight - 50);
    width: expression(document.body.offsetWidth - 200);
}
```

Now I can finally explain the JavaScript portion of the example, which is surprisingly concise and simple. The first part of the JavaScript attaches `mousedown` events to each of the children `<div>` elements residing within the `<div>` element with ID name *hCalendarControls*. This portion handles the mousedown states for each of the buttons at the bottom, making the CSS sprites functional. First, the code checks to see that the <div> element the user has begun a click on is not a separator. If the <div> element isn't a separator, a child <div> element is added to it and its preceding and following sibling elements. This causes the mousedown state of the button defined in the style sheet to become active for the button and the separators immediately before and after it.

```
    $('div#hCalendarControls > div').mousedown(
      function() {
        if (!$(this).hasClass('hCalendarSeparator')) {
          $(this).html("<div></div>");
          $(this).prev().html("<div></div>");
          $(this).next().html("<div></div>");
        }
      }
)
```

When you add the child <div> element, you trigger one of the rules like the following, depending on which button you pressed:

```
div div#hCalendarControlWeek div {
    background-position: -71px -50px;
}
```

The style sheet has already set up rules for each child <div> element, making the background of each correspond with the last row of images in the master sprite file. So from jQuery all you have to do is dynamically add or remove a child <div> element from each button to reveal the button pressed, mousedown style. In the next bit of JavaScript, you complete the button effects. When the user releases the mouse button, as mouseup, first you check to see that the button element is not a separator, then you check to see if the button <div> element has the class name *hCalendarControlToggle,* indicating that it's one of the three buttons — Day, Week, or Month — that can be toggled on or off. If the button element does have this class name, that means that you want the button to remain *on* after it's been pressed. In terms of style, that means that it should display the images present in the second row of the master CSS sprite image file.

```
    .mouseup(
      function() {
        if (!$(this).hasClass('hCalendarSeparator')) {
          if ($(this).hasClass('hCalendarControlToggle')) {
            $('div#hCalendarControls div').not(this).empty();
            $(this).find('div').addClass('hCalendarControlOn');
            $(this).prev().html("<div></div>");
            $(this).next().html("<div></div>");
          } else {
            $(this).empty();

            if (!$(this).prev().prev().find('div').length) {
              $(this).prev().empty();
            }

            if (!$(this).next().next().find('div').length) {
              $(this).next().empty();
            }

            var $isNext = ($(this).attr('id').indexOf('Next') != -1);

            $('div#hCalendar').load(
```

```
                'Example%207-2%20' + ($isNext? 'Next' : 'Previous') + '.html'
            );
          }
        }
      }
    );
```

To make sure the button stays on, you do the following. First, you remove the child <div> element from every sibling element except the one that's being pressed. You do this by using jQuery's `not()` method, and passing `this` (the element that's been pressed) to be excluded from the selection. Then you call the `empty()` method to remove any children or descending elements. That makes sure that the other buttons don't remain *on* when the current button is set to *on*, since only one of Day, Week, or Month can be activated but not more than one.

```
$('div#hCalendarControls div').not(this).empty();
```

To set the current button's style to toggled *on*, you add the class name *hCalendarControlOn* to the current button's child <div> element. That's the same <div> element that you dynamically added when the button was first pressed with the `mousedown` event.

```
$(this).find('div').addClass('hCalendarControlOn');
```

Now all that's left to complete the "toggled on" effect is to style the adjacent separators, so that they complement the "toggled on" button. This is done simply by adding a child <div> element to the immediately preceding and following separators just like you did in the `mousedown` portion of the code.

```
  $(this).prev().html("<div></div>");
$(this).next().html("<div></div>");
```

Otherwise, if the button being pressed does not have the class name *hCalendarControlToggle*, that means you're dealing with the Next or Previous buttons, which do not have a toggled *on* state, and once you have pressed one of these buttons, the button should revert back to its *off* state. To do this, you simply remove the child <div> element from the button being pressed to remove the style.

```
$(this).empty();
```

Then, you remove the style from the adjacent separator, but only if the adjacent button is not toggled on, because if you remove the style from the adjacent separator and the adjacent button is toggled on, you'll mess up its style. To tell if the adjacent button is toggled on, you traverse to it using two calls to either `prev()` or `next()`, then look inside that element (two elements over from the Next or Previous button) with the `find()` method to see if it has a child <div> element. If it has one, that means that it's on, and you don't want to remove style from the adjacent separator.

```
if (!$(this).prev().prev().find('div').length) {
  $(this).prev().empty();
}

if (!$(this).next().next().find('div').length) {
  $(this).next().empty();
}
```

And lastly, since you are dealing with pressing the Next or Previous button, this is also the place to place your AJAX Request to change the main calendar to the previous or following month.

```
var $isNext = ($(this).attr('id').indexOf('Next') != -1);

$('div#hCalendar').load(
  'Example%207-2%20' + ($isNext? 'Next' : 'Previous') + '.html'
);
```

As I mentioned previously, this example only crudely simulates what a script hooking into a real server-side script would do. First, you determine whether the button being pressed is the Next or Previous button, then you load up the file Example 7-2 Next.html or Example 7-2 Previous.html, depending on what is actually the case. By chaining the call to `load()` onto the end of a selection, you are telling jQuery to replace the `innerHTML` of the element or elements in the selection with the HTML being requested from the server. For this example, you've crafted HTML structurally identical to the calendar that's present in the main file in the `<table>` element for the months preceding and following September 2008, allowing you to simulate one click forward or one click backward.

Dynamically Loading JavaScript

Another useful and innovative feature of jQuery is its ability to dynamically and asynchronously load JavaScript documents using its AJAX API. As I covered in Chapter 1, it is a recommended best practice to split JavaScript development into smaller, easier-to-digest modules that have narrowly focused tasks. Another technique that goes hand-in-hand with modular JavaScript development is loading the minimal required JavaScript at the initial page load and dynamically loading additional JavaScript via AJAX as it is needed to save page load time and to make applications more responsive.

Besides modular JavaScript development, another reason you may want to load JavaScript via AJAX is to have JavaScript that changes dynamically, depending on user actions, or when you have need of loading more-complex applications that vary depending on user input or context.

Whatever use you find for this functionality, in this section, I walk you through the API that jQuery provides for loading JavaScript via its AJAX interface using its `$.getScript()` method. The following example demonstrates how to load jQuery's Color API asynchronously and then use that API to produce an animation that transitions between two colors. To demonstrate this, you add a few lines of JavaScript to the calendar you made in Example 7-2.

```
$(document).ready(
  function() {
    $('div#hCalendarControls > div').mousedown(
      function() {
        if (!$(this).hasClass('hCalendarSeparator')) {
          $(this).html("<div></div>");
          $(this).prev().html("<div></div>");
          $(this).next().html("<div></div>");
        }
      }
    ).mouseup(
      function() {
```

```
          if (!$(this).hasClass('hCalendarSeparator')) {
            if ($(this).hasClass('hCalendarControlToggle')) {
              $('div#hCalendarControls div').not(this).empty();
              $(this).find('div').addClass('hCalendarControlOn');
              $(this).prev().html("<div></div>");
              $(this).next().html("<div></div>");
            } else {
              $(this).empty();

              if (!$(this).prev().prev().find('div').length) {
                $(this).prev().empty();
              }

              if (!$(this).next().next().find('div').length) {
                $(this).next().empty();
              }

              var $isNext = ($(this).attr('id').indexOf('Next') != -1);

              $('div#hCalendar').load(
                'Figure%207-8%20' + ($isNext? 'Next' : 'Previous') + '.html'
              );
            }
          }
        }
      );

      $.getScript(
        '../../../Source Code/jQuery/jQuery.color.js',
        function() {
          $('table.hCalendar td').click(
            function() {
              $(this)
                .animate({backgroundColor: 'lightgrey'}, 1000)
                .animate({backgroundColor: 'lightblue'}, 1000);
            }
          );
        }
      );
    }
  );
```

The new JavaScript demonstrates how an external script is loaded via jQuery's `$.getScript()` method. The `$.getScript()` method takes two arguments, the path to the script that you want to load, and like jQuery's other AJAX Request method, it also allows a callback function, which is executed when the script has been loaded and successfully executed.

The screenshot in **Figure 7-8** shows a snapshot after the animation that takes place when you click on a day in the calendar. The colors shift between all the variations of blue between the `lightgrey` and `lightblue` color keywords. I cover jQuery's `animate()` method in more detail in Chapter 19.

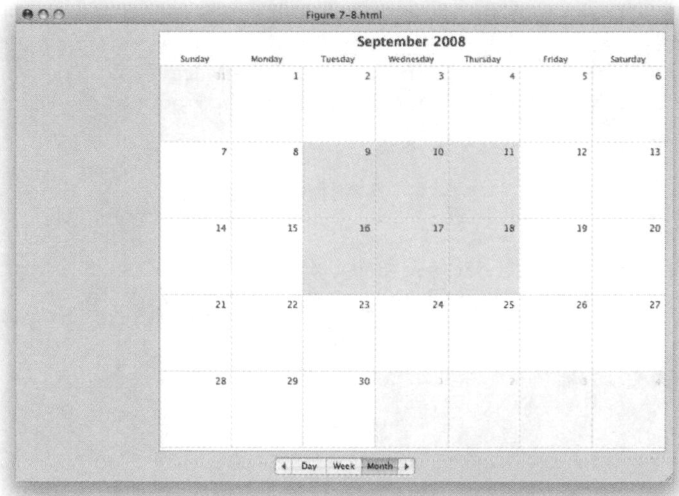

Figure 7-8

The script that you load for the example, jQuery.color.js, along with the source code for the example itself, is available with this book's source code download materials at `www.wrox.com`.

This example is inspired via a similar concept that appears in jQuery's official documentation at `www.jquery.com`.

The JavaScript being loaded via the `$.getScript()` method is merely an example of loading additional script from JavaScript via the `$getScript()` method; should you take this example further, you could perhaps modify the script to not request that JavaScript until it is actually needed, such as the first time you click on one of the days in the calendar, for example.

AJAX Events

In this section, I cover what jQuery calls *AJAX Events*. *AJAX Events* are milestones that occur during an AJAX Request that can give you feedback about the status of your request or allow you to execute code when each milestone occurs. Examples of milestones are when a request starts, when a request stops, when a request has been sent, when a request has failed, when a request is completed, and when a request is completely successful. I don't go into exhaustive detail about each of these events, but Appendix G has a full listing of all of the AJAX methods, properties, and AJAX Events supported by jQuery.

But one example is how to show a "Loading" message while some remote content is being fetched. There are three ways to do this. One method allows you to globally set AJAX Events for all AJAX Requests, and there are two ways to set AJAX Events per individual request using jQuery's `ajax()` method or jQuery's individual AJAX Event methods. In this section, I describe how to make a loading message using each of these methods.

Adding jQuery AJAX Events globally is very easy — all you have to do is call jQuery's `ajaxSetup()` method. To demonstrate how this is done, I've modified the Finder example from **Figure 7-5**. First, you need an activity indicator to show that something is taking place. Typically, an animated GIF is good enough to get the job done. In the following snippet from the Finder example, I've added an animated GIF to display while activity is taking place:

```
        <li class='hFinderTreeDirectoryBranch'>
          <div class='hFinderTreeDirectory' id='hFinderTreeDirectory-5185'
               title='/Users'>
            <div class='hFinderTreeIcon'></div>
            <span>Users</span></div>
            <img src='../../../Images/Finder/Right.png' class='hFinderTreeHasChildren'
                 id='hFinderTreeIcon-5185' alt='+' title='Click to expand.' />
            <div class='hFinderTreeBranchWrapper'>
          </div>
        </li>
      </ul>
    </li>
  </ul>
  <div id='hFinderActivity'>
    <img src='../../../Images/Activity.gif' alt='Activity Indicator' />
  </div>
      </div>
    </body>
  </html>
```

Then, some CSS is added to the example to put the activity indicator in the lower-right-hand part of the window.

```
div.hFinderTreeIcon {
    background: url('../../../Images/Finder/Folder.png') no-repeat left;
    width: 16px;
    height: 16px;
    margin: 0 5px 0 0;
    float: left;
}
div.hFinderTreeBranchWrapper {
    display: none;
}
div#hFinderActivity {
    position: absolute;
    bottom: 5px;
    right: 5px;
    display: none;
}
```

Then finally, the JavaScript is modified so that the activity indicator is dynamically revealed when an AJAX Request takes place and hidden when the request concludes:

```
$.ajaxSetup({
  beforeSend : function() {
    $('div#hFinderActivity').show();
  },
  success : function() {
```

```
      $('div#hFinderActivity').hide();
    }
  });

  $(document).ready(
    function() {
      $('img.hFinderTreeHasChildren').click(
        function() {
          if (!$(this).next().children('ul').length) {
            $(this).next().load(
              'AJAX%20Request%20Documents/' +
                $(this).prev().attr('id').split('-').pop() + '.html',
              function() {
                $(this).show();
                $(this).prev().attr(
                  'src',
                  '../../../Images/Finder/Down.png'
                );
              }
            );
          } else {
            $(this).next().toggle();

            $(this).attr(
              'src',
              '../../../Images/Finder/' +
                ($(this).attr('src').indexOf('Down') != -1? 'Right' : 'Down') + '.png'
            );
          }
        }
      );
    }
  );
```

This modification looks like what you see in **Figure 7-9**, when you make an AJAX Request. Since you're requesting a file from your own local computer, the activity indicator will be revealed and hidden almost instantaneously. So this technique is obviously better suited for requesting content from a remote server where there may be some latency.

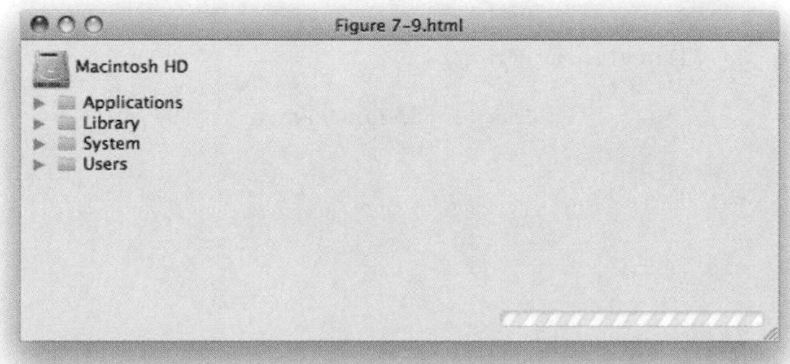

Figure 7-9

In the JavaScript, you make a call to `$.ajaxSetup()` to define an event called `beforeSend` and another one called `success`. Each of these events is defined inside a JavaScript object literal that is passed to the `$.ajaxSetup()` method. By attaching a callback function to the `beforeSend` property, you are telling jQuery to execute the specified function before every AJAX Request. In this case, you cause the activity indicator to be displayed by calling jQuery's `show()` method. Then, once the request has completed successfully, you hide the activity indicator by attaching a callback function to the `success` property, which, in turn, is executed upon a successful request. These are but a few of the properties that you can specify using this method to define AJAX defaults globally for jQuery. All of the options that can be specified here are outlined in detail in Appendix G.

You are not, of course, limited to this use of jQuery's AJAX Events. jQuery's AJAX Events can also be used to modify the HTTP headers that will be used in the request or to do other low-level things with jQuery's AJAX API.

The preceding example defined how to define events globally using the `$.ajaxSetup()` method. In the following example (which produces **Figure 7-10**, not shown here) I demonstrate how to do the same using individual jQuery AJAX Event methods. This time only the JavaScript has been modified, and the remainder is the same as shown in **Figure 7-9**.

```
$(document).ready(
  function() {
    $('img.hFinderTreeHasChildren').click(
      function() {
        if (!$(this).next().children('ul').length) {
          $(this).next()
            .ajaxSend(
              function() {
                $('div#hFinderActivity').show();
              }
            )
            .ajaxSuccess(
              function() {
                $('div#hFinderActivity').hide();
              }
            )
            .load(
              'AJAX%20Request%20Documents/' +
                $(this).prev().attr('id').split('-').pop() + '.html',
              function() {
                $(this).show();
                $(this).prev().attr(
                  'src',
                  '../../../Images/Finder/Down.png'
                );
              }
            );
        } else {
          $(this).next().toggle();

          $(this).attr(
            'src',
```

```
                '../../../Images/Finder/' +
                  ($(this).attr('src').indexOf('Down') != -1? 'Right' : 'Down') + '.png'
              );
            }
          }
        );
      }
    );
```

The preceding modification gives you the same outcome demonstrated in **Figure 7-9**, only this time the functions that reveal and hide the activity indicator are limited to occurring on the specific AJAX Requests associated with fetching the contents of each folder. To achieve the same result, you moved the callback function for the `beforeSend` property to inside the call to the `ajaxSend()` method, and the callback function for the `success` property to inside the call to the `ajaxSuccess()` method. And those methods, are, of course, chainable like most of jQuery's other methods.

The last way that you can attach events is via a call to jQuery's more low-level `ajax()` method. The `ajax()` method is used internally, within jQuery, to construct AJAX Requests for jQuery's other AJAX Request methods, like `$.get()`, `$getJSON()`, `$.post()`, and so on. jQuery's `$.ajax()` method gives you the ability to set as many low-level AJAX Request options as you like. The following example demonstrates how to use `$.ajax()` to mimic the same results as the preceding two examples:

```
$(document).ready(
  function() {
    $('img.hFinderTreeHasChildren').click(
      function() {
        if (!$(this).next().children('ul').length) {
          var self = $(this);

          $.ajax({
            beforeSend : function() {
              $('div#hFinderActivity').show();
            },
            success : function() {
              $('div#hFinderActivity').hide();
            },
            complete : function($response, $status) {
              if ($status == "success" || $status == "notmodified" ) {
                self.next().html($response.responseText);

                self.next().show();
                self.attr(
                  'src',
                  '../../../Images/Finder/Down.png'
                );
              }
            },
            url : 'AJAX%20Request%20Documents/' +
                  self.prev().attr('id').split('-').pop() + '.html'
          });
        } else {
```

```
                $(this).next().toggle();

                $(this).attr(
                  'src',
                  '../../../Images/Finder/' +
                    ($(this).attr('src').indexOf('Down') != -1? 'Right' : 'Down') + '.png'
                );
              }
            }
          );
        }
      );
```

The preceding example (which produces **Figure 7-11**, not shown here) is functionally identical to the last two examples that you've seen in this section. Just like those other two examples, you are requesting the contents of each folder with each AJAX Request, and you're showing an activity indicator that appears while the AJAX Request is taking place and is hidden when it completes. Since the `$.ajax()` method works by calling that method of the jQuery object directly, you have to change your approach from using the `load()` method. First, since you want to load HTML, you need to remember what element you want to load that HTML into.

```
var self = $(this);
```

`this` is assigned to a variable called `self` so that you can reference the variable `self` from within the callback functions that you assign to the various options of the `$.ajax()` method. If you remember from **Figure 7-5**, `this` refers to the `<img>` element containing the arrows that appear beside each folder. The `$.ajax()` method itself takes various options defined as an object literal, which again are documented in Appendix G. You again define the `beforeSend` and `success` options that contain functions that reveal and hide the activity indicator, but this time in the context of the AJAX Request that you're making instead of globally. The complete option defines a callback function that is executed upon completion of the AJAX Request ... this would be the callback function that was executed for jQuery's other AJAX Request methods like `load()`, `$.get()`, or `$.post()`. The callback function that you define is more low level, though, since you pass the `XMLHttpRequest` response object in the first argument and the status of the request in the second argument. If the `$status` variable is `success` or `notmodified`, that means your request was successful; the rest of the code carries on like the code from **Figure 7-5**, and the `<img>` element is contained in the variable `self`. The `responseText` property contains the text content of the response, in this case, the HTML snippet containing all the subfolders. If this were an XML request, you'd be interested in working with the `responseXML` object. The HTML snippet is loaded into the next sibling `<div>` element that appears after the `<img>` element, then that `<div>` element is made visible with the `show()` method, and then the orientation of the arrow is changed by swapping the arrow image from `Right.png` to `Down.png`.

jQuery's `$.ajax()` method is intended for use internally within jQuery or when you need to make lots of low-level modifications to how the request will carry on and the default methods don't do the trick.

Making an AJAX-Style File Upload

I've decided to throw this topic in along with my discussion of jQuery's AJAX Request methods, because many novice programmers do not know that it isn't possible to upload a file from a client via an AJAX Request. It is, however, possible to make a file upload look as though it completed via an

AJAX Request, seamlessly and without requiring your document to reload. Prior to the ubiquitous AJAX XMLHttpRequest API, you could still do AJAX-like interaction with a server, but if you wanted to do it in a cross-browser-compatible way, you had to simulate what would happen with an AJAX Request with a hidden `<iframe>` element. This, of course, didn't offer much in the way of the low-level HTTP request-tweaking that is possible with the XMLHttpRequest API, but it let you update content in a document without reloading the document. The XMLHttpRequest API, however, does not account in any way for file uploads. The primary reason for this is that it's a security risk. You can't upload files from the user's computer without the user specifically initiating the file upload. I would imagine that some future revision of the XMLHttpRequest API might find a way to offer AJAX file uploads without compromising the user's security. Until then we're stuck with an ad hoc method that involves targeting a `<form>` element to a hidden `<iframe>` element. This method keeps security, since the user still must specifically initiate the file upload, but it also lets you keep the Web 2.0, AJAXy desktop application feel, by allowing the file upload to take place without causing the user's page to reload. In the following example, I demonstrate the client-side components that you would need for such an application, but I am obviously unable to demonstrate how the server-side component works, since different languages work with file uploads differently, and that portion of the discussion is outside the scope of this book.

```
<!DOCTYPE html PUBLIC "-//W3C//DTD XHTML 1.0 Strict//EN"
    "http://www.w3.org/TR/xhtml1/DTD/xhtml1-strict.dtd">
<html xmlns='http://www.w3.org/1999/xhtml' xml:lang='en'>
  <head>
    <meta http-equiv='content-type' content='text/html; charset=utf-8' />
    <meta http-equiv='content-language' content='en-us' />
    <title></title>
    <script type='text/javascript'
            src='../../../Source Code/jQuery/jQuery.js'></script>
    <script type='text/javascript' src='Figure 7-12.js'></script>
    <link type='text/css' href='Figure 7-12.css' rel='stylesheet' />
  </head>
  <body>
     <iframe src='about:blank' name='hFinderUpload'
            id='hFinderUpload'></iframe>
     <form action='Figure 7-12 Upload.html' method='post'
           enctype='multipart/form-data' target='hFinderUpload'>
       <fieldset>
         <legend>Upload a File</legend>
       <div id='hFinderUploadFileWrapper'>
         <label for='hFinderUploadFile'>File:</label>
         <input type='file' name='hFinderUploadFile'
                id='hFinderUploadFile' size='25' />
       </div>
       <div id='hFinderButtonWrapper'>
         <input type='submit' id='hFinderButton'
                name='hFinderButton' value='Upload File' />
       </div>
       </fieldset>
     </form>
  </body>
</html>
```

In the preceding HTML, you see a bare-bones recipe for a file upload. You include a `<form>` element with the `enctype` attribute set to `multipart/form-data`, and an `<input>` element with the `type` attribute set to `file`. The `<form>` element has its `target` attribute set to `hFinderUpload`, which is the name of the `<iframe>` element. When you submit the form, it will post its results to the URL specified in the `action` attribute, and the response from that request will load in the `<iframe>` element.

In the style sheet, you hide the `<iframe>` element with the declaration `display: none;`:

```
body {
    font: 16px sans-serif;
}
fieldset {
    background: #93cdf9;
    border: 1px solid rgb(200, 200, 200);
}
fieldset div {
    padding: 10px;
    margin: 5px;
}
fieldset label {
    float: left;
    width: 200px;
    text-align: right;
    padding: 2px 5px 0 0;
}
div#hFinderButtonWrapper {
    text-align: right;
}
iframe {
    display: none;
    position: absolute;
    bottom: 5px;
    right: 5px;
}
```

The file Figure 7-12 Upload.html simulates what your server might provide as a response to the file upload:

```
<!DOCTYPE html PUBLIC "-//W3C//DTD XHTML 1.0 Strict//EN"
    "http://www.w3.org/TR/xhtml1/DTD/xhtml1-strict.dtd">
<html xmlns='http://www.w3.org/1999/xhtml' xml:lang='en'>
  <head>
    <meta http-equiv='content-type' content='text/html; charset=utf-8' />
    <meta http-equiv='content-language' content='en-us' />
    <title></title>
  </head>
  <body>
  <p>
    This file would load upon requesting your form.
    <script type='text/javascript'>
      top.hFinder.onFileUpload();
    </script>
  </p>
  </body>
</html>
```

In the HTML, there is embedded JavaScript that calls the `top` object, which references the parent document of the document loaded into the `<iframe>`. Back in the main HTML file, you included a JavaScript, Figure 7-12.js, which has the following script inside it:

```
var hFinder = {
  onFileUpload : function()
  {
    alert('File uploaded!');
  }
};
```

The preceding is executed after the file is successfully uploaded, via the response you sent from the server. As you can see, without discussing the server-side portion of a file upload, it is relatively painless to simulate an AJAX Request for a file upload.

This example gives you results similar to what you see in **Figure 7-12**.

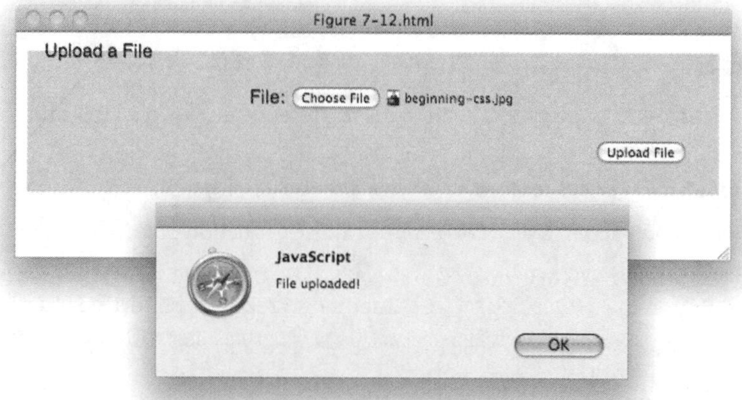

Figure 7-12

Summary

In this chapter, I took you on a tour of jQuery's built-in AJAX capabilities. You saw the differences between a GET and a POST HTTP request, learning that a GET request has a limit on its length, in addition to being semantically suited for requests that result in no lasting modification or effect on the server. POST requests, in contrast, should be reserved for requests that shouldn't be arbitrarily repeated and do have some kind of lasting impact on the server. In terms of AJAX, GET requests have a slight performance advantage.

jQuery offers the `$.get()` method to make GET requests and the `$.post()` method to make POST requests. When you're working with XML, jQuery makes it super-easy to extract information from an XML document by giving you full access to jQuery's various selection methods for querying your XML responses. The JSON format can be even easier to work with, but extra care must be taken to ensure that you don't make yourself vulnerable to a cross-site forgery. For working with JSON data, jQuery offers the `$getJSON()` method.

The `load()` method can be used to insert HTML snippets requested from the server into elements that you select with jQuery.

I also presented a complex real-life-oriented example in which you used jQuery in conjunction with CSS and markup to create a cross-platform, AJAX-driven calendar that uses CSS sprites for buttons and jQuery's `load()` method to change the calendar's month.

I described how to load script asynchronously with jQuery's `$.getScript()` method. This was demonstrated by loading jQuery's color script, which was applied to the calendar you made in Example 7-2, and provided a nifty animated effect when you clicked on the various days in the calendar.

I talked about jQuery's AJAX Events and described the different ways you can use AJAX Events to add an activity indicator to the Finder example that you saw in **Figure 7-5**.

Finally, I described how you can simulate an AJAX style of request for a file upload via the use of a hidden `<iframe>` element.

Exercises

1. In terms of an AJAX Request, is there any difference between a GET and a POST HTTP request?
2. How would you provide extra data with a request using jQuery's `$.get()` method?
3. How would you access a JSON object in a callback function provided to the `$.getJSON()` method?
4. Given the following XML, how would you access the contents of the `<response>` element, assuming you used jQuery's `$.get()` method to request the XML document?

```
<?xml version="1.0" encoding="UTF-8" standalone="yes"?>
<response>Yes!</response>
```

5. If you wanted to load an HTML snippet into a selection of elements, what jQuery method would you use?
6. In the following JavaScript, describe what happens:

```
$.ajaxSetup({
  beforeSend : function() {
    $('div#hFinderActivity').show();
  },
  success : function() {
    $('div#hFinderActivity').hide();
  }
});
```

7. If you wanted to attach AJAX Events to apply only in the context of an individual AJAX Request, rather than globally, what methods does jQuery provide to attach events in this way?
8. What jQuery method would you use if you wanted to get the value of every input element within a form?

8

Effects

Up to this point, you've been learning about jQuery's nuts and bolts. jQuery does a lot to make the life of a developer easier, but jQuery does not stop at making it easier to traverse the DOM, or manipulate, or iterate, or all of the other very cool things you've learned about in the preceding chapters. It also gives you the tools to make your documents look very polished, professional, and sophisticated via animation and some rudimentary special effects. In this chapter, I present how to work with the API that jQuery provides for dealing with effects.

As you've seen in examples in previous chapters, jQuery can toggle the display of elements between hidden and displayed states using its `show()` and `hide()` methods. What you may not have already learned is that those methods also have the ability to animate between hidden and displayed states via a short animation.

jQuery also gives you the ability to animate an element between hidden and displayed states by animating an element's height, in addition to the ability to fade elements on and off via an animation of an element's opacity, all with a simple and trivial function call.

Finally, jQuery also has the ability to animate objects in your document between arbitrary numeric styles, which gives you the ability to create your own, custom animations.

Showing and Hiding Elements

jQuery provides three methods for showing and hiding elements — `show()`, `hide()`, and `toggle()`. You've seen examples of `show()` and `hide()` in previous chapters. Those two methods simply make an object visible or invisible by toggling that element's CSS `display` property. These methods simply make it easier to turn elements on or off. What you haven't learned about these properties already is that you can also supply arguments to these methods that make elements fade on and off, by animating the element's opacity, in combination with an animation of the element's width and height. You can also supply a callback function in the second argument, which is executed when the animation completes. The following document demonstrates how to show and hide documents using jQuery's `show()` and `hide()` methods:

```
<!DOCTYPE html PUBLIC "-//W3C//DTD XHTML 1.0 Strict//EN"
    "http://www.w3.org/TR/xhtml1/DTD/xhtml1-strict.dtd">
<html xmlns='http://www.w3.org/1999/xhtml' xml:lang='en'>
  <head>
    <meta http-equiv='content-type' content='text/html; charset=utf-8' />
    <meta http-equiv='content-language' content='en-us' />
    <title></title>
    <script type='text/javascript'
            src='../../../Source Code/jQuery/jQuery.js'></script>
    <script type='text/javascript' src='Figure 8-1.js'></script>
    <link type='text/css' href='Figure 8-1.css' rel='stylesheet' />
  </head>
  <body>
     <input type='submit' id='tmpOpen' value='Open Dialogue' />
     <div id='tmpDialogue'>
       <p>
         Lorem ipsum dolor sit amet, consectetuer adipiscing elit. Ut
         vestibulum ornare augue. Fusce non purus vel libero mattis aliquet.
         Vivamus interdum consequat risus. Integer feugiat fringilla est.
         Vivamus libero. Vestibulum imperdiet arcu vitae nunc. Nunc est velit,
         varius sed, faucibus quis,
       </p>
       <div id='tmpButtons'>
         <input type='submit' id='tmpClose' value='Close Dialogue' />
       </div>
     </div>
  </body>
</html>
```

The following style sheet is applied to the preceding markup document:

```
body {
    font: 16px sans-serif;
}
div#tmpDialogue {
    display: none;
    position: absolute;
    top: 50%;
    left: 50%;
    width: 500px;
    height: 200px;
    margin: -101px 0 0 -251px;
    background: rgb(233, 233, 233);
    border: 1px solid rgb(128, 128, 128);
}
div#tmpDialogue p {
    padding: 5px;
    margin: 5px;
}
div#tmpButtons {
    position: absolute;
    bottom: 5px;
    right: 5px;
}
```

The following script demonstrates the animations provided by jQuery's `show()` and `hide()` methods:

```
$(document).ready(
  function() {
    $('input#tmpOpen').click(
      function($e) {
        $('div#tmpDialogue').show('slow');
      }
    );

    $('input#tmpClose').click(
      function($e) {
        $('div#tmpDialogue').hide(5000);
      }
    );
  }
);
```

In the preceding script, you see how jQuery's `show()` method can take a string argument indicating the speed at which jQuery should animate revealing the element. There are four possible arguments that you can pass to indicate the speed of the animation for the `show()`, `hide()`, or `toggle()` method: `"slow"`, `"normal"`, or `"fast"`, or the time in milliseconds. **Figure 8-1** displays a screenshot of the preceding example as it appears in Safari.

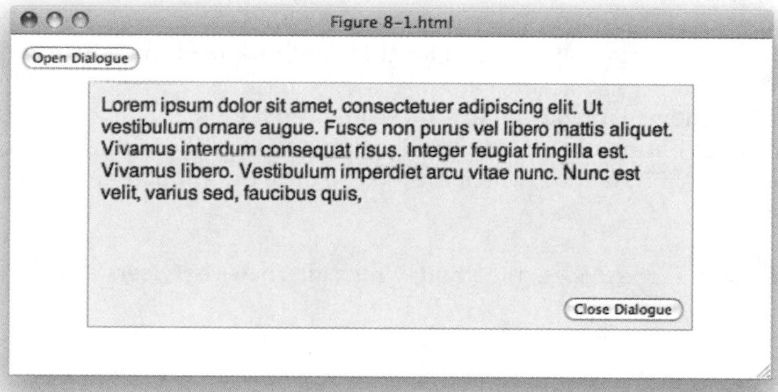

Figure 8-1

Sliding Elements

jQuery also provides the ability to animate an element by sliding. *Sliding* is defined in jQuery as animating an element's height. So, *sliding down* means to animate an element's height from nothing to its normal height. *Sliding up*, on the other hand, means to animate an element's height from its normal height to nothing. Sliding is another way to reveal and hide elements. You're just using different animation to accomplish the task. jQuery's `slideDown()` and `slideUp()` methods are demonstrated in the following script, which is applied to the same markup document in **Figure 8-1**:

```
$(document).ready(
  function() {
    $('input#tmpOpen').click(
      function($e) {
        $('div#tmpDialogue').slideDown('slow');
      }
    );

    $('input#tmpClose').click(
      function($e) {
        $('div#tmpDialogue').slideUp(5000);
      }
    );
  }
);
```

The preceding script results in the same document that you see in **Figure 8-1** and can be accessed in the free source code download materials available for this book at `www.wrox.com`, in the folder named *Figure 8-2*.

When you click on the input button labeled *Open Dialogue*, you see that the `<div>` with ID name *tmpDialogue* has its height animated slowly from nothing until it reaches its full height. When you click on the button labeled *Close Dialogue*, the `<div>` element with ID name *tmpDialogue* again has its height animated, but this time in reverse, from full height to nothing, over the course of 5 seconds.

The speeds that are allowed are the same as those allowed for jQuery's `show()` and `hide()` methods. Additionally, you can optionally provide a callback function in the second argument passed to the `slideDown()` or `slideUp()` method, which is executed once the animation completes, once for each element selected.

Finally, there is also a `slideToggle()` method, which alternates between `slideUp()` and `slideDown()`.

Fading Elements

Fading elements is yet another variation that jQuery offers for revealing and hiding elements. The API is the same as the methods of the preceding two sections; only the names of those methods and the animation used by those methods are different. jQuery's `fadeIn()` method reveals an element by animating its opacity from fully transparent, to fully opaque; and jQuery's `fadeOut()` method, of course, does the same thing in reverse, animating an element from fully opaque to fully transparent.

```
$(document).ready(
  function() {
    $('input#tmpOpen').click(
      function($e) {
        $('div#tmpDialogue').fadeIn('slow');
      }
```

```
      );

      $('input#tmpClose').click(
        function($e) {
          $('div#tmpDialogue').fadeOut(5000);
        }
      );
    }
  );
```

Again, just like the `hide()`, `show()`, `slideUp()`, and `slideDown()` methods, you have the option of specifying two arguments — the speed of the animation and a callback function that is executed when the animation completes. The preceding script can be found in the source code download as *Figure 8-3*.

Custom Animation

jQuery also provides an API that facilitates custom animation, in the method called `animate()`. jQuery's animate method intuitively transitions CSS properties with numeric values over a specified duration. For example, if you have a `<div>` element and that `<div>` element has a width of 300 pixels (300px), when you call jQuery's `animate()` method with a width of 500px and a duration of 3 seconds, the animate method will automatically adjust the `<div>` element's width from 300px to 500px smoothly over a period of 3 seconds. The `animate()` method is demonstrated in the following document:

```
<!DOCTYPE html PUBLIC "-//W3C//DTD XHTML 1.0 Strict//EN"
    "http://www.w3.org/TR/xhtml1/DTD/xhtml1-strict.dtd">
<html xmlns='http://www.w3.org/1999/xhtml' xml:lang='en'>
  <head>
    <meta http-equiv='content-type' content='text/html; charset=utf-8' />
    <meta http-equiv='content-language' content='en-us' />
    <title></title>
    <script type='text/javascript'
            src='../../../Source Code/jQuery/jQuery.js'></script>
    <script type='text/javascript' src='Figure 8-4.js'></script>
    <link type='text/css' href='Figure 8-4.css' rel='stylesheet' />
  </head>
  <body>
      <div id='tmpDialogue'>
        <p>
          Lorem ipsum dolor sit amet, consectetuer adipiscing elit. Ut
          vestibulum ornare augue. Fusce non purus vel libero mattis aliquet.
          Vivamus interdum consequat risus. Integer feugiat fringilla est.
          Vivamus libero. Vestibulum imperdiet arcu vitae nunc. Nunc est velit,
          varius sed, faucibus quis,
        </p>
        <div id='tmpButtons'>
          <input type='submit' id='tmpAnimate' value='Animate Dialogue' />
        </div>
      </div>
  </body>
</html>
```

The following style sheet is applied to the preceding markup document. Take note of the width (500px) and left margin (-251px) of the <div> with ID name *tmpDialogue*.

```
body {
    font: 16px sans-serif;
}
div#tmpDialogue {
    position: absolute;
    top: 50%;
    left: 50%;
    width: 500px;
    height: 200px;
    margin: -101px 0 0 -251px;
    background: rgb(233, 233, 233);
    border: 1px solid rgb(128, 128, 128);
}
div#tmpDialogue p {
    padding: 5px;
    margin: 5px;
}
div#tmpButtons {
    position: absolute;
    bottom: 5px;
    right: 5px;
}
```

The preceding script demonstrates how the `animate()` method is used to transition between two style properties with numeric values.

```
$(document).ready(
  function() {
    $('input#tmpAnimate').click(
      function($e) {
        $('div#tmpDialogue').animate({
            width: '600px',
            marginLeft: '-301px'
          }, 3000
        );
      }
    );
  }
);
```

In the preceding script, you animate the <div> element with ID name *tmpDialogue* upon pressing the button labeled *Animate Dialogue*. Two arguments are provided to the `animate()` method. In the first argument, an object literal consisting of styles is provided. The two properties specified in that object literal are a width of 600px and a left margin of -301px. When the `animate()` method is executed, the script takes the starting value of 500px for the `width` property and animates that width until the value of 600px is reached, all the while doing the same with the `marginLeft` property. It begins with a value of -251px and animates until it reaches the value -301px. The value 3,000 is provided in the second parameter passed to the `animate()` method, which is the length of the animation in milliseconds (ms): 3,000 ms = 3 seconds. **Figure 8-4** shows the beginning state of the <div> element, and **Figure 8-5** shows the ending state of the <div> element.

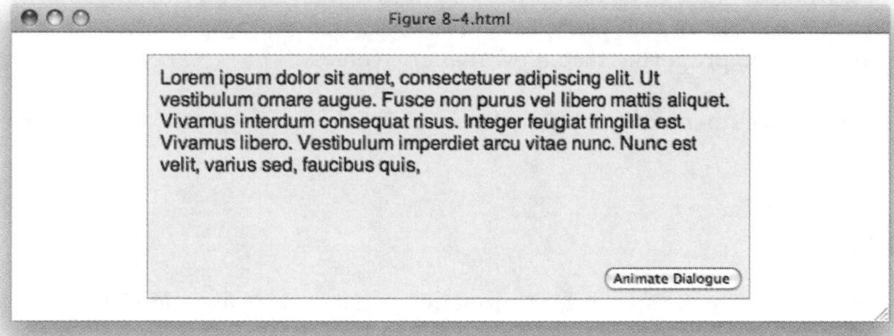

Figure 8-4

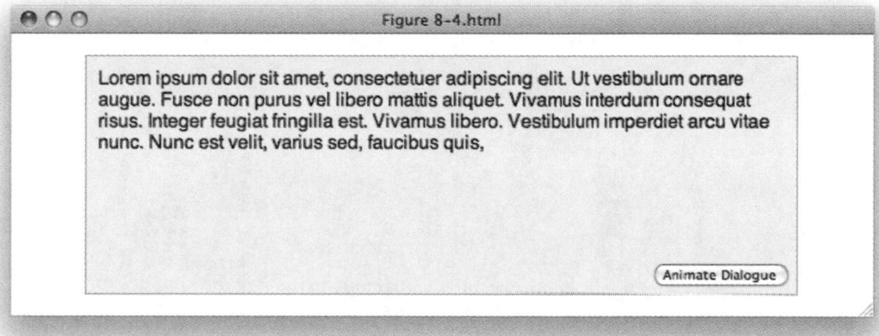

Figure 8-5

Summary

In this chapter, you learned how jQuery's animation elements work to hide and display elements, either by using jQuery's various built-in animations or by making a custom animation.

You learned how jQuery's `hide()` and `show()` methods can be provided a speed in their first argument, which can be `"slow"`, `"normal"`, or `"fast"`, or the time specified in milliseconds. When used without any arguments specified, jQuery's `show()` and `hide()` methods simply show and hide an element by toggling the CSS `display` property. Specifying the first argument causes these methods to use an animation to transition between the hidden and displayed states.

jQuery offers a few alternative animations that essentially provide the same function, toggling between a hidden and displayed state. jQuery's `slideDown()`, `slideUp()`, and `slideToggle()` methods animate an element's height to hide and display an element. jQuery's `fadeIn()` and `fadeOut()` methods animate an element's opacity to hide and display an element.

Finally, you learned about jQuery's `animate()` method, which lets you transition between the styles an element already has to styles that you specify. The styles that can be animated are, at the time of this writing, limited to CSS properties that allow numeric values.

jQuery Effects are documented in detail in Appendix M.

Exercises

1. When specifying the speed of an animation, what options are allowed?
2. What does jQuery's `slideDown()` method do?
3. What method would you use to display an element using an animation of that element's opacity?
4. What method would you use to create a custom animation?
5. How is jQuery's `animate()` method limited at the time of this writing?

Plugins

Beyond making many scripting tasks much easier, jQuery also makes itself very easy to extend with new functionality. This is done with a very easy-to-understand Plugin API. Using jQuery's Plugin API, you can make your own chainable jQuery methods and even write entire complex client-side applications completely as jQuery plugins.

There are lots of things you can do with plugins. Some of the more useful and prominent examples of jQuery plugins are found in the jQuery UI library, which I begin discussion of in Chapter 10. Plugins in the jQuery UI library help you to implement functionality like drag-and-drop or selecting elements, and a variety of other functionality. There is also a thriving third-party development community for jQuery that produces plugins for just about anything you can think of. jQuery's thriving plugin community exists largely thanks to how ridiculously easy it is to write plugins for jQuery.

In this chapter, I demonstrate how to use jQuery's Plugin API and cover the basic concepts you'll need to understand to start writing plugins of your own. Beyond what you learn about jQuery plugin basics in this chapter, you'll also see more examples that use jQuery's Plugin API later in the book.

Writing a Plugin

jQuery plugins are very easy to implement. All you need to do is pass an object literal containing the methods you want to extend jQuery with to the `$.fn.extend()` method. The following code demonstrates how this is done:

```
<!DOCTYPE html PUBLIC "-//W3C//DTD XHTML 1.0 Strict//EN"
    "http://www.w3.org/TR/xhtml1/DTD/xhtml1-strict.dtd">
<html xmlns='http://www.w3.org/1999/xhtml' xml:lang='en'>
  <head>
    <meta http-equiv='content-type' content='text/html; charset=utf-8' />
    <meta http-equiv='content-language' content='en-us' />
```

```
    <title></title>
    <script type='text/javascript'
            src='../../../Source Code/jQuery/jQuery.js'></script>
    <script type='text/javascript'
            src='../../../Source Code/jQuery/jQueryUI.js'></script>
    <script type='text/javascript' src='Figure 9-1.js'></script>
    <link type='text/css' href='Figure 9-1.css' rel='stylesheet' />
  </head>
  <body>
    <h4>John Candy Movies</h4>
    <ul>
      <li>The Great Outdoors</li>
      <li>Uncle Buck</li>
      <li>Who's Harry Crumb</li>
      <li>Canadian Bacon</li>
      <li>Home Alone</li>
      <li>Space Balls</li>
      <li>Plans, Trains, and Automobiles</li>
    </ul>
    <p>
      <a href='javascript:void(0);'>Select All</a>
    </p>
  </body>
</html>
```

The following CSS document is used to style the preceding markup document:

```
body {
    font: 12px "Lucida Grande", Arial, sans-serif;
    background: #fff;
    color: rgb(50, 50, 50);
    margin: 0;
    padding: 0;
}
h4 {
    margin: 5px;
}
ul {
    list-style: none;
    margin: 5px;
    padding: 5px;
}
li {
    padding: 3px;
}
li.tmpSelected {
    background: yellow;
}
p {
    text-align: right;
    padding: 5px;
}
```

The following JavaScript demonstrates how to use jQuery's Plugin API to write custom plugins for jQuery:

```
$.fn.extend({
  Select: function() {
    return $(this).addClass('tmpSelected');
  },
  Unselect: function() {
    return $(this).removeClass('tmpSelected');
  },
  MyApplication: {
    Ready: function() {
      $('p a').click(
        function($e) {
          $e.preventDefault();
          $('li').Select();
        }
      );

      $('li').click(
        function() {
          $(this).hasClass('tmpSelected')?
            $(this).Unselect() : $(this).Select();
        }
      );
    }
  }
});

$(document).ready(
  function() {
    $.fn.MyApplication.Ready();
  }
);
```

The preceding code results in the screenshot that you see in **Figure 9-1** when you click on individual movie titles.

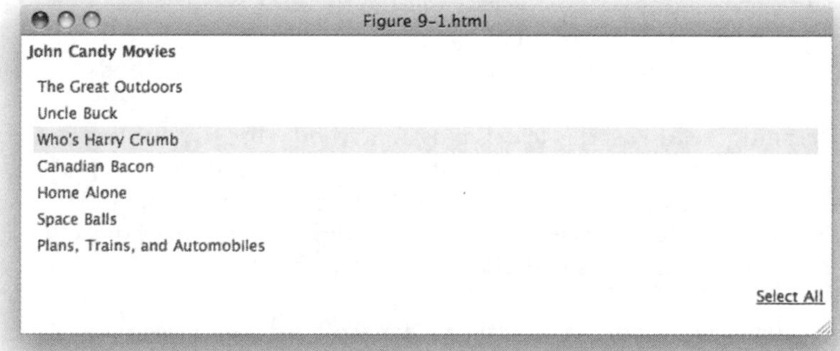

Figure 9-1

And you get the result that you see in **Figure 9-2** when you click on the "Select All" link.

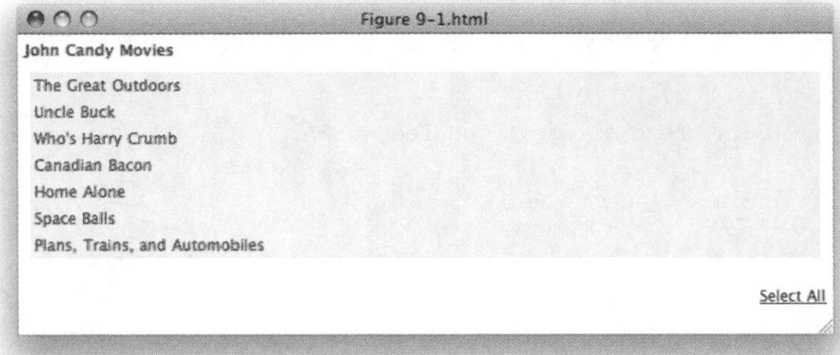

Figure 9-2

In the preceding example, you see how jQuery plugins are written using the `$.fn.extend()` method. A jQuery plugin is passed as an object literal to the `$.fn.extend()` method. Some plugins are written to be called directly on element objects. For example, you make a selection with jQuery like `$('li')` or `$(this)` and then call the plugin method, like `$('li').Select()`. When the method is called, the selection of elements that you've made is passed to the plugin method as an array, in the `this` keyword.

```
Select: function() {
  return $(this).addClass('tmpSelected');
},
```

In the preceding snippet, the `Select()` method is a custom jQuery plugin, and it expects an array of element objects to be present in the `this` keyword. The `this` keyword is wrapped in a call to jQuery, then the `addClass()` method is called, which adds a class name to one or more items … allowing the `Select()` method to work whether one item is passed or several. Then at the end of your plugin method, you return the jQuery object, so that you preserve chainability of methods.

There are two components that are universally applicable to jQuery plugin development: The `this` keyword contains an array of one or more items, and the function returns the jQuery object. These two components let you include your custom plugin just like any other jQuery function call and allow you to make a selection, call your custom method, then chain additional methods onto that function call.

Another way that plugins are used is to call plugin methods directly. In the preceding example, you see an object called `MyApplication`, which contains a method called `Ready()`. The `Ready()` method is called directly at the jQuery `ready()` event by using the code `$.fn.MyApplication.Ready()`. The call to `$.fn.MyApplication.Ready()` is an example of a plugin that is called directly rather than via a chain to a selection, as was the case with the `Select()` method.

In the following "Try It Out," you try writing a jQuery plugin for yourself:

Try It Out Writing a jQuery Plugin

Example 9-1

To write your first jQuery plugin, follow these steps.

1. Key in the following HTML document:

```
<!DOCTYPE html PUBLIC "-//W3C//DTD XHTML 1.0 Strict//EN"
    "http://www.w3.org/TR/xhtml1/DTD/xhtml1-strict.dtd">
<html xmlns='http://www.w3.org/1999/xhtml' xml:lang='en'>
  <head>
    <meta http-equiv='content-type' content='text/html; charset=utf-8' />
    <meta http-equiv='content-language' content='en-us' />
    <title></title>
    <script type='text/javascript'
            src='../../../Source Code/jQuery/jQuery.js'></script>
    <script type='text/javascript'
            src='../../../Source Code/jQuery/jQueryUI.js'></script>
    <script type='text/javascript' src='Example 9-1.js'></script>
    <link type='text/css' href='Example 9-1.css' rel='stylesheet' />
  </head>
  <body>
    <div>
      <p>
        jQuery plugins give you the ability to extend jQuery's functionality,
        quickly and seamlessly.  In this example you see how to make a context
        menu plugin, that handles everything you need to make a context menu
        widget in self-contained jQuery plugin.
      </p>
      <ul>
        <li>This is  a context menu item.</li>
      </ul>
    </div>
  </body>
</html>
```

2. Save the preceding HTML document as *Example 9-1.html.*
3. Enter the following CSS document:

```
body {
    font: 12px "Lucida Grande", Arial, sans-serif;
    background: #fff;
    color: rgb(50, 50, 50);
}
body,
html {
    width: 100%;
    height: 100%;
    margin: 0;
    padding: 0;
}
div {
    position: absolute;
```

```
    width: 100%;
    height: 100%;
}
p {
    padding: 5px;
}
ul.tmpContextMenu {
    list-style: none;
    margin: 0;
    padding: 5px;
    border: 1px solid rgb(200, 200, 200);
    position: absolute;
    top: 0;
    left: 0;
    background: lightblue;
    width: 200px;
    min-height: 200px;
    display: none;
}
li {
    padding: 3px;
}
```

4. Save the preceding style sheet as *Example 9-1.css.*

5. Enter the following JavaScript document:

```
$.fn.extend({
  ContextMenu: function() {
    this.each(
      function() {
        $(this).addClass('tmpContextMenu');

        $(this).hover(
          function() {
            $.data(this, 'ContextMenu', true);
          },
          function() {
            $.data(this, 'ContextMenu', false);
          }
        );

        // Only attach the following event once.
        if (!$.data(document, 'MouseDown')) {
          $.data(document, 'MouseDown', true);
          $(document).mousedown(
            function() {
              $('.tmpContextMenu').each(
                function() {
                  if (!$.data(this, 'ContextMenu')) {
                    $(this).hide();
                  }
                }
              );
            }
```

```
    );
}

$(this).parent().bind(
  'contextmenu',
  function($e) {
    $e.preventDefault();

    // The contextmenu doesn't work in Opera.
    // Guess those four users will just have to do without.
    var $menu = $(this).find('.tmpContextMenu');

    $menu.show();

    // The following bit gets the dimensions of the viewport
    var $vpx, $vpy;

    if (self.innerHeight) {
      // all except Explorer
      $vpx = self.innerWidth;
      $vpy = self.innerHeight;
    } else if (document.documentElement &&
               document.documentElement.clientHeight) {
      // Explorer 6 Strict Mode
      $vpx = document.documentElement.clientWidth;
      $vpy = document.documentElement.clientHeight;
    } else if (document.body) {
      // other Explorers
      $vpx = document.body.clientWidth;
      $vpy = document.body.clientHeight;
    }

    // Reset offset values to their defaults
    $menu.css({
      top:    'auto',
      right:  'auto',
      bottom: 'auto',
      left:   'auto'
    });

    /**
    * If the height or width of the context menu is greater than the amount
    * of pixels from the point of click to the right or bottom edge of the
    * viewport adjust the offset accordingly
    */
    if ($menu.outerHeight() > ($vpy - $e.pageY)) {
      $menu.css('bottom', ($vpy - $e.pageY) + 'px');
    } else {
      $menu.css('top', $e.pageY + 'px');
    }

    if ($menu.outerWidth() > ($vpx - $e.pageX)) {
      $menu.css('right',  ($vpx - $e.pageX) + 'px');
    } else {
```

```
                    $menu.css('left', $e.pageX + 'px');
                  }
                }
              );
            }
          );

          return $(this);
        },
        MyApplication: {
          Ready: function() {
            $('ul').ContextMenu();
          }
        }
      });

      $(document).ready(
        function() {
          $.fn.MyApplication.Ready();
        }
      );
```

6. Save the preceding document as *Example 9-1.js*. The preceding code results in the image that you see in **Figure 9-3**.

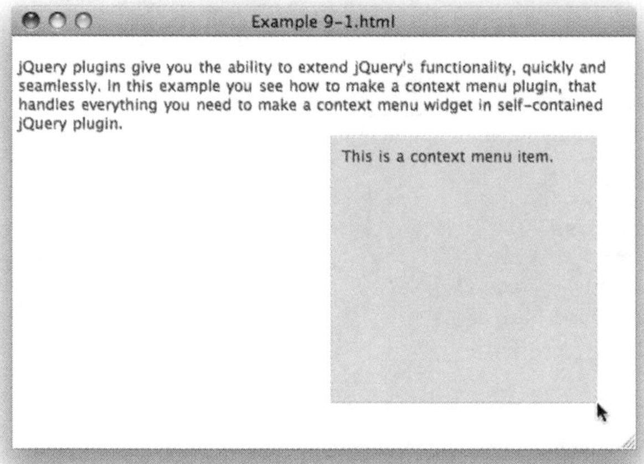

Figure 9-3

In Example 9-1, you took the context menu example that you learned about in Chapter 6 and learned how to turn that into an extensible, reusable jQuery plugin called *ContextMenu*. The plugin that you made allows you to make any item in a document into a context menu by simply calling the `ContextMenu()` method on that item and defining a few styles in your style sheet.

The math and logic that take place in this example do expect a context menu that's positioned relative to the viewport, but you begin to see how you might make a reusable jQuery plugin that attempts to do as much of the grunt work as possible, leaving you with just the aesthetic details.

The plugin that you create expects to make whatever elements you select into context menus. Those elements' parent element is automatically affixed with the `contextmenu` event. The context menu logic causes the item that you make into a context menu to be revealed as the context menu whenever a right click is made on that element's parent element.

You begin by defining your plugin with the `$.fn.extend()` method. In this example, you pass an object literal to that method, which contains two items, a `ContextMenu()` method and a `MyApplication` object. When the ready event fires, the `Ready()` method of the `MyApplication` object is executed.

```
$(document).ready(
  function() {
    $.fn.MyApplication.Ready();
  }
);
```

In the `Ready()` method of the `MyApplication` object, all `<ul>` elements in the document are made into context menus. First, all `<ul>` elements are selected, then the `ContextMenu()` method is called.

```
  MyApplication: {
    Ready: function() {
      $('ul').ContextMenu();
    }
  }
```

The call to the `ContextMenu()` method conjures up your home-brewed jQuery plugin. The first bits of logic that occur within the `ContextMenu()` method immediately begin an iteration using jQuery's `each()` method, iterating over the one or more items present in the `this` keyword. The `this` keyword at this point is expected to contain just one `<ul>` element, but you could have selected multiple `<ul>` elements, and the plugin logic supports that scenario as well.

```
$.fn.extend({
  ContextMenu: function() {
    this.each(
      function() {
```

Each item selected to be a context menu is given the class name *tmpContextMenu*, which gives you the ability to style your context menu with CSS.

```
        $(this).addClass('tmpContextMenu');
```

The next block adds a jQuery `hover` event to your context menu that's used to track whether the mouse cursor is over the context menu or not. To keep track of whether the mouse cursor is over your context menu, you use jQuery's `$.data()` method, which is provided by jQuery for temporarily storing data associated with an object or element. To store a value, the `$.data()` method takes three arguments: the element you want the data associated with, the name you want to associate with the data you're storing, and the value you want to store. You can think of this feature like adding a custom property or attribute to an element. In this case, you use jQuery's `hover` event to set the value of `ContextMenu` to `true` when the mouse cursor is over the context menu, and conversely, you set the value of `ContextMenu` to `false` when the mouse cursor leaves the context menu.

```
$(this).hover(
  function() {
    $.data(this, 'ContextMenu', true);
  },
  function() {
    $.data(this, 'ContextMenu', false);
  }
);
```

As you did in Chapter 6 by setting a global variable called `tmpContextMenu` to `true` or `false`, the preceding snippet of code provides the same functionality, but allows you to have multiple context menus, since it associates the toggle with each context menu individually, rather than a single global variable. Tracking the position of the mouse cursor helps you to implement closing the context menu when the user clicks anywhere in the document outside the context menu. Closing an inactive context menu is handled by the next snippet of code.

In the following snippet of code, you first check to see if the value of `MouseDown` is `false`, and if it is, you set it to `true`, then you attach a new `mousedown` event. Setting `MouseDown` to `true` prevents the `mousedown` event from being attached more than once, since this event only needs to be attached once per document regardless of how many context menus you add to the document.

```
// Only attach the following event once.
if (!$.data(document, 'MouseDown')) {
  $.data(document, 'MouseDown', true);
  $(document).mousedown(
    function() {
      $('.tmpContextMenu').each(
        function() {
          if (!$.data(this, 'ContextMenu')) {
            $(this).hide();
          }
        }
      );
    }
  );
}
```

When a `mousedown` event occurs, the preceding code iterates through each context menu element and checks the value of `ContextMenu` as attached to each of those elements using the `$.data()` method. If the value of `ContextMenu` is `false`, that means the mouse cursor is not over the context menu element, which means the user has clicked on the document outside the context menu, meaning the context menu should be closed.

The final bits of code handle the `contextmenu` event and positioning the context menu itself. The logic within the following code expects you to right-click on the context menu's parent element to trigger the context menu, and from the standpoint of logic and math, it also expects the context menu to be positioned relative to the viewport, rather than relative to its parent. This is typically how you want an application to work. Context menus are positioned globally with respect to your viewport; however, you'll have to take this into account while laying out your document, as you won't be able to absolutely position those parent elements, lest you change the positioning of the context menu. If you don't like that idea, it's easy to come up with new logic that expects you to make all context menus children of the `<body>` element, and specify the elements you want that context menu to be used on.

```
$(this).parent().bind(
  'contextmenu',
  function($e) {
    $e.preventDefault();
```

The logic and math behind the positioning of the context menu itself remains basically the same as you saw in Chapter 6.

Good Practice for jQuery Plugin Development

There are just a few things you should keep in mind while developing your own jQuery plugins:

- When developing jQuery plugins, it's considered good practice to always expect one or more items to be passed to your plugin, and to always return the jQuery object, whenever it makes sense and is possible to do so.
- I name my jQuery plugins using capital letters to avoid potential naming conflicts with other jQuery plugins. If you plan on using third-party jQuery plugins, you'll want to consider namespacing your own plugins in some way, so that your naming choices don't conflict with those of third-party plugins. I capitalize my plugin names because I find that capitalizing plugin names isn't very common among third-party developers and naturally lends itself to distinguishing my own local plugins from the ones obtained through third-party sources. Of course, this may not be enough, or you might not like that approach.
- If you're interested in developing official third-party jQuery plugins that follow all the recommended best practices put out by jQuery's developers, see the document located at `http://docs.jquery.com/Plugins/Authoring`.
- Finally, I'm not a big fan of having to write `$.fn` to refer to my plugin methods, so I choose to alias that to two dollar signs. So instead of writing `$.fn.MyApplication`, I write `$$.MyApplication`, which is made possible by writing `var $$ = $.fn`. I use this in the preceding chapters of this book, but this is another thing that I like doing personally that you may not like doing. I advocate doing whatever makes sense to you.

Summary

In this chapter, you learned the basic concepts needed to author your own jQuery plugin. You learned how jQuery plugins are created by passing an object literal to jQuery's `$.fn.extend()` method.

You learned how jQuery plugins expect to have one or more items passed to them, which are always present in the `this` keyword.

When you write jQuery plugins, you should return the jQuery object (when it makes sense and is possible to do so), since this preserves jQuery's magical ability to chain method calls onto one another.

Exercises

1. What method do you use to add a plugin to jQuery?
2. How are items you've selected with jQuery made available in your custom plugin?
3. What value should your plugin return?

Part II
jQuery UI

Implementing Drag-and-Drop

Beginning with this chapter, I shift discussion to the jQuery UI library. The *jQuery UI library* is a collection of reusable components that let you make user-interface functionality more quickly. The jQuery UI library handles a variety of tasks, like making elements in a document draggable or making a list of items that you can rearrange by drag-and-drop, and many other UI tasks that you learn about in the remaining chapters of this book.

The jQuery UI library is functionality that exists outside jQuery's core framework that you've been using and learning about throughout the preceding chapters of this book. The jQuery UI library is a series of jQuery plugins that each handles these different UI tasks, which in the spirit of jQuery's API, makes certain UI tasks much easier to implement.

You can download jQuery UI library components from `http://ui.jquery.com/download`. The website lets you customize your download based on which UI components you want to use, and it offers this customization so that you can add the least amount of JavaScript possible, which, in turn, reduces overhead like file size and bandwidth. The source code download for this book available free from `www.wrox.com` includes the entire jQuery UI package, which comprises all jQuery UI library plugins. For testing and learning purposes, this is fine; however, if you want to use UI library components in a real, production website, you should customize your jQuery UI library download to include only the components that you will use in your application, since the entire library is a sizable file weighing in at 229.56 KB packed (all white space, comments, and line breaks removed), or 347.82 KB fully unpacked and uncompressed … a fairly large file download.

In this chapter, I begin coverage of the jQuery UI library with the *Draggable* library. The Draggable library gives you the ability to make any element on a page draggable. In the most rudimentary sense, that means you can move elements around in a document with your mouse and arrange those elements however you like.

Making Elements Draggable

The jQuery UI library provides the ability to drag elements around in a document via its *Draggables* plugin. Making an element draggable is really easy: First, you need to include the UI library that includes the Draggables plugin; then, once you've made a selection with jQuery, you simply chain the method `draggable()` to the selection, like so:

```
$('div#tmpSomeElement').draggable();
```

The preceding code makes the `<div>` element with ID name *tmpSomeElement*, a draggable element, which means that you can move the element anywhere in the document with your mouse. The ability to make elements draggable gives you more options in terms of how your applications function, giving you many of the same options that you have developing desktop applications.

The actual code behind the scenes, enabling the drag operation, isn't too terribly complex, but it's yet another thing that jQuery allows you to take several lines of code and compress them into very little code. In this case, it's a simple function call!

To let you grasp just how easy it is to make an element draggable, the following "Try It Out" presents an example in which you create a file manager that looks like Mac OS X Leopard's Finder.

Try It Out — Implementing Drag-and-Drop Folders

Example 10-1

To try out jQuery's Draggables plugin, follow these steps:

1. Create the following markup document as *Example 10-1.html*:

```
<!DOCTYPE html PUBLIC "-//W3C//DTD XHTML 1.0 Strict//EN"
    "http://www.w3.org/TR/xhtml1/DTD/xhtml1-strict.dtd">
<html xmlns='http://www.w3.org/1999/xhtml' xml:lang='en'>
  <head>
    <meta http-equiv='content-type' content='text/html; charset=utf-8' />
    <meta http-equiv='content-language' content='en-us' />
    <title></title>
    <script type='text/javascript'
            src='../../../Source Code/jQuery/jQuery.js'></script>
    <script type='text/javascript'
            src='../../../Source Code/jQuery/jQueryUI.js'></script>
    <script type='text/javascript' src='Example 10-1.js'></script>
    <link type='text/css' href='Example 10-1.css' rel='stylesheet' />
    <!--[if lt IE 7]>
      <link type='text/css' href='Example 10-1.IE.css' rel='stylesheet' />
    <![endif]-->
  </head>
  <body>
    <div id="hFinderFiles">
      <div class="hFinderDirectory" title="/Applications">
        <div class="hFinderIcon"><div></div></div>
        <div class="hFinderDirectoryName">
          <span>Applications</span>
        </div>
      </div>
```

```
        <div class="hFinderDirectory" title="/Library">
          <div class="hFinderIcon"><div></div></div>
          <div class="hFinderDirectoryName">
            <span>Library</span>
          </div>
        </div>
        <div class="hFinderDirectory" title="/Network">
          <div class="hFinderIcon"><div></div></div>
          <div class="hFinderDirectoryName">
            <span>Network</span>
          </div>
        </div>
        <div class="hFinderDirectory" title="/Sites">
          <div class="hFinderIcon"><div></div></div>
          <div class="hFinderDirectoryName">
            <span>Sites</span>
          </div>
        </div>
        <div class="hFinderDirectory" title="/System">
          <div class="hFinderIcon"><div></div></div>
          <div class="hFinderDirectoryName">
            <span>System</span>
          </div>
        </div>
        <div class="hFinderDirectory" title="/Users">
          <div class="hFinderIcon"><div></div></div>
          <div class="hFinderDirectoryName">
            <span>Users</span>
          </div>
        </div>
      </div>
    </body>
  </html>
```

2. Add the following style sheet as *Example 10-1.css*:

```
html,
body {
    width: 100%;
    height: 100%;
}
body {
    font: 12px "Lucida Grande", Arial, sans-serif;
    background: rgb(189, 189, 189)
      url('../../../Images/Finder/Bottom.png') repeat-x bottom;
    color: rgb(50, 50, 50);
    margin: 0;
    padding: 0;
}
div#hFinderFiles {
    border-bottom: 1px solid rgb(64, 64, 64);
    background: #fff;
    position: absolute;
    top: 0;
    right: 0;
    bottom: 23px;
    left: 0;
```

```
        overflow: auto;
    }
    div.hFinderDirectory {
        float: left;
        width: 150px;
        height: 100px;
        overflow: hidden;
    }
    div.hFinderIcon {
        height: 56px;
        width: 54px;
        margin: 10px auto 3px auto;
    }
    div.hFinderIcon div {
        background: url('../../../Images/Finder/Folder 48x48.png')
          no-repeat center;
        width: 48px;
        height: 48px;
        margin: auto;
    }
    div.hFinderIconSelected {
        background-color: rgb(196, 196, 196);
        -moz-border-radius: 5px;
        -webkit-border-radius: 5px;
    }
    div.hFinderDirectoryName {
        text-align: center;
    }
    span.hFinderDirectoryNameSelected {
        background: rgb(56, 117, 215);
        -moz-border-radius: 8px;
        -webkit-border-radius: 8px;
        color: white;
        padding: 1px 7px;
    }
```

3. Create the following document as *Example 10-1.IE.css*:

```
div#hFinderFiles {
    height: expression(document.body.offsetHeight - 23);
    width: expression(document.body.offsetWidth);
}
div.hFinderIcon div {
    background: none;
    filter: progid:DXImageTransform.Microsoft.AlphaImageLoader
      (src='../../../Images/Finder/Folder 48x48.png', sizingMethod='crop');
}
```

4. Create the following document as *Example 10-1.js*.

```
$(document).ready(
  function() {
    $('div.hFinderDirectory').mousedown(
      function() {
        $('div.hFinderDirectory').not(this)
          .find('div.hFinderIcon')
```

```
                .removeClass('hFinderIconSelected');

            $('div.hFinderDirectory').not(this)
              .find('div.hFinderDirectoryName span')
                .removeClass('hFinderDirectoryNameSelected');

            $(this).find('div.hFinderIcon')
              .addClass('hFinderIconSelected');

            $(this).find('div.hFinderDirectoryName span')
              .addClass('hFinderDirectoryNameSelected');
          }
        )
        .draggable();
    }
);
```

The preceding source code results in the document that you see in **Figure 10-1**.

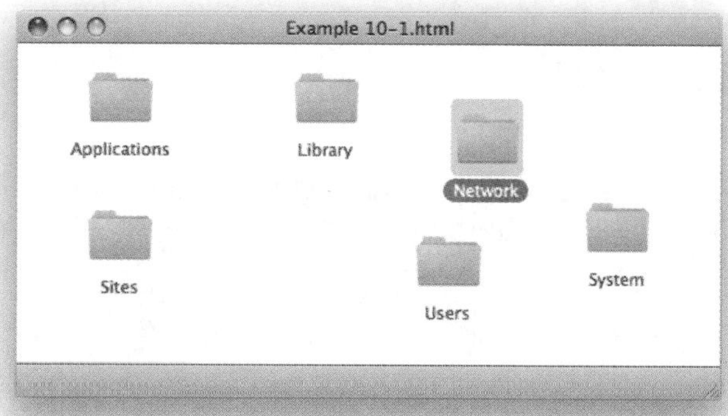

Figure 10-1

In the preceding example, you created a layout of folders that resembles Mac OS X Finder in Leopard. The only difference you'll notice between browsers is that the rounded-corner effect present on selected folders only comes through on WebKit and Gecko browsers, while IE and Opera show square corners. This is because I've used the experimental CSS properties `-moz-border-radius` and `-webkit-border-radius` to produce this effect, which only works in Gecko and WebKit browsers, respectively. If I were to go the extra mile and produce that effect in all browsers, I would have to use static background images and possibly still more markup. Additionally, highlighting the filename with rounded corners would be more difficult, if not impossible to pull off, since this requires the rounded corners to be applied to inline elements, like the `<span>` element in this example, where if the name of the folder wraps to a new line, you have the background applied to each line and only to the background of the text. In other words, the background *hugs* the text, like you see in **Figure 10-2**.

Figure 10-2

In **Figure 10-2**, you see that the blue background with rounded corners hugs the text, causing the width of the background to vary with the width of the text. **Figure 10-2** shows what Safari does with its rounded corners, and even this is inconsistent with what the real Finder does, which is shown in **Figure 10-3**.

Figure 10-3

So, given that making the look true to the real Finder is a bit of a tall order and, given the limitations of the browsers involved, to avoid that complication, I simply accept that IE and Opera have square boxes.

In a nutshell, the gist of this example allows you to select a single folder at a time and drag those folders around to any position in the window.

To make the elements draggable, you included the jQuery UI library, which includes all of the jQuery UI plugins, including the Draggables plugin.

```
<script type='text/javascript'
        src='../../../Source Code/jQuery/jQueryUI.js'></script>
```

The markup in this example is pretty straightforward. The individual folders are all contained in the `<div>` element with ID name *hFinderFiles*; this container element is needed to assist in controlling the presentation of the folders.

```
<div id="hFinderFiles">
```

Each folder resides in a container `<div>` element with the class name *hFinderDirectory*, with the path to the directory being contained in the `title` attribute, which could then be used to implement AJAX functionality, where the path of the folder is submitted asynchronously to the server and the server responds with the contents of that folder. Each folder has an icon and a name, so markup is put in place for each of these. The reasoning behind this specific structure makes more sense once you examine the style sheet, but you create one `<div>` element for the icon, which contains a nested `<div>` element. The outer `<div>` element controls the position of the icon and sets the dimensions for the highlighted style. Then the name of the folder is contained in another `<div>` element, which has the name of the folder nested in a `<span>` element. The `<span>` element is used so that the when the folder is highlighted, the background is applied to an inline element, and the background hugs the text, even if the text takes up multiple lines, as you saw in **Figure 10-1**.

```
<div class="hFinderDirectory" title="/Applications">
  <div class="hFinderIcon"><div></div></div>
  <div class="hFinderDirectoryName">
    <span>Applications</span>
  </div>
</div>
```

The style sheet does all the work of making this raw lump of structural markup into a Finder-imitating document. The following reviews each rule in the style sheet and explains why each is needed:

In this example, you put each folder in a container `<div>` element, which will be absolutely positioned later in the style sheet. The styles that position that `<div>` element rely on the specification of opposing offset properties to imply width and height, and as you already saw in the iCal-clone that I presented in Chapter 7, that technique doesn't work in IE6. So, as you did in that example, you must give the `<html>` and `<body>` elements 100 percent width and height, so that the presentation in IE can be fixed. This is needed because, in the IE style sheet that you made, the container `<div>` element is given dimensions that are based on the dimensions of the `<body>` element, and for that to work, you need the `<body>` element to take up the entire viewport, which is why you apply the following rule:

```
html,
body {
    width: 100%;
    height: 100%;
}
```

In the next rule, you give the Finder a Lucida Grande font, which is a Mac font used for many Mac applications. If that font isn't around, you fall back on Arial, which is present on Windows, or otherwise, if that font is not present, you fall back on the generic sans-serif font. The `background` is set to gray, then an image is tiled across the bottom of the window so that this document looks just like the real Finder. The font `color` is set to a very dark gray, and finally, the default `padding` and `margin` are removed from the `<body>` element.

```
body {
    font: 12px "Lucida Grande", Arial, sans-serif;
    background: rgb(189, 189, 189)
      url('../../../Images/Finder/Bottom.png') repeat-x bottom;
    color: rgb(50, 50, 50);
    margin: 0;
    padding: 0;
}
```

The next rule positions the `<div>` element with ID name *hFinderFiles*, which contains all the folders. This `<div>` element is positioned absolutely and is set to take up the entire viewport, except the bottom 23 pixels, and that is done by specifying opposing offset properties to imply width and height. The `background` is set to white, there is a dark gray border placed across the bottom of the container, and finally, the `overflow: auto;` declaration is added so that when you have more folders and files than the container can hold, a scrollbar appears so you can access everything.

```
div#hFinderFiles {
    border-bottom: 1px solid rgb(64, 64, 64);
    background: #fff;
    position: absolute;
    top: 0;
    right: 0;
    bottom: 23px;
    left: 0;
    overflow: auto;
}
```

The remaining style-sheet declarations set up the folders themselves. The next rule puts the folders side-by-side and gives each fixed dimensions. The `overflow: hidden;` declaration prevents long folder names from extending outside the bounds of the container.

```
div.hFinderDirectory {
    float: left;
    width: 150px;
    height: 100px;
    overflow: hidden;
}
```

The next two rules handle the display of the folder icon. You need an inner and an outer `<div>` to display the folder icon. This could actually be done with a single `<div>` element, if it weren't for the fact that IE6 doesn't handle PNG transparency, and, to force IE into displaying the PNG image correctly, you have to use IE's proprietary filter property, which doesn't allow you to center the image. So, the outer `<div>` element sets the dimensions of the icon with the highlighting effect in mind, and the gray background applied to a selected folder is applied to this outer `<div>` element. The inner `<div>` element has the same dimensions of the background image that's being loaded, the folder icon, and it is centered within the outer `<div>` element using the `margin: auto;` declaration. The result is a folder icon that looks like the real Finder in Mac OS X.

```
div.hFinderIcon {
    height: 56px;
    width: 54px;
    margin: 10px auto 3px auto;
}
div.hFinderIcon div {
    background: url('../../../Images/Finder/Folder 48x48.png')
      no-repeat center;
    width: 48px;
    height: 48px;
    margin: auto;
}
```

The following rule defines the style for a selected folder. The class name *hFinderIconSelected* is applied to the `<div>` element with class name *hFinderIcon* dynamically using jQuery.

```
div.hFinderIconSelected {
    background-color: rgb(196, 196, 196);
    -moz-border-radius: 5px;
    -webkit-border-radius: 5px;
}
The next rule centers the name of the folder.
div.hFinderDirectoryName {
    text-align: center;
}
```

And finally, the last rule sets the style for the selected folder's name. A blue background, a little padding, white text, and rounded corners are added to make the folder name look more like the real Finder.

```
span.hFinderDirectoryNameSelected {
    background: rgb(56, 117, 215);
    -moz-border-radius: 8px;
    -webkit-border-radius: 8px;
```

```
        color: white;
        padding: 1px 7px;
    }
```

The IE style sheet fixes a couple of display glitches in IE6. The first rule sets the dimensions of the `div#hFinderFiles` so that the `<div>` element has dimensions based on those of the `<body>` element, which you previously made take up the entire viewport with 100 percent width and height, removing both default padding and margin. This is because some browsers apply default padding to `<body>` and others apply default margin to `<body>`. The width and height of the `<div>` are set by using a CSS expression, which is IE-proprietary. CSS expressions should be used sparingly, if used at all, since they can affect performance and lead to difficult-to-locate JavaScript errors. JavaScript errors occurring in CSS expressions come up in an alert in IE, complaining about an error in the main HTML file, at line 1, instead of the relevant line of the CSS file in which the error appears. You may be better off correcting glitches like this from JavaScript, instead of CSS. On the other hand, this fix is limited to IE6 — a browser that is becoming obsolete (let's hope as soon as possible). In any case, if you do use CSS expressions, just remember to check your IE style sheet if you see that JavaScript error.

```
div#hFinderFiles {
    height: expression(document.body.offsetHeight - 23);
    width: expression(document.body.offsetWidth);
}
```

The second rule in the IE style sheet fixes the PNG transparency of the folder icon by using IE's proprietary filter property. The background image is removed, and the filter is applied using the same image. This gets rid of the light-blue/gray background around the folder icon, making that part of the image transparent.

```
div.hFinderIcon div {
    background: none;
    filter: progid:DXImageTransform.Microsoft.AlphaImageLoader
      (src='../../../Images/Finder/Folder 48x48.png', sizingMethod='crop');
}
```

And as you've no doubt come to expect, the JavaScript portion of this example is very simple. You start with the code that's required to make a folder selectable, which is done by adding a `mousedown` event. A `mousedown` event is used instead of, say, a `click` event, because you want a selection to take place even if the user moves the mouse cursor outside the boundaries of the folder while the button is pressed. If the user moves the cursor while the button is pressed, that causes the element to be dragged, and because of that, you want the folder to be selected to show the user that the folder they are dragging is selected.

```
        $('div.hFinderDirectory').mousedown(
          function() {
          }
        )
```

Inside that `mousedown` event, you write some logic for selecting the folder. This is done by selecting every folder except the one that's being clicked on, and removing the class name *hFinderIconSelected* from the `div.hFinderIcon` element inside each folder. Then you make the same selection again, but this time, you remove the class name *hFinderDirectoryNameSelected* from the `div.hFinderDirectoryName span` of every folder, except the one that's being clicked on. Then you add those same class names to the `div.hFinderIcon` and `div.hFinderDirectoryName span` of the folder that's being selected.

```
$('div.hFinderDirectory').not(this)
  .find('div.hFinderIcon')
    .removeClass('hFinderIconSelected');

$('div.hFinderDirectory').not(this)
  .find('div.hFinderDirectoryName span')
    .removeClass('hFinderDirectoryNameSelected');

$(this).find('div.hFinderIcon')
  .addClass('hFinderIconSelected');

$(this).find('div.hFinderDirectoryName span')
  .addClass('hFinderDirectoryNameSelected');
```

Then, finally, you made each folder draggable, by chaining the method `draggable()` to the call to `mousedown()`. The jQuery UI `draggable()` method lets you move the folders in the document to any position you like, kind of how Mac OS X's Finder works by default, allowing you to arrange the folders however you like. But the jQuery UI `draggable()` method lets you do much more than just this.

Making Elements Draggable with Ghosting

Let's say that you want to make the folder icons in Example 10-1 behave in a more sane and useful way, as, for example, if you wanted to make your folders so that you can drag-and-drop one folder onto another. The jQuery UI `draggable()` method lets you do this too. In fact, the jQuery UI `draggable()` method has a lot of options that you can tinker with to customize how a drag operation works. Like the `$.ajax()` method that you saw in Chapter 7 or the `css()` method that you saw in Chapter 6, you can pass an object literal to the `draggable()` method, which defines options that tweak how the `draggable()` method works.

One option that you have available to use is called *ghosting*. *Ghosting* occurs when you start dragging an element, and instead of moving the original element, a clone of the original element is created, with the same dimensions and look and feel, and that element is dragged instead. One example of this is when you open Finder, or Explorer on Windows, and move a folder. When you drag a folder, a semitransparent copy of the folder is created, and you can drag that image around, usually, to drop it on another folder icon so that you move the folder to a new location. **Figure 10-4** shows an example of ghosting in Leopard's Finder.

To add the ghosting effect to your faux Finder, the JavaScript you need looks like this:

```
$('div.hFinderDirectory').draggable({
  helper: 'clone',
  opacity: 0.5
});
```

You need to specify two options — `helper` and `opacity`. The `helper` option can take one of two string values, *`original`* or *`clone`*. The value *`original`* produces the same effect that you observed in Example 10-1, which lets you move the elements around the document. The value *`clone`* causes the drag to produce the ghosting effect that you see in **Figure 10-4**, where a copy of the item is made. The other option, `opacity`, controls the transparency of the element you're dragging. Just like the CSS `opacity` property supported by various browsers, this option takes a float between 0, which is fully transparent, and 1, which is fully opaque. A value of 0.5 produces 50 percent transparency. The following "Try It Out" adds this code to your Finder clone:

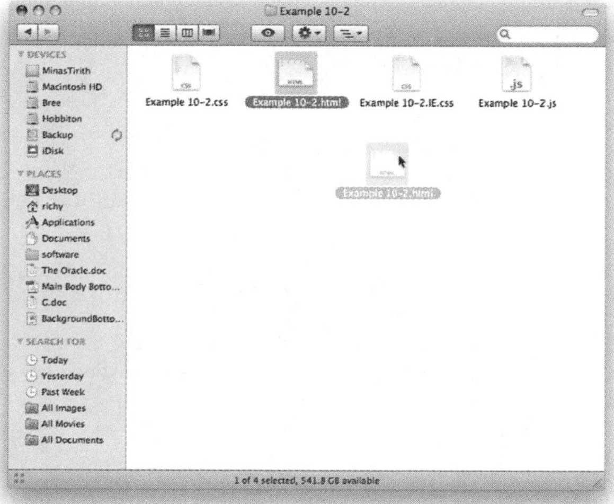

Figure 10-4

Try It Out — Adding a Ghosting Effect to Your Finder

Example 10-2

To add ghosting to your Finder, follow these steps:

1. Copy the files from Example 10-1 to Example 10-2.html, Example 10-2.css, Example 10-2.IE.css, Example 10-2.js, and so on.
2. In the newly copied Example 10-2.html, update the file references to Example 10-2.

```
<!DOCTYPE html PUBLIC "-//W3C//DTD XHTML 1.0 Strict//EN"
    "http://www.w3.org/TR/xhtml1/DTD/xhtml1-strict.dtd">
<html xmlns='http://www.w3.org/1999/xhtml' xml:lang='en'>
  <head>
    <meta http-equiv='content-type' content='text/html; charset=utf-8' />
    <meta http-equiv='content-language' content='en-us' />
    <title></title>
    <script type='text/javascript'
            src='../../../Source Code/jQuery/jQuery.js'></script>
    <script type='text/javascript'
            src='../../../Source Code/jQuery/jQueryUI.js'></script>
    <script type='text/javascript' src='Example 10-2.js'></script>
    <link type='text/css' href='Example 10-2.css' rel='stylesheet' />
    <!--[if lt IE 7]>
      <link type='text/css' href='Example 10-2.IE.css' rel='stylesheet' />
    <![endif]-->
  </head>
  <body>
```

3. Modify Example 10-2.js, adding new code to the call to `draggable()`:

```
$(document).ready(
  function() {
    $('div.hFinderDirectory').mousedown(
      function() {
        $('div.hFinderDirectory').not(this)
          .find('div.hFinderIcon')
            .removeClass('hFinderIconSelected');

        $('div.hFinderDirectory').not(this)
          .find('div.hFinderDirectoryName span')
            .removeClass('hFinderDirectoryNameSelected');

        $(this).find('div.hFinderIcon')
          .addClass('hFinderIconSelected');

        $(this).find('div.hFinderDirectoryName span')
          .addClass('hFinderDirectoryNameSelected');
      }
    )
    .draggable({
      helper: 'clone',
      opacity: 0.5
    });
  }
);
```

The preceding improvements result in what you see in **Figure 10-5**.

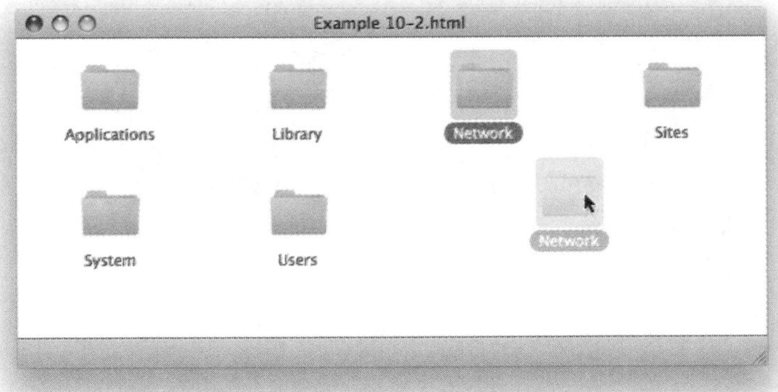

Figure 10-5

In the preceding example, you see the first part of what you need to make a drag-and-drop user interface for a file manager, which, at this point comes to exactly four lines of code in your application, and the inclusion of the jQuery UI Draggables plugin. The `helper` option, with a value of `clone`, gives you the same ghosting effect that you observe in your Operating System's native file manager. This is combined with the `opacity` option, which lets your effect mirror the native file manager's effect. And that's all there is to it!

Dragging between Windows in Safari

As I was preparing the material for this chapter, I noticed that the jQuery UI Draggables plugin fails to use Safari on Mac OS X's native Drag-and-Drop API. The only reason that I feel this is worth mentioning, is Safari's native Drag-and-Drop API lets you do something very cool: It lets you drag-and-drop items not only within the same browser window, but also between completely separate browser windows. This capability lets you have web-based file management that really mimics native OS file management in just about every way. And beyond just file management, it also makes for some other interesting UI scenarios, for example, dragging and dropping image thumbnails from one window to another to manage content.

The simple elegance of this technique is also too juicy to pass on, because it requires ridiculously minimal modifications to take advantage of. Unfortunately, for you Windows folks and even users of browsers other than Safari on the Mac, there is no comparable technique available. However, I thought the concept was worth presenting all the same in the hopes of raising awareness that we as developers need features like this to make truly compelling and usable web-based applications, and just because you can't use the technique in all browsers doesn't mean that you can't provide the sugar for the browser that does support it … simply out of convenience to those users.

The following "Try It Out" shows you how to make the drag portion of a drag-and-drop implementation work between windows in Safari. Unfortunately, this technique is incompatible with the jQuery UI Draggables implementation, so if you want to offer this feature, you'll need to work around this in your code. The following shows you how to do this:

Try It Out — Implementing Safari's Native Drag-and-Drop API

Example 10-3

To implement Safari's native Drag-and-Drop API, follow these steps:

1. Copy the files you made for Example 10-2 to Example 10-3.html, Example 10-3.css, Example 10-3.IE.css, and Example 10-3.js.
2. Modify the Example 10-3.html file you just created, so that the file references each point to the right file.

```
<!DOCTYPE html PUBLIC "-//W3C//DTD XHTML 1.0 Strict//EN"
    "http://www.w3.org/TR/xhtml1/DTD/xhtml1-strict.dtd">
<html xmlns='http://www.w3.org/1999/xhtml' xml:lang='en'>
  <head>
    <meta http-equiv='content-type' content='text/html; charset=utf-8' />
    <meta http-equiv='content-language' content='en-us' />
    <title></title>
    <script type='text/javascript'
            src='../../../Source Code/jQuery/jQuery.js'></script>
    <script type='text/javascript'
            src='../../../Source Code/jQuery/jQueryUI.js'></script>
```

```
    <script type='text/javascript' src='Example 10-3.js'></script>
    <link type='text/css' href='Example 10-3.css' rel='stylesheet' />
    <!--[if lt IE 7]>
      <link type='text/css' href='Example 10-3.IE.css' rel='stylesheet' />
    <![endif]-->
  </head>
  <body>
```

3. Modify the style sheet, Example 10-3.css. The modifications that you make will enable Safari's native Drag-and-Drop API.

```
div.hFinderDirectory {
    float: left;
    width: 150px;
    height: 100px;
    overflow: hidden;
    -khtml-user-drag: element;
}
div.hFinderDirectory:-khtml-drag {
    opacity: 0.5;
}
```

4. Modify Example 10-3.js like so:

```
$(document).ready(
  function() {
    $('div.hFinderDirectory').mousedown(
      function() {
        $('div.hFinderDirectory').not(this)
          .find('div.hFinderIcon')
            .removeClass('hFinderIconSelected');

        $('div.hFinderDirectory').not(this)
          .find('div.hFinderDirectoryName span')
            .removeClass('hFinderDirectoryNameSelected');

        $(this).find('div.hFinderIcon')
          .addClass('hFinderIconSelected');

        $(this).find('div.hFinderDirectoryName span')
          .addClass('hFinderDirectoryNameSelected');
      }
    );

    if (!($.browser.safari && navigator.appVersion.indexOf('Mac') != -1)) {
      $('div.hFinderDirectory').draggable({
        helper: 'clone',
        opacity: 0.5
      });
    }
  }
);
```

These modifications make it so that you can drag a folder from one browser window to another, which you see in **Figure 10-6**.

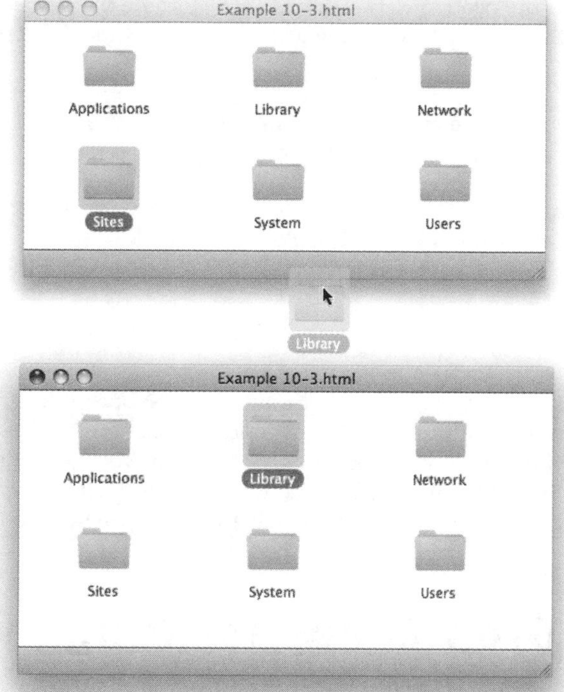

Figure 10-6

In Example 10-3, you enable Safari's native Drag-and-Drop API. Unfortunately, this API only works in the Mac version of Safari and doesn't work in the Windows version of Safari, or Google Chrome. I expect that will change with some future iteration of WebKit. Using Safari's native Drag-and-Drop API gives you one big advantage for users of that browser on a Mac, in that it lets you drag elements between multiple windows, instead of confining you to only one browser window. The implementation is very easy, so it's not too much of a hassle to make the added functionality available, and users of other browsers still get the jQuery UI Draggables plugin. The first thing you did to enable this functionality is add a single declaration to the following rule:

```
div.hFinderDirectory {
    float: left;
    width: 150px;
    height: 100px;
    overflow: hidden;
    -khtml-user-drag: element;
}
```

The declaration `-khtml-user-drag: element;` makes each folder draggable. Then, to style the element being dragged, you added a new rule:

```
div.hFinderDirectory:-khtml-drag {
    opacity: 0.5;
}
```

The preceding rule uses the pseudo-class `:-khtml-drag` to style the element being dragged; the style you apply is the same that you applied for the `draggable()` method, 50 percent opacity via the declaration `opacity: 0.5`.

In the JavaScript, you wrap some browser detection around the call to the `draggable()` method so that method is executed for every browser except Safari Mac.

```
if (!($.browser.safari && navigator.appVersion.indexOf('Mac') != -1)) {
  $('div.hFinderDirectory').draggable({
    helper: 'clone',
    opacity: 0.5
  });
}
```

jQuery lets you detect the browser via `$.browser` and then a subproperty. `$.browser.safari` checks for not only Safari, but any WebKit browser. Then you look inside the `navigator.appVersion` string to see what OS the script is executing on, looking for the string *Mac*. And thus it is that you allow Safari's native Drag-and-Drop API in Safari on OS X, and use the jQuery UI Draggables plugin for all the other browsers. The modifications needed were extremely minimal, just six additional lines of code.

Delegating Drop Zones for Dragged Elements

Typically when you implement dragging on elements in your document, you want to delegate somewhere else for the elements being dragged to be dropped. jQuery UI provides another plugin for handling the drop portion, called *Droppables*. The jQuery UI Droppables plugin lets you create and manipulate a variety of things associated with dropping one element onto another, including what happens while you're dragging one element over a drop zone and what happens when a drop takes place. jQuery allows you to have precision control over drag-and-drop, which lets you create a very basic drag-and-drop implementation or a very polished drag-and-drop implementation.

As you've already seen for the Draggables API, jQuery UI provides a concise, easy-to-use API for handling the drop side. To make an element into a droppable element, all you have to do is make a selection and call the `droppable()` method with the appropriate options. Like the `draggable()` method, options are provided via an object literal consisting of key, value pairs. The following example shows you what a droppable implementation looks like in the context of the Finder clone you've been building throughout this chapter:

```
$('div.hFinderDirectory').draggable({
  helper: 'clone',
  opacity: 0.5
})
.droppable({
  accept: 'div.hFinderDirectory',
  hoverClass: 'hFinderDirectoryDrop'
});
```

In the preceding code example, you have a really basic implementation of the Droppables API. Each `<div>` element with the class name *hFinderDirectory* is made into a drop zone, so that any directory can be dragged and dropped onto any other directory. To make the drop portion function properly, you pass some options to the `droppable()` method. The `accept` option lets you specify a selector that will be used to match what elements you want to allow to be dropped onto the drop zone; in this case, you only want to allow `<div>` elements with the class name *hFinderDirectory* to be dropped. Using this filter, you can add other drag-and-drop functionality in the same document, without having conflict between different drag-and-drop implementations. The `hoverClass` option allows you to change the style of the drop zone as a draggable element is being dragged over the droppable element. You simply specify a class name as the value, then set up the appropriate styles in your style sheet.

In the following "Try It Out," you take the basic concept of the Droppables API that I just demonstrated and apply the `droppable()` method to the Finder clone you've been building, complete with hacks for Internet Explorer 6 and an independently implemented Drag-and-Drop API for Safari on Mac OS X:

Try It Out Adding Drop Zones

Example 10-4

To add droppable functionality to the Finder clone, follow these steps:

1. Copy the files you made for Example 10-3 to Example 10-4.html, Example 10-4.css, Example 10-4.IE.css, and Example 10-4.js.

2. Modify the Example 10-4.html file you just created, so that the file references each point to the right file.

```
<!DOCTYPE html PUBLIC "-//W3C//DTD XHTML 1.0 Strict//EN"
    "http://www.w3.org/TR/xhtml1/DTD/xhtml1-strict.dtd">
<html xmlns='http://www.w3.org/1999/xhtml' xml:lang='en'>
  <head>
    <meta http-equiv='content-type' content='text/html; charset=utf-8' />
    <meta http-equiv='content-language' content='en-us' />
    <title></title>
    <script type='text/javascript'
            src='../../../Source Code/jQuery/jQuery.js'></script>
    <script type='text/javascript'
            src='../../../Source Code/jQuery/jQueryUI.js'></script>
    <script type='text/javascript' src='Example 10-4.js'></script>
    <link type='text/css' href='Example 10-4.css' rel='stylesheet' />
    <!--[if lt IE 7]>
      <link type='text/css' href='Example 10-4.IE.css' rel='stylesheet' />
    <![endif]-->
  </head>
  <body>
```

3. Make the following modifications to Example 10-4.css:

```
html,
body {
    width: 100%;
    height: 100%;
}
body {
    font: 12px "Lucida Grande", Arial, sans-serif;
    background: rgb(189, 189, 189)
      url('../../../Images/Finder/Bottom.png') repeat-x bottom;
    color: rgb(50, 50, 50);
```

```
    margin: 0;
    padding: 0;
}
div#hFinderFiles {
    border-bottom: 1px solid rgb(64, 64, 64);
    background: #fff;
    position: absolute;
    top: 0;
    right: 0;
    bottom: 23px;
    left: 0;
    overflow: auto;
}
div.hFinderDirectory {
    float: left;
    width: 150px;
    height: 100px;
    overflow: hidden;
    -khtml-user-drag: element;
}
div.hFinderDirectory:-khtml-drag {
    opacity: 0.5;
}
div.hFinderIcon {
    height: 56px;
    width: 54px;
    margin: 10px auto 3px auto;
}
div.hFinderIcon div {
    background: url('../../../Images/Finder/Folder 48x48.png')
      no-repeat center;
    width: 48px;
    height: 48px;
    margin: auto;
}
div.hFinderIconSelected,
div.hFinderDirectoryDrop div.hFinderIcon {
    background-color: rgb(196, 196, 196);
    -moz-border-radius: 5px;
    -webkit-border-radius: 5px;
}
div.hFinderDirectoryDrop div.hFinderIcon div {
    background-image:
      url('../../../Images/Finder/Open Folder 48x48.png');
}
div.hFinderDirectoryName {
    text-align: center;
}
span.hFinderDirectoryNameSelected,
div.hFinderDirectoryDrop span {
    background: rgb(56, 117, 215);
    -moz-border-radius: 8px;
    -webkit-border-radius: 8px;
    color: white;
    padding: 1px 7px;
}
```

4. Modify Example 10-4.js like so:

```
$(document).ready(
  function() {
    $('div.hFinderDirectory').mousedown(
      function() {
        $('div.hFinderDirectory').not(this)
          .find('div.hFinderIcon')
            .removeClass('hFinderIconSelected');

        $('div.hFinderDirectory').not(this)
          .find('div.hFinderDirectoryName span')
            .removeClass('hFinderDirectoryNameSelected');

        $(this).find('div.hFinderIcon')
          .addClass('hFinderIconSelected');

        $(this).find('div.hFinderDirectoryName span')
          .addClass('hFinderDirectoryNameSelected');
      }
    );

    if (!($.browser.safari && navigator.appVersion.indexOf('Mac') != -1)) {
      $('div.hFinderDirectory').draggable({
        helper: 'clone',
        opacity: 0.5
      })
      .droppable({
        accept: 'div.hFinderDirectory',
        hoverClass: 'hFinderDirectoryDrop',
        over: function(e, ui) {
          if ($.browser.msie && $.browser.version == 6.0) {
            $(this).find('div.hFinderIcon div').css({
              background: 'none',
              filter:
              "progid:DXImageTransform.Microsoft.AlphaImageLoader" +
              "(src='../../../Images/Finder/Open Folder 48x48.png'," +
                "sizingMethod='crop')"
            });
          }
        },
        out: function(e, ui) {
          if ($.browser.msie && $.browser.version == 6.0) {
            $(this).find('div.hFinderIcon div').css({
              background: 'none',
              filter:
                "progid:DXImageTransform.Microsoft.AlphaImageLoader" +
                "(src='../../../Images/Finder/Folder 48x48.png'," +
                  "sizingMethod='crop')"
            });
          }
        },
        drop: function(e, ui) {
          var $path = ui.draggable.attr('title');
          // Do something with the path

          // Remove the element that was dropped.
```

```
          ui.draggable.remove();
        }
      });
    } else {
      // Safari Mac OS X Native API
      var dragElement;

      $('div.hFinderDirectory').each(
        function() {
          // jQuery's event API does not provide the dataTransfer
          // object.
          this.addEventListener(
            'dragstart',
            function($e) {
              // The setData method lets you save some data
              // for the element being dragged.
              $e.dataTransfer.setData('Text', $(this).attr('title'));

              // Remeber the drag element.
              dragElement = $(this);
            }, false
          );

          this.addEventListener(
            'dragenter',
            function($e) {
              // Browser default behavior is canceled.
              $e.preventDefault();
            }, false
          );

          this.addEventListener(
            'dragover',
            function($e) {
              $e.preventDefault();
              // Add the style for the folder being dragged over
              // But not if the drag element is being dragged over itself.
              if (dragElement.attr('title') != $(this).attr('title')) {
                $(this).addClass('hFinderDirectoryDrop');
              }
            }
          );

          this.addEventListener(
            'dragleave',
            function($e) {
              $e.preventDefault();
              // Remove the style when the drag item leaves the
              // drop zone.
              $(this).removeClass('hFinderDirectoryDrop');
            }
          );

          this.addEventListener(
```

```
                    'drop',
                    function($e) {
                      var $path = $e.dataTransfer.getData('Text');
                      // Do something with the path

                      // Delete the drag element.
                      dragElement.remove();
                      $e.preventDefault();
                    }, false
                  );
                }
              );
            }
          }
        );
```

The preceding source code gives you output like you see in **Figure 10-7**, in Safari on Mac OS X.

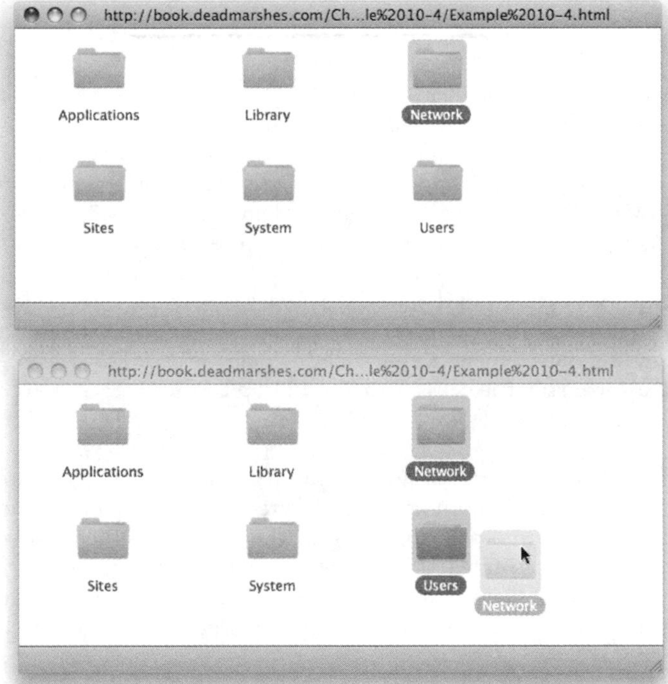

Figure 10-7

Figure 10-8 shows you what this example looks like in Internet Explorer 8 Beta 2 on Windows Vista.

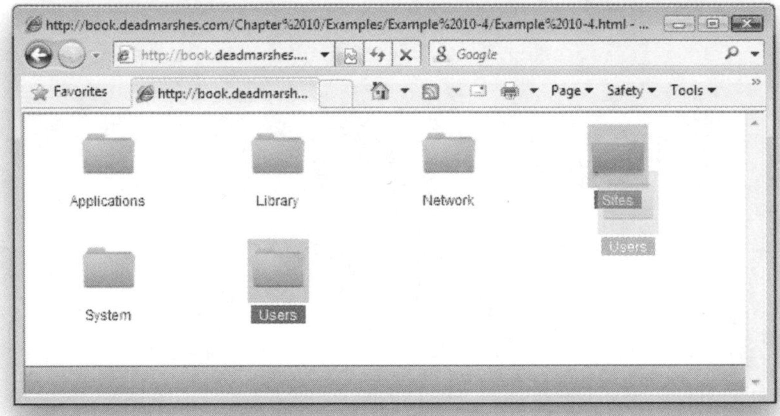

Figure 10-8

In the preceding example, you added the jQuery UI `droppable()` method to the Finder clone, which lets you delegate areas where draggable elements can be dropped, and a series of methods that use Safari's native Drag-and-Drop API for Safari on Mac OS X. Of course, you don't have to use Safari's native API, if you don't want to. The jQuery UI Draggables and Droppables plugins both work in Safari (however, jQuery UI uses its own API); the only reason I've implemented the native Drag-and-Drop API is so that folders can be dragged and dropped between completely separate browser windows on that platform.

In order to set up the document for the Droppables library, you added a few rules to the style sheet, which define what an element looks like while you're dragging one element over another. From here on, I refer to the action of dragging one element over another element as the `dragover` event. jQuery UI simply refers to this event as `over`, but the native Drag-and-Drop API in IE and Safari both call this event `dragover`.

In essence, the style that you use for `dragover` is simply the same style that you're already using to highlight a folder to indicate its selection, with just one difference: You swap out the default folder icon with an open folder icon. In the JavaScript portion, changing the `dragover` style in the style sheet is made possible by the addition of the class name, *hFinderDirectoryDrop*. This class name is added to the `<div>` element with class name *hFinderDirectory*. jQuery dynamically adds or removes the *hFinderDirectoryDrop* class name to or from this `<div>` element, allowing you to define a different style upon `dragover`.

So, you're reusing the "selected folder style" for folders where the `dragover` event is taking place. Reusing that style is done simply by adding additional selectors that reference the `<div>` element with the `dragover` class name *hFinderDirectoryDrop* to the style sheet.

```
div.hFinderIconSelected,
div.hFinderDirectoryDrop div.hFinderIcon {
    background-color: rgb(196, 196, 196);
    -moz-border-radius: 5px;
    -webkit-border-radius: 5px;
}
```

```
div.hFinderDirectoryDrop div.hFinderIcon div {
    background-image:
      url('../../../Images/Finder/Open Folder 48x48.png');
}
div.hFinderDirectoryName {
    text-align: center;
}
span.hFinderDirectoryNameSelected,
div.hFinderDirectoryDrop span {
    background: rgb(56, 117, 215);
    -moz-border-radius: 8px;
    -webkit-border-radius: 8px;
    color: white;
    padding: 1px 7px;
}
```

The preceding reuses the selected folder style for dragover elements. To replace the default folder icon with an open folder icon, you use a more specific selector. The following selector is used to add the default folder icon:

```
div.hFinderIcon div
```

The following selector overrides the preceding selector when a `dragover` event is taking place, providing an open folder icon instead of the default folder icon:

```
div.hFinderDirectoryDrop div.hFinderIcon div
```

The IE style sheet, Example 10-4.IE.css, doesn't add a similar style-sheet rule, though. If you recall from the preceding examples in this chapter, IE6 doesn't properly display transparent PNG images without a hack that makes use of its proprietary CSS `filter` property. It turns out that if you add a new rule mirroring what you've done in the main style sheet, IE6 encounters some kind of internal style-sheet parsing bug and does not render the folder icons correctly. To work around this, you swap out the folder icon directly from JavaScript using browser detection. Unfortunately, in this case, IE6 makes it impossible to keep its styles in the style sheet and out of your JavaScript.

The IE hack makes use of some of the other options that jQuery UI allows for working with Droppable elements. If you recall from earlier in this section, you saw how you can pass an object literal to the `droppable()` method. Within the object literal, you specify options via key, value pairs, which, in turn, give you fine-grained control over how a drop operation works. In the portion of JavaScript that calls `droppable()`, you have options like accept, which as you saw previously in this section, lets you filter which elements are allowed in the drop zone by specifying a selector.

```
        .droppable({
          accept: 'div.hFinderDirectory',
```

The next option specifies the class name that is added to the drop element when a `dragover` event takes place. As you already saw, this option causes the class name *hFinderDirectoryDrop* to be added to the `<div>` element with class name *hFinderDirectory* when a `dragover` event takes place.

```
          hoverClass: 'hFinderDirectoryDrop',
```

The following option lets you set a callback function that is executed when a `dragover` event takes place; the name of this option is simply `over`. This callback function specified here fixes the IE6 glitch that prevents you from putting the `dragover` style in the IE style sheet. Since IE produces a bug when you add a new rule to the IE style sheet with a new filter image for `dragover`, you have to fix that manually with JavaScript. So the following JavaScript checks to see that the browser is IE6; then it queries for the `<div>` element that houses the folder image, removes the `background`, and applies the transparent PNG image via IE's proprietary `filter` property. This hack lets you use PNG images with transparent parts in IE6, which doesn't support transparency in PNG images natively. IE7, on the other hand, does implement support for transparency in PNG images, so you don't have to apply the fix to newer versions of Internet Explorer.

```
over: function(e, ui) {
  if ($.browser.msie && $.browser.version == 6.0) {
    $(this).find('div.hFinderIcon div').css({
      background: 'none',
      filter:
      "progid:DXImageTransform.Microsoft.AlphaImageLoader" +
      "(src='../../../Images/Finder/Open Folder 48x48.png'," +
        "sizingMethod='crop')"
    });
  }
},
```

The next option specifies a function that occurs at the `dragleave` event, when the dragged element has left the boundaries of a drop zone. jQuery UI calls the option for specifying this event `out`. The code within this callback function finishes the IE6 hack by restoring the default folder image, again using IE's proprietary `filter` property.

```
out: function(e, ui) {
  if ($.browser.msie && $.browser.version == 6.0) {
    $(this).find('div.hFinderIcon div').css({
      background: 'none',
      filter:
        "progid:DXImageTransform.Microsoft.AlphaImageLoader" +
        "(src='../../../Images/Finder/Folder 48x48.png'," +
          "sizingMethod='crop')"
    });
  }
},
```

In the last option passed to the `droppable()` method, you specify a function that occurs at the `drop` event, which occurs when an element has been dragged over a drop zone and the mouse button released. Within this function is where you'll want to do whatever it is the act of dragging and dropping is intended to provide. In this case, you'd want to remove the folder being dropped, then make an AJAX call to the server, where on the server side you'd have code that actually moves the folder to the new location.

```
    drop: function(e, ui) {
      var $path = ui.draggable.attr('title');
      // Do something with the path

      // Remove the element that was dropped.
      ui.draggable.remove();
    }
  });
```

In the preceding drop event, you are able to access properties associated with the drag-and-drop operation by specifying a second argument in your callback function. In the preceding examples, the second argument is named ui; then the ui.draggable object gives you access to the element that has been dragged and dropped on this element. In the example, you access the title attribute of the element being dragged, which contains the folder's absolute path, which you could then send to the server, along with the path to the folder that the folder has been dropped on, and actually move that folder to the new location programmatically. The function ends with the dragged element being deleted, which would be the final operation that you would do upon implementing a drag-and-drop folder UI.

The preceding described what you need to do to use the jQuery UI Droppable library. The remaining JavaScript code deals with implementing Safari's native Drag-and-Drop API on Mac OS X, which has a slightly different approach. For the native API implementation, you first declare a variable that is used to remember the element being dragged. This is used so that you can access the element being dragged from the various events that fire on the element acting as a drop zone. Unlike jQuery, the native Drag-and-Drop API does not provide the draggable element in either the event object or another argument passed to the callback functions.

```
var dragElement;

$('div.hFinderDirectory').each(
  function() {
    // jQuery's event API does not provide the dataTransfer
    // object.
```

First, you set up the dragstart event. This event fires when a drag on an element begins. Safari and IE both support drag-and-drop events; however, IE does not provide support for drag-and-drop via CSS, as you saw previously in this chapter with the -khtml-user-drag property. Aside from the events themselves, another feature shared by the IE and Safari implementations is the dataTransfer object, which lets you store data in a clipboard for the drag-and-drop operation. You can set data at any point in the process, but you may only access data in the clipboard when a drop event has taken place.

```
    this.addEventListener(
      'dragstart',
      function($e) {
        // The setData method lets you save some data
        // for the element being dragged.
        $e.dataTransfer.setData('Text', $(this).attr('title'));

        // Remeber the drag element.
        dragElement = $(this);
      }, false
    );
```

In the callback function for the dragstart event, the path to the folder being dragged is saved to the clipboard using the setData() method of the dataTransfer object. While I'm not going to go into great detail about the setData() method, I will summarize its purpose by saying that Safari lets you pass plain text, whereas you specify the type of data in the first argument, as Text, and the data in the second argument. Another type of data that you can specify is a URL. These are the two data types supported by both Internet Explorer and Safari. Safari also supports specifying MIME types in the first argument, such as text/plain or image/jpeg. MIME, short for *Multipurpose Internet Mail Extension*, is a standard, similar to file extensions, that is used for identifying data within a file. For example, a PNG image has the extension .png, but also has the MIME type `image/png`. So, in Safari, it is also possible to transmit data using the `setData()` method, where you are able to provide a MIME type for the data you're transmitting, and thus not be limited to plain text or a URL.

In the preceding code, the data passed to the `setData()` method is the path of the folder being dragged. You don't really need to pass this data since you also set the variable `dragElement` with a reference to the element being dragged. I have provided the `setData()` method simply to let you know about its existence.

Next, you attach a `dragenter` event. Nothing is really happening with this event, except the default action of the browser is being canceled. This is done so that you don't inadvertently conflict with something the browser supports by default with a drag-and-drop operation.

```
this.addEventListener(
  'dragenter',
  function($e) {
    // Browser default behavior is canceled.
    $e.preventDefault();
  }, false
);
```

In the next snippet of code, you attach a `dragover` event. Here, basically, you're reproducing the same thing that's going on with the jQuery UI code. You check to see if the folder is being dragged over itself; if it is, you do nothing; if it isn't, you apply the *hFinderDirectoryDrop* class name to the drop folder. This does the same thing that you saw with the `droppable()` method's `hoverClass` option, giving the drop folder the selected style, in addition to swapping out the default folder icon with an open folder icon. And you again prevent the default action of the browser with a call to `preventDefault()` so that you don't conflict with something the browser does by default when the user does a drag-and-drop.

```
this.addEventListener(
  'dragover',
  function($e) {
    $e.preventDefault();
    // Add the style for the folder being dragged over
    // But not if the drag element is being dragged over itself.
    if (dragElement.attr('title') != $(this).attr('title')) {
      $(this).addClass('hFinderDirectoryDrop');
    }
  }
);
```

The next event that you attach is the `dragleave` event, when the dragged element leaves the boundaries of the drop element; you remove the class *hFinderDirectoryDrop* from the folder and, again, prevent the default action.

```
this.addEventListener(
  'dragleave',
  function($e) {
    $e.preventDefault();
```

```
            // Remove the style when the drag item leaves the
            // drop zone.
            $(this).removeClass('hFinderDirectoryDrop');
          }
        );
```

Finally, you come to the drop event, which is where you will complete the drag-and-drop operation. You can get the path that you passed to the dataTransfer.getData() method, by specifying the same type of data that you set when you saved that data to the clipboard. Again, you are only able to call the getData() method from the drop event, which is a security precaution that prevents you from having arbitrary access to the user's system clipboard. Here is where you might make an AJAX Request to the server, sending both the drag-and-drop path so that the folder move is completed. Finally, you also prevent the browser's default action again.

```
        this.addEventListener(
          'drop',
          function($e) {
            var $path = $e.dataTransfer.getData('Text');
            // Do something with the path

            // Delete the drag element.
            dragElement.remove();
            $e.preventDefault();
          }, false
        );
      }
    );
  }
```

In the preceding example, you've seen how the jQuery UI droppable() method works in a real-life-oriented demonstration of a drag-and-drop implementation. You've also seen how the jQuery UI droppable() method, which works in all popular browsers, contrasts with Safari and IE's native drag-and-drop capabilities, which if the work going on in HTML5 is any indication, will soon become the universal Drag-and-Drop API standard supported by all browsers. No doubt when that occurs, jQuery will be adjusted to take advantage of the native API, keeping with its vision of letting you do more with less code.

A comprehensive jQuery UI Draggable and Droppable reference is available in Appendix J, including all of the options that you can pass to both the `draggable()` and `droppable()` methods, and the `ui` object that you can optionally specify in the second argument to draggable and droppable event handlers.

Summary

In this chapter, you learned how to use the jQuery UI Draggables and Droppables plugins, which you are able to download à la carte from `www.jquery.com`. The jQuery website provides à la carte downloading for UI components so that you can include only the plugins that you need to use, which, in turn, helps keep your applications lean and efficient.

Throughout this chapter, you worked on building a clone of Mac OS X's Finder and saw how you are able to make folders into draggable elements. You also learned how to use Safari's native Drag-and-Drop API in Safari on Mac OS X, which is based on IE's Drag-and-Drop API, with some compelling and useful extensions. You saw how you are able to control the nuisances of a drag-and-drop implementation via the options that jQuery UI allows you to pass to both the `draggable()` and `droppable()` methods, which help you to control what kind of drag operation you want, what the `drag` element looks like, what the `drop` element looks like, and the event handlers you can specify to execute code during specific events that take place during a drag-and-drop operation.

In the next chapter, I present another drag-and-drop UI concept that jQuery provides, called *Sortables*.

Exercises

1. If you wanted to have a UI that allows users to drag elements around in a document and position those elements wherever they like, what would you use? (Hint: what function call?)
2. If you wanted to create draggable elements that work similarly to your Operating System's file manager, where the original element remains in place, but when a drag operation starts, you drag around a clone of that element, how would you do that with jQuery UI? (Hint: what function call?)
3. If you wanted to make an element into a drop zone for draggable elements, what function call would you use?
4. Write the function call that you would use to add a class name to a drop zone while an element was being dragged over the top of it.
5. What option would you provide to the `droppable()` method if you wanted to limit the drag elements that can be dropped on the `drop` element? Also, what type of value would you provide to that option?
6. List the events that you would use for a native drag-and-drop implementation.

Drag-and-Drop Sorting

In Chapter 10, I introduced how jQuery UI provides plugins that make implementing drag-and-drop UI very easy to implement. In this chapter, I present another jQuery UI plugin called *Sortables*, which enables you to make items in a list of some kind sortable, or "rearrangable."

The need for sorting items comes up often in Website Development. There's always going to be, through either need or convenience, the desire to change the order that items appear in. An example would be the order in which products appear in a navigation or side menu.

Without drag-and-drop, it's still possible to give users the ability to tweak the order of items. You can offer up or down arrows for shifting items in a list, for example, but drag-and-drop sorting is the fastest, most intuitive way to implement this type of user interface.

Making a List Sortable

As you've seen throughout this book, jQuery takes complex programming tasks and makes them easy. Sometimes you can do a lot by adding just one line of code or even chaining one addition function call to a selection! Once you experience how easy jQuery makes common programming tasks, it becomes near impossible to return to boring, bloated, plain-vanilla JavaScript. In Chapter 10, you saw how making elements draggable amounts to making a selection, then making a single function call. Making a list of items sortable via drag-and-drop is just as easy — you make a selection of elements, then you make a single function call. The function that you call in this case is called `sortable()`. Like the drag-and-drop examples that I presented in Chapter 10, you have the ability to tweak element sortability via fine-grained options that you can pass to the `sortable()` method via a JavaScript object literal. Each of the options that jQuery UI provides for the Sortables plugin is defined in detail in Appendix K.

The following code demonstrates a very remedial example of making elements sortable by drag-and-drop and how ridiculously easy jQuery UI makes this task. The following markup shows a simple unordered list of elements:

```
<!DOCTYPE html PUBLIC "-//W3C//DTD XHTML 1.0 Strict//EN"
    "http://www.w3.org/TR/xhtml1/DTD/xhtml1-strict.dtd">
<html xmlns='http://www.w3.org/1999/xhtml' xml:lang='en'>
  <head>
    <meta http-equiv='content-type' content='text/html; charset=utf-8' />
    <meta http-equiv='content-language' content='en-us' />
    <title></title>
    <script type='text/javascript'
            src='../../../Source Code/jQuery/jQuery.js'></script>
    <script type='text/javascript'
            src='../../../Source Code/jQuery/jQueryUI.js'></script>
    <script type='text/javascript' src='Figure 11-1.js'></script>
    <link type='text/css' href='Figure 11-1.css' rel='stylesheet' />
  </head>
  <body>
    <h4>Delicious nutty snacks</h4>
    <ul>
      <li>Almonds</li>
      <li>Cashews</li>
      <li>Peanuts</li>
      <li>Walnuts</li>
      <li>Pine nuts</li>
    </ul>
  </body>
</html>
```

The preceding markup is accompanied by the following CSS:

```
body {
    font: 12px "Lucida Grande", Arial, sans-serif;
    background: #fff;
    color: rgb(50, 50, 50);
    margin: 0;
    padding: 0;
}
h4 {
    margin: 5px;
}
ul {
    list-style: none;
    width: 250px;
    margin: 5px;
    padding: 0;

}
li {
    background: lightblue;
    padding: 3px;
    width: 250px;
    border: 1px solid #90c5d6;
}
```

And the following JavaScript completes the example:

```
$(document).ready(
  function() {
    $('ul').sortable();
  }
);
```

The preceding example shows you just how easy it is to make a sortable list. The CSS and markup are pretty routine, nothing particularly exciting or interesting. The JavaScript included in the example gives you the ability to sort the items within the `<ul>` element via drag-and-drop in any browser. All you needed to make this possible was to include the relevant jQuery UI plugin, Sortables, then make a selection with jQuery and chain a call to the function `sortable()` onto that selection. The Sortables plugin requires that you select the container element, whose immediate children will be sortable by drag-and-drop. The container is, of course, the `<ul>` element, and the sortable children are the `<li>` elements contained within that element. You should see output similar to what you see in **Figure 11-1** when you load this example and try sorting.

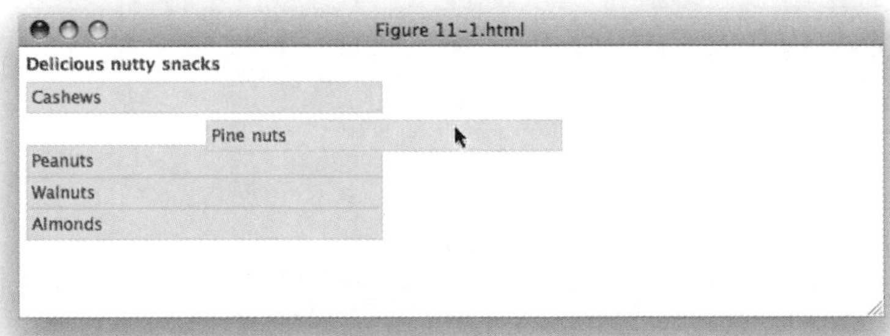

Figure 11-1

And naturally, this functionality works in all modern browsers — IE6, IE7, IE8, Firefox, Safari, and Opera.

In the preceding example, you see that utilizing the Sortables plugin is really very easy. In the following "Try It Out," I put the concept of sortability into context with a more real-world-oriented application, where you are sorting files through a GUI interface, which you might use in a corporate Content Management System (CMS), to control things like sorting links in a sidebar or dropdown menu, or the order products appear in a catalog. You'll also return to this example throughout this chapter to examine other aspects of file sorting that jQuery UI provides through its Sortables plugin.

Try It Out — Implementing a Sortable List

Example 11-1

To make a list of sortable files, follow these steps:

1. Create the following markup document as *Example 11-1.html*:

```
<!DOCTYPE html PUBLIC "-//W3C//DTD XHTML 1.0 Strict//EN"
    "http://www.w3.org/TR/xhtml1/DTD/xhtml1-strict.dtd">
<html xmlns='http://www.w3.org/1999/xhtml' xml:lang='en'>
```

```
<head>
  <meta http-equiv='content-type' content='text/html; charset=utf-8' />
  <meta http-equiv='content-language' content='en-us' />
  <title></title>
  <script type='text/javascript'
          src='../../../Source Code/jQuery/jQuery.js'></script>
  <script type='text/javascript'
          src='../../../Source Code/jQuery/jQueryUI.js'></script>
  <script type='text/javascript' src='Example 11-1.js'></script>
  <link type='text/css' href='Example 11-1.css' rel='stylesheet' />
  <!--[if lt IE 7]>
    <link type='text/css' href='Example 11-1.IE.css' rel='stylesheet' />
  <![endif]-->
</head>
<body>
  <ul id='hFinderCategoryFiles'>
    <li class="hFinderCategoryFile">
      <div class="hFinderCategoryFileIcon"></div>
      <h5 class="hFinderCategoryFileTitle">
        Using CoreImage to Resize and Change Formats on the Fly
      </h5>
      <div class="hFinderCategoryFilePath">
        <a href="/Blog/apple/CoreImage.html">
          /Blog/apple/CoreImage.html
        </a>
      </div>
    </li>
    <li class="hFinderCategoryFile">
      <div class="hFinderCategoryFileIcon"></div>
      <h5 class="hFinderCategoryFileTitle">
        Exploring Polymorphism in PHP
      </h5>
      <div class="hFinderCategoryFilePath">
        <a href="/Blog/php/Polymorphism.html">
          /Blog/php/Polymorphism.html
        </a>
      </div>
    </li>
    <li class="hFinderCategoryFile">
      <div class="hFinderCategoryFileIcon"></div>
      <h5 class="hFinderCategoryFileTitle">
        A PHP Shell Script for Backups
      </h5>
      <div class="hFinderCategoryFilePath">
        <a href="/Blog/php/Backup%20Script.html">
          /Blog/php/Backup Script.html
        </a>
      </div>
    </li>
    <li class="hFinderCategoryFile">
      <div class="hFinderCategoryFileIcon"></div>
      <h5 class="hFinderCategoryFileTitle">
        HTML 5 DOCTYPE
      </h5>
```

```
          <div class="hFinderCategoryFilePath">
            <a href="/Blog/web/html5_doctype.html">
              /Blog/web/html5_doctype.html
            </a>
          </div>
        </li>
        <li class="hFinderCategoryFile">
          <div class="hFinderCategoryFileIcon"></div>
          <h5 class="hFinderCategoryFileTitle">
            First Impressions of IE 8 Beta 2
          </h5>
          <div class="hFinderCategoryFilePath">
            <a href="/Blog/web/ie8_beta2.html">
              /Blog/web/ie8_beta2.html
            </a>
          </div>
        </li>
      </ul>
    </body>
  </html>
```

2. Create the following style sheet as *Example 11-1.css*:

```
html,
body {
    width: 100%;
    height: 100%;
}
body {
    font: 12px "Lucida Grande", Arial, sans-serif;
    background: rgb(189, 189, 189)
      url('../../../Images/Finder/Bottom.png') repeat-x bottom;
    color: rgb(50, 50, 50);
    margin: 0;
    padding: 0;
}
ul#hFinderCategoryFiles {
    position: absolute;
    top: 0;
    bottom: 22px;
    left: 0;
    width: 300px;
    border-bottom: 1px solid rgb(64, 64, 64);
    border-right: 1px solid rgb(64, 64, 64);
    background: #fff;
    list-style: none;
    margin: 0;
    padding: 0;
}
li.hFinderCategoryFile {
    clear: both;
    padding: 5px 5px 10px 5px;
    min-height: 48px;
    width: 290px;
}
```

```
li.hFinderCategoryFile h5 {
    font: normal 12px "Lucida Grande", Arial, sans-serif;
    margin: 0;
}
div.hFinderCategoryFileIcon {
    float: left;
    width: 48px;
    height: 48px;
    background: url('../../../Images/Finder/Safari Document.png') no-repeat;
}
h5.hFinderCategoryFileTitle,
div.hFinderCategoryFilePath {
    padding-left: 55px;
}
li.hFinderCategoryFileSelected {
    background: rgb(24, 67, 243)
      url('../../../Images/Backgrounds/Selected Item.png') repeat-x bottom;
    color: white;
}
li.hFinderCategoryFileSelected a {
    color: lightblue;
}
```

3. Create the following style sheet as *Example 11-1.IE.css*:

```
ul#hFinderCategoryFiles {
    height: expression(document.body.offsetHeight - 23);
}
div.hFinderCategoryFileIcon {
    background: none;
    filter: progid:DXImageTransform.Microsoft.AlphaImageLoader
      (src='../../../Images/Finder/Safari Document.png',
sizingMethod='crop');
}
```

4. Create the following JavaScript document as *Example 11-1.js*:

```
$(document).ready(
  function() {
    $('li.hFinderCategoryFile').mousedown(
      function() {
        $('li.hFinderCategoryFile').not(this)
          .removeClass('hFinderCategoryFileSelected');

        $(this).addClass('hFinderCategoryFileSelected');
      }
    );

    $('ul#hFinderCategoryFiles').sortable();
  }
);
```

The preceding source code gives you results like those you see in **Figure 11-2**.

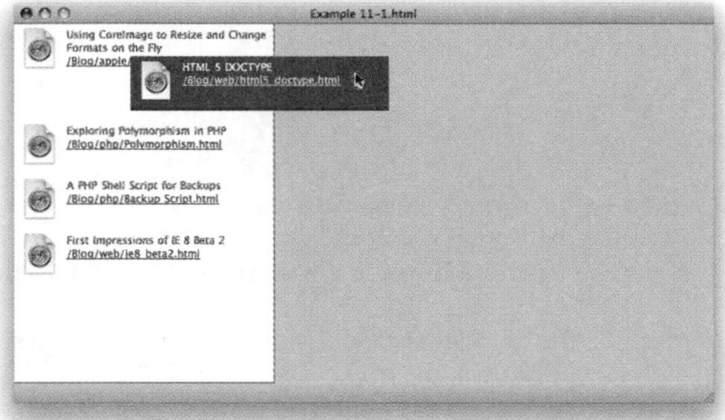

Figure 11-2

In the preceding example, you have a more realistic demonstration of the jQuery UI Sortables plugin, with an application that provides file sorting, which can have a variety of applications, as I mentioned just prior to presenting the "Try It Out" example.

In this example, you have five files. Each has a file icon, a title, and a clickable link to the file. I have, again, borrowed from Mac OS X for the look and feel, to make an application that feels more like a native desktop application. If I were to extend this concept, I could also provide alternative templates that mirror the look and feel of other operating systems. A server-side language that can detect the user's operating system, combined with different style sheets for each OS, makes that a viable option, which will make your users feel more at home with your web-based application.

In the markup, you set things up so that the content can be styled with CSS. Each file item is represented as a `<li>` element. Since you're working with a list of items, semantically speaking, it makes the most sense to set up your sortable list as a `<ul>` element, with each list item, `<li>`, representing each file.

The file icon is placed in a `<div>` element. You use a `<div>` so that you can provide the icon via the CSS `background` property, and because I am using a PNG image with variable alpha transparency, this also helps you to hack IE6 so that it properly handles transparency in the PNG image. This approach is similar to what you used in Chapter 10 for the Finder clone that you created.

The text content is wrapped within an `<h5>` and a `<div>` element so that you are able to control the margin and padding using block elements, instead of inline elements like `<span>`. You'll see how this is helpful as I explain how the style sheet works in this example. Then, you also gratuitously give each element class names, which makes it much easier to apply style or behavior to those specific elements, in addition to making it easier to identify the purpose of the element from the standpoint of semantics. Each class name is chosen so that it conveys the exact purpose of the element.

```
<li class="hFinderCategoryFile">
  <div class="hFinderCategoryFileIcon"></div>
  <h5 class="hFinderCategoryFileTitle">
    Using CoreImage to Resize and Change Formats on the Fly
  </h5>
  <div class="hFinderCategoryFilePath">
```

```
            <a href="/Blog/apple/CoreImage.html">
              /Blog/apple/CoreImage.html
            </a>
          </div>
        </li>
```

The application is designed so that sortable elements are contained in a single column that spans the left side, and the column is created by using the `top` and `bottom` offset properties in tandem to imply height, which, in turn, lets you have a stretchy column that will re-size fluidly with the size of the viewport.

Just as you did in Chapter 10 for the Finder example, you must set the scene so that IE6 and IE7 can also be whipped into shape, presentationally speaking. First, you give the `<html>` and `<body>` elements 100 percent `width` and `height`, and remove any default `margin` or `padding` from the `<body>` element (some browsers apply default `margin`, some apply default `padding`). This is an essential part of making the column display correctly in IE6 and IE7. You saw a similar hack in Chapter 10 in the Finder example.

```
html,
body {
    width: 100%;
    height: 100%;
}
body {
    font: 12px "Lucida Grande", Arial, sans-serif;
    background: rgb(189, 189, 189)
      url('../../../Images/Finder/Bottom.png') repeat-x bottom;
    color: rgb(50, 50, 50);
    margin: 0;
    padding: 0;
}
```

In the next style-sheet rule, you create the left column by styling the `<ul>` element with ID name *hFinderCategoryFiles* so that it spans the height of the left side of the document. The declaration `top: 0;` combined with the declaration `bottom: 22px;` causes the `<ul>` element to span the entire height of the viewport, except for the bottom 22 pixels, which has a gradient background applied to that space. The `<ul>` element is given a fixed width of 300 pixels; otherwise, you would have shrink-to-fit width, since the `<ul>` element is absolutely positioned.

```
ul#hFinderCategoryFiles {
    position: absolute;
    top: 0;
    bottom: 22px;
    left: 0;
    width: 300px;
    border-bottom: 1px solid rgb(64, 64, 64);
    border-right: 1px solid rgb(64, 64, 64);
    background: #fff;
    list-style: none;
    margin: 0;
    padding: 0;
}
```

As you did in Chapter 10, you have to apply a hack for IE6 so that the column correctly spans the height of the viewport, since it does not support specifying offset properties in tandem. This is done in a separate style sheet that specifically targets IE6. In that style sheet, you use an IE proprietary CSS expression to fix the height of the column. The CSS expression defines the height of the column by getting the `offsetHeight` of the <body> element and subtracting 23 pixels from that height.

```
ul#hFinderCategoryFiles {
    height: expression(document.body.offsetHeight - 23);
}
```

It should be noted that IE's proprietary CSS expressions have been discontinued in IE8; however, the fringe use cases, like this, that might call for the use of this feature have thankfully been fixed. IE7 does support specifying opposing offset properties to imply height, but it has some bugs and does not correctly handle this particular use case until the <body> and <html> elements are each given 100 percent width and height, which is contrary to the CSS2.1 specification.

Each `<li>` element first has the declaration `clear: both` applied, which is needed to clear the left floating of each file icon (the <div> element with class name *hFinderCategoryFileIcon*). Without this declaration, you'd have a jumbled unintelligible mess, as each `<li>` element tried to float up to the right of the icon of the preceding `<li>` element, and the `<li>` element preceding that one, float up to the right of the icon of the `<li>` element before that one, and so on. The `clear: left` declaration cancels floating, so that the icon floats to the left, and only the text content within the `<li>` element floats up to the right of that icon.

Each `<li>` element is given a fixed `width` of 290 pixels. You do this because when you drag a `<li>` element, the element loses its width and shrinks. It does that because without an explicit width, each `<li>` element's width is based on the parent, <ul>, element's width. When you drag a `<li>` element, its parent is no longer the <ul> element, but the <body> element. The `<li>` element is moved with the mouse cursor through CSS; it is positioned absolutely, relative to the viewport, and its position is constantly updated based on where the mouse cursor is going via the jQuery UI Sortables plugin. Otherwise, as an absolutely positioned element, the `<li>` element would have shrink-to-fit width, so by giving the `<li>` element a fixed width, you allow it to maintain its dimensions as it is dragged from one point to another. The `min-height` property keeps the spacing within the `<li>` element consistent, but also allows each `<li>` element to expand vertically to accommodate additional text content.

```
li.hFinderCategoryFile {
    clear: both;
    padding: 5px 5px 10px 5px;
    min-height: 48px;
    width: 290px;
}
```

The next item of interest in the style sheet is the icon, which is defined by the following rule:

```
div.hFinderCategoryFileIcon {
    float: left;
    width: 48px;
    height: 48px;
    background: url('../../../Images/Finder/Safari Document.png') no-repeat;
}
```

The file icon is set to have a width and height of 48 pixels, which is a size that is consistent with the settings and icons offered by operating systems. In fact, the Safari icon that you see is the same icon that Safari actually uses for HTML documents on Mac OS X. It has just been converted to PNG and sized down to 48 by 48 pixels. Staying consistent with desktop OS icons lets you reuse desktop OS icons, if you want to, or to even use one of the many free icon packages available on the Internet. In the preceding rule, the `<div>` element is floated to the left with the declaration `float: left;`. That declaration causes the text content to float to the right of the icon, as I explained previously. The `clear: both;` declaration of the previous rule that I explained cancels this declaration on each `<li>` element, so that only the text content is affected. The icon is set as the background using the `background` property. This approach to displaying the icon does a few things for you. An `<img />` element is more verbose and causes more redundancy in code, and it lets you easily use transparent PNG images, since this approach lends itself to easy hacking for IE6, which unfortunately can't properly display transparent PNG images by default. In the IE style sheet, transparency in the PNG image is fixed with the following rule:

```
div.hFinderCategoryFileIcon {
    background: none;
    filter: progid:DXImageTransform.Microsoft.AlphaImageLoader
      (src='../../../Images/Finder/Safari Document.png', sizingMethod='crop');
}
```

The last items of interest in the style sheet define the look for selected files. That's done in the following two rules:

```
li.hFinderCategoryFileSelected {
    background: rgb(24, 67, 243)
      url('../../../Images/Backgrounds/Selected Item.png') repeat-x bottom;
    color: white;
}
li.hFinderCategoryFileSelected a {
    color: lightblue;
}
```

The preceding two rules are for `<li>` elements with the class name *hFinderCategoryFileSelected*. This class name is dynamically added and removed from `<li>` elements by JavaScript with jQuery. This addition of this class name lets your users see which file is currently selected. Beyond providing a visual cue for selection, this also lets you implement the ability to add a Delete button, which when pressed would remove the selected item or implement some other functionality that is contingent on the selection of an element.

The JavaScript for this example is very lean and to the point. The JavaScript basically does two things. It provides the ability to select a `<li>` element by adding and removing the class name *hFinderCategoryFileSelected* as appropriate to indicate selection. And it makes the `<li>` elements sortable using the jQuery UI Sortables plugin.

When the DOM is ready, the first task is to attach a `mousedown` event to each `<li>` element. You'll use this event to implement an indication of which element is selected.

```
$('li.hFinderCategoryFile').mousedown(
  function() {
    $('li.hFinderCategoryFile').not(this)
```

```
            .removeClass('hFinderCategoryFileSelected');

          $(this).addClass('hFinderCategoryFileSelected');
        }
    );
```

The script selects every <li> element with class name *hFinderCategoryFile*. The class name is added to the selection, even though as it stands, you could just select every <li> element without a class name and get the same result, so that your application can be easily extended. You might bring in more functionality that involves adding <li> elements that are completely unrelated to what you're doing here. Adding the class name to the selector makes the selection more specific and gives you the ability to expand your application's functionality more effortlessly. So every <li> element with class name *hFinderCategoryFile* is selected, then the <li> element on which the `mousedown` event is taking place is filtered out using `.not(this)`, and the class name *hFinderCategoryFileSelected* is removed from every <li> element, except the <li> element on which the `mousedown` event is taking place.

This is actually not the most efficient way to implement selection, especially if you have a very long list. Selecting every <li> element is inefficient and can make your script slow if you have a lot of items in the list. So having showed you the wrong way to do selection, a better approach is to create a global variable, and every time a selection is made, store the currently selected element in that variable. The following code is what this approach looks like in the context of Example 11-1:

```
$(document).ready(
  function() {
    var $selectedFile;

    $('li.hFinderCategoryFile').mousedown(
      function() {
        if ($selectedFile && $selectedFile.length) {
          $selectedFile.removeClass('hFinderCategoryFileSelected');
        }

        $selectedFile = $(this);
        $selectedFile.addClass('hFinderCategoryFileSelected');
      }
    );

    $('ul#hFinderCategoryFiles').sortable();
  }
);
```

The selected item is stored in the variable `$selectedItem`. When the `mousedown` event fires, the script first checks to see if there is an element stored in the `$selectedItem` variable; if there is, the *hFinderCategoryFileSelected* class name is removed from that element, since that element is the previously selected element.

Then the element on which the `mousedown` event is being fired, referenced by the `this` keyword, is made into a jQuery object by wrapping this in a call to the dollar sign function, and the class name *hFinderCategoryFileSelected* is added to the element on which the `mousedown` event is being fired. Presto, you have a leaner, more efficient selection API.

Then the last item that happens in the script (and the point of this example) is every `<li>` element being made sortable with a call to the `sortable()` method:

```
$('ul#hFinderCategoryFiles').sortable();
```

Customizing Sortables

In this section, I talk about some of the visual tweaks that you can make to sortable lists and how you link one list to another, so that you have sorting between multiple, separate lists. The jQuery UI `sortable()` method, like `draggable()` and `droppable()`, also allows you to specify an object literal as its first argument, which lets you tweak how sorting works, in addition to providing callback functions that are executed during specific events that occur as sorting is taking place. I discuss just a few of the options that jQuery UI exposes for its Sortables plugin in this section; however, you can find a complete list of options in the API reference for Sortables that appears in Appendix K.

The first option I present is called `placeholder`. The `placeholder` option gives you the ability to style the placeholder that appears within a sortable list as a drag is taking place to indicate where the item will be dropped, if the mouse is released. By default, from Example 11-1, you can see that the `placeholder` is simply empty white space, sized relatively to the element being dragged. The `placeholder` option accepts a class name as its value, which, in turn, is applied to the `placeholder` element.

The second option I present describes how you can customize the element being dragged; the process for doing this can also be applied to the jQuery UI `draggable()` method. By default, jQuery UI displays the element the user picked for sorting as the element that the user drags, which, of course, makes sense for most scenarios. You do, however, have the option of using a completely different element for display as the drag element, if you so choose. Customizing the element that's displayed during a drag is done with the `helper` option. In jQuery UI, *helper*, as applied to *drag-and-drop*, whether in the Sortables plugin or the Dragables plugin, or other plugins, is the term used for the element that is displayed while a drag is taking place. The `helper` option takes two arguments: The first argument is the event object, and the second argument references the element the user picked for sorting. Aside from completely replacing the element displayed during the `drag` event, you can also use this option to simply tweak the display of the element that the user picked. The following example demonstrates how to use the `placeholder` and `helper` options.

```
<!DOCTYPE html PUBLIC "-//W3C//DTD XHTML 1.0 Strict//EN"
    "http://www.w3.org/TR/xhtml1/DTD/xhtml1-strict.dtd">
<html xmlns='http://www.w3.org/1999/xhtml' xml:lang='en'>
  <head>
    <meta http-equiv='content-type' content='text/html; charset=utf-8' />
    <meta http-equiv='content-language' content='en-us' />
    <title></title>
    <script type='text/javascript'
            src='../../../Source Code/jQuery/jQuery.js'></script>
    <script type='text/javascript'
            src='../../../Source Code/jQuery/jQueryUI.js'></script>
    <script type='text/javascript' src='Figure 11-3.js'></script>
    <link type='text/css' href='Figure 11-3.css' rel='stylesheet' />
  </head>
  <body>
    <h4>Lord of the Rings Characters</h4>
    <ul>
```

```
        <li>Frodo</li>
        <li>Sam</li>
        <li>Pippin</li>
        <li>Meriadoc</li>
        <li>Gandalf</li>
        <li>Aragorn</li>
        <li>Arwen</li>
        <li>Gimli</li>
        <li>Legolas</li>
        <li>Boromir</li>
        <li>Faramir</li>
        <li>Gollum</li>
      </ul>
    </body>
  </html>
```

The preceding markup is linked to the following style sheet:

```
body {
    font: 12px "Lucida Grande", Arial, sans-serif;
    background: #fff;
    color: rgb(50, 50, 50);
    margin: 0;
    padding: 0;
}
h4 {
    margin: 5px;
}
ul {
    list-style: none;
    width: 250px;
    margin: 5px;
    padding: 0;
    border: 1px solid rgb(110, 59, 28);
    border-bottom: none;
}
li {
    background: rgb(218, 191, 162);
    padding: 3px;
    width: 244px;
    border-bottom: 1px solid rgb(110, 59, 28);
}
li.tmpPlaceholder {
    background: rgb(110, 59, 28);
    height: 22px;
}
li.tmpHelper {
    border: 1px solid rgb(110, 59, 28);
}
```

Then, the following JavaScript document is also included in the preceding markup document:

```
$(document).ready(
  function() {
    $('ul').sortable({
```

```
            placeholder: 'tmpPlaceholder',
            helper: function(e, element) {
              return $(element).clone().addClass('tmpHelper');
            }
          });
        }
      );
```

The preceding example provides the result you see in **Figure 11-3** when loaded into a browser.

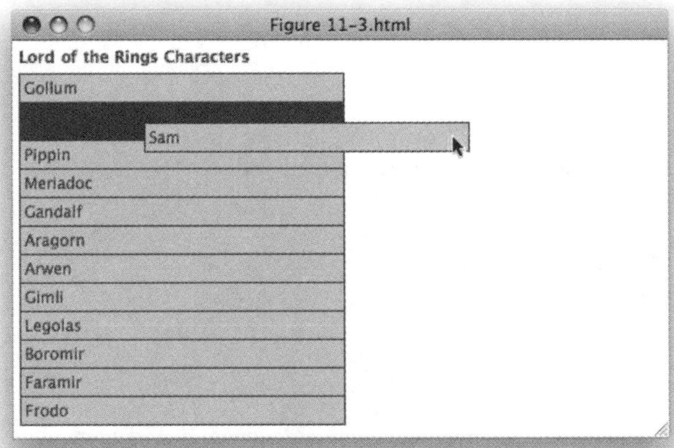

Figure 11-3

In the preceding example, you saw how the `placeholder` and `helper` options can be used to tweak the presentation of the dynamic components of a sortable list. In the example, you set the `placeholder` option with the class name *tmpPlaceholder*. This class name can then be used in the style sheet to tweak the look of the element that acts as a `placeholder` for sortable items while a sort is taking place. In the style sheet, the `placeholder` is given a dark-brown background and a fixed height.

Then, the `helper` option is provided with a callback function, which has two arguments: The first argument references the event object, and the second argument, `element`, references the element that the user picked for sorting. In the JavaScript, the element the user picked for sorting is cloned, then the class name *tmpHelper* is added to the clone, and the clone is returned from the callback function. Adding this class name lets you control the style of the `helper` element from the style sheet. It is necessary to add a class name in this way because jQuery UI does not have an option to set the class name of the `helper` element, as you saw with the `placeholder` option.

Adding a class name to the `helper` element lets you control its style. In the context of the previous example, this is beneficial for the way the border is applied to each `<li>` element. In the style sheet, only a bottom border is specified. This is combined with a left, right, and top border applied to the `<ul>` element, and that's done so that only 1 pixel of border surrounds each `<li>` element. Adding the *tmpHelper* class name to the helper element is used to change the border so that the border is applied to all sides of the `helper` element, rather than just the bottom, which makes the `helper` element look more natural.

As I mentioned previously, you don't have to use the element that the user picked as the element displayed for the `helper` element. You can, if you so choose, return a completely different element from that callback function, and that will be the element that the user drags around on the screen.

In the following "Try It Out," you extend the file-sorting application that you created in Example 11-1, with some options, like the `placeholder` and `helper` options that you learned about in this section. You also add another option that gives you the ability to sort elements between multiple lists.

Try It Out — Customizing Sortable Lists

Example 11-2

To see how multiple sortable lists are implemented, follow these steps:

1. Using Example 11-1.html as the basis, create the following markup document as *Example 11-2.html*:

```
<!DOCTYPE html PUBLIC "-//W3C//DTD XHTML 1.0 Strict//EN"
    "http://www.w3.org/TR/xhtml1/DTD/xhtml1-strict.dtd">
<html xmlns='http://www.w3.org/1999/xhtml' xml:lang='en'>
  <head>
    <meta http-equiv='content-type' content='text/html; charset=utf-8' />
    <meta http-equiv='content-language' content='en-us' />
    <title></title>
    <script type='text/javascript'
            src='../../../Source Code/jQuery/jQuery.js'></script>
    <script type='text/javascript'
            src='../../../Source Code/jQuery/jQueryUI.js'></script>
    <script type='text/javascript' src='Example 11-2.js'></script>
    <link type='text/css' href='Example 11-2.css' rel='stylesheet' />
    <!--[if lt IE 8]>
      <link type='text/css' href='Example 11-2.IE.css' rel='stylesheet' />
    <![endif]-->
  </head>
  <body>
    <div id='hFinderCategoryFileWrapper'>
      <ul id='hFinderCategoryFiles'>
        <li class="hFinderCategoryFile">
          <div class="hFinderCategoryFileIcon"></div>
          <h5 class="hFinderCategoryFileTitle">
            Using CoreImage to Resize and Change Formats on the Fly
          </h5>
          <div class="hFinderCategoryFilePath">
            <a href="/Blog/apple/CoreImage.html">
              /Blog/apple/CoreImage.html
            </a>
          </div>
        </li>
        <li class="hFinderCategoryFile">
          <div class="hFinderCategoryFileIcon"></div>
          <h5 class="hFinderCategoryFileTitle">
            Exploring Polymorphism in PHP
          </h5>
          <div class="hFinderCategoryFilePath">
            <a href="/Blog/php/Polymorphism.html">
```

```
              /Blog/php/Polymorphism.html
            </a>
          </div>
        </li>
        <li class="hFinderCategoryFile">
          <div class="hFinderCategoryFileIcon"></div>
          <h5 class="hFinderCategoryFileTitle">
            A PHP Shell Script for Backups
          </h5>
          <div class="hFinderCategoryFilePath">
            <a href="/Blog/php/Backup%20Script.html">
              /Blog/php/Backup Script.html
            </a>
          </div>
        </li>
        <li class="hFinderCategoryFile">
          <div class="hFinderCategoryFileIcon"></div>
          <h5 class="hFinderCategoryFileTitle">
            HTML 5 DOCTYPE
          </h5>
          <div class="hFinderCategoryFilePath">
            <a href="/Blog/web/html5_doctype.html">
              /Blog/web/html5_doctype.html
            </a>
          </div>
        </li>
        <li class="hFinderCategoryFile">
          <div class="hFinderCategoryFileIcon"></div>
          <h5 class="hFinderCategoryFileTitle">
            First Impressions of IE 8 Beta 2
          </h5>
          <div class="hFinderCategoryFilePath">
            <a href="/Blog/web/ie8_beta2.html">
              /Blog/web/ie8_beta2.html
            </a>
          </div>
        </li>
      </ul>
      <ul id='hFinderOtherCategoryFiles'>
      </ul>
    </div>
  </body>
</html>
```

2. Using the style sheet in Example 11-1.css, make the following modifications and save the results in a new file, as *Example 11-2.css*:

```
html,
body {
    width: 100%;
    height: 100%;
}
body {
    font: normal 12px "Lucida Grande", Arial, sans-serif;
    background: rgb(189, 189, 189)
      url('../../../Images/Finder/Bottom.png') repeat-x bottom;
```

```
    color: rgb(50, 50, 50);
    margin: 0;
    padding: 0;
}
div#hFinderCategoryFileWrapper {
    position: absolute;
    top: 0;
    right: 0;
    bottom: 23px;
    left: 0;
}
ul#hFinderCategoryFiles,
ul#hFinderOtherCategoryFiles {
    float: left;
    height: 100%;
    width: 300px;
    border-bottom: 1px solid rgb(64, 64, 64);
    border-right: 1px solid rgb(64, 64, 64);
    background: #fff;
    list-style: none;
    margin: 0;
    padding: 0;
}
li.hFinderCategoryFile {
    clear: both;
    padding: 5px 5px 10px 5px;
    min-height: 48px;
    width: 290px;
}
li.hFinderCategoryFile h5 {
    font: normal 12px "Lucida Grande", Arial, sans-serif;
    margin: 0;
}
div.hFinderCategoryFileIcon {
    float: left;
    width: 48px;
    height: 48px;
    background: url('../../../Images/Finder/Safari Document.png') no-repeat;
}
h5.hFinderCategoryFileTitle,
div.hFinderCategoryFilePath {
    padding-left: 55px;
}
li.hFinderCategoryFileSelected {
    background: rgb(24, 67, 243)
      url('../../../Images/Backgrounds/Selected Item.png') repeat-x bottom;
    color: white;
}
li.hFinderCategoryFileSelected a {
    color: lightblue;
}
.hFinderCategoryFilePlaceholder {
    background: rgb(230, 230, 230);
    height: 58px;
}
```

3. Starting with Example 11-1.IE.css, create the following style sheet and save the modified style sheet as *Example 11-2.IE.css*:

```
ul#hFinderCategoryFiles,
ul#hFinderOtherCategoryFiles {
    height: expression(document.body.offsetHeight - 23);
}
div.hFinderCategoryFileIcon {
    background: none;
    filter: progid:DXImageTransform.Microsoft.AlphaImageLoader
      (src='../../../Images/Finder/Safari Document.png',
sizingMethod='crop');
}
```

4. Starting with the JavaScript file you created in Example 11-1.js, make the following modifications and save the new JavaScript file as *Example 11-2.js*:

```
$(document).ready(
  function() {
    var $selectedFile;

    $('li.hFinderCategoryFile').mousedown(
      function() {
        if ($selectedFile && $selectedFile.length) {
          $selectedFile.removeClass('hFinderCategoryFileSelected');
        }

        $selectedFile = $(this);
        $selectedFile.addClass('hFinderCategoryFileSelected');
      }
    );

    $('ul#hFinderCategoryFiles').sortable({
      connectWith : [
        'ul#hFinderOtherCategoryFiles'
      ],
      placeholder: 'hFinderCategoryFilePlaceholder',
      opacity: 0.8,
      cursor: 'move'
    });

    $('ul#hFinderOtherCategoryFiles').sortable({
      connectWith : [
        'ul#hFinderCategoryFiles'
      ],
      placeholder: 'hFinderCategoryFilePlaceholder',
      opacity: 0.8,
      cursor: 'move'
    });
  }
);
```

The preceding gives you something similar to what you see in **Figure 11-4**.

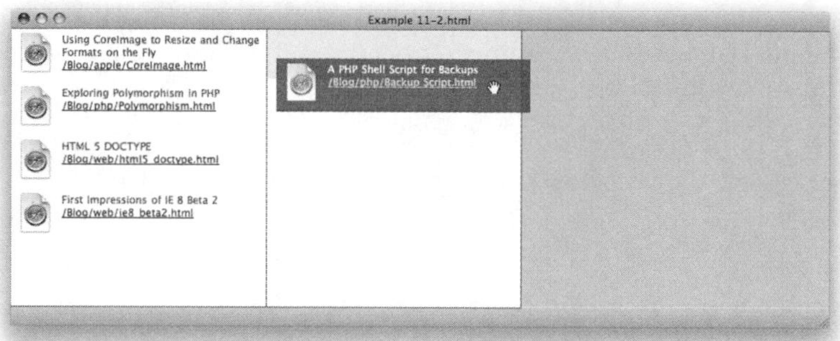

Figure 11-4

In Example 11-2, you added a few options to the `sortable()` method and tweaked the presentation of the document to accommodate multiple lists.

Presentationally speaking, there was one unique challenge in having the correct rendering in IE6 and IE7 as you have in other browsers. In Example 11-1, the files are contained in a `<ul>` element, and that element is made into an absolutely positioned column. It turns out that IE z-index bugs prevent you from using that technique to make columns with sortable lists. This can also be a bug in the Sortables plugin, but the gist of the matter is that, with absolutely positioned columns, it is impossible for the draggable elements to have the right z-index with respect to the other column, even after explicitly setting a z-index on each absolutely positioned column. What happens when you try this approach is, when dragging an element to a separate list, the `drag` element goes behind the list, instead of staying on top, as it is supposed to do. To work around this bug, I took a different approach for making columns, using CSS floating rather than positioning. The first step in implementing the alternative approach is to create a wrapper element in the markup that contains both columns.

```
<div id='hFinderCategoryFileWrapper'>
<ul id='hFinderCategoryFiles'>
```

The `<div>` element contains two `<ul>` elements; each, in turn, is a sortable list. Each `<ul>` element is also made into a column that spans the height of the `<div>` element. The following CSS is used to prepare the `<div>` element so that the `<ul>` elements within it can become columns.

```
div#hFinderCategoryFileWrapper {
    position: absolute;
    top: 0;
    right: 0;
    bottom: 23px;
    left: 0;
}
```

The `<div>` element is positioned absolutely, and the four offset properties are used to imply width and height, causing the `<div>` element to take up the entire viewport, save the bottom 23 pixels. Then syles are applied to each `<ul>` element. Each `<ul>` element is floated to the left and given fixed dimensions.

This styling manages to turn both <ul> elements into columns, matching the visual look and feel that you saw in Example 11-1, but also managing to work around the annoying IE z-index bug that rears its ugly head when you try to sort between the two lists.

```
ul#hFinderCategoryFiles,
ul#hFinderOtherCategoryFiles {
    float: left;
    height: 100%;
    width: 300px;
    border-bottom: 1px solid rgb(64, 64, 64);
    border-right: 1px solid rgb(64, 64, 64);
    background: #fff;
    list-style: none;
    margin: 0;
    padding: 0;
}
```

Going back to the JavaScript, the scripting portion should be pretty straightforward. The `connectWith` option, which accepts a selector as its value, lets you connect one list to another so that you have the ability to sort items between multiple lists.

Then, the other options — `placeholder`, `opacity`, and `cursor` — are each used to tweak the presentation of each sortable list. The `placeholder` option, as you already learned, lets you add a custom class name to the element that acts as a placeholder during sorting. The `opacity` option is used to control the opacity of the `helper` element, and it takes a standard CSS 3 `opacity` property value (that works in IE too). The `cursor` option is used to change the cursor while the helper is being dragged, and it takes any value that the CSS `cursor` property can take.

```
$('ul#hFinderCategoryFiles').sortable({
    connectWith : [
      'ul#hFinderOtherCategoryFiles'
    ],
    placeholder: 'hFinderCategoryFilePlaceholder',
    opacity: 0.8,
    cursor: 'move'
});
```

In the preceding snippet of code, the <ul> list with ID name *hFinderCategoryFiles* is connected to the <ul> list with ID name *hFinderOtherCategoryFiles*. The `connectWith` option specified for this list sets up a one-way connection from the first <ul> element to the second, which lets you drag items from the first list to the second, but not vice versa. To have two-way sorting, you need to set options on the second <ul> list, which you see in the following snippet:

```
$('ul#hFinderOtherCategoryFiles').sortable({
    connectWith : [
      'ul#hFinderCategoryFiles'
    ],
    placeholder: 'hFinderCategoryFilePlaceholder',
    opacity: 0.8,
    cursor: 'move'
});
```

You set basically the same options on the other `<ul>` element, except for the `connectWith` option, where you use a selector to reference the first `<ul>` element.

Again, I have presented just a few of the options that you can set for Sortables. All options for Sortables are documented in Appendix K.

Saving the State of Sorted Lists

The Sortables API in jQuery UI wouldn't be complete without one last detail — saving the state of a sorted list. This too is covered by the Sortables plugin. In Chapter 7, you learned about jQuery's `serialize()` method, which automatically takes a selection of input elements for a form and serializes the data in those input elements into a string of data that you can then submit to a server-side script with an AJAX Request. The Sortables plugin provides a similar mechanism for retrieving data from a sortable list. But instead of retrieving input form values, the Sortables plugin retrieves a specific attribute from each sortable element. By default, the Sortables plugin will retrieve the value of the `id` attribute. So in the context of the examples you've completed in this chapter, you'd give each `<li>` element an `id` attribute, then use the Sortables plugin's mechanism for serializing the data present in each `id` attribute into a string that you can pass on to an AJAX Request to a server-side script, so you can save the sort. The following code snippet shows the code you'd use on the JavaScript side:

```
var $data = $('ul').sortable(
  'serialize', {
    key: 'listItem[]'
  }
);
```

In the preceding code, to serialize the data present in the `id` attribute of each `<li>` element, you call the `sortable()` method, with the first argument set to `'serialize'`, and for the second argument, you specify an object literal of options. The `key` option specifies the name you want to use for each query string argument. I've used the name `listItem[]`, which in PHP and some other server-side scripts will cause the query string of sorted items to be translated into an array or hash.

To better illustrate how you serialize data using the `sortable()` method, the following document demonstrates how that works:

```
<!DOCTYPE html PUBLIC "-//W3C//DTD XHTML 1.0 Strict//EN"
    "http://www.w3.org/TR/xhtml1/DTD/xhtml1-strict.dtd">
<html xmlns='http://www.w3.org/1999/xhtml' xml:lang='en'>
  <head>
    <meta http-equiv='content-type' content='text/html; charset=utf-8' />
    <meta http-equiv='content-language' content='en-us' />
    <title></title>
    <script type='text/javascript'
            src='../../../Source Code/jQuery/jQuery.js'></script>
    <script type='text/javascript'
            src='../../../Source Code/jQuery/jQueryUI.js'></script>
    <script type='text/javascript' src='Figure 11-5.js'></script>
    <link type='text/css' href='Figure 11-5.css' rel='stylesheet' />
  </head>
  <body>
    <h4>Lord of the Rings Characters</h4>
```

```
    <ul>
      <li id='tmpFrodo'>Frodo</li>
      <li id='tmpSam'>Sam</li>
      <li id='tmpPippin'>Pippin</li>
      <li id='tmpMeriadoc'>Meriadoc</li>
      <li id='tmpGandalf'>Gandalf</li>
      <li id='tmpAragorn'>Aragorn</li>
      <li id='tmpArwen'>Arwen</li>
      <li id='tmpGimli'>Gimli</li>
      <li id='tmpLegolas'>Legolas</li>
      <li id='tmpBoromir'>Boromir</li>
      <li id='tmpFaramir'>Faramir</li>
      <li id='tmpGollum'>Gollum</li>
    </ul>
  </body>
</html>
```

This document uses the same CSS as **Figure 11-3**, so I won't repeat that portion. The following JavaScript demonstrates how the `id` attribute of each `<li>` element is serialized:

```
$(document).ready(
  function() {
    $('ul').sortable({
      placeholder: 'tmpPlaceholder',
      helper: function(e, element) {
         return $(element).clone().addClass('tmpHelper');
      },
      update : function(e, ui) {
        alert(
          $(this).sortable(
            'serialize', {
              key: 'list[]',
              expression: /^(.*)$/
            }
          )
        )
      }
    });
  }
);
```

The preceding results in the screenshot you see in **Figure 11-5**, once you try sorting an item.

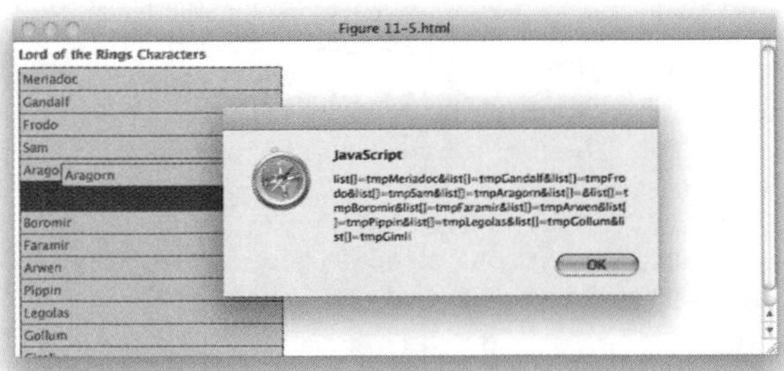

Figure 11-5

The serialized data is popped up on screen in a JavaScript alert.

In the preceding JavaScript, you add a new option to the configuration for the sortable list — the `update` option. The `update` option takes a callback function that is executed every time a sort is completed. From within the callback function that you assign to the update method, you can retrieve data from the sortable list, then forward that data onto a server-side script, allowing you to save sortable list data as it is sorted, in real time. To retrieve the data, you call the `sortable()` method, with the first argument set to `'serialize'`; then you provide a few options in the second argument. The `key` option defines what name to give the data for submission to a server-side script. The other option, `expression`, lets you define a regular expression that is applied to the attribute you're getting data from. The expression that I have used, `/^(.*)$/`, says to get whatever value the attribute has, that is, the whole value, not a subset of the value. You can use a more sophisticated regular expression to get a string from within the `id` attribute. Once this method is executed, the following is the data it returns:

```
list[]=tmpMeriadoc&list[]=tmpGandalf&list[]=tmpFrodo&list[]=tmpAragorn&list[]=tmpSa
m&list[]=tmpBoromir&list[]=tmpFaramir&list[]=tmpArwen&list[]=tmpPippin&list[]=&list
[]=tmpLegolas&list[]=tmpCollum&list[]=tmpGimli
```

You see that you have a long query string of data that includes the value of each `<li>` element's `id` attribute. This data can then be directly included in the `data` argument of a jQuery AJAX Request.

In the following "Try It Out," you apply the concepts you've just learned to the sortable files example that you've been working on throughout this chapter:

Try It Out — How to Save the State of a Sorted List

Example 11-3

To see how to save the state of a sorted list, follow these steps.

1. Using Example 11-2.html as the basis, copy the contents of that file into a new document, and save that document as *Example 11-3.html*; then add a `title` attribute to each `<li>` element, as you see in the following markup. Don't forget to update each file reference to Example 11-3.

```
<!DOCTYPE html PUBLIC "-//W3C//DTD XHTML 1.0 Strict//EN"
    "http://www.w3.org/TR/xhtml1/DTD/xhtml1-strict.dtd">
<html xmlns='http://www.w3.org/1999/xhtml' xml:lang='en'>
  <head>
    <meta http-equiv='content-type' content='text/html; charset=utf-8' />
    <meta http-equiv='content-language' content='en-us' />
    <title></title>
    <script type='text/javascript'
            src='../../../Source Code/jQuery/jQuery.js'></script>
    <script type='text/javascript'
            src='../../../Source Code/jQuery/jQueryUI.js'></script>
    <script type='text/javascript' src='Example 11-3.js'></script>
    <link type='text/css' href='Example 11-3.css' rel='stylesheet' />
    <!--[if lt IE 8]>
      <link type='text/css' href='Example 11-3.IE.css' rel='stylesheet' />
    <![endif]-->
  </head>
  <body>
    <div id='hFinderCategoryFileWrapper'>
```

```
<ul id='hFinderCategoryFiles'>
  <li class="hFinderCategoryFile" title="/Blog/apple/CoreImage.html">
    <div class="hFinderCategoryFileIcon"></div>
    <h5 class="hFinderCategoryFileTitle">
      Using CoreImage to Resize and Change Formats on the Fly
    </h5>
    <div class="hFinderCategoryFilePath">
      <a href="/Blog/apple/CoreImage.html">
        /Blog/apple/CoreImage.html
      </a>
    </div>
  </li>
  <li class="hFinderCategoryFile" title="/Blog/php/Polymorphism.html">
    <div class="hFinderCategoryFileIcon"></div>
    <h5 class="hFinderCategoryFileTitle">
      Exploring Polymorphism in PHP
    </h5>
    <div class="hFinderCategoryFilePath">
      <a href="/Blog/php/Polymorphism.html">
        /Blog/php/Polymorphism.html
      </a>
    </div>
  </li>
  <li class="hFinderCategoryFile" title="/Blog/php/Backup Script.html">
    <div class="hFinderCategoryFileIcon"></div>
    <h5 class="hFinderCategoryFileTitle">
      A PHP Shell Script for Backups
    </h5>
    <div class="hFinderCategoryFilePath">
      <a href="/Blog/php/Backup%20Script.html">
        /Blog/php/Backup Script.html
      </a>
    </div>
  </li>
  <li class="hFinderCategoryFile" title="/Blog/web/html5_doctype.html">
    <div class="hFinderCategoryFileIcon"></div>
    <h5 class="hFinderCategoryFileTitle">
      HTML 5 DOCTYPE
    </h5>
    <div class="hFinderCategoryFilePath">
      <a href="/Blog/web/html5_doctype.html">
        /Blog/web/html5_doctype.html
      </a>
    </div>
  </li>
  <li class="hFinderCategoryFile" title="/Blog/web/ie8_beta2.html">
    <div class="hFinderCategoryFileIcon"></div>
    <h5 class="hFinderCategoryFileTitle">
      First Impressions of IE 8 Beta 2
    </h5>
    <div class="hFinderCategoryFilePath">
      <a href="/Blog/web/ie8_beta2.html">
        /Blog/web/ie8_beta2.html
      </a>
```

```
        </div>
      </li>
    </ul>
    <ul id='hFinderOtherCategoryFiles'>
    </ul>
  </div>
</body>
</html>
```

2. Copy Example 11-2.css to a new file, and save that file as *Example 11-3.css*.
3. Copy Example 11-2.IE.css to a new file, *Example 11-3.IE.css*.
4. Copy Example 11-2.js to a new file, *Example 11-3.js*, and make the following modifications:

```
$(document).ready(
  function() {
    var $selectedFile;

    $('li.hFinderCategoryFile').mousedown(
      function() {
        if ($selectedFile && $selectedFile.length) {
          $selectedFile.removeClass('hFinderCategoryFileSelected');
        }

        $selectedFile = $(this);
        $selectedFile.addClass('hFinderCategoryFileSelected');
      }
    );

    var saveUpdate = function(e, ui) {
      var $data = $(this).sortable(
        'serialize', {
          attribute: 'title',
          expression: /^(.*)$/,
          key: 'categoryFiles[]'
        }
      );

      alert($data);

      // Here you could go on to make an AJAX request
      // to save the sorted data on the server, which
      // might look like this:
      //
      // $.get('/path/to/server/file.php', $data);
    };

    $('ul#hFinderCategoryFiles').sortable({
      connectWith : [
        'ul#hFinderOtherCategoryFiles'
      ],
      placeholder: 'hFinderCategoryFilePlaceholder',
      opacity: 0.8,
      cursor: 'move',
      update: saveUpdate
```

```
        });

        $('ul#hFinderOtherCategoryFiles').sortable({
          connectWith : [
            'ul#hFinderCategoryFiles'
          ],
          placeholder: 'hFinderCategoryFilePlaceholder',
          opacity: 0.8,
          cursor: 'move',
          update: saveUpdate
        });
      }
    );
```

The preceding document gives you something similar to the screenshot that you see in **Figure 11-6**.

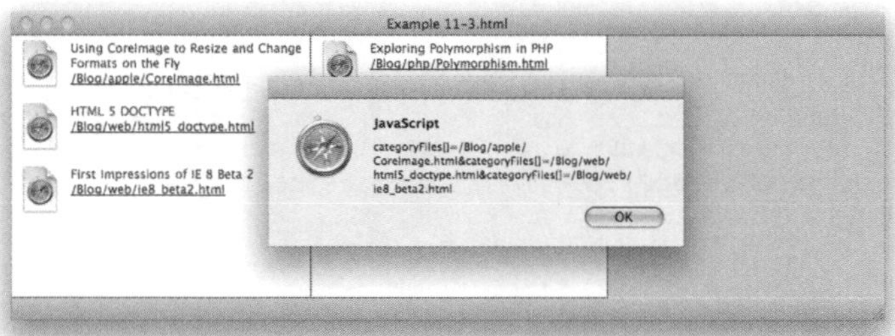

Figure 11-6

In Example 11-3, you add some code that retrieves data from each `<li>` element. However, instead of getting data from the `id` attribute, which is what jQuery UI uses by default, you're getting data from the `title` attribute.

```
var saveUpdate = function(e, ui) {
  var $data = $(this).sortable(
    'serialize', {
      attribute: 'title',
      expression: /^(.*)$/,
      key: 'categoryFiles[]'
    }
  );

  alert($data);

  // Here you could go on to make an AJAX request
  // to save the sorted data on the server, which
  // might look like this:
  //
  // $.get('/path/to/server/file.php', $data);
};
```

You start this project by defining a new function that will act as the callback function for the `update` option; this function is named `saveUpdate`. Within the `saveUpdate` function, you retrieve data from each `<li>` element by calling the `sortable()` method, with the `serialize` option. Then, in the options you pass in the second argument to that method, you change the attribute that jQuery UI serializes data from by using the `attribute` option and setting the value of that option to `title`. The rest is the same: You use the `expression` option to retrieve the `title` attribute's entire value, from beginning to end, rather than just a substring within that value. And the `key` option is set to `categoryFiles[]`, which is used to name the data in the serialized string.

You could then go on to submit that data to the server, automatically, giving you the ability to save the sort as a list is sorted.

Summary

In this chapter, you learned how to make sortable lists with the jQuery UI Sortables plugin. Using the Sortables plugin, you are able to offer a drag-and-drop sorting API very effortlessly. jQuery UI provides a plethora of options that you can use for fine-grained control.

You learned how to use options like `placeholder`, `helper`, `cursor`, and `opacity` to control the look and feel of a sortable list. The `placeholder` option, you saw, takes a class name, which allows you to use CSS to customize the look of the space that's reserved for a sortable element as sorting is taking place. You saw how the `helper` option can be provided with a callback function, where you can return the element that the user drags around. And you saw how the `opacity` and `cursor` options both take the same values of the CSS `opacity` and `cursor` properties.

You saw how multiple lists can be connected to each other using the `connectWith` option, which you provide with a selector that indicates which list you want that sortable list to be able to exchange items with. The `connectWith` option creates a one-way link to another list, which means that you can only drag items to the other list, but not back to the original. To create a two-way link, you can also add the `connectWith` option to the other list, with a selector that references the first list.

You've also learned how to save the state of sorted lists, which is also done with the `sortable()` method. In the first argument, you provide the string `'serialize'`, then in the second argument, you can provide options that determine how serialization works — for example, you provide the `attribute` option if you want to get the value of any attribute other than the `id` attribute. Another option you can use is the `expression` option, which takes a JavaScript regular expression as its value. Then, the `key` option is used to name the data that's serialized.

You also learned how the `update` option can be provided to sortable lists, which takes a callback function that executes once a sort is completed.

Exercises

1. What method do you use to make a list sortable?
2. What kind of value do you provide to the `placeholder` option?
3. What is the purpose of the `placeholder` option?
4. If you want to change the cursor displayed as a sort is taking place, which option would you use?
5. What is the purpose of the `helper` option?
6. Which option do you use to connect multiple sortable lists to one another?
7. What kind of value do you provide to the `connectWith` option?
8. How do you save the state of a sortable list after every sort takes place?

Selection by Drawing a Box

In this chapter, I present the jQuery UI Selectables plugin. The Selectables plugin fills more of a niche need for UI functionality. I say that because you probably won't use this functionality very much in your applications. The functionality provided by the Selectables plugin is the ability to select elements by drawing a box, something you've probably done a few times in your operating system's file manager or a graphical editor like Photoshop.

The Selectables plugin's status as niche functionality is evident in its scant documentation on the official jQuery website at `www.jquery.com` and by the fact that there aren't as many customization options for this plugin as there are for the plugins covered in the previous two chapters.

Nonetheless, the Selectables plugin can be very useful, and I'll show you in this chapter at least one practical application of this plugin — a continuation of the Mac OS X Finder clone that you started in Chapter 10.

Introducing the Selectables Plugin

The Selectables plugin works similarly to the Sortables plugin that I presented in Chapter 11, and all jQuery UI plugins, as you'll have recognized by now, share a clean and consistent API that is implemented in pretty much the same way from plugin to plugin.

To make elements into Selectable elements, you call the `selectable()` method on any element that contains a list of elements that you want to be selectable by drawing a box with your mouse. In the following example, I present a very remedial proof-of-concept demonstration of the Selectables functionality.

```
<!DOCTYPE html PUBLIC "-//W3C//DTD XHTML 1.0 Strict//EN"
    "http://www.w3.org/TR/xhtml1/DTD/xhtml1-strict.dtd">
<html xmlns='http://www.w3.org/1999/xhtml' xml:lang='en'>
  <head>
    <meta http-equiv='content-type' content='text/html; charset=utf-8' />
    <meta http-equiv='content-language' content='en-us' />
    <title></title>
    <script type='text/javascript'
            src='../../../Source Code/jQuery/jQuery.js'></script>
    <script type='text/javascript'
            src='../../../Source Code/jQuery/jQueryUI.js'></script>
```

```
      <script type='text/javascript' src='Figure 12-1.js'></script>
      <link type='text/css' href='Figure 12-1.css' rel='stylesheet' />
    </head>
    <body>
      <h4>The Beatles</h4>
      <ul>
        <li>John Lennon</li>
        <li>Paul McCartney</li>
        <li>George Harrison</li>
        <li>Ringo Starr</li>
      </ul>
    </body>
  </html>
```

The following style sheet is included in the preceding markup document:

```
body {
    font: 12px "Lucida Grande", Arial, sans-serif;
    background: #fff;
    color: rgb(50, 50, 50);
    margin: 0;
    padding: 0;
}
h4 {
    margin: 5px;
}
ul {
    list-style: none;
    margin: 0;
    padding: 15px 5px;
}
li {
    background: gold;
    padding: 3px;
    width: 244px;
    margin: 1px;
}
li.tmpSelected {
    background: yellow;
}
```

The following JavaScript is also included in the preceding markup document:

```
$(document).ready(
  function() {
    $('ul').selectable({
      selecting: function(e, ui) {
        $(ui.selecting).addClass('tmpSelected');
      },
      unselecting: function(e, ui) {
        $(ui.unselecting).removeClass('tmpSelected');
      }
    });
  }
);
```

The preceding example results in the screenshot that you see in **Figure 12-1** when you try drawing a box within the boundaries of the <ul> element.

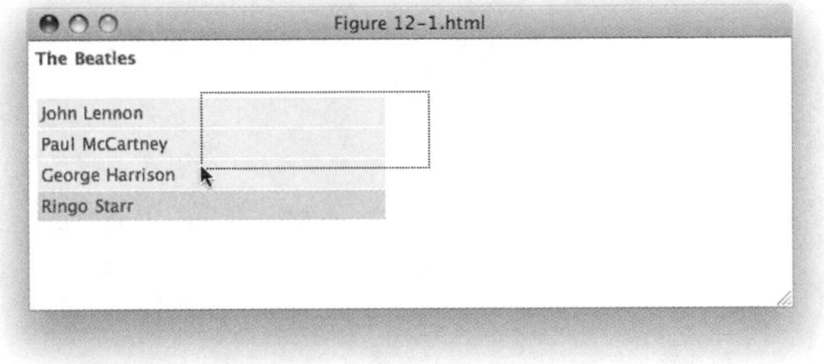

Figure 12-1

In the preceding example, you see how easy it is to use the jQuery UI Selectables plugin. The `selectable()` method is called on an element containing a list of elements that you want to be selectable. Naturally, in this example, the `selectable()` method is called on a <ul> element, so that you can select one or more of its child <li> elements by drawing a box. The Selectables plugin, like the other jQuery UI plugins that I've presented so far, accepts an object literal in its first argument, which is used to provide options for how the plugin works. You see two options here, the `selecting` and the `unselecting` options. The `selecting` option specifies a callback function that is executed as a selection is made, on each element added to the selection. The element added to the selection is available in the second argument, `ui`, as `ui.selecting`. The `unselecting` option, conversely, provides a callback function that executes as elements are removed from the selection. Like the selecting option, the element being removed from the selection is also available in the second, `ui`, argument, as `ui.unselecting`. In this example, these two options are used to add and remove the class name from <li> elements as they are included and removed from the selection.

To put the Selectables plugin into real-world context, in the following "Try It Out," you apply the Selectables plugin to the Mac OS X Finder clone that you last worked on in Example 10-4, expanding the Finder clone so that you have the ability to select multiple folders by drawing a box, just as your desktop OS does.

Try It Out — Adding Selectability to Your Finder Clone

Example 12-1

To see how you apply the jQuery UI Selectables plugin to your Finder clone, follow these steps.

1. Copy the markup document that you made in Example 10-4.html to a new document, and make the following modifications:

```
<!DOCTYPE html PUBLIC "-//W3C//DTD XHTML 1.0 Strict//EN"
    "http://www.w3.org/TR/xhtml1/DTD/xhtml1-strict.dtd">
<html xmlns='http://www.w3.org/1999/xhtml' xml:lang='en'>
  <head>
    <meta http-equiv='content-type' content='text/html; charset=utf-8' />
    <meta http-equiv='content-language' content='en-us' />
    <title></title>
```

```
    <script type='text/javascript'
            src='../../../Source Code/jQuery/jQuery.js'></script>
    <script type='text/javascript'
            src='../../../Source Code/jQuery/jQueryUI.js'></script>
    <script type='text/javascript' src='Example 12-1.js'></script>
    <link type='text/css' href='Example 12-1.css' rel='stylesheet' />
    <!--[if lt IE 7]>
      <link type='text/css' href='Example 12-1.IE.css' rel='stylesheet' />
    <![endif]-->
  </head>
  <body>
    <div id="hFinderFiles">
      <div class="hFinderDirectory" title="/Applications">
        <div class="hFinderIcon"><div></div></div>
        <div class="hFinderDirectoryName">
          <span>Applications</span>
        </div>
      </div>
      <div class="hFinderDirectory" title="/Library">
        <div class="hFinderIcon"><div></div></div>
        <div class="hFinderDirectoryName">
          <span>Library</span>
        </div>
      </div>
      <div class="hFinderDirectory" title="/Network">
        <div class="hFinderIcon"><div></div></div>
        <div class="hFinderDirectoryName">
          <span>Network</span>
        </div>
      </div>
      <div class="hFinderDirectory" title="/Sites">
        <div class="hFinderIcon"><div></div></div>
        <div class="hFinderDirectoryName">
          <span>Sites</span>
        </div>
      </div>
      <div class="hFinderDirectory" title="/System">
        <div class="hFinderIcon"><div></div></div>
        <div class="hFinderDirectoryName">
          <span>System</span>
        </div>
      </div>
      <div class="hFinderDirectory" title="/Users">
        <div class="hFinderIcon"><div></div></div>
        <div class="hFinderDirectoryName">
          <span>Users</span>
        </div>
      </div>
    </div>
  </body>
</html>
```

2. Save the preceding markup document as *Example 12-1.html.*

3. Copy the CSS document that you made in Example 10-4.css to a new document, and make the following modifications:

```
html,
body {
    width: 100%;
    height: 100%;
    overflow: hidden;
}
body {
    font: 12px "Lucida Grande", Arial, sans-serif;
    background: rgb(189, 189, 189)
      url('../../../Images/Finder/Bottom.png') repeat-x bottom;
    color: rgb(50, 50, 50);
    margin: 0;
    padding: 0;
}
div#hFinderFiles {
    border-bottom: 1px solid rgb(64, 64, 64);
    background: #fff;
    position: absolute;
    top: 0;
    right: 0;
    bottom: 23px;
    left: 0;
    overflow: auto;
}
div.hFinderDirectory {
    float: left;
    width: 150px;
    height: 100px;
    overflow: hidden;
}
div.hFinderIcon {
    height: 56px;
    width: 54px;
    margin: 10px auto 3px auto;
}
div.hFinderIcon div {
    background: url('../../../Images/Finder/Folder 48x48.png')
      no-repeat center;
    width: 48px;
    height: 48px;
    margin: auto;
}
div.hFinderIconSelected,
div.hFinderDirectoryDrop div.hFinderIcon {
    background-color: rgb(196, 196, 196);
    -moz-border-radius: 5px;
    -webkit-border-radius: 5px;
}
div.hFinderDirectoryDrop div.hFinderIcon div {
    background-image:
      url('../../../Images/Finder/Open Folder 48x48.png');
}
```

```
div.hFinderDirectoryName {
    text-align: center;
}
span.hFinderDirectoryNameSelected,
div.hFinderDirectoryDrop span {
    background: rgb(56, 117, 215);
    -moz-border-radius: 8px;
    -webkit-border-radius: 8px;
    color: white;
    padding: 1px 7px;
}
div.ui-selectable-helper {
    background: rgb(128, 128, 128) !important;
    border: 1px solid black !important;
    opacity: 0.25;
    /* IE6 and IE7 */
    filter: alpha(opacity=25);
    /* IE8 standards mode */
    -ms-filter: "alpha(opacity=25)";
}
```

4. Save the preceding document as *Example 12-1.css.*
5. Copy the file you made in Example 10-4.IE.css to a new file called *Example 12-1.IE.css.*
6. Copy the JavaScript file you made in Example 10-4.js, and make the following modifications:

```
var $$ = $.fn;

$$.extend({
  SelectElement: function() {
    $(this).find('div.hFinderIcon')
      .addClass('hFinderIconSelected');

    $(this).find('div.hFinderDirectoryName span')
      .addClass('hFinderDirectoryNameSelected');

    $.each(
      this,
      function() {
        if ($.inArray(this, $$.Finder.SelectedElements) == -1) {
          $$.Finder.SelectedElements.push(this);
        }
      }
    );

    return $;
  },

  UnselectElement: function() {
    $(this).find('div.hFinderIcon')
      .removeClass('hFinderIconSelected');

    $(this).find('div.hFinderDirectoryName span')
      .removeClass('hFinderDirectoryNameSelected');

    // Don't remove the item from the array, unless it is
```

```
      // being unselected individually (as opposed to
      // all elements being unselected)
      if (arguments[0]) {
        // Alias the selection to elements, so you can reference it
        // from within the anonymous function passed to grep.
        var elements = this;

        if ($$.Finder.SelectedElements.length) {
          $$.Finder.SelectedElements = $.grep(
            $$.Finder.SelectedElements,
            function(item, i) {
              // If the item isn't in the selection, it should
              // be kept.
              return $.inArray(item, elements) == -1;
            }
          );
        }
      }

      return $;
    },

    Finder: {
      SelectingElements: false,
      SelectedElements: [],

      UnselectSelected: function() {
        $.each(
          $$.Finder.SelectedElements,
          function() {
            $(this).UnselectElement();
          }
        );

        $$.Finder.SelectedElements = [];
      },
      FolderOver: {
        background: 'none',
        filter:
          "progid:DXImageTransform.Microsoft.AlphaImageLoader" +
          "(src='../../../Images/Finder/Open Folder 48x48.png'," +
            "sizingMethod='crop')"
      },
      FolderOut: {
        background: 'none',
        filter:
          "progid:DXImageTransform.Microsoft.AlphaImageLoader" +
          "(src='../../../Images/Finder/Folder 48x48.png'," +
            "sizingMethod='crop')"
      },
      Ready: function() {
        $('div.hFinderDirectory')
          .mousedown(
            function() {
              if (!$$.Finder.SelectingElements) {
                // Unselect all selected
```

```
          $$.Finder.UnselectSelected();

          // Select this element.
          $(this).SelectElement();
        }
      }
    )
    .draggable({
      helper: 'clone',
      opacity: 0.5
    })
    .droppable({
      accept: 'div.hFinderDirectory',
      hoverClass: 'hFinderDirectoryDrop',
      over: function(e, ui) {
        if ($.browser.msie && $.browser.version == 6.0) {
          $(this).find('div.hFinderIcon div').css(
            $$.Finder.FolderOver
          );
        }
      },
      out: function(e, ui) {
        if ($.browser.msie && $.browser.version == 6.0) {
          $(this).find('div.hFinderIcon div').css(
            $$.Finder.FolderOut
          );
        }
      },
      drop: function(e, ui) {
        var $path = ui.draggable.attr('title');
        // Do something with the path

        // Remove the element that was dropped.
        ui.draggable.remove();
      }
    });

  // Make it possible to select folders and files by
  // drawing a box with the mouse.
  $('div#hFinderFiles').selectable({
    start: function(e, ui) {
      // Selection has started, prevent the selection
      // of individual elements
      $$.Finder.SelectingElements = true;

      // Unselect anything already selected
      $$.Finder.UnselectSelected();
    },
    stop: function(e, ui) {
      // Allow the individual selection of elements again.
      $$.Finder.SelectingElements = false;
    },
    selecting: function(e, ui) {
```

```
                if (ui.selecting) {
                  $(ui.selecting).SelectElement();
                }
              },
              unselecting: function(e, ui) {
                $(ui.unselecting).UnselectElement(true);
              }
            });
          }
        }
      });

      $(document).ready($$.Finder.Ready);
```

7. Save the preceding document as *Example 12-1.js*.

The preceding source code comes together to give you the document that you see in **Figure 12-2**.

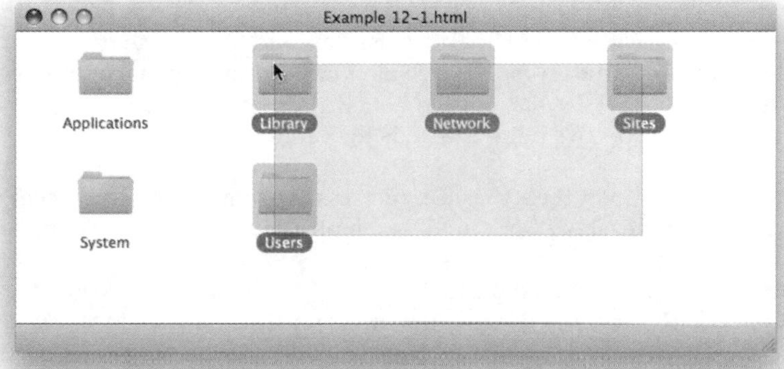

Figure 12-2

While this example teaches you how to draw a selection box, you'll note that you're not able to drag the selection once it is made, even though you have implemented drag-and-drop on the individual folders. While this is possible, it is beyond the scope of this example.

In this example, you applied the Selectables plugin to the Mac OS X Finder Clone that you worked on in Chapter 10. This example drops the native Safari Drag-and-Drop API that I discussed in Chapter 10, to make the example smaller and more focused. This example also incorporates a lot of jQuery functionality that you learned about in previous chapters to better demonstrate how you apply jQuery in a realistic example.

You made a few changes to the style sheet. Besides dropping Safari's native Drag-and-Drop API from there, you added one additional rule that gives you the ability to customize the box that's drawn when a selection is made. jQuery's default selection box looks like the one used in older operating systems, like

Windows 98, which just provides a dotted box to indicate where the box is being drawn. In this example, you changed the style of that box to look more like the selection box in Mac OS X.

```
div.ui-selectable-helper {
    background: rgb(128, 128, 128);
    border: 1px solid black !important;
    opacity: 0.25;
    /* IE6 and IE7 */
    filter: alpha(opacity=25);
    /* IE8 standards mode */
    -ms-filter: "alpha(opacity=25)";
}
```

The selection box must be customized with the same selector that you see here, as jQuery UI does not provide a mechanism for customizing the style of the selection box via an option. The class name *ui-selectable-helper* is the class name that jQuery UI applies to the selection box internally, so the customization that you see simply exploits that fact.

The style provides a gray background and a black border, then the box is made semitransparent via the standard `opacity` property supported by Safari, Firefox, and Opera; the proprietary `filter` property supported by IE6 and IE7; and the proprietary `-ms-filter` property that's supported by IE8 (when in super-standards mode). The IE8 syntax for the `filter` property is the same as previous versions; it just puts quotes around the property's value and adds the vendor-specific `-ms-` prefix.

Aside from those modifications, the style sheet remains the same as the style sheet you made in Chapter 10. The brunt of the elbow work in this example occurs in the JavaScript.

In this example, you re-write the example that you saw in Example 10-4 so that it leverages jQuery's Plugin API, and you add some functionality that deals with keeping track of selected folders.

First you alias jQuery's plugin functionality, which you normally refer to as `$.fn`, to `$$`, or double dollar sign, which, as I mentioned in Chapter 9, is the way that I prefer to work with jQuery's Plugin API and is a "take it or leave it" preference. You may prefer to simply use `$.fn`, or something else entirely; I think `$$` makes the Plugin API more intuitive to work with.

```
var $$ = $.fn;
```

Then you call jQuery's `extend()` method to add your own functionality to jQuery. You add three items to jQuery — `SelectElement()`, `UnselectElement()`, and the `Finder` object.

```
$$.extend({
```

The `SelectElement()` method is called when you want to select a folder or a file. Since you've implemented this function as an extension to jQuery, you can call this function using jQuery when you make a selection or wrap a DOM node with a call to jQuery. For example, you can call `SelectElement()` with `$(this).SelectElement()` or `$('div.hFinderDirectory').SelectElement()`. Since `SelectElement()` is a plugin, it's designed to work just as jQuery's built-in methods work. You can select one or many elements at once.

Within the `SelectElement()` method, you select the folder or file by adding the *hFinderIconSelected* class name to the `<div>` with the class name *hFinderIcon*, which resides within each `<div>` representing a folder or file. Then, you add the *hFinderDirectoryNameSelected* class name to the `<span>` element that resides within the `<div>` with class name *hFinderDirectoryName*.

You did the same thing back in Chapter 10; however, this time, you've modified the selection process so that you have the ability to select multiple files and folders, and, of course, to use jQuery's plugin capabilities. In Chapter 10, you didn't have the ability to reuse the selection functionality, since it was included within the anonymous function executed at the `mousedown` event. This time around, you've made the selection functionality reusable, so that you can take advantage of that functionality not just from within your Finder clone, but also from completely separate applications. And you begin to see how a jQuery application can evolve and how you should think about things like reusing code you've already written and making your applications as extensible as possible.

Why did I add *Directory* to the class name of the element? Wouldn't this template apply to files as well? I add *Directory* to the class name for two reasons. One, I might want to have the ability to style directories differently from files; and two, I need some way of distinguishing directories from files, so that if a user double-clicks on a file, I can have one action take place, like opening or downloading the file, and when a user double-clicks on a directory, I can replace the contents of the window with the contents of that directory. Of course, there are several ways that you can approach this, and you might have a better way of doing it. Having said that, I often do find a better way of doing things after writing an implementation, but for the sake of argument, that's my reasoning behind the naming.

After the class names are added, each selected item is added to the `$$.Finder.SelectedElements` array. I discuss the `Finder` object, how that works, and why I made it later in this section, but the `SelectedElements` array exists to keep track of what directories and files are selected, so that they can easily be referenced in whatever other functionality that I might write that would need to know which items the user selected. Since you can be adding one or more items to the array, and since jQuery always applies actions to one or more items, wherever possible, and wherever it makes sense to do so, you iterate over the selection using jQuery's `each()` method. And as you learned in Chapter 9, jQuery makes the selection available to a plugin using the `this` keyword. Then, as you learned in Chapter 5, the anonymous function provided to `$.each()` is executed for each item in the array passed to it, and each item from the array is available within the anonymous function using the `this` keyword.

Thus, you have to account for the possibility that you are working with one or more items, which are always passed to your plugin in array form, and you want the ability to select one or more items. So, you iterate over the selection with `$.each()`, and each item is added to the `SelectedElements` array using `push()`. You ensure that the array doesn't contain duplicate items by checking to see if the item is in the array before actually adding the item to the array, and you do that with jQuery's `$.inArray()` method, which you learned about in Chapter 8.

Then the function returns the jQuery object, which gives you the ability to chain method calls, as you would with any other jQuery method.

```
SelectElement: function() {
  $(this).find('div.hFinderIcon')
    .addClass('hFinderIconSelected');

  $(this).find('div.hFinderDirectoryName span')
    .addClass('hFinderDirectoryNameSelected');

  $.each(
    this,
```

```
            function() {
              if ($.inArray(this, $$.Finder.SelectedElements) == -1) {
                $$.Finder.SelectedElements.push(this);
              }
            }
          );

          return $;
        },
```

The next function is the `UnselectElement()` function. This function removes the *hFinderIconSelected* and *hFinderDirectoryNameSelected* class names from the relevant elements, removing the "selected" style. Then, it removes that/those item(s) from the `SelectedElements` array. Like the `SelectElement()` function, the `UnselectElement()` function is able to handle one or more items passed to it.

Removing items from the `SelectedElements` array is triggered when the first argument to the function is specified in a call and has any value other than `false` or `null`. This trigger is put in place to account for situations in which all items are unselected at once, which is done in the `$$.Finder.UnselectSelected()` function. Without that toggle, you run into a chicken/egg scenario — within the `UnselectSelected()` function, you iterate over the `SelectedElements` array to unselect every item in it, but in the `UnselectElement()` function, you remove items from the `SelectedElements` array. Doing both at the same time results in a breakdown because in the `UnselectSelected()` method, you can't iterate over an array that's constantly being changed. The toggle in the `UnselectElement()` method lets you control whether the item is removed from the `SelectedElements` array or not, preserving your ability to unselect all elements at once.

Within the section of code that removes items from the `SelectedElements` array, the first thing that you do is alias the selection, which is available in the `this` keyword, to the variable named `elements`. You alias the selection because when you filter the `SelectedElements` array with `$.grep()`, you need to be able to reference the selection from within the anonymous function passed to that method, and once you're working within that anonymous function, the `this` keyword has a different meaning. As you've seen throughout this book, jQuery typically gives the `this` keyword a value that is meaningful in relation to what you're doing. In a plugin, the `this` keyword refers to the elements you've selected with jQuery through the `$()` method or the countless other methods that let you modify a selection. Also, as you learned in Chapter 5, in jQuery's `$.each()` method, in the function you pass to `$.each()`, each item in the array is passed to a function, which you declare in the second argument, where the `this` keyword refers to an individual item within an array. Then, within the context of events, as you learned in Chapter 3, the `this` keyword refers to the node or element on which the event is taking place, whereas if you add a `click` event to a `<div>` element and you click on that element, in the function you've added as an event handler, the `this` keyword refers to the `<div>` element. Thus, the `this` keyword changes depending on what context you're using it in. In this example, you have two different contexts — the `this` keyword as it applies to the `UnselectElement()` method, which refers to the selection; and the `this` keyword as it applies to the anonymous function passed to the `$.grep()` method, which is undefined. To make the selection available from within that anonymous function, you assign it to the `elements` variable.

The `$.grep()` method, as you learned in Chapter 5, is used to filter an array. In the application that you see in this example, the `$.grep()` method takes two arguments — the array you want to filter and a function that determines whether each item should be in the array. If the function returns a `true` value, that is, Boolean `true`, or a value other than false, null, or zero, then that item should remain in the array;

and if the function returns a `false` value (false, null, or zero), that item should not remain in the array. In this example, you iterate over the entire list of items in the `SelectedElements` array and check to see if an item is present in the selection passed to the `UnselectElement` method, which is now present in the `elements` variable. If the item is present in the `elements` variable, then it should be removed from the `SelectedElements` array. To determine whether the item is present in the `elements` variable, you use `$.inArray()`. If the value returned is –1, the item isn't present, and the function returns `true` (by virtue of the == expression). If the item is present, an `$.inArray()` returns a value other than –1, and the function returns `false`, which causes `$.grep()` to remove that item from the `SelectedElements` array.

Once `$.grep()` has finished executing the anonymous function for each item in the `SelectedElements` array, it returns a filtered array that is now missing the unselected items, and that new array is assigned as the new value of `SelectedElements`.

```
UnselectElement: function() {
  $(this).find('div.hFinderIcon')
    .removeClass('hFinderIconSelected');

  $(this).find('div.hFinderDirectoryName span')
    .removeClass('hFinderDirectoryNameSelected');

  // Don't remove the item from the array, unless it is
  // being unselected individually (as opposed to
  // all elements being unselected)
  if (arguments[0]) {
    // Alias the selection to elements, so you can reference it
    // from within the anonymous function passed to grep.
    var elements = this;

    if ($$.Finder.SelectedElements.length) {
      $$.Finder.SelectedElements = $.grep(
        $$.Finder.SelectedElements,
        function(item, i) {
          // If the item isn't in the selection, it should
          // be kept.
          return $.inArray(item, elements) == -1;
        }
      );
    }
  }

  return $;
},
```

The next thing that you do in this code is define a new object called `Finder`. The `Finder` object contains all of the logic related to your Finder clone. I have created the `Finder` object as a jQuery plugin, which is a technique that lends itself naturally to the concept of namespacing your code and limiting your impact on the global namespace, which I discussed in Chapter 1. You want to limit your impact on the global namespace because you want to increase the portability of your application so that you can drop your code into a document and not worry so much about your naming choices having conflicts with whatever naming is already present in that document. Or vice versa, you want to be able to include third-party applications in your application without worrying about naming conflicts. By writing your applications as jQuery plugins, you limit possible naming conflicts to jQuery's Plugin API. Of course, lots of people write jQuery plugins, and you might want to use third-party plugins from time to time, so you should also take that into consideration and name your plugins intelligently. I use capitalized names for my plugins to limit the possibility of conflict with other plugins. You may also want to use a prefix of some kind, like `tmp` or `h` (as I sometimes use, `tmp` being short for template and `h` referring to my own Hierophant framework, respectively). In the Finder clone, I don't expect to be using many third-party plugins, if any at all, so I'm sticking to simply capitalizing my names. You'll want to choose whatever naming convention makes the most sense to you.

As you've already seen, properties and methods within the `Finder` object are available using the `$$.Finder` prefix. Thus, to access the `SelectedElements` array, I'd use `$$.Finder.SelectedElements`, or to execute the `UnselectSelected()` function, I'd use `$$.Finder.UnselectSelected()`. If you don't like the `$$` alias for `$.fn`, you'll want to change those references accordingly, for example, `$.fn.Finder.SelectedElements`.

```
    Finder: {
```

The following property, `$$.Finder.SelectingElements`, is a Boolean that's used to keep track of when the user is selecting multiple folders by drawing a box using the jQuery UI Selectables plugin. When this property is `true`, a selection is taking place. You'll see how this property is useful later in this section.

```
      SelectingElements: false,
```

Then, as you've already learned, the `$$.Finder.SelectedElements` property contains an array of all of the items that are currently selected, which makes it easier for this and other applications to grab the current selection.

```
      SelectedElements: [],
```

The `$$.Finder.UnselectSelected()` method is used to remove all selected elements from a selection, that is, to re-set Finder to a completely unselected state. To do this, the `UnselectSelected` method iterates over the `SelectedElements` array, calling the `UnselectElement()` method for each item in that array. Then it re-sets the `SelectedElements` array to an empty array.

```
      UnselectSelected: function() {
        $.each(
          $$.Finder.SelectedElements,
          function() {
            $(this).UnselectElement();
          }
        );

        $$.Finder.SelectedElements = [];
      },
```

The next two items move CSS hacks that you wrote for IE back in Example 10-4 into two objects, `$$.Finder.FolderOver` and `$$.Finder.FolderOut`, which each specifies CSS for the folder over (or open) state and the default state (FolderOut). These were moved for two reasons: one, because of the possibility that you might want to reuse these styles; and two, because it made these lines of code shorter, which, in turn, made it easier to fit these into this book, where space is limited.

```
FolderOver: {
  background: 'none',
  filter:
    "progid:DXImageTransform.Microsoft.AlphaImageLoader" +
    "(src='../../../Images/Finder/Open Folder 48x48.png', sizingMethod='crop')"
},
FolderOut: {
  background: 'none',
  filter:
    "progid:DXImageTransform.Microsoft.AlphaImageLoader" +
    "(src='../../../Images/Finder/Folder 48x48.png', sizingMethod='crop')"
},
```

The next function, `$$.Finder.Ready()`, is executed when the DOM is fully loaded by virtue of the following line, which appears at the end of the JavaScript document:

```
$(document).ready($$.Finder.Ready);
```

The `Ready()` function contains all of the code that you want to be executed when the DOM is fully loaded and available:

```
Ready: function() {
```

The next section of code includes the drag-and-drop functionality that you saw in Chapter 10, with a few tweaks to accommodate the selection of multiple elements and using jQuery's Plugin API, and it also includes the ability to select individual folders.

The `mousedown()` event executes a function every time a user presses his or her mouse button while over a <div> element with class name *hFinderDirectory.* At present, you only want to allow an individual folder or file to be selected on `mousedown` when the user isn't making a selection by drawing a box. So, to limit actions to when a selection isn't being made via the Selectables plugin, you check to see if `$$.Finder.SelectingElements` is `false`. If it is `false`, no selection is taking place. Then, to select an individual folder or file, you first unselect anything already selected, by calling `$$.Finder.UnselectSelected()`, then you select the element the user is clicking on by calling `$(this).SelectElement()`.

```
$('div.hFinderDirectory')
  .mousedown(
    function() {
      if (!$$.Finder.SelectingElements) {
        // Unselect all selected
        $$.Finder.UnselectSelected();

        // Select this element.
        $(this).SelectElement();
      }
    }
  )
```

```
        .draggable({
          helper: 'clone',
          opacity: 0.5
        })
```

In the following block of code, one thing that is done differently from Chapter 10 is when you call jQuery's `css()` method. You include references to the objects stored in `$$.Finder.FolderOver` and `$$.Finder.FolderOut`, instead of defining those objects directly.

```
        .droppable({
          accept: 'div.hFinderDirectory',
          hoverClass: 'hFinderDirectoryDrop',
          over: function(e, ui) {
            if ($.browser.msie && $.browser.version == 6.0) {
              $(this).find('div.hFinderIcon div').css(
                $$.Finder.FolderOver
              );
            }
          },
          out: function(e, ui) {
            if ($.browser.msie && $.browser.version == 6.0) {
              $(this).find('div.hFinderIcon div').css(
                $$.Finder.FolderOut
              );
            }
          },
          drop: function(e, ui) {
            var $path = ui.draggable.attr('title');
            // Do something with the path

            // Remove the element that was dropped.
            ui.draggable.remove();
          }
        });
```

The last block of code makes folders and files selectable via the jQuery UI Selectables plugin. To make the folders selectable, you call the `selectable()` method on the element that contains the folder elements, which in this case is the `<div>` with ID name *hFinderFiles.*

You provide four options to the `selectable()` method: `start`, `stop`, `selecting`, and `unselecting`, each providing a callback function for a selection event.

The `start` option lets you provide a callback function that is executed once a selection is initiated. Within the callback function provided to the `start` option, you toggle the variable `$$.Finder.SelectingElements` to `true`, to indicate that a selection is taking place. That variable, as you've already learned, is used to prevent individual selection of folders and files via the `mousedown` event that you attached to each folder and file element. Once that variable is toggled, anything that's already selected is cleared and re-set to an unselected state by calling `$$.Finder.UnselectSelected()`. Calling that method removes any existing selection once a new selection is initiated.

```
      // Make it possible to select folders and files by
      // drawing a box with the mouse.
      $('div#hFinderFiles').selectable({
```

```
          start: function(e, ui) {
            // Selection has started, prevent the selection
            // of individual elements
            $$.Finder.SelectingElements = true;

            // Unselect anything already selected
            $$.Finder.UnselectSelected();
          },
```

The `stop` option lets you provide a callback function that is executed when a selection is completed (when the selection box has been drawn and the user releases the mouse button). Within the callback function provided to the `stop` option, you simply toggle the variable `$$.Finder.SelectingElements` to `false` to indicate that a selection is no longer taking place, which again allows the individual selection of files and folders.

```
          stop: function(e, ui) {
            // Allow the individual selection of elements again.
            $$.Finder.SelectingElements = false;
          },
```

The `selecting` option, as you've already learned, allows you to specify a callback function that is executed once for every element added to a selection, in real time, as elements are added to the selection by expanding the selection box. Within the callback function here, you check to see if the `ui.selecting` object exists, which refers to the object added to the selection. If the object exists, you call the `SelectElement()` method on it, so that that folder is properly styled to indicate its selection.

```
          selecting: function(e, ui) {
            if (ui.selecting) {
              $(ui.selecting).SelectElement();
            }
          },
```

The `unselecting` option, conversely, specifies a callback function that is executed once for each element removed from a selection or as elements are removed from a selection by shrinking the selection box. Here, each element is present in the second argument, as `ui.unselecting`. The `UnselectElement()` method is called on each element to remove the selected style.

```
          unselecting: function(e, ui) {
            $(ui.unselecting).UnselectElement(true);
          }
        });
      }
    }
  });
```

Complete API documentation for the Selectables plugin is available in Appendix L.

Summary

In this chapter, you learned about the jQuery UI Selectables plugin, which provides functionality for making selections by drawing a box with your mouse cursor. You saw how the Selectables plugin can be applied to a remedial `<ul>` list and to the more complex Finder clone that you made in Chapter 10.

The Selectables plugin, like jQuery UI's other plugins, accepts an object literal of options that are specified in key, value form. The Selectables plugin lets you specify callback functions for selectable events. Callback functions provided to the options `start` and `stop` are executed when a selection begins and ends, respectively. Callback functions provided to the options `selecting` and `unselecting` are executed as items are added and removed from a selection while a selection is taking place.

Exercises

1. Which option do you use to execute callback function when a selection begins?
2. What options do you use to execute callback functions when items are added or removed from a selection (while a selection is taking place)?
3. When using the selected and unselected options, how do you access each element added and removed from the selection?
4. What selector would you add to a style sheet to customize the look and feel of the selection box?

Accordion UI

So far you've learned about how jQuery makes dragging and dropping very easy to implement, and you've learned how jQuery makes it a breeze to select items by drawing a box. And you've also seen how ridiculously easy it is to implement drag-and-drop sorting with jQuery. In this chapter, I present another very cool jQuery UI plugin, called *Accordion*.

The jQuery UI Accordion plugin makes it very easy to implement content that expands and folds like your favorite polka instrument, the accordion.

Accordion UI widgets can be seen on popular websites like `www.apple.com/mac`. In this chapter, you'll find out how to use the jQuery UI Accordion plugin to make your very own Accordion widget and customize its look.

Building an Accordion UI

In this section, I discuss how to make an Accordion UI. An *Accordion UI*, by definition, is a collection of content panes that each has its own header, where only one content pane is visible at a time. When you click on the other content panes, a smooth animation transitions the visible pane to closed by animating its height, leaving only its header visible, and animates the other element's height, expanding that element until it is fully visible.

Having briefly explained what an Accordion UI is, the following document begins with a basic implementation of the jQuery UI Accordion plugin:

```
<!DOCTYPE html PUBLIC "-//W3C//DTD XHTML 1.0 Strict//EN"
    "http://www.w3.org/TR/xhtml1/DTD/xhtml1-strict.dtd">
<html xmlns='http://www.w3.org/1999/xhtml' xml:lang='en'>
  <head>
    <meta http-equiv='content-type' content='text/html; charset=utf-8' />
    <meta http-equiv='content-language' content='en-us' />
    <title></title>
    <script type='text/javascript'
            src='../../../Source Code/jQuery/jQuery.js'></script>
```

```
    <script type='text/javascript'
            src='../../../Source Code/jQuery/jQueryUI.js'></script>
    <script type='text/javascript' src='Figure 13-1.js'></script>
    <link type='text/css' href='Figure 13-1.css' rel='stylesheet' />
  </head>
  <body>
    <h4>The Beatles</h4>
    <ul>
      <li>
        <a href='#'>John Lennon</a>
        <p>
          Lorem ipsum dolor sit amet, consectetuer adipiscing elit.
          Vestibulum luctus rutrum orci. Praesent faucibus tellus
          faucibus quam. Aliquam erat volutpat. Nam posuere.
        </p>
      </li>
      <li>
        <a href='#'>Paul McCartney</a>
        <p>
          Lorem ipsum dolor sit amet, consectetuer adipiscing elit.
          Vestibulum luctus rutrum orci. Praesent faucibus tellus
          faucibus quam. Aliquam erat volutpat. Nam posuere.
        </p>
      </li>
      <li>
        <a href='#'>George Harrison</a>
        <p>
          Lorem ipsum dolor sit amet, consectetuer adipiscing elit.
          Vestibulum luctus rutrum orci. Praesent faucibus tellus
          faucibus quam. Aliquam erat volutpat. Nam posuere.
        </p>
      </li>
      <li>
        <a href='#'>Ringo Starr</a>
        <p>
          Lorem ipsum dolor sit amet, consectetuer adipiscing elit.
          Vestibulum luctus rutrum orci. Praesent faucibus tellus
          faucibus quam. Aliquam erat volutpat. Nam posuere.
        </p>
      </li>
    </ul>
  </body>
</html>
```

The following style sheet is applied to the preceding markup document:

```
body {
    font: 12px "Lucida Grande", Arial, sans-serif;
    background: #fff;
    color: rgb(50, 50, 50);
    margin: 0;
    padding: 0;
}
```

```
h4 {
    margin: 5px;
}
ul {
    list-style: none;
    margin: 0;
    padding: 15px 5px;
}
li {
    background: gold;
    padding: 3px;
    width: 244px;
    margin: 1px;
}
```

The following script makes the <ul> element in the markup document into an accordion with a simple function call:

```
$(document).ready(
  function() {
    $('ul').accordion();
  }
);
```

Figure 13-1 shows that, while the accordion has been created, your work here is not yet done.

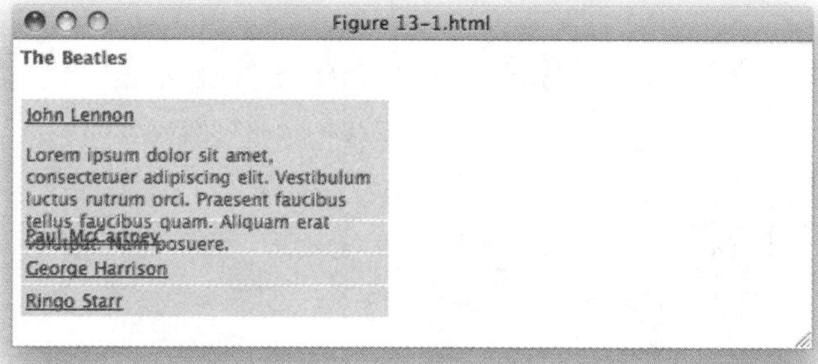

Figure 13-1

In **Figure 13-1**, the height of each element is not correct and you can see content overflowing each <li> element. In the next section, I describe how to correct this problem when you see it.

Structurally speaking, jQuery's Accordion plugin wants to be applied to a collection of elements; like a <ul> element, it automatically recognizes each <a> element as being the header portion of each content pane. Later in this chapter, I discuss in more detail how to approach styling an accordion.

Setting Auto-Height

In **Figure 13-1**, you saw that the content of the first pane didn't fit within that pane, and when you try the example in a browser, you see that the bottom of each content pane is clipped. jQuery's Accordion plugin, like the Selectable, Draggable, Droppable, and other plugins, lets you supply options to the method via an object literal that you pass as the first argument to a call to the `accordion()` method. In this section, I describe how to use Accordion's `autoHeight` option.

The `autoHeight` option can be provided with a Boolean value, and its value is `true`, by default. The value `true` causes the Accordion plugin to calculate and apply height to each content pane, based on the highest content, which does not always provide the results you may be looking for.

Setting the value of `autoHeight` to `false` changes the way that the Accordion UI handles height with each content pane. The following demonstrates how to modify the `autoHeight` option:

```
$(document).ready(
  function() {
    $('ul').accordion({
      autoHeight: false
    });
  }
);
```

The preceding script is applied to the same document that I presented in **Figure 13-1**; in **Figure 13-2**, you can see that the height problem that you observed in **Figure 13-1** has been corrected.

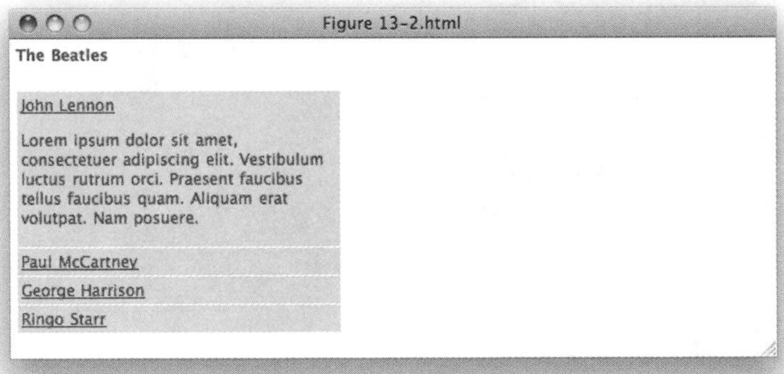

Figure 13-2

Setting `autoHeight` *has no effect in Internet Explorer or Firefox. The preceding effect is only observable in Safari.*

Changing the Default Pane

At this point, you have a functioning Accordion UI. In this section, I show you how to change the content pane that's displayed by default. Out-of-the-box, the Accordion plugin displays the first content pane, but using the `active` option, you can force a different content pane to be displayed. The following markup document demonstrates this concept; note the application of the class name *tmpSelected* to the <a> element wrapping the text *George Harrison*:

```
<!DOCTYPE html PUBLIC "-//W3C//DTD XHTML 1.0 Strict//EN"
    "http://www.w3.org/TR/xhtml1/DTD/xhtml1-strict.dtd">
<html xmlns='http://www.w3.org/1999/xhtml' xml:lang='en'>
  <head>
    <meta http-equiv='content-type' content='text/html; charset=utf-8' />
    <meta http-equiv='content-language' content='en-us' />
    <title></title>
    <script type='text/javascript'
            src='../../../Source Code/jQuery/jQuery.js'></script>
    <script type='text/javascript'
            src='../../../Source Code/jQuery/jQueryUI.js'></script>
    <script type='text/javascript' src='Figure 13-3.js'></script>
    <link type='text/css' href='Figure 13-3.css' rel='stylesheet' />
  </head>
  <body>
    <h4>The Beatles</h4>
    <ul>
      <li>
        <a href='#'>John Lennon</a>
        <p>
          Lorem ipsum dolor sit amet, consectetuer adipiscing elit.
          Vestibulum luctus rutrum orci. Praesent faucibus tellus
          faucibus quam. Aliquam erat volutpat. Nam posuere.
        </p>
      </li>
      <li>
        <a href='#'>Paul McCartney</a>
        <p>
          Lorem ipsum dolor sit amet, consectetuer adipiscing elit.
          Vestibulum luctus rutrum orci. Praesent faucibus tellus
          faucibus quam. Aliquam erat volutpat. Nam posuere.
        </p>
      </li>
      <li>
        <a href='#' class='tmpSelected'>George Harrison</a>
        <p>
          Lorem ipsum dolor sit amet, consectetuer adipiscing elit.
          Vestibulum luctus rutrum orci. Praesent faucibus tellus
          faucibus quam. Aliquam erat volutpat. Nam posuere.
        </p>
      </li>
```

```
        <li>
          <a href='#'>Ringo Starr</a>
          <p>
            Lorem ipsum dolor sit amet, consectetuer adipiscing elit.
            Vestibulum luctus rutrum orci. Praesent faucibus tellus
            faucibus quam. Aliquam erat volutpat. Nam posuere.
          </p>
        </li>
      </ul>
    </body>
  </html>
```

The following style sheet is applied to the preceding markup document:

```
body {
    font: 12px "Lucida Grande", Arial, sans-serif;
    background: #fff;
    color: rgb(50, 50, 50);
    margin: 0;
    padding: 0;
}
h4 {
    margin: 5px;
}
ul {
    list-style: none;
    margin: 0;
    padding: 15px 5px;
}
li {
    background: gold;
    padding: 3px;
    width: 244px;
    margin: 1px;
}
```

In the following script, you see that the selector `a.tmpSelected` is provided to the `active` option, which causes the `<li>` element that contains the `<a>` element with that class name in the markup document to be used as the default content pane:

```
$(document).ready(
  function() {
    $('ul').accordion({
      autoHeight: false,
      active: 'a.tmpSelected'
    });
  }
);
```

In **Figure 13-3**, you see that the content under *George Harrison* is now the default content.

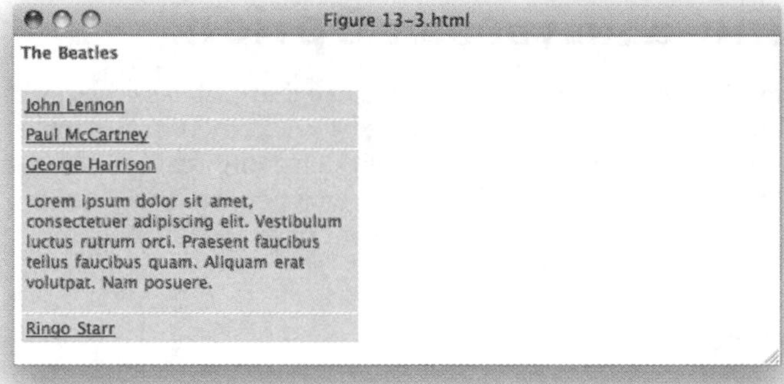

Figure 13-3

You can also set the option `active` to `false`, which makes no content open by default; this is demonstrated in the following script:

```
$(document).ready(
  function() {
    $('ul').accordion({
      autoHeight: false,
      active: false
    });
  }
);
```

In **Figure 13-4**, you see that setting the option to `false` causes no content to be visible by default, just the headings.

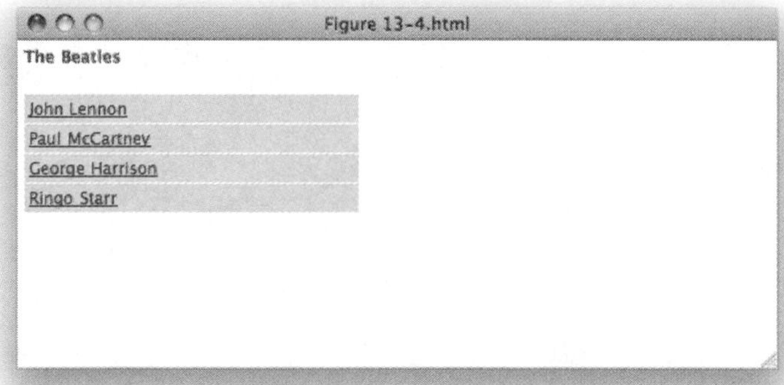

Figure 13-4

Toggling the `alwaysOpen` Option

The Accordion plugin's `alwaysOpen` option is a Boolean that dictates whether a content pane has to be open. By default, the Accordion plugin forces at least one content pane to be open. If you click on the open item's header, nothing happens; and if you click on a different header, the Accordion plugin transitions the open one to closed, and the clicked-on item to open via an animation. The `alwaysOpen` option provides you with the ability to close the open content pane by clicking on its header. The following is a demonstration of the `alwaysOpen` option:

```
$(document).ready(
  function() {
    $('ul').accordion({
      autoHeight: false,
      active: false,
      alwaysOpen: false
    });
  }
);
```

When the `alwaysOpen` option is set to `false`, you are able to close the active element by clicking on its header, which gives you the same screenshot that you see in **Figure 13-4**.

The preceding example is available in the code download as *Figure 13-5*, but not shown here.

Changing the Accordion Event

Upon setup, Accordion content panes are transitioned when you click on a header. You have the option of changing the event that triggers the transition using the `event` option. The following script shows you how to change the event to a `mouseover` event, from a `click` event:

```
$(document).ready(
  function() {
    $('ul').accordion({
      autoHeight: false,
      active: false,
      alwaysOpen: false,
      event: 'mouseover'
    });
  }
);
```

The preceding modification makes no visible change, so you see a document that looks similar to the one you see in **Figure 13-4**, but when you load it in a browser, you are able to transition between content panes using a `mouseover` event instead of a `click` event.

The preceding example is available in the source materials as *Figure 13-6*, but is not shown here.

Filling the Height of the Parent Element

The next option, called `fillSpace`, changes the way the Accordion plugin handles height. Setting the `fillSpace` option to `true` causes each `<li>` element that contains content to fill the height of its parent `<ul>` element.

```
$(document).ready(
  function() {
    $('ul').accordion({
      fillSpace: true,
      event: 'mouseover',
      active: 'a.tmpSelected'
    });
  }
);
```

The height of the `<ul>` element is recorded prior to each content element being collapsed, the space is then divided between the closed content panes, and the remaining open content pane receives the remaining space. The screenshot in **Figure 13-7** shows a screenshot that illustrates what happens when you set the `fillSpace` option to `true`.

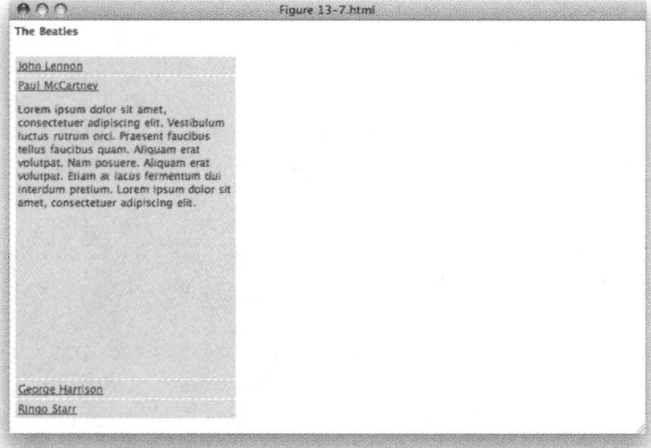

Figure 13-7

Setting the Header Elements

By default, the Accordion uses the `<a>` element as a header within each `<li>` element. You don't have to use an `<a>` element as the header; however, the following example illustrates how to use an `<h4>` element instead of an `<a>` element:

```
<!DOCTYPE html PUBLIC "-//W3C//DTD XHTML 1.0 Strict//EN"
    "http://www.w3.org/TR/xhtml1/DTD/xhtml1-strict.dtd">
<html xmlns='http://www.w3.org/1999/xhtml' xml:lang='en'>
```

```
  <head>
    <meta http-equiv='content-type' content='text/html; charset=utf-8' />
    <meta http-equiv='content-language' content='en-us' />
    <title></title>
    <script type='text/javascript'
            src='../../../Source Code/jQuery/jQuery.js'></script>
    <script type='text/javascript'
            src='../../../Source Code/jQuery/jQueryUI.js'></script>
    <script type='text/javascript' src='Figure 13-8.js'></script>
    <link type='text/css' href='Figure 13-8.css' rel='stylesheet' />
  </head>
  <body>
    <h4>The Beatles</h4>
    <ul>
      <li>
        <h4>John Lennon</h4>
        <p>
          Lorem ipsum dolor sit amet, consectetuer adipiscing elit.
          Vestibulum luctus rutrum orci.
        </p>
      </li>
      <li>
        <h4>Paul McCartney</h4>
        <p>
          Lorem ipsum dolor sit amet, consectetuer adipiscing elit.
          Vestibulum luctus rutrum orci. Praesent faucibus tellus
          faucibus quam. Aliquam erat volutpat. Nam posuere. Aliquam
          erat volutpat. Etiam at lacus fermentum dui interdum pretium.
          Lorem ipsum dolor sit amet, consectetuer adipiscing elit.
        </p>
      </li>
      <li>
        <h4 class='tmpSelected'>George Harrison</h4>
        <p>
          Lorem ipsum dolor sit amet, consectetuer adipiscing elit.
          Vestibulum luctus rutrum orci. Praesent faucibus tellus
          faucibus quam. Aliquam erat volutpat. Nam posuere.
        </p>
      </li>
      <li>
        <h4>Ringo Starr</h4>
        <p>
          Lorem ipsum dolor sit amet, consectetuer adipiscing elit.
          Vestibulum luctus rutrum orci. Praesent faucibus tellus
          faucibus quam. Aliquam erat volutpat. Nam posuere.
        </p>
      </li>
    </ul>
  </body>
</html>
```

The following style sheet is applied to the preceding markup document:

```
body {
    font: 12px "Lucida Grande", Arial, sans-serif;
    background: #fff;
    color: rgb(50, 50, 50);
    margin: 0;
    padding: 0;
}
h4 {
    margin: 5px;
}
ul {
    list-style: none;
    margin: 0;
    padding: 15px 5px;
}
ul h4,
ul p {
    margin: 5px;
}
li {
    background: gold;
    padding: 3px;
    width: 244px;
    margin: 1px;
}
```

In the following script, you change the element that's used as the header for each content pane by providing a selector to the header option, in this case `h4`, which causes the `<h4>` element of each `<li>` element to be used as a header, rather than the `<a>` element:

```
$(document).ready(
  function() {
    $('ul').accordion({
      fillSpace: true,
      event: 'mouseover',
      active: 'h4.tmpSelected',
      header: 'h4'
    });
  }
);
```

In the preceding script, take note that you also have to change the selector provided to the `active` option, since now you want to have a content pane that uses an `<h4>` header to be open by default.

The screenshot shown in **Figure 13-8** demonstrates that the `<h4>` element is used instead of an `<a>` element.

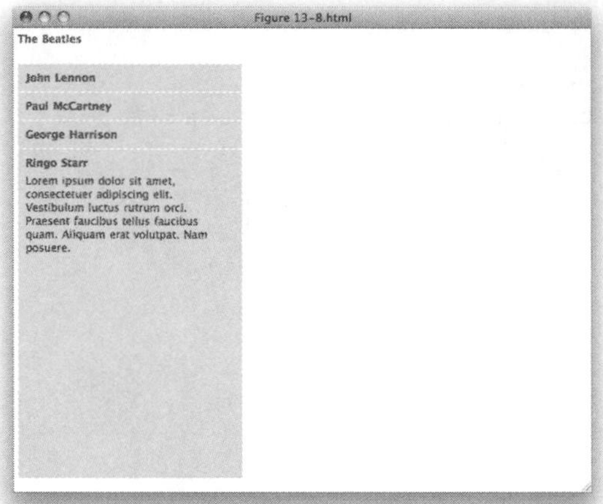

Figure 13-8

Styling Selected Panes

The next option that I present is the `selectedClass` option, which lets you specify a class name for the active content pane, allowing you to style the active content pane by attaching a class name to it. The following document demonstrates how to style the active content pane using the `selectedClass` option:

```
<!DOCTYPE html PUBLIC "-//W3C//DTD XHTML 1.0 Strict//EN"
    "http://www.w3.org/TR/xhtml1/DTD/xhtml1-strict.dtd">
<html xmlns='http://www.w3.org/1999/xhtml' xml:lang='en'>
  <head>
    <meta http-equiv='content-type' content='text/html; charset=utf-8' />
    <meta http-equiv='content-language' content='en-us' />
    <title></title>
    <script type='text/javascript'
            src='../../../Source Code/jQuery/jQuery.js'></script>
    <script type='text/javascript'
            src='../../../Source Code/jQuery/jQueryUI.js'></script>
    <script type='text/javascript' src='Figure 13-9.js'></script>
    <link type='text/css' href='Figure 13-9.css' rel='stylesheet' />
  </head>
  <body>
    <h4>The Beatles</h4>
    <ul>
      <li>
        <h4>John Lennon</h4>
        <p>
          Lorem ipsum dolor sit amet, consectetuer adipiscing elit.
          Vestibulum luctus rutrum orci.
        </p>
      </li>
```

```
        <li>
          <h4>Paul McCartney</h4>
          <p>
            Lorem ipsum dolor sit amet, consectetuer adipiscing elit.
            Vestibulum luctus rutrum orci. Praesent faucibus tellus
            faucibus quam. Aliquam erat volutpat. Nam posuere. Aliquam
            erat volutpat. Etiam at lacus fermentum dui interdum pretium.
            Lorem ipsum dolor sit amet, consectetuer adipiscing elit.
          </p>
        </li>
        <li>
          <h4 class='tmpSelected'>George Harrison</h4>
          <p>
            Lorem ipsum dolor sit amet, consectetuer adipiscing elit.
            Vestibulum luctus rutrum orci. Praesent faucibus tellus
            faucibus quam. Aliquam erat volutpat. Nam posuere.
          </p>
        </li>
        <li>
          <h4>Ringo Starr</h4>
          <p>
            Lorem ipsum dolor sit amet, consectetuer adipiscing elit.
            Vestibulum luctus rutrum orci. Praesent faucibus tellus
            faucibus quam. Aliquam erat volutpat. Nam posuere.
          </p>
        </li>
      </ul>
    </body>
  </html>
```

In the following style sheet, which is applied to the preceding markup, the rule beginning with the selector `li.tmpContentSelected` defines the styles for the active content pane:

```
body {
    font: 12px "Lucida Grande", Arial, sans-serif;
    background: #fff;
    color: rgb(50, 50, 50);
    margin: 0;
    padding: 0;
}
h4 {
    margin: 5px;
}
ul {
    list-style: none;
    margin: 0;
    padding: 15px 5px;
}
ul h4,
ul p {
    margin: 5px;
}
```

```
li {
    background: gold;
    padding: 3px;
    width: 244px;
    margin: 1px;
}
li.tmpContentSelected {
    background: yellow;
    border: 1px solid #000;
    width: 242px;
}
```

In the following script, the option `selectedClass` has the value *tmpContentSelected*. This class name is applied to the `<li>` and `<h4>` elements of the active content, giving you the ability to style the active content differently from inactive content.

```
$(document).ready(
  function() {
    $('ul').accordion({
      fillSpace: true,
      event: 'mouseover',
      active: 'h4.tmpSelected',
      header: 'h4',
      selectedClass: 'tmpContentSelected'
    });
  }
);
```

Figure 13-9 shows a screenshot of the document with this new modification applied, and you see that the selected content has a yellow background with a black border, with a width that's 2 pixels shorter to accommodate the border.

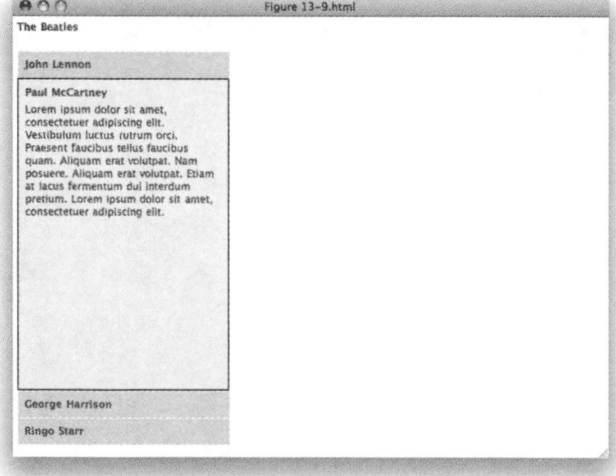

Figure 13-9

Selecting a Content Pane by Location

jQuery also gives you the ability to change the default content pane depending on location, by having jQuery automatically compare the URLs to content present in the Accordion, in the `href` attribute of each <a> element, to the document's `location.href` property. The following document demonstrates how to change the Accordion's default content pane, depending on location:

```
<!DOCTYPE html PUBLIC "-//W3C//DTD XHTML 1.0 Strict//EN"
    "http://www.w3.org/TR/xhtml1/DTD/xhtml1-strict.dtd">
<html xmlns='http://www.w3.org/1999/xhtml' xml:lang='en'>
  <head>
    <meta http-equiv='content-type' content='text/html; charset=utf-8' />
    <meta http-equiv='content-language' content='en-us' />
    <title></title>
    <script type='text/javascript'
            src='../../../Source Code/jQuery/jQuery.js'></script>
    <script type='text/javascript'
            src='../../../Source Code/jQuery/jQueryUI.js'></script>
    <script type='text/javascript' src='Figure 13-10.js'></script>
    <link type='text/css' href='Figure 13-10.css' rel='stylesheet' />
  </head>
  <body>
    <h4>The Beatles</h4>
    <ul>
      <li>
        <a href='john.html'>John Lennon</a>
        <p>
          Lorem ipsum dolor sit amet, consectetuer adipiscing elit.
          Vestibulum luctus rutrum orci.
        </p>
      </li>
      <li>
        <a href='paul.html'>Paul McCartney</a>
        <p>
          Lorem ipsum dolor sit amet, consectetuer adipiscing elit.
          Vestibulum luctus rutrum orci. Praesent faucibus tellus
          faucibus quam. Aliquam erat volutpat. Nam posuere. Aliquam
          erat volutpat. Etiam at lacus fermentum dui interdum pretium.
          Lorem ipsum dolor sit amet, consectetuer adipiscing elit.
        </p>
      </li>
      <li>
        <a href='george.html'>George Harrison</a>
        <p>
          Lorem ipsum dolor sit amet, consectetuer adipiscing elit.
          Vestibulum luctus rutrum orci. Praesent faucibus tellus
          faucibus quam. Aliquam erat volutpat. Nam posuere.
        </p>
      </li>
      <li>
        <a href='ringo.html'>Ringo Starr</a>
```

```
          <p>
            Lorem ipsum dolor sit amet, consectetuer adipiscing elit.
            Vestibulum luctus rutrum orci. Praesent faucibus tellus
            faucibus quam. Aliquam erat volutpat. Nam posuere.
          </p>
        </li>
      </ul>
      <h1>John Lennon</h1>
    </body>
  </html>
```

The preceding markup document is named *john.html,* and similar markup documents are created and named *paul.html, george.html,* and *ringo.html.* The following style sheet is applied to all four markup documents:

```
body {
    font: 12px "Lucida Grande", Arial, sans-serif;
    background: #fff;
    color: rgb(50, 50, 50);
    margin: 0;
    padding: 0;
}
h4 {
    margin: 5px;
}
ul {
    list-style: none;
    margin: 0;
    padding: 15px 5px;
    clear: left;
}
h4,
ul {
    float: left;
}
ul a {
    margin: 5px;
    font-weight: bold;
    display: block;
}
ul p {
    margin: 5px;
}
li {
    background: gold;
    padding: 3px;
    width: 244px;
    margin: 1px;
}
li.tmpContentSelected {
    background: yellow;
```

```
        border: 1px solid #000;
        width: 242px;
    }
    h1 {
        margin-left: 280px;
    }
```

In the following script, you see how the `navigation` and `navigationFilter` options are used to change the default content pane depending on the `location.href` property's value:

```
$(document).ready(
  function() {
    $('ul').accordion({
      fillSpace: true,
      event: 'mouseover',
      selectedClass: 'tmpContentSelected',
      navigation: true,
      navigationFilter: function() {
        return(
          decodeURIComponent(this.href).toLowerCase() ==
          decodeURIComponent(location.href.toLowerCase())
        );
      }
    });
  }
);
```

In the preceding example, when you click on any of the four links, you see that the default content pane changes depending on which document you navigate to, and this is done by comparing the value of the `href` attribute of each `<a>` element to the `location.href` property. Triggering a location comparison is done by setting the `navigation` option to `true`. By default, the Accordion plugin uses the following logic to compare the location specified in each `href` attribute to the `location.href` property:

```
navigationFilter: function() {
  return this.href.toLowerCase() == location.href.toLowerCase();
}
```

The `navigationFilter` option gives you the ability to modify the logic that's used for matching the location with your own logic. I noticed in my own test, for example, that there were URL-encoded characters present in the `href` attribute of each `<a>` element. Each space character was replaced with the URL-encoded equivalent, `%20`, for example. But these same characters were not URL-encoded in the browser's `location.href` property. To fix this, I provided my own callback function to the `navigationFilter` option, which decodes URL-encoded characters using JavaScript's `decodeURIComponent()` method before attempting a comparison. You can also use the `navigationFilter` option to compare location in other ways, such as by looking for a query string argument instead of the document's path. You simply have to have your callback function return `true` to indicate a match, and return `false` otherwise. **Figure 13-10** shows a screenshot of the john.html page of the preceding example, where you see that the content pane "John Lennon" is open by default in the Accordion.

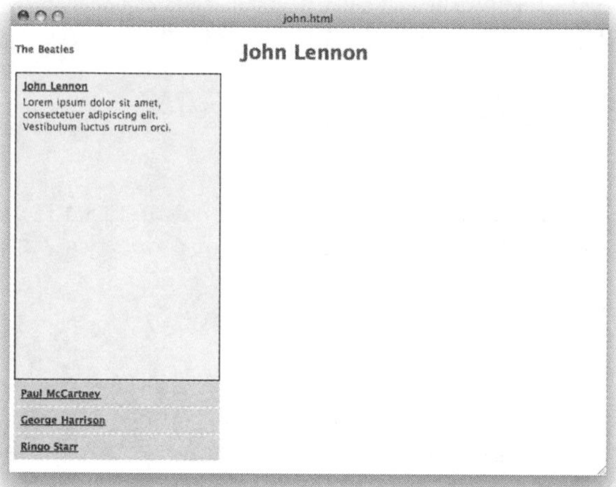

Figure 13-10

Summary

In this chapter, you learned how to create an Accordion UI and the various options that you can use to tweak an Accordion UI implementation. You learned that the Accordion plugin takes a list of elements, such as a `<ul>` element, and makes the items in that list into smoothly animated content panes, which transition one to the other by animating the height of each item in the list. By default, headers for each content pane are provided as `<a>` elements, but you can change the header element to something else by supplying a selector to the `header` option.

The `active` option can be used to change the default content pane that's displayed when the page first loads. Alternatively, you can have the default content pane change dynamically using the `navigation` and `navigationFilter` options, and if you so choose, you can have no default content pane at all by setting the `active` option to `false`. If no default content pane is specified, the first element in the list will be used.

Normally, the Accordion plugin requires at least one content pane to be open; the `alwaysOpen` option can be used to allow closing the open content pane.

The `autoHeight`, `clearStyle`, and `fillSpace` options can each be used to tweak how the Accordion plugin defines the height for each content pane. The `autoHeight` option takes the highest content and uses that height as the height for all other content panes, which may not always provide the right look and feel. The `clearStyle` option clears `height` and `overflow` limitations set by the Accordion plugin during an animation after an animation completes.

The `event` option is used to change the event that's used to trigger a content pane transition; `click` is the default event.

Finally, the `selectedClass` option can be used to provide a class name for the active content pane, which allows you to provide a different look and feel for active content as opposed to inactive content.

A quick reference of the Accordion plugin and its options appears in Appendix N.

Exercises

1. Which option would you provide to the `accordion()` method to change the default content pane?
2. What does the `alwaysOpen` option do?
3. Which three options would you consider using to change how the `accordion()` method handles height?
4. What option would you use to make the `accordion()` method trigger a content transition using a `mouseover` event, instead of a `click` event?
5. What option would you use to change the header element to an `<h3>` element?
6. How would you customize the logic used to dynamically change the default content pane depending on the value of the `location.href` property?
7. What option would you use to style the active content pane differently from inactive content panes?

Datepicker

jQuery UI offers a sophisticated and feature-rich UI component for inputting dates into a form field in its Datepicker plugin.

The jQuery UI Datepicker plugin provides a graphical calendar that can be set to pop up anywhere you might need a date keyed into a form. The calendar can be customized in its look and feel. The date format it produces can be set to mirror local customs. The text it labels fields with can be swapped out with whatever text you like, translated into a foreign language, or otherwise … making the plugin fully capable of localization.

In this chapter, I describe how to use and customize the Datepicker plugin.

Implementing a Datepicker

A barebones implementation of the Datepicker plugin doesn't look like much; it's unstyled, but it works, more or less, from the standpoint of functionality.

The following document is a demonstration of what a basic implementation of the jQuery UI Datepicker plugin looks like:

```
<!DOCTYPE html PUBLIC "-//W3C//DTD XHTML 1.0 Strict//EN"
    "http://www.w3.org/TR/xhtml1/DTD/xhtml1-strict.dtd">
<html xmlns='http://www.w3.org/1999/xhtml' xml:lang='en'>
  <head>
    <meta http-equiv='content-type' content='text/html; charset=utf-8' />
    <meta http-equiv='content-language' content='en-us' />
    <title></title>
    <script type='text/javascript'
            src='../../../Source Code/jQuery/jQuery.js'></script>
    <script type='text/javascript'
            src='../../../Source Code/jQuery/jQueryUI.js'></script>
    <script type='text/javascript' src='Figure 14-1.js'></script>
    <link type='text/css' href='Figure 14-1.css' rel='stylesheet' />
  </head>
  <body>
    <form action='javascript:void(0);' method='post'>
      <fieldset>
```

```
            <legend>Appointment Form</legend>
            <div>
              <label for='tmpDate'>Date:</label>
              <input type='text' id='tmpDate' size='25' value='' />
            </div>
          </fieldset>
        </form>
      </body>
    </html>
```

The following style sheet provides a little bit of styling for the preceding markup document:

```
body {
    font: 12px "Lucida Grande", Arial, sans-serif;
    background: #fff;
    color: rgb(50, 50, 50);
}
fieldset {
    border: none;
}
input {
    background: lightblue;
}
```

In the following script, the `datepicker()` method is called on the `<input>` element in the markup document, which causes a calendar to dynamically pop up for date selection whenever the `<input>` element receives focus:

```
$(document).ready(
  function() {
    $('input#tmpDate').datepicker();
  }
);
```

As you can see in **Figure 14-1**, the Datepicker plugin provides an unstyled calendar that is provided each time the `<input>` field it is associated with is activated.

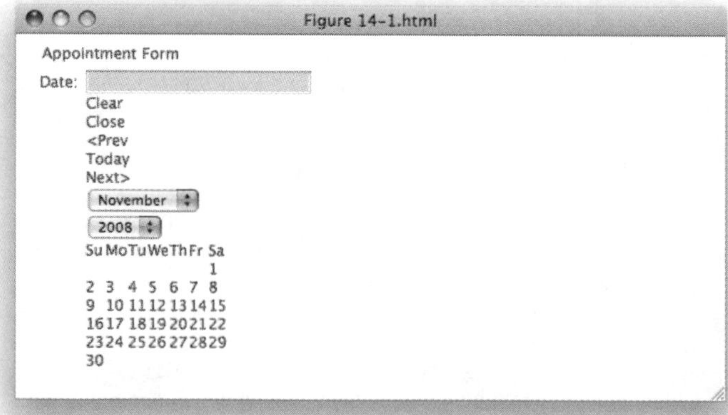

Figure 14-1

Styling the Datepicker

By default, the Datepicker plugin doesn't provide much styling. In this section, I present how to style the Datepicker calendar. Before you can set out to style the Datepicker widget, however, you need to understand how the widget is structured. A comprehensive list of customization options and a list of class names appear in Appendix O.

The following markup is the structure used by default for the Datepicker widget:

```
<div  id="ui-datepicker-div">
  <div class="ui-datepicker-control">
    <div class="ui-datepicker-clear">
     <a>Clear</a>
    </div>
    <div class="ui-datepicker-close">
      <a>Close</a>
    </div>
  </div>
  <div class="ui-datepicker-links">
    <div class="ui-datepicker-prev">
      <a>&lt;Prev</a>
    </div>
    <div class="ui-datepicker-current">
      <a>Today</a>
    </div>
    <div class="ui-datepicker-next">
      <a>Next&gt;</a>
    </div>
  </div>
  <div class="ui-datepicker-one-month ui-datepicker-new-row">
    <div class="ui-datepicker-header">
      <select class="ui-datepicker-new-month">
        <option value="0">January</option>
        <option value="1">February</option>
        <option value="2">March</option>
        <option value="3">April</option>
        <option value="4">May</option>
        <option value="5">June</option>
        <option value="6">July</option>
        <option value="7">August</option>
        <option value="8">September</option>
        <option value="9">October</option>
        <option value="10" selected="selected">November</option>
        <option value="11">December</option>
      </select>
      <select class="ui-datepicker-new-year">
        <option value="1998">1998</option>
        <option value="1999">1999</option>
        <option value="2000">2000</option>
        <option value="2001">2001</option>
        <option value="2002">2002</option>
        <option value="2003">2003</option>
        <option value="2004">2004</option>
        <option value="2005">2005</option>
        <option value="2006">2006</option>
```

```
        <option value="2007">2007</option>
        <option value="2008" selected="selected">2008</option>
        <option value="2009">2009</option>
        <option value="2010">2010</option>
        <option value="2011">2011</option>
        <option value="2012">2012</option>
        <option value="2013">2013</option>
        <option value="2014">2014</option>
        <option value="2015">2015</option>
        <option value="2016">2016</option>
        <option value="2017">2017</option>
        <option value="2018">2018</option>
     </select>
    </div>
    <table class="ui-datepicker" cellpadding="0" cellspacing="0">
      <thead>
        <tr class="ui-datepicker-title-row">
          <td class="ui-datepicker-week-end-cell">
            <a title="Sunday">Su</a>
          </td>
          <td>
            <a title="Monday">Mo</a>
          </td>
          <td>
            <a title="Tuesday">Tu</a>
          </td>
          <td>
            <a title="Wednesday">We</a>
          </td>
          <td>
            <a title="Thursday">Th</a>
          </td>
          <td>
            <a title="Friday">Fr</a>
          </td>
          <td class="ui-datepicker-week-end-cell">
            <a title="Saturday">Sa</a>
          </td>
        </tr>
      </thead>
      <tbody>
        <tr class="ui-datepicker-days-row">
          <td class="ui-datepicker-days-cell
                     ui-datepicker-week-end-cell
                     ui-datepicker-other-month
                     ui-datepicker-unselectable"> </td>
          <td class="ui-datepicker-days-cell
                     ui-datepicker-other-month
                     ui-datepicker-unselectable"> </td>
          <td class="ui-datepicker-days-cell
                     ui-datepicker-other-month
                     ui-datepicker-unselectable"> </td>
          <td class="ui-datepicker-days-cell
                     ui-datepicker-other-month
                     ui-datepicker-unselectable"> </td>
```

```
    <td class="ui-datepicker-days-cell
               ui-datepicker-other-month
               ui-datepicker-unselectable"> </td>
    <td class="ui-datepicker-days-cell
               ui-datepicker-other-month
               ui-datepicker-unselectable"> </td>
    <td class="ui-datepicker-days-cell ui-datepicker-week-end-cell">
      <a>1</a>
    </td>
  </tr>
  <tr class="ui-datepicker-days-row">
    <td class="ui-datepicker-days-cell ui-datepicker-week-end-cell">
      <a>2</a>
    </td>
    <td class="ui-datepicker-days-cell">
      <a>3</a>
    </td>
    <td class="ui-datepicker-days-cell">
      <a>4</a>
    </td>
    <td class="ui-datepicker-days-cell">
      <a>5</a>
    </td>
    <td class="ui-datepicker-days-cell">
      <a>6</a>
    </td>
    <td class="ui-datepicker-days-cell">
      <a>7</a>
    </td>
    <td class="ui-datepicker-days-cell ui-datepicker-week-end-cell">
      <a>8</a>
    </td>
  </tr>
  <tr class="ui-datepicker-days-row">
     <td class="ui-datepicker-days-cell ui-datepicker-week-end-cell">
       <a>9</a>
    </td>
    <td class="ui-datepicker-days-cell">
      <a>10</a>
    </td>
    <td class="ui-datepicker-days-cell">
      <a>11</a>
    </td>
    <td class="ui-datepicker-days-cell">
      <a>12</a>
    </td>
    <td class="ui-datepicker-days-cell">
      <a>13</a>
    </td>
    <td class="ui-datepicker-days-cell">
      <a>14</a>
    </td>
    <td class="ui-datepicker-days-cell ui-datepicker-week-end-cell">
      <a>15</a>
    </td>
  </tr>
```

```
<tr class="ui-datepicker-days-row">
  <td class="ui-datepicker-days-cell ui-datepicker-week-end-cell">
    <a>16</a>
  </td>
  <td class="ui-datepicker-days-cell">
    <a>17</a>
  </td>
  <td class="ui-datepicker-days-cell">
    <a>18</a>
  </td>
  <td class="ui-datepicker-days-cell">
    <a>19</a>
  </td>
  <td class="ui-datepicker-days-cell">
    <a>20</a>
  </td>
  <td class="ui-datepicker-days-cell">
    <a>21</a>
  </td>
  <td class="ui-datepicker-days-cell ui-datepicker-week-end-cell">
    <a>22</a>
  </td>
</tr>
<tr class="ui-datepicker-days-row">
  <td class="ui-datepicker-days-cell ui-datepicker-week-end-cell">
    <a>23</a>
  </td>
  <td class="ui-datepicker-days-cell">
    <a>24</a>
  </td>
  <td class="ui-datepicker-days-cell">
    <a>25</a>
  </td>
  <td class="ui-datepicker-days-cell">
    <a>26</a>
  </td>
  <td class="ui-datepicker-days-cell">
    <a>27</a>
  </td>
  <td class="ui-datepicker-days-cell ui-datepicker-today">
    <a>28</a>
  </td>
  <td class="ui-datepicker-days-cell ui-datepicker-week-end-cell">
    <a>29</a>
  </td>
</tr>
<tr class="ui-datepicker-days-row">
  <td class="ui-datepicker-days-cell ui-datepicker-week-end-cell">
    <a>30</a>
  </td>
  <td class="ui-datepicker-days-cell
             ui-datepicker-other-month
             ui-datepicker-unselectable"> </td>
  <td class="ui-datepicker-days-cell
             ui-datepicker-other-month
             ui-datepicker-unselectable"> </td>
```

```
          <td class="ui-datepicker-days-cell
                     ui-datepicker-other-month
                     ui-datepicker-unselectable"> </td>
          <td class="ui-datepicker-days-cell
                     ui-datepicker-other-month
                     ui-datepicker-unselectable"> </td>
          <td class="ui-datepicker-days-cell
                     ui-datepicker-other-month
                     ui-datepicker-unselectable"> </td>
          <td class="ui-datepicker-days-cell
                     ui-datepicker-week-end-cell
                     ui-datepicker-other-month
                     ui-datepicker-unselectable"> </td>
        </tr>
      </tbody>
    </table>
  </div>
  <div style="clear: both;"></div>
</div>
```

The preceding markup produces *Figure 14-2* (not shown).

In the following “Try It Out,” I present one way you might approach styling the Datepicker widget:

Try It Out Styling the Datepicker

Example 14-1

To style the Datepicker, follow these steps.

1. Create the following markup document:

```
<!DOCTYPE html PUBLIC "-//W3C//DTD XHTML 1.0 Strict//EN"
    "http://www.w3.org/TR/xhtml1/DTD/xhtml1-strict.dtd">
<html xmlns='http://www.w3.org/1999/xhtml' xml:lang='en'>
  <head>
    <meta http-equiv='content-type' content='text/html; charset=utf-8' />
    <meta http-equiv='content-language' content='en-us' />
    <title></title>
    <script type='text/javascript'
            src='../../../Source Code/jQuery/jQuery.js'></script>
    <script type='text/javascript'
            src='../../../Source Code/jQuery/jQueryUI.js'></script>
    <script type='text/javascript' src='Example 14-1.js'></script>
    <link type='text/css' href='Example 14-1.css' rel='stylesheet' />
    <!--[if IE 6]>
      <link type='text/css' href='Example 14-1.IE6.css' rel='stylesheet' />
    <![endif]-->
  </head>
  <body>
    <form action='javascript:void(0);' method='post'>
      <fieldset>
        <legend>Appointment Form</legend>
        <div>
          <label for='tmpDate'>Date:</label>
```

```
            <input type='text' id='tmpDate' size='25' value='' />
          </div>
        </fieldset>
      </form>
    </body>
  </html>
```

2. Save the preceding document as *Example 14-1.html*.
3. Create the following style sheet:

```
body {
    font: 12px "Lucida Grande", Arial, sans-serif;
    background: #fff;
    color: rgb(50, 50, 50);
}
fieldset {
    border: none;
}
input {
    background: lightblue;
}
#ui-datepicker-div {
    width: 300px;
    border: 1px solid rgb(128, 128, 128);
    padding: 5px;
    background: lightgreen;
    display: none;
}
div.ui-datepicker-control {
    position: relative;
    height: 25px;
    background: forestgreen;
}
div.ui-datepicker-control div {
    padding: 5px;
}
div.ui-datepicker-control div a {
    color: #fff;
}
div.ui-datepicker-links {
    position: relative;
    height: 20px;
    padding: 5px 0 0 0;
    background: darkgreen;
    border-bottom: 1px solid green;
    text-align: center;
}
div.ui-datepicker-links div {
    padding: 5px;
}
div.ui-datepicker-links div a {
    color: #fff;
}
div.ui-datepicker-clear,
```

```
div.ui-datepicker-prev {
    position: absolute;
    top: 0;
    left: 0;
}
div.ui-datepicker-close,
div.ui-datepicker-next {
    position: absolute;
    top: 0;
    right: 0;
}
div.ui-datepicker-current {
    display: inline;
}
div.ui-datepicker-header {
    margin-top: 5px;
    text-align: center;
}
div.ui-datepicker-header select {
    margin: 0 3px;
}
table.ui-datepicker {
    width: 250px;
    border-collapse: collapse;
    margin: 10px 0 0 0;
}
table.ui-datepicker td {
    padding: 3px;
    border: 1px solid green;
}
table.ui-datepicker thead td {
    text-align: center;
    font-weight: bold;
    background: green;
    color: lightgreen;
}
td.ui-datepicker-today {
    background: #dff6e4;
}
td.ui-datepicker-current-day {
    background: darkgreen;
    color: #fff;
}
```

4. Save the preceding style sheet as *Example 14-1.css.*
5. Create the following style sheet for IE6:

```
.ui-datepicker-cover {
    display: none; /*sorry for IE5*/
    display/**/: block; /*sorry for IE5*/
    position: absolute; /*must have*/
    z-index: -1; /*must have*/
    filter: mask(); /*must have*/
    top: -4px; /*must have*/
```

```
        left: -4px; /*must have*/
        width: 193px; /*must have to match width and borders*/
        height: 200px; /*must have to match maximum height*/
    }
    #ui-datepicker-div {
        z-index: 10; /* must have */
    }
```

6. Save the preceding style sheet as *Example 14-1.IE6.css.*

7. Create the following JavaScript:

```
$(document).ready(
  function() {
    $('input#tmpDate').datepicker();
  }
);
```

8. Save the preceding JavaScript as *Example 14-1.js.*

The preceding example results in something like the screenshot that you see in **Figure 14-3** when you load up the markup document in a browser.

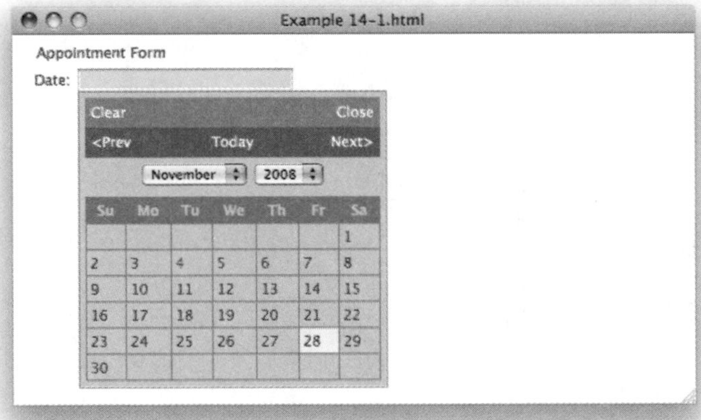

Figure 14-3

In the preceding example, you learned more about how to style the default Datepicker widget. Other aspects of the Datepicker concerning what dates you are allowed to pick from, how dates are formatted, and what controls are present in the widget may also be customized, but you learn more about these things later in the chapter.

In order to style the Datepicker, you reference the markup that I provided just before Example 14-1, using the various class names to create styling for the pop-up calendar. Some corrections have to be made for IE6; the corrections provided are the same recommended in the official documentation appearing at www.jquery.com for the Datepicker plugin. The IE6 corrections are provided in a separate style sheet, so that your main style sheet doesn't have to be increased in size to accommodate IE6's shortcomings. IE7 and IE8 Beta 2, on the other hand, are able to properly display the Datepicker widget out-of-the-box without any further modification.

The styles provided are nothing particularly extraordinary, just run-of-the-mill CSS.

Setting the Range of Allowed Dates

By default, the jQuery UI Datepicker plugin allows you to select from a range of dates that goes 10 years into the future and 10 years into the past. You can customize the range of dates that are allowed by the widget, however, by specifying the range via an option.

The following script demonstrates how to limit the range of selectable dates:

```
$(document).ready(
  function() {
    $('input#tmpDate').datepicker({
        minDate: new Date(2000, 0, 1),
        maxDate: new Date(2002, 0, 1)
    });
  }
);
```

The preceding script is applied to the document that you created in Example 14-1, and **Figure 14-4** shows the effects of the preceding options when viewed in a browser.

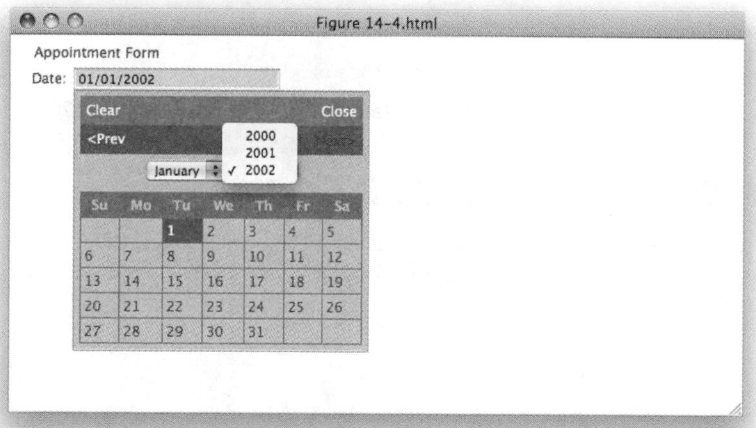

Figure 14-4

In the preceding example, you set a minimum and a maximum date. The date is supplied using a `Date()` object, where you specify the year, the month offset from zero, and the day. The minimum date is passed to the option minDate, and the maximum is passed to the option maxDate. The date is supplied as Date(yy, mm, dd), and again, for the month, January is numbered zero, and February is number one, and so on. This results in having dates selectable from January 1, 2000 until January 1, 2002; the widget won't allow selection of January 2, 2002, for example.

Otherwise, instead of the minDate and maxDate options, you can also set a range of allowed dates via another option called yearRange. The yearRange option sets the range of selectable dates based on which years you want to be selectable. Whereas the minDate and maxDate options allow you fine-grained control down to the day, the yearRange option allows you to specify the selectable date only by the year. The option allows two different ways of specifying a range of years. The following script shows you the default range:

```
$(document).ready(
  function() {
    $('input#tmpDate').datepicker({
      yearRange: "-10:+10"
    });
  }
);
```

The preceding sets a range relative to today's date, setting a range of years from 10 years in the past to 10 years in the future. Aside from setting the range of years relative to today's date, you can also set an arbitrary range of years, which the following script demonstrates:

```
$(document).ready(
  function() {
    $('input#tmpDate').datepicker({
      yearRange: "1900:2020"
    });
  }
);
```

The preceding script sets a range of selectable dates from 1900 until the year 2020.

Allowing a Date Range to Be Selected

You can also allow the user to select a range of dates within the widget, that is, select a beginning date and an ending date. The following script shows how to enable the selection of a range of dates by setting the rangeSelect option to true.

```
$(document).ready(
  function() {
    $('input#tmpDate').datepicker({
        rangeSelect: true
    });
  }
);
```

The preceding script is applied to the document that you created in Example 14-1. **Figure 14-5** shows that the widget now allows you to select a beginning date and an ending date.

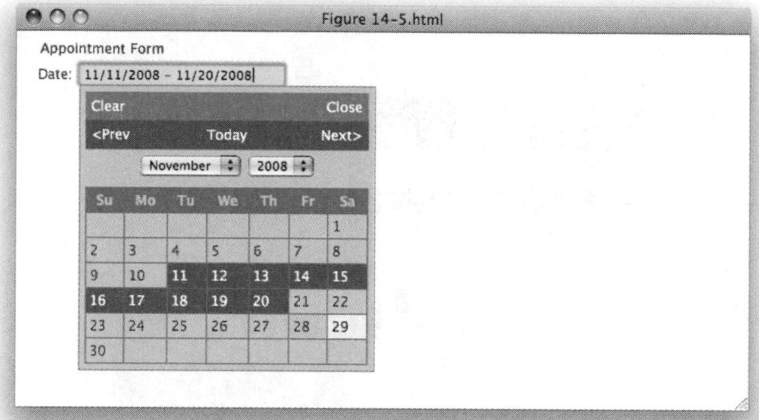

Figure 14-5

The characters that are used to separate the range are also customizable using the `rangeSeparator` option; by default, the `rangeSeparator` option uses a space followed by a hyphen followed by a space.

Localizing the Datepicker

The Datepicker plugin has many localization options that allow you to completely change how the calendar looks, the text that it uses, the date format that it uses, and the weekday the calendar starts on. In the following sections, I describe how to localize a Datepicker implementation.

Setting the Date Format

The date format displayed as the value of the `<input>` element can be changed to whatever format you like. The following script demonstrates how to change the date format so that the day is placed before the month as is done with dates in much of the world:

```
$(document).ready(
  function() {
    $('input#tmpDate').datepicker({
        dateFormat: 'dd/mm/yy'
    });
  }
);
```

In the preceding script, you see that the date format is set using the `dateFormat` option; in this case, it specifies the day, month, and year — the day and month with leading zeros and the year in four-digit format. A full list of options is available in Appendix O, under "Format Options." **Figure 14-6** shows that the day appears first, then the month, then the year.

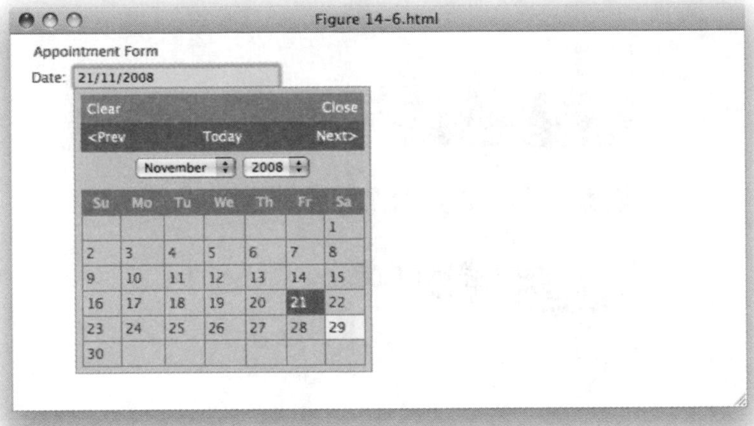

Figure 14-6

Localizing Datepicker Text

The following options can be used to localize, customize, or translate an implementation of Datepicker:

- `clearText` — The text to display for the clear link. The default is `"Clear"`.
- `clearStatus` — The text to display in the status bar for the clear link. The default is `"Erase the current date"`.
- `closeText` — The text to display for the close link. The default is `"Close"`.
- `closeStatus` — The text to display in the status bar for the close link. The default is `"Close without change"`.
- `prevText` — The text to display for the previous month link. The default is `"Prev"`.
- `prevStatus` — The text to display in the status bar for the previous month link. The default is `"Show the previous month"`.
- `nextText` — The text to display for the next month link. The default is `"Next>"`.
- `nextStatus` — The text to display in the status bar for the next month link. The default is `"Show the next month"`.
- `currentText` — The text to display for the current day link. The default is `"Today"`.
- `currentStatus` — The text to display in the status bar for the current day link. The default is `"Show the current month"`.
- `monthNames` — The list of full month names, as used in the month header on each Datepicker and as requested via the `dateFormat` setting. The default is `["January", "February", "March", "April", "May", "June", "July", "August", "September", "October", "November", "December"]`.

- `monthNamesShort` — The list of abbreviated month names, for use as requested via the `dateFormat` setting. The default is `["Jan", "Feb", "Mar", "Apr", "May", "Jun", "Jul", "Aug", "Sep", "Oct", "Nov", "Dec"]`.
- `monthStatus` — The text to display in the status bar for the month dropdown list. The default is `"Show a different month"`.
- `yearStatus` — The text to display in the status bar for the year dropdown list. The default is `"Show a different year"`.
- `weekHeader` — The column header for the week of the year (see `showWeeks`). The default is `"wk"`.
- `weekStatus` — The text to display in the status bar for the week of the year. The default is `"Week of the year"`.
- `dayNames` — The list of long day names, starting from Sunday, for use as requested via the `dateFormat` setting. Day names also appear as pop-up hints when hovering over the corresponding column headings. The default is `["Sunday", "Monday", "Tuesday", "Wednesday", "Thursday", "Friday", "Saturday"]`.
- `dayNamesShort` — The list of abbreviated day names, starting from Sunday, for use as requested via the `dateFormat` setting. The default is `["Sun", "Mon", "Tue", "Wed", "Thu", "Fri", "Sat"]`.
- `dayNamesMin` — The list of minimized day names, starting from Sunday, for use as column headers within the Datepicker. The default is `["Su", "Mo", "Tu", "We", "Th", "Fr", "Sa"]`.
- `dayStatus` — The text to display in the status bar for the day of the week links. Use *DD* for the full name of the day or *D* for its short name. The default is `"Set DD as first week day"`.
- `initStatus` — The text to display in the status bar when the Datepicker is first opened. The default is `"Select a date"`.

Changing the Starting Weekday

In some places in the world, the calendar begins with Monday and ends with Sunday. Whichever day you want to use as the starting weekday is also customizable via the `firstDay` option. The following script demonstrates how to change the starting weekday:

```
$(document).ready(
  function() {
    $('input#tmpDate').datepicker({
        dateFormat: 'dd/mm/yy',
        firstDay: 1
    });
  }
);
```

In the preceding script, the `firstDay` option is used to change the starting calendar day from Sunday (which is number zero) to Monday (which is number one). **Figure 14-7** shows the result of the change.

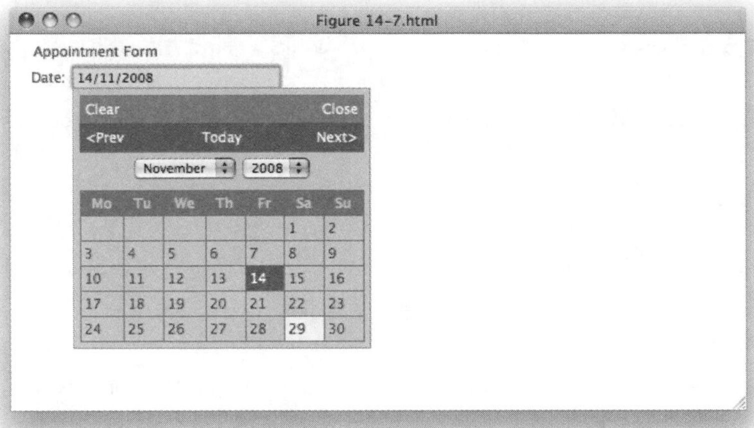

Figure 14-7

Summary

In this chapter, you learned a little about what the jQuery UI Datepicker plugin has to offer. This chapter covered only some of the options that are allowed, owing to constraints on resources; however, a comprehensive reference containing all of the options that you can use with the `datepicker()` method appears in Appendix O.

In this chapter, you learned that the Datepicker plugin does not come with much styling, and whatever styling you want must be implemented by yourself. You saw how the widget's markup is structured, and a sample style sheet that could be applied to it.

You learned that the Datepicker can limit the range of selectable dates. For fine-grained, down-to-the-day control, the `minDate` and `maxDate` options can be used. For an arbitrary range of years, the `yearRange` option can be used.

You learned a little about the options that are available to you for localizing the Datepicker — you can change the date format, you can change any of the text labels, and you can change the starting weekday that's displayed in the calendar.

Exercises

1. Name three options that you could potentially use to limit the range of selectable dates provided in the calendar, and describe the differences between them.
2. What option would you use to change the date format?
3. Does the Datepicker plugin give you the ability to translate its text into Spanish?
4. What option would you use to change the starting weekday?

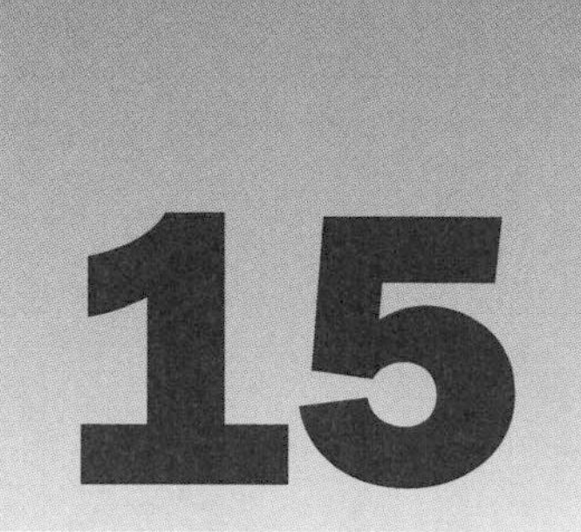

Dialogs

In this chapter, I present how to work with the jQuery UI Dialog plugin, which provides pseudo-pop-up windows that are created using purely markup, CSS, and script.

Unlike pop-up windows, which require that you open a new document in a separate browser window that is increasingly saddled with security limitations, such as being unable to hide the URL of the document and being unable to hide the status bar at the bottom of the window, dialogs that are created using markup, CSS, and script can be styled in any way that you like and can impose any limitations that you like, for example, the ability to make a modal dialog, which provides a dialog and prevents the user from continuing to interact with the document until the dialog is closed.

Another difference between pop-up windows and *dialogs* (as I will now refer to this widget for the remainder of this chapter — without reiterating the fact that they are generated by markup, CSS, and script) is that dialogs are unable to leave the browser window in which they reside, so a dialog cannot be minimized to your operating system's taskbar, although you could possibly create your own minimization script so that the dialog can be minimized within the browser window.

As with many of the things that you've learned about in this book, jQuery UI again leaves very little to be desired in its own spare-no-function implementation of dialogs.

Implementing a Dialog

As with every other jQuery UI plugin, I begin the discussion of the Dialog plugin by presenting a barebones, unconfigured, and unstyled implementation of what the plugin looks like. The following document demonstrates the out-of-the-box implementation:

Lipsum text can be copied and pasted from www.lipsum.com.

```
<!DOCTYPE html PUBLIC "-//W3C//DTD XHTML 1.0 Strict//EN"
    "http://www.w3.org/TR/xhtml1/DTD/xhtml1-strict.dtd">
<html xmlns='http://www.w3.org/1999/xhtml' xml:lang='en'>
```

```
  <head>
    <meta http-equiv='content-type' content='text/html; charset=utf-8' />
    <meta http-equiv='content-language' content='en-us' />
    <title></title>
    <script type='text/javascript'
            src='../../../Source Code/jQuery/jQuery.js'></script>
    <script type='text/javascript'
            src='../../../Source Code/jQuery/jQueryUI.js'></script>
    <script type='text/javascript' src='Figure 15-1.js'></script>
    <link type='text/css' href='Figure 15-1.css' rel='stylesheet' />
  </head>
  <body>
    <div id='tmpExample' title='Lorem Ipsum'>
      <p>
        Lorem ipsum dolor sit amet, consectetuer adipiscing elit. In
        sagittis commodo ipsum. Donec est. Mauris eget arcu. Suspendisse
        tincidunt aliquam velit. Maecenas libero. Aliquam dapibus
        tincidunt eros. Donec suscipit tincidunt odio. Maecenas congue
        tortor non ligula. Phasellus vel elit. Suspendisse potenti. Nunc
        odio quam, hendrerit ac, imperdiet sit amet, venenatis sed, enim.
      </p>
    </div>
  </body>
</html>
```

The following style sheet is applied to the preceding markup document:

```
body {
    font: 12px "Lucida Grande", Arial, sans-serif;
    background: #fff;
    color: rgb(50, 50, 50);
}
```

In the following script, you see how the `<div>` element with ID name *tmpExample* is made into a dialog by selecting that `<div>` element and then calling the `dialog()` method:

```
$(document).ready(
  function() {
    $('div#tmpExample').dialog();
  }
);
```

In **Figure 15-1**, you can see that the dialog doesn't look like much out-of-the-box. The styling is in some desperate need of attention. The title of the dialog is set by placing the title in the `title` attribute of the element that you want to transform into a dialog. The title of the dialog may also be set by passing a `title` option to the `dialog()` method; either method of setting the title can be used.

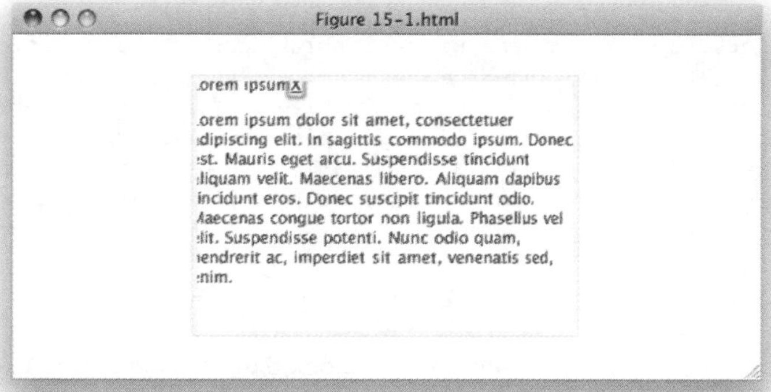

Figure 15-1

Examining a Dialog's Markup

Before you can learn how to style a dialog, you need to see how its underbelly is constructed and assembled in markup. The following markup is the basic structure used for a run-of-the-mill jQuery UI dialog:

```
<div tabindex="-1" class="ui-dialog ui-draggable ui-resizable">
  <div class="ui-dialog-container">
    <div unselectable="on" class="ui-dialog-titlebar">
      <span unselectable="on" class="ui-dialog-title">
        This is my title
      </span>
      <a unselectable="on" href="#" class="ui-dialog-titlebar-close">
        <span unselectable="on">X</span>
      </a>
    </div>
    <!-- Begin Dialog Content -->
    <div class="ui-dialog-content" id="tmpExample">
      <p>
        Lorem ipsum dolor sit amet, consectetuer adipiscing elit. In
        sagittis commodo ipsum. Donec est. Mauris eget arcu. Suspendisse
        tincidunt aliquam velit. Maecenas libero. Aliquam dapibus
        tincidunt eros. Donec suscipit tincidunt odio. Maecenas congue
        tortor non ligula. Phasellus vel elit. Suspendisse potenti. Nunc
        odio quam, hendrerit ac, imperdiet sit amet, venenatis sed, enim.
      </p>
    </div>
    <!-- End Dialog Content -->
  </div>
  <div class="ui-dialog-buttonpane"></div>
  <div unselectable="on" class="ui-resizable-handle ui-resizable-n"></div>
```

```
    <div unselectable="on" class="ui-resizable-handle ui-resizable-e"></div>
    <div unselectable="on" class="ui-resizable-handle ui-resizable-s"></div>
    <div unselectable="on" class="ui-resizable-handle ui-resizable-w"></div>
    <div unselectable="on" class="ui-resizable-handle ui-resizable-se"></div>
    <div unselectable="on" class="ui-resizable-handle ui-resizable-sw"></div>
    <div unselectable="on" class="ui-resizable-handle ui-resizable-ne"></div>
    <div unselectable="on" class="ui-resizable-handle ui-resizable-nw"></div>
</div>
```

The preceding markup produces *Figure 15-2* (not shown).

The preceding shows what the dialog source might look like, minus the HTML comments that I added to show where content is inserted.

In the following "Try It Out," you apply styling to the dialog to jazz it up a bit:

Try It Out Styling a Dialog

Example 15-1

To style a dialog, follow these steps.

1. Create the following markup document:

```
<!DOCTYPE html PUBLIC "-//W3C//DTD XHTML 1.0 Strict//EN"
    "http://www.w3.org/TR/xhtml1/DTD/xhtml1-strict.dtd">
<html xmlns='http://www.w3.org/1999/xhtml' xml:lang='en'>
  <head>
    <meta http-equiv='content-type' content='text/html; charset=utf-8' />
    <meta http-equiv='content-language' content='en-us' />
    <title></title>
    <script type='text/javascript'
            src='../../../Source Code/jQuery/jQuery.js'></script>
    <script type='text/javascript'
            src='../../../Source Code/jQuery/jQueryUI.js'></script>
    <script type='text/javascript' src='Example 15-1.js'></script>
    <link type='text/css' href='Example 15-1.css' rel='stylesheet' />
    <!--[if IE 6]>
      <link type='text/css' href='Example 15-1.IE6.css' rel='stylesheet' />
    <![endif]-->
  </head>
  <body>
    <div id='tmpExample' title='Lorem Ipsum'>
      <p>
        Lorem ipsum dolor sit amet, consectetuer adipiscing elit. In
        sagittis commodo ipsum. Donec est. Mauris eget arcu. Suspendisse
        tincidunt aliquam velit. Maecenas libero. Aliquam dapibus
        tincidunt eros. Donec suscipit tincidunt odio. Maecenas congue
        tortor non ligula. Phasellus vel elit. Suspendisse potenti. Nunc
        odio quam, hendrerit ac, imperdiet sit amet, venenatis sed, enim.
      </p>
    </div>
  </body>
</html>
```

2. Save the preceding markup document as *Example 15-1.html*.

3. Create the following style sheet. Images referenced in the style sheet are available in this book's free source code download materials available from `www.wrox.com`.

```
body {
    font: 12px "Lucida Grande", Arial, sans-serif;
    background: #fff;
    color: rgb(50, 50, 50);
}
div.ui-dialog {
    overflow: visible !important;
}
div.ui-dialog-titlebar {
    height: 23px !important;
    background: url('../../../Images/Dialog/titlebarRight.png')
      no-repeat top right;
    position: relative;
    z-index: 10 !important;
}
span.ui-dialog-title {
    display: block;
    font-size: 13px;
    text-align: center;
    margin: 0 9px;
    padding: 4px 0 0 0;
    height: 19px !important;
    background: url('../../../Images/Dialog/titlebar.png')
      repeat-x top;
    position: relative;
    z-index: 10;
}
div.ui-dialog-container {
    background: #fff url('../../../Images/Dialog/titlebarLeft.png')
      no-repeat top left;
}
a.ui-dialog-titlebar-close {
    position: absolute;
    width: 14px;
    height: 15px;
    top: 5px;
    left: 10px;
    background: url('../../../Images/Dialog/closeOff.png')
      no-repeat top left;
    z-index: 10;
}
a.ui-dialog-titlebar-close:hover {
    background: url('../../../Images/Dialog/closeOn.png')
      no-repeat top left;
}
a.ui-dialog-titlebar-close span {
    display: none;
}
a.ui-dialog-titlebar-close:focus {
    border: none;
    outline: none;
}
```

```
div.ui-dialog-content  {
    padding: 10px;
    background: #fff !important;
    width: auto !important;
    height: auto !important;
    z-index: 10 !important;
    position: absolute !important;
    top: 23px;
    left: 0;
    bottom: 0;
    right: 0;
}
div.ui-resizable-handle {
    border: none !important;
    z-index: -1 !important;
}
div.ui-resizable-nw {
    background: url('../../../Images/Dialog/Shadow/shadow_01.png')
      no-repeat top right !important;
    width: 117px !important;
    height: 112px !important;
    top: -50px !important;
    left: -60px !important;
}
div.ui-resizable-n {
    background: url('../../../Images/Dialog/Shadow/shadow_02.png')
      repeat-x top !important;
    height: 112px !important;
    top: -52px !important;
}
div.ui-resizable-ne {
    background: url('../../../Images/Dialog/Shadow/shadow_03.png')
      no-repeat top left !important;
    width: 115px !important;
    height: 112px !important;
    top: -50px !important;
    right: -60px !important;
}
div.ui-resizable-w {
    background: url('../../../Images/Dialog/Shadow/shadow_04.png')
      repeat-y top left !important;
    width: 115px !important;
    left: -60px !important;
    top: 62px !important;
    bottom: 51px !important;
    height: auto !important;
}
div.ui-resizable-e {
    background: url('../../../Images/Dialog/Shadow/shadow_06.png')
      repeat-y top left !important;
    width: 117px !important;
    right: -60px !important;
    top: 62px !important;
```

```
    bottom: 51px !important;
    height: auto !important;
}
div.ui-resizable-sw {
    background: url('../../../Images/Dialog/Shadow/shadow_07.png')
      no-repeat top right !important;
    width: 115px !important;
    height: 111px !important;
    bottom: -60px !important;
    left: -60px !important;
}
div.ui-resizable-s {
    background: url('../../../Images/Dialog/Shadow/shadow_08.png')
      repeat-x bottom !important;
    height: 111px !important;
    bottom: -60px !important;
    width: auto !important;
    left: 55px !important;
    right: 57px !important;
}
div.ui-resizable-se {
    background: url('../../../Images/Dialog/Shadow/shadow_14.png')
      no-repeat top right !important;
    width: 117px !important;
    height: 111px !important;
    bottom: -60px !important;
    right: -60px !important;
}
```

4. Save the preceding document as *Example 15-1.css*.
5. Create the following style sheet separately to fix some IE6 bugs:

```
div.ui-resizable-handle {
    border: none !important;
    background: #fff !important;
    filter: alpha(opacity=99);
}
div.ui-dialog-content {
    border: 1px solid rgb(128, 128, 128);
    border-top: none;
    padding: 10px 14px 10px 10px;
}
a.ui-dialog-titlebar-close {
    background: none;
    filter: progid:DXImageTransform.Microsoft.AlphaImageLoader
      (src="../../../Images/Dialog/closeOff.png", sizingMethod="crop");
}
a.ui-dialog-titlebar-close:hover {
    background: none;
    filter: progid:DXImageTransform.Microsoft.AlphaImageLoader
      (src="../../../Images/Dialog/closeOn.png", sizingMethod="crop");
}
```

6. Save the preceding document as *Example 15-1.IE6.css*.

7. Create the following script:

```
$(document).ready(
  function() {
    $('div#tmpExample').dialog();
  }
);
```

8. Save the preceding script as *Example 15-1.js*.

The preceding results in styling the jQuery UI Dialog similar to a Mac OS X Leopard application window, which features a semitransparent drop shadow in every browser but IE6, which is unable to produce a drop shadow, using PNG images, that is repeated in the background. Screenshots of the styled dialog in Safari 3.2 and IE6 appear in **Figure 15-3**.

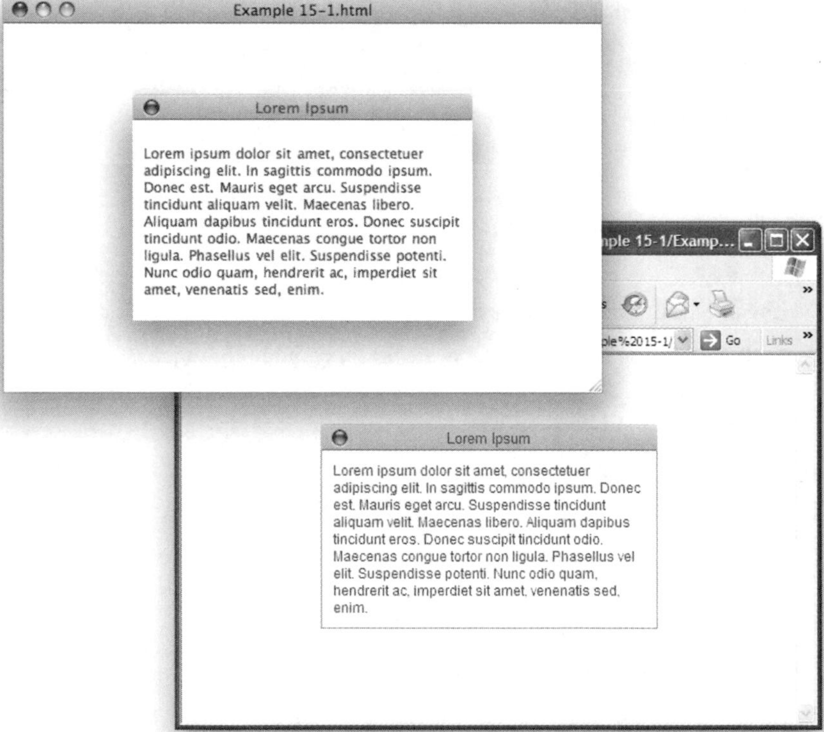

Figure 15-3

In the preceding example, you learned how to apply an ambitious styling to the jQuery UI Dialog plugin, which is made to resemble the look of application windows found on Mac OS X Leopard. Certainly, you can do a lot without necessarily making the styling this complex, but you're able to get an idea of how far you can take styling a dialog.

The example that you saw in Example 15-1 works great in every browser, although there is no drop shadow in IE6, which is not capable of repeating a semitransparent PNG background. Unfortunately, IE6 PNG hacks may only be applied to non-repeating backgrounds. So, rather than a drop shadow in IE6, you see a solid gray border. On the other hand, the dialog renders fine in IE7.

jQuery UI itself applies some styling of its own, and you see that many of the declarations in the style sheet include `!important`, which is used to override the cascade and force the application of the rules that `!important` is attached to.

Making a Modal Dialog

A *modal dialog*, as I mentioned in the chapter opening, is a dialog that, upon activation, prevents interaction with the document until the dialog is closed. The following script demonstrates how to make a jQuery UI Dialog into a modal dialog, which is demonstrated with the following HTML:

```
<!DOCTYPE html PUBLIC "-//W3C//DTD XHTML 1.0 Strict//EN"
    "http://www.w3.org/TR/xhtml1/DTD/xhtml1-strict.dtd">
<html xmlns='http://www.w3.org/1999/xhtml' xml:lang='en'>
  <head>
    <meta http-equiv='content-type' content='text/html; charset=utf-8' />
    <meta http-equiv='content-language' content='en-us' />
    <title></title>
    <script type='text/javascript'
            src='../../../Source Code/jQuery/jQuery.js'></script>
    <script type='text/javascript'
            src='../../../Source Code/jQuery/jQueryUI.js'></script>
    <script type='text/javascript' src='Figure 15-4.js'></script>
    <link type='text/css' href='Figure 15-4.css' rel='stylesheet' />
    <!--[if IE 6]>
      <link type='text/css' href='Figure 15-4.IE6.css' rel='stylesheet' />
    <![endif]-->
  </head>
  <body>
    <p>
      Lorem ipsum dolor sit amet, consectetuer adipiscing elit. In
      sagittis commodo ipsum. Donec est. Mauris eget arcu. Suspendisse
      tincidunt aliquam velit. Maecenas libero. Aliquam dapibus
      tincidunt eros. Donec suscipit tincidunt odio. Maecenas congue
      tortor non ligula. Phasellus vel elit. Suspendisse potenti. Nunc
      odio quam, hendrerit ac, imperdiet sit amet, venenatis sed, enim.
    </p>
    <div id='tmpExample' title='Lorem Ipsum'>
```

```
      <p>
        Lorem ipsum dolor sit amet, consectetuer adipiscing elit. In
        sagittis commodo ipsum. Donec est. Mauris eget arcu. Suspendisse
        tincidunt aliquam velit. Maecenas libero. Aliquam dapibus
        tincidunt eros. Donec suscipit tincidunt odio. Maecenas congue
        tortor non ligula. Phasellus vel elit. Suspendisse potenti. Nunc
        odio quam, hendrerit ac, imperdiet sit amet, venenatis sed, enim.
      </p>
    </div>
  </body>
</html>
```

The preceding HTML document uses the same CSS document that you made in Example 15-1 and the following JavaScript:

```
$(document).ready(
  function() {
    $('div#tmpExample').dialog({
      modal: true,
      overlay : {
        background: '#fff',
        opacity: '0.7'
      }
    });
  }
);
```

In the preceding script, you turn on the `modal` option by setting it to `true`. When you set the `modal` option to `true`, you disable interaction with background content while the dialog is open. The second option, `overlay`, styles the overlay that's used to disable interaction with background content so that the user has a visual cue that the content is disabled. The `overlay` option accepts style properties in key, value pairs, similarly to jQuery's `css()` method discussed in Chapter 6.

In **Figure 15-4**, you see that the background is draped in a semitransparent white background to indicate that it is disabled.

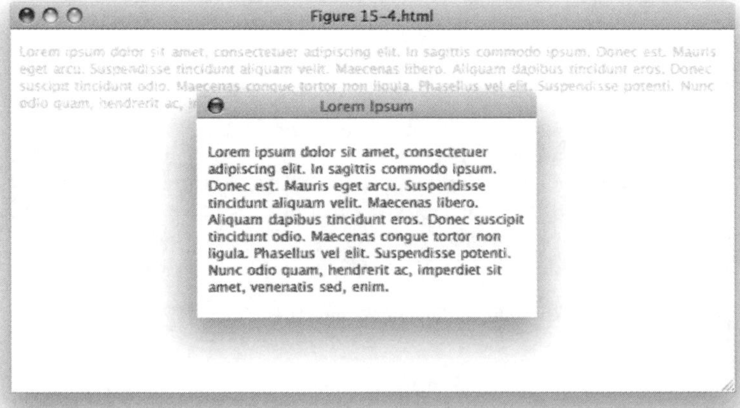

Figure 15-4

Auto-Opening the Dialog

By default, upon calling the `dialog()` method, the dialog is automatically opened. This is easily controlled by setting the `autoOpen` option to `false`. Once the `autoOpen` option is set to `false`, you can programmatically open a dialog by calling the `dialog()` method with the string `'open'` in its first argument. This is demonstrated in the following document:

```
<!DOCTYPE html PUBLIC "-//W3C//DTD XHTML 1.0 Strict//EN"
    "http://www.w3.org/TR/xhtml1/DTD/xhtml1-strict.dtd">
<html xmlns='http://www.w3.org/1999/xhtml' xml:lang='en'>
  <head>
    <meta http-equiv='content-type' content='text/html; charset=utf-8' />
    <meta http-equiv='content-language' content='en-us' />
    <title></title>
    <script type='text/javascript'
            src='../../../Source Code/jQuery/jQuery.js'></script>
    <script type='text/javascript'
            src='../../../Source Code/jQuery/jQueryUI.js'></script>
    <script type='text/javascript' src='Figure 15-5.js'></script>
    <link type='text/css' href='Figure 15-5.css' rel='stylesheet' />
    <!--[if IE 6]>
      <link type='text/css' href='Figure 15-5.IE6.css' rel='stylesheet' />
    <![endif]-->
  </head>
  <body>
    <p>
      Lorem ipsum dolor sit amet, consectetuer adipiscing elit. In
      sagittis commodo ipsum. Donec est. Mauris eget arcu. Suspendisse
      tincidunt aliquam velit. Maecenas libero. Aliquam dapibus
      tincidunt eros. Donec suscipit tincidunt odio. Maecenas congue
      tortor non ligula. Phasellus vel elit. Suspendisse potenti. Nunc
      odio quam, hendrerit ac, imperdiet sit amet, venenatis sed, enim.
    </p>
    <input type='submit' id='tmpOpen' value='Open Dialog' />
    <div id='tmpExample' title='Lorem Ipsum'>
      <p>
        Lorem ipsum dolor sit amet, consectetuer adipiscing elit. In
        sagittis commodo ipsum. Donec est. Mauris eget arcu. Suspendisse
        tincidunt aliquam velit. Maecenas libero. Aliquam dapibus
        tincidunt eros. Donec suscipit tincidunt odio. Maecenas congue
        tortor non ligula. Phasellus vel elit. Suspendisse potenti. Nunc
        odio quam, hendrerit ac, imperdiet sit amet, venenatis sed, enim.
      </p>
    </div>
  </body>
</html>
```

The CSS documents that you created in Example 15-1 are applied to the preceding markup document, along with the following script:

```
$(document).ready(
  function() {
    $('div#tmpExample').dialog({
      autoOpen: false
```

```
      });

      $('input#tmpOpen').click(
        function($e) {
          $('div#tmpExample').dialog('open');
        }
      );
    }
  );
```

In the preceding script, you prevent the dialog from being opened automatically by setting the `autoOpen` option to `false`. To open the dialog, you attach a `click` event to the `<input>` element, and when that event takes place, you make a call to `$('div#tmpExample').dialog('open')` to open the dialog programmatically. **Figure 15-5** shows a screenshot of the preceding example.

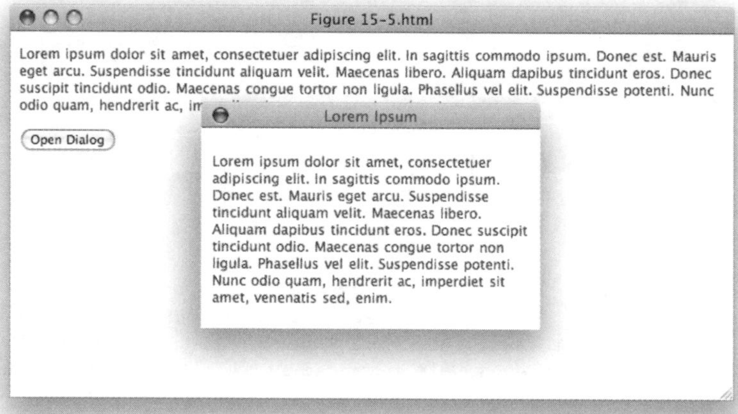

Figure 15-5

Controlling Dynamic Interaction

By default, the jQuery UI Dialog plugin allows you to re-size and drag the Dialog window. Both types of dynamic interaction with a dialog can be disabled by passing options to the `dialog()` method; for example, the `draggable` option can be set to `false` to disable dragging the dialog, and the `resizable` option can also be set to `false` to disable re-sizing a dialog. Disabling these options is demonstrated in the following script:

```
$(document).ready(
  function() {
    $('div#tmpExample').dialog({
      resizable: false,
      draggable: false
    });
  }
);
```

The preceding script results in something like what you see in **Figure 15-6**.

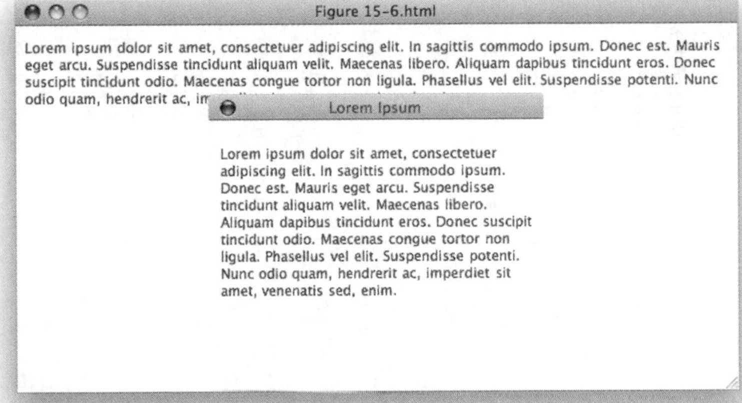

Figure 15-6

In **Figure 15-6**, you see that the drop shadow that you applied in Example 15-1 has disappeared, and that's because you disabled re-sizing the dialog. The re-sizing portion of the markup, however, is where you applied each drop shadow slice. So, in order to use styling like what I presented in Example 15-1, re-sizing must be preserved.

Animating the Dialog

Opening or closing a dialog can also be animated using one of the effects listed in Appendix M. Animation can be introduced by providing an effect to the `show` option.

The following script demonstrates how to do this:

```
$(document).ready(
  function() {
    $('div#tmpExample').dialog({
      autoOpen: false,
      show: 'explode'
    });

    $('input#tmpOpen').click(
      function($e) {
        $('div#tmpExample').dialog('open');
      }
    );
  }
);
```

The preceding script applies an animation upon opening the dialog using the jQuery `explode` effect. **Figure 15-7** shows what this looks like in a browser.

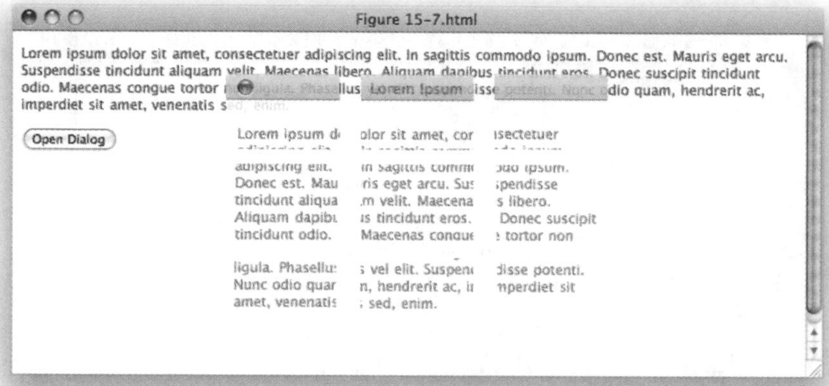

Figure 15-7

In **Figure 15-7**, you see that upon clicking on the "Open Dialog" button, the dialog is opened with an animation that has the dialog sliced into nine pieces coming together.

Working with Dialog Events

The Dialog plugin supports a variety of events. You can set up events that are executed when the dialog is opened, when the dialog is focused, when the dialog is re-sized, when the dialog is dragged, or when the dialog is closed. The following document demonstrates attaching a `close` event to the dialog, but a full list of events is available in Appendix P:

```
$(document).ready(
  function() {
    $('div#tmpExample').dialog({
      autoOpen: false,
      show: 'explode',
      close: function(e, ui) {
        alert(this.id);
      }
    });

    $('input#tmpOpen').click(
      function($e) {
        $('div#tmpExample').dialog('open');
      }
    );
  }
);
```

The preceding script demonstrates the attachment of the `close` option to the dialog, which causes a callback function to be executed when the dialog is closed. The callback function is executed within the context of the dialog element it is attached to, making that element available in the `this` keyword, which results in the screenshot that you see in **Figure 15-8**.

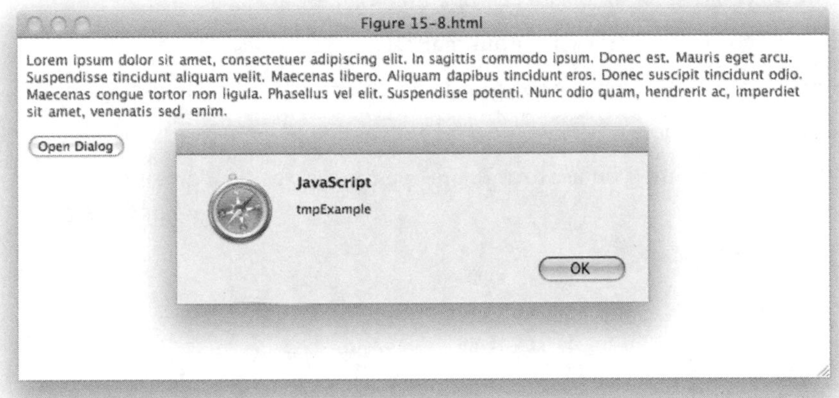

Figure 15-8

Summary

In this chapter, you learned how to implement a dialog using the jQuery UI Dialog plugin. You learned that the Dialog plugin doesn't come with much styling, so you learned how the markup is structured and implemented your own styling for a dialog.

You learned how to make a modal dialog using the `modal` and `overlay` options: The `modal` option can be used to prevent interaction with the document in the background, and the `overlay` option can be used to style the element that's used to disable interaction with the background to give the user a visual indication that interaction with the document is disabled.

You learned how to disable automatically opening a dialog using the `autoOpen` option. After automatically opening a dialog has been disabled, you can programmatically open a dialog by calling `dialog('open')`.

You can disable re-sizing a dialog and dragging a dialog using the `resizable` and `draggable` options, but disabling re-sizing removes the drop shadow that you added to the Dialog window in Example 15-1, since that drop shadow was tied to the markup elements that are added for re-sizing.

If you so choose, you can animate opening and closing a dialog by providing an effect (documented in Appendix M) to the `show` option.

Finally, there are a variety of events associated with a dialog that you can attach callback functions to. You saw an example of the `close` event, but a full list of options can be found in Appendix P.

Exercises

1. What option would you use to disable interaction with the document while a dialog is open?
2. What option would you use to style the overlay used to disable a document while a dialog is open?
3. How do you disable automatically opening a dialog?
4. How do you open a dialog programmatically?
5. How do you close a dialog programmatically. (Hint: see Appendix P.)
6. How do you disable re-sizing and dragging a dialog?
7. What option would you use to animate opening or closing a dialog?

Tabs

In this, the final installment of my introduction to jQuery and jQuery UI, I present how to work with the jQuery UI Tabs plugin, a plugin that makes it easier to implement tabbed functionality, in which you click on a series of tabs that toggles the display of content that either already exists in the document or is loaded via an AJAX Request.

jQuery UI provides all the functional aspects that you would need to implement a tabbed user interface, but does not provide any of the presentational aspects — you are expected to BYOSS ("Bring Your Own Style Sheet").

Implementing tabbed user interface, like many of the plugin functionality that jQuery UI offers, is very easy. You need only learn about a few fundamentals, such as how to structure markup destined to become tabs and, of course, the various options that the Tabs plugin offers to allow tweaking the implementation.

In this chapter, I cover how to implement and style a tabbed user interface, and I cover a few of the options offered by the Tabs plugin that you're most likely to use.

Implementing Tabs

To get started, I present a barebones implementation of the jQuery UI Tabs plugin, which is the purpose of the following document:

```
<!DOCTYPE html PUBLIC "-//W3C//DTD XHTML 1.0 Strict//EN"
    "http://www.w3.org/TR/xhtml1/DTD/xhtml1-strict.dtd">
<html xmlns='http://www.w3.org/1999/xhtml' xml:lang='en'>
  <head>
    <meta http-equiv='content-type' content='text/html; charset=utf-8' />
    <meta http-equiv='content-language' content='en-us' />
    <title></title>
    <script type='text/javascript'
            src='../../../Source Code/jQuery/jQuery.js'></script>
    <script type='text/javascript'
            src='../../../Source Code/jQuery/jQueryUI.js'></script>
```

```
    <script type='text/javascript' src='Figure 16-1.js'></script>
    <link type='text/css' href='Figure 16-1.css' rel='stylesheet' />
  </head>
  <body>
    <div id="tmpTabExample">
      <ul>
        <li><a href="#tmpTab-1"><span>First Tab</span></a></li>
        <li><a href="#tmpTab-2"><span>Second Tab</span></a></li>
        <li><a href="#tmpTab-3"><span>Third Tab</span></a></li>
      </ul>
      <div id="tmpTab-1">
        <p>
          First tab is activated by default.
        </p>
      </div>
      <div id="tmpTab-2">
        <p>
          Lorem ipsum dolor sit amet, consectetuer adipiscing elit. Suspendisse
          id sapien. Suspendisse rutrum libero sit amet dui. Praesent pede elit,
          tincidunt pellentesque, condimentum nec, mollis et, lacus. Donec nulla
          ligula, tempor vel, eleifend ut, luctus nec, est. Duis imperdiet sapien
          condimentum est. Curabitur euismod. Vestibulum magna. Vivamus massa
          erat, tristique at, congue in, fringilla sed, massa. Duis posuere justo
          ac magna. Lorem ipsum dolor sit amet, consectetuer adipiscing elit.
          Donec ac dolor mollis lectus posuere convallis.
        </p>
      </div>
      <div id="tmpTab-3">
        <p>
          Lorem ipsum dolor sit amet, consectetuer adipiscing elit. Suspendisse
          id sapien. Suspendisse rutrum libero sit amet dui. Praesent pede elit,
          tincidunt pellentesque, condimentum nec, mollis et, lacus. Donec nulla
          ligula, tempor vel, eleifend ut, luctus nec, est. Duis imperdiet sapien
          condimentum est. Curabitur euismod. Vestibulum magna. Vivamus massa
          erat, tristique at, congue in, fringilla sed, massa. Duis posuere justo
          ac magna. Lorem ipsum dolor sit amet, consectetuer adipiscing elit.
          Donec ac dolor mollis lectus posuere convallis.
        </p>
      </div>
    </div>
  </body>
</html>
```

The preceding document is styled with the following style sheet:

```
body {
    font: 12px "Lucida Grande", Arial, sans-serif;
    background: #fff;
    color: rgb(50, 50, 50);
}
div#tmpTab-1 {
    background: lightblue;
    padding: 5px;
}
```

```
div#tmpTab-2 {
    background: lightgreen;
    padding: 5px;
}
div#tmpTab-3 {
    background: yellow;
    padding: 5px;
}
```

The following script demonstrates a call to the jQuery UI's `tabs()` method:

```
$(document).ready(
  function() {
    $('div#tmpTabExample > ul').tabs();
  }
);
```

Figure 16-1 shows that the preceding actually doesn't look like much so far.

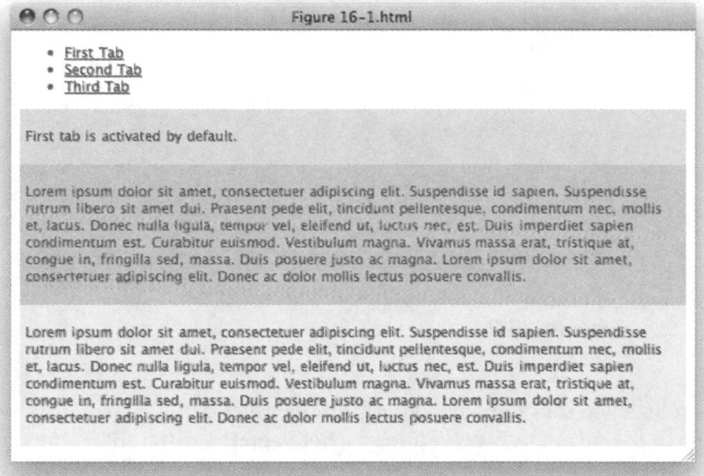

Figure 16-1

The preceding doesn't even appear to have created any tabs. However, appearances are deceitful. You don't appear to have achieved any results because the Tabs plugin doesn't do any presentational styling of tabbed content … it only handles the functional aspects of tabs. To get something closer to a bare-bones implementation, you have to add a rule to the style sheet, so that the style sheet looks like this:

```
body {
    font: 12px "Lucida Grande", Arial, sans-serif;
    background: #fff;
    color: rgb(50, 50, 50);
}
```

```
div#tmpTab-1 {
    background: lightblue;
    padding: 5px;
}
div#tmpTab-2 {
    background: lightgreen;
    padding: 5px;
}
div#tmpTab-3 {
    background: yellow;
    padding: 5px;
}
.ui-tabs-hide {
    display: none;
}
```

The addition of the last rule to the style sheet hides the inactive tabs, and you get a result like what you see in **Figure 16-2**.

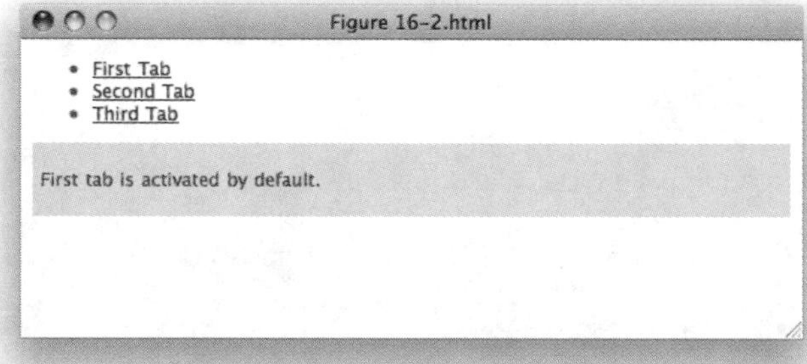

Figure 16-2

In **Figure 16-2**, you can see that the second and third content panels have been hidden, and when you click on the labels in the `<ul>` element, you toggle between the different content panels. You have the freedom to style the tabs however you like, and I will describe a possible styling scenario later in this chapter. Making tabs requires some structural rules. First, you have a list of items, and in that list you have hyperlinks to anchors.

```
<ul>
  <li><a href="#tmpTab-1"><span>First Tab</span></a></li>
  <li><a href="#tmpTab-2"><span>Second Tab</span></a></li>
  <li><a href="#tmpTab-3"><span>Third Tab</span></a></li>
</ul>
```

In the preceding snippet of markup, each hyperlink links to an anchor that appears elsewhere in the document, by including a pound sign, followed by that element's ID name. Structuring the document in this way makes your scripting unobtrusive. If scripting is disabled, the user will still be able to navigate the tabs by clicking on a link to an anchor, instead of toggling the display of a content pane.

Following the list, you have three <div> elements, each having an ID name that corresponds to the anchor link, which makes those elements anchors.

```
<div id="tmpTab-1">
  <p>
    First tab is activated by default.
  </p>
</div>
```

When you call the tabs() method, jQuery looks at the list and automatically pulls the ID names from the hyperlinks, and it automatically attaches the class name *ui-tabs-hide* to every tab but the first, which is considered the active tab by default. That class name can then be used to hide inactive tabs, but as you saw in Figure 16-2, you have to explicitly hide inactive tabs of your own accord.

Since you basically decide the structure of your tabs for yourself, rather than having the structure generated for you, you have more freedom with how to style your tabs. In the following "Try It Out," I present how to apply basic styling to your new jQuery UI–enabled tabs:

Try It Out Styling Tabs

Example 16-1

To style the tabs example, follow these steps.

1. Create the following document. The "Lorem Ipsum" filler text that you see in these documents can be copied and pasted from www.lipsum.com.

```
<!DOCTYPE html PUBLIC "-//W3C//DTD XHTML 1.0 Strict//EN"
    "http://www.w3.org/TR/xhtml1/DTD/xhtml1-strict.dtd">
<html xmlns='http://www.w3.org/1999/xhtml' xml:lang='en'>
  <head>
    <meta http-equiv='content-type' content='text/html; charset=utf-8' />
    <meta http-equiv='content-language' content='en-us' />
    <title></title>
    <script type='text/javascript'
            src='../../../Source Code/jQuery/jQuery.js'></script>
    <script type='text/javascript'
            src='../../../Source Code/jQuery/jQueryUI.js'></script>
    <script type='text/javascript' src='Example 16-1.js'></script>
    <link type='text/css' href='Example 16-1.css' rel='stylesheet' />
  </head>
  <body>
    <div id="tmpTabExample">
      <ul>
        <li><a href="#tmpTab-1"><span>First Tab</span></a></li>
        <li><a href="#tmpTab-2"><span>Second Tab</span></a></li>
        <li><a href="#tmpTab-3"><span>Third Tab</span></a></li>
      </ul>
      <div id="tmpTab-1">
        <p>
          First tab is activated by default.
        </p>
      </div>
```

```
        <div id="tmpTab-2">
          <p>
            Lorem ipsum dolor sit amet, consectetuer adipiscing elit. Suspendisse
            id sapien. Suspendisse rutrum libero sit amet dui. Praesent pede elit,
            tincidunt pellentesque, condimentum nec, mollis et, lacus. Donec nulla
            ligula, tempor vel, eleifend ut, luctus nec, est. Duis imperdiet sapien
            condimentum est. Curabitur euismod. Vestibulum magna. Vivamus massa
            erat, tristique at, congue in, fringilla sed, massa. Duis posuere justo
            ac magna. Lorem ipsum dolor sit amet, consectetuer adipiscing elit.
            Donec ac dolor mollis lectus posuere convallis.
          </p>
        </div>
        <div id="tmpTab-3">
          <p>
            Lorem ipsum dolor sit amet, consectetuer adipiscing elit. Suspendisse
            id sapien. Suspendisse rutrum libero sit amet dui. Praesent pede elit,
            tincidunt pellentesque, condimentum nec, mollis et, lacus. Donec nulla
            ligula, tempor vel, eleifend ut, luctus nec, est. Duis imperdiet sapien
            condimentum est. Curabitur euismod. Vestibulum magna. Vivamus massa
            erat, tristique at, congue in, fringilla sed, massa. Duis posuere justo
            ac magna. Lorem ipsum dolor sit amet, consectetuer adipiscing elit.
            Donec ac dolor mollis lectus posuere convallis.
          </p>
        </div>
      </div>
    </body>
  </html>
```

2. Save the preceding markup document as *Example 16-1.html.*

3. Enter the following style sheet in a new document in your text editor:

```
body {
    font: 12px "Lucida Grande", Arial, sans-serif;
    background: #fff;
    color: rgb(50, 50, 50);
}
div#tmpTab-1 {
    background: lightblue;
    padding: 5px;
}
div#tmpTab-2 {
    background: lightgreen;
    padding: 5px;
}
div#tmpTab-3 {
    background: yellow;
    padding: 5px;
}
.ui-tabs-hide {
    display: none;
}
div#tmpTabExample ul {
    list-style: none;
    padding: 0;
```

```
        margin: 0;
        height: 22px;
        border-bottom: 1px solid darkgreen;
    }
    div#tmpTabExample ul li {
        float: left;
        height: 17px;
        padding: 4px 10px 0 10px;
        margin-right: 5px;
        border: 1px solid rgb(200, 200, 200);
        border-bottom: none;
        position: relative;
        background: yellowgreen;
    }
    div#tmpTabExample ul li a {
        text-decoration: none;
        color: black;
    }
    div#tmpTabExample ul li.ui-tabs-selected {
        background: darkgreen;
    }
    div#tmpTabExample ul li.ui-tabs-selected a {
        color: white;
    }
```

4. Save the preceding document as *Example 16-1.css*.
5. Create the following document in your text editor:

```
$(document).ready(
  function() {
    $('div#tmpTabExample > ul').tabs();
  }
);
```

6. Save the preceding document as *Example 16-1.js*.

Figure 16-3 shows the stylistic adjustments.

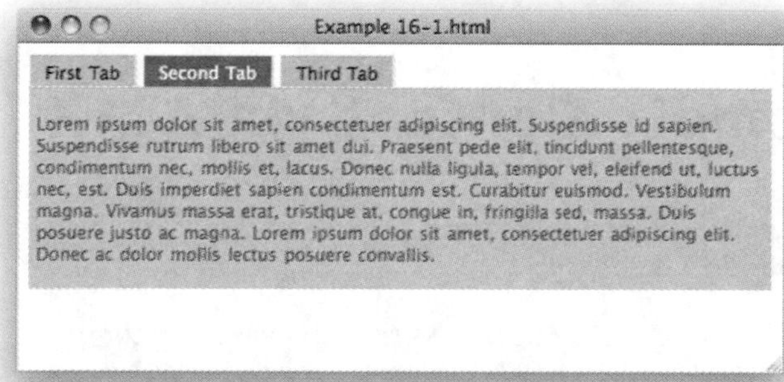

Figure 16-3

In Example 16-1, you see a very remedial styling of the tabbed user interface. Since you're able to provide your own structure, you can make your tab implementation as basic or as fancy as you like.

In the example, you see basic styling of the tabs, which are floated beside each other. There is nothing particularly complex from the standpoint of the styles that are applied.

You do add a new class name to the style sheet that is generated by the Tabs plugin for the selected tab.

```
div#tmpTabExample ul li.ui-tabs-selected {
    background: darkgreen;
}
```

The preceding selector is written the way that it is — instead of, for example, something like this:

```
li.ui-tabs-selected {
    background: darkgreen;
}
```

because you have already applied a background to each `<li>` element using a more specific selector with the following rule:

```
div#tmpTabExample ul li {
    float: left;
    height: 17px;
    padding: 4px 10px 0 10px;
    margin-right: 5px;
    border: 1px solid rgb(200, 200, 200);
    border-bottom: none;
    position: relative;
    background: yellowgreen;
}
```

Therefore, you need to use an even more specific selector to override the background applied in the preceding rule, so that the selected tab receives a `darkgreen` background instead of a `yellowgreen` background. If you'd like to learn more about the concept of specificity as it is used in CSS, I cover this topic in greater detail in my book *Beginning CSS: Cascading Style Sheets for Web Design*, 2nd ed. (Wiley, 2007). Otherwise, the styles that are applied are basic, run-of-the-mill CSS.

Loading Remote Content via AJAX

Loading remote content instead of local content is very easy to do. The following document shows an example of how to set up a tab that loads remote content using AJAX, instead of having that content already loaded in your document:

```
<!DOCTYPE html PUBLIC "-//W3C//DTD XHTML 1.0 Strict//EN"
    "http://www.w3.org/TR/xhtml1/DTD/xhtml1-strict.dtd">
<html xmlns='http://www.w3.org/1999/xhtml' xml:lang='en'>
  <head>
```

```
    <meta http-equiv='content-type' content='text/html; charset=utf-8' />
    <meta http-equiv='content-language' content='en-us' />
    <title></title>
    <script type='text/javascript'
            src='../../../Source Code/jQuery/jQuery.js'></script>
    <script type='text/javascript'
            src='../../../Source Code/jQuery/jQueryUI.js'></script>
    <script type='text/javascript' src='Figure 16-4.js'></script>
    <link type='text/css' href='Figure 16-4.css' rel='stylesheet' />
  </head>
  <body>
    <div id="tmpTabExample">
      <ul>
        <li><a href="#tmpTab-1"><span>First Tab</span></a></li>
        <li><a href="#tmpTab-2"><span>Second Tab</span></a></li>
        <li><a href="#tmpTab-3"><span>Third Tab</span></a></li>
        <li><a href="tab.html" title="tmpTab-4"><span>Fourth Tab</span></a></li>
      </ul>
      <div id="tmpTab-1">
        <p>
          First tab is activated by default.
        </p>
      </div>
      <div id="tmpTab-2">
        <p>
          Lorem ipsum dolor sit amet, consectetuer adipiscing elit. Suspendisse
          id sapien. Suspendisse rutrum libero sit amet dui. Praesent pede elit,
          tincidunt pellentesque, condimentum nec, mollis et, lacus. Donec nulla
          ligula, tempor vel, eleifend ut, luctus nec, est. Duis imperdiet sapien
          condimentum est. Curabitur euismod. Vestibulum magna. Vivamus massa
          erat, tristique at, congue in, fringilla sed, massa. Duis posuere justo
          ac magna. Lorem ipsum dolor sit amet, consectetuer adipiscing elit.
          Donec ac dolor mollis lectus posuere convallis.
        </p>
      </div>
      <div id="tmpTab-3">
        <p>
          Lorem ipsum dolor sit amet, consectetuer adipiscing elit. Suspendisse
          id sapien. Suspendisse rutrum libero sit amet dui. Praesent pede elit,
          tincidunt pellentesque, condimentum nec, mollis et, lacus. Donec nulla
          ligula, tempor vel, eleifend ut, luctus nec, est. Duis imperdiet sapien
          condimentum est. Curabitur euismod. Vestibulum magna. Vivamus massa
          erat, tristique at, congue in, fringilla sed, massa. Duis posuere justo
          ac magna. Lorem ipsum dolor sit amet, consectetuer adipiscing elit.
          Donec ac dolor mollis lectus posuere convallis.
        </p>
      </div>
      <div id="tmpTab-4">
      </div>
    </div>
  </body>
</html>
```

In the preceding markup document, there are a few minor modifications made to add a new tab that has content loaded via AJAX. You set up the tab with the `href` attribute referencing the document that you want to load by AJAX and place the ID of the element, into which you want to load that content, in the `title` attribute.

In the following style sheet, you add new styling for the new tab that you've added:

```
body {
    font: 12px "Lucida Grande", Arial, sans-serif;
    background: #fff;
    color: rgb(50, 50, 50);
}
div#tmpTab-1 {
    background: lightblue;
    padding: 5px;
}
div#tmpTab-2 {
    background: lightgreen;
    padding: 5px;
}
div#tmpTab-3 {
    background: yellow;
    padding: 5px;
}
div#tmpTab-4 {
    background: pink;
    padding: 5px;
}
.ui-tabs-hide {
    display: none;
}
div#tmpTabExample ul {
    list-style: none;
    padding: 0;
    margin: 0;
    height: 22px;
    border-bottom: 1px solid darkgreen;
}
div#tmpTabExample ul li {
    float: left;
    height: 17px;
    padding: 4px 10px 0 10px;
    margin-right: 5px;
    border: 1px solid rgb(200, 200, 200);
    border-bottom: none;
    position: relative;
    background: yellowgreen;
}
div#tmpTabExample ul li a {
    text-decoration: none;
    color: black;
}
```

```
div#tmpTabExample ul li.ui-tabs-selected {
    background: darkgreen;
}
div#tmpTabExample ul li.ui-tabs-selected a {
    color: white;
}
```

The following is what appears in the tab.html file. Using a server-side script, you could also add logic at the server side that presents this content within your normal template depending on whether scripting is enabled on the client side. To do that, what you would do is, by default, make the link `tabs.html?noscript=true`. Then, in your JavaScript, automatically remove the query string portion `?noscript=true` at page load, which would then signal your server-side script to serve only the content, rather than the content within your template.

Then the following script is also included, which you can see has remained unchanged:

```
$(document).ready(
  function() {
    $('div#tmpTabExample > ul').tabs();
  }
);
```

The preceding example results in the screenshot that you see in **Figure 16-4**.

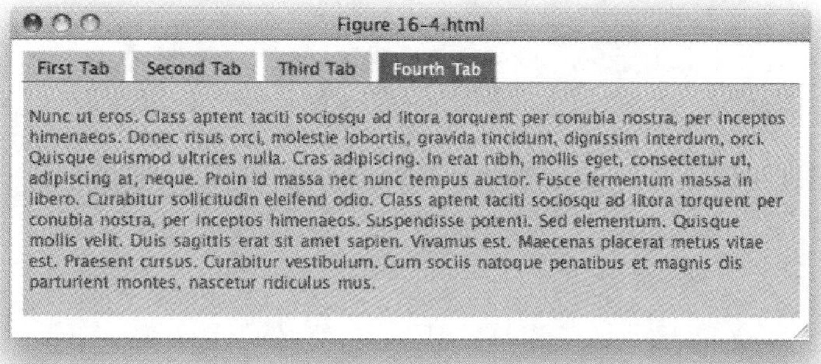

Figure 16-4

There are also a few options that you can pass to the `tabs()` method that configure AJAX loading. The option `spinner` is used to display content in the tab label of AJAX content while that content is loading; you can specify plain text or HTML content.

Additionally, the option `ajaxOptions` can be passed an object of AJAX options to configure the AJAX Request. See Appendix G for a full list of options.

Animating Tab Transitions

Most things in jQuery UI's plugin arsenal can be provided with fancy animated effects, and the Tabs plugin is no exception. The following script demonstrates how to animate a tab transition:

```
$(document).ready(
  function() {
    $('div#tmpTabExample > ul').tabs({
      fx: {
        opacity: 'toggle',
        duration: 'slow'
      }
    });
  }
);
```

The preceding animates the opacity, fading out the tab being closed and fading in the tab being opened. **Figure 16-5** shows a screenshot of this effect in midstream.

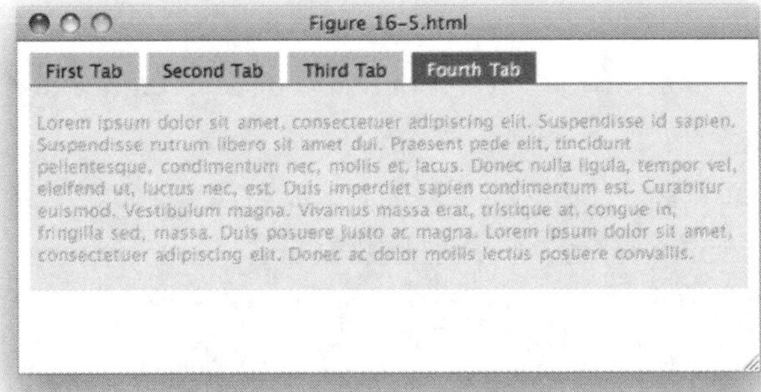

Figure 16-5

You can also animate the height, creating a sliding effect, or both `height` and `opacity`, which create a sliding effect while fading. The following script demonstrates combining both `height` and `opacity` animation:

```
$(document).ready(
  function() {
    $('div#tmpTabExample > ul').tabs({
      fx: {
        opacity: 'toggle',
        height: 'toggle',
        duration: 'slow'
      }
    });
  }
);
```

The preceding script adds a height option, with a value of `'toggle'`; the screenshot that you see in **Figure 16-6** shows the effect produced by this script in midstream.

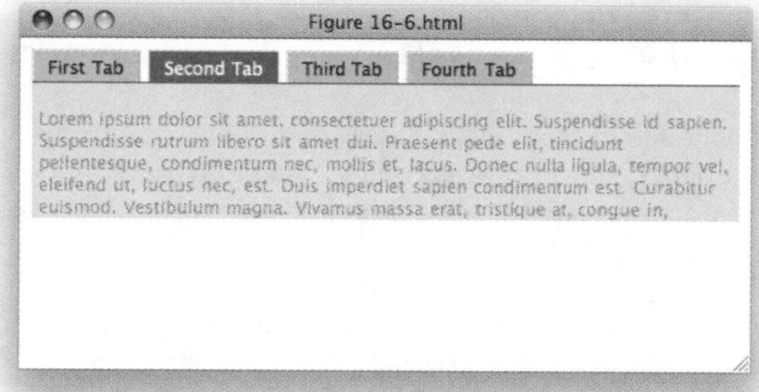

Figure 16-6

Summary

Several additional options can also be used with a tabs implementation; I've covered some of the more useful options in this chapter, and you'll find a full reference of all options available for the Tabs plugin in Appendix Q.

In this chapter, you learned how to implement a tabbed user interface using the jQuery UI Tabs plugin. By default, the Tabs plugin offers no presentational styling whatsoever and only offers the functionality portion of a tabbed user interface. You learned how to approach styling a tabbed user interface with a fairly basic example.

You learned that the Tabs plugin supports loading content remotely using AJAX; you need only minimal modifications to accomplish this.

And finally, you also learned that the Tabs plugin supports animated transitions between tabs and supports animating the opacity or the height, or both, and the duration that an animation takes place.

What Next?

You learned a lot about jQuery and jQuery UI in this book. You've seen that jQuery and jQuery UI provide a comprehensive, robust, and stable API to build web applications on top of. jQuery takes care of a lot of cross-browser development headaches that have presented as frustrating roadblocks to web development in the past. It helps you fix events in JavaScript with an intuitive API of its own that actually works. It helps you build applications with a rich, consistent API that strives to minimize the number of lines of code that you need to write an application wherever possible. jQuery UI makes common UI tasks much easier, helping you with drag-and-drop, with selection, and with dialogs and tabs.

There are two plugins, Re-sizables and Slider, that I wasn't able to include coverage for in the body of this book owing to resource constraints. I have, however, included API documentation for these plugins in Appendixes R and S.

Beyond what is officially offered by jQuery at the jQuery website at `www.jquery.com`, there is also a thriving community of third-party jQuery plugins, which you can learn more about at `plugins.jquery.com`.

I have tried to include as much of the official jQuery documentation in the appendixes of this book as possible, for your convenience; however, it's possible that I may have missed some material. If that is the case, the official jQuery documentation can be found at `docs.jquery.com`, where you'll find documentation, code examples, and FAQ.

Going forward, I recommend that you have a look at Nicholas C. Zakas's books: *Professional JavaScript for Web Developers* (Wiley, 2005; 2nd ed., 2009) and *Professional Ajax*, 2nd ed. (Wiley 2007), by Nicholas C. Zakas, Jeremy McPeak, and Joe Fawcett, which provide excellent, critically acclaimed coverage of advanced JavaScript programming topics.

Exercises

1. What class name do you have to create a rule for in a style sheet to hide inactive content?
2. What class name do you have to create a rule for in a style sheet to change the styling of the active tab?
3. What do you have to do to load content via an AJAX call?
4. What option can you use to animate a tab transition?

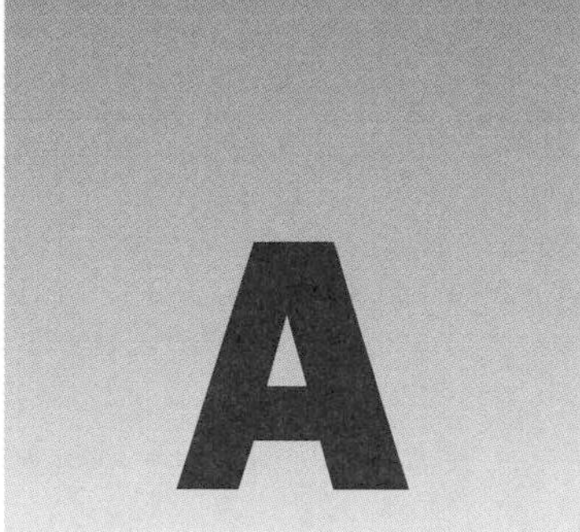

Answers to Exercises

Chapter 2

1. CSS and XPath are both acceptable answers.
2. `parents()`
3. `prev()`
4. `find()` or `children()`, depending on where the element exists in the hierarchy: `children()` can be used for immediate children of the element, and `find()` can be used for either immediate children or descendents.
5. `not()`
6. You would use the `eq()` method and supply the position of the element within the selection offset from zero as the first argument.
7. `siblings()`, `prev()`, `next()`, `prevAll()`, `nextAll()`
8. Using the `add()` method
9. Yes

Chapter 3

1. It is not possible to attach multiple events of the same type to the same element using the traditional event model; however, some very keen programming creativity could overcome this limitation, if one were so inclined.
2. The ability to attach multiple events of the same type to the same element. There are other items addressed in the W3C's API, but I consider this to be the biggest.
3. In the traditional event model, and Microsoft's event model, each event is named with an *on* prefix, for example, `onclick`, `onsubmit`, `onchange`, and so on. In the W3C's event model, the *on* prefix is dropped, but the names are otherwise the same.
4. The `bind()` method. It has a shorter name, and it drops the third `useCapture` argument used in the W3C's Event API. Bonus points if you referred to the `useCapture` argument as "mostly useless."

5. You can use the `trigger('focus')` method, or you can call the `focus()` method without any arguments. Bonus points if you looked in Appendix D and discovered the `triggerHandler()` method, which is just like the `trigger()` method but cancels the browser's default action for any given event.

6. jQuery's `hover()` method takes two handlers, one for `mouseover`, and one for `mouseout`, in that order.

Chapter 4

1. One possibility:

```
$('input').attr(
            'value' : 'Some Value'.
            'class' : 'someClass'
         );
```

   Another possibility:

```
$('input').addClass('someClass').val('Some Value');
```

2. It might look like this:

```
$('a').attr('href', 'http://www.example.com');
```

3. `removeAttr()`
4. `hasClass()`
5. No, HTML tags will not be present in the return value, only the element's text content.
6. Yes, HTML tags will be escaped and treated like text content.
7. One bug that jQuery's `append()` and `prepend()` methods work around in IE is how IE makes `innerHTML` Read Only on `<table>` elements.
8. One bug that jQuery's `append()` and `prepend()` methods work around in Firefox is how Firefox occasionally loses form input values when appending or prepending HTML content using `innerHTML`.
9. `insertBefore()`
10. `wrapAll()`
11. `outerHTML`
12. `remove()`
13. `clone(true)`

Chapter 5

1. It might look like this:

```
$($elements).each(
          function() {
          }
        );

         $.each(
           $elements,
           function() {
           }
         );
```

2. `return false;`

3. The items referenced by the selector are kept in the selection; items not referenced by the selector are discarded.

4. Keeps the current item in the selection; returning `false` removes the current item from the selection.

5. A value that evaluates to `true`. Returning `false` will remove an item from the array.

6. It replaces the value of the item passed to the callback function during that iteration.

7. `-1` means that the value does not exist within the array; a return value of zero or greater means that the value exists within the array.

8. The `$.unique()` method is used to remove duplicate elements from an array consisting of all elements.

Chapter 6

1. `$('div').css('color');`

2. Specifying any color in the second argument, the code would look something like this:

```
$('body').css('backgroundColor', 'yellow');
```

3.
```
$('div').css({
  padding: '5px',
  margin: '5px',
  border: '1px solid grey'
});
```

4. `offsetWidth()`

5. `offsetHeight({margin: true})`

Chapter 7

1. When in the context of an AJAX request, the only real difference between GET and POST requests is that a GET request has a concrete limitation on the amount of data you can pass; the actual limit varies from browser to browser. A GET request can also be slightly more efficient.
2. An optional second argument to the `$.get()` method allows you to pass data along with the request, either as a query string or as a JavaScript object literal.
3. You access the JSON object in the variable that you assign to the first argument of the callback function that you specify for the `$.getJSON()` method. This variable can have any name you like.
4. Accessing the contents of the `<response>` element looks something like this:

```
$.get(
  '/url/to/request.xml',
  function(xml) {
    alert($(xml).text());
  }
);
```

5. The `load()` method
6. In the JavaScript, jQuery sets AJAX Events globally via a call to the `$.ajaxSetup()` method, which takes a list of options that are formatted as a JavaScript object literal. The `beforeSend` property specifies a callback function that is executed before every AJAX request. The `success` property specifies a callback function that is executed upon every successful AJAX request. Within the callback function specified for `beforeSend`, the `<div>` element with ID name *hFinderActivity* is made visible with a call to the `show()` method. Within the callback function specified for success, the same `<div>` element is made invisible with a call to the `hide()` method.
7. One method is by using jQuery's AJAX Event methods like `ajaxStart()` and `ajaxSuccess()`; another is via jQuery's `$.ajax()` method.
8. Select the form elements you want to get the values of, then call the `serialize()` method.

Chapter 8

1. `slow`, `normal`, `fast`, or the time specified in milliseconds
2. The `slideDown()` method animates an element's height from nothing to its normal height.
3. `fadeIn()`
4. `animate()`
5. You can only animate CSS properties that have a numeric value.

Chapter 9

1. `$.fn.extend()` or `jQuery.fn.extend()`
2. The selection can be accessed using the `this` keyword. You can use `this.each()` to iterate over multiple methods.
3. Whenever possible, you should return the jQuery object to preserve chainability.

Chapter 10

1. Make a selection with jQuery, then apply the `draggable()` method, such as:

```
$('div.someElement').draggable();
```

2. Make a selection with jQuery, then apply the `draggable()` method with the `helper` option specified, giving the `helper` option a value of `clone`, similar to this:

```
$('div.someElement').draggable({
helper: 'clone'
});
```

3. Make a selection with jQuery, then apply the `droppable()` method, for example:

```
$('div.someElement').droppable();
```

4. To add a class name to a drop element while a drag element is over that element, you make a call to the `droppable()` method, with the `hoverClass` option specified. The value you specify for the `hoverClass` option is the class name you want added. This looks similar to the following code:

```
$('div.someElement').droppable({
    hoverClass: 'someClassName'
});
```

5. You'd use the `accept` option, providing a selector as the value, similar to what you see in the following code:

```
$('div.someElement').droppable({
    accept: 'div.someDragElementYouWant'
});
```

6. `dragstart`, `dragenter`, `dragover`, `dragleave`, `drop`

Chapter 11

1. The `sortable()` method
2. A class name
3. The `placeholder` option takes a class name that gives you the ability to style with CSS, the white space that's reserved as a sort takes place.
4. The `cursor` option
5. The `helper` option gives you the ability to change the element that the user drags during a sort.
6. The `connectWith` option
7. A selector
8. You specify the `update` option on a sortable list, with a callback function as its value. Then in the callback function, you do something similar to the following code:

```
var $data = $('ul').sortable(
  'serialize', {
    key: 'list'
  }
);

$.get('/path/to/server/side/script.php', $data);
```

Chapter 12

1. The `start` option
2. The `selecting` and `unselecting` options
3. By specifying a second argument for the callback function (in this book's examples and documentation, the second argument for callback functions for Selectable events is named `ui`). Then you can access each element as `ui.selected` and `ui.unselected`. The property that you use to access each element that's added or removed always goes by the same name as the option.
4. `div.ui-selectable-helper`

Chapter 13

1. `active`
2. The `alwaysOpen` option gives you the ability to dictate whether the open content pane can be closed.
3. `autoHeight`, `clearStyle`, and `fillSpace`
4. `event`
5. `header: "h3"`

6. Set the `navigation` option to `true`, then provide a callback function to the `navigationFilter` option. Within the callback function, you can provide your own logic to determine whether the `href` attribute of a given `<a>` element matches the `location.href` property, thus making that content pane displayed by default.
7. `selectedClass`

Chapter 14

1. The `minDate` and `maxDate` options can be used to limit the range of selectable dates, down to the day. The `yearRange` option can be used to limit the range of selectable dates between an arbitrary set of years.
2. The `dateFormat` option, of course!
3. Yes, the Datepicker plugin provides fine-grained customization of every text label.
4. The `firstDay` option

Chapter 15

1. The `modal` option set to `false`
2. The `overlay` option
3. Set the `autoOpen` option to `false`.
4. Select the dialog you want to open, then call `dialog('open')`.
5. Select the dialog you want to close, then call `dialog('close')`.
6. Set `resizable` and `draggable` options to `false`.
7. The `show` option

Chapter 16

1. `ui-tabs-hide`
2. `ui-tabs-selected`
3. First, you create a tab in a `<li>` element. In the `<a>` element that you put inside of that `<li>` element, you reference the document that you want to load in the `href` attribute, and put the ID of the element that content will be loaded into in the `title` attribute. Then you create the content pane, like normal, with an `id` attribute containing the name that you specified in the `title` attribute. The only thing that you do differently is not include any content, since it's being loaded externally.
4. The `fx` option

Selectors Supported by jQuery

The following table contains the selector syntax that you are able to use with jQuery's Selector API:

Selector	Description
Simple Selectors	
`#id`	Selects a single element via the ID name specified in the element's `id` attribute.
`element`	Selects one or more elements by the element name, for example, `form`, `div`, `input`, and so on.
`.className`	Selects one or more elements via a class name present in the element's `class` attribute. Individual elements may also have multiple class names.
`*`	The universal or wildcard selector; selects all elements.
`grouping, multiple, selectors`	Selects one or more elements by chaining multiple selectors together with commas.
Hierarchy	
`ancestor descendent`	Selects one or more elements based on an ancestral relationship.
`parent > child`	Selects one or more elements based on a parent, child relationship.
`sibling + nextAdjacentSibling`	Selects the sibling immediately following an element.
`sibling ~ anyProceedingSibling`	Selects any siblings immediately following an element.

Selector	Description
Basic Filters	
`:first`	Selects the first element.
`:last`	Selects the last element.
`:not(selector)`	Selects elements based on what you don't want.
`:even`	Selects only elements falling within even numbering. Since jQuery calculates position offset from zero, this actually results in the odd-numbered items being returned. Item one would be considered number zero, item two would be considered number one, and so on; so `even` matches numbers zero, two, four, and so on.
`:odd`	Selects only elements falling within odd numbering. Since jQuery calculates position offset from zero, this actually results in even-numbered items being returned (see `:even`).
`:eq(index)`	Selects a single element based on its index; for example, what number (offset from zero) the element would be given when it and all of its siblings are tallied and each assigned a number.
`:gt(index)`	Selects all elements where each element's index is greater than the number specified.
`:lt(index)`	Selects all elements where each element's index is less than the number specified.
`:header`	Selects all elements that are headers, for example, `h1`, `h2`, `h3`, `h4`, `h5`, or `h6`.
`:animated`	Selects all elements that are currently being animated.
Content Filters	
`:contains(text)`	Selects elements based on whether the text specified is present among the element's content.
`:empty`	Selects elements that have no children (including text nodes).
`:has(selector)`	Selects elements that match the specified selector.
`:parent`	Selects all elements that are parents, for example, elements that have text or other elements as children.

Selector	Description
Visibility Filters	
`:hidden`	Selects all elements that are hidden, or `<input>` elements that are of `type="hidden"`.
`:visible`	Selects all elements that are visible.
Attribute Filters	
`[attribute]`	Selects all elements where the specified attribute is present.
`[attribute=value]`	Selects all elements where the attribute has the specified value.
`[attribute!=value]`	Selects all elements where the attribute does not have the specified value.
`[attribute^=value]`	Selects all elements where the attribute's value begins with the specified string.
`[attribute$=value]`	Selects all elements where the attribute's value ends with the specified string.
`[attribute*=value]`	Selects all elements where the attribute's value contains the specified string anywhere within the value.
`[attribute][attribute][attribute]`	Selects all elements where the element has each attribute; for example, you can chain any of the preceding attribute selectors together to look at multiple attributes.
Child Filters	
`:nth-child(index/even/odd/equation)`	Selects all elements where the element is a certain index (see `:eq`), or an odd, or an even child. Unlike jQuery's `eq`, this one counts offset from one instead of zero.
`:first-child`	Selects all elements where the element is a first child of its parent.
`:last-child`	Selects all elements where the element is a last child of its parent.
`:only-child`	Selects all elements where the element is an only child of its parent.

Selector	Description
Forms	
`:input`	Selects all `<input>`, `<select>`, `<textarea>`, and `<button>` elements.
`:text`	Selects all `<input>` elements where `type="text"`.
`:password`	Selects all `<input>` elements where `type="password"`.
`:radio`	Selects all `<input>` elements where `type="radio"`.
`:checkbox`	Selects all `<input>` elements where `type="checkbox"`.
`:submit`	Selects all `<input>` elements where `type="submit"`.
`:image`	Selects all `<input>` elements where `type="image"`.
`:reset`	Selects all `<input>` elements where `type="reset"`.
`:button`	Selects all `<button>` elements and `<input>` elements where `type="button"`.
`:file`	Selects all `<input>` elements where `type="file"`.
`:hidden`	Selects all elements that are hidden, or `<input>` elements where `type="hidden"`.
Form Filters	
`:enabled`	Selects all elements that are enabled.
`:disabled`	Selects all elements that are disabled.
`:checked`	Selects all elements that are checked, for example, check-box and radio inputs.
`:selected`	Selects all elements that are selected, for example, options in a Select dropdown.

Selecting and Filtering

The following methods are provided by jQuery for selecting and filtering elements as documented at `www.jquery.com`.

Method/Property	Description	Return Value
jQuery Core		
`$(`*`selector`*`)`	Makes a selection from the document.	jQuery
`jQuery(`*`selector`*`)`	An alternative name for the preceding, dollar sign method	jQuery
`length`	The number of selected elements	Number
`get()`	Returns all selected elements as an array, rather than as a jQuery object.	Array
`get(`*`index`*`)`	Returns a single element from the selection; the `index` argument is the element's position in the selection, offset from zero.	Element
`index(`*`subject`*`)`	Searches the selection for the specified element and returns that element's position in the selection offset from zero.	Number
Filtering		
`eq(`*`index`*`)`	Reduce a selection to a single element, where `index` is the number representing the element's position in the selection offset from zero.	jQuery
`filter(`*`selector`*`)`	Removes all elements that do not match the specified selector.	jQuery

Method/Property	Description	Return Value
filter(*function*)	The filter() method may alternatively accept a function as its first argument, which works identically to the jQuery $.each() method. The function is executed for each item selected. The function must return a Boolean value, where true indicates that the element should remain in the result set, and false indicates that the element should be removed from the result set.	jQuery
not(*selector*)	Removes elements from the selection that match the specified selector.	jQuery
slice(*indexStart*, *indexEnd*)	Selects a subset of the selection, where each index is a number representing the element's position in the selection offset from zero.	jQuery
Finding		
add(*selector*)	Adds more elements to the selection.	jQuery
children(*selector*)	Makes a selection within the context of the matched elements' children. The selector argument is optional; to select all children of all the selected elements, simply omit the selector argument.	
find(*selector*)	Makes a selection within the context of matched elements' descendents.	jQuery
next(*selector*)	Selects the next sibling element; the selector argument is optional.	jQuery
nextAll(*selector*)	Selects all subsequent sibling elements; the selector argument is optional.	jQuery
prev(*selector*)	Selects the previous sibling element; the selector argument is optional.	jQuery
prevAll(*selector*)	Selects all preceding sibling elements; the selector argument is optional.	jQuery
siblings(*selector*)	Selects all sibling elements; the selector argument is optional.	jQuery
parents(*selector*)	Selects all ancestor elements; the selector argument is optional.	jQuery
parent(*selector*)	Selects all immediate parent elements; the selector argument is optional.	jQuery
Chaining		
andSelf()	Adds the previous selection to the current selection.	jQuery

Events

The following table contains all of the event methods supported by jQuery as listed in jQuery's official documentation at `www.jquery.com`.

All of the event methods return the jQuery object.

Method	Description
Page Load	
`ready(`*`function`*`)`	Attaches a function that is executed when the DOM is completely loaded, that is, all markup, CSS, and JavaScript are loaded, but not necessarily images.
Event Handling	
`bind(`*`event, function`*`)`	Attach a function that is executed when the event occurs. Multiple events can be specified in the event argument; if you specify multiple events, each event must be separated with a single space.
`bind(`*`event, data, function`*`)`	The `bind()` method accepts an optional data argument. The data argument is an object that is passed to the `event` object of the attached function as `event.data`.
`one(`*`event, function`*`)`	Attaches a function to be fired for the specified event. The function is only executed once. Subsequent events will not execute the specified function.
`one(`*`event, data, function`*`)`	The `one()` method accepts an optional data argument. The data argument is an object that is passed to the `event` object of the attached function as `event.data`.
`trigger(`*`event`*`)`	Triggers the specified event on matched elements.
`trigger(`*`event, data`*`)`	The `trigger()` method accepts an optional data argument. The data argument is an object that is passed to `event` object functions being triggered as `event.data`.
`triggerHandler(`*`event`*`)`	Triggers the specified event on matched elements while canceling the browser's default action for any given event.

Method	Description
`triggerHandler(`*`event, data`*`)`	The `triggerHandler()` method accepts an optional data argument. The data argument is an object that is passed to event object functions being triggered as `event.data`.
`unbind(`*`event, function`*`)`	Removes the event and function.
Event Helpers	
`hover(`*`mouseover, mouseout`*`)`	Attaches a function for `mouseover`, and a function for `mouseout` to the same element.
`toggle(`*`function1, function2, function3...`*`)`	Upon first click, the first function is executed; upon second click, the second function is executed; upon third click, the third function is executed, and so on. A minimum of two functions must be specified; an unlimited number of total functions may be specified.
Event Methods	
`blur()`	Triggers the `blur` event of each selected element.
`blur(`*`function`*`)`	Attaches a function to the `blur` event of each selected element.
`change()`	Triggers the `change` event of each selected element.
`change(`*`function`*`)`	Attaches a function to the `change` event of each selected element.
`click()`	Triggers the `click` event of each selected element.
`click(`*`function`*`)`	Attaches a function to the `click` event of each selected element.
`dblclick()`	Triggers the `dblclick` (double-click) event of each selected element.
`dblclick(`*`function`*`)`	Attaches a function to the `dblclick` event of each selected element.
`error()`	Triggers the `error` event of each selected element.
`error(`*`function`*`)`	Attaches a function to the `error` event of each selected element.
`focus()`	Triggers the `focus` event of each selected element.
`focus(`*`function`*`)`	Attaches a function to the `focus` event of each selected element.
`keydown()`	Triggers the `keydown` event of each selected element.
`keydown(`*`function`*`)`	Attaches a function to the `keydown` event of each selected element.
`keyup()`	Triggers the `keyup` event of each selected element.
`keyup(`*`function`*`)`	Attaches a function to the `keyup` event of each selected element.
`load(`*`function`*`)`	Attaches a function to the `load` event of each selected element.
`mousedown(`*`function`*`)`	Attaches a function to the `mousedown` event of each selected element.

Method	Description
mousemove(*function*)	Attaches a function to the mousemove event of each selected element.
mouseout(*function*)	Attaches a function to the mouseout event of each selected element.
mouseover(*function*)	Attaches a function to the mouseover event of each selected element.
mouseup(*function*)	Attaches a function to the mouseup event of each selected element.
resize(*function*)	Attaches a function to the resize event of each selected element.
scroll(*function*)	Attaches a function to the scroll event of each selected element.
select()	Triggers the select event of each selected element.
select(*function*)	Attaches a function to the select event of each selected element.
submit()	Triggers the submit event of each selected element.
submit(*function*)	Attaches a function to the submit event of each selected element.
unload(*function*)	Attaches a function to the unload event of each selected element.

Event Object Normalization

jQuery provides the following in the event object passed as the first argument to every function acting as an event handler, in every browser, even those that wouldn't support these otherwise:

Method/Property	Description
event.type	Provides the type of event, for example, click, mouseover, keyup, and so on.
event.target	The DOM element that triggered the event
event.pageX, event.pageY	The mouse coordinates relative to the document
event.preventDefault()	Prevents the browser's default action for a given event, for example, submitting a form, or navigating to the href attribute of an <a> element.
event.stopPropagation()	Stops the propagation of an event from a child or descendent element to its parent or ancestor elements, which prevents the same event from running on the later ancestor elements.
event.data	An object passed to the function acting as an event handler. See the data argument specified for various methods under "Event Handling" in the previous table.

Manipulating Attributes and Data Caching

Method/Property	Description	Return Value
attr()		
`attr(name)`	Returns the attribute value for the specified attribute from the first element present in a selection. If no element is present, the method returns "undefined."	Object
`attr(properties)`	Allows you to set attributes via the specification of key, value pairs. For example: `attr({ id: 'someIDName', href: '/example.html', title: 'Some tooltip text.' });`	jQuery
`attr(key, value)`	Allows you to specify an attribute by providing the name of the attribute in the `key` argument and its value in the `value` argument.	jQuery
`attr(key, function)`	Sets an attribute's value depending on the return value of the callback function that you specify. The callback function is executed within the context of each selected element, where each selected element can be accessed within the function via `this`.	jQuery
`removeAttr(name)`	Removes the specified attribute from the element(s).	jQuery
Class Names		
`addClass(class)`	Adds the specified class name to each selected element. Elements can have one or more class names.	jQuery
`hasClass(class)`	Returns `true` if the specified class name is present on at least one of the selected elements.	Boolean

Method/Property	Description	Return Value
`removeClass(class)`	Removes the specified class name from each selected element.	jQuery
`toggleClass(class)`	Adds the specified class name if it is not present, and removes the specified class name if it is present.	jQuery
HTML		
`html()`	Returns the HTML contents, or `innerHTML`, of the first element of the selection. This method does not work on XML documents, but does work on XHTML documents.	String
`html(value)`	Sets the HTML contents of every selected element. This method does not work on XML documents, but does work on XHTML documents.	jQuery
Text		
`text()`	Returns the text content of each selected element.	String
`text(value)`	Sets the text content of each selected element. HTML source code will not be rendered.	jQuery
Value		
`val()`	Returns the contents of the `value` attribute for the first element of the selection. For `<select>` elements with attribute `multiple="multiple"`, an array of selected values is returned.	String, Array
`val(value)`	When providing a single value, this method sets the contents of the `value` attribute for each selected element.	jQuery
`val(values)`	When providing multiple values, this method checks or selects radio buttons, checkboxes, or select options that match the set of values.	jQuery
Data Caching		
jQuery has the ability to store data with an element, which works similarly to how you would manipulate attributes.		
`data(name)`	Returns data stored for an element by the specified name for the selected elements.	Any
`data(name, value)`	Stores data by the specified name with the selected elements, and also returns the value.	Any
`removeData(name)`	Removes the data by the specified name from the selected elements.	jQuery

Manipulating Content

Method/Property	Description	Return Value
HTML		
`html()`	Returns the HTML contents, or `innerHTML`, of the first element of the selection. This method does not work on XML documents, but does work on XHTML documents.	String
`html(`*`value`*`)`	Sets the HTML contents of every selected element. This method does not work on XML documents, but does work on XHTML documents.	jQuery
Text		
`text()`	Returns the text content of each selected element.	String
`text(`*`value`*`)`	Sets the text content of each selected element. HTML source code will not be rendered.	jQuery
Inserting Inside		
`append(`*`content`*`)`	Appends the specified content to the inside of every selected element.	jQuery
`appendTo(`*`selector`*`)`	Appends all of the selected elements to the elements specified by the `selector` argument.	jQuery
`prepend(`*`content`*`)`	Prepends the specified content to the inside of each selected element.	jQuery
`prependTo(`*`selector`*`)`	Prepends all of the selected elements to the elements specified by the `selector` argument.	jQuery
Inserting Outside		
`after(`*`content`*`)`	Inserts the specified content after each selected element.	jQuery
`insertAfter(`*`selector`*`)`	Inserts the selected elements after the elements specified by the `selector` argument.	jQuery

Method/Property	Description	Return Value
`before(content)`	Inserts the specified content before each selected element.	jQuery
`insertBefore(selector)`	Inserts the selected elements before the selectors specified by the `selector` argument.	jQuery
Inserting Around		
`wrap(html)`	Wraps each selected element with the specified HTML content.	jQuery
`wrap(element)`	Wraps each selected element with the specified element from the DOM.	jQuery
`wrapAll(html)`	Wraps all of the selected elements with a single wrapper specified as HTML.	jQuery
`wrapAll(element)`	Wraps all of the selected elements with the specified element from the DOM.	jQuery
`wrapInner(html)`	Wraps the inner contents of each selected element with the specified HTML.	jQuery
`wrapInner(element)`	Wraps the inner contents of each selected element with the specified element from the DOM.	jQuery
Replacing		
`replaceWith(content)`	Replaces each selected element with the specified HTML or DOM elements. This method returns the jQuery object including the element that was replaced.	jQuery
`replaceAll(selector)`	Replaces the elements specified in the `selector` argument with the selected elements.	jQuery
Removing		
`empty()`	Removes all child nodes from the selected elements.	jQuery
`remove(selector)`	Removes the selected elements from the DOM.	jQuery
Copying		
`clone()`	Clones the selected elements; returns the jQuery object including the clones you created.	jQuery
`clone(true)`	Clones the selected elements and their event handlers; returns the jQuery object including the clones you created.	jQuery

AJAX Methods

Method	Description	Return Value
AJAX Requests		
`jQuery.ajax(options)` `$.ajax(options)`	Allows you to pass an object literal specifying various options in key, value pairs. For the complete list of options, see the "Options" section. This method is used by jQuery's other AJAX methods to make AJAX requests. You should only use this method if you require finer-grained control over an AJAX request than is possible with jQuery's other methods.	XMLHttpRequest
`load(url, [data], [function])`	Loads HTML from a remote file and inserts the HTML inside of the selected elements. The `data` argument (optional) is specified as an object literal, defining the data you want to pass to the server in key, value pairs. The `function` argument (also optional) is the callback method that will handle the data once it is returned from the server.	jQuery
`jQuery.get(url, [data], [function], [type])` `$.get(url, [data], [function], [type]))`	Initiates an HTTP request using the GET method.	XMLHttpRequest
`jQuery.getJSON(url, [data], [function])` `$.getJSON(url, [data], [function])`	Initiates an HTTP request using the GET method, in which the response will be JSON-formatted data.	XMLHttpRequest
`jQuery.getScript(url, [function])` `$.getScript(url, [function])`	Loads and executes a new JavaScript file via the GET method asynchronously.	XMLHttpRequest

Method	Description	Return Value
`jQuery.post(url, [data], [function], [type])` `$.post(url, [data], [function], [type])`	Initiates an HTTP request using the POST method.	XMLHttpRequest
AJAX Events		
`ajaxComplete(function)`	Attaches a function to be executed when an AJAX request is completed.	jQuery
`ajaxError(function)`	Attaches a function to be executed when an AJAX request fails.	jQuery
`ajaxSend(function)`	Attaches a function to be executed before an AJAX request is sent.	jQuery
`ajaxStart(function)`	Attaches a function to be executed when an AJAX request begins (if not already active).	jQuery
`ajaxStop(function)`	Attaches a function to be executed when an AJAX request ends.	jQuery
`ajaxSuccess(function)`	Attaches a function to be executed when an AJAX request has completed successfully.	jQuery
Miscellaneous		
`jQuery.ajaxSetup(options)` `$.ajaxSetup(options)`	Configures the default options for AJAX requests. The `option` argument is passed as an object literal, in key, value pairs. See the "Options" section.	jQuery
`serialize()`	Serializes a set of input elements into a string of data.	jQuery
`serializeArray()`	Serializes all forms and form elements into a JSON structure.	jQuery

Options

Option	Description	Type
`async`	By default, jQuery sends all AJAX requests asynchronously. To send a synchronous request, set this property to `false`.	Boolean
`beforeSend`	The function you specify for this option is executed before the AJAX request is sent.	Function

Option	Description	Type
`cache`	Whether or not the AJAX request should be cached. The default is `true`, `false` for `dataType` `script`.	Boolean
`complete`	This option allows you to specify a function that is executed when the AJAX request has completed.	Function
`contentType`	The MIME type of data being sent to the server. The default is `application/x-www-form-urlencoded`.	String
`data`	The data to be sent to the server with a GET or POST request. Can be specified as either a string of ampersand-delimited arguments or as an object literal in key, value pairs.	Object, String

`dataFilter`	A function to be used to handle the raw response data of `XMLHttpRequest`. This is a pre-filtering function to sanitize the response. You should return the sanitized data. The function has two arguments: the raw data returned from the server and the type parameter (see `dataType`):
	`function (data, type) {`
	`  // do something`
	`  // return the sanitized data`
	`  return data;`
	`}`
		Function

`dataType`	The type of data that you expect to receive in your response from the server. jQuery automatically determines whether to pass `responseText` or `responseXML` to the callback function handling the response, depending on the MIME type of the data returned by the server. See the "Types" section for a list of allowed data types.	String
`error`	A function that is executed if the AJAX request fails	Function
`global`	Whether or not to trigger the global AJAX event handlers for the request, for example, the handlers set by the various AJAX Event methods. The default is `true`.	Boolean
`ifModified`	Allows the request to be successful only if the request has been modified since the last request. This is determined by checking the time specified in the `Last-Modified` HTTP header. The default is `false` (ignore the Last-Modified header).	Boolean
`jsonp`	Overrides the callback function name in a jsonp request. This value will be used instead of `'callback'` in the `'callback=?'` part of the query string in the URL for a GET or the data for a POST. So `{jsonp:'onJsonPLoad'}` would result in `onJsonPLoad=?` passed to the server.	String
`password`	A password to use in response to an HTTP access authentication request	String

Option	Description	Type
processData	By default, data passed in to the data option will be processed and transformed into a query string, fitting to the default content-type application/x-www-form-urlencoded. If you want to send DOMDocuments or other non-processed data, set this option to false. The default is true.	Boolean
scriptCharset	For GET requests where the dataType is set to script or jsonp. Forces the request to be interpreted with the specified charset. This is only needed if the charset of local content is different from the remote content being loaded.	String
success	A function that is executed upon success of the AJAX request	Function
timeout	Sets the amount of time in milliseconds (ms) to allow before a time-out will occur.	Number
type	The type of HTTP request, one of GET or POST. You can also specify PUT or DELETE. However, those methods are not supported by all browsers.	String
url	The URL to request	String
username	A username to specify in response to an HTTP authentication required request	String
xhr	Callback for creating the XMLHttpRequest object. Defaults to the ActiveXObject when available (IE), the XMLHttpRequest otherwise. Override to provide your own implementation for XMLHttpRequest or enhancements to the factory.	Function

Types (allowed for the dataType option, or type argument)

Type	Description
xml	Returns an XML document that can be processed with jQuery.
html	Returns HTML as plain text. <script> elements are evaluated upon inserting into the DOM.
script	Evaluates the response as JavaScript and returns the script as plain text to the callback function. Disables caching unless the cache option is used. Note: This type of request will make POST requests into GET requests.
json	Evaluates the response as JSON and returns a JavaScript object.
jsonp	Loads in a JSON block using JSONP. Will add an extra ?callback=? to the end of your URL to specify the callback.
text	Returns the server response as a plain text string.

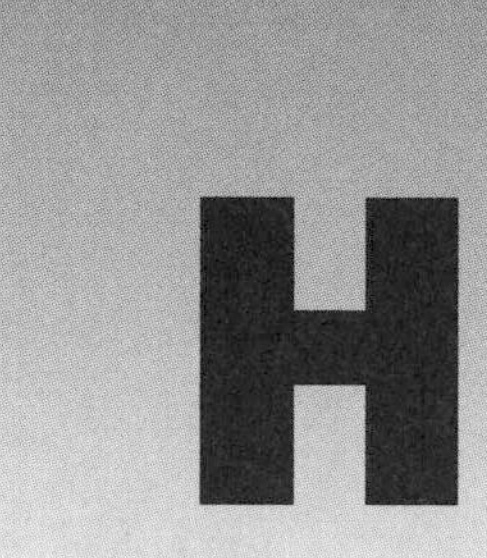

CSS

<table>
<tr><th>Method</th><th>Description</th><th>Return Value</th></tr>
<tr><td colspan="3">CSS</td></tr>
<tr><td><code>css(property)</code></td><td>Returns the specified CSS property value from the first selected element, for example:
<code>$('div').css('background-color')</code></td><td>String</td></tr>
<tr><td><code>css(properties)</code></td><td>Sets the specified CSS properties. The <code>properties</code> argument is defined as an object literal of key, value pairs, for example:
<code>$('div').css({</code>
<code> backgroundColor: 'red',</code>
<code> marginLeft: '10px'</code>
<code>});</code></td><td>jQuery</td></tr>
<tr><td><code>css(property, value)</code></td><td>Sets the specified CSS property value, for example:
<code>$('div').css('background', 'red');</code></td><td>jQuery</td></tr>
<tr><td colspan="3">Positioning</td></tr>
<tr><td><code>offset()</code></td><td>Returns the offset position of the first selected element relative to the viewport.
<code>var $offset = $('div').offset();</code>
<code>alert('Left: ' + $offset.left);</code>
<code>alert('Top: ' + $offset.top);</code></td><td>Object</td></tr>
<tr><td colspan="3">Height and Width</td></tr>
<tr><td><code>height()</code></td><td>Returns the pixel height (CSS height, excluding borders and padding) of the first selected element.</td><td>Integer</td></tr>
<tr><td><code>height(value)</code></td><td>Sets the pixel height (CSS height) of the first selected element. If no unit of measurement is provided, px (pixels) is used.</td><td>jQuery</td></tr>
<tr><td><code>width()</code></td><td>Returns the pixel width (CSS width, excluding borders and padding) of the first selected element.</td><td>Integer</td></tr>
</table>

Method	Description	Return Value
`width(value)`	Sets the pixel width (CSS width) of the first selected element. If no unit of measurement is provided, px (pixels) is used.	jQuery
`outerHeight(options)`	Returns the `offsetHeight` (includes the pixel height, borders, and padding) of the first selected element. The `options` argument is a JavaScript object literal of options. See the "Options" section for more information.	Integer
`outerWidth(options)`	Returns the `offsetWidth` (includes the pixel width, borders, and padding) of the first selected element. The `options` argument is a JavaScript object literal of options. See the "Options" section for more information.	Integer

Options

Option	Description	Type
`margin`	When set to `true`, the margin will be included in the calculation for `offsetWidth` or `offsetHeight`.	Boolean

Utilities

Method/Property	Description	Return Value/Type
Browser Detection		

`$.browser`
`jQuery.browser`
	Contains properties for determining the make of the browser. Each of the following are Boolean values depending on what browser you use to access the property:
	`$.browser.safari`
	`$.browser.opera`
	`$.browser.msie`
	`$.browser.mozilla`
	One additional property provides the browser version:
	`$.browser.version`
		Object

`$.boxModel` `jQuery.boxModel`	Provides whether the browser is using the standard W3C box model.	Boolean
Array and Object Operations		
`$.each(`*object, function*`)` `jQuery.each(`*object, function*`)`	A function that iterates over the contents of an array or object, passing each item to a callback function.	Object
`$.extend(`*target, object1...*`)` `jQuery.extend(`*target, object1...*`)`	Extends the target object with one or more specified objects. Returns the original, unmodified object.	Object

Method/Property	Description	Return Value/Type
`$.grep(array, function, invert)` `jQuery.grep(array, function, invert)`	Filters items out of an array using a callback function. If the optional *invert* argument is `false` or not provided, `grep` returns an array of items where the callback function has returned `true` for each of those items. If the *invert* argument is `true`, it returns an array where the callback function for each item has returned `false`.	Array
`$.makeArray(object)` `jQuery.makeArray(object)`	Turns anything into an array (as opposed to an Object or a StaicNodeList).	Array
`$.map(array, function)` `jQuery.map(array, function)`	Translate the items in the specified array to another array via logic provided in the callback function.	Array
`$.inArray(value, array)` `jQuery.inArray(value, array)`	Determines whether the specified value appears in the specified array.	Array
`$.unique(array)` `jQuery.unique(array)`	Removes duplicate values from the specified array.	Array
Test Operations		
`$.isFunction(item)` `jQuery.isFunction(item)`	Determines if the specified item is a function.	Boolean
String Operations		
`$.trim(string)` `jQuery.trim(string)`	Removes white space (newline characters, spaces, tabs, carriage returns) from the beginning and end of a string.	String

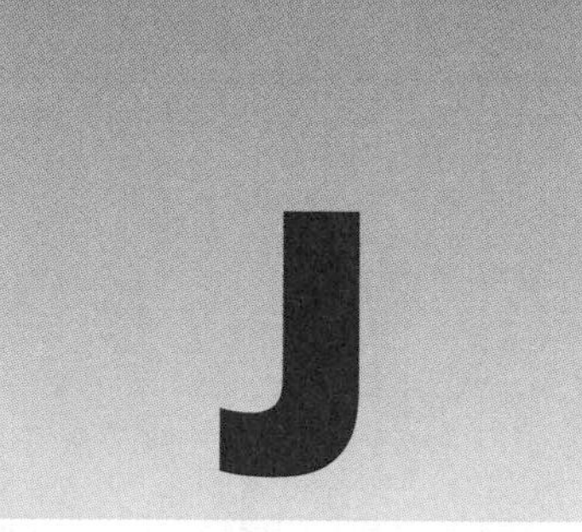

Draggables and Droppables

Draggable and Droppable Methods

Method	Description	Return Value
`draggable(`*`options`*`)`	Makes the selected element(s) draggable. Options can be specified by passing an object literal as the first argument using key, value pairs. For a complete list of options, see the "Draggables Options" section later in this Appendix.	jQuery
`draggable('disable')`	Disables draggable functionality on the selected element(s).	jQuery
`draggable('enable')`	Enables draggable functionality on the selected element(s).	jQuery
`draggable('destroy')`	Completely removes draggable functionality from the selected element(s).	jQuery
`droppable(`*`options`*`)`	Makes the selected element(s) droppable. Options can be specified by passing an object literal as the first argument using key, value pairs. For a complete list of options, see the "Droppable Options" section later in this Appendix.	Dropset
`droppable('disable')`	Disables droppable functionality on the selected element(s).	jQuery
`droppable('enable')`	Enables droppable functionality on the selected element(s).	jQuery
`droppable('destroy')`	Completely removes droppable functionality from the selected element(s).	jQuery

Draggables Options

Option	Description	Type
`appendTo`	For a draggable with a `helper` option specified, the matched element passed to the `appendTo` option will be used as the helper's container. If not specified, the helper is appended to the same container as the draggable.	Element, Selector
`axis`	Contains dragging to an *X*- or *Y*-axis. Defaults to `false`.	String
`cancel`	Prevents dragging, if you start on elements matching the selector.	Selector
`containment`	Contains dragging within the bounds of the specified element or selection.	Element, Selector
`cursor`	The CSS `cursor` to be used during the operation	String
`cursorAt`	Moves the dragging element/helper so the cursor always appears to drag from the same position. Coordinates can be given as an object literal using the keys: `top`, `left`, `right`, `bottom`.	Object, Array
`delay`	Time in milliseconds (ms) to delay the start of a drag. This helps prevent unwanted dragging from occurring when clicking on an element.	Integer
`distance`	Tolerance in pixels for when dragging should start. Prevents dragging from taking place until the mouse cursor has reached the pixel distance from the point the drag began.	Integer
`grid`	Snaps the dragging element or helper to a grid.	Integer x, Integer y
`handle`	Restricts the drag start to the specified element. This lets you make a large element draggable, but only when a smaller element within it is used as the "handle."	Element, Selector
`helper`	Allows for a `helper` element to be used for dragging display. The `clone` option will produce a ghosting effect. Possible values: `original` and `clone`. The default value is `original`. If you supply a function, it must return a valid DOM node.	String, Function
`opacity`	The CSS `opacity` for the element being dragged	CSS Opacity

Option	Description	Type
`revert`	If set to `true`, the element will return to its start position when dragging stops. Also accepts the strings `valid` and `invalid`. If set to `invalid`, revert will only occur if the draggable has not been dropped on a droppable. If set to `valid`, it's the other way around.	Boolean
`revertDuration`	The duration of the revert animation; stable since version 1.6.	Integer
`scroll`	If set to `true`, the draggable's container auto-scrolls while dragging.	Boolean
`scrollSensitivity`	Distance in pixels from the edge of the viewport after which the viewport should scroll. Distance is relative to the pointer, not the draggable.	Integer
`scrollSpeed`	The speed at which the window should scroll once the mouse pointer gets within the `scrollSensitivity` distance	Integer
`snap`	If set to a selector or to `true` (same as selector `.ui-draggable`), the new draggable will snap to the edges of the selected elements when coming to an edge of the element.	Boolean, Selector
`snapMode`	If set, the dragged element will only snap to the outer edges or to the inner edges of the element. Possible values are `inner` and `outer`.	String
`snapTolerance`	The distance in pixels from the snapping elements before the snapping should occur	Integer
`refreshPositions`	If set to `true`, all droppable positions are calculated on every `mousemove`. Caution: This solves issues on highly dynamic pages, but dramatically decreases performance.	Boolean
`zIndex`	The `z-index` value for the helper element, while it is being dragged.	Integer
`start`	A function that is executed when the element begins a drag	function(e, ui)
`drag`	A function that is executed while the element is being dragged	function(e, ui)
`stop`	A function that is executed when the element's drag ends	function(e, ui)

Draggable UI Object Options

The callback functions specified for various draggable options specify in the second argument, a `ui` object. Following are the properties exposed in the `ui` object:

Option	Description	Type
`ui.options`	Options used to initialize the draggable element	Object
`ui.helper`	The jQuery object representing the `helper` being dragged	Object
`ui.position`	The current position of the `helper` as an object literal, relative to the offset element	Object {top, left}
`ui.absolutePosition`	The current absolute position of the `helper`, relative to the page	Object {top, left}

Droppable Options

Option	Description	Type
`accept`	A function that is executed each time a draggable is dropped on a droppable. This lets you filter which elements can be dropped. The function should return `true` if the dragged element should be accepted, and `false` if it should not.	function(draggable)
`accept`	All draggables that match the specified selector will be accepted by the droppable.	Selector
`activeClass`	A class name that is added to the droppable element while a draggable element is being dragged	className
`greedy`	If `true`, this property prevents event propagation on nested droppables. The default value is `false`.	Boolean
`hoverClass`	A class name that is added to the droppable element while a draggable element is being dragged over the droppable element	className
`tolerance`	Specifies which method to use for determining whether a draggable element is over a droppable element. Possible values are `fit`, `intersect`, `pointer`, or `touch`. The default value is `intersect`.	String
`activate`	A function that is executed any time an acceptable draggable element begins a drag	function(e, ui)

Option	Description	Type
`deactivate`	A function that is executed any time an acceptable draggable element's drag ends	function(e, ui)
`over`	A function that is executed when an acceptable draggable element is dragged over a droppable element ("over" is defined by the `tolerance` option)	function(e, ui)
`out`	A function that is executed when an acceptable draggable element leaves a droppable element ("leave" is defined by the `tolerance` option.)	function(e, ui)
`drop`	A function that is executed when an accepted draggable element is dropped on a droppable element ("on" is defined by the `tolerance` option). Within the function, `this` refers to the droppable element, and `ui.draggable` refers to the draggable element.	function(e, ui)

Droppable UI Object Options

The callback functions specified for various droppable options specify in the second argument, a `ui` object. Following are the properties exposed by the `ui` object:

Option	Description	Type
`ui.options`	The options used to initialize the droppable element	Object
`ui.position`	The current position of the draggable `helper`	Object {top, left}
`ui.absolutePosition`	The current absolute position of the draggable `helper`	Object {top, left}
`ui.draggable`	The current draggable element	Object
`ui.helper`	The current draggable helper	Object

Sortables

Method	Description	Return Value
Sortable Methods		
`sortable(`*`options`*`)`	Makes the selected element(s) sortable. Options can be specified by passing an object literal as the first argument using key, value pairs. For a complete list of options, see the "Sortable Options" section later in this Appendix.	jQuery
`sortable('disable')`	Disables sortable functionality on the selected element(s).	jQuery
`sortable('enable')`	Enables sortable functionality on the selected element(s).	jQuery
`sortable('destroy')`	Completely removes sortable functionality from the selected element(s).	jQuery
`sortable('serialize',` *`options`*`)`	Returns a string of serialized IDs for each sortable item, which can then be used in an AJAX request or input form. For a complete list of options, see the "Serialize Options" section later in this Appendix.	String
`sortable('refresh')`	Refreshes the sortable items.	jQuery
`sortable('refreshPositions')`	Refreshes the cached positions of sortable items.	jQuery

Sortable Options

Option	Description	Type
appendTo	Defaults to the parent; defines where the helper that moves with the mouse is being appended to during the drag (e.g., to resolve overlap/zIndex issues).	String
axis	If specified, the items can only be dragged along either the *X*- or *Y*-axis. Only allows the values *x* or *y*.	One of *x* or *y*
cancel	Prevents sorting from beginning on elements that match the selector.	Selector
connectWith	Accepts an array of selectors, where the selector(s) match elements that are sortable elements. If this option is specified, the sortable element that the option is applied to is connected one-way to the sortable elements specified by the selector(s).	Array
containment	Constrains the dragging of sortable elements within the bounds of the specified element. Possible values are *parent* or *document*.	One of *parent* or *document*
cursor	Specifies the cursor that should be shown while sortable elements are being dragged.	CSS cursor
delay	Defines a delay time in milliseconds (ms), which helps to prevent unwanted drags. The default is 0.	Integer
distance	A tolerance in pixels, for where the threshold sorting should take place. If this option is specified, sorting won't take place until the mouse cursor is dragged beyond the specified distance. The default is 1.	Integer
dropOnEmpty	If set to true, this option allows a sortable item to be dropped from a linked selectable. The default is true.	Boolean
handle	See the handle option under the "Draggables Options" section in Appendix J.	Selector, element
forcePlaceholderSize	If true, this option forces the placeholder for the sortable to have a size. The default is false.	Boolean
grid	Snaps the dragging element/helper to a grid, every *x* and *y* pixel.	Object {x, y}
helper	This option allows a helper element to be displayed while dragging is taking place. If a callback function is specified, it should return a valid DOM node that can be used for display.	Element, function(e, element)

Option	Description	Type
`tolerance`	This option defines how reordering behaves during a `drag` event. The default value is *`guess`*. The *`guess`* value automatically guesses whether to use *`intersect`* or *`tolerance`*. In some applications, *`pointer`* is more appropriate.	One of *`guess`*, *`intersect`*, *`tolerance`*, or *`pointer`*
`items`	Which items sorting should be applied to. The default value is "> *" (all children elements).	Selector
`opacity`	Defines the opacity of the helper while sorting using a CSS 3 `opacity` value, where `0` is fully transparent, `1` is fully opaque, and floating points between are semitransparent. For example, `0.5` would be half-transparent (or half-opaque). The default is `1`.	CSS 3 Opacity
`placeholder`	Applies a class name to the placeholder element (which would otherwise be empty white space).	className
`revert`	This option triggers the dragged item to be reverted back to its original position using a smooth animation. The default is `true`.	Boolean
`scroll`	This option causes the page to scroll when a dragged element comes to an edge. The default is `true`.	Boolean
`scrollSensitivity`	This option defines how close to an edge a dragged element must be before scrolling occurs. Measured in pixels, the default is `20`.	Integer
`scrollSpeed`	This option defines the distance an element is scrolled. Measured in pixels, the default is `20`.	Integer
`zIndex`	The z-index for the `drag` element	Integer
`start`	A function that executes when sorting begins	function(e, ui)
`sort`	A function that executes while sorting is taking place	function(e, ui)
`change`	A function that executes when a change in sorting takes place	function(e, ui)
`stop`	A function that executes when sorting ends	function(e, ui)
`beforeStop`	A function that executes when sorting ends, but while the `placeholder` or `helper` is still available	function(e, ui)
`update`	A function that executes when sorting ends and the DOM position of the dragged element has changed	function(e, ui)
`receive`	A function that executes when an item from a connected (separate) sortable list is dragged to this sortable list	function(e, ul)

Option	Description	Type
remove	A function that executes when an item from this sortable list is dragged to a connected (separated) sortable list	function(e, ui)
over	A function that executes when an item is moved over a connected list	function(e, ui)
activate	A function that executes when a drag on a sortable item begins. This function propagates to all connected lists.	function(e, ui)
deactivate	A function that executes when sorting ends. This function propagates to all connected lists.	function(e, ui)

Serialize Options

Option	Description	Type
attribute	The attribute value that is retrieved from each sortable element. The default is `id`.	String
expression	A regular expression used to extract a string from within the attribute value. The default is `/(.+)[-=_](.+)/`.	Regular expression
key	The key in the URL hash. If not specified, it will take the first result of the expression.	String

Selectables

Method	Description	Return Value
Sortable Methods		
`selectable(options)`	Turns the children of selected element(s) into selectable elements. Options can be specified by passing an object literal as the first argument using key, value pairs. For a complete list of options, see the "Selectable Options" section later in this Appendix.	jQuery
`selectable('disable')`	Disables selectable functionality on the selected element(s).	jQuery
`selectable('enable')`	Enables selectable functionality on the selected element(s).	jQuery
`selectable('refresh')`	Refreshes the position and size of each selected element.	jQuery
`selectable('toggle')`	Toggles selectability (between enabled and disabled).	jQuery
`selectable('destroy')`	Completely removes the selectable functionality.	jQuery

Selectable Options

Option	Description	Type
`autoRefresh`	This option determines whether to refresh (the cached) the position and size of each selectable element at the beginning of a select operation. If you have experienced performance degradation (as you would if you have lots of selectable elements), you might want to set this option to `false` and refresh positions manually, as needed. The default value is `true`.	Boolean

Option	Description	Type
`filter`	The matching child elements will be made into selectable elements. The default value is `*` (all children elements).	Selector
`selected`	This function is executed at the end of a select operation (when the mouse button has been released), on each element added to the selection. Selected elements are available in the `ui` argument as `ui.selected`. The `this` keyword refers to the parent selectable element.	function(e, ui)
`selecting`	This function is executed as elements are selected during a select operation (while the selection box is being drawn). Selected elements are available in the `ui` argument as `ui.selecting`. The `this` keyword refers to the parent selectable element.	function(e, ui)
`start`	This function is executed at the beginning of a select operation (when the mouse button is first pressed down). The `this` keyword refers to the parent selectable element.	function(e, ui)
`stop`	This function is executed at the end of a select operation (when the mouse button is released). The `this` keyword refers to the parent selectable element.	function(e, ui)
`unselected`	This function is executed at the end of a select operation (when the mouse button has been released), for each element removed from the selection. The element removed from the selection is available in the `ui` argument as `ui.unselected`. The `this` keyword refers to the parent selectable element.	function(e, ui)
`unselecting`	This function is executed during a select operation (while the selection box is being drawn). Selected elements are available in the `ui` argument as `ui.unselecting`. The `this` keyword refers to the parent selectable element.	function(e, ui)

Notes

In the `ui` argument of each of the callback functions documented here, the parent selectable element is also available as `ui.selectable`.

The Selectables plugin currently does not provide a way to customize the box being drawn, by adding a class name to it via a Selectables option, for example. Despite this limitation, you do have the ability to customize the selection box, however, and you can do that by adding a rule to your style sheet that references the selector, `div.ui-selectable-helper`. If you want to override the jQuery UI styling of the box, like the dashed border, for example, you must add `!important` to override style-sheet declarations.

Effects

Speed

In the following table, the `speed` argument of each method means that any one of `"slow"`, `"normal"`, `"fast"`, or the time specified in milliseconds can be specified for that argument.

Callback Function

An optional callback function may be provided in the second argument. If a callback function is provided, it is executed when the animation completes.

Method	Description	Return Value
Showing and Hiding Methods		
`show()`	Displays each selected element if the element is hidden.	jQuery
`show(`*`speed, function`*`)`	Displays each selected element using an animation (see "Speed" and "Callback Function").	jQuery
`show(`*`effect, options, speed,`*` function)`	Uses a specific effect on an element to show the element if the first argument is an `effect` string (see "Effects").	jQuery
`hide()`	Hides each selected element if the element is not already hidden.	jQuery
`hide(`*`speed, function`*`)`	Hides each selected element using an animation (see "Speed" and "Callback Function").	jQuery
`hide(`*`effect, options, speed, function`*`)`	Uses a specific effect on an element to hide the element if the first argument is an `effect` string (see "Effects").	jQuery
`toggle()`	Toggles each selected element between displayed and hidden.	jQuery

Method	Description	Return Value
`toggle(`*`speed, function`*`)`	Toggles each selected element between displayed and hidden using an animation (see "Speed" and "Callback Function").	jQuery
`toggle(`*`effect, options, speed, function`*`)`	Uses a specific effect on an element to toggle the element if the first argument is an `effect` string (see "Effects").	jQuery
`effect(`*`effect, options, speed, function`*`)`	Uses a specific effect on an element (without the show/hide logic) (see "Effects").	jQuery
Sliding Methods		
`slideDown(`*`speed, function`*`)`	Displays each selected element if the element is hidden by animating the element's height from nothing to its normal height (see "Speed" and "Callback Function").	jQuery
`slideUp(`*`speed, function`*`)`	Hides each selected element if the element is displayed by animating the element's height from its normal height to nothing (see "Speed" and "Callback Function").	jQuery
`slideToggle(`*`speed, function`*`)`	Toggles each selected element between displayed and hidden by animating the element's height (see "Speed" and "Callback Function").	jQuery
Fading Methods		
`fadeIn(`*`speed`*`, function)`	Fades in each selected element by adjusting the element's opacity (see "Speed" and "Callback Function").	jQuery
`fadeOut(`*`speed, function`*`)`	Fades out each selected element by adjusting the element's opacity (see "Speed" and "Callback Function").	jQuery
`fadeTo(`*`speed, opacity, function`*`)`	Fades each selected element to the specified opacity (see "Speed" and "Callback Function").	jQuery
Custom Animation Methods		
`animate(`*`styles, duration, easing, function`*`)`	Animates an element's styles, from the styles an element begins with, to the styles specified in an object literal provided to the first argument. At the time of this writing, only CSS properties with numeric values are supported (animating color transitions is not supported). The `easing` argument accepts two possible values, `"linear"` and `"swing"`.	jQuery

Method	Description	Return Value
`animate(styles, options)`	See the "Animate Options" section.	jQuery
`stop()`	Stops all the currently running animations on all the specified elements.	jQuery
`queue()`	Returns a reference to the first element's queue (which is an array of functions).	Array (Function)
`queue(function)`	Adds a new function to be executed onto the end of the queue of all selected elements.	jQuery
`queue(queue)`	Replaces the queue of all matched elements with this new queue (the array of functions).	jQuery
`dequeue()`	Removes a queued function from the front of the queue and executes it.	jQuery

Animate Options

Option	Description	Type
`duration`	Any one of `"slow"`, `"normal"`, `"fast"`, or the time specified in milliseconds (ms).	String, number
`easing`	The name of the easing effect that you want to use (plugin required). There are two built-in values, `"linear"` and `"swing"`.	String
`complete`	A function to be executed when the animation completes	Function
`step`	*	Callback
`queue`	Setting this to `false` will make the animation skip the queue and begin running immediately.	Boolean

*No description is available in the jQuery documentation for the step option at the time of this writing.

Effects

Option	Description
Effects that can be used with Show/Hide/Toggle:	
`blind`	Blinds the element away or shows it by blinding it in.
`clip`	Clips the element on or off, vertically or horizontally.
`drop`	Drops the element away or shows it by dropping it in.
`explode`	Explodes the element into multiple pieces.
`fold`	Folds the element like a piece of paper.

Option	Description
`puff`	Scale and fade out animations create the puff effect.
`slide`	Slides the element out of the viewport.
`scale`	Shrinks or grows an element by a percentage factor.
`size`	Re-sizes an element to a specified width and height.
`pulsate`	Pulsates the opacity of the element multiple times.

Effects that can only be used stand-alone:

`bounce`	Bounces the element vertically or horizontally *n*-times.
`highlight`	Highlights the background with a defined color.
`shake`	Shakes the element vertically or horizontally *n*-times.
`transfer`	Transfers the outline of an element to another.

Accordion

Method	Description	Return Value
Showing and Hiding Methods		
`accordion(`*`options`*`)`	Makes the selected elements into accordions (see "Accordion Options").	jQuery
`accordion('activate', index)`	Activates a content part of the accordion programmatically.	jQuery
`accordion('enable')`	Enables the selected accordion.	jQuery
`accordion('disable')`	Disables the selected accordion.	jQuery
`accordion('destroy')`	Destroys the selected accordion.	jQuery

Accordion Options

Option	Description	Type
`active`	Used to set the default content pane. If a selector is provided, it must reference the element used for a header. If the value `false` is provided, no element will be used as the default content pane. The default value is the first element.	Boolean, selector, element, number, jQuery
`alwaysOpen`	By default, there is always one content pane open, and the open content pane cannot be closed. If this open is set to `false`, the user is given the ability to toggle the open content pane open or closed. The default value is `true`.	Boolean
`animated`	If set to `false`, animation is disabled. If the jQuery UI Easing plugin is installed, you may use the values *`bounceslide`* or *`easeslide`*. The default value is *`slide`*.	Boolean, *`slide`*, *`bounceslide`*, or *`easeslide`*

Option	Description	Type
autoHeight	If set to true, the highest content pane is used as a height reference for every pane. The default value is true.	Boolean
clearStyle	If set, clears height and overflow styles after finishing an animation, which enables accordions to work with dynamic content. Won't work with the autoHeight option. The default value is false.	Boolean
event	The event used to trigger the accordion. The default value is *click*.	Event name
fillSpace	If set, the accordion completely fills the height of the accordion container element (the element that you call the accordion() method on). The default value is false.	Boolean
header	Selector referencing the element to use for the header element for each content pane. The default value is "a" (<a> elements).	Selector, element, jQuery
icons	Icons to use for headers	header or headerSelected
navigation	Makes the accordion content pane that contains an <a> element, whose href value matches the location.href of the window (the document's current location). Allows the accordion to adjust the default pane dynamically depending on location. The default value is false.	Boolean
navigationFilter	Overrides the default location.href matching used by the Accordion plugin with logic that you provide in your own callback function.	Function
selectedClass	A class name that is applied to active content panes, giving you the ability to style the active content pane differently from inactive content panes. The default value is *selected*.	Class name

Datepicker

Method	Description	Return Value
Datepicker Methods		
`datepicker(`*`options`*`)`	Makes the selected elements into datepickers (see "Datepicker Options").	jQuery
`datepicker("option", `*`settings`*`)`	Changes settings for a previously attached datepicker.	jQuery
`datepicker("dialog", `*`dateText`*`, `*`onSelect`*`, `*`settings`*`)`	Opens a datepicker in a dialogue box.	jQuery
`datepicker("disable")`	Disables a datepicker.	jQuery
`datepicker("enable")`	Enables a datepicker.	jQuery
`datepicker("isDisabled")`	Determines whether a datepicker field has been disabled.	Boolean
`datepicker("hide", speed)`	Closes a previously open datepicker.	jQuery
`datepicker("show")`	Calls up a previously attached datepicker.	jQuery
`datepicker("destroy")`	Disconnects the datepicker functionality from its associated control.	jQuery
`datepicker("getDate")`	Retrieves the current date(s) for a datepicker.	Date or Date[2]
`datepicker("setDate", `*`date`*`, `*`endDate`*`)`	Sets the current date(s) for a datepicker.	jQuery

Datepicker Options

Option	Description	Type
clearText	The text to display for the clear link. The default is "Clear".	String
clearStatus	The text to display in the status bar for the clear link. The default is "Erase the current date".	String
mandatory	true if a date must be selected, causing the Clear link to be removed. false if the date is not required. The default is false.	Boolean
closeText	The text to display for the close link. The default is "Close".	String
closeStatus	The text to display in the status bar for the close link. The default is "Close without change".	String
closeAtTop	If set to true, the Clear/Close links are positioned at the top; otherwise, if set to false, these links are positioned to the bottom. The default is true.	Boolean
prevText	The text to display for the previous month link. The default is "<Prev".	String
prevStatus	The text to display in the status bar for the previous month link. The default is "Show the previous month".	String
nextText	The text to display for the next month link. The default is "Next>".	String
nextStatus	The text to display in the status bar for the next month link. The default is "Show the next month".	String
hideIfNoPrevText	By default, the previous and next links are disabled with not applicable; setting this attribute to true hides them altogether. The default is false.	Boolean
currentText	The text to display for the current day link. The default is "Today".	String
currentStatus	The text to display in the status bar for the current day link. The default is "Show the current month".	String
gotoCurrent	If true, the current day link moves to the currently selected date instead of *today*. The default is false.	Boolean
navigationAsDateFormat	When set to true, the formatDate function is applied to the prevText, nextText, and currentText values before display, allowing them to display the target month names, for example. The default is false.	Boolean

Option	Description	Type
monthNames	The list of full month names, as used in the month header on each datepicker and as requested via the `dateFormat` setting. The default is `["January", "February", "March", "April", "May", "June", "July", "August", "September", "October", "November", "December"]`.	Array
monthNamesShort	The list of abbreviated month names, for use as requested via the `dateFormat` setting. The default is `["Jan", "Feb", "Mar", "Apr", "May", "Jun", "Jul", "Aug", "Sep", "Oct", "Nov", "Dec"]`.	Array
changeMonth	Allows you to change the month by selecting from a dropdown list. You can disable this feature by setting this attribute to `false`. The default is `true`.	Boolean
monthStatus	The text to display in the status bar for the month drop-down list. The default is `"Show a different month"`.	String
yearRange	Controls the range of years displayed in the year drop-down. Sets a range of years relative to the current year `"-nn:+nn"` , where `n` is the number of years forward or backward; or an arbitrary range of years `"nnnn:nnnn"`, where `n` is the beginning and ending year. The default is `"-10:+10"`.	String
changeYear	Allows you to change the year by selecting from a dropdown list. You can disable this feature by setting this option to `false`. The default is `true`.	Boolean
yearStatus	The text to display in the status bar for the year drop-down list. The default is `"Show a different year"`.	String
weekHeader	The column header for the week of the year (see `showWeeks`). The default is `"wk"`.	String
weekStatus	The text to display in the status bar for the week of the year. The default is `"Week of the year"`.	String
dayNames	The list of long day names, starting from Sunday, for use as requested via the `dateFormat` setting. Day names also appear as pop-up hints when hovering over the corresponding column headings. The default is `["Sunday", "Monday", "Tuesday", "Wednesday", "Thursday", "Friday", "Saturday"]`.	Array
dayNamesShort	The list of abbreviated day names, starting from Sunday, for use as requested via the `dateFormat` setting. The default is `["Sun", "Mon", "Tue", "Wed", "Thu", "Fri", "Sat"]`.	Array

Option	Description	Type
dayNamesMin	The list of minimized day names, starting from Sunday, for use as column headers within the Datepicker. The default is ["Su", "Mo", "Tu", "We", "Th", "Fr", "Sa"].	Array
firstDay	Sets the first day of the week: Sunday is 0, Monday is 1. The default is 0.	Number
changeFirstDay	Allows you to click on the day names to have the week start on that day. You can disable this feature by setting this option to false. The default is true.	Boolean
dayStatus	The text to display in the status bar for the day of the week links. Use DD for the full name of the day, or D for its short name. The default is "Set DD as first week day".	String
highlightWeek	If true, the entire week row is highlighted when the mouse hovers over a day. The default is false.	Boolean
showOtherMonths	Displays dates in other months (non-selectable) at the start or end of the current month. The default is false.	Boolean
dateStatus	The text to display in the status bar for the date links. Use any of the dateFormat characters (see "Format Options"). The default is "Select DD, M d".	String
showWeeks	Displays the week of the year alongside each month. The column header is specified by the weekHeader setting. The week number is calculated based on the first date shown in each row in the Datepicker, and thus may not apply to all days in that row. The calculateWeek setting allows you to change the week of the year calculation from the default ISO 8601 implementation. The default is false.	Boolean
calculateWeek	Performs the week of the year calculation. This function accepts a Date as a parameter and returns the number of the corresponding week of the year. The default implementation uses the ISO 8601 definition of a week: Weeks start on a Monday, and the first week of the year contains January 4. This means that up to three days from the previous year may be included in the first week of the current year, and that up to three days from the current year may be included in the last week of the previous year. The default is $.datepicker.iso8601Week.	Function
numberOfMonths	Sets how many months to show at once. The value can be a straight integer, or it can be a two-element array to define the number of rows and columns to display. The default is 1.	Number, Number[2]

Option	Description	Type
stepMonths	Sets how many months to move when clicking the Previous/Next links. The default is 1.	Number
rangeSelect	Sets to true to allow the selection of a date range on the one date picker, or false to just select a single date. For a date range, the first click sets the start date, and a second click sets the end date. The default is false.	Boolean
rangeSeparator	Sets the text to use to separate the two dates in a date range via the onSelect function. The default is " - ".	String
defaultDate	Sets the date to display on first opening if the field is blank. Specifies either an actual date via a Date object, or relative to today with a number (e.g., +7) or a string of values and periods ('y' for years, 'm' for months, 'w' for weeks, 'd' for days; e.g., '+1m +7d'), or null for today. The default is null.	Number, string
minDate	Sets a minimum selectable date via a Date object, or relative to today with a number (e.g., +7) or a string of values and periods ('y' for years, 'm' for months, 'w' for weeks, 'd' for days; e.g., '-1y -1m'), or null for no limit. The default is null.	Number, string
maxDate	Sets a maximum selectable date via a Date object, or relative to today with a number (e.g., +7) or a string of values and periods ('y' for years, 'm' for months, 'w' for weeks, 'd' for days; e.g., '+1m +1w'), or null for no limit. The default is null.	Number, string
dateFormat	The format for parsed and displayed dates. For a full list of the possible formats, see "Format Options."	String
shortYearCutoff	Sets the cutoff year for determining the century for a date (used in conjunction with dateFormat 'y'). If a numeric value (0–99) is provided, then this value is used directly. If a string value is provided, then it is converted to a number and added to the current year. Once the cutoff year is calculated, any dates entered with a year value less than or equal to it are considered to be in the current century, while those greater than it are deemed to be in the previous century. The default is "+10".	String, number
initStatus	The text to display in the status bar when the Datepicker is first opened. The default is "Select a date".	String
showStatus	true if a status bar should be shown within the Datepicker indicating what each control does. false if no status bar is required. The default is false.	Boolean

Option	Description	Type
statusForDate	The function to call to determine the status text for a date within the Datepicker. The default function uses the dateStatus value and substitutes in information from the current date. The default is this.dateStatus.	Function
appendText	The text to display after each date field, for example, to show the required format. The default is "".	String
duration	Controls the speed at which the Datepicker appears. It may be a time in milliseconds (ms), a string representing one of the three pre-defined speeds ("slow", "normal", "fast"), or '' for immediately. The default is "normal".	String, number
showOn	Has the Datepicker appear automatically when the field receives focus, 'focus'; appear only when a button is clicked, 'button'; or appear when either event takes place, 'both'. The default is "focus".	focus, button, or both
showAnim	Sets the name of the animation used to show/hide the Datepicker. Uses 'show' (the default), 'slideDown', 'fadeIn', or any of the show/hide jQuery UI effects. The default is "show".	String
showOptions	If using one of the jQuery UI effects for showAnim, you can provide additional settings for that animation via this option. The default is {}.	Options
buttonText	The text to display on the trigger button. Use in conjunction with showOn equal to 'button' or 'both'. The default is "...".	String
buttonImage	The URL for the pop-up button image. If set, button text becomes the alt value and is not directly displayed. The default is "".	String
buttonImageOnly	Set to true to place an image after the field to use as the trigger without it appearing on a button. The default is false.	Boolean
beforeShow	Can be a function that takes an input field and current Datepicker instance and returns a settings (anonymous) object to update the Datepicker with. It is called just before the Datepicker is displayed. The default is null.	Function

Option	Description	Type
`beforeShowDay`	The function takes a date as a parameter and must return an array, with `[0]` equal to `true/false` indicating whether or not this date is selectable, `[1]` equal to a CSS class name(s), or `''` for the default presentation. It is called for each day in the Datepicker before it is displayed. The default is `null`.	Function
altField	The jQuery selector for another field that is to be updated with the selected date from the Datepicker. Use the `altFormat` setting below to change the format of the date within this field. Leave as blank for no alternate field. The default is `""`.	String
`altFormat`	The `dateFormat` to be used for the `altField` above. This allows one date format to be shown to the user for selection purposes, while a different format is actually sent behind the scenes. The default is `""`.	String
`onSelect`	Allows you to define your own event when the Datepicker is selected. The function receives the selected date(s) as text and the Datepicker instance as parameters. `this` refers to the associated input field. The default is `null`.	Function
`onChangeMonthYear`	Allows you to define your own event when the Datepicker moves to a new month and/or year. The function receives the date of the first day of the first displayed month and the Datepicker instance as parameters. `this` refers to the associated input field. The default is `null`.	Function
`onClose`	Allows you to define your own event when the Datepicker is closed, whether or not a date is selected. The function receives the selected date(s) as a date or array of dates and the Datepicker instance as parameters. `this` refers to the associated input field. The default is `null`.	Function
`isRTL`	`true` if the current language is drawn from right to left. The default is `false`.	Boolean
`constrainInput`	`true` if the input field is constrained to the current date format. The default is `true`.	Boolean

Datepicker Utilities

Method	Description	Return Value
`$.datepicker .setDefaults(options)`	Changes the default settings for all datepickers. For the options argument, see "Datepicker Options."	Datepicker
`$.datepicker .formatDate(format, date, options)`	Formats a date into a string value with a specified format. For the `format` argument, see "Format Options." The optional `options` argument can be provided an object literal of settings that include the `dayNamesShort`, `dayNames`, `monthNamesShort`, or `monthNames` options.	String
`$.datepicker .iso8601Week(date)`	Determines the week of the year for a given date: 1 to 53.	Number
`$.datepicker .parseDate(format, value, options)`	Extracts a date from a string value with a specified format. For the `format` option, see "Format Options." The optional `options` argument can be provided an object literal that includes the `shortYearCutoff`, `dayNamesShort`, `dayNames`, `monthNamesShort`, or `monthNames` options.	Date

`$datePicker.formatDate()` Format Options

Option	Description
`d`	Day of the month with no leading zero
`dd`	Day of the month with leading zero
`D`	Day name short
`DD`	Day name long
`m`	Month of the year with no leading zero
`mm`	Month of the year with leading zero
`M`	Month name short
`MM`	Month name long
`y`	Two-digit year
`yy`	Four-digit year
`@`	UNIX timestamp (seconds elapsed since 01/01/1970)
...	Literal text
`''`	Single quote

Option	Description
`Anything else.`	Literal text
`ATOM`	yy-mm-dd (same as RFC 3339 / ISO 8601)
`COOKIE`	D, dd M yy
`ISO_8601`	yy-mm-dd
`RFC_822`	D, d M y
`RFC_850`	DD, dd-M-y
`RFC_1036`	D, d M y
`RFC_1123`	D, d M yy
`RFC_2822`	D, d M yy
`RSS`	D, d M y
`TIMESTAMP`	UNIX timestamp (seconds elapsed since 01/01/1970)
`W3C`	yy-mm-dd (same as ISO 8601)

Datepicker Styling

ID	Description
`ui-datepicker-div`	The container that wraps around the entire Datepicker. This element is shared by all pop-up datepickers. Inline datepickers have their own instances with IDs in the format `ui-datepicker-div-nn`, where `nn` is the ID of the associated input field or division.
Class	**Description**
`ui-datepicker-multi`	Indicates that the Datepicker shows multiple months.
`ui-datepicker-rtl`	Indicates that the Datepicker uses a right-to-left rendered language.
`ui-datepicker-inline`	Container for the Datepicker if it is displayed inline
`ui-datepicker-prompt`	The row for a prompt when displayed in a dialog
`ui-datepicker-control`	The row containing the Clear and Close links
`ui-datepicker-clear`	The division containing the Clear link
`ui-datepicker-close`	The division containing the Close link
`ui-datepicker-links`	The row containing the Prev, Next, and Current links

Class	Description
ui-datepicker-prev	The division containing the Prev link
ui-datepicker-current	The division containing the Current link
ui-datepicker-next	The division containing the Next link
ui-datepicker-one-month	The container for a single month
ui-datepicker-new-row	The start of a new row of months
ui-datepicker-header	The row containing the month and year
ui-datepicker-new-month	Dropdown menu for selecting months
ui-datepicker-new-year	Dropdown menu for selecting years
ui-datepicker	The table for a single month
ui-datepicker-title-row	The header row of the table containing day names
ui-datepicker-days-row	A row of day numbers on the calendar
ui-datepicker-week-over	Highlight for the hovered row of day numbers on the calendar
ui-datepicker-week-col	The week of the year column
ui-datepicker-days-cell	A standard day number
ui-datepicker-days-cell-over	Mouseover state for a selectable day
ui-datepicker-current-day	Highlights the currently selected date.
ui-datepicker-today	Highlights today's date.
ui-datepicker-week-end-cell	Contains a weekend date.
ui-datepicker-other-month	Dates before and after the days in the current month
ui-datepicker-unselectable	Days that are deactivated for users to select
ui-datepicker-status	The status bar for the Datepicker
ui-datepicker-cover	IFRAME that only displays in Internet Explorer 6 or below

Dialog

Method	Description	Return Value
Dialog Methods		
`dialog(options)`	Makes the selected elements into dialog boxes.	jQuery
`dialog("open")`	Opens the specified dialog box(es).	jQuery
`dialog("IsOpen")`	Determines if the dialog is open.	Boolean
`dialog("moveToTop")`	Moves the specified dialog on top of the dialogs stack.	jQuery
`dialog("close")`	Closes the specified dialog box(es).	jQuery
`dialog("destroy")`	Completely removes the dialog.	jQuery

Dialog Options

Option	Description	Type
`autoOpen`	When set to `true`, the dialog will open automatically when dialog is called. If set to `false`, it will stay hidden until `dialog("open")` is called on it. The default is `true`.	Boolean
`bgiframe`	When `true`, the `bgiframe` plugin will be used, to fix the issue in IE6 where select boxes show on top of other elements, regardless of `zIndex`. Requires including the `bgiframe` plugin. Future versions may not require a separate plugin. The default is `false`.	Boolean
`buttons`	Specifies which buttons should be displayed on the dialog. The property key is the text of the button. The value is the callback function for when the button is clicked. The context of the callback is the dialog element; if you need access to the button, it is available as the target of the `event` object.	Object
`dialogClass`	The specified class name(s) will be added to the dialog, for additional styling.	String

Option	Description	Type
draggable	When set to true, the resulting dialog will be draggable. If false, the dialog will not be draggable. The default is true.	Boolean
height	The height of the dialog, in pixels. The default is 200.	Number
hide	The effect to be used when the dialog is closed	String
maxHeight	The maximum height to which the dialog can be re-sized, in pixels	Number
maxWidth	The maximum width to which the dialog can be re-sized, in pixels	Number
minHeight	The minimum height to which the dialog can be re-sized, in pixels. The default is 100.	Number
minWidth	The minimum width to which the dialog can be re-sized, in pixels. The default is 150.	Number
modal	When modal is set to true, the dialog will have modal behavior; other items on the page will be disabled (i.e., cannot be interacted with). Modal dialogs create an overlay below the dialog but above other page elements. Custom style values for the overlay (e.g., changing its color or opacity) can be provided with the overlay option. The default is false.	Boolean
overlay	Key/value object of style properties for the overlay to display behind the dialog (but above other page elements)	Options
position	Specifies where the dialog should be displayed. Possible values: 'center', 'left', 'right', 'top', 'bottom', or an array containing a coordinate pair (in pixel offset from top-left of viewport) or the possible string values (e.g., ['right','top'] for top-right corner). The default is "center".	"center", "left", "right", "top", "bottom", Array
resizable	Specifies whether the dialog will be re-sizable. The default is true.	Boolean
show	The effect to be used when the dialog is opened (see "Effects" in Appendix M)	String
stack	Specifies whether the dialog will stack on top of other dialogs. This will cause the dialog to move to the front of other dialogs when it gains focus. The default is true.	Boolean
title	Specifies the title of the dialog. The title can also be specified by the title attribute on the dialog source element.	String

Option	Description	Type
width	The width of the dialog, in pixels. The default is 300.	Number
open	Function that's executed at the dialog open event. The function gets passed two arguments in accordance with the triggerHandler interface. The data passed is the opened dialog options object.	function(event, ui)
focus	Function that's executed at the dialog focus event. The function gets passed two arguments in accordance with the triggerHandler interface. The data passed is the focused dialog options object.	function(event, ui)
dragStart	Function that's executed when a dialog is at the beginning of a dialog drag	function(event, ui)
drag	Function that's executed while a dialog is being dragged	function(event, ui)
dragStop	Function that's executed when a dialog drag ends	function(event, ui)
resizeStart	Function that's executed when a dialog re-size is begun	function(event, ui)
resize	Function that's executed during a dialog re-size	function(event, ui)
resizeStop	Function that's executed when a dialog re-size ends	function(event, ui)
close	Function that's executed when a dialog is closed	function(event, ui)

Dialog Styling

Class	Description
ui-dialog-container	The whole dialog window
ui-dialog-titlebar	The titlebar
ui-dialog-titlebar-close	The close button (the top-right "X")
ui-dialog-titlebar-hover	The Close button's hover style
ui-dialog-content	Additional style for dialog contents
ui-dialog-buttonpane	The container for the dialog buttons (like "Yes," "No," "Cancel")

Class Names Inherited from ui.resizable
ui.resizable, ui-resizable-handle, ui-resizable-disabled, ui-resizable-autohide, ui-resizable-n, ui-resizable-s, ui-resizable-e, ui-resizable-w, ui-resizable-se, ui-resizable-sw, ui-resizable-nw, ui-resizable-ne

Tabs

Method	Description	Return Value
Tab Methods		
`tabs(options)`	Makes the selected elements into tabs (see "Tab Options").	jQuery
`tabs("add", url, label, index)`	Adds a new tab.	jQuery
`tabs("remove", index)`	Removes a tab.	jQuery
`tabs("enable", index)`	Enables a previously disabled tab.	jQuery
`tabs("disable", index)`	Disables a tab.	jQuery
`tabs("select", index)`	Selects a tab (simulates a click programmatically).	jQuery
`tabs("load", index)`	Reloads the content of an AJAX tab programmatically.	jQuery
`tabs("url", index, url)`	Changes the URL from which an AJAX (remote) tab will be loaded.	jQuery
`tabs("destroy")`	Destroys Tabs interface and reverts HTML to the state before creating tabs.	jQuery
`tabs("length")`	Retrieves the number of tabs of the first matched Tab pane.	Number
`tabs("rotate", ms, continuing)`	Sets up an automatic rotation through tabs of a Tab pane.	jQuery

Tab Options

Option	Description	Type
`selected`	Zero-based index of the tab to be selected upon initialization. To set all tabs to unselected, set this option to `null`. The default is `0`.	Number
`unselect`	Allows a currently selected tab to become unselected upon clicking. The default is `false`.	Boolean
`event`	The type of event to be used for selecting a tab. The default is `"click"`.	String
`disabled`	An array containing the position of the tabs (zero-based) that should be disabled upon initialization. The default is `[]`.	Array
`cookie`	Stores the latest active (clicked) tab in a cookie. The cookie is used to determine the active tab on the next page load. Requires Cookie plugin. The object needs to have key/value pairs of the form the Cookie plugin expects as options. Available options are `{expires: 7, path: '/', domain: 'jquery.com', secure: true}`.	Object
`spinner`	The HTML content of this string is shown in a tab title while remote content is loading. Pass in empty string to deactivate that behavior. The default is `Loading…`.	String
`cache`	Whether or not to cache remote tabs content; for example, load only once or with every click. Cached content is being lazyloaded; for example, once and only once for the first click. Note that to prevent the actual AJAX requests from being cached by the browser, you need to provide an extra `cache: false` flag to `ajaxOptions`. The default is `false`.	Boolean
`ajaxOptions`	Additional AJAX options to consider when loading tab content (see "Options" in Appendix G).	Object
`idPrefix`	If the remote tab (i.e., its anchor element) has no `title` attribute to generate an ID from, an ID/fragment identifier is created from this prefix, and a unique ID is returned by `$.data(element);` for example, `"ui-tabs-54"`. The default is `ui-tabs-`.	String

Option	Description	Type
fx	Enables animations for hiding and showing Tab panels. The duration option can be a string representing one of the three pre-defined speeds ("slow", "normal", "fast") or the duration in milliseconds (ms) to run an animation. The default is "normal".	Object
tabTemplate	HTML template from which a new tab is created and added. The placeholders #{href} and #{label} are replaced with the URL and tab label that are passed as arguments to the add method. The default is: <li> <a href="#{href}"> <span>#{label}</span> </a> </li>	String
panelTemplate	HTML template from which a new Tab panel is created in case of adding a tab with the add method or when creating a panel for a remote tab on the fly. The default is <div></div>.	String
select	Function that's executed upon clicking on a tab	function(event, ui)
load	Function that's executed after content for a remote tab has been loaded	function(event, ui)
show	Function that's executed when a tab is shown	function(event, ui)
add	Function that's executed when a tab was added	function(event, ui)
remove	Function that's executed when a tab was enabled	function(event, ui)
enable	Function that's executed when a tab is enabled	function(event, ui)
disable	Function that's executed when a tab is disabled	function(event, ui)

Tab Styling

Class	Description
ui-tabs-nav	This is the whole menu. Use this as a base class.
ui-tabs-selected	This is the current tab. It's very important to create a strong visual indication which tab is the current one.
ui-tabs-unselect	This is the class for all the tabs that are not selected but selectable.

Class	Description
ui-tabs- deselectable	This is the class for all tabs that can be de-selected.
ui-tabs-disabled	For when a tab is disabled. Highly recommended to appear somewhat transparent or disabled. This is often done by graying the color.
ui-tabs-panel	These are the boxes that will have their visibility toggled.
ui-tabs-hide	This class hides the boxes (perhaps the most important class).
Element	**Description**
<span>	<span> elements are there to facilitate tricks like rounded corners and re-sizable backgrounds.

Re-Sizables

Method	Description	Return Value
Dialog Methods		
`resizable(`*`options`*`)`	Makes the selected elements into re-sizable elements (see "Re-Sizable Options").	jQuery
`resizable('disable')`	Temporarily disables re-sizable functionality.	jQuery
`resizable('enable')`	Enables re-sizable functionality.	jQuery
`resizable('destroy')`	Completely removes re-sizable functionality.	jQuery

Re-Sizable Options

Option	Description	Type
`animate`	Animates to the final size after re-sizing. The default is `false`.	Boolean
`animateDuration`	Duration time for animating. Accepts the time in milliseconds (ms), or one of `"slow"`, `"normal"`, or `"fast"`. The default is `"slow"`.	`slow`, `normal`, `fast`, or Integer
`animateEasing`	Easing effect for animation. The default is `"swing"`.	String
`alsoResize`	Re-sizes these elements synchronously when re-sizing. The default is `false`.	Selector, Boolean
`aspectRatio`	When set to `true`, re-sizing is constrained by the original aspect ratio. If an alternate ratio is desired, you can submit a number and then the aspect ratio will be constrained by height\width. The default is `false`.	Boolean, number
`autoHide`	When set to `true`, automatically hides the handles except when the mouse hovers over the element. The default is `false`.	Boolean

Option	Description	Type
`cancel`	Prevents re-sizing if you start on elements matching the selector. The default is `":input"`.	Selector
`containment`	Constrains re-sizing to within the bounds of the specified element. This can be a DOM element, `'parent'`, `'document'`, or a selector. The default is `false`.	Element, selector, Boolean
`delay`	Time in milliseconds (ms) to define when dragging should start. It helps prevent unwanted drags when clicking on an element. The default is `0`.	Integer
`disableSelection`	When set to `true`, stops users from selecting handles and helpers. Default is `true`	Boolean
`distance`	Tolerance in pixels, for when re-sizing should start. If specified, re-sizing will not start until after the mouse is moved beyond the specified distance. The default is `1`.	Integer
`ghost`	When set to `true`, a substitute element is displayed while re-sizing. The default is `false`.	Boolean
`grid`	Snaps the re-sizing element to a grid size, every x and y pixel. The default is `false`.	Array[x, y]
`handles`	Each handle string (if specified) should be a jQuery selector matching the child element of the re-sizable to use as the handle. If the handle is not a child of the re-sizable, you can pass in the DOM node or a valid jQuery object directly. Options are `{n, e, s, w, ne, se, sw, nw, all}`.	Object
`helper`	This is the CSS class that will be added to a proxy element to outline the re-size during the drag of the re-size handle. Once the re-size is complete, the original element is sized. The default is `null`.	String
`knobHandles`	Uses square handlebars as re-size handles, rather than the default border. The default is `false`.	Boolean
`maxHeight`	This is the maximum height the re-sizable should be allowed to re-size to. The default is `null`.	Integer
`maxWidth`	This is the maximum width the re-sizable should be allowed to re-size to. The default is `null`.	Integer
`minHeight`	This is the minimum height the re-sizable should be allowed to re-size to. The default is `10`.	Integer

Option	Description	Type
minWidth	This is the minimum width the re-sizable should be allowed to re-size to. The default is 10.	Integer
preserveCursor	Sets whether the direction cursors are used when re-sizing an element. The default is true.	Boolean
preventDefault	Whether or not to prevent Safari's default re-sizing on <textarea> elements. The default is true.	Boolean
proportionallyResize	Advanced option that allows other elements to get proportionally re-sized together with the original one. Just specify jQuery string in this array or directly insert DOM nodes. The default is false.	Array, Boolean
transparent	Whether the element is transparent when re-sizing. The default is false.	Boolean
start	This function is called at the start of a re-size operation.	function(event, ui)
resize	This function is called during the re-size, on the drag of the re-size handler.	function(event, ui)
stop	This function is called at the end of a re-size operation.	function(event, ui)

Resizable Class Names
ui.resizable, ui-resizable-handle, ui-resizable-disabled, ui-resizable-autohide, ui-resizable-n, ui-resizable-s, ui-resizable-e, ui-resizable-w, ui-resizable-se, ui-resizable-sw, ui-resizable-nw, ui-resizable-ne

Sliders

Method	Description	Return Value
Dialog Methods		
`slider(`*`options`*`)`	Make the selected elements into slider elements (see "Slider Options").	jQuery
`slider("moveTo",` *`value, index`*`)`	Moves a slider's handle to the given position.	jQuery
`slider("value",` *`index`*`)`	Retrieves a handle's value.	jQuery
`slider("disable")`	Temporarily disables the slider.	jQuery
`slider("enable")`	Enables the slider.	jQuery
`slider("destroy")`	Completely removes the sliding functionality.	jQuery

Slider Options

Option	Description	Type
`animate`	Whether slide handles smoothly when the user clicks outside the handle on the bar. The default is `false`.	Boolean
`axis`	Normally you don't need to set this option because the plugin detects the slider orientation automatically. If the orientation is not correctly detected, you can set this option to `'horizontal'` or `'vertical'`.	`horizontal` or `vertical`
`handle`	The jQuery selector to use for the handle(s) of the slider. The default is `".ui-slider-handle"`.	Selector

Option	Description	Type
`handles`	Specifies boundaries for one or more handles. Format: `[{start:Integer, min:Integer, max:Integer, id:String} [, ..]]`. Only `start` is required. If the slider doesn't have handles already, they are automatically created.	Object
`max`	The maximum value of the slider. Useful for tracking values via callback, and to set steps. The default is `100`.	Integer
`min`	The minimum value of the slider. Useful for tracking values via callback, and to set steps. The default is `0`.	Integer
`range`	If set to `true`, the slider will detect if you have two handles and create a stylable range element between these two. You now also have access to `ui.range` in your callbacks to get the amount of the range. The default is `false`.	Boolean
`startValue`	The value that the handle will have first.	Integer
`stepping`	If defined, the new value has to be dividable through this number, so the slider jumps from step to step.	Integer
`steps`	Alternative to stepping, this defines how many steps a slider will have, instead of how many values to jump, as in stepping. The default is `0`.	Integer
`start`	Function that gets called when the user starts sliding	function(event, ui)
`slide`	Function that gets called on every mouse move during the slide. Takes arguments `e` and `ui`, for event and user interface, respectively. Use `ui.value` (single-handled sliders) to obtain the value of the current handle, `$(..).slider('value', index)` to get another handle's value.	function(event, ui)
`change`	Function that gets called on slide stop, but only if the slider position has changed. Takes arguments `e` and `ui`, for event and user interface, respectively. Use `ui.value` (single-handled sliders) to obtain the value of the current handle, `$(..).slider('value', index)` to get another handle's value.	function(event, ui)
`stop`	Function that gets called when the user stops sliding	function(event, ui)

Index

A

D

E

F

G

J

N

O

P

S

T

U

V

W